Biblical Ar

Volume I

An Introduction with Recent Discoveries that Support the Reliability of the Bible

SECOND EDITION

David E. Graves, Ph.D.

EMC Electronic Christian Media
Toronto, Canada
2018

Biblical Archaeology. Vol. 1: An Introduction with Recent Discoveries that Support the Reliability of the Bible. SECOND EDITION
Includes bibliographic references and indexes.

Revision March 2018
Published by Electronic Christian Media
Toronto, Ontario, Canada M2J 4T4

ISBN-13: 978-1985349087
ISBN-10: 1985349086

1. Bible–Evidences, authority, etc. 2. Bible–Antiquities 3. Bible-Archaeology. I. Graves, David E. II. Title

Interior Book Design: David E. Graves
Cover Design: David E. Graves

Front Page Background: Dead Sea Scroll Messianic Testimony (4Q175) located in the Amman Museum, Jordan. God's Name, Yahweh is represented by four dots. Ammon Museum. Photo by David E. Graves

Center: Relief of Assyrian King Sennacherib, 705–681 BC, (2 Kgs 18:13; Isa 36:1; 37:17, and 2 Chron 32:1) from the walls of the Temple of Nabu in the city of Khorsabad (Dur-Sherrukin), the capital of the Assyrian Empire. Oriental Institute Museum of the University of Chicago, IL. Photo by David E. Graves.

Bottom Left: Iron age oil lamp from the time of Solomon (ca. 750 BC). Photo by David E. Graves.

Bottom Right: Bronze sestertius coin (65 AD) of Nero (54-68 AD). Laureate head right. The inscription reads "NERO CLAVD CAESAR AVG GER P M TR P IMP P P." Courtesy of CNG.

Top border: Stone tile floors of the porticos of the Jewish Temple built by King Herod. Created by Frankie Snyder from *opus sectile* recovered during the Temple Mount Salvage operation. Courtesy of Fankie Snyder.

Bottom border: scarab seal of Amenhotep II, *ca.* 1485–1418 BC discovered at Khirbet el-Maqatir in 2013. Photo by Michael C. Luddeni.

Back Page Background: Assyrian Court scene (ca. 865–860 BC), from Nimrud, North-West Palace, Room G, panels 2-4 portraying King Ashurnasirpal II (883–859 BC) with attendants. Original is in the British Museum, copy from Pushkin Museum, Moscow Russia. Photo by David E. Graves.

Picture Acknowledgements

All photographs are by the author, unless otherwise indicated. For the credits of the photographs used in the charts see *Credits and Permissions.*

Charts

David E. Graves: all charts

Maps

David E. Graves: Nos. 1, 2, 3, 4, 5, 6, 7, 8
Ritmeyer Archaeological Design: No. 9

Printed in the United States of America.

To my daughters
Jessica and Rebecca

Intentionally Left Blank

Acknowlegements

This book owes a great debt of gratitude to many friends and family whose profession and passion for the Bible and archaeology have contributed to its completion. First is Steven Collins, who has allowed me to have the priviledge of working as a field supervisor at Tall el-Ḥammâm and discovering many amazing artifacts. Another individual not to be forgotten is Scott Stripling, a friend and colleague who dug with me at Tall el-Ḥammâm, Jordan, for several seasons and is now the director of the excavation at Khirbet el-Maqatir. His insights, over the years, have been greatly appreciated.

Also, to my good friend and editor Glen Ruffle-thanks for your patience and wisdom during this project. His eye to detail and prompt attention to minor issues is much appreciated. I could not have done it without your help.

I wish to thank Kimberly Day, the resource sharing librarian, at the Jerry Falwell Library for her help in locating journal articles and books for my research.

I also wish to express my gratitude to Leen Reitmyer, Michael C. Luddeni, John Bondarchuck, Casey Olsen, Mark Wilson, Frankie Snyder and Todd Bolen for their permission to use their fine work in photographs, illustrations, and images.

Lastly, I wish to express my thankfulness to my loving wife Irina for her helpful comments, deep love, care, and patience during the long hours of writing and editing this work. Her editing skills and keen eye to detail were deeply appreciated.

Sola Deo Gloria
2018

Table of Contents

Index of Images

ABBREVIATIONS

This work will conform to the abbreviations and general format conventions set out by *The SBL Handbook of Style: for Ancient Near Eastern, Biblical and Early Christian Studies* by Patrick H. Alexander, et al. eds. second printing (Peabody, MA: Hendrickson, 2002) for general literary conventions, Bible translations, biblical books, Dead Sea scrolls, pseudepigraphical, early patristic books, targumic material, *Mishnah*, Talmud, other Rabbinic works, *Nag Hammadi* tractates, commonly used periodicals, reference works and serials. Unless otherwise indicated the references to the works of ancient sources reflect the Loeb Classical Library numbering system and Latin abbreviations. Note that there are several spelling variations for most sites especially as used by early explorers, since they spell the Arabic words as they sound.

OLD TESTAMENT

Gen	Genesis
Exod	Exodus
Lev	Leviticus
Num	Numbers
Deut	Deuteronomy
Judg	Judges
Josh	Joshua
1–2 Sam	1–2 Samuel
1–2 Kgs	1–2 Kings
1–2 Chr	1–2 Chronicles
Neh	Nehemiah
Esth	Esther
Job	Job
Ps/Pss	Psalms
Prov	Proverbs
Eccl	Ecclesiastes
Isa	Isaiah
Jer	Jeremiah
Lam	Lamentations
Ezek	Ezekiel
Dan	Daniel
Obad	Obadiah
Jonah	Jonah
Mic	Micah
Nah	Nahum
Hab	Habakkuk
Zeph	Zephaniah
Mal	Malachi

NEW TESTAMENT

Matt	Matthew
Rom	Romans
1–2 Cor	1–2 Corinthians
Gal	Galatians
Eph	Ephesians
Phil	Philippians
Col	Colossians
1–2 Thess	1–2 Thessalonians
1–2 Tim	1–2 Timothy
Phlm	Philemon
Heb	Hebrews
Jas	James
1–2 Pet	1–2 Peter
1–2–3 John	1–2–3 John
Rev	Revelation

APOCRYPHA

1–2 Macc	1–2 Maccabees
Sir	Sirach/Ecclesiasticus
Wis	Wisdom of Solomon

OT PSEUDEPIGRAPHA

1 En.	*1 Enoch* (Ethiopic Apocalypse)
2 Bar.	*2 Baruch* (Syriac Apocalypse)
3 Bar.	*3 Baruch* (Greek Apocalypse)
3 En.	*3 Enoch* (Hebrew Apocalypse)
3 Macc.	*3 Maccabees*
4 Macc.	*4 Maccabees*

Apoc. El. *Apocalypse of Elijah*
Apoc. Mos. *Apocalypse of Moses*
As. Mos. *Assumption of Moses*
Ascen. Isa. *Martyrdom and Ascension of Isaiah 6–11*
Ep. Arist. *The Letter of Aristeas*
Jub. *Jubilees ca.* 200–150 BC
Odes Sol. *Odes of Solomon*
Sib. Or. *Sibylline Oracles*
T. Jud. *Testament of Judah*
T. Levi *Testament of Levi*

DEAD SEA SCROLLS

11Q5 Psalms, 11QPs[a] Sanders, *The Psalms Scroll of Qumran Cave 11.* DJD 4. (1965).
1QapGen Excavated frags. from cave col. XXI (frag. pulled from side of scroll).
1QH *Hodayoth* or *Thanksgiving Hymns* from Qumran Cave 1. Sukenik, *The Dead Sea Scrolls of the Hebrew University* (1955), pls. XXXV–LVIII.
1QIsa[a] *The Great Isaiah Scroll.* Kutscher, *The Language and Linguistic Background of the Isaiah Scroll: I QIsaa.* (1974).
1QIsa[b] Isaiah[b] Scroll. Kutscher, *The Language and Linguistic Background of the Isaiah Scroll: I QIsaa.* (1974).
IQIsa[d] Isaiah[d] Scroll. Kutscher, *The Language and Linguistic Background of the Isaiah Scroll: I QIsaa.* (1974).
1QS *Serek ha-Yahad* or *Rule of the Community, Manual of Discipline*, Trever, *Scrolls from Qumran Cave I* (1974).
4Q175 4QTest; *Testimonia* from Qumran Cave 4
4Q186 *Horoscope*, Allegro, *Qumran Cave 4.I,* DJD 5 (1968), pl. XXXI.
4QIsa[d] *Isaiah[d] Scroll.* Kutscher, *The Language and Linguistic Background of the Isaiah Scroll: I QIsaa.* (1974).
5Q12 *Cairo Damascus Document,* (Genizah text), *Covenant of Damascus.* Baillet, Milik, and de Vaux, eds. *Les "petites grottes" de Qumrân.* DJD 3. (1962), pl. XXXVIII.
DSS Dead Sea Scrolls

APOSTOLIC FATHERS

FrgPol. *Fragments on Polycarp. ANF*
Ign. *Phld.* Ignatius of Antioch, *To the Philadelphians. ANF*
Mart. Pol. *Martyrdom of Polycarp. ANF*
Herm. *Sim.* Shepherd of Hermas, *Similitude. ANF*
Herm. *Vis.* Shepherd Hermas, *Vision. ANF*

ANCIENT SOURCES

Abr. Philo, *De Abrahamo, A Treatise on the Life of the Wise Man Made Perfect by Instruction or, On the Unwritten Law, That Is To Say, On Abraham*, LCL 289
Ag. Ap. Josephus, *Contra Apionem, Against Apion,* LCL 186
Anat. Admin. Galen. *De anatomicis administrationibus, On Anatomical Procedures* (trans. Singer 1956)
Ann. Tacitus, *Annales, Annals,* LCL 249, 312, 322
Ant. Josephus, *Antiquitates judaicae, Jewish Antiquities,* LCL 242, 281, 365, 410, 433, 456, 489
Arch. Vitruvius. *De architectura, The Ten Books on Architecture.* LCL 251, 280
Ascen. Isa. *Martyrdom and Ascension of Isaiah 6–11* (OTP)
Att. Cicero, *Epistulae ad Atticum, Letters to Atticus,* LCL 7
b. (before rabb. txt.) Babylonian Talmud, Rodkinson, ed. *New Edition of the Babylonian Talmud:*

	Original Text (1918)
b. Qidd.	Babylonian Talmud tractate *Qiddušin, Qiddushin*
b. Sem.	Babylonian Talmud tractate *Semahot, Semaḥot* or *Ebel Rabbati, Great Mouning,* Zlotnick (1966)
b. Yoma	Babylonian Talmud tractate *Yoma* (= *Kippurim*)
b. ʿErub.	Babylonian Talmud tractate, *ʿErubin, Eruvin*
Bacch.	Plautus. *Bacchides, The Two Bacchises.* LCL 60
Bell. civ.	Appian of Alexandria. *Bella civilia, Civil Wars.* LCL 5
Chron.	Pamphilus Eusebius, *Chronicon, Chronicle,* Fotheringham, ed. *The Bodleian Manuscript of Jerome's Version of the Chronicles of Eusebius* (2012)
Claud.	Suetonius, *Divus Claudius, The Deified Claudius,* LCL 38
Com.	Theodoret, *Haereticarum fabularum compendium, Compendium of Heretical Accounts* NPNF^2
Comm. Apoc.	Victorinus of Pettau, *Commentary on the Apocalypse,* Weinrich (2012); *ANF* 7
Comm. in Ep. Paul	Jerome. *Commentary on Epistles of Paul, NPNF*^{2}
Comm. Matt.	Origen of Alexandria, *Commentary on Matthew, ANF* 9
Congr.	Philo, *De congressueru ditionis gratia, On Mating with the Preliminary Studies* LCL 261
Cor.	Demosthenes, *De corona, On the Crown,* LCL 155
Ctes.	Aeschines, *In Ctesiphonem, Against Ctesiphon,* LCL 106
Curc.	Plautus, Titus Maccius. *Curculio.* LCL 61
Deipn.	Athenaeus. *Deipnosophistae, The Learned Banqueters.* LCL 204
Descr.	Pausanias. *Graeciae description, Description of Greece.* LCL 93, 188
Dig.	Ulpian, *Digest of Justinian* (ed. Watson, 1998)
Dom.	Suetonius, *Domitianus, Domitian,* LCL 38
DSS	Dead Sea Scrolls
Ep.	Pliny the Younger, *Epistulae, Letters,* LCL 59
Eph. Tale	Xenophon of Ephesus. *The Ephesian Tale of Anthia and Habrocomes.* LCL 69
Epig.	Martial, Marcus Valerius. *Epigrammata, Epigrams,* LCL 94, 480
Fam.	Cicero, *Epistulae ad familiares, Letters to Friends,* LCL 230
Flac.	Cicero, *Pro Flacco, Valerius Flaccus, In Defense of Lucius,* LCL 324
Geogr.	Strabo, *Geographica, Geography,* LCL 211, 223
Good Person	Philo, *Quod omnis probus liber sit, That Every Good Man Is Free* LCL 363
Haer.	Irenaeus, *Adversus haereses, Against Heresies, ANF* 1
Hell.	Xenophon, *Hellenica, Hellenic Writings,* LCL 88
Hist.	Herodotus, *Historiae, The Histories of the Persian Wars,* LCL 117, 119, 120
Hist.	Polybius, *Historiae, The Histories* or *The Rise of the Roman Empire,* LCL 161
Hist. eccl.	Pamphilus Eusebius, *Historia ecclesiastica, Ecclesiastical History, NPNF*^{2}; LCL 153, 265
Hist. Rom.	Dio Cassius, *Historia Romana, Roman History,* LCL 175, 176
Hom. Od.	Eustathius, Archbishop of Thessalinica. *Commentarii Ad Homeri Iliadem et Odysseam, Commentaries On Homer's Iliad and Odyssey* (4 vols. ed. Stallbaum, 1970)
Hypoth.	Philo, *Hypothetica, Hypothetical Discourse.* Under *Fragments of Lost Works.* Yonge (2007)
I.Eph.	*Die Inschriften von Ephesos, Inscriptions of Ephesus* (8 vols. ed. Wankel et al., 1979–1984)
I.Laod.	*Die Inschriften von Laodikeia am Lykos* (ed. Corsten, 1997)
I.Phil.	*Tituli Lydiae Linguis Graeca et Latina Conscripti: Fasciculus III, Philadelpheia et Ager Philadelphenus. TAM V,3.* (ed. Petzl, 2007)

I.Sard. — *Sardis: Greek and Latin Inscriptions* (eds. Buckler and Robinson, 1932).

I.Thyat. — Inscriptions from Thyatira, in *Tituli Lydiae Linguis. TAM V, 2.* (ed. Hermann 1989)

Icar. — Lucian of Samosata. *Icaromenippus, The Sky-man.* LCL 54

IG X 2.1 — *Inscriptiones graecae X: Inscriptiones Epiri, Macedoniae, Thraciae, Scythiae. Pars II, fasc. 1: Inscriptiones Thessalonicae et viciniae* (2 vols. ed. Edson, 1972)

IG XII 2 — *Inscriptiones graecae XII: Inscriptiones Insularum Maris Aegaei Praeter Delum: 2. Inscriptiones Lesbi, Nesi, Tenedi* (ed. Paton, 1899)

Il. — Homer, *Iliad,* LCL 171

J.W. — Josephus, *Bellum judaicum, Jewish War,* LCL 203, 210, 487

Laps. — Cyprian, *De lapsis, Concerning the Lapsed, ANF* 5

Legat. — Philo, *Legatio ad Gaium, On the Embassy to Gaius* (Yonge, trans. *The Works of Philo,* 2007); LCL 379

Lex. — Lucian of Samosata. *Lexiphanes.* LCL 302

Lib. Mem. — Ampelius, Lucius. *Liber Memorialis, Memorial Book* (trans. Assmann, 1935)

Luct. — Lucian, *De luctu, Funerals,* LCL 162

m. — *The Mishnah* (ed. Eugene J. Lipman)

m. Sanh. — *Mishnah* tractate *Sanhedrin*

Mart. Pionii — *Martyrdom of Pionius, The Acts of the Christian Martyrs* (ed. Musurillo, 1972)

Merc. cond. — Lucian of Samosata, *De mercede conductis, Salaried Posts in Great Houses,* LCL 130

Metam. — Apuleius, *Metamorphoses, The Golden Ass,* LCL 453

Metam. — Ovid, *Metamorphoses,* LCL 42

Mid. — *Talmud* tractate, *Middot*

Midr. — Rabbinic writing, *Midrash*

Mor. — Plutarch. *Moralia, Moral Essays.* LCL 245

Mos. — Philo, *De vita Mosis I, II, On the Life of Moses 1, 2,* Trans. Yonge, *The Works of Philo,* LCL 289

Nat. quaest. — Seneca, Lucius Annaeus. *Naturales Quaestiones, Natural Questions.* LCL 450

Nat. — Pliny the Elder, *Naturalis historia, Natural History,* LCL 330, 352, 370, 394, 418, 419

NPNF[1] — *Nicene and Post-Nicene Fathers, Series 1* (eds. Roberts et al. 14 vols. 1994)

NPNF[2] — *Nicene and Post-Nicene Fathers, Series 2* (eds. Roberts et al., 14 vols. 1994)

Oct. — Marcus Minucius Felix. *Octavius.* LCL 250

On. — Eusebius, *Onomasticon, On the Place-Names in the Holy Scripture,* Freeman-Grenville, and Taylor, eds. (2003) or Trans. Wolf

Orat. — Aelius Aristides. *Orations* (2 Vols. trans. Behr 1981, 1986)

P.Mich. — *Michigan Papyri,* Libellus of the Decian Persecution, Knipfing, trans. (1923)

P.Oxy. — *Oxyrhynchus Papyri,* Grenfell and Hunt, trans. 75 vols. (2009)

Paed. — Clement of Alexandria, *Paedagogus, Christ the Educator, ANF*

Pan. — Epiphanius of Salamis, *Panarion (Adversus haereses), Refutation of All Heresies,* Williams, trans. (1993)

Phil. — Cicero, *Orationes philippicae, Consisting of 14 tirades against Mark Anthony (Antonian Orations),* LCL 507

Pneum. — Heron of Alexandria. *Pneumatica* (Schmidt 1976)

Praec. ger. publ. — Plutarch. *Praecepta gerendae rei publicae, Precepts of Statecraft.* LCL 321

Praep. Ev. — Eusebius, *Praeparatio evangelica, Preparation for the Gospel.* Gifford (1981)

Praescr. — Tertullian, *De praescriptione haereticorum, Prescription against Heretics, ANF* 3

Prob. — Philo, *Quod omnis probus liber sit, Good Person That Every Good Person is Free,* LCL 363

Rab.	*Rabbah*, rabbinic writing usually on one of the books of the Pentateuch (i.e., *Genesis Rabbah*)
Resp.	Plato. *Respublica, Republic.* LCL 237
Rhod.	Dio Chrysostom, *Rhodiaca (Or. 31), To the People of Rhodes,* LCL 358
Rosc. Amer.	Cicero. *Pro Sexto Roscio Amerino, For Sextus Roscius of Ameria.* LCL 240
Rud.	Plautus. *Rudens, The Rope.* LCL 260
Sat.	Seneca Petronius, *Satyricon, Satyrica,* LCL 15
Siege	Aeneas Tacticus, *How to Survive under Siege. Aeneas Tacticus, Asclepiodotus, and Onasander.* LCL 156
Sifra	*Sipra,* The Halakic *Midrash* to Leviticus, Finkelstein
Silv.	Statius, *Silvae,* LCL 206
Somn. 1, 2	Philo, *De somniis I, II, On Dreams 1 and 2.* LCL 275
Strom.	Clement of Alexandria, *Stromata, Miscellanies or Patchwork, ANF* 2, *ANF* 1
t.	The *Talmudic* tractates of the *Tosefta,* Goldwurm and Scherman, eds. *Talmud.* 73 vols. Schottenstein Edition (1990)
Theog.	Hesiod. *Theogonia, Theogony.* LCL 57
Thuc.	Dionysius of Halicarnassus, *De Thucydide, On the Character of Thucydides,* LCL 465
Tim. Frag.	Theopompus. *Timaei Fragmenta* (Müller, 1841)
Top.	Theodosius, *De Situ Terrae Sanctae or Topografia, Topography of the Holy Land* (ed. Wilkinson, 2002)
Vir. ill.	Jerome, *De viris illustribus, On Illustrious Men,* Halton, ed. (1999)
Vit. Apoll.	Flavius Philostratus, *De Vita Apollonii, Life of Apollonius of Tyana,* LCL 16, 17
Vita	Josephus, *Vita, The Life,* LCL 186

MODERN SOURCES

§	section
AASOR	*The Annual of the American Schools of Oriental Research*
AB	The Anchor Bible
abbr.	abbreviation
ABD	*The Anchor Yale Bible Dictionary* (eds. Freedman et al., 1996)
ADAJ	*Annual of the Department of Antiquities of Jordan*
AE	*L'Année épigraphique* (Merlin, 1909–2010)
AEHL	*The Archaeological Encyclopedia of the Holy Land* (Negev, 3rd ed. 1996)
AESM	Archaeological Exploration of Sardis
AF	*Apostolic Fathers*
AGRW	*Associations in the Greco-Roman World* (eds. Ascough, Harland, and Kloppenborg, 2012)
AJA	*American Journal of Archaeology*
AJEC	Ancient Judaism and Early Christianity
ANE	ancient Near East
ANET	*The Ancient Near Eastern Texts Relating to the Old Testament* (ed. Pritchard, 1969)
ANEVT	ancient Near Eastern vassal treaties (treaty)
ANF	*The Ante-Nicene Fathers* (eds. Roberts et al., 10 vols, 1994)
ANRW	*Aufstieg und Niedergang der römischen Welt: Geschichte und Kultur Roms im Spiegel der neueren Forschung* (eds. Haase and Temporini, 1972–1995)

AS	*Anatolian Studies*
AUSS	*Andrews University Seminary Studies*
AYBC	*The Anchor Yale Bible Commentaries* (40 vols. eds. Freedman et al., 1996)
BA	*The Biblical Archaeologist*
BABesch	Bulletin antieke beschaving Supplement
BAFCS	Book of Acts in Its First-Century Setting Series
BAR	*Biblical Archaeology Review*
BARI	British Archaeological Reports International Series
BASOR	*Bulletin of the American Schools of Oriental Research*
BCH	*Bulletin de correspondance hellénique*
BDAG	*Greek-English Lexicon of the New Testament and Other Early Christian Literature.* (eds. Bauer, Danker, Arndt, and Gingrich)
BDB	*A Hebrew and English Lexicon of the Old Testament* (Briggs, Driver, and Brown, 1907)
BECNT	Baker Exegetical Commentary on the New Testament
BeD	Bâb edh-Dhrâʿ
BJRL	*Bulletin of the John Rylands University Library of Manchester*
BJS	*Brown Judaic Studies*
BN	*Biblische Notizen*
BRB	*Biblical Research Bulletin*
BrillPauly	*Brill's New Pauly, Antiquity Volumes Online* (22 vols. eds. Cancik, and Schneider. Trans. Salazar and Gentry, 2006)
BS	*Bible and Spade*
BSac	*Bibliotheca sacra*
Byz.	Byzantine
BZAW	*Beihefte zur Zeitschrift für die alttestamentliche Wissenschaft*
ca.	Lat. *circa*, "around, about."
cal BP	calibrated years before the present
CamCS	Cambridge Classical Studies
CBQ	*Catholic Biblical Quarterly*
CBR	*Currents in Biblical Research*
CCS	Cincinnati Classical Studies
cent.	century
ch.	chapter (s)
CIG	*Corpus Inscriptionum Graecarum* (4 vols. eds. Böeckh et al., 1828–1877)
CIIP	*Corpus Inscriptionum Iudaeae/Palaestinae: Vol. 2 Caesarea and the Middle Coast: Nos. 1121–2160* (eds. Ameling, et al. 7 vols., 2011)
CIJ	*Corpus inscriptionum judaricarum* (Frey, vol. 3, 1936)
CIL	*Corpus inscriptionum latinarum* (20 vols., ed., Mommsen, 1974)
CNG	Classical Numismatic Group, Inc. www.cngcoins.com
CNT	Commentary on the New Testament Series
CSNTM	The Center for the Study of New Testament Manuscripts
DBib	*Dictionary of the Bible* (eds. Hastings and Selbie, 1 vol. 1909)
DBib5	*A Dictionary of the Bible: Dealing with Its Language, Literature and Contents Including the Biblical Theology* (eds. Hastings and Selbie, 5 vols. 1911)

DGRA	*Dictionary of Greek and Roman Antiquities* (2 Vols, ed. Smith, Wayte, and Marindin, 1890–1891)
DJD	Discoveries in the Judaean Desert
DJG	*Dictionary of Jesus and the Gospels* (eds. Green, McKnight, and Marshall, 1992)
DNA	Deoxyribonucleic acid
DNTB	*Dictionary of New Testament Background: A Compendium of Contemporary Biblical Scholarship* (eds. Evans and Porter, 2000)
DOA	Department of Antiquities (Jordan
e.g.	exempli gratia, for example
EAEHL	*Encyclopedia of Archaeological Excavations in the Holy Land* (eds, Avi-Yonah and Stern, 3rd ed., 4 vols. 1996)
EB	Early Bronze
EBA	Early Bronze Age
EBC	The Expositor's Bible Commentary
ECAM	Early Christianity in Asia Minor
ed(s).	editor(s), edited by
EDB	*Eerdmans Dictionary of the Bible* (eds., Freedman, Myers, and Beck, 2000)
EDEJ	*The Eerdmans Dictionary of Early Judaism* (eds. Collins and Harlow, 2010)
EDSP	Expedition to the Dead Sea Plain
EDT	*Evangelical Dictionary of Theology* (ed. Elwell, 2001)
EJ	*Encyclopedia Judaica* (eds., Berenbaum and Skolnik, 2nd ed., 22 vols., 2006)
ESCJ	Studies in Christianity and Judaism/Études sur le christianisme et le judaïsme
ESV	English Standard Version
et al.	et alii, and others
etc.	et cetera, and the rest
ExpTim	*The Expository Times*
Fr.	French
ft.	feet
Ger.	German
GPR	Ground Pentrating Radar
GPS	Global Positioning System
Gr.	Greek
GTCEC	The Greek Testament: A Critical and Exegetical Commentary
Heb.	Hebrew
HNT	Handbuch zum neuen Testament
HTR	*Harvard Theological Review*
HTS	*Harvard Theological Studies*
i.e.	id est, that is
IAA	Israel Antiquities Authority
IEJ	*Israel Exploration Journal*
IGR	*Inscriptiones graecae ad res romanas pertinentes* (4 vols., eds. Lafaye, Toutain, Henry, and Cagnat, 1911–1927). Vol 1: (nos. 1–1518; ed. Cagnat, Toutain, and Jouguet, 1911); Vol 2: never published; Vol 3: ed. Cagnat and Lafaye, 1906); Vol. 4: Asia (nos. 1–1764; ed. Lafaye, 1927)
IGSK	Inschriften griechischer Städte aus Kleinasien

Int	*Interpretation*
ISBE2	*The International Standard Bible Encyclopedia* (ed., Bromiley, 4 vols., 1995).
JAC	Jahrbuch Für Antike Und Christentum
JBL	*Journal of Biblical Literature*
JDAI	Jahrbuch des kaiserlich-deutschen archäologischen Instituts
JE	*The Jewish Encyclopedia* (ed. Singer. 12 vols. 1906)
JEA	*The Journal of Egyptian Archaeology*
JETS	*Journal of the Evangelical Theological Society*
JJS	*Journal of Jewish Studies*
JNES	*Journal of Near Eastern Studies*
JÖAI	Jahreshefte des Österreichischen archäologischen Instituts
JPOS	*Journal of the Palestine Oriental Society*
JRA	*Journal of Roman Archaeology*
JRS	*The Journal of Roman Studies*
JSNT	*Journal for the Study of the New Testament*
JSNTSup	Journal for the Study of the New Testament: Supplement Series
JSOT	*Journal for the Study of the Old Testament*
JSQ	*Jewish Studies Quarterly*
JTS	*Journal of Theological Studies*
Kh.	Khirbet
KJV	King James Version
km	kilometer
KZNT	Kommentar Zum Neuen Testament
Lat.	Latin
LB	Late Bronze
LBA	Late Bronze Age
LCL	Loeb Classical Library
LEC	Library of early Christianity
loc. cit.	*loco citato,* in the place cited
LTQ	*Lexington Theological Quarterly*
LXX	The Septuagint (the Greek OT)
m	meter
MB	Middle Bronze
MBA	Middle Bronze Age
MNTC	The Moffatt New Testament Commentary
MT	Masoretic Text
NBD	*New Bible Dictionary* (eds., Marshall et al., 3rd ed., 1996)
NCB	New Century Bible Commentary
NCE	*The New Catholic Encyclopedia* (eds. Carson, 15 vols. 2003)
NDT	New Dictionary of Theology (eds. Wright, and Ferguson, 1988)
NEA	*Near Eastern Archaeology*
NEAEHL	*The New Encyclopedia of Archaeological Excavations in the Holy Land* (eds., Stern, Levinson-Gilboa, and Aviram, 4 vols., 1993)
NEASB	*Near East Archaeological Society Bulletin*

NewDocs	*New Documents Illustrating Early Christianity* (10 vols. eds. Horsley, and Llewelyn, 1981–2012)
NICNT	New International Commentary on the New Testament
NIDBA	*The New International Dictionary of Biblical Archaeology* (eds., Blaiklock and Harrison, 1983)
NIGTC	New International Greek Testament Commentary
NIV	New International Version
NovT	*Novum Testamentum*
NovTSup	Novum Testamentum Supplements
NPNF	*Nicene and Post-Nicene Fathers, Series II* (eds., Roberts et al., 14 vols., 1994)
NST	northern Sodom theory
NTC	New Testament Commentary
NTOA	Novum Testamentum et Orbis Antiquus
NTS	*New Testament Studies*
NumC	*Numismatic Chronicle*
NZ	*Numismatische Zeitschrift*
OCD	*The Oxford Classical Dictionary* (eds. Hornblower and Spawforth, 2003)
OEAGR	*The Oxford Encyclopedia of Ancient Greece and Rome* (7 vols. ed. Gagarin, 2010)
OEANE	*The Oxford Encyclopedia of Archaeology in the Near East* (ed., Meyers, 5 vols., 1997)
OGIS	*Orientis Graeci Inscriptiones Selectae, Supplementum Sylloges Inscriptionum Graecarum* (eds., Dittenberger et al., 4 vols., 1915)
OIM	Oriental Institute Museum, University of Chicago
op. cit.	*opere citato*, in the work cited
OSRE	Oxford Studies on the Roman Economy
𝔓	papyrus
P.Oxy.	Oxyrhynchus Papyri
PD	Public Domain
PECS	*The Princeton Encyclopedia of Classical Sites* (eds., Stillwell, MacDonald, and McAllister, 1976)
PEF	Palestine Exploration Fund
PEFSt	*Palestine Exploration Fund: Quarterly Statement*
PEQ	*Palestine Exploration Quarterly*
PHI	Packard Humanities Institute numbers for Greek inscriptions. Cornell University and Ohio State University. http://epigraphy.packhum.org/inscriptions
pls.	plates
rabb.	rabbinic
RB	*Revue Biblique*
RE Supp	Realencyklopädie für protestantische Theologie und Kirche Supplement
RevExp	*Review and Expositor*
RPC	*Roman Provincial Coinage* (9 Vol. ed. Burnett, 2003)
SEG	*Supplementum Epigraphicum Graecum* (eds. Chaniotis, et al. 23 vols. 1923)
SFSHJ	South Florida Studies in the History of Judaism
sic	"so, thus, in this manner" meaning the error was in the original
SIG	*Sylloge inscriptionum graecarum* (4 vols., ed. Dittenberger, 3rd ed. 1915–1924)
SJLA	Studies in Judaism in Late Antiquity
SNTS	Society for New Testament Studies Monograph Series

SST	southern Sodom theory
SUNT	Studien zur Umwelt des Neuen Testaments
TAD	*Türk Arkeoloji Dergisi*
TAM III	*Tituli Asiae Minoris, III* (Heberdey, 1941)
TAM V	*Titula Asiae Minoris, V* (Vol. 1, nos. 1-825; Vol. 2, nos. 826-1414, ed. Hermann 1989)
TB	*Tyndale Bulletin*
TDNT	*Theological Dictionary of the New Testament* (eds., Kittel and Friedrich, 10 vols., 1985)
TeH	Tall el-Ḥammâm or Tall al-Hammâm
TeHEP	Tall el-Ḥammâm Exploration Project
Tg.	Targum
TWOT	*Theological Wordbook of the Old Testament* (eds., Harris, Archer, Jr., and Waltke, 2 vols., 1980)
TynBul	*Tyndale Bulletin*
UF	*Ugarit Forschungen*
Vg.	Vulgate
VT	*Vetus Testamentum*
VTSup	*Supplements to Vetus Testamentum*
WBC	Word Biblical Commentary
WUNT	Wissenschaftliche Untersuchungen Zum Neuen Testament
ZDPV	*Zeitschrift des deutschen Palästina-Vereins*
ZECNT	Zondervan Exegetical Commentary on the New Testament
ZHB	*Zondervan Handbook to the Bible* (eds., Alexander and Alexander, 1999)
ZNW	*Zeitschrift für die neutestamentliche Wissenschaft und die Kunde der älteren Kirche*
ZPE	*Zeitschrift für Papyrologie und Epigraphik*
ZPEB	*Zondervan Pictorial Encyclopedia of the Bible* (eds., Tenney and Silva, 5 vols., 2009)

Intentionally Left Blank

Preface

We live in a time when an unprecedented number of excavations are happening in the Lands of the Bible, producing fascinating research and discoveries. Never before have so many new sites been opened and artifacts and inscriptions brought to the attention of the world. While there have been many exciting discoveries made in the past by famous archaeologists such as Petrie, Rawlinson, Layard, Woolley, Kenyon, and others, many new discoveries have surfaced in recent years that directly relate to the biblical text. These new discoveries needed a voice and venue to make them accessible to non-specialist students.

My interest in archaeology goes back over 35 years (1979) to my first archaeology course while a student at Ontario Bible College (now Tyndale University College and Seminary). Since that time I have had the privilege to teach archaeology in various settings to undergraduate students, travel through the lands of the Bible and visit firsthand many archaeological sites. In addition I have been working at Tall el-Ḥammâm, Jordan since 2009, uncovering artifacts in the Chalcolithic, Early Bronze, Middle Bronze, Iron Age and Roman Byzantine periods. During this time I closely followed, with interest, the new discoveries that have been made. What I observed is that, unfortunately, the modern media does not normally present the facts relevant to new archaeological discoveries of the Bible, and "revisionist" scholars seek to undermine and downplay the relevance of many of the discoveries. For the minimalists, Sodom never existed, the Exodus never happened, Jericho never fell to the Israelites, and David was never a great king. But so often the archaeological material essential for a meaningful dialogue over the reliability of the Bible is confined to academic journals and conference papers. While there are many good older works on biblical archaeology available on the market, few dealt with both the Old and New Testament together in one volume, with an introduction to archaeological methods, a concise history of archaeology, descriptions of the manuscripts, and the recent archaeological discovery and finds. For students just being introduced to archaeology, all of these elements are important and necessary for a good grasp of biblical archaeology. Thus, this book was born out of necessity and a desire to deliver an accessible single-volume work for approaching up-to-date research in biblical archaeology.

The discoveries of the last 20 years, presented in this work, are not meant to be an exhaustive treatment of the subject, nor presented as a technical discussion and the final conclusion of archaeological research. As with all archaeological investigations, many of the conclusions are ongoing. However, they are presented here in a summary introduction for undergraduate students to appreciate the availability of relevant discoveries and some of the possible implications for understanding the biblical text. Some of the most significant and promising finds have been selected to demonstrate the historical reliability of the people and events of the Bible. This work is intended to fill the void in providing an accessible and collective work on the subject of biblical archaeology and the reliability of the Bible.

The advantage of such a text is that it provides a collective source of material for students that would otherwise take a long time to assemble or be inaccessible. Of help for the student are 140 photographs, charts, timelines, maps, and a glossary, which will facilitate the difficult task of understanding the unfamiliar lands of the Bible. Numerous footnotes and an academic bibliography are provided to give students the tools for doing further research. It is my hope that those who use this work will find it useful and develop a love and passion, like the author, for the fascinating field of biblical archaeology. Students can read the Bible with confidence that the details of its geography and facts are accurate and be encouraged in their faith that the Bible is reliable.

The archaeolgocial dates (i.e., EB1, IB1, MB2, or LB2A) represented in the New Chronology (see Chart 1 and 2) will be used throughout the work, although the old dating system (i.e., EB I, EB IV, MB II, etc) will be used when dealing with works that refer to the older dating system.

The artifacts listed in Charts 1-8 are dealt with in *Biblical Archaeology: Famous Discoveries That Support the Reliability of the Bible*. Vol. 2. Toronto, Can.: Electronic Christian Media, 2015. Chart 2 is dealt with in *The Location of Sodom: Key Facts for Navigating the Maze of Arguments for the Location of the Cities of the Plain*. Toronto, Ont.: Electronic Christian Media, 2016.

The online *Biblical Archaeology* companion website is free for everyone and accessible through this link http://biblicalarchaeologygraves.blogspot.com. The website provides photos from the book, enlarged and in color, external web links, and an extended bibliography for research, along with additional bonus material that could not be put into the book due to space limitations and to keep the cost down for students.

David E. Graves, PhD
Toronto, Canada
February 10, 2014

Preface to Second Edition

While the Bible does not change, the same cannot be said for archaeological finds. There is a continual release of archaeolgical information each year that demands the need to update the discoveries for the public in a format that is both informative and understandable. Thus, this second edition was completed to provide the most up-to-date archaeological material and also make the material available in both black and white and color. The layout has been refreshed using a single column and many new images were added. It is the hope and prayer of the author that those who read these discoveries would be blessed and encouraged in their faith and that know that the Bible is historically accurate so they can better understand what is being said.

David E. Graves, PhD
Toronto, Canada
January 17, 2018

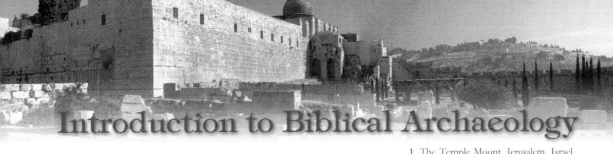

Introduction to Biblical Archaeology

1. The Temple Mount, Jerusalem, Israel. Excavations on the SE corner of the Temple Mount have revealed stonework, which may date back to the time of Zerubbabel, who led the first group to return from exile and started to rebuild the temple.

Photo by B. Crawford/Wikimedia Commons

This book is about archaeology and its contribution to our understanding of the Bible. The word "archaeology" conjures up many romantic images of what this discipline is all about. The Hollywood-inspired image of Indiana Jones is often what comes to mind; but this is far from reality!

I once asked a family: "What's the different between me and Indiana Jones? They all thought for a moment and then one young boy spoke up and said.... "you don't carry a gun". While it is true that archaeologists do not need to carry a gun, they often do have armed tourist police present on site, especially if they are working in the Middle East. The answer to the question however is Jones worked alone (although usually with a beautiful lady), while we work as a team. Nevertheless, we all wear hats like Jones to be protected from the hot sun!

Because there are many misconceptions about archaeology and archaeologists, this introduction will provide a basic overview of the discipline and lay a foundation for the discoveries to follow in the remaining chapters.

Assumptions

This book rests on four assumptions:

1. History is Reliable

This material is presented from a Judeo-Christian worldview and assumes that the Scriptures of both the Old and New Testaments (OT/NT) are historically true and reliable.[1] While it is possible to misunderstand the meaning of the text, this is an issue with our interpretation and not with the objective facts in the text.

2. Pluralistic Audience

This material also assumes that the readers have come from a variety of faith backgrounds and experiences. As such, material is presented with respect for other positions.

3. Selective Scope

It should be understood that not all recent excavations and discoveries are listed here. Those selected are intentional and generally from the last 15-20 years. Many earlier discoveries, while sometimes mentioned, can be examined in more detail in other standard works[2] and in *Biblical*

---

[1] Craig L. Blomberg, *Making Sense of the New Testament: Three Crucial Questions* (Grand Rapids: Baker Academic, 2004), 17; James E. Taylor, *Introducing Apologetics: Cultivating Christian Commitment* (Grand Rapids: Baker Academic, 2006), 174.

[2] G. Ernest Wright, *Biblical Archaeology*, Abridged (Philadelphia, PA: Westminster, 1960); Merrill F. Unger, *Archaeology and the Old Testament* (Grand Rapids: Zondervan, 1954); Merrill F. Unger, *Archaeology and the New Testament* (Grand Rapids: Zondervan, 1975); Edwin M Yamauchi, *The Archaeology of New Testament Cities in Western Asia Minor* (Grand Rapids: Baker, 1980); J. Randall Price and H. Wayne House, *Zondervan Handbook of Biblical Archaeology: A Book by Book Guide to Archaeological Discoveries Related to the Bible* (Grand Rapids: Zondervan, 2018); John McRay, *Archaeology and the New Testament* (Grand Rapids: Baker, 1991); Amihai Mazar, *Archaeology of the Land of the Bible: 10,000-586 B.C.E.*, vol. 1, The Anchor Yale Bible Reference Library (New Haven, CT: Yale University Press, 1992); Alfred J. Hoerth, *Archaeology and the Old Testament* (Grand Rapids: Baker, 1999).

Archaeology Vol. 2.[3]

4. Unable to Please Everyone

The assumption is made that not everyone will agree with everything written in this book or with the choice of selected sites. We may personally find some of the opinions that we encounter objectionable and offensive. Because neutrality is a myth (see *Fallacy of Neutrality)* and many have differing opinions on various subjects and none of us agrees with everyone, it is important to have tolerance for one another (see *Tolerance* below).

DEFINITION OF BIBLICAL ARCHAEOLOGY

The term "archaeology" comes from two Greek words: *arkhaios* (ἀρχαῖος) meaning old or ancient + *logos* (λόγος) meaning word, speech, or study. Thus, the Greek word *archaiologia* (ἀρχαιολογία) means the study of the material culture of past civilizations.[4] Definitions of archaeology may vary depending the presuppositions and goals of a particular archaeologist.[5]

While the Greek term is used by Plato (about Lacedaemonians), Thucydides (about Greece), Dionysius of Halicarnassus (about Rome), and Josephus (about Jews), it appears in English for the first time in 1607, when it is used by Bishop Hall of Norwick.

Classical Archaeology generally involves the classical sites around the Mediterranean Sea, while Near East Archaeology deals with sites in the Middle East. The term "Biblical Archaeology," while challenged by some,[6] is the discipline involved with biblical sites from these two regions. Dever prefers the term "Syro-Palestinian archaeology,"[7] although he is still not sure what to call it.[8] Amihai Mazar professor at the Institute of Archaeology of the Hebrew University of Jerusalem, responds that:

> "Biblical archaeology" is still a justified term for this field of inquiry. Whatever term will be used for defining the discipline, the archaeology of Palestine and that of the related countries are unique and ever increasing resources for reconstructing the social, environmental, and cultural background from which the Hebrew Bible emerged. Thus biblical archaeology, like many branches of knowledge, lends itself to changes and new contents.[9]

As Hoffmeier and Millard pointed out: "Biblical archaeology is interdisciplinary in nature, and thus is not Syro-Palestinian archaeology, nor Assyriology, nor a branch of such fields. Rather, its focus is on the times and places, the physical remains and written documents from across the Near East that relate to the biblical text either as background and context or by more direct contact."[10]

---

[3] David E. Graves, *Biblical Archaeology: Famous Discoveries That Support the Reliability of the Bible*, vol. 2 (Toronto, Can.: Electronic Christian Media, 2015).

[4] Catherine Soanes and Angus Stevenson, *Concise Oxford English Dictionary*, 11th ed. (Oxford: Oxford University Press, 2005), s.v.

[5] Guy E. Gibbon, *Critically Reading the Theory and Methods of Archaeology: An Introductory Guide* (Lanham, MD: AltaMira, 2014), 7–9.

[6] In 1999 after 60 years the American Schools of Oriental Research (ASOR) replaced the name of its journal *Biblical Archaeologist*, with the new title *Near Eastern Archaeology*.

[7] William G. Dever, "The Impact of the 'New Archaeology' on Syro-Palestinian Archaeology," *Bulletin of the American Schools of Oriental Research*, no. 242 (April 1, 1981): 15–29; "Retrospects and Prospects in Biblical and Syro-Palestinian Archeology," *BA* 45, no. 2 (April 1, 1982): 103; "Syro-Palestinian and Biblical Archaeology Ca. 1945–1980," in *The Hebrew Bible and Its Modern Interpreters*, ed. Douglas A. Knight and Gene M. Tucker (Chicago, IL: Scholars Press, 1985), 31–74; *What Did the Biblical Writers Know, and When Did They Know It?* (Grand Rapids: Eerdmans, 2001), 61–62.

[8] William G. Dever, "Whatchmacallit: Why It's So Hard to Name Our Field," *BAR* 29, no. 4 (2003): 56–61.

[9] Mazar, *Archaeology of the Land of the Bible*, 1:32–33.

[10] James Karl Hoffmeier and Alan R. Millard, eds., *The Future of Biblical Archaeology: Reassessing Methodologies and Assumptions*, The Proceedings of a Symposium, August 12-14, 2001 at Trinity International University (Grand Rapids: Eerdmans, 2004), xi.

McRay, retired professor of NT at Wheaton College Graduate School, agrees and points out that: "We must also bear in mind that "biblical archaeology" does not have reference to an independent discipline nor to a methodology peculiar to the Bible. Like classical archaeology, biblical archaeology exists not as a separate discipline, but as a field of inquiry within the general discipline of archaeology."[11]

It is not merely about pottery and digging but seeks to retrace man's footsteps into the past and recognize and understand the intersection of turf and text. The prominent biblical archaeologist and late Harvard professor, G. Ernest Wright, observed:

> Biblical archaeology is a special 'armchair' variety of general archaeology. The Biblical Archaeologist may or may not be an archaeologist himself, but he studies the discoveries of the excavations in order to glean from every fact that throws a direct, indirect or even diffused light upon the Bible. He must be intelligently concerned with stratigraphy and typology, upon which the methodology of modern archaeology rests. . . .Yet his chief concern is not with methods or pots or weapons in themselves alone. His central and absorbing interest is the understanding and exposition of the Scriptures. The intensive study of the Biblical archaeologist is thus the fruit of the vital concern for history which the Bible has instilled in us. We cannot, therefore, assume that the knowledge of Biblical history is unessential to the faith. Biblical theology and Biblical archaeology must go hand in hand, if we are to comprehend the Bible's meaning.[12]

SHORT HISTORY OF BIBLICAL ARCHAEOLOGY

Archaeology is a relatively new discipline, which slowly developed over the past 250 years. Fascination with the past has intrigued people throughout the centuries (i.e., Nabonidus [556-539 BC]; Herodotus [*ca.* 484-425 BC]; Berosus, a Babylonian priest [340-278 BC]; Manetho, an Egyptian priest; Eusebius *Onomasticon*; and Josephus [37-100 AD]).

Antiquarians

The early antiquarians of the seventeenth century, looking for hidden treasures, were more treasure hunters, looters and grave-robbers rather than what we might consider "archaeologists" in the true scientific sense. Perhaps the first real scientific excavation was at Herculaneum in 1738, under the direction of Rocque Joaquin de Alcubierre (Spanish) and Marcello di Venuti (Italian), closely followed by Pompeii in 1748 when it was properly identified with what the locals called *la Civita* ("the city"). It was identified by the German antiquarian Lucas Holstenius and Karl Jakob Weber, who supervised the excavations from 1750 to 1765.[13]

Nationalism

Following these important excavations, the British established the Society of Antiquities in 1751 to promote artifacts through their journal, a monthly publication. The British Museum (London) was founded in 1753-59 from the private collection of Sir Hans Sloane and charged an entrance fee. Shortly after, in 1793, the Louvre (Paris) was founded, but with a new twist: the public were admitted free (today the reverse is the case for both). Museums that began with their private

---

[11] McRay, *Archaeology and the NT*, 20.

[12] Wright, *Biblical Archaeology*, 17. For his latest view on biblical archaeology see "The 'New' Archaeology," *Biblical Archaeologist* 38, no. 3–4 (September 1, 1975): 104–15.

[13] Niccolò Marcello marchese Venuti, *A Description of the First Discoveries of the Ancient City of Heraclea*, trans. Wickes Skurray (London: Baldwin, 1750); Christopher Charles Parslow, *Rediscovering Antiquity: Karl Weber and the Excavation of Herculaneum, Pompeii and Stabiae* (Cambridge: Cambridge University Press, 1998), 19; Lale Özgenel, "A Tale of Two Cities: In Search of Ancient Pompeii and Herculaneum," *Middle East Technical University Journal of the Faculty of Architecture METU JFA* 2008, no. 25 (1-25): 8; Alfred Hoerth and John McRay, *Bible Archaeology: An Exploration of the History and Culture of Early Civilizations* (Grand Rapids: Baker, 2006), 12.

collections were now propelled by a strong spirit of nationalism to fill their museums with grander show pieces.

2. The Rosetta Stone.
British Museum (EA 24).
© Hans Hillewaert / Wikimedia Commons

Rosetta Stone

The discovery of the large Rosetta[14] Stone by Boussard–one of Napoleon's soldiers–in 1799 was the key to the decipherment of Egyptian hieroglyphics. The stone was moved to Cairo, where Napoleon had it copied, but when the French surrendered Egypt to the British in 1801, the Rosetta stone also passed into British hands and is presently exhibited in the British Museum.[15] Some consider this the beginning of scientific archaeology,[16] others not. Irrespective, it was certainly a momentous breakthrough for archaeology.

The tablet contained two languages: Egyptian Hieroglyphic, (top 14 lines) with an Egyptian shorthand script called Demotic (Gr. "people of the town", middle 32 lines), and Koine Greek (bottom 54 lines) which makes the script bilingual and not trilingual. Scholars could read the Greek and thus decipher the Egyptian and Demotic.

3. Nineteenth cent. oil portrait by Leon Cogniet of Jean-François Champollion (1831).
Wikimedia Coomons

The first attempts to decipher the scripts from the stone before 1800 were unsuccessful, as the pictures were believed to be composed of mystic symbols. In 1802 some progress was made by the French scholar A. I. Silvestre de Sacy and the Swedish diplomat, Jean David Akerblad, when they identified a number of proper names in the Demotic text by comparing it with the Greek.[17]

Further work was carried out by Thomas Young, an accomplished linguist, who discovered that the royal names were written within ovals called cartouches, and worked out from these a phonetic alphabet. In 1814, he established the way in which the birds and animals in the pictorial script faced. Difficulty came when he failed to recognise that the Demotic and Hieroglyphic were paraphrases and not literal translations. As a result, not all of the characters lined up

[14] It is named after the town of Rosetta, Rashid in the delta region of Egypt where it was discovered.

[15] E. A. Wallis Budge, *Rosetta Stone in the British Museum* (Whitefish, MT: Kessinger, 2003), 44.

[16] Richard S. Hess, "Archaeology," in *Zondervan Pictorial Encyclopaedia of the Bible*, ed. Merrill C. Tenney and Moisés Silva, Revised, Full-Color Edition, vol. 1 (Grand Rapids: Zondervan, 2009), 300; J. Randall Price, *The Stones Cry Out: What Archaeology Reveals About the Truth of the Bible* (Eugene, OR: Harvest House, 1997), 26. The Italian excavations at the Bay of Naples, Pompeii, Herculaneum and Stabiae were approximately fifty years earlier.

[17] J. D. Ray, *The Rosetta Stone and the Rebirth of Ancient Egypt* (Cambridge, MA: Harvard University Press, 2007), 98.

4. From a German edition of Austen Layard's *A Popular Account of Discoveries at Nineveh*. The image depicts the transport of the human headed winged bull at Nimrod.

Wikimedia Coomons / colorized by David E. Graves

equally.[18]

Jean-François Champollion (1790–1832) continued the work with the discovery that the hieroglyphic text was the translation of the Greek, not the reverse as had been thought. On September 17, 1822 Champollion read his *Lettre a M. Dacier* and exhibited his "Hieroglyphic Alphabet", with its Greek and Demotic equivalents, before the Academy of Inscriptions in Paris. He further developed his system in a series of memoirs called *Precis du systeme hieroglyphique des anciens Egyptiens*, which he read in the Academy of Inscriptions in 1823. Champollion was assisted in his work when he had the opportunity to travel to Egypt and copy 2,000 pages of inscriptions in his own hand writing. Working from his meagre alphabet and skillfully applying his knowledge of Coptic and of the Rosetta stone, he successfully deciphered them.[19]

Until 1822, Egyptian history, as derived from inscriptions on the walls of tombs and tablets, lay silent in a mystical sequence of fascinating pictures. The brilliant work of Champollion and others with the Rosetta stone opened the way into 3,000 years of written Egyptian history, essential for the study of the humanities and biblical studies.[20] The true significance of the Rosetta Stone cannot be determined by the message inscribed upon it but rather in the use of the letters to decipher other Egyptian hieroglyphic documents.

Filling Museums

The demand for museum antiquities might be seen as the origin of a new wave of treasure hunters which brought the Elgin Marbles from the Parthenon to the British Museum during the

[18] R. B. Parkinson *et al.*, *Cracking Codes: The Rosetta Stone and Decipherment* (Berkeley: University of California Press, 1999), 33.

[19] Henry Salt, Jean-François Champollion, and Thomas Young, *Essay on Dr. Young's and M. Champollion's Phonetic System of Hieroglyphics: With Some Additional Discoveries* (London: Londman, Hurst, Rees, Orme, Brown & Green, 1823), 7 ff.; Parkinson *et al.*, *Cracking Codes*, 35.

[20] Ray, *The Rosetta Stone and the Rebirth of Ancient Egypt*, 142–45.

5. Sir Austen Henry Layard (1817–1894), oil on canvas.

Wikimedia Commons

years 1803–1812. Lord Elgin (Thomas Bruce, British Ambassador to the Sultan in Istanbul) saved the Marbles from being burned for lime, to his everlasting credit, though he has since been condemned for theft and destruction of part of the edifice.[21]

Mesopotamian Expeditions

Expeditions were also dispatched to Mesopotamia around this time. In 1817 Henry Salt, the British Consul-General to Egypt, hired the Italian engineer Giovanni Battista Belzoni (1778–1823) to collect antiquities for the British Museum. And his exploits were successful, floating the colossal 7.25 ton stone bust of Ramesses II (1270 BC) down the Nile to the British Museum.

The French sent Paul-Émile Botta (1802–1870), Eugene Napoleon Flandin (1809–1876), and Victor Place (1822–1875), to Khorsabad in Iraq on behalf of the Louvre in Paris, to fill it with treasures from the Assyrian capital of king Sargon II (see image on front cover).[22] Two of these expeditions in 1855 had the unfortunate experience of losing a boatload of 308 cases of sculptures to the bottom of the Tigris River.[23] Not to be outdone, the British dispatched Sir Austin Henry Layard (1817–1894; see Fig. 5) to Nineveh in Iraq to collect monuments from the reign of Ashurnasirpal II with greater success than the French.[24] He is credited with the recovery of a statue of Ashurnasirpal II; the Black Obelisk of Shalmaneser III (1846; see Fig. 71); the *Gilgamesh* and *Atrahasis Epics* (which recount a Babylonian creation and flood story); the *Enuma Elish* (a creation epic); and the Lachish Reliefs, just to name a few of his achievements.

Deciphering the Tablets

Many of the early archaeologists were working at the European consuls in the remote locations of Baghdad and Mosul in Mesopotamia.[25] Claudius James Rich (1787–1821) was the first British

---

[21] John Romer, *The History of Archaeology: Great Excavations of the World* (New York: Checkmark, 2001), 72–73; William St Clair, *Lord Elgin and the Marbles: The Controversial History of the Parthenon Sculptures*, 3rd ed. (Oxford: Oxford University Press, 1998); Marc Fehlmann, "Casts & Connoisseurs: The Early Reception of the Elgin Marbles," *Apollo* 165, no. 544 (June 2007): 44–51; Christopher Casey, "'Grecian Grandeurs and the Rude Wasting of Old Time': Britain, the Elgin Marbles, and Post-Revolutionary Hellenism," *Foundation* 3, no. 1 (2008): 31–64; Dana Facaros and Linda Theodorou, *Greece*, Country & Regional Guides - Cadogan (London: Cadogan Guides, 2003), 55.

[22] Paul-Émile Botta and Étienne Flandin, *Monument de Ninive découvert et décrit par M. P.-É. Botta, mesuré et dessiné par M. E. Flandin...* (Paris: Impr. nationale, 1849).

[23] Henry O. Thompson, *Biblical Archaeology: The World, the Mediterranean, the Bible* (New York: Paragon, 1987), 61.

[24] Austen Henry Layard, "Nineveh and Its Remains," *The Southern Quarterly Review* 16, no. 31 (1849): 1–31; *Nineveh and Its Remains: A Narrative of an Expedition to Assyria During the Years 1845, 1846 and 1847* (London: J. Murray, 1867); *The Monuments of Nineveh: From Drawings Made on the Spot* (Piscataway, NJ: Gorgias, 2004); Mogens Trolle Larsen, *The Conquest of Assyria: Excavations in an Antique Land* (New York: Routledge, 1996); Frederick N. Bohrer, "Layard, Austen Henry," in *OEANE*, ed. Eric M. Meyers, vol. 3, 5 vols. (Oxford: Oxford Biblical Studies Online, 1997), n.p., http://www.oxfordbiblicalstudies.com/article/opr/t256/e621; Frederic J. Goldsmid, "Obituary: The Right Honourable Sir Henry Austen Layard, G. C. B.," *The Geographical Journal* 4, no. 4 (October 1, 1894): 370–73.

[25] Brian M. Fagan, *Return to Babylon: Travelers, Archaeologists and Monuments in Mesopotamia* (Boston, MA: Little, Brown & Co., 1979), 8.

6. Sir Henry Creswicke Rawlinson.

Photo by Lock & Whitfield. Wellcome Library, London/Wikimedia Commons

consul at Baghdad and in 1811 he mapped and excavated part of Babylon.[26] It was Rich who introduced his successor, Sir Henry Creswicke Rawlinson (1810–1895; see Fig. 6), to the complexities of cuneiform script.[27] Thus amid the plundering of ancient sites, during Rawlinson days off (1837), he would travel to the remote site, and with the help of a Kurdish boy, he was able to reach an inaccessible inscription and take a paper mache cast, from which he deciphered (1842) the mysterious trilingual cuneiform Persian inscriptions of the Behistun Relief of Darius I.[28] This has been compared to the achievement of breaking the code of the Rosetta Stone. Now the world of cuneiform texts in the Old Persian language was made available to scholars. It would not be long before the ancient Elamite and Akkadian languages would be deciphered, making available some 500,000 stone and clay tablets of the Assyrian and Babylonian kingdoms.[29]

As Fagan points out: "The early archaeologists had to pursue their work in the midst of constant political change, of emerging Iraqi nationalism and eventual political independence…The heroic days of Mesopotamian archaeology are gone forever, but their passing, however nostalgically regarded, only benefited serious scholarship: the pioneers often did irrevocable damage with their picks and huge gangs of workmen."[30]

Palestine Surveys

Since the region of Palestine (modern Israel, Jordan, and Syria) was missing significant monuments for the museum race, the London based Palestine Exploration Fund (PEF)[31] dispatched British military officers, Charles Wilson (1836–1905), Charles Warren (1840–1927), Claude R. Conder (1848–1910), and Horatio Herbert Kitchener (1850–1916) to carry out geographic surveys of the region. German (Ulrich Seetzen and Johan Ludwig Burckhardt) and American (Edward Robinson and Eli Smith) scholars were also involved.[32] Levy points out that: "Condor and Kitchener's geographical survey of Western Palestine, started in 1872, recorded more than 10,000 sites. The survey was published in seven volumes, together with a giant map covering an area of some 6,000 square miles. It remained the basis of all topographic maps down

[26] Claudius James Rich, *Narrative of a Journey to the Site of Babylon in 1811* (London: Duncan & Malcolm, 1839).

[27] Fagan, *Return to Babylon*, 9.

[28] Henry C. Rawlinson, *The Persian Cuneiform Inscription at Behistun, Decyphered and Translated; With a Memoir on Persian Cuneiform Inscriptions in General, and on That of Behistun in Particular* (Journal of the Royal Asiatic Society of Great Britain and Ireland, 1848); Edward E. Salisbury, "Colonel Rawlinson's Outlines of Assyrian History, Derived from His Latest Readings of Cuneiform Inscriptions," *Journal of the American Oriental Society* 3 (January 1, 1853): 486–90.

[29] Hoerth and McRay, *Bible Archaeology*, 14.

[30] Fagan, *Return to Babylon*, 4.

[31] http://www.pef.org.uk/history/

[32] John James Moscrop, *Measuring Jerusalem: The Palestine Exploration Fund and British Interests in the Holy Land* (London: Leicester University Press, 2000), 1–5.

7. Portrait of Sir Flinders Petrie *ca.* 1930's.
Wikimedia Commons

to the establishment of the state of Israel in 1948."[33]

Some excavations in Palestine were carried out by F. de Saulcy, Charles Clermont (both French) and Charles Warren (British officer in the Royal Engineers), but their excavation techniques would be considered unscientific compared with modern procedures and had no way to determine dating.

Development of Egyptian Controversy

In 1858 the Egyptians created a new position for the Frenchman Auguste Mariette (1821–1881) of "Conservator of Egyptian Monuments," and he quickly created an unpopular policy that only France could excavate in Egypt.

By 1860, Mariette had set up some 35 new dig sites, but his methods were not without their critics.[34] Sir William Matthew Flinders Petrie (1853–1942; see Fig. 7), the famous Egyptologist,[35] who was living and working in Egypt at the time, criticized Mariette's work and stated: "Nothing was done with any uniform plan, work is begun and left unfinished, no regard is paid to future requirements of exploration and no civilized or labor-saving appliances are used. It is sickening to see the rate at which everything is being destroyed, and the little regard paid to preservation."[36]

Petrie was one of a kind and rather excentric, as Thompson points out: "He never went to school because of chronic asthma. Yet he was professor of Egyptology of University College, London, for forty-one years (1892–1933) and was knighted in 1923....A highly controversial figure in retrospect, he has been called a quiet little man who spent his first two years in Egypt living in a tomb."[37]

When he was eight years old he set out his theory of digging, "the earth ought to be pared away inch by inch to see all that is in it and how it lies."[38] He set in motion the predominant method of archaeological procedure that was followed by many of the great archaeologist after him.

Although Petrie was not without his critics,[39] he laid the foundation for the scientific use of stratigraphy earning him the nick name of " Father of pots"[40] and the distinguished title of

---

[33] Thomas E. Levy, "From Camels to Computers: A Short History of Archaeological Method," *BAR* 22, no. 4 (1995): 44–45.

[34] Auguste Mariette and Alphonse Mariette, *The Monuments of Upper Egypt, a Translation of the "Itinéraire de La Haute Égypte", of Auguste Mariette-Bey* (Cairo: A. Mourès, 1877); Auguste Mariette, *Catalogue général des monuments d'Abydos découverts pendant les fouilles de cette ville* (Paris: L'Impr. nationale, 1880); Brian Fagan, *The Rape of the Nile: Tomb Robbers, Tourists, and Archaeologists in Egypt*, Revised and Updated (New York: Basic Books, 2009), 191–204.

[35] Margaret S. Drower, *Flinders Petrie: A Life in Archaeology* (Madison, Wisc.: University of Wisconsin Press, 1995).

[36] Robert Silverberg, *Great Adventures in Archaeology* (Lincoln, Neb.: University of Nebraska Press, 1964), 34.

[37] Thompson, *Biblical Archaeology*, 86.

[38] Silverberg, *Great Adventures in Archaeology*, 34.

[39] G. I. Davies, "British Archaeologists," in *Benchmarks in Time and Culture: An Introduction to Palestinian Archaeology*, ed. Joel F. Drinkard, Gerald L. Mattingly, and J. Maxwell Miller, ASOR/SBL Archaeology And Biblical Studies (Atlanta, Ga.: Scholars Press, 1988), 49; Mortimer Wheeler, *Archaeology From The Earth* (New Delhi, India: Munshiram Manoharlal, 2004), 29–34.

[40] Drower, *Flinders Petrie*, 91.

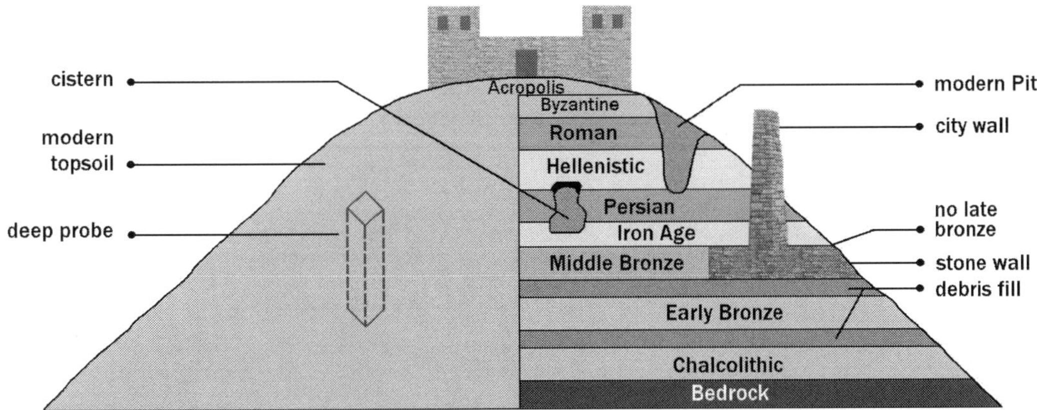

8. Typical stratigraphy of a Tell. The well or cistern is dug in the Hellenistic period and penetrates the previous Persian and Iron Age periods. When features are cut into previous periods, like digging modern pits, graves or foundations, this can make reading the pottery difficult, as there can be later pottery down in earlier strata. Sometimes a probe is used to get a sense of what periods lie below the surface.

the "Father of Modern Egyptology."[41]

Petrie and Stratigraphy

In 1890, while working at Tel el-Hesi (Palestine), Petrie, "ushered in the era of modern scientific archaeology"[42] by employing his new theory of stratigraphy. Petrie predicted: "If I do nothing else, I shall at least have established a scale of pottery which will enable any future explorer to date all the tells and khirbets,"[43] and then, after just six weeks of excavation, he found that he had accomplished his goal. His method, sometimes called "sequence dating" (S.D.),[44] is simply the observation that, like a layer cake, the top levels or strata, with their artifacts, are the most recent periods while the lower strata contain the earlier periods (see Fig. 8). But it must be remembered that not all strata are to be found at the same depth, so each stata must be carefully examined and dated. In addition, pottery types can be compared between sites to cross reference the dates and occupation.

Hoerth described the process best when he explained that Petrie:

> observed that each layer in the tell contained its own unique type of ceramic pottery. By carefully recording the pottery in each layer one could observe the changes in cultural occupation. He saw that some of the pottery had different forms, which he recognized from his work in Egypt. There he had found similar pottery in contexts which could be dated from inscriptions found at the levels in which the pottery was discovered.[45]

William F. Albright further developed and refined Petrie's methods while working at Tell

[41] Okasha El Daly, *Egyptology: The Missing Millennium. Ancient Egypt in Medieval Arabic Writings* (London: Cavendish, 2005), 12.

[42] Shlomo Bunimovitz, "How Mute Stones Speak, Interpreting What We Dig Up," *BAR* 21, no. 2 (1995): 60.

[43] Thomas W. Davis, *Shifting Sands: The Rise and Fall of Biblical Archaeology: The Rise and Fall of Biblical Archaeology* (Oxford: Oxford University Press, 2004), 29.

[44] Colin Renfrew and Paul G. Bahn, *Archaeology: Theories, Methods, and Practice*, 6th ed. (New York: Thames & Hudson, 2012), 122.

[45] Hoerth and McRay, *Bible Archaeology*, 15.

9. The author, standing in front of a cut-away section of the city wall at Tall el-Ḥammâm, in season 1 (2006) exposing the stratigraphy of the tall. The military cut a road through the wall and exposed this cross section, which was later clarified. At his feet is the location of a 0.5 m (1.6 ft.) thick MB burn layer in the mudbrick section of the city wall (Sodom?), dated by a MB handle (inset photo) at the same location. The IA stone wall was built over the earlier burned MB mudbrick wall.

Beit Mirsim (1926–1932).[46] Today the work of refining the methods of Petrie and Albright continues.[47] While the chronological evolution is clearly evident in all types of pottery, perhaps

[46] William F. Albright, *The Excavation of Tell Beit Mirsim in Palestine, Vol. 1, The Pottery of the First Three Campaigns*, AASOR 12 (Cambridge, MA: American Schools of Oriental Research, 1932); "New Light from Egypt on the Chronology and History of Israel and Judah," *BASOR* 130 (April 1, 1953): 4–11.

[47] Paul W. Lapp, *Palestinian Ceramic Chronology, 200 B.C.-A.D. 70*, ASOR (New Haven, CT: American Schools of Oriental Research, 1961); Ruth Amiran, *Ancient Pottery of the Holy Land: From Its Beginnings in the Neolithic Period to the End of the Iron Age* (New Brunswick, NJ: Rutgers University Press, 1970); John W. Hayes, *Late Roman Pottery* (Rome: British School at Rome, 1972); *A Supplement to Late Roman Pottery* (Rome: British School at Rome, 1980); Bryant G. Wood, *The Sociology of Pottery in Ancient Palestine: The Ceramic Industry and the Diffusion of Ceramic Style in the Bronze and Iron Ages*, The Library of Hebrew Bible/OT Studies (New York: T&T Clark, 2009); Carroll M. Kobs, *The Tall Al-Hammam Excavation Project 2005–2013: Volume One: Seven Seasons of Ceramics, Eight Seasons of Artifacts* (Albuquerque, N.M.: TSU Press, 2014).

the most noticeable changes in ceramics can be identified in the domestic oil lamps of Palestine (see Fig. 18).[48]

Archaeology and Intelligence Work

Over the years, archaeology has had an intriguing relationship with politics and intelligence work. The PEF and the British Museum were used as a front for intelligence work in 1912–14. As Moscrop describes: "The Wilderness of Zin Survey, conducted by T. E. Lawrence [of Arabia] and Charles L. Woolley, was nothing but a cover for the mapping work conducted by Captain Newcomb in the same area."[49]

10. Archaeologist Prof. Nelson Glueck in Israel, 1956.

The telegraph from the British Museum dated December 1913 sent Woolley and Lawrence on a six-week survey to "look at the Biblical, Nabatean and Byzantine sites in the northern Sinai and the southern Negev deserts for the Palestine Exploration Fund"[50] with Captain Stewart Newcombe of the Royal Engineers in Beersheva. The underlying reason for the expedition was to spy on the Turks and to see their defenses in an area of southern Palestine, which was only about a hundred miles from the Suez Canal. As Tabachnick points out, "The surprising thing is that this rushed book,[51] designed as a cover for a relatively brief spying survey, remains of permanent importance in Biblical studies."[52]

Later, during World War II, Rabbi Nelson Glueck helped the Office of Strategic Services (OSS) to come up with a plan to retreat from the Germans if necessary. He was useful because of his experience and study of the Palestine region. Glueck was part of a small, secret team that mapped an escape strategy in case there was a German victory demanding an escape route for

---

[48] Robert Houston Smith, "The Household Lamps of Palestine in Old Testament Times," *BA* 27, no. 1 (February 1, 1964): 2–31; "The Household Lamps of Palestine in Intertestamental Times," *BA* 27, no. 4 (December 1, 1964): 101–24; "The Household Lamps of Palestine in New Testament Times," *BA* 29, no. 1 (February 1, 1966): 2–27; J. W Hayes, *Ancient Lamps in the Royal Ontario Museum a Catalogue. 1 Greek and Roman Clay Lamps* (Toronto: Royal Ontario Museum, 1980); Donald Michael Bailey, *A Catalogue of the Lamps in the British Museum*, 4 vols. (London: British Museum, 1975); Noam Adler, *Oil Lamps of the Holy Land from the Adler Collection* (Jerusalem: Old City, 2005); Eric Christian Lapp, "The Archaeology of Light: The Cultural Significance of the Oil Lamp from Roman Palestine" (Ph.D., Duke University, 1997); Stanislao Loffreda, *Light and Life: Ancient Christian Oil Lamps of the Holy Land*, Studium Biblicum (Jerusalem: Franciscan, 2001); Varda Sussman, *Ornamented Jewish Oil Lamps: From the Destruction of the Second Temple through the Bar-Kokhba Revolt*, Reprint, Ancient Near East (Jerusalem: Aris & Phillips, 1983); *Roman Period Oil Lamps in the Holy Land: Collection of the Israel Antiquities Authority* (Oxford: British Archaeological Reports, 2012).

[49] Moscrop, *Measuring Jerusalem*, 4.

[50] Stephen Ely Tabachnick, "Lawrence of Arabia as Archaeologist," *Biblical Archaeology Society* 23, no. 5 (1997): 40–47, 70–71.

[51] C. Leonard Woolley and T. E. Lawrence, *The Wilderness of Zin*, 2nd Revised (London: Stacey International, 2003).

[52] Tabachnick, "Lawrence of Arabia as Archaeologist," 45.

Britain out of Palestine. On March 23, 1942 Glueck went to the OSS, an arm of the CIA, to begin working with the agency as a Lt. Colonel. He arrived in Cairo on May 4th 1942 undercover under the guise of archaeological reconnaissance.[53]

UNDERSTANDING DATES IN ARCHAEOLOGY

While there are some dates given in the Bible (i.e., third reign of King...), these are not presented according to modern calendars, and few period benchmarks from before the Iron Age I period. The first Pharaoh mentioned in the Bible is Sheshonq (Shishak) in 1 Kings 11:40 (see Chart 5) who invaded Palestine in 925 BC (1 Kgs 14:25). The chronologicla dates are derived from correlating the biblical chronology with other extrabiblical data (i.e., Assyrian, Hittite, Egyptian, Babylonian, etc.) and modern conventional dates.

Approach to Numbers

One issue that affects chronology is the set of different methods used when handling biblical numbers. Some conservative scholars propose a literal chronology using base-10 hard numbers.[54] Bryant Wood states that he bases his dating scheme on "a straightforward reading of the chronological data in the Old Testament."[55]

By contrast, other conservative scholars use a different method of accounting for numbers, where they treat the years as "formulaic/honorific" or authentic.[56] Collins states: "I do take the number [440] as formulaic and not literal in the arithmetic sense, and I rely on historical synchronisms to link the Exodus to Egyptian history."[57] Collins goes on to explain "in terms of its original cultural context. . . . Authentic may equate to literal if that's what the writer intended."[58] For example, this explains why even conservative scholars arrive at conclusions with such a large spread between the dates of the patriarchs (see Chart 14).

Egyptian Chronology

A large part of the chronology of the OT is derived from correlating the reign of the Egyptian Pharaoh's with the events described in the Bible.[59] In the third cent. BC, Manetho, an Egyptian

---

[53] Floyd S. Fierman, "Rabbi Nelson Glueck: An Archaeologist's Secret Life in the Service of the OSS," *BAR* 12, no. 5 (1986): 18–22.

[54] Bryant G. Wood, "Locating Sodom: A Critique of the Northern Proposal," *BS* 20, no. 3 (2007): 81; Eugene H. Merrill, *Kingdom of Priests: A History of Old Testament Israel*, 2nd ed. (Grand Rapids: Baker Academic, 2008), 83–96; "Fixed Dates in Patriarchal Chronology," *BSac* 137, no. 547 (1980): 241–51; "Texts, Talls, and Old Testament Chronology: Tall el-Hammam as a Case Study," *Artifax* 27, no. 4 (2012): 20–21; Thiele, *Mysterious Numbers of the Hebrew Kings.*

[55] Wood, "Locating Sodom: A Critique of the Northern Proposal," 81.

[56] David M. Fouts, "A Defense of the Hyperbolic Interpretation of Large Numbers in the Old Testament," *JETS* 40 (1997): 377–87; "The Demographics of Ancient Israel," *BRB* 7, no. 2 (2007): 1–10; Carol A. Hill, "Making Sense of the Numbers of Genesis," *Perspectives on Science and Christian Faith* 55, no. 4 (2003): 239–51; Andrew E. Steinmann, "The Mysterious Numbers Of the Book of Judges," *JETS* 48 (2005): 491–500; James K. Hoffmeier, "What Is the Biblical Date for the Exodus? A Response to Bryant Wood," *JETS* 50, no. 2 (2007): 235–39; Steven Collins, "Tall el-Hammam Is Still Sodom: Critical Data-Sets Cast Serious Doubt on E. H. Merrill's Chronological Analysis," *BRB* 13, no. 1 (2013): 4; "Tall el-Hammam Is Sodom: Billington's Heshbon Identification Suffers from Numerous Fatal Flaws," *Artifax* 27, no. 3 (Summer 2012): 6; Craig Olson, "A Proposal for a Symbolic Understanding of the Patriarchal Lifespans" (Dallas Theological Seminary, 2017); "How Old Was Father Abraham? Re-Examining the Patriarchal Lifespans in Light of Archaeology," in *Evangelical Theological Society* (Evangelical Theological Society, Boston, MA, 2017), 1–26.

[57] Collins, "Tall el-Hammam Is Still Sodom," 8.

[58] Steven Collins and Latayne C. Scott, *Discovering the City of Sodom: The Fascinating, True Account of the Discovery of the Old Testament's Most Infamous City* (New York: Simon & Schuster, 2013), 138.

[59] Kenneth A. Kitchen, "Egyptian Interventions in the Levant in Iron Age II," in *Symbiosis, Symbolism, and the Power of the Past: Canaan, Ancient Israel, and Their Neighbors from the Late Bronze Age Through Roman Palaestina*, ed. William G. Dever and Seymour Gitin (Winona Lake, IN: Eisenbrauns, 2003), 113–32.

priest, recorded thirty Egyptian dynasties in his work *Aegyptiaka* (*History of Egypt* in Greek), which have become useful in creating the Egyptian chronology.[60] However, even with his help this is not an exact science and while dates for the Kingdoms are generally agreed upon, there is much debate over the exactitude of the rule of individual Pharaohs.[61]

As Kitchen explains:

> Unfortunately, the lengths of a good number of reigns are not completely known, or not known at all, and in the "intermediate periods", national unity broke down with rival lines of kings reigning contemporaneously. However, a variety of resources exist by use of which one may largely overcome these gaps and obscurities, particularly from the second millennium BC onwards.[62]

But recent archaeology has assisted in refining the dates. Kitchen explains: "Decipherment of the Egyptian scripts and language brought us king-lists almost a thousand years earlier than Manetho–and a multitude of original sources contemporary with many of the rulers named in the lists."[63]

A new chronology has been proposed by David M. Rohl and others, who attempt to lower dates by several hundred years to align the dates better with the biblical account (see Chart 9).[64] However, Kitchen is not impressed with his arguments and states: "a recent "crank-chronologist," Rohl (1995), whose attempts to down-date Egyptian and ancient Near Eastern chronology by 250/300 year are 100% nonsense, considering the full array of evidence we are privileged to have these days."[65]

For a scholarly evaluation of the discussion one should consult Hornung *et al.*, *Ancient Egyptian Chronology*.[66] However, Kitchen has summarized the approach best. He states:

> The chronology of ancient Egypt can only be recovered (and then, inexactly) by combining several approaches. These include the sequences of kings and reigns, grouped into dynasties and larger periods. Original documents and interstate synchronisms (plus genealogical data) permit considerable control. To some extent, if their ambiguities can be overcome, lunar and 'Sothic' dates from astronomy can help. Other science-based techniques (e.g., radiocarbon) are not precise enough to help, except in the prehistoric epoch. The margin of error of c. 200 years in early third millennium BC sinks to 20/10 years during the second millennium, and to zero in 664 BC.[67]

---

[60] Manetho, *History of Egypt and Other Works*, trans. W. G. Waddell, Loeb Classical Library 350 (Cambridge, MA: Harvard University Press, 1940).

[61] Renfrew and Bahn, *Archaeology*, 132; Nicolas Grimal, *A History of Ancient Egypt* (Oxford: Wiley-Blackwell, 1994), 389–95; Erik Hornung, Rolf Krauss, and David A. Warburton, *Ancient Egyptian Chronology*, Handbook of Oriental Studies Section One: The Near and Middle East 83 (Leiden: Brill Academic, 2006), 13; Kenneth A. Kitchen, "The Basics of Egyptian Chronology in Relation to the Bronze Age," in *High, Middle Or Low?: Acts of an International Colloquium on Absolute Chronology Held at the University of Gothenburg, 20th-22nd August, 1987*, ed. Paul Åström, vol. 1, 3 vols., Studies in Mediterranean Archaeology and Literature (Gothenburg: Åström, 1987), 37–55; "Regnal and Genealogical Data of Ancient Egypt (Absolute Chronology I) The Historical Chronology of Ancient Egypt, A Current Assessment," in *Synchronisation of Civilisations in Eastern Mediterranean in the Second Millennium B.C. II*, ed. Manfred Bietak, Contributions to the Chronology of the Eastern Mediterranean: Denkschriften Der Gesamtakademie 29 (Vienna: Austrian Academy of Sciences, 2003), 39–52; "Egyptian Interventions in the Levant in Iron Age II," 113–32; "The Chronology of Ancient Egypt," *World Archaeology* 23, no. 2 (October 1, 1991): 201–8; *The Third Intermediate Period in Egypt, 1100-650 BC*, 2nd ed., Egyptology (Warminster: Aris & Phillips, 1996).

[62] Kitchen, "The Chronology of Ancient Egypt," 201.

[63] Kitchen, "Regnal and Genealogical Data of Ancient Egypt (Absolute Chronology I) The Historical Chronology of Ancient Egypt, A Current Assessment," 39.

[64] David M. Rohl, *A Test Of Time: Volume One-The Bible-From Myth to History* (London: Arrow, 2001), 159–74; *Pharaohs and Kings: A Biblical Quest* (New York: Three Rivers, 1997); *From Eden to Exile: The Five-Thousand-Year History of the People of the Bible* (Lebanon, TN: Greenleaf, 2009); *The Lords Of Avaris: Uncovering the Legendary Origins of Western Civilisation* (Hawthorn, Australia: Cornerstone Digital, 2010); R. Morkot *et al.*, *Centuries of Darkness: A Challenge to the Conventional Chronology of Old World Archaeology* (New Brunswick, NJ: Rutgers University Press, 1991).

[65] Kitchen, "Egyptian Interventions in the Levant in Iron Age II," 122.

[66] Hornung, Krauss, and Warburton, *Ancient Egyptian Chronology*, 13.

[67] Kitchen, "The Chronology of Ancient Egypt," 208.

Old Testament Chronology

Dating and chronology are further complicated by how ancient people calculated the reigns of kings. In the 1950's Edwin R. Thiele demonstrated, in his dissertation at the University of Chicago, that the chronological practice in the ANE was also used in the OT.[68] For example, when a king died they would wait until the end of the year to include this period in the years of his reign (accession year system). Depending on the system practiced at the time, the next king would either wait until the following year to begin counting his reign (accession year system) or he would include the partial year as the first year of his reign (non-accession year system). In the non-accession calculation both kings are given credit for the same year, creating an overlap in their reign.

Thiele further identified that occasionally the ANE kings would allow their sons to join them on the throne (coregency system) and both father and son were granted the full years of their coregency, duplicating the calculation. Taking these anomalies into consideration, Thiele created his widely accepted chronology of the kings of Israel and Judah. Although many conservative and liberal scholars use his chronology, Kaiser points out: "Despite that fact of scholarly dedication, neither Thiele's carefully argued University of Chicago dissertation, nor anyone else's, has achieved as yet universal acceptance."[69]

New Dating Chronology

Recently a new calibration of relative dates for the early Bronze Age has been proposed based on some 420 calibrated radiocarbon dates taken from 57 sites in Israel and Jordan.[70] This was deemed necessary as the southern Levant does not have its own historical chronology and normally scholars would depend on the chronologies of neighboring countries such as Egypt, however, as Regev *et al.*, points out: "The chronological framework of Egypt has been amply discussed by scholars (Kitchen 1987, 1991; Hornung *et al.* 2006) and recently by Dee *et al.* (2009), but there is a controversy over its accuracy for the third millennium BCE."[71]

This study synthesizes the dates from various sites using relative and absolute dates and creates a plausible chronology of the EB period in the Levant (see Chart 9).

New Testament Chronology

Birth and Death of Jesus

Luke states that Jesus lived during the rule of Caesar Augustus, and that he was the emperor of Rome from 27 BC until AD 14 (Luke 2:1). The year can further be narrowed because Herod the Great was present during the visit of the Magi at the nativity (Matt 2:1) and we know that he died in the spring of 4 BC.[72] Josephus tells us that Herod died after a lunar eclipse (Josephus *Ant.* 17.6.4) and before the springtime Passover of the Jews.[73] Therefore most scholars

[68] Edwin Richard Thiele, *The Mysterious Numbers of the Hebrew Kings: A Reconstruction of the Chronology of the Kingdoms of Israel and Judah*, revised (Grand Rapids: Kregel Academic & Professional, 1994).

[69] Walter C. Kaiser, Jr., *History of Israel* (Nashville, TN: Broadman & Holman, 2010), 293; J. Gordon McConville, *Exploring the Old Testament, Volume 4: A Guide to the Prophets* (Downers Grove, IL: IVP Academic, 2008), viii.

[70] Johanna Regev *et al.*, "Chronology of the Early Bronze Age in the Southern Levant: New Analysis for a High Chronology," *Radiocarbon* 3–4 (2012): 528.

[71] Ibid., 525.

[72] Barnes, "The Date of Herod's Death"; Bernegger, "Affirmation of Herod's Death in 4 B.C."

[73] Mark Kidger, *The Star of Bethlehem: An Astronomer's View* (Princeton, NJ: Princeton University Press, 1999), 46.

understand the date of Jesus' birth to be between 6 and 4 BC.[74]

It is known that there were four lunar eclipses between 7 and 1 BC.[75] Most scholars favor the eclipse of 4 BC,[76] placing the birth of Jesus in *ca.* 6 BC, while a few have challenged this date[77] preferring 1 BC for the eclipse and placing the birth of Jesus in 3 or 2 BC.[78]

Maier argues for "late 5 BC as the most probable time for the first Christmas."[79] The early Church Father, Clement of Alexandria (*ca.* 200 AD), gives a date for the birth of Jesus according to the Egyptian calendar (25 Pachon or May 20th; *Strom.* 1.21) which, according to the Gregorian calendar, converts to the 14th of May, 6 BC.

While there is no certainty for the date of Jesus' birth, as Franz points out, the spring date in May is "consistent with the material culture of Luke 2."[80] Franz continues with several examples:

> the shepherds would have been out in the Wilderness of Judah during the winter months and not around the fields surrounding Bethlehem. The farmers do not want the sheep in their fields while the wheat and barley is growing. However, after the barley harvest (after Passover, usually in April or early May), the farmer wants the sheep in his harvested fields to eat the stubble as well as fertilize the fields for next season. After Pentecost (usually in May or early June) the wheat harvest begins. The May 14th date is consistent with the account in Luke's gospel.[81]

Luke records that Jesus began his ministry at the age of thirty (Luke 3:23) and ministered for three years, evident from the number of Passovers listed in the Gospel of John. Jesus was crucified under the orders of Pontius Pilate, the Roman governor of Judea (Matt 27:27–61, Mark 15:1–47, Luke 23:25–54 and John 19:1–38; Josephus *Ant.* 18.3; Tacitus *Ann.* 15.44), and he governed from 26 AD–37 AD.[82] This would mean that Jesus died around AD 30 which fits the time period of Pilate.

Chronology of Paul's Life

The majority of the chronology of the NT is based on the life of Paul found in the book of Acts and his letters. McRay has described efforts to establish a chronology[83] of the dates for the

---

[74] Dunn, *Jesus Remembered*, 324; Finegan, Vardaman, and Yamauchi, *Chronos, Kairos, Christos*, 97–117; Bailey, *Jesus Through Middle Eastern Eyes*.

[75] Kidger, *The Star of Bethlehem*, 48–49; Manfred Kudlek and Erich H. Mickler, *Solar and Lunar Eclipses of the Ancient Near East from 3000 B.C. to 0 with Maps* (Neukirchen-Vluyn: Butzon & Bercker, 1971).

[76] Hoehner, "The Date of the Death of Herod the Great"; Emil Schürer, *The History of the Jewish People in the Age of Jesus Christ (175 BC–AD 135)*, ed. G. Vermes, F. Miller, and M. Black, Rev (Edinburgh: T&T Clark, 1979), 1:326–28 n. 165; F. F. Bruce, *New Testament History*, 2nd ed. (New York: Doubleday, 1980), 23.

[77] Ernest L. Martin, "The Nativity and Herod's Death," in *Chronos, Kairos, Christos*, ed. Jack Finegan, Jerry Vardaman, and Edwin M. Yamauchi (Winona Lake, IN: Eisenbrauns, 1989), 86; W. E. Filmer, "The Chronology of the Reign of Herod the Great," *JTS* 17 (1966): 283–98.

[78] This later date has been challenged by Barnes and Johnson who again favor the 4 BC date. Barnes, "The Date of Herod's Death," 204–209; Douglas Johnson, "The Star of Bethlehem Reconsidered: A Refutation of the Mosley/Martin Historical Approach," *Planetarian* 10, no. 1 (1981): 14–16.

[79] Paul L. Maier, "The Date of the Nativity and the Chronology of Jesus' Life," in *Chronos, Kairos, Christos*, ed. Jack Finegan, Jerry Vardaman, and Edwin M. Yamauchi (Winona Lake, IN: Eisenbrauns, 1989), 113.

[80] Gordon Franz, "The Birth Date of Jesus," *BS* 26, no. 1 (2013): 2.

[81] Ibid.

[82] Warren Carter, *Pontius Pilate: Portraits of a Roman Governor*, Interfaces Series (Collegeville, Minn.: Liturgical, 2003), 44–45; Everett Ferguson, *Backgrounds of Early Christianity*, 3rd ed. (Grand Rapids: Eerdmans, 2003), 416.

[83] Thomas H. Campbell, "Paul's 'Missionary Journeys' as Reflected in His Letters," *Journal of Biblical Literature* 74, no. 2 (1955): 80–87; Karl Paul Donfried, "Chronology: New Testament," ed. David Noel Freedman *et al.*, *ABD* (New York: Doubleday, 1996), 1:1012–1013; Rainer Riesner, *Paul's Early Period: Chronology, Mission Strategy, Theology*, trans. Douglas W. Stott (Grand Rapids: Eerdmans, 1998); F. F Bruce, *Paul, Apostle of the Heart Set Free* (Grand Rapids: Eerdmans, 2000), 318–19; Andrew E. Steinmann, *From Abraham to Paul: A Biblical Chronology* (St. Louis, Miss.: Concordia, 2011).

events of Paul's life as "one of the most baffling problems of New Testament study."[84] Donfried also cautions that: "it must be acknowledged that no matter from what perspective one views the data, *there can be no absolutely definite chronology of this period*; all attempts must be tentative and subject to correction and revision (emphasis added)."[85]

However, in determining dates there are certain markers that assist in the chronology of events in the book of Acts:

- Acts 9:25; 2 Cor 11:32: The death of the Nabatean King Aretas IV Philopatris, between AD 37–40,[86] who was the client king of the Romans and whose capital was in Petra, Jordan (Josephus *Ant.* 13.387–92; *J.W.* 1.99–103). Aretas was the father-in-law of Herod Antipas who controlled Galilee and Perea. Antipas was first married to Aretas' daughter Phasaelis but later divorced her (AD 36) to marry his brother Philip's wife Herodias (Matt 14:3–4; Mark 6:17–18; Luke 3:19–20). The divorce caused friction between Aretas and Antipas that led to Aretas invading Antipas' territory, which included Bantanaea, south of Damascus (Josephus *Ant.* 18.109–25; *J.W.* 2.94–95). Aretas' power reached as far north as Damascus, where he appointed an ethnarch (Gr. *ethnarches*, from *ethnos* "nation" + *arkhein* "to rule") over the city.[87] With the accession of the Roman emperor Caligula (AD 37–41), a new policy of tolerance for client kings was proposed and it is assumed that Damascus was not under Nabatean control before AD 37. Campbell concludes "we can claim with some confidence that Aretas did not control the city beyond early 37 C.E....and [it would have been] largely impossible during the reign of Philip over the Decapolis, that is, up to 34 C.E....We know, moreover, that in late 36 C. E. Aretas launched a successful military strike against Antipas, ruler of Galilee."[88] Vardaman builds a case based on microletters[89] on the coins of Aretas, for the control of Damascus being passed from Aretas IV to Tiberius after AD 33/34,[90] towards the end of Tiberius' career in AD 37.[91] While it is unlikely that Paul's departure from Damascus (2 Cor 11:32; Acts 9) took place as early as AD 34, the general consensus of scholars is that the events of Acts 9 must have taken place between AD 36 and 37.[92]
- Acts 11:28; Acts 18:2: On January 24th AD 41, Caligula (AD 37–41) was assassinated and Claudius Caesar (AD 41–54) came to the throne (Suetonius *Claud.* 10, 25; Josephus *Ant.* 19.212–20).
- Acts 12:20–23: the death of Herod Agrippa I in AD 44 (Josephus *Ant.* 19.343–50; *J.W.* 2.219).
- Acts 13:6–12: Sergius Paulus [Gr. *Sergios Paulos*] was Proconsul of Cyprus in AD 41–54[93] during the time of Claudius Caesar (Pliny *Nat.* 2.113; see Fig. 95).[94]

---

[84] John McRay, *Paul: His Life and Teaching* (Grand Rapids: Baker Academic, 2007), 60.

[85] Donfried, "Chronology: NT," 1:1017.

[86] Gerald F. Hawthorne, Ralph P. Martin, and Daniel G. Reid, eds., *Dictionary of Paul and His Letters* (Downers Grove, IL: InterVarsity, 1993), 117; Lee Martin MacDonald, "Acts," in *The Bible Knowledge Background Commentary: Acts-Philemon*, ed. Craig A. Evans and Isobel A. Combes (Colorado Springs, Colo.: Cook, 2004), 72; E. Jerry Vardaman, "Jesus' Life: A New Chronology," in *Chronos, Kairos, Christos*, ed. Jack Finegan, E. Jerry Vardaman, and Edwin M. Yamauchi (Winona Lake, IN: Eisenbrauns, 1989), 72.

[87] Douglas A. Campbell, "An Anchor for Pauline Chronology: Paul's Flight from 'The Ethnarch of King Aretas' (2 Corinthians 11:32-33)," *Journal of Biblical Literature* 121, no. 2 (2002): 281 n. 7; G. W. Bowersock, *Roman Arabia* (Cambridge, MA: Harvard University Press, 1998), 65–69; Steinmann, *From Abraham to Paul*, 302.

[88] Campbell, "An Anchor for Pauline Chronology," 296–97.

[89] "Microletters are very samll inscriptions placed on coins and other objects. They are so small that a magnifying glass is required to see them and, in case you may be wondering, magnifying glasses were indeed used in antiquity." Arthur E. Palumbo, *The Dead Sea Scrolls and the Personages of Earliest Christianity* (New York: Algora, 2004), 175.

[90] Schürer, *History of the Jewish People*, 1:852 n. 25.

[91] Vardaman, "Jesus' Life: A New Chronology," 71–73.

[92] George Ogg, *The Chronology of the Life of Paul* (London: Epworth, 1968), 22–23; Robert Jewett, *A Chronology of Paul's Life* (Minneapolis, MN: Fortress, 1979), 30–33; Ralph P. Martin, *2 Corinthians*, ed. David A Hubbard and Glenn W Barker, Word Biblical Commentary 40 (Dallas, Tex.: Word Books, 1998), 385–86; Campbell, "An Anchor for Pauline Chronology," 296–97.

[93] Bastian Van Elderen, "Some Archaeological Observations on Paul's First Missionary Journey," in *Apostolic History and The Gospel Biblical and Historical Essays Presented to F. F. Bruce on His 60th Birthday*, ed. W. Ward Gasque (Exeter: Paternoster, 1970), 155; Thomas W. Martin, "Paulus, Sergius (Person)," ed. David Noel Freedman *et al.*, *ABD* (New York: Doubleday, 1996), 5:205; Emilio Gabba, *Iscrizioni Greche E Latine per Lo Studio Della Bibba* (Torino: Marietti, 1958), 71–73.

- Acts 24:27; 25:12: Felix's reign as the procurator of Judea was succeeded (Josephus *Ant.* 20.8.7, 9; *J.W.* 2.13.7) by Porcius Festus in about AD 59 (Josephus *J.W.* 2.14.1; *Ant.* 20.8.9–11) until his death in AD 62 when he was succeeded by Lucceius Albinus.[95]
- Paul composed his theological writings between AD 50 and 68.[96]

One must keep in mind (as Donfried has reminded us): "Any attempt to reconstruct the chronology of the NT must be tentative at best. The primary intention of the Gospels and other NT writings is not historical or biographical—they are documents of faith intended to proclaim, teach, and encourage the various early Christian communities."[97]

Köstenberger recommends that the best approach "relies primarily on Paul's letters for the chronology of Paul's life and supplements that chronology with data from Acts."[98] This allows for the possibility that Luke may have arranged some of his material topically.[99] However, the details of the events that Luke provided are none the less historical and accurate. See Chart 12.

Three-Age Dating System

Archaeologists have developed a three-age method of generalizing the dating periods through the identification of ancient technologies. The first to propose the three-age dating system for the region of Palestine was the Danish archaeologist Christian Jürgensen Thomsen (1788–1865). He identified the age by reference to the materials – stone, bronze, and iron – used to manufacture the artifacts in each period (see Chart 9).[100]

- Stone Age - 8500 BC–3600 BC
- Bronze Age - 3600 BC–1500 BC
- Iron Age - 1500 BC–586 BC

In 1865 Sir John Lubbock divided the Stone Age into sub-epochs and for the first time coined the terms "Palaeolithic" and "Neolithic" to identify the Old and New Stone Ages.[101] However, the notion of a Stone Age civilization existing purely through the use of stones is a relative fantasy. All metals were used to greater or lesser degree throughout the ages.[102] For example, in the tomb of King Tutankhamun, who lived in the Late Bronze Age (1300 BC), an iron dagger was found. While there is debate over the origin of the iron (meteorite or smelted),[103] the evidence remains that it was being used in the LBA. The Early Bronze Age used

---

[94] Douglas A. Campbell, "Possible Inscriptional Attestation to Sergius Paulus (Acts 13:6–12) and the Implications for Pauline Chronology," *JTS* 56, no. 1 (2005): 1–29.

[95] Bruce, *New Testament History*, 345; Joel B Green, "Festus, Porcius (Person)," ed. David Noel Freedman *et al.*, *ABD* (New York: Doubleday, 1992), 794–95.

[96] Darrell L. Bock, *Breaking The Da Vinci Code: Answers to the Questions Everyone's Asking* (New York: Nelson, 2006).

[97] Donfried, "Chronology: NT," 1:1012–1013.

[98] Andreas J. Köstenberger, L. Scott Kellum, and Charles L Quarles, *The Cradle, the Cross, and the Crown: An Introduction to the New Testament* (Nashville, TN: Broadman & Holman Academic, 2009), 397; Campbell, "Paul's 'Missionary Journeys'"; Joseph A Fitzmyer, "The Pauline Letters and the Lucan Account of Paul's Missionary Journeys," *Society of Biblical Literature Seminar Papers* 27 (1988): 82–89.

[99] L. C. A. Alexander, "Chronology of Paul," ed. Gerald F. Hawthorne, Ralph P. Martin, and Daniel G. Reid, *Dictionary of Paul and His Letters* (Downers Grove, IL: InterVarsity, 1993), 115–23.

[100] Peter Rowley-Conwy, *From Genesis to Prehistory: The Archaeological Three Age System and Its Contested Reception in Denmark, Britain, and Ireland*, Oxford Studies in the History of Archaeology (Oxford: Oxford University Press, 2007), 298–301.

[101] Sir John Lubbock, *Pre-Historic Times, as Illustrated by Ancient Remains, and the Manners and Customs of Modern Savages*, 2nd ed. (London: Williams & Norgate, 1869), 2–3.

[102] Graham Connah, *Writing about Archaeology* (Cambridge: Cambridge University Press, 2010), 62–63.

[103] Alfred Lucas and J. R. Harris, *Ancient Egyptian Materials and Industries* (Mineola, NY: Dover, 1962), 239–241; John Coleman Darnell and Colleen Manassa, *Tutankhamun's Armies: Battle and Conquest During Ancient Egypt's Late Eighteenth Dynasty* (Hoboken, NJ: Wiley, 2007), 77; Jack Ogden, "Metals," in *Ancient Egyptian Materials and Technology*, ed. Ian Shaw and Paul T. Nicholson (Cambridge

very little bronze but preferred copper (Chalcolithic), and bronze was used in the Iron Age and even through the Roman period.[104] Recently (2014), a copper awl was discovered in a Middle Chalcolithic tomb at Tel Tsaf, Israel, providing evidence that imported cast metal technology was introduced to the Jordan Valley region as early as the late sixth millennium BC.[105]

Thus the identification of periods according to materials used in those periods is rather arbitrary, but these are the accepted terms used in biblical archaeology, although the dates are well-established for these periods since they are correlated with the datable chronology of Ancient Egypt. Certainly scholars continue to debate the dates of the sub-periods attached to these periods, but as Princeton professor Peter Bogucki states: "Although modern archaeologists realize that this tripartite division of prehistoric society is far too simple to reflect the complexity of change and continuity, terms like 'Bronze Age' are still used as a very general way of focusing attention on particular times and places and thus facilitating archaeological discussion."[106]

Dating Abbreviations

BC and AD

The abbreviation BC means "before Christ," while AD means *anno Domini* (Lat. "in the year of our Lord").[107] From the relative birth of Christ, BC counts backward and AD counts forward. There is no year 0. It must be acknowledged that the dates used still do not perfectly coincide with the birth of Christ, since it is known that Jesus was born between 6 and 4 BC[108], because Matthew writes that he was "born in Bethlehem of Judea in the days of Herod the king" (Matt 2:1), and Herod the Great died in 4 BC.[109]

The origin of this dating system dates back to Dionysius Exiguus (ca. AD 470–ca. AD 544) who was known as the inventor of the Anno Domini (AD) era, used to number the years of both the Gregorian calendar and the (Christianised) Julian calendar.[110] Their general acceptance is described by Feeney, who points out: "Only in 1627 did Domenicus Petavius, in his *Opus De Doctrina Temprum*, expound the B.C./A.D. system as a basis for a universal time line for scholars and historians, on the understanding that the reference point of the birth of Christ represented 'not the actual event but an agreed upon point from which all real events could be dated.'"[111]

England: Cambridge University Press, 2009), 166–68; Lloyd Weeks, "Metallurgy," in *A Companion to the Archaeology of the Ancient Near East*, ed. D. T. Potts (Hoboken, NJ: Wiley & Sons, 2012), 298.

[104] Weeks, "Metallurgy," 302.

[105] Yosef Garfinkel *et al.*, "The Beginning of Metallurgy in the Southern Levant: A Late 6th Millennium Cal BC Copper Awl from Tel Tsaf, Israel," *PLoS ONE* 9, no. 3 (March 26, 2014): e96882.

[106] Peter Bogucki, "Europe, Northern and Western: Bronze Age," in *Encyclopedia of Archaeology*, ed. Deborah M. Pearsall, vol. 1 (San Diego, CA: Academic Press, 2008), 1216.

[107] Bonnie Blackburn and Leofranc Holford-Strevens, *The Oxford Companion to the Year: An Exploration of Calendar Customs and Time-Reckoning* (Oxford: Oxford University Press, 2003), 782.

[108] James D. G. Dunn, *Jesus Remembered* (Grand Rapids: Eerdmans, 2003), 324; Jack Finegan, E. Jerry Vardaman, and Edwin M. Yamauchi, eds., *Chronos, Kairos, Christos* (Winona Lake, IN: Eisenbrauns, 1989), 97–117; Kenneth E. Bailey, *Jesus Through Middle Eastern Eyes: Cultural Studies in the Gospels* (Downers Grove, IL: IVP Academic, 2008).

[109] Timothy David Barnes, "The Date of Herod's Death," *Journal of Theological Studies* 19, no. 1 (1968): 204–19; P. M. Bernegger, "Affirmation of Herod's Death in 4 B.C.," *Journal of Theological Studies* 34, no. 2 (1983): 526–31; Harold W. Hoehner, "The Date of the Death of Herod the Great," in *Chronos, Kairos, Christos*, ed. Jack Finegan, Jerry Vardaman, and Edwin M. Yamauchi (Winona Lake, IN: Eisenbrauns, 1989), 101–32.

[110] J. Rambaud-Buhot, "Dionysius, Exiguus," *NCE* 4:754; Georges Declercq, *Anno Domini: The Origins of the Christian Era*, Brepols Essays in European Culture 1 (Turnhout, Belgium: Brepols, 2000).

[111] Denis Feeney, *Caesar's Calendar: Ancient Time and the Beginnings of History* (Oakland, Calf.: University of California Press, 2007), 7; Donald J. Wilcox, *The Measure of Times Past: Pre-Newtonian Chronologies and the Rhetoric of Relative Time* (Chicago, IL: University of Chicago Press, 1989), 207.

But the system did not become popular until the eighteenth century and is often used by Christian scholars who wish to convey a Christian worldview. It is the terminology used in this publication.

C.E. and B.C.E.

The abbreviation B.C.E. means "Before the Common Era" and means the same as BC, while C.E. means "Common Era", "Christian Era", or "Current Era." These abbreviations are often preferred by those who do not want to refer to religious titles, however, the actual use of the dates are the same for both sets of abbreviations (i.e. B.C.E./BC or C.E./AD). This theologically neutral system is now used by secular, Jewish and Christian scholars who exavate in Bible lands and is the accepted academic terminology for archaeology.

BP

Since the Muslims and Jews also have a dating system, scientists who work with radiocarbon dating (C-14) prefer an international standard and count the years backward from the present (BP; see below *Dating a Tel: Radiocarbon Dating*). This date is not counted from the point of Jesus' birth, but rather the birth of radiocarbon dating, thus "before 1950."[112] This is a very confusing dating method and it is best to convert all dates to BC or AD.

CHARACTERISTICS OF ARCHAEOLOGY

Archaeology, as a scientific endeavour, is distinguished by several distinctive characteristics.

1. A Team Player

As opposed to Indiana Jones, who acts alone, archaeologists work with many wonderful people, including professional scientists, volunteers, and local representatives from the respective country. The success of the excavation is dependent on many diverse and talented specialists. Hoerth and McRay best describe the hierarchy of an excavation:

> One or more directors initiate an archaeology dig. An administrator handles such details as travel arrangements for the tea, on-site transportation, housing, and meals. Normally a site will have several areas under excavation at the same time, and each area will have a supervisor. The supervisor will direct the work of the volunteers, who do much of the actual excavation. Field architects and photographers record the daily progress, while other specialists such as botanists, geologists, linguists, and paleontologists, study the excavated materials.[113]

2. A Volunteer Enterprise

Most excavations are dependent on volunteers to join their projects. While young college students are the typical volunteer, you will find people of all ages. Typically a trained archaeologist called a "Square Supervisor" oversees a small group in a square (6m by 6m). The square supervisor does the paperwork. On occasion some projects hire local workers to assist with the heavy lifting.

3. A Destructive Science

It is noteworthy that archaeology is a destructive science. Douglas Edwards has described it as

---

[112] Renfrew and Bahn, *Archaeology*, 114.

[113] Hoerth and McRay, *Bible Archaeology*, 16.

"Organized Vandalism."[114] In the past archaeologists were accused of many destructive practices and certainly they were much more careless than today. However, recently many improvements have been made in the precision and computerized documentation of a site that has raised the level of care. But still, once a site is dug up, it is forever destroyed, and if good records and documentation are not properly kept, then the site is actually destroyed twice.

4. A Potsherd is Their Text

In reality the biblical archaeologist handles two texts, the Bible and the material remains.[115] The Bible is ordered, many believe, by inspiration; while the material culture is ordered by providence. Past cultures have left a logical sequence of occupation that, like a written text, can be read. Steven M. Ortiz explains that:

> The text of the archaeologist is the potsherd. From this small piece of material culture [potsherd] we derive interpretations, models, and historical reconstructions of the past. Pottery continues to be one of the basic building blocks for the archaeologists. Therefore, the future of biblical archaeology is rooted in its past – ceramic analysis.[116]

While ceramics are certainly an important part of the text which is read, there is much more that makes up the material remains of an excavation and demands experts in various fields. Archaeologist also encounter human (bioarchaeology or palaeo-osteology and anthropologists), plant (paleobotany and ethnobotany), and animal remains (zooarchaeology).

The importance of these disciplines is illustrated by the discovery in 1963–1965 of a number of 2000 year old date seeds excavated at Masada.[117] In 2005 their first century date was confirmed by carbon-14 testing and three of the seeds were handed over, by Ehud Netzer, to paleobotanists, who were able to successfully germinate the seeds. From DNA samples it was determined that the endemic date plants of the region were not the same as the California dates that now grow in Israel.[118]

In addition archaeologists periodically recover buildings, earthworks, coins (numismatics), tablets, inscriptions (epigraphy), manuscripts, tools, weapons, mosaics, and objects of art and religion.

5. A Preoccupation with Squares

Looking over an excavation site one might wonder if ancient people lived in square holes in the ground as the landscape is covered in tidy 6-metre squares.[119] But this is the remnants of the Wheeler-Kenyon method of doing archaeology in the Middle East. The prominent feature of this method is the use of 6-metre by 6-metre squares. While it is not the only method used in archaeology, it dominates biblical archaeology. But usually this only indicates a small part of the entire site. Of the more than thirteen thousand excavation squares marked off by the surveyor at

---

[114] Douglas Edwards, "Galilean Archaeology and the Historical Jesus Quest," in *Biblical Archaeology: From the Ground Down: DVD*, ed. Hershel Shanks (Atlanta, Ga.: Biblical Archaeology Society, 2003), n.p.

[115] Davis, "Theory and Method in Biblical Archaeology," 26.

[116] Steven M. Ortiz, "Deconstructing and Reconstructing the United Monarchy: House of David or Tent of David (Current Trends in Iron Age Chronology)," in *The Future of Biblical Archaeology: Reassessing Methodologies and Assumptions*, ed. James Karl Hoffmeier and Alan R. Millard, The Proceedings of a Symposium, August 12-14, 2001 at Trinity International University (Grand Rapids: Eerdmans, 2004), 121.

[117] Yigael Yadin, "The Excavation of Masada—1963/64: Preliminary Report," *IEJ* 15, no. 1/2 (January 1, 1965): 16, 45.

[118] John Roach, "2,000-Year-Old Seed Sprouts, Sapling Is Thriving," *National Geographic News*, November 22, 2005, http://news.nationalgeographic. com/news/2005/11/1122_051122_old_seed.html; S. Sallon *et al.*, "Germination, Genetics, and Growth of an Ancient Date Seed," *Science* 320, no. 5882 (June 13, 2008): 1464.

[119] Davis, "Theory and Method in Biblical Archaeology," 27–28.

the Tall el-Ḥammâm site in Jordan, only about eighty of them had been opened after seven seasons.[120] There is so much more to learn and waiting to be uncovered, even though in those seven seasons "pottery sherds representing all or part of forty thousand separate vessels have been brought out of the soil."[121]

6. An Obsession with Documentation

Proper documentation is vital to preserving the site on paper as soil is methodically removed from the square. Central to accurate records and data collection is the use of GPS and an electronic theodolite or transit called the "Total Station" used by the site surveyor.[122] Once all the paperwork has been compiled, it is necessary to publish the findings.

7. A Need for Funding

There is always a need for funding to carry out an excavation. Typically an excavation project will be underwritten by universities, museums, foundations, or individuals. Few excavations are fully funded by governments in the Middle East. Usually volunteers pay their own way or receive scholarships to help underwrite the expenses.

THE ROLE OF ARCHAEOLOGY IN BIBLICAL STUDIES

But what exactly is the value of biblical archaeology for biblical studies? Some people believe that archaeology can be used to confirm, authenticate, substantiate or even prove the Bible true. This view goes back to the nineteenth century when the liberal critics began to use archaeology in an attempt to disprove the Bible. For example, in 1872, George E. Smith translated the Mesopotamian flood story and found parallels with the biblical record. The critics quickly came to the conclusion that the Genesis account was borrowed from the Mesopotamian account and was not inspired by God.

When archaeologists found no trace of the Hittite civilization, the biblical critics made the claim that the Hittite people were imaginary.[123] In 1876 Archibald H. Sayce delivered a lecture to the Society of Biblical Archaeology in London, making a startling claim that the Hittites were a vast empire, but the capital was yet to be discovered.[124] In 1906, when the Hittite civilization was discovered by Hugo Winckler along with the royal archive of 10,000 tablets during his excavations at Boğazköy (*Ḫattuša*), this brought a new zeal to archaeology and its use for defending the Bible.[125] Believers began to think that archaeology had validated their faith.

But as Hoerth states:

> Even if every historical statement in the Bible could be proven true – confirmed – this would still not prove the theological message of the Bible…It can be proved that historical conditions were such that Solomon could have been as powerful a king as the Bible says he was; but this does not prove that God gave Solomon wisdom. It can be fairly well substantiated that there was a census when Jesus was born;

[120] Collins and Scott, *Discovering the City of Sodom*, 33.

[121] Ibid.

[122] Barry F. Kavanagh and S. J. Glenn Bird, *Surveying: Principles and Applications*, 4th ed. (Englewood Cliffs, NJ: Prentice Hall College Division, 1995), 257–64.

[123] Francis William Newman, *A History of the Hebrew Monarchy: From the Administration of Samuel to the Babylonish Captivity* (London: Chapman, 1853), 179 n.2.

[124] Trevor Bryce, *Life and Society in the Hittite World* (Oxford: Oxford University Press, 2004), 2; A. H. Sayce, *The Hittites the Story of a Forgotten Empire*, Classic Reprint (Charleston, SC: Forgotten Books, 2012).

[125] Bryce, *Life and Society in the Hittite World*, 2.

11. Author standing in the Lion Gate of the Hittite capital *Ḫattuša (Boğazköy)* founded in the Old Kingdom period by Hattushili I *ca.* 1586–1556 BC.

but this confirmation hardly proves his divinity. No archaeological evidence will prove the atonement.[126]

It is interesting that eminent archaeologist William F. Albright was lead more towards a respect for the historicity of the Bible, but was increasingly more liberal in his theology.[127] One must be careful not to assume too much from archaeology.

No archaeological evidence can verify the atonement or the virgin birth. As Vaux pointed out: "This spiritual truth can neither be proven nor contradicted, nor can it be confirmed or invalidated by the material discoveries of archaeology."[128] Albright also cautions that:

> Though archaeology can thus clarify the history and geography of ancient Palestine, it cannot explain the basic miracle of Israel's faith, which remains a unique factor in world history. But archaeology can help enormously in making the miracle rationally plausible to an intelligent person whose vision is not shortened by a materialistic world view.[129]

Hoerth summarizes Yamauchi and points out that: "no one questioned the historicity of either Pontius Pilate or Herod the Great, yet neither were found in inscriptions until the early 1960's. It is a mistake to insist that traditions – including the Old Testament stories – must interlock with other evidences before they can be believed."[130]

But this is not a division between history and faith, because it is impossible to separate faith from history. The problem lies not with the evidence but with our faith. Even if we were to prove every Bible story as historically accurate by referencing archaeological evidence, this still would not solve the dilemma of sinful human nature. This in essence is what Jesus taught in the account of the rich man and Lazarus (Luke 16:27–31; see *Quotes from Antiquity*).

The question of sufficient evidence is certainly not at issue here, since the resurrection by itself offers abundant evidence for belief in the gospel. The Bible records that Jesus rose from the dead and there were hundreds of witnesses to the resurrection, but people continue to doubt. The problem is not in the lack of evidence but because of the human condition of spiritual blindness and the unbelief of the human heart (Luke 16:27–31; 1 Cor 2:14). Humanity needs a changed heart and nature, not more evidence. Archaeology does not change hearts, only the landscape. As Charlesworth put it: "Archaeology cannot form faith, but it can help inform

---

[126] Hoerth, *Archaeology and the Old Testament*, 20.

[127] William F. Albright, "Toward a More Conservative View: Interview with W. F. Albright," *Christianity Today*, January 18, 1963, 3–5; "Archaeological Discovery and the Scriptures," *Christianity Today* 12, no. 19 (June 21, 1968): 3–5; William G. Dever, "What Remains of the House That Albright Built?," *BA* 56, no. 1 (March 1993): 25–35.

[128] Roland de Vaux, "On Right and Wrong Uses of Archaeology," in *Near Eastern Archaeology in the Twentieth Century: Essays in Honor of Nelson Glueck*, ed. James A. Saners (New York: Doubleday, 1970), 68.

[129] William F. Albright, *The Archaeology of Palestine* (London: Penquin, 1956), 255.

[130] Hoerth, *Archaeology and the Old Testament*, 21; Edwin Yamauchi, *The Stones and the Scriptures: An Introduction to Biblical Archaeology* (Grand Rapids: Baker, 1981).

faith."[131] God may use archaeology to change our hearts, but this is not its main purpose.

> ***Quotes from Antiquity***
>
> **Jesus on Evidence**
>
> And he said, 'Then I beg you, father [Abraham], to send him [Lazarus] to my father's house— for I have five brothers—so that he may warn them, lest they also come into this place of torment.' But Abraham said, 'They have Moses and the Prophets; let them hear them.' And he said, 'No, father Abraham, but if someone goes to them from the dead, they will repent.' He said to him, 'If they do not hear Moses and the Prophets, neither will they be convinced if someone should rise from the dead' (Luke 16:27–31).

Raymond uses a helpful illustration of the radio station, which transmits the signal properly, but the radio at the other end cannot pick up the signal because there is something wrong with the radio's aerial, not the transmission.[132]

The Bible does not need proving true as it is self-authenticating, but archaeology can help shed light on the text. Therefore, the value of archaeology is not apologetic but hermeneutic. It increases our understanding of the Bible and its world. Hoerth describes the various uses for archaeology: "The most important contributions of archaeology to biblical studies are the various ways it illuminates the cultural and historical setting of the Bible; adds to our knowledge of the people, places, things and events in the Bible; and aids in translation and exegesis of biblical passages."[133]

The new information we acquire to advance our knowledge of the biblical text only comes from the discipline of archaeology. The role of archaeology in our understanding of the text is immeasurable. Through the discovery of local references we better understand the geography, religions, traditions, history and text of the Bible. The ground and text work together to further our awareness of what is in the Bible.

LIMITATIONS OF ARCHAEOLOGY

1. Old Does Not Make It True

Just because something has been discovered in antiquity does not mean we understand it correctly. For example, it does not follow that because we have discovered an inscription that talks about Yahweh and his wife,[134] that God must be "married" and our theology is incorrect. Differing views and falsehoods have been around throughout history; they are not a modern phenomenon.

2. To Err is Human

Historians, who interpret the data, do make mistakes. They often can and do make correct conclusions, but archaeology is a speculative science and all archaeologists are fallible.

3. We Have Only Scratched The Surface

Rarely is a site completely excavated, meaning that much remains underground and the complete

---

[131] James H. Charlesworth, "Archaeology, Jesus, and Christian Faith," in *What Has Archaeology to Do with Faith?*, ed. James H. Charlesworth and Walter P. Weaver, Faith & Scholarship Colloquies (Philadelphia, PA: Trinity Press International, 1992), 19.

[132] Robert L. Reymond, *A New Systematic Theology of the Christian Faith*, 2nd ed. (Nashville, TN: Nelson, 1998), 81.

[133] Hoerth, *Archaeology and the Old Testament*, 17.

[134] Richard S. Hess, "Yahweh's 'Wife' and Belief in One God in the Old Testament," in *Do Historical Matters Matter to Faith?: A Critical Appraisal of Modern and Postmodern Approaches to Scripture*, ed. James K. Hoffmeier and Graham A. Magary (Wheaton, IL: Crossway Books, 2012), 459–76.

picture of a site or civilization remains to be fully discovered. There is still so much to learn.

But Yamauchi also reminds us of the fragmentary nature of the evidence.

A). Existence: Very little of what was made or written in antiquity has survived to this day due to erosion and looting. Perhaps one-tenth.

B). Surveyed: Very few of the ancient sites have been surveyed or even found. Osborne points out that "the number of sites rose from 300 in 1944 to 5,000 in 1963 to 7,000 by 1970."[135] Perhaps six-tenths of those found have been surveyed.

C). Excavated: Probably less than two-percent of the known sites have been meaningfully excavated. Osborne calculates that "of the 5,000 in Palestine in 1963 only 150 had been excavated in part and only 26 had become major sites."[136] Perhaps one-fiftieth of that excavated.

D). Examined: Few of these sites have been more than touched, due to the high cost of excavation and amount of time involved. Yigael Yadin calculated that it would take him eight hundred years to complete the excavation of Hazor, which is about 200 acres (MB period sizes: Ashkelon 150 acres, Tall el-Ḥammâm 62 acres, Gezer 40 acres, Megiddo 20 acres, Jericho 10 acres). Perhaps one-tenth of all discovered sites have been examined.[137]

E). Published: Only a fraction of the fraction that has been excavated have been published and became available to the scholarly world. Many finds are still stored away in museum basements. There are 30,000 cuneiform tablets stored in the British Museum alone which have not been translated. Perhaps only half of them have been published.[138]

This translates into the claim that only about .006 percent of the evidence is available.[139] This should cause archaeologists to be cautious about making categorical claims and approach their theories with humility.

4. We See Through a Glass Darkly

We only know part of the picture due to incomplete data and our vantage point of having to look back into a vague historical past. As Tzaferis reminds us: "Archaeology is not an exact science."[140] Therefore, many archaeological conclusions are based on incomplete information.

5. We All Have Presuppositions

The conclusions of what we do know are often clouded by our own presuppositions. It is a fallacy to believe that we are neutral and completely objective (see *the Fallacy of Neutrality*). This is illustrated in the minimalist and maximalist debate (see *Minimalist vs Maximalist Approach* below).

6. A Subjective Interpretation

While the collection of data is both scientific and objective, because of the archaeologist's presuppositions and biases (see Archaeological Fallacies), they do not always agree with the interpretation of that data.[141] What you believe about the Bible will influence how you interpret

---

135 Grant R Osborne, *The Hermeneutical Spiral: A Comprehensive Introduction to Biblical Interpretation* (Downers Grove, IL: InterVarsity, 2006), 160.

136 Ibid.

137 David E. Graves, *Key Facts for the Location of Sodom Student Edition: Navigating the Maze of Arguments* (Moncton, NB: Electronic Christian Media, 2014), 107.

138 Yamauchi, *The Stones and the Scriptures*, 146–58.

139 Osborne, *The Hermeneutical Spiral*, 160.

140 Vassilios Tzaferis, "Archaeological Views: From Monk to Archaeologist," *BAR* 32, no. 4 (2006): 22.

141 Ibid.

it. If you don't believe that miracles can happen, then you are going to interpret the miracles in such a way that the supernatural is removed. For Rudolph Bultmann the supernatural presented in the Gospels was unnecessary, leaving behind only an existential theology.[142] This leads to archaeology becoming a rather controversial discipline as "experts" share varying interpretations of the same data from their own presuppositions.

7. Politics Play a Role

Whether one is talking about the conflict in Iraq, where Islamic militants, known as ISIS, destroyed several religious monuments (i.e., the Tomb of Jonah in 2014), or the Palestinian Arab/Israelis controversy in Israel, where connections to ancient Israel are either emphasised or downplayed in order to prove/disprove the Jewish people's historic ties to the land, politics affects archaeology.

8. The Scourge of Looters

Most sites suffer from the onslaught of the proverbial "night diggers" and looters. Many articles have been written on the problem of illegal and unprovenanced pieces coming to market for sale. The *Follow the Pots* project[143] is part of the Expedition to the Dead Sea Plain's (EDSP) exploration, monitoring the epidemic in Jordan at the site of several ancient cemeteries at the Early Bronze Age sites of Bâb edh-Dhrâʿ, Fifa, eṣ-Ṣafi, Khirbet Khanazir, Naqa, and Numayra (or Numeira). The project monitors the "life as looted objects, illegally removed from cist and shaft graves, and charnel houses in order to supply the burgeoning demand for objects from the Holy Land."[144]

MINIMALIST VS MAXIMALIST APPROACH

Before proceeding we must differentiate between what is meant by a minimalist and a maximalist in the context of archaeology, as these terms are commonly used in both the debate over the historical reliability of the Bible and in the remaining chapters.

Minimalist View

In archaeology, a *minimalist*[145] (The Copenhagen School, also called "nihilists,"[146] and "deconstructionists"[147]) or "revisionist,"[148] as they sometimes call themselves, is one who finds that the Bible contributes little or not at all to our understanding of the history of Palestine before about 500 BC (that is before Israel's return from exile). They accept the minimal amount of biblical history in relation to the archaeolgical inquiry. The leading spokespersons for this view are P. Davies,[149] G. Garbini,[150] J. Van Seters,[151] I. Finkelstein,[152] N. Lemche,[153] and T.

---

[142] Rudolph Bultmann, *Jesus Christ and Mythology* (Upper Saddle River, NJ: Prentice Hall, 1981).

[143] http://followthepotsproject.org

[144] Meredith S. Chesson and Morag M. Kersel, "Tomato Season In The Ghor Es-Safi: A Lesson in Community Archaeology," *NEA* 76, no. 3 (2013): 159.

[145] Baruch Halpern, "Erasing History: The Minimalist Assault on Ancient Israel," *Bible Review* 11, no. 6 (December 1995): 26–35.

[146] Anson F. Rainey, "The 'House of David' and the House of the Deconstructionists," *BAR* 20, no. 6 (1994): 47.

[147] Gary N. Knoppers, "The Vanishing Solomon: The Disappearance of the United Monarchy from Recent Histories of Ancient Israel," *JBL* 116, no. 1 (April 1, 1997): 20.

[148] William G. Dever, "The Current School of Revisionist and Their Nonhistories of Ancient Israel," in *What Did the Biblical Writers Know, and When Did They Know It?* (Grand Rapids: Eerdmans, 2001), 23.

[149] Philip R. Davies, *In Search of "Ancient Israel": A Study in Biblical Origins*, The Library of Hebrew Bible/OT Studies (London: Continuum International, 2006), 57–71.

Thompson,[154] among others.[155] They argue that the primary OT characters, like the patriarchs, Moses, David, and Solomon, did not exist except in the minds of the Israelites. Davies, a professed revisionist, explains it this way:

> There is no way in which history automatically reveals itself in a biblical text; there are no literary criteria for believing David to be more historical than Joshua, Joshua more historical than Abraham, and Abraham more historical than Adam. An additional problem, in fact, is that there is no non-literary way of making this judgment either, since none of these characters has left a trace outside the biblical text![156]

According to Ronald S. Hendel, Professor of Hebrew Bible and Jewish Studies in the Department of Near Eastern Studies at the University of California, Berkeley:

> Archaeology did not illumine the times and events of Abraham, Moses and Joshua. Rather, it helped to show that these times and events are largely unhistorical. The more we know about the Bronze and early Iron Ages, the more the Biblical portrayals of events in this era appear to be a blend of folklore and cultural memory, in which the details of historical events have either disappeared or been radically reshaped. The stories are deeply meaningful, but only occasionally historical. Archaeological research has—against the intentions of most of its practitioners—secured the non-historicity of much of the Bible before the era of the kings.[157]

Dever, who does not consider himself to be a minimalist although most would place him in this camp, summarizes their position:

> There was no "ancient" or "biblical" Israel. These are all late "intellectual constructs," forced back upon an imagined past by centuries of Jewish and Christian believers. The notion of "ancient Israel" stems ultimately from the Bible itself; but the Bible is "pious fiction," not historical fact. The Bible, too, is a late literary construct, written in and reflecting the realities of the Persian-Hellenistic era (*ca.* fifth–first centuries BC), not the Iron Age of Palestine (*ca.* 12th–sixth centuries) that purports to be its setting.[158]

In addition, minimalists look to the date of the earliest discovered manuscripts of the Dead Sea Scrolls (DSS), written sometime after the second cent. BC, to provide the date for the writing of the OT books. For the minimalist, the biblical books were originally composed just before the time of the DSS (fourth–third cent. BC). Kenneth Kitchen reveals the implications of this view: "With that late date they would couple an ultralow view of the reality of that history, dismissing virtually the whole of it as pure fiction, as an attempt by the puny Jewish community in Palestine to write themselves an imaginary past large, as a form of national propaganda."[159]

Others were already involved in this practice, setting the precedent for Israel. Both Manetho's (Egyptian priest, third cent. BC) *Aegyptiaka*[160] and Berossus' (Babylonian priest of

---

[150] Giovanni Garbini, *Myth and History in the Bible*, The Library of Hebrew Bible/OT Studies (London: Sheffield Academic Press, 2003), 1–10.

[151] John Van Seters, *In Search of History: Historiography in the Ancient World and the Origins of Biblical History* (Winona Lake, IN: Eisenbrauns, 1997); *The Biblical Saga of King David* (Winona Lake, IN: Eisenbrauns, 2009).

[152] Israel Finkelstein and Nadav Na'aman, eds., *From Nomadism to Monarchy: Archaeological and Historical Aspects of Early Israel* (Jerusalem: Israel Exploration Society, 1994); Israel Finkelstein and Neil Asher Silberman, *The Bible Unearthed: Archaeology's New Vision of Ancient Israel* (New York: Touchstone, 2002); Israel Finkelstein and Amihai Mazar, *The Quest for the Historical Israel*, ed. Brian B. Schmidt, Archaeology and Biblical Studies 17 (Atlanta, Ga.: SBL, 2007).

[153] Hershel Shanks *et al.*, "Face to Face: Biblical Minimalists Meet Their Challenge," *BAR* 23, no. 4 (1997): 26–42, 66; *The Israelites in History and Tradition*, Library of Ancient Israel (Louisville, KY: Westminster/Knox, 1998), 166.

[154] Thomas L. Thompson, *The Bible in History: How Writers Create a Past* (London: Jonathan Cape, 1999); *The Mythic Past: Biblical Archaeology And The Myth Of Israel* (New York: Basic Books, 2000), 77–82; *Early History of the Israelite People: From the Written & Archaeological Sources* (Leiden: Brill, 2000).

[155] Robert B. Coote and Keith W. Whitelam, *The Emergence of Early Israel in Historical Perspective*, Social World of Biblical Antiquity Series (Sheffield: Sheffield Phoenix, 2010).

[156] Davies, *In Search of "Ancient Israel": A Study in Biblical Origins*, 12.

[157] Ronald S. Hendel, "Biblical Views: Is There a Biblical Archaeology?," *BAR* 32, no. 4 (2006): 20.

[158] Dever, *What Did the Biblical Writers Know, and When Did They Know It?*, 4.

[159] Kenneth A. Kitchen, *On the Reliability of the Old Testament* (Grand Rapids: Eerdmans, 2003), 2.

[160] Manetho, *Manetho.*

Marduk) *Chaldaika*[161] were written as political propaganda. However, the OT books were written in Hebrew for their own nation, not as political propaganda for others. The Greek translation of the OT (LXX) was produced years later and then only for their own community.

The minimalists have even gone so far as to campaign against the use of the term *biblical archaeology* and replace it with *Near-Eastern archaeology*. Holden and Geisler explain their motivation behind this change:

> Their [Minimalists] contempt for any title associated with the Bible appears to be driven by its perceived association to biased research, antiquated methodology, rigid ideology, lack of objectivity, and contempt for the scientific method. (However, this notion seems to be shortsighted since it requires archaeologists to discriminate against the Bible as a valid primary-source document originating from the ancient Near-Eastern world.)[162]

Kitchen asks several important questions which deserve answering:

> Were the Old Testament books all composed within circa 400–200 BC? And are they virtually pure fiction of that time, with few or no roots in the real history of the Near East during circa 2000–400 BC? . . . Are they purely fiction, containing nothing of historical value, or of major historical content and value, or a fictional matrix with a few historical nuggets embedded?
>
> Merely sitting back in a comfy armchair just wondering or speculating about the matter will achieve us nothing. Merely proclaiming one's personal convictions for any of the three options just mentioned (all, nothing, or something historical) simply out of personal belief or agenda, and not from firm evidence on the question, is also a total waste of time.[163]

12. Pottery jar handles stamped with seals reading *lmlk* (belonging to the King). Upper right: two-winged icon with only one word in the top register. Upper left: two-winged icon with divided words in both registers. Center: two-winged icon with divided word in the top but an undivided word in the bottom. Lower left: four-winged icon with a professional carved inscription. Lower right: four-winged icon with an amateurish, cursory inscription. Such stamps are specific to the reign of Hezekiah of Judah (716–687 BC).

Courtesy of George M. Grena

Maximalist View

By contrast the *maximalists* are those who generally accept the biblical text as historically accurate and see a significant correspondence between the Bible and the archaeological data. They accept the maximum amount of biblical history in relation to the archaeolgical inquiry. They find that the Bible contributes significantly to our understanding of the history of Palestine and generally agree with the early dates for the authorship of the OT books. Kitchen lays out significant evidence for such an early date in his life's work entitled *On the Reliability of the Old Testament*.[164]

---

[161] Stanley Mayer Burstein, *The Babyloniaca of Berossus*, 2nd ed., vol. 1, 5 vols., Sources from the Ancient Near East 1 (Malibu: Undena Publications, 1978).

[162] Norman L Geisler and Joseph M. Holden, *The Popular Handbook of Archaeology and the Bible* (Eugene, OR: Harvest House, 2013), 183.

[163] Kitchen, *Reliability of the OT*, 2–3.

[164] Ibid., 283–99.

There is not always agreement on the exact dates between these scholars, as dates can be very difficult to verify with pinpoint accuracy.

Leading maximalist scholars would include Kitchen, Hoerth, Hoffmeier, Millard, Price, Ortiz, McRay, Yamauchi, and others.[165] While some would place William Dever in this camp, he would not consider himself either a maximalist or a minimalist but a middleist, placing himself somewhere in the middle. From his own statements, most evangelicals would not consider him to be a maximalist. Dever states:

> We cannot turn the clock back on the time when archaeology allegedly "proved the Bible." We must allow archaeology as it is practiced today to challenge, as well as to confirm, the Bible's stories. Some things described there really did happen, but ***others did not.*** The Biblical narratives about Abraham, Moses, Joshua and Solomon probably do reflect some historical memories of actual people and places, but the "larger-than-life" portraits of the Bible are ***unrealistic*** and are, in fact, ***contradicted by the archaeological evidence.*** Some of Israel's ancestors probably did come out of Egyptian slavery, but there was ***no military conquest of Canaan***, and most early Israelites were displaced Canaanites (emphasis added).[166]
>
> What the revisionists seem to mean by "biblical" Israel is the Israel of mythic proportions. This is the Israel reflected in numerous "stories" that are ***embellished with exaggerations*** and ***fanciful features*** such as miracles, compiled partly from sagas, legends, folk-tales, and outright inventions. Above all, it is the story of an Israel that is set in an over-arching theocratic framework whose intent is always didactic. It aims not at historical narrative per se, but at elucidating the hidden theological meaning of events and their moral significance. Of course this "Israel" is ***not historical***, except for revealing something of the historical context of its writers and final editors. But then few modern readers except Fundamentalists ever thought that it was (emphasis added).[167]

While he is often very critical of the minimalists, he himself clearly does not believe that the Bible is historical, and thus Dever is a minimalist. However, Dever has criticised scholars for holding the view that every historical event in the Bible should be "assumed to be false" unless supported by archaeological evidence. On this point maximalists would agree with Dever.

It is apparent that the distinction is not as simple as saying that Minimalists are theological liberals and Maximalists are theological conservatives. A person, like Dever, may deny the miracles of the OT, attributing such biblical accounts to the superstitious nature of people in biblical days, and still believe that the overall history of Israel is accurately portrayed in the Bible. Likewise, a person may not believe in the miracles of the Bible, such as the Resurrection, but may still be a maximalist and believe that the majority of the Bible's history is true.

The minimalist approaches the biblical text from the viewpoint that it contains a minimal amount of real history, as opposed to the maximalist viewpoint that holds to a more conservative position and embraces the maximum amount of history. Davis observes the difference between the two in that "where the combatants disagree is on the value placed on the biblical record."[168] While these are broad generalizations, most archaeologists would fall somewhere between these two approaches to biblical history.

---

[165] Kitchen, *Reliability of the OT*; *Ancient Orient and Old Testament* (Wheaton, IL: Tyndale, 1966); Hoerth and McRay, *Bible Archaeology*, Hoerth, *Archaeology and the Old Testament*; James K. Hoffmeier, ed., *The Archaeology of the Bible: Reassessing Methodologies and Assumptions* (Oxford: Lion Hudson, 2008); Edwin M Yamauchi, "Homer and Archaeology: Minimalists and Maximalists in Classical Context," in *The Future of Biblical Archaeology: Reassessing Methodologies and Assumptions*, ed. James K. Hoffmeier and Alan R. Millard (Grand Rapids: Eerdmans, 2008), 69–90; Hoffmeier and Millard, *The Future of Biblical Archaeology*, McRay, *Archaeology and the NT*; J. Randall Price and H. Wayne House, Zondervan Handbook of Biblical Archaeology: A Book by Book Guide to Archaeological Discoveries Related to the Bible (Grand Rapids: Zondervan, 2018).

[166] William G. Dever, "The Western Cultural Tradition Is At Risk," *BAR* 32, no. 2 (2006): 76.

[167] Dever, *What Did the Biblical Writers Know, and When Did They Know It?*, 46.

[168] Davis, "Theory and Method in Biblical Archaeology," 26.

Direct and Indirect Evidence

13. Reproduction of a seal (bulla) of King Hezekiah of Judah. A total of eight bullae have been discovered bearing the name of Hezekiah. Six picture a two-winged scarab (dung beetle) pushing a ball of mud or dung (see above), and two bullae picture a two-winged sundisk. All have the identical inscription: "Belonging to Hezekiah [son of] Ahaz, King of Judah."

The maximalist need not put his head in the sand and ignore the evidence. There is ample evidence all around, but sometimes it is hard to see (see *The Fallacy of Negative Proof*). Evidence can be broken down into two categories, direct and indirect, and both are valid forms of verification. An example of explicit, or direct evidence would be the royal seals with the names of the kings of Judah on them (see Fig. 12).[169] Seal-impressions (bullae) exist that verify the rule of Judah's kings e.g., "Belonging to Yotham" (739–735 BC; 2 Kgs 14:22; see Fig. 22); "Belonging to Ahaz (son of Yotham) king of Judah" (735–716 BC; 2 Kgs 15:38; "Belonging to Hezekiah (son of Ahaz) king of Judah" (715–687 BC; 2 Kgs 16:20; see Fig. 13)[170] and "Belonging to Manasseh, son of the king" (687–643 BC; 2 Kgs 20:21). There is also the famous Megiddo lion seal "to Shema (Heb. *Lšmc*) Servant of Jeroboam" (1 Kgs 12–14).[171]

The more difficult evidence to understand is the implicit or indirect evidence, but it is still valuable. This type of evidence is exemplified in the comparison of the price of a slave or the covenant structure in the biblical text with their counterparts in ancient tablets.

For example, the age of the tablets and the cost of a slave are known from the archaeological period (strata). Joseph was sold into slavery for 20 shekels (Gen 37:28). In the early second millennium the cost of a slave, according to the Code of Hammurabi (§§116, 214, 252),[172] the Mari tablets,[173] and other documents, averaged 22 shekels.[174] Inflation was in operation as it is today and so the cost of a slave gradually increased. In the Third Dynasty of Ur the cost was 10 shekels,[175] while after the eighteenth cent. it was 30 shekels (Moses, Lev 27:2) until in the first millennium the price of a slave rose to as much as 50–60 shekels (Menahem, 2 Kgs 15:20).[176] During the Persian Empire prices reached 90–120 shekels.[177] This graph of

[169] George M. Grena, *LMLK--A Mystery Belonging to the King*, vol. 1 (Redondo Beach, CA: 4000 Years of Writing History, 2004); "What Are Lmlk Stamps and What Were They Used For?," *Bible and Spade* 18, no. 1 (2005): 19–24.

[170] Nahman Avigad, *Hebrew Bullae from the Time of Jeremiah: Remnants of a Burnt Archive*, trans. Rafi Grafman (Jerusalem: Israel Exploration Society, 1986). Another seal was uncovered in 2009 by Eilat Mazar at the Ophel excavations in Jerusalem, and the only one found by archaeologists in a provenanced context. https://www.biblicalarchaeology.org/daily/biblical-sites-places/jerusalem/king-hezekiah-in-the-bible-royal-seal-of-hezekiah-comes-to-light.

[171] Avraham Negev and Shimon Gibson, eds., *Archaeological Encyclopedia of the Holy Land*, 3rd ed. (New York: Continuum International, 1996), 452–54.

[172] James Bennett Pritchard, *Ancient Near Eastern Texts Relating to the Old Testament with Supplement*, 3rd ed. (Princeton, NJ: Princeton University Press, 1969), 170, 175–76.

[173] André Parrot, Georges Dossin, and Georges Boyer, *Archives Royales de Mari: Publiées Sous La Direction de André Parrot et Georges Dossin. Textes Juridiques: Transcrits, Traduits et Commentés Par Georges Boyer*, vol. 8 (Paris: Imprimerie Nationale, 1958), 23, no. 10:1–4.

[174] A. Falkenstein, *Die Neusumerische Gerichtsurkunden*, vol. I (Munich: Beck, 1956), 88 n. 5.

[175] Ibid., I:88–90; Isaac Mendelsohn, *Slavery in the Ancient Near East; A Comparative Study of Slavery in Babylonia, Assyria, Syria, and Palestine From the Middle of the Third Millennium to the End of the First Millennium* (Oxford: Oxford University Press, 1949), 117, 155 n. 164.

[176] C. H. W. Johns, *Assyrian Deeds and Documents Recording the Transfer of Property, Including the So-Called Private Contracts, Legal Decisions and Proclamations Preserved* (Cambridge: Cambridge University Press, 1924), 542–46.

[177] Mendelsohn, *Slavery in the ANE*, 117, 155 n. 174.

inflation for the price of a slave creates a parallel track useful in dating each of the biblical events. The date for writing the biblical text corresponds to the discovered tablets by comparing the price of a slave.

The covenant structure also evolved over time and displays a unique pattern in the second and first millennium BC that Kitchen uses for dating the biblical material. According to Kitchen "the sequence of covenants is consistent, reliable and securely dated"[178] and useful for dating.

Tolerance

In a controversial discipline like archaeology how does one interact with those of differing opinions? The general response is tolerance. But what does tolerance mean? Does it mean that their views are also true and valid? Does it mean that we must accept their views as our own in order to be tolerant? Unfortunately, this is often the postmodern understanding of tolerance.[179]

The *Oxford American Dictionary & Thesaurus* defines tolerance and toleration as: "Tolerance: A willingness or ability to tolerate; forbearance. . . Toleration: The process or practice of tolerating, esp. the allowing of differences in religious opinion without discrimination."[180]

Webster's Unabridged Dictionary defines toleration as: "The endurance of the presence or actions of objectionable persons, or of the expression of offensive opinions."[181]

The definition of tolerance deals with how people are treated and how people interact with others. There are many misconceptions about tolerance in the postmodern world. Tolerance does not mean accepting that two opposing views are both valid or embracing their views. It does not mean accepting their views as correct. It means fairly representing a differing opinion. Tolerance means treating those who differ with us with respect and fairness. Stetson defines it as "patience toward a practice or opinion one disapproves of."[182]

Debate is a sound academic exercise, but must be done with respect for the person because everyone is created in the image of God (Gen 1:26–27; John 13:35). Debate must involve fairly representing the opposing views. Thus, it is important to represent an opposing view as accurately and fairly as possible. If one creates a caricature of the views of others and soundly demolishes the caricature, then you have not successfully countered their arguments.

ARCHAEOLOGICAL FALLACIES

As with many disciplines there are many fallacies commonly practiced in the discipline of archaeology. Here are a few of the more common mistakes and fallacies that deal with the archaeological method.

1. The Fallacy of Neutrality

When it comes to ideas there is no neutrality. Everyone has certain assumptions when approaching archaeology and no one is completely objective. This is seen in the debate between

---

178 Kitchen, *Reliability of the OT*, 4.

179 Josh McDowell and Bob Hostetler, *The New Tolerance: How a Cultural Movement Threatens to Destroy You, Your Faith, and Your Children* (Wheaton, IL: Tyndale, 1998), 19.

180 Christine A. Lindberg, Katherine M. Isaacs, and Ruth Handlin Manley, eds., *Oxford American Dictionary & Thesaurus*, 2nd ed. (New York: Oxford University Press, USA, 2009), 1607.

181 Daniel Webster, *Random House Webster's Unabridged Dictionary* (New York: Random House Reference, 1999), NP.

182 Brad Stetson and Joseph G. Conti, *The Truth About Tolerance: Pluralism, Diversity and the Culture Wars* (Downers Grove, IL: InterVarsity, 2005), 140; Arthur F. Holmes, *All Truth Is God's Truth* (Downers Grove, IL: InterVarsity, 1983); James W. Sire, *The Universe Next Door: A Basic Worldview Catalog* (Downers Grove, IL: InterVarsity, 1997).

minimalists and maximalists (see Minimalists vs Maximalists Approach). Whether we decide that the history recorded in the Bible is accurate or just myths, we still have a view. Everyone comes with an opinion, and if we say we have no opinion, then we have the opinion of no opinion. The issue is whether we are honest about our presuppositions and assumptions. No one can say that they take a neutral position.

2. The Fallacy of Seeing More Than is There

There is a real danger of seeing more in the archaeological evidence than is there and then championing the discovery as something that was there in the ground from the beginning. Sometimes archaeologists make claims that go beyond the evidence. For example: I have heard it said that the new discovery of the Pool of Siloam proves that Jesus healed the blind man in John 9. However, all that archaeological evidence proves is that a pool was discovered in Jerusalem (see The Pool of Siloam) and that it is likely the same pool that is mentioned in John 9. The archaeological evidence has not proven anything about Jesus healing a blind man. All one can claim is that John was accurate in describing a pool. While the probability is high, scholars cannot be certain that this is Siloam's pool as there was no inscription.

3. The Fallacy that Archaeology is an Exact Science

While archaeology is a science, it is not an exact science[183] and as Hoerth and McRay point out, not "capable of producing irrefutable evidence for a given hypothesis."[184] The inexact nature of this field of study is evident from the incomplete information that is available for a site and period. Many of the dates, that are used, are still relative dates and not exact.

In addition, once the excavation is finished, it is impossible to repeat the experiment. [185] After the season of excavation all that is left are notes, photographs, and artifacts, but the strata is gone.

But all is not lost as, Hoerth and McRay explain: "If properly conducted, however; it is a unique and comprehensive method of research that employs scientific technology in the excavation, investigation, and evaluation of cultural data."[186]

4. The Fallacy that Archaeology is a Monologue

Archaeology is a dialogue with the text of the ground. An excavation is not an exercise in pure science, where the remains are looked at as typical of all sites. Instead the artifacts tell a story of the lives of real people. However, looking at the artifacts, it is difficult to understand their lives. As Davis points out:

> We do ***not*** know what meanings a specific object or even a site carried in its own lifetime. What we may see as primary in an artifact's importance may have been unknown to the original users. . . . Wright was right when he warned the "pure scientists" that archaeology deals with human beings and thus must remain a humanistic discipline.[187]

Archaeology also requires dialogue with other scholars and disciplines which may include: photographers, artists, linguists, Egyptologists, historians, geologists, physicists, architects, botanists, zoologists, metallurgists, skin-divers, pottery and computer imagery experts, just to

---

[183] Tzaferis, "From Monk to Archaeologist," 22; Hoerth and McRay, *Bible Archaeology*, 16.

[184] Hoerth and McRay, *Bible Archaeology*, 16.

[185] Davis, "Theory and Method in Biblical Archaeology," 27.

[186] Hoerth and McRay, *Bible Archaeology*, 16.

[187] Davis, "Theory and Method in Biblical Archaeology," 26.

mention a few. In this sense, as Wright reminded us, it is not a pure science:

> I believe archaeology is far too restricted when treated as a discipline in and of itself, whether by those who presume to be pure scientists, or by those who belong to other wings of anthropology or fine arts. In my opinion, archaeology must use all of the science that it can, but in the final analysis it is dealing with human beings, and therefore it can never be anything other than one among the several branches of cultural and humanistic history.[188]

5. The Fallacy that the *a priori* Method is Bad Science

If archaeology is a dialogue, then each excavation must begin with a question or hypothesis, and in this sense we begin with an *a priori* approach.[189] The *a priori* approach is a standard method used by archaeologists for all sites. All good scientists, including archaeologists, begin with a working hypothesis and then excavate to test their hypothesis against the data collected.

For example, James K. Hoffmeier, the Egyptologist and professor of Old Testament and Ancient Near Eastern History at Trinity Evangelical Divinity School, illustrates this method for his research on Migdol. He argues: "We believe that Gardiner's proposed association of Migdol of Egyptian texts with Migdol of the Exodus narratives is a reasonable one, and thus accept it as our working hypothesis."[190]

Thus the methods used in the field are directed by the hypothesis, though there must be guards in place to stop them imposing answers on the research. This is a delicate dialogue, but one that must be followed.[191]

6. The Fallacy that the Simplest is Always the Best Answer

A governing principle in science states: "simplicity is a virtue in scientific theories and that, other things being equal, simpler theories should be preferred to more complex ones"[192] (Lat. *Entita non sunt rnultiplicanda, praeter necessitatem*). Known as Occam's Razor (also spelled Ockham; Lat. *lex parsimoniae*),[193] it is commonly used by archaeologists with some success,[194] but it must be applied with caution.[195] As we all know, the world is much more complex than first believed. It is too simplistic to suggest that the early Babylonians were not cultured after witnessing the sophisticated discoveries at Ur by Woolley and his team. It is also too simplistic to suggest that literacy never developed until after the tenth century BC. As Gary Rendsburg points out: "Taken together, the Tel Zayit abecedary, the Khirbet Qeiyafa inscription and the Gezer calendar (see Fig. 24) demonstrate that writing was well-established in tenth-century Israel— certainly sufficiently so for many of the works later incorporated into the Hebrew Bible to have been

---

188 George Ernest Wright, "The 'New' Archaeology: An Address Prepared to Be given at Idalion, Summer, 1974," *BA* 38, no. 3–4 (September 1, 1975): 115.

189 The *Webster's New World College Dictionary* defined *a priori* as a theory which is determined "before examination or analysis." Michael E. Agnes, *Webster's New World College Dictionary*, 4th ed. (Cleveland, Ohio: Webster's New World, 1999), op. cit.

190 James K. Hoffmeier, "The North Sinai Archaeological Project's Excavations at Tell El-Borg (Sinai): An Example of the 'New' Biblical Archaeology?," in *The Future of Biblical Archaeology: Reassessing Methodologies and Assumptions*, ed. James K. Hoffmeier and Alan R. Millard (Grand Rapids: Eerdmans, 2004), 61.

191 Davis, "Theory and Method in Biblical Archaeology," 27.

192 Simon Fitzpatrick, "Simplicity of the Philosophy of Science," *Internet Encyclopedia of Philosophy: A Peer-Reviewed Academic Resource*, August 13, 2014, n.p., http://www.iep.utm.edu/simplici.

193 Kevin T. Kelly, "Justification as Truth-Finding Efficiency: How Ockham's Razor Works," *Minds and Machines* 14 (2004): 485–505.

194 Collins, "Tall el-Hammam Is Still Sodom," 22.

195 William M. Thorburn, "The Myth of Occam's Razor," *Mind*, New Series, 27, no. 107 (July 1, 1918): 345–53; Elliott Sober, "Let's Razor Ockham's Razor," in *From a Biological Point of View: Essays in Evolutionary Philosophy*, ed. Elliott Sober, Cambridge Studies in Philosophy and Biology (Cambridge: Cambridge University Press, 1994), 136–57.

composed at this time."[196]

7. The Fallacy of Fitting a Square Peg Into a Round Hole

As Davis has pointed out "The flaws of a model are not fatal to the source. Too often, the biblical narrative has been forced to conform to an archaeological model."[197] As an example he mentioned the archaeological research and model of W. F. Albright and G. E. Wright, who used a selective archaeological approach which they equated with the biblical account. There are often errors in the archaeological model which may not reflect the true historical picture. Here are some helpful guidelines:

- Do not dismiss the history and geography of the Bible. The Bible is a reliable ancient text.
- Do not minimize problems or stretch interpretation of data to explain things away.
- Do not make claims beyond what the data can support. Be honest with the findings.
- Do not place upon archaeology the burden of "proving" the Bible (see the role of archaeology).

8. The Fallacy of Negative Proof

Archaeological data can be acquired either from what archaeologists have found (evidence), or not found (non-evidence). Often both of these types of evidence are mingled together to interpret the results, and both are treated as valid evidence, when in reality the only true evidence is that which has been found. Finding nothing is not valid evidence. This is called "the fallacy of negative proof" and defined by the historian, David H. Fischer, as "an attempt to sustain a factual proposition merely by negative evidence."[198] Geisler and Holden call it "the argument from silence."[199] This fallacy was applied to archaeology by Hoffmeier[200] and Merling.[201] As Merling explained: "Data not collected or not found constitute nonevidence [fallacious evidence], an argument from silence which does not have the same weight as data that are found."[202] As Hoffmeier illustrated "The absence of direct evidence for Joseph, of course, does not disprove his existence because negative evidence proves nothing."[203]

Sometimes the idea is expressed by the phrase "absence of evidence is not evidence of absence,"[204] but as Moreland and Craig explained: "Per the traditional aphorism, "absence of evidence is not evidence of absence", positive evidence of this kind is distinct from a lack of evidence or ignorance of that which should have been found already, had it existed."[205]

As Merling explained: "to admit that one has no information does not prove the information does not exist."[206] Perhaps the evidence will eventually be discovered in another

---

196 Gary A. Rendsburg, "Review of Literate Culture and Tenth-Century Canaan: The Tel Zayit Abecedary in Context by Ron E. Tappy; P. Kyle McCarter," *BASOR* 359 (August 1, 2010): 91.

197 Davis, "Theory and Method in Biblical Archaeology," 28.

198 David Hackett Fischer, *Historians' Fallacies: Toward a Logic of Historical Thought* (New York: Harper & Row, 1970), 47.

199 Geisler and Holden, *Popular Handbook of Archaeology and the Bible*, 233.

200 James K. Hoffmeier, *Israel in Egypt: The Evidence for the Authenticity of the Exodus Tradition* (Oxford: Oxford University Press, 1999), 34, 53.

201 David Merling, "The Book of Joshua, Part I: Its Evaluation by Nonevidence," *Andrews University Seminary Studies* 39, no. 1 (2001): 64–65; David Merling, "The Relationship Between Archaeology and Bible: Expectations and Reality," in *The Future of Biblical Archaeology: Reassessing Methodologies and Assumptions*, ed. James Karl Hoffmeier and Alan R. Millard, The Proceedings of a Symposium, August 12-14, 2001 at Trinity International University (Grand Rapids: Eerdmans, 2004), 33–34.

202 Merling, "The Book of Joshua, Part I," 64–65.

203 Hoffmeier, *Israel in Egypt*, 97.

204 Kenneth A. Kitchen, "The Patriarchal Age: Myth or History?," *BAR* 21, no. 2 (1995): 48; Price, *The Stones Cry Out*, 332.

205 James Porter Moreland and William Lane Craig, *Philosophical Foundations for a Christian Worldview* (InterVarsity, 2003), 155–56.

206 Merling, "The Book of Joshua, Part I," 65.

excavation or season. Fisher states it as: "Not knowing that something exists is simply not knowing."[207] There is so much more to discover and perhaps archaeologists are looking in the wrong place. As Holden and Geisler point out "one should recognize that the absence of evidence—when there has been a diligent search for it—*is* evidence of the absence of the event in the area searched."

For example, this fallacy is illustrated in the interpretation of data from Khirbet et-Tell by Miller and Dever. They used nonevidence (no MB or LB evidence) of the archaeological excavations at et-Tell (See Ai in Chapter Three) to conclude that the biblical story of Ai (considered to be et-Tell) is erroneous[208] because according to Miller there is "negative archaeological evidence" thus "archaeology denies" the biblical account.[209] But all that is known is that archaeologists have found no evidence of MB or LBA at the site of et-Tell. And certainly, as Miller points out, "absence of crucial sherds or occupational strata—in site identifications is that even the most thoroughly conducted archaeological surveys and excavations produce only samplings of evidence."[210] The Associates for Biblical Research have sought the location of Ai elsewhere and found good positive evidence for a more likely candidate at Khirbet el-Maqatir (see Ai in Chapter Three).[211]

The lack of archaeological evidence cannot support or deny the reliability of a biblical story because it says nothing about *why* there is a lack of data, and there may be other explanations for the absence of evidence. The silent evidence speaks more about the archaeological interpretation, than it does about the accuracy of the biblical story.

9. The Fallacy that the Geography of the Bible is Unreliable

Some believe that the history of the biblical text is a myth[212] implying that the geography of the Bible is also unreliable. For example, Thompson and Irwin's statement about the "ahistorical nature of the tales which make up the Pentateuch"[213] conveys the sentiment of some biblical scholars. Kitchen has answered the arguments well for the historicity of the patriarchal narrative.[214] Using Greek history as another example, Dever points out: "A generation ago, even a decade ago, Classicists and ancient historians would have dismissed Homer as a mythical figure and would have argued that the tales of the Trojan Wars were mainly "invented" by much later Greek writers."[215]

Yamauchi has marshaled compelling evidence that demonstrated that although Homer's

---

[207] Fischer, *Historians' Fallacies*, 48.

[208] William G. Dever, *Archaeology and Biblical Studies: Retrospects and Prospects: William C. Winslow Lectures, 1972* (Evanston, IL: Seabury-Western Theological Seminary, 1974), 41, 46; Merling, "The Book of Joshua, Part I: Its Evaluation by Nonevidence," 65; J. Maxwell Miller, "Archaeology and the Israelite Conquest of Canaan: Some Methodological Observations," *PEQ* 109, no. 2 (July 1977): 89.

[209] Merling, "The Book of Joshua, Part I," 65.

[210] J. Maxwell Miller, "Site Identification: A Problem Area in Contemporary Biblical Scholarship," *Zeitschrift Des Deutschen Palästina-Vereins (1953-)* 99 (January 1, 1983): 121.

[211] For another explanation for the lack of evidence at et-Tell see Merling, "Relationship Between Archaeology and Bible," 35–41.

[212] Dorothy Irwin, *Mytharion: The Comparison of Tales from the Old Testament and the Ancient Near East*, Alter Orient Und Altes Testament 32 (Neukirchen-Vluyn: Neukirchener Verlag, 1978); Thompson, *The Mythic Past*; *The Historicity of the Patriarchal Narratives: The Quest for the Historical Abraham* (Valley Forge, PA: Trinity Press International, 2002); John Van Seters, *Abraham in History and Tradition* (New Haven, CT: Yale University Press, 1975); Donald B. Redford, *A Study of the Biblical Story of Joseph: Genesis 37-50* (Leiden: Brill, 1970); *Egypt, Canaan, and Israel in Ancient Times* (Princeton, NJ: Princeton University Press, 1993).

[213] Thomas L. Thompson and Dorothy Irwin, "The Joseph and Moses Narratives," in *Israelite and Judaean History*, ed. John H. Hayes and J. Maxwell Miller (Philadelphia, PA: Westminster, 1977), 210.

[214] Kitchen, "Patriarchal Age," 48–57, 89–95.

[215] Dever, *What Did the Biblical Writers Know, and When Did They Know It?*, 279.

Iliad and *Odyssey* are literary creations, they "nonetheless preserve accurate historical memories."[216] Yamauchi concluded: "This raises an intriguing possibility: If the Hellenic world could have kept alive accurate historical details in an oral tradition lasting many centuries, couldn't the Biblical world have done so too?"[217]

As Dever concludes: "If Homer can in a sense be 'historical,' why not the Hebrew Bible?"[218] Since Homer has been shown to be a historical figure, how much more should the Bible be given consideration as a historically accurate document? If Heinrich Schliemann could use the *Iliad* and *Odyssey*, which was considered a myth, to locate Troy, why can we not use the Bible, even if it is considered a myth by some, to locate cities mentioned in this ancient text? What is clear is that the serial geography used by these ancient writers was accurate. The biblical text is an ancient primary source that it would be irresponsible *not* to consult for geographical clues for the identification of ancient sites.[219] Monson points out: "Routes, agriculture, building materials, settlement patterns, and trade all factor into the flow of events described in the Hebrew Bible and New Testament. When events are overlaid upon geographical regions, a previously unnoticed pattern emerges and locations become what Walter Brueggemann would describe as a 'storied place.'"[220]

10. The Fallacy that Most Biblical Sites Have Been Identified Using an Inscription

Of all the biblical cities on our Bible maps today only Dan, Gezer, Gibeon, Hazor, Hebron, Shiloh, and Jerusalem have a secondary inscription identifying their location.[221] Collins points out "only one identified biblical site – Ekron – has such an identifying, in situ, in-period, unquestioned inscription naming the city."[222]

Collins defines an OT primary inscription as: "one found in situ in a sealed archaeological context [locus], specifically providing the name of the site in question. Further, the inscription must date from the Old Testament period, i.e., either the Bronze Age or Iron Age. It must also be unquestionable as to translation."[223]

Shanks notes that the city of "Gezer was the first biblical city to be identified by an [secondary] inscription found at the site. . . . In 1873, the great French scholar Clermont-Ganneau found a boundary inscription dating from the Herodian period which reads in Hebrew script, 'boundary of Gezer.'"[224]

---

[216] Edwin M. Yamauchi, "Historic Homer: Did It Happen?," *BAR* 33, no. 2 (2007): 37; "Homer and Archaeology: Minimalists and Maximalists in Classical Context," 69–90; John K. Davies, "The Reliability of the Oral Tradition," in *The Trojan War: Its Historicity and Context*, ed. Lin Foxhall and John Kenyon Davies, Papers of the First Greenbank Colloquium, Liverpool, 1981 (Bristol: Bristol Classical, 1984), 101.

[217] Yamauchi, "Historic Homer: Did It Happen?," 29.

[218] Dever, *What Did the Biblical Writers Know, and When Did They Know It?*, 279.

[219] Yohanan Aharoni, *The Land of the Bible: A Historical Geography*, trans. Anson F. Rainey, 2nd ed. (Louisville, KY: Westminster/Knox, 1981); Anson F. Rainey, "Historical Geography," in *Benchmarks in Time and Culture: An Introduction to Palestinian Archaeology*, ed. Joel F Drinkard, Gerald L Mattingly, and J. Maxwell, Callaway, Joseph A Miller, ASOR/SBL Archaeology And Biblical Studies (Atlanta, Ga.: Scholars Press, 1988), 353–68; Aharoni, *The Land of the Bible*; Anson F Rainey and R. Steven Notley, *The Sacred Bridge: Carta's Atlas of the Biblical World* (Jerusalem: Carta, 2005).

[220] John M. Monson, "The Role of Context and the Promise of Archaeology in Biblical Interpretation," in *The Future of Biblical Archaeology: Reassessing Methodologies and Assumptions*, ed. James Karl Hoffmeier and Alan R. Millard, The Proceedings of a Symposium, August 12-14, 2001 at Trinity International University (Grand Rapids: Eerdmans, 2004), 323; Walter Brueggermann, *The Land*, Overtures to Biblical Theology (Philadelphia, PA: Fortress, 1977), 185.

[221] Appendix C, "How are Biblical Cities and Towns Identified and Placed on Bible Maps? Collins and Scott, *Discovering the City of Sodom*, 273–96.

[222] Ibid., 142.

[223] Ibid., 277.

[224] Hershel Shanks, "The Sad Case of Tell Gezer," *BAR* 9, no. 4 (1983): 30–42.

Since the odds of an inscription appearing, which will absolutely identify a site, are like winning the lottery, how do scholars identify biblical sites? Usually archaeologists use geographic indicators to identify a city's location. These indicators can be as simple as by the Jordan River, below Mount Nebo, near Jerusalem, etc.[225] Thus, proper use of geographical indicators rather than waiting for an inscription to appear is the common approach for identifying biblical sites. The method relied on by all scholars is to use the geography of ancient texts to locate the site, unless they are fortunate enough to locate an inscription. If Heinrich Schliemann used the text of Homer's *Iliad* to locate ancient Troy[226] surely we can use the text of the Bible to locate biblical sites such as Ur, Sodom, Ai, Jericho and Ephraim.

11. The Fallacy that a Surface Survey is the Same as an Excavation

This may seem obvious, but an archaeological surface survey consists of walking across a tell and identifying the various visible pottery sherds lying on the surface. This can give archaeologists an idea of what lies beneath the surface but is quite different from the archaeological excavation itself.

For example: *The East Jordan Valley Survey,* conducted in 1995–1996, reported that there were few EB-MB sherds at Tall el-Ḥammâm (site 190)[227] although they did identify Iron 1–3 sherds. However, the excavation reports from 2005–2014 clearly show that there are many EB and MB sherds and also architectural walls and structures.[228] Out of the 1,951 diagnostic pottery sherds read, up to the fourth season in 2009, 8% were EB, 38% were MB, and 32% were 1A 2.[229] The Iron Age ruins were lying on the surface of the upper Tell and visible to those conducting the surface survey, while the EB and MB structures and sherds were buried underground.

One must not rely on a surface survey as the definitive word on the presence or absence of an archaeological period.[230] LB pottery lying on the ground does not mean that there are archaeological structures below; while the absence of EB/MB sherds does not mean that there are no EB/MB structures lying under the ground.

Surface surveys are an important guide for initial identification, but are always trumped by excavations with excavation reports.

12. The Fallacy that All Archaeologists Use the Same Date System

See *Dating Systems and Chronology* above.

EXCAVATION METHODS

The methods used for excavation have developed significantly over the years. Every site is

---

[225] Rainey, "Historical Geography," 353–68.

[226] Susan Heuck Allen, *Finding the Walls of Troy: Frank Calvert and Heinrich Schliemann at Hisarlik* (Berkeley, CA: University of California Press, 1999), 1.

[227] Khair Yassine, Moawiyah M. Ibrahim, and James A. Sauer, "The East Jordan Valley Survey 1975 (Part Two)," in *The Archaeology of Jordan: Essays and Reports*, ed. Khair Yassine (Amman: Department of Archaeology, University of Jordan, 1988), 192.

[228] Steven Collins *et al.*, "Tall el-Hammam Season Eight, 2013: Excavation, Survey, Interpretations and Insights," *BRB* 13, no. 2 (2013): 13–14.

[229] Steven Collins, Khalil Hamdan, and Gary A. Byers, "Tall el-Hammam: Preliminary Report on Four Seasons of Excavation (2006–2009)," *ADAJ* 53 (2009): 406.

[230] Richard Hope-Simpson, "The Limitation of Surface Surveys," in *Archaeological Survey in the Mediterranean Area*, ed. Donald R. Keller and D. W. Rupp, Bar International 155 (Oxford: British Archaeological Reports, 1983), 45–48; "The Analysis of Data from Surface Surveys," *Journal of Field Archaeology* 11, no. 1 (April 1, 1984): 115–17.

unique and to a certain extent each site required its own unique combination of methods, but there are basic methods used in most excavations. One must decide which site to excavate, survey the site, excavate the site, including collecting and dating the finds, then publish what has been discovered.

For a more detailed explanation of excavation methods one can consult the available books,[231] field manuals, [232] and articles.[233] A basic outline of excavation methods is provided here.

14. Tall el-Ḥammâm on the eastern side of the Jordan Valley. The tall rises to 45m (150 ft.) although the occupation levels sit on top of the natural hill and around the base of the tall. The white arrows indicate the location of two hot springs that provided year-round water for irrigation.

Identifying a Tel

A Tel is fundamental to archaeology in the ancient Near East. The spelling of Tel or Tall is determined by its location. In Arab countries the term is spelled Tal or Tall (Arabic "mound or hill" from the Babylonian *tillu*, which meant "ruin heap."[234]; i.e., Tall el-Ḥammâm in Jordan. See Fig. 13). In Israel Tel or Tell (Heb.) is used derieved from the Hebrew (i.e., Tel Dan).

A Tell is an unnatural mound created by the repeated destruction and rebuilding of ancient cities on the same site from the pre-Hellenistic period (sites from classical antiquity are low level sites and generally not considered tells, like Rome, Corinth, Ephesus, Caesarea, Jerash, etc.). Joshua mentions the tel in his description of the conquest of Canaan and that: "none of the cities that stood on mounds [tells] did Israel burn, except Hazor alone; that Joshua burned" (Josh 11:13). A "Tel" is a pile of ruins which are completely buried in a mound, while a "Khirbet" refers to ruins that are still visible with only one or a few periods of occupation. The average size of a Tell averages 7–20 acres with the smallest measuring .5 acre with the largest at Hazor at over 200 acres. Some have as many as 20 layers of occupation.

How does an archaeologist select a site to excavate? As mentioned above, if one were looking for a new virgin Tell, such as a particular site mentioned in the Bible, then geographical

---

[231] William S. Dancey, *Archaeological Field Methods: An Introduction* (Minneapolis, MN: Burgess, 1981); Joel F. Drinkard, Gerald L. Mattingly, and J. Maxwell Miller, eds., *Benchmarks in Time and Culture: An Introduction to Palestinian Archaeology*, ASOR/SBL Archaeology And Biblical Studies (Atlanta, Ga.: Scholars Press, 1988); Philip Barker, *Techniques of Archaeological Excavation*, 3rd ed. (London: Routledge, 1993); Steve Roskams, *Excavation*, Cambridge Manuals in Archaeology (Cambridge: Cambridge University Press, 2001); Suzanne Richard, ed., *Near Eastern Archaeology: A Reader* (Winona Lake, IN: Eisenbrauns, 2003); Renfrew and Bahn, *Archaeology*; Jane Balme and Alistair Paterson, eds., *Archaeology in Practice: A Student Guide to Archaeological Analyses* (Hoboken, NJ: Wiley & Sons, 2014).

[232] William G. Dever and H. Darrell Lance, eds., *A Manual of Field Excavation: Handbook for Field Archaeologists* (Jerusalem: Hebrew Union College Press, 1978); Larry G. Herr *et al.*, *Excavation Manual: Madaba Plains Project*, revised (Berrien Springs, Mich.: Andrews University Press, 1998); Steven Collins, Carroll Kobs, and Phillip J. Silvia, *Tall el-Hammam Excavation Project Field Manual* (Albuquerque, N.M.: TSU Press, 2013).

[233] Kathleen M. Kenyon, "Excavation Methods in Palestine," *PEQ* 71, no. 1 (1939): 29–37; Peter R. S. Moorey, "Kathleen Kenyon and Palestinian Archaeology," *PEQ* 111, no. 1 (1979): 3–10; Henry O. Thompson, "Thoughts On Archeological Method," *BAR* 3, no. 3 (1977): 225–27; John W. Betylon, "Numismatics and Archaeology," *BA* 48 (1985): 162–65.

[234] William F. Albright, *The Archaeology of Palestine* (London: Taylor & Francis, 1956), 18.

indicators would be used, (see *Fallacy* no. 10 above). But more often than not, the Tell is selected first, since it is visible from the surface, and then research is carried out to determine its identification, usually employing linguistics. It is also common to continue to excavate an already excavated site, since only small sections are worked on at any given time, and there are often large areas that have gone untouched.

15. An *in situ* Iron Age 2A hippo storage jar, excavated from a storage room behind a domestic kitchen at Tall e-Hammam in Season 2, January 8, 2007. This turned out to be a complete vessel (see insert and Fig. 16), something which is rare in excavations. There were six similar jars all broken beside it with a portion of one still visible.

The Tells Utilitarian Essentials

All ancient settlements need a combination of several vital things to exist at one time to allow people to live in a particular place. Without this combination, most settlements would cease to exist; and disruptions to this combination in many cases led to the disappearance of ancient settlements.

- **Sufficient land:** population growth and expansion necessitated a suitable location for development.
- **Sufficient food:** People must eat and so food must either be grown or traded. This would necessitate either suitable agricultural land or reliable roads.
- **Sufficient water:** one cannot live in most places in the Middle East without water. Water was vital for daily life and essential if the city was under siege. The challenge was how to get water on top of a hill. Cisterns, vertical shafts, and reservoirs were used to supply water and in the NT period aqueducts were used to transport large quantities of water from reliable sources. Water was collected from rivers (*wadi,* but seasonal), fresh water springs (rare), and runoff from seasonal rains.

- **Defensible position:** settlements must be strategically located and defensible from one's enemy. This was usually accomplished by building on a natural hill with a good view of an approaching enemy.
- **Good infrastructure:** Cities needed access to efficient roads for trade and communication. Two examples of these were the King's Highway along the ridge above the Jordan valley and the *Via Maris* (Lat. "the way of the Sea") that ran from Mesopotamia to Egypt along the coast of Palestine.

Permits

Next, one must obtain a dig permit from the local authorities. In Israel this is the Israel Antiquities Authority (IAA) and in Jordan it is the Jordanian Department of Antiquities (DOA). With a permit the work can begin.

Surveying the Site

Once the site has been selected, a survey is carried out on the site to determine where to excavate, since the entire site is rarely excavated due to the size and time involved. This can be as general as a surface survey (see Fallacy No. 11 above), but will most certainly involve an intensive survey by a surveyor. All features of the site are noted including visible structures, roads, cemeteries, water features, agricultural areas, and so on. The surveyor lies out the tel in a grid pattern, assigning numbers and letters to each grid. All measurements are in the metric system in archaeology. Ground Penetrating Radar (GPR) is also used as an unobtrusive method of surveying below the surface before excavations begin, so archaeologists can decide where to begin excavations. Often aerial or satellite photography is carried out on the site to provide the big picture.

Excavating a Tel

Phases

There are three general phases to every excavation.

1) Data Collection

First is the collection of the data from the stratigraphy of the squares or structures. This involves measuring from the benchmark all material remains or artifacts that have come to light in the excavation process.

2) Analysis

Second is the study of the material remains and artifacts to determine their date and use. This will involve the reading of each piece (pottery, objects, coins, etc.) to determine its age. This is performed by experts in different periods of study.

3) Reconstruction

From the information gathered an attempt is made to reconstruct the human culture from this site. What can be learned from the date and the excavation?

Excavation Methods

The process of collecting data is achieved by means of excavation methods. In archaeology there are three approaches used in Palestine since 1948.

1. The British Method (Wheeler-Kenyon)

This approach was developed by Sir. Mortimer Wheeler in England at Verulamium (1930–1935),[235] and adapted to Near Eastern archaeology by Kathleen Kenyon at Jericho (1952–1958).[236] It uses a grid of 6m-by-6m squares with the north and east metre unexcavated and left in place through most of the excavation as a standing baulk that can be read for the various occupational periods (i.e., reading the baulk). Only the 5m by 5m square is excavated, and all features are carefully drawn on graph paper (see Fig. 16) and documented. The soil is carefully removed similar to lowering the water in a bathtub to expose all various types of loci and artifacts which are documented, measured and then removed. The vertical stratigraphy is central to this approach more than the horizontal architectural features that lay outside the square.[237]

2. The American Method (Architectural)

The American method was pioneered by George Reisner, W. F. Albright, and G. E. Wright and is considered a compromise between the British and Israeli methods. This approach focuses on the architectural remains and the horizontal exposure of complete architectural units based on the relationship of wall and floor levels. As Mazar and Bar-Yosef observe, this method is: "an effort to expose large parts of ancient settlements basing the stratigraphy on observations of the architectural development of the structures."[238] Albright emphasised the need for daily ceramic analysis along with the integration of other scientific disciplines such as zoology, botany and geology. Also Reisner emphasised photography and a meticulous numbering system.[239]

3. The Israeli Method

The founders of the Israeli method are such scholars as E. L. Sukenik, B. Mazar, I. Ben-Dor, S. Yeivin and M. Avi-Yonah – who started their careers during the 1930s and 1940s. It was further developed by Immanuel (Munya) Dunayevsky.[240]

According to Mazar and Bar-Yosef, the Israeli method was

> based on general Near Eastern tradition, of exposing selected large areas and establishing the stratigraphy by relating successions of buildings and floors to one another. The method did not differ much from that known at the large excavations of the 1930s; however, the work was done with much more care, involving many staff. The selection of the excavation areas was meticulous, taking into consideration many components to enable the construction of a stratigraphic sequence of the whole of this huge mound. Each one of the areas was big enough to allow the study of large architectural units, so that the principles of urban development during various periods could be studied. Although the use of baulks to establish the stratigraphy was almost unknown at Hazor (except in one area, dug by the French prehistorian J . Perrot), the general stratigraphic observations have since proved to be reliable. In processing the finds, a special emphasis was given to the restoration of pottery vessels from fragments

---

235 Mortimer Wheeler, *Archaeology from the Earth* (Oxford: Clarendon, 1956), 15, 113, 149, 152, 182, 195.

236 Kenyon, "Excavation Methods in Palestine," 29, 37; Joseph A. Callaway, "Dame Kathleen Kenyon, 1906 -1978," *BA* 42, no. 2 (1979): 122–125.

237 Thompson, "Thoughts On Archeological Method," 225–27; William G. Dever, "Two Approaches to Archaeological Method-the Architectural and the Stratigraphic," *Eretz-Israel* 11 (1973): 1–8.

238 Amihai Mazar and Ofer Bar-Yosef, "Israeli Archaeology," *World Archaeology* 13, no. 3 Regional Traditions of Archaeological Research II (February 1, 1982): 311.

239 Dever, "Two Approaches to Archaeological Method-the Architectural and the Stratigraphic," 1–8; Peter Douglas Feinman, "Methodism and the Origins of Biblical Archaeology: The William Foxwell Albright Story," *AUSS* 47, no. 1 (2009): 61–72; *William Foxwell Albright and the Origins of Biblical Archaeology* (Berrien Springs, Mich.: Andrews University Press, 2004); Wright, *Biblical Archaeology*, Albright, *The Archaeology of Palestine*, 21–22.

240 Yohanan Aharoni and Ruth Amiran, "A New Scheme for the Sub-Division of the Iron Age in Palestine," *Israel Exploration Journal* 8, no. 3 (January 1, 1958): 171–84; Yohanan Aharoni, "The Israeli Method," *Eretz Israel* 11 (1973): 48–53; Anson F. Rainey, "Yohanan Aharoni: The Man and His Work," *Biblical Archaeology Review* 2, no. 4 (1976): 39–40, 48; Yigael Yadin, ed., *Jerusalem Revealed: Archaeology In The Holy City, 1968-1974* (Jerusalem: Israel Exploration Society, 1976), 21, 63, 131, 137; Bar-Yosef and Mazar, "Israeli Archaeology," 310–25.

> found in proximity and to the publication of homogeneous groups.[241]

As Mazar and Bar-Yosef observed:

> This combination of the general Near Eastern "architectural" tradition with the Wheeler-Kenyon method of stratigraphic excavation brought significant results and is in fact the current basis for Israeli field methods. The Israeli method of digging, therefore, may be defined as emphasizing both the horizontal and the vertical dimensions with a declared goal of uncovering selected large parts of ancient settlements and the study of their planning as well as their detailed stratigraphic development.[242]

In addition, the daily baskets of pottery are identified by a series of two numbers: the basket number and loci number. The Israeli method is the basis for most excavation today.

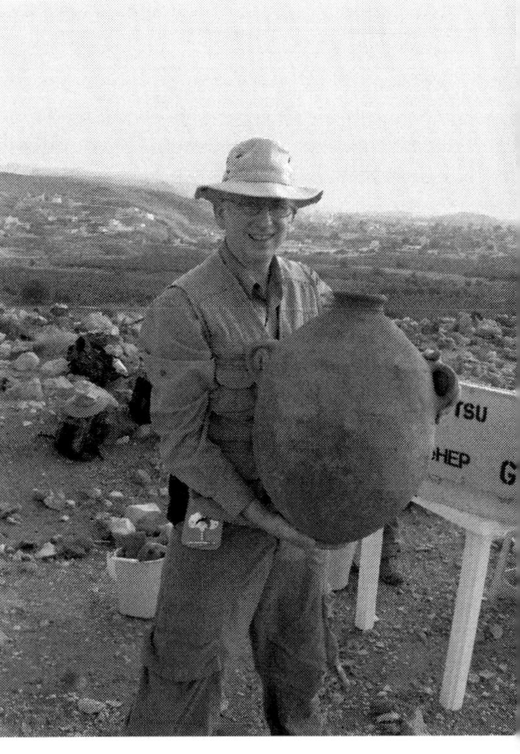

16. The author holding the extricated Iron Age 2A hippo storage jar from the Tall el-Ḥammâm, Season 2 (see Fig. 15).

Setting Up the Work Area

This involves cleaning the area of all rock and debris from the area to be excavated. If the 6m-by-6m square method is being used, then these squares need to be laid out (opening or re-opening a square). Usually the surveyor will choose two corners and a benchmark to get you started. The "primary" benchmark is a point on a high secure surface that is set by the surveyor at the start of the excavation with an assigned and recorded elevation reference. This is the mark used to take all level readings within the square. It may be assigned to one of the corner markers (i.e. stakes) of the square. From the two corners provided by the surveyor the 5m-by-5m square is easy to lie out. The diagonal measurement from corner to corner is 8.485 meters. Although the square is 6m-by-6m, only a 5m-by-5m area is excavated, leaving a 1 m wide baulk on the north and east sides of the square. Stakes are placed at all four corners with a bright coloured string lining the square. Either stones or sand bags are used to line the outside edge of the string to protect the strings and prevent volunteers from kicking things into the square once the excavation has begun, which would contaminate the site. (i.e., the archaeolgoists would not know if an object found in the square was unearthed or kicked in from outside). A Roman piece of pottery kicked into an Iron Age square is difficult to explain during pottery reading! The top 5 cm of soil is contaminated and some do not consider it to be the first locus.

The Work of Excavation

The term "excavation" comes from two Latin words *ex* meaning "out" and *cavare* meaning "to make hollow." This is a slow and methodical exercise in patience and observation of removing soil and arifacts from the ground. The trowel and dustpan are the implements of choice for taking down the levels of soil. As the volunteer pulls his trowel across the soil, he listens for the

---

[241] Mazar and Bar-Yosef, "Israeli Archaeology," 314.
[242] Ibid., 315.

change in sound from soil hitting his tool, as pottery sounds much different from rock when one comes in contact with it. When pottery is found it is not dug out but the soil around it is lowered gradually until the artifact appears at the top of the soil like a child's toy appears after letting out the water in a bath tub. The artifact must be recorded *in situ* before it is removed. The location of the artifact is documented by measuring its distance from the benchmark and distance from the benchmark level.

Tools of the Trade

The archaeologist's tool box is full of simple tools. The most basic tools are the tape measure and trowel ("Marshalltown," available in various sizes, is the brand of choice). A small handpick, called a pastiche, is used to break up the ground, with the flat end being used to trim the baulks. The dirt is collected in a rubber bucket (Arabic *goupha*) or wheelbarrow and taken to a location outside the square to be sifted for the collection of small objects, like coins, beads, or seals.

Other tools may include a compass, line level, plumb line, leaf trowels, and dental picks for fine work. A dust pan and various paint brushes for clearing soil from around artifacts are also useful. A kneeling pad is a recommended item for kneeling in the square.

Documenting a Tel

All the data is collected on a series of specially prepared forms. The most common forms that relate to the square are the: a) locus log, b) pottery reading summary, and c) weekly supervisor log. The most common forms that relate to the locus are the: a) soil locus form, b) architectural locus form, c) functional surface locus form, d) installation locus form, e) skeleton/burial locus form, f) identification tag for objects in bags, and g) pottery tag for sherds in buckets. Soil samples are taken of each locus with the help of a Munsell soil kit. The hue, value, and chroma color charts from the kit are compared with the soil sample to determine its scientific color which is recorded on the forms. For example, 5YR4/3 describes a soil with a hue of 5YR, value of 4 and chroma of 3. This soil material would be a "reddish brown" color. This is useful when comparing similar areas in two different squares, for example a burn layer or a glacis that runs through multiple squares.

Drawings

The square supervisor will normally perform the locus, baulk, and square drawings of the square (see Fig. 16) drawn to 1:25 scale ready for publication. For excavations carried out below sea level (i.e. Tall el-Ḥammâm, Jericho, Qumran, etc.) the level number will be negative and the bottom level will be larger than the top level.

Records and Photographs

Reports are submitted to the director of excavations for compilation with fieldwork and square reports to be archived. Official photographs are taken by the excavation photographer with metre sticks and compass arrows pointing north. A boom shoot may be taken of the square from a ladder or elevated pole. Today hot air balloons and model planes or drones are used to take aerial shots.

Pottery Washing

Material remains arrive from the excavation site in bags, boxes or buckets. Pottery is collected in tagged buckets and objects (bone, metal, seeds, unidentified objects, etc.) are either collected in a

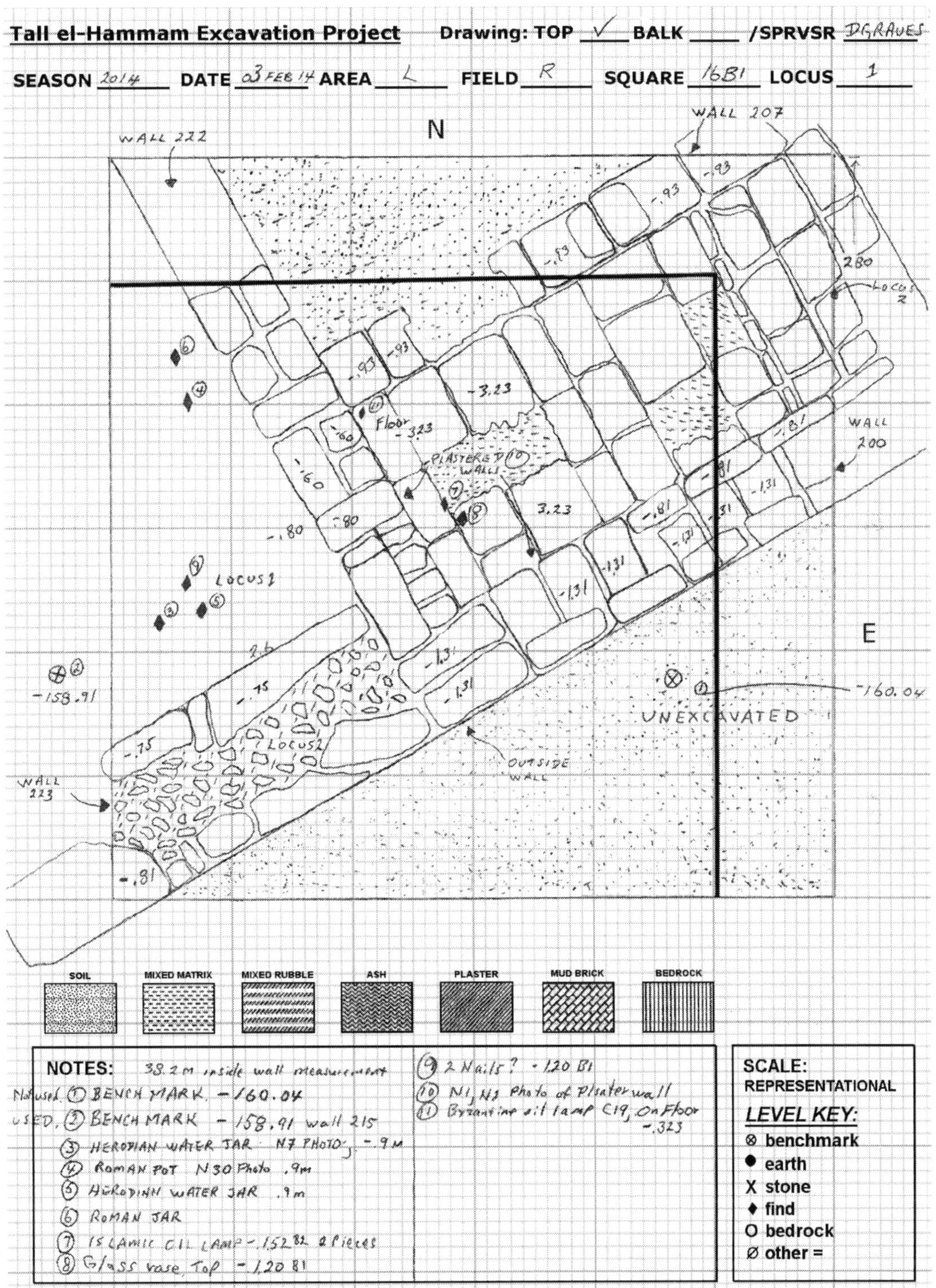

17. Scale drawing of square 16B1 in the Roman bath complex at Tall el-Ḥammâm from 2014 season. Notice that the one meter N & E baulks were removed to expose the artitectural features. Also, note that all the levels are negative numbers, as Tall el-Ḥammâm is in the Jordan Valley below sea level. Drawn to 1:25 scale.

marked envelope or tagged net bag. At the end of the dig day these are collected and taken to the pottery washing facility, where the objects are registered and the pottery is washed to revealany inscriptions, markings or unusual features. The tag is transferred to a drying basket where the cleaned pottery is placed to dry for several hours or overnight.

Dating a Tel

Two types of dating are used in combination with each other to date an archaeological site, *relative* and *absolute*.

> *Example of Absolute and Relative Dating*
>
> **Absolute Dating:** I have been teaching for Liberty since 2009. This is an exact date.
>
> **Relative Dating:** I started teaching for Liberty after my oldest daughter was born. She is 30 years old. This is relative and only tell you that I have worked for Liberty less than 30 years.

Ralative Dating

In archaeology "relative dates" are determined by relating a stucture or event to other known chronological sequences, usually in the same strata. For archaeologists it is not so essential to know the exact date that an event occurred (absolute dating), but just to know which event happened before and after another, known as chronology. It is based on what is located at the top of the tel (most current date) compared with what is at the bottom (the earliest date). Pottery, coins, but rarely inscriptions, can give a relative date for a specific stratum. Coins and pottery have been catalogued in such large quantities that a significant datebase is available to provide a close approximation of the date (usually to within 50 years). Coin dating is limited due to the late production of coins (seventh cent. BC).

This technique, called "ceramic typology",[243] has become widely used in biblical archaeology for dating stratigraphic levels. Pottery is prolifically found on archaeological sites for a number of reasons. Pottery was inexpensive to manufacture and easily broken. Cooking pots broke only after a few usages from the high heat. With so much available pottery it was often disposed of as filler in walls, grout for aqueducts, and household decorations. Because clay (*terra cotta*) pottery is virtually imperishable, it has become the most prolifically found artifact in any archaeological excavation square, almost anywhere on earth.

A helpful illustration is the evolution of the Coca-Cola container. From 1899–1902 Hutchinson glass bottles were short cylinder style; from 1900–1916 they were brown glass bottles with raised logos and triangle glued labels; in 1957 they were green glass bottles with raised logos and green glass bottles with white logos; in 1961 they were contour clear bottles with raised logos; in 1991 they were green glass bottles with white logos; in 1994 they were plastic litre bottles; and in 1955 to the present they were aluminum cans.[244] The style easily identifies the manufacturing period. In a similar way the occupational period (strata) can be dated by the style of the ancient clay pottery. Oil lamp styles are a good example and dateable to a specific period (see Fig. 18).

Also, some jar handles even have seal impressions with the specific name of a king (*lmlk* see Fig. 12)

---

[243] Davis, *Shifting Sands*, 73; Carla M. Sinopoli, *Approaches to Archaeological Ceramics* (Berlin: Springer Science & Business Media, 1991); J. N. Hill and Evans, "A Model for Classification and Typology," in *Models in Archaeology*, ed. David L. Clarke (London: Methuen, 1972), 231–74; R. Whallon, *Essays on Archaeological Typology* (Evanston, Ill: Center for Amer Archeology Pr, 1982).

[244] http://www.coca-cola.co.uk/125/coca-cola-bottles-history.html

18. Pottery styles identify the periods (top row, from left): Iron Age 2A, Bronze Age/Iron Age/and Hasmonean (Maccabean) period, Herodian; bottom row, from left to right, Late Roman, Byzantine, Islamic.

Baulk Reading

Once the square has been excavated the baulk can be read for the stratigraphy (see *Petrie and Stratigraphy*) of the site. Care must be given to the fact that not all periods are found in the same horizontal level and graves, garbage pits, backfill, modern agricultural/military activity may affect the location of objects in the strata. Large administrative building may have remained in use for several generations, while some of the dwellings could have been reoccupied and rebuilt. The streets around the house may have changed over time. It is not always easy to read the baulk and obtain a clear picture of the changes and development of a site.

Absolute Dating

"Absolute dating" (chronometric) is determined by correlating known dates, usually obtained from the period of the Pharaoh's of Eygpt, with the cultural indicators in the biblical text and the chronology of the Kings of Israel and Judah given in the books of Chronicles and Kings (see *Example of Absolute and Relative Dating*).

Radiocarbon Dating (C-14)

The radiocarbon (C-14) dating method of dating (sometimes called "absolute dating"[245]) analysed using accelerator mass spectrometry (AMS) is frequently used by archaeologists to date

[245] Ian Tattersall and Winfried Henke, eds., *Handbook of Paleoanthropology* (New York: Springer, 2007), 1:312.

finds that contain carbon (organic material, i.e., wood, bone, seeds, textiles etc.).[246] In 1949, the inventor of radiocarbon dating Willard F. Libby, and his colleagues at the University of Chicago, used a piece of wood, for which the age was known from an ancient Egyptian artifact dating to 1850 BC, to demonstrate the accuracy of this method.[247] The method is based on the belief that C-14 (an isotope of common carbon) deteriorates (radioactive decay) into carbon-12 at a measurable rate, thus allowing scientists to calculate the age of samples. While it belongs to what archaeologists call absolute dating, it is far from being unqualified.

Radiocarbon dating appears in this formula: 3500 ±100 BP (OxA 1735). The first figure of 3500 is the radiocarbon date BP (before the present date of 1950, see BP dating above) followed by the error measurement that should be added to either side of the date. Following the date the code of the laboratory which performed the testing is given in parenthesis. In this example OxA represents Oxford, England.[248] The date would be calculated between 3200–3700 BP (not 3400–3600), as the 100 is doubled in carbon dating.

Due to many variables such as nuclear testing, environment, and human contact, which affects the level of radiocarbon, the measurement is not consistent and requires calibration. Although the equipment used to date radioactive materials has become more sophisticated over time, basic problems, originally discovered by Willard Libby the inventor of the C-14 dating method, still exist. According to the journal *Science News*, "The older an artifact is, the less certain scientists can be about its age."[249] Despite the use of formulas to adjust the calibration (Bayesian methods and software models), this method is not accurate prior to 3000 BC according to Libby, the inventor of the process. He states:

> The first shock Dr. Arnold and I had was that our advisors informed us that history extended back only 5,000 years. We read books and find statements that such and such a society or archaeological site is [said to be] 20,000 years old. We learned rather abruptly that these numbers, these ancient ages, are not known; in fact, it is about the time of the first dynasty in Egypt that the last [earliest] historical date of any real certainty has been established.[250]

Davis makes a similar claim and points out the implications of this difficulty: "Radioactive dating methods cannot be calibrated with known dates before 5,000 years ago. A date given as 880 BC ±60 means an equally valid date range from 940 BC to 820 BC. Finkelstein and Silberan do not seem aware of this in their discussion about David and Solomon. The dates from Megiddo need to be seen in this light. An average means nothing, but an overlap range does have meaning."[251]

While there are additional methods for dating being used today, such as tree-ring dating (dendrochronology),[252] obsidian hydration, potassium-argon (K-Ar), uranium-series (U-series),

---

[246] Willard F. Libby, *Radiocarbon Dating* (Chicago, IL: University of Chicago Press, 1952); R. E. Taylor, *Radiocarbon Dating an Archaeological Perspective* (Amsterdam: Academic Press, 1987); James M. Weinstein, "Radiocarbon Dating," in *Benchmarks in Time and Culture: An Introduction to Palestinian Archaeology*, ed. Joel F. Drinkard, Gerald L. Mattingly, and J. Maxwell Miller, ASOR/SBL Archaeology And Biblical Studies (Atlanta, Ga.: Scholars Press, 1988), 235–60; Sheridan Bowman, *Radiocarbon Dating* (Berkeley, CA: University of California Press, 1990); Thomas E. Levy and Thomas Higham, eds., *The Bible and Radiocarbon Dating: Archaeology, Text and Science* (London: Routledge, 2014).

[247] J. R. Arnold, and Willard F. Libby. "Age Determinations by Radiocarbon Content: Checks with Samples of Known Age." *Science* 110 (1969): 678–80.

[248] Renfrew and Bahn, *Archaeology*, 136–45.

[249] Carolyn Barry, "Rolling Back the Years: Radiocarbon Dating Gets a Remake," *Science News* 172, no. 22 (2007): 344.

[250] Willard F. Libby, "Perspectives: Radiocarbon Dating" *American Scientist* 44 no. 1 (1956): 107.

[251] Thomas W. Davis, "Theory and Method in Biblical Archaeology," in *The Future of Biblical Archaeology: Reassessing Methodologies and Assumptions*, ed. James K. Hoffmeier and Alan R. Millard (Grand Rapids: Eerdmans, 2008), 27.

[252] V. C. LaMarche and T. P. Harlan, "Accuracy of Tree Ring Dating of Bristlecone Pine For Calibration of the Radiocarbon Time Scale," *Journal of Geophysical Research* 78 (1973): 8849–8858; Harold S. Gladwin, "Dendrochronology, Radiocarbon, and Bristlecones," *Creation Research Society Quarterly* 15 (1978): 24–26; M. G. L. Baillie, *Tree-Ring Dating and Archaeology* (Chicago, IL:

thermoluminescence dating (TL), and electron spin resonance (ESR),[253] they also suffer from the same problem of calibration and should be viewed cautiously, particularly for older dates. The correlation of volcanic eruptions (tephrachronology), such as Thera, has also proven helpful in dating.[254]

Pottery Reading

Once the pottery is dry it is counted, sorted, then read to determine the style of the original vessel and the period it was manufactured (EB, MB, IA, Roman, etc.). Diagnostic sherds are pieces of pottery, such as rims, handles, bases, and painted sherds, which identify the structure of the whole vessel. A variety of different dating techniques, both relative (e.g., stratigraphy, pottery) and absolute (e.g., radiocarbon, obsidian hydration, potassium-argon, coins), are used to place events in time. Pottery can be dated to within 50 years from the shape while absolutedating is less accurate (see Radiocarbon Dating). The pottery is coded and placed in a registry. Some items, that are exceptional, are marked as publishable, which are then photographed and chosen for dating evidence. These may be used in later published articles or books. Some finds are sent to specialists for analysis. Tzaferis explains that from his experience good archaeology must verify the results, stating: "the final conclusions need to be substantiated through multi-disciplinary collaboration."[255] As archaeology begins as a team effort, it also finishes in the same way.

Publishing the Finds

Once the season is over the process of publishing the finds should begin. Unfortunately, during the excavation, much of the physical evidence is destroyed. Except for objects and pottery, most scholars only have the published reports to reproduce the work of the excavation.

Robert J. Braidwood has put it well when he described the dual aspects of archaeology: "Archaeology is that science or art – it can be maintained that it is both – which is concerned with the material remains of man's past. There are two aspects to the archaeologist's concern. The first of these is the discovery and reclamation of the ancient remains; this usually involves field excavation or at least surface collecting. The second concern is the analysis, interpretation and publication of the findings."[256]

Both aspects are vital to the work of an archaeologist if the site is to be of value to humanity.

One of the deficiencies in Kenyon's work was the publication of her finds. While she did publish a popular work on Jericho in 1957 called *Digging Up Jericho* and two massive volumes in 1960 and 1964, the overwhelming task of publishing the excavation material had to be tackled piecemeal alongside her other commitments. The four final volumes, which appeared posthumously between 1981 and 1983, were achieved only by Kenyon's editor Thomas A. Holland, who compiled and reworked her excavation reports. Holland summarized the apparent results as follows: "Kenyon concluded, with reference to the military conquest theory and the Late Bronze Age walls, that there was no archaeological data to support the thesis that the town

University of Chicago Press, 1982), 23; Walter E. Lammerts, "Are the Bristlecone Pine Trees Really So Old?," *Creation Research Society Quarterly* 20 (1983): 108–115.

[253] Renfrew and Bahn, *Archaeology*, 145–56.

[254] B. V. Alloway *et al.*, "Tephrochronology," in *Encyclopedia of Quaternary Science*, ed. Scott Elias and Cary Mock, 2nd ed., vol. 4 (Edinburgh: Elsevier, 2013), 277–304.

[255] Tzaferis, "From Monk to Archaeologist," 22.

[256] Braidwood, quoted in Hoerth, *Archaeology and the Old Testament*, 14.

19. The author standing in front of the Middle Bronze age wall (W20) that his team conserved at Shiloh, January 2017.
Photo courtesy of Leen Ritmeyer

had been surrounded by a wall at the end of LB (*ca.* 1400 BCE….)."[257]

Some of her findings are challenged by Bryant G. Wood of the Associates for Biblical Research, who is an expert in Philistine "*bichrome*" pottery.[258] Wood, in examining her reports, discovered evidence from the pottery she had excavated that seemed to refute her own conclusions on the dating of the conquest and Jericho's destruction.

Publishing the finds is thus a vital component in the archaeological process and sadly it is often neglected for the pleasures of doing field work.

Conservation

In some cases conservation is carried out on fragile or decayed finds that have had enough pieces recovered to put the vessel together. A water-based glue is used to mend pottery as it can easily be separated by soaking it in water if the pieces do not fit properly or a mistake is made. Void areas are recovered with the use of modeling clay (see Fig. 89).

Vulnerable structures, such as walls, may also be reinforced to preserve them. In 2017 the author was part of the conservation of a Middle Bronze Age city wall (W18–21 in square AE-30

[257] Thomas A. Holland, "Jericho," in *OEANE*, ed. Eric M. Meyers, vol. 1 (Oxford: Oxford University Press, 1997), 223.

[258] Bryant G. Wood, "Did the Israelites Conquer Jericho? A New Look at the Archaeological Evidence," *BAR* 16, no. 2 (1990): 44–58.

and W23 in square AG-28) at Shiloh, that had been excavated earlier that season.

The basic process of conservation is first to remove all loose soil from between the stones with small instruments and water. Missing stones were replaced with available stones of the same size. Then a special mortar mixture is prepared that consisted of imported heat-treated NHL 5 natural hydraulic lime, Class M2.5 (cement-free). To the 25 kg bag of mortar is added a shovel of quarry sand for texture and half a shovel of sifted soil for coloration. To help bind the mortar to the surface, the stones were first brushed with water, then the mortar mixture was injected into creveses between the stones and brushed to a smooth finish (see Fig. 78). If there were large gaps smaller stones were placed into the mortar to take up the loose space. Once the mortar has set the exposed stones are brushed of the excess mortar. This helps to preserve the authentic look of the ancient walls (see Fig. 19).

CHART 1: MANUSCRIPT DISCOVERIES

MANUSCRIPTS[1]					
Discovery	**Image**	**Place and Discoverer**	**Origin Date /Year Found**	**Biblical Passage**	**Significance**
Ketef Hinnom Silver Scroll		Ketef Hinnom southwest of Jerusalem by Gabriele Barkay and Gordon Franz	ca. 600 BC 1979 2016	Exod 20:6; Deut 5:10; 7:9; Num 6:24–26	Earliest biblical text and mention of Yahweh
Jerusalem papyrus		Judean desert cave (Israel) but confiscated by IAA officials	ca. 650 BC 2016	Gen 14:18; Josh 10:1	Earliest mention of Jeursalem in a non-biblical document
Dead Sea Scrolls		Bedouin shepherds discovered 981 scrolls in Qumran caves	225 BC–AD 68 1947–1953	OT Manuscripts	Messianic concept, Essene sect
Nash Papyrus		Fayyum, Egypt by Antiquitiy dealer	150-100 BC 1902	Exod 20; Deut 5; 6:4–5	Until the discovery of the DSS it was the oldest copy of the Hebrew Bible
Oxyrhynchus Papyri		Oxyrhaynchus, Egypt by Bernard Grenfell and Arthur S. Hunt	AD 6–104 1897–1900	Luke 1–2	Census parallel to Luke and Acts, Koine Greek was common in the NT

[1] The most up to date and reliable list of NT papyri is provided online by the Münster Institut für textkritische Textforschung, maintained at: http://ntvmr.uni-muenster.de/liste. Another reliable online list is provided by Wieland Wilker: http://www-user.uni-bremen.de/~wie/texte/Papyri-list.html.

Discovery	Image	Place and Discoverer	*Origin Date /Year Found*	Biblical Passage	Significance
Magdalen Papyrus ($\mathfrak{P}^{64}$)		Luxor, Egypt	*ca.* AD 70–100 AD 150–175 1901	Matt 26:23, 31	Oldest copy of Matthew
Rylands Papyrus ($\mathfrak{P}^{31}$, $\mathfrak{P}^{32}$, and $\mathfrak{P}^{52}$)	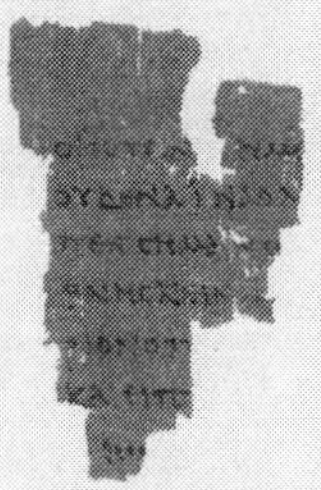	Egytian aniquities market by Bernard Grenfell	*ca.* AD 125 1920	($\mathfrak{P}^{52}$) John 18:31–33, 37–38	($\mathfrak{P}^{52}$) Earliest extant fragment of the Gospels
Chester Beatty Papyri ($\mathfrak{P}^{45}$, $\mathfrak{P}^{46}$, and $\mathfrak{P}^{47}$)		Aphroditopoli, Egypt?	*ca.* mid first cent. AD 200 1930–1931	Portions of OT, NT Gospels, Pauline Epistles, and Rev.	Early circulation of Pauline writing
Martin Bodmer Papyri ($\mathfrak{P}^{66}$, $\mathfrak{P}^{72}$, $\mathfrak{P}^{73}$, $\mathfrak{P}^{74}$, and $\mathfrak{P}^{75}$)		Pabau, Egypt	*ca.* AD 200 1952	Luke 3–24 and John 1–15, Jude, 1&2 Peter	($\mathfrak{P}^{66}$) oldest copy of John; ($\mathfrak{P}^{72}$) oldest copy of Jude, 1 and 2 Peter; ($\mathfrak{P}^{75}$) oldest fragments of Luke and John
Codex Vaticanus (**B**)	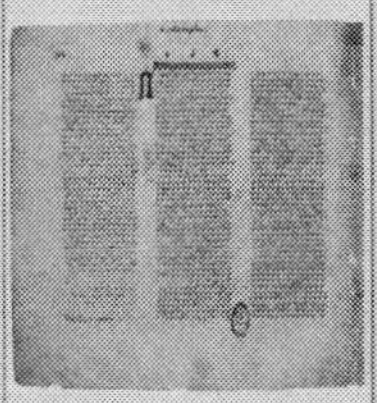	? Rome, Alexandria, or Caesarea	*ca.* AD 325–350 1475	Most of the OT and NT	Among the oldest extant Greek uncial codices

Discovery	Image	Place and Discoverer	Origin Date /Year Found	Biblical Passage	Significance
Codex Sinaiticus (**א**)		Saint Catherine's Monastery in the Sinai Peninsula, Egypt by Constantine von Tischendorf	*ca.* AD 330–360 1844	NT	Earliest complete NT
Codex Alexandrinus (**A**)		Mount Athos, then taken to Alexandria, Egypt	*ca.* AD 400–440 1616	Majority of the Septuagint and the NT	One of the early codices
Codex Ephraemi Rescriptus (**C**)		Egypt by Constantine von Tischendorf	*ca.* AD 450/1453 1843–1845	145 NT and 64 OT pages	One of the four great uncial codices
Nag Hammadi Papyri (Gospel of Judas)		Egypt by Muhammed al-Samman	*ca.* fourth–fifth cent. AD 1945	Gnostic beliefs	NT and Gnostic texts

Archaeology and the Text

The Bible contains 66 books written by around 24 authors over a period of 2000–3500 years. The Old Testament (OT) consists of 39 books, while the New Testament (NT) contains 27 books. With so many documents it is surprising that so little discussion is provided in biblical archaeology textbooks to the processes of archaeology and to biblical texts and manuscripts. This chapter will introduce the major discoveries of biblical texts and manuscripts that have provided the basis for the English Bible.

20. A photographic reproduction of part of the Isaiah Scroll discovered among the Dead Sea Scrolls from cave one. It is the best preserved of the biblical scrolls found at Qumran and contains the entire Book of Isaiah in Hebrew (second Cent. BC).

Languages of the Bible

Originally God communicated his revelation in three languages: Hebrew, Aramaic, and Greek. Thus, biblical texts can be found in all three of these languages, as well as translated into other languages, such as Copitc, Latin, Syriac, and etc.

Semitic Languages

Hebrew and Aramaic are *Semitic* languages, named after the descendants of Shem (Gen 10). Other Semitic languages include Phoenician, Assyrian, Arabic, Akkadian, Ethiopic, Sumerian (see Fig. 21), Ugaritic, Moabite, and Babylonian. All of these languages are read from right to left except Akkadian and Ethiopic, which were the first languages to indicate vowels. There is a common cultural life because of the common language. Sumerian, Greek and English are Indo-European languages and not Semitic.

21. The Sumerian pictograph tablet. This tablet is one of the first pieces of writing recovered, dating to 3100–2900 BC.

Cast of the original at the University of Pennsylvania Museum.

Cuneiform Script

The cuneiform (cursive wedge-shaped) script can be traced back to Egyptian hieroglyphs, though the phonetic values are dependent on the *acrophonic* principle of the Proto-Canaanite alphabet (LBA). For example, the letter A, represents the sound "a", while the pictogram representing an ox is pronounced as *'alp*. Ancient Hebrew and Phoenician are based on the Proto-Canaanite language (see Fig. 21, 22, 85, and 88) and this family of languages are the first to adopt a Semitic alphabet.

One might wonder why sometimes the spelling of the names in the inscriptions differs from the way they are spelled in the Bible. The main reason is that the ancient languages were more spoken than written. People spelled words the way they sounded, and because of different accents similar words with the same meaning were often spelled a bit differently. There was no standardisation of spelling, much like it is today with British and American words (colour and color). Thus, it is difficult to know if the person or place names in the tablets are the same as in the Bible. One good example is found in the Ebla tablets.

22. Reproduction of a seal (bulla) with the eighth cent. BC inscription "Belonging to Ahaz (son of) Yotham King of Judah" written in the Paleo-Hebrew script.
Housed in the Shlomo Moussaieff Collection, London.

Ebla Tablets

In 1974 and 1975 some 1,757 clay tablets (with some 4,875 fragments), now known as the Ebla tablets, were discovered under the direction of Paolo Matthiae of the University of Rome, during the excavations of the ancient city of Tell Mardikh (Ebla, Syria). They date to between 2500 BC and the destruction of the city in *ca.* 2250 BC and contain about 1,000 place names from the ancient Near East.[1] Some scholars argue that *si-da-mu*[2] and *è-ma-ra*[3] are the same cities[4] as Sodom and Gomorrah mentioned in the Bible (Gen 19), while others argue they are not.[5] It is difficult to know for sure.

Mari Tablets

During the French excavation in 1933 at Mari (Tell Hariri, Syria), led by André Parrot for the Louvre Museum, a palace, ziggurat and royal archive of 23,000 cuneiform tablets were uncovered.

The tablets were written primarily in the Akkadian language (Semitic dialect) although a few were bilingual, also written in Hurrian and Sumerian. The tablets were primarily from the second millennium (*ca.* 1800–1750 BC) and contained treaty documents between Iasmah-Adad and Zimri-Lim as well as between Zimri-Lim and Hammurabi. While the text dealt largely with financial, administrative and business transactions, they mention personal and place names with striking parallels to the patriarchal records in Genesis. The customs, practices and names reflected in the Mari texts also illustrate practices during patriarchal times that are similar to those mentioned by Abraham, Isaac, and Jacob.

For example, treaties and covenants were ratified by the killing of an ass, as described in the pact between the Shechemites and Jacob (Gen 33:19; 34:1–3). Yahweh's name appears in the

---

[1] Alfonso Archi, "The Epigraphic Evidence from Ebla and the Old Testament," *Biblica* 60, no. 4 (1979): 556–66; "The Archives of Ebla," in *Cuneiform Archives and Libraries*, ed. Klaas R. Veenhof, Papers Read at the 30e Rencontre Assyriologique Internationale, Leiden, 4-8 July 1983 (Leiden: Netherlands Institute for the Near East, 1986), 78.

[2] Giovanni Pettinato and A. Alberti, *Catalogo Dei Testi Cuneiformi Di Tell Mardikh-Ebla*, Materiali Epigrafici Di Ebla 1 (Naples: Istituto Universitario Orientale di Napoli, 1979), Catalog No. 6522; 76. G. 524; Catalog No. 75. G. 2377, obverse IV.8; Catalog No. 2379 reverse 1.5.

[3] Ibid., Catalog No. 1671; 75. G. 2233; Catalog No. 1008; 75. G. 1570 obverse 111.

[4] Clifford Wilson, *Ebla Tablets: Secrets of a Forgotten City: Revelations of Tell Mardikh, Third, Enlarged and Updated* (San Diego, CA: Creation-Life, 1981).

[5] Mark W. Chavalas and K. Lawson Younger, eds., *Mesopotamia and the Bible: Comparative Explorations* (Grand Rapids: Baker Academic, 2002), 41.

tables, but while not likely worshipped at Mari, appears to be known among the Yawi names like the OT name Yawi-El (Joel). The practice of dedication to destruction or the ban (Heb. *ḥērem*) that was placed on life and property of conquests, proclaimed at Jericho (Josh 6), is also described in the Mari tablets as the *asakkum*. Among the similarities both accounts describe severe penalties for violating the ban (*ḥērem* see p. 148 n.85).

The discovery of these tablets also greatly increased our understanding of many Biblical words. For example, the Hebrew word *'ed* in Gen 2:6 is translated by the KJV as "mist." From the context within Sumerian and Akkadian languages the same word is translated as "river" or "river god." The word "river" fits the context of Genesis 2:6.

Again in Proverbs 26:23 the KJV translates the Hebrew word *sîg* "like a potsherd covered with *silver dross*." From Ugaritic the word *spsg* means "glaze." Thus, the ESV translates Proverbs 26:23 "like the *glaze* covering an earthen vessel."[6] While the theological reliability of the text is unaffected, the meaning is clearer.

History of Hebrew

The majority of the OT was written in Hebrew with small portions written in Aramaic (Gen 31:47b; Jer 10:11b; Ezra 4–7; Dan 2–7; See Aramaic). One of the earliest Hebrew inscriptions yet discovered is by Yosef Garfinkel, the Israeli director of the Khirbet Qeiyafa excavation (2007). It dates to around 1,000–975 BC (see Khirbet Qeiyafa ostracon).[7]

For Jews, Hebrew was "the language of sanctity, the holy tongue" (*m. Sotah* 7:2). This fact helps to explain the reason for the care exercised by the scribes to ensure the precision of the Hebrew text down through the generations.

23. The Siloam inscription (facsimile) records the construction of Hezekiah's tunnel in the eighth cent. BC and demonstrates one of the oldest examples of the ancient Paleo-Hebrew alphabet. In the nineteenth century, it was damaged when thieves cut it from the tunnel wall, but it was recovered and repaired.

The original is located in the Istanbul Archaeological Museum.

Writing was well-established in Palestine while Israel was ruling there, evident from the many inscriptions that have been discovered from that period (see Paleo-Hebrew inscriptions below).[8] Diringer indicated that the Bible has "as many as 429 references to writing or written documents."[9] An early criticism of the Bible was that it could not have been written as early as it stated because writing was not used until much later. However, according to Diringer in 1934 there were "about 300 Early Hebrew inscriptions, ostraca, seals [*ca.* 150+], jar-handle-stamps [*ca.* 600+], weights [*ca.*

[6] Charles F. Pfeiffer, *Wycliffe Dictionary of Biblical Archaeology* (Peabody, MA: Hendrickson, 2000), 65.

[7] Gershon Galil, "The Hebrew Inscription from Khirbet Qeiyafa/Neta'im: Script, Language, Literature and History," *UF* 41 (2009): 193–242; S. H. William, "The Qeiyafa Ostracon," *UF* 41 (2009): 601–10; Haggai Misgav, Yosef Garfinkel, and Saar Ganor, "The Ostracon," in *Khirbet Qeiyafa: Excavation Report 2007-2008*, ed. Yosef Garfinkel and Saar Ganor, vol. 1 (Jerusalem, Israel: Israel Exploration Society, 2010), 143–60; Hershel Shanks, "Prize Find: Oldest Hebrew Inscription Discovered in Israelite Fort on Philistine Border," *BAR* 36, no. 2 (April 2010): 51–55; Christopher A. Rollston, "The Khirbet Qeiyafa Ostracon: Methodological Musings and Caveats," *Journal of the Institute of Archaeology of Tel Aviv University* 38, no. 1 (2011): 67–82; Aaron Demsky, "An Iron Age IIA Alphabetic Writing Exercise from Khirbet Qeiyafa," *IEJ* 62, no. 2 (2012): 186–99; Israel Finkelstein and Alexander Fantalkin, "Khirbet Qeiyafa: An Unsensational Archaeological and Historical Interpretation," *Tel Aviv* 39 (2012): 38–63.

[8] Alan R. Millard, "An Assessment of the Evidence for Writing in Ancient Israel," in *Biblical Archaeology Today, Proceedings of the International Congress on Biblical Archaeology, Jerusalem*, ed. Avraham Biran (Jerusalem: Israel Exploration Society, 1985), 98.

[9] David Diringer, "The Biblical Scripts," in *The Cambridge History of the Bible*, ed. Peter R. Ackroyd and Craig F. Evans, vol. 1, From the Beginnings to Jerome (Cambridge: Cambridge University Press, 1975), 13.

100+], and so on."[10] Today there are hundreds more.

Paleo-Hebrew

Also known as Old Hebrew or Archaic Biblical Hebrew (tenth to sixth cent. BC), Paleo-Hebrew is descended from the Canaanite (Phoenician) alphabet.[11] Diringer explains that: "We may assume that about 1000 BC, after the united kingdom had been established and its centralised administation organised by King David with a staff of secretaries (see, for instance, 2 Sam 8:17 and 20:25), the Early Hebrew alphabet had begun its autonomous development."[12]

By the fifth cent. it was no longer used by the Jews, who had adopted the Aramaic alphabet for their system of writing. However, a small group of modern Samaritan still use a derivative of the old Paleo-Hebrew script known as the Smaritan alphabet. Some examples of this early Hebrew script can be found in the Siloam Tunnel Inscription[13] (1880, lapidary style *ca.* 700 BC; see Fig. 23), the Gezer Calendar[14] (1908; see Fig. 24), the Lachish Letters or ostraca[15] (1935–1938, cursive style sixth cent. BC), Lachish Step inscription (1938), Tel Dan stele[16] (1993–94), and Tel Zayit Abecedary (2006). It is also unlikely that reading and writing were only confined to the professional scribe, as Albright states:

> Since the forms of the letters are very simple, the 22 letter alphabet could be learned in a day or two by a bright student and in a week or two by the dullest; hence it could spread with great rapidity. I do not doubt for a moment that there were many urchins . . . who could read and write as early as the time of the Judges, although I do not believe that the script was used for formal literature until later.[17]

24. The Gezer tablet (tenth cent. BC). The limestone agricultural calender, written in Paeo-Hebrew, is only 4 inches (10 cm) high and lists the seasons and thier associated agricultural activities.

Archaeological Museum Istanbul (no. 2089 T). Photo courtesy of Greg Gulbrandsen

[10] Ibid.; *Le Iscrizioni Antico-Ebraiche Palestinesi* (Florence, Italy: Le Monnier, 1934).

[11] Edward Yechezkel Kutscher, *A History of the Hebrew Language* (Jerusalem: The Hebrew University Magnes Press, 1982), 1; Angel Sáenz-Badillos, *A History of the Hebrew Language*, trans. John Elwolde (Cambridge: Cambridge University Press, 1996), 1–45; Benjamin Sass, *The Alphabet at the Turn of the Millennium: West Semitic Alphabet CA 1150-850 BCE*, Tel Aviv Occasional Publications 4 (Tel-Aviv: Institute of Archaeology, 2009).

[12] Diringer, "The Biblical Scripts," 13; Alan R. Millard, "The Practice of Writing in Ancient Israel," *Biblical Archaeologist* 35, no. 4 (1972): 98–111.

[13] C. Schick, "Phoenician Inscription in the Pool of Siloam," *PEQ* 12, no. 4 (1880): 238–39; Robert B. Coote, "Siloam Inscription," ed. David Noel Freedman *et al.*, *ABD* (New York: Doubleday, 1996), 6:23–24; Mitchell J. Dahood, "Siloam Inscription," *NCE*, 13:120; R. I. Altman, "Some Notes on Inscriptional Genres and the Siloam Tunnel Inscription," *Antiquo Oriente* 5 (2007): 35–88.

[14] Daniel Sivan, "The Gezer Calendar and Northwest Semitic Linguistics," *IEJ* 48, no. 1–2 (1998): 101–105; William F. Albright, "The Gezer Calendar," *BASOR* 92 (1943): 16–26.

[15] André LeMaire, *Inscriptions Hébraïques. I. Les Ostraca.*, vol. 1, Littératures Anciennes Du Proche-Orient 9 (Paris: Les Éditions du Cerf, 1977); Anson F. Rainey, "Watching for the Signal Fires of Lachis," *PEQ* 119 (1987): 149–51.

[16] Rainey, "The 'House of David' and the House of the Deconstructionists," 47; André LeMaire, "'House of David' Restored in Moabite Inscription," *BAR* 20, no. 3 (1994): 30–37; Alan R. Millard, "The Tell Dan Stele," in *The Context of Scripture: Canonical Compositions from the Biblical World*, ed. William W. Hallo and K. Lawson Younger, vol. 2 (Leiden: Brill Academic, 2002), 2:161–62; Lester L. Grabbe, *Ahab Agonistes: The Rise and Fall of the Omri Dynasty* (New York: Continuum International, 2007), 333.

[17] William F. Albright and Benno Landsberger, "Scribal Concepts of Education," in *City Invincible: A Symposium on Urbanization and Cultural Development in the Ancient Near East. Held at the Oriental Institute of the University of Chicago, December 4-7, 1958*, ed. Carl H. Kraeling and Robert M. Adams (Chicago, IL: University of Chicago Press, 1960), 123.

Classical Biblical Hebrew

Classical Biblical Hebrew flourished during the Babylonian Exile in the sixth cent. BC. The influence of the Greeks and Persians is evident from the presence of Persian and Greek loanwords in Hebrew. However, by the fifth cent. BC, the Jews gradually stopped using it and adopted the Aramaic alphabet and writing system. The present Hebrew alphabet ("square-script") is descended from these.

25. Dead Sea Scroll reproduction.
Qumran Visitors Center, Qumran, Israel.

Late Biblical Hebrew

A slight variation of the classical biblical Hebrew that corresponds to the Persian Period was used in the sixth–fourth cent. BC. It used the Imperial Aramaic script.

Qumran Hebrew

The Hebrew script of the Hellenistic and Roman Periods before 70 AD (third cent. BC–AD first cent.) used the Hebrew square script (Assyrian or literary style script), and it is still in use today.[18] The script is used in many of the Dead Sea Scroll (DSS) manuscripts discovered in the caves around Khirbet Qumran in 1946 and 1947.[19] Portions of approximately 931 manuscripts were recovered from eleven caves on the west side of the Jordan valley (*kikkār*). A twelfth cave (53)[20] that once contained DSS was identified in January 2017. A small unmarked leather scroll was found among broken Qumran pottery.[21]

26. Storage jar in which the Dead Sea Scrolls were stored with their unique lid.
Used with permission of Oriental Institute Museum

The DSS's dated from approximately 300 BC to AD 40 with the majority of them identified as Zealot correspondence from the Second Jewish Revolt[22] and the Essene monastic community.[23] But among the manuscripts discovered were copies of all of the Hebrew Bible.[24] Although the book of Esther has often been claimed to not appear in the Dead Sea Scrolls, some claim that a small DSS fragment

---

[18] Ernst Würthwein, *The Text of the Old Testament: An Introduction to the Biblia Hebraica*, trans. Erroll F. Rhodes, 2nd ed. (Grand Rapids: Eerdmans, 1994), 1.

[19] Sáenz-Badillos, *A History of the Hebrew Language*, 112–46; James C. VanderKam, *The Dead Sea Scrolls Today*, 2nd ed. (Grand Rapids: Eerdmans, 2010), 2–28.

[20] Rudolf Cohen and Yigal Yisraeli, "The Excavations of Rock Shelter XII/50 and in Caves XII/52-53," *Atiqot* 41, no. 2 (2002): 207–13.

[21] Oren Gutfeld and J. Randall Price, "Hebrew University Archaeologists Find 12th Dead Sea Scrolls Cave," *The Hebrew University of Jerusalem*, February 8, 2017, https://new.huji.ac.il/en/article/33424.

[22] J. Randall Price, *The Dead Sea Scrolls Pamphlet: The Discovery Heard around the World* (Torrance, CA: Rose, 2005), 2.

[23] VanderKam, *The Dead Sea Scrolls Today*, 99–120.

[24] F. Garcia Martinez and W. G. E. Watson, *The Dead Sea Scrolls Translated: The Qumran Texts in English*, 2nd ed. (Leiden: Brill Academic, 1997); James H. Charlesworth, *The Dead Sea Scrolls: Hebrew, Aramaic, and Greek Texts With English Translations* (Louisville, KY: Westminster/Knox, 2000); Martin G. Abegg, Jr., Michael O. Wise, and Edward M. Cook, *The Dead Sea Scrolls: A New Translation* (San Francisco, Calf.: HarperCollins, 2005).

27. Qumran Cave number 4.

(4Q267 or 4Qproto-Esther) is linked to Esther.[25] Up until the discovery of the DSS no substantial copies of any of the Hebrew Scriptures were known from before the tenth cent. AD (Aleppo Codex AD 935, Leningrad Codex Masoretic Text AD 1008).[26] The dates have been confirmed by archaeology,[27] paleography, and radiocarbon dating.[28]

There were twenty-one scroll fragments from Isaiah recovered. The most famous, *The Great Isaiah Scroll* (1QIsa[a]), is the only recovered intact OT book.[29] It was written on 17 sheets of leather stitched together, and measured 7.16 m (23.5 feet) long with 54 columns which orthographers date to between 125 and 100 BC.[30] The scrolls of Isaiah were over 1,000 years older than any previous copy and confirm the scrolls as the oldest example of Hebrew writing on papyrus. This scroll strongly confirmed the accuracy of the copies. The text of the scroll differs very little (1%) from the newer Masoretic (*Textus Receptus*) Hebrew text.[31] Vanderkam and Flint point out one very interesting variant from Isaiah 53:11: "Here a difficult reading in the traditional [Masoretic] text ("*He shall see* of the travail of his soul") is transformed by an additional word in three Isaiah scrolls [1QIsa[a], 1QIsa[b], and 4QIsa[d]] ("Out of the suffering of his soul *he will see light")*."[32]

They observe that this early reading of "light" is also found in the Septuagint (abbr. LXX see detail below) and "shows that the early Hebrew text used by the Septuagint translators actually contained the word *light*, and provides a new reading for exegesis of the passage."[33]

Another significant find is the missing verse in the KJV from the Acrostic Psalm 145. Each verse in Psalm 145 begins with a different letter of the 22 characters of the Hebrew alphabet;

---

[25] Shemarayahu Talmon, "Was the Book of Esther Known at Qumran?," *Dead Sea Discoveries* 2, no. 3 (November 1995): 249–68; Sidnie White Crawford, "Has Esther Been Found at Qumran? 4QProto-Esther and the Esther Corpus," *Revue de Qumrân* 17, no. 1/4 (65/68) (November 1996): 307–25; "Has Every Book of the Bible Been Found Among the Dead Sea Scrolls?," *Bible Review* 12 (October 1996): 28–33, 56; Jonathan Ben-Dov, "A Presumed Citation of Esther 3:7 in 4Qdb," *Dead Sea Discoveries* 6, no. 3 (1999): 401–22; Kristin De Troyer, "Once More, the So-Called Esther Fragments of Cave 4," *Revue de Qumrân* 19, no. 3 (75) (June 2000): 401–22.

[26] Price and House, *Zondervan Handbook of Biblical Archaeology*, 222–23.

[27] Lawrence H. Schiffman, ed., *Archaeology and History in the Dead Sea Scrolls: The New York University Conference in Memory of Yigael Yadin*, vol. JSOT/ASOR Monographs 2, Journal for the Study of the Pseudepigrapha Supplement Series 8 (Sheffield: JSOT Press, 1990); Jodi Magness, *The Archaeology of Qumran and the Dead Sea Scrolls* (Grand Rapids: Eerdmans, 2003).

[28] James C. VanderKam and Peter W. Flint, *The Meaning of the Dead Sea Scrolls: Their Significance for Understanding the Bible, Judaism, Jesus, and Christianity* (San Francisco, Calf.: Harper, 2002), 27–32; Georges Bonani *et al.*, "Radiocarbon Dating of the Dead Sea Scrolls," *Tigot* 20 (1991): 27–32; Georges Bonani *et al.*, "Radiocarbon Dating of Fourteen Dead Sea Scrolls," *Radiocarbon* 34, no. 3 (2006): 843–49; G. Doudna, "Dating the Scrolls on the Basis of Radiocarbon Analysis," in *Dead Sea Scrolls After Fifity Years*, ed. Peter W. Flint and James C. VanderKam, vol. 1 (Leiden: Brill Academic, 1999), 1:430–71.

[29] VanderKam, *The Dead Sea Scrolls Today*, 126–27.

[30] VanderKam and Flint, *Meaning of the Dead Sea Scrolls*, 131; R. K. Harrison and Martin G. Abegg, Jr., "Dead Sea Scrolls," in *ZPEB*, 2:64.

[31] VanderKam, *The Dead Sea Scrolls Today*, 127–29.

[32] Vanderkam and Flint, *Meaning of the Dead Sea Scrolls*, 133.

[33] Ibid.

however the KJV only has 21 verses. The *nun* verse is missing. The DSS Psalm 145, found in cave 11, includes the missing verse: "God is faithful in his words, and gracious in all his deeds"(11Q5, 11Q5Ps[a]).

Jerusalem Papyrus

28. Reproduction of Jerusalem Papyrus.

A controversial find that dates to October 26, 2016 concerns the announcement by the Israel Antiquities Authority (IAA) of a 2,700-year-old papyrus that mentions the city of Jerusalem. Its provenance is unknown but is believed to have come from one of the caves in the Judean Desert on the western shore of the Dead Sea and was confiscated from black market sellers by the Israeli robbery prevention unit.

The small scroll (4.3 in ×1.3 in [10.9cm × 3.2cm]) only contains three lines but has been translated as "From the king's maidservant, from Naharata, jars of wine, to Jerusalem."[34] Some read Naharata as "from his cave" or "from To-Maarat" or "from To-Naarat" (as in the Bible, Josh 10:36).[35]

Forgery of papyrus is a common practice and difficult to refute due to the availability of blank papyrus on the black market. A small piece of blank papyrus was discovered in cave 53 now identified as Q12) by the author's team led by Oren Gutfeld of Hebrew University and Randall Price on January 16, 2017. Forgers acquire a piece of blank papyrus and forge an significant message to receive a high price on the black market. But as the epigrapher Christopher Rollston points out "The fact that the papyrus itself has been carbon dated to the 7th century BCE certainly does not mean that the writing on the papyrus is ancient. . . In fact, it really means nothing."[36] The important analysis is the ink that was used but as Prof. Gideon Avny, head of the Antiquities Authority's Archaeological Division and a lecturer at the Hebrew University's Institute of Archaeology points out, it is difficult to accurately analyze the date of ink. The style of writing appears to be authentic but the use of a margin of a sheet of papyrus, the *modus operandi* of forgers, brings the authenticity of the discovery into question.

Writing Yahweh

Because Jews would not say God's special name–*Yahweh* (*YHWH tetragrammaton*)–scribes would insert a substitute series of letters or symbols into the text of the manuscript.

Examples of this practice can be found in the DSS Messianic Testimonia (4Q175; see Fig. 24) quoting from Deut 5:28–9, 18:18–19, 33:8–11, and Numbers 24:15–17[37] where the Messiah is described as prophet, priest, and king and *Yahweh* is described using four dots, each representing the consonants *YHWH* (*tetragrammaton*). Another DSS fragment of the Psalms

---

[34] Daniel K. Eisenbud, "IAA Refutes Authenticity Accusations of 'Jerusalem' Papyrus Inscription," *The Jerusalem Post*, October 30, 2016, http://www.jpost.com/Israel-News/IAA-refutes-authenticity-accusations-of-Jerusalem-papyrus-inscription-471239.

[35] Michael Langlois, "How a 2,700-Year-Old Piece of Papyrus Super-Charged the Debate over UNESCO and Jerusalem," *The Conversation*, November 15, 2016, http://theconversation.com/how-a-2-700-year-old-piece-of-papyrus-super-charged-the-debate-over-unesco-and-jerusalem-68376.

[36] Eisenbud, "IAA Refutes Authenticity."

[37] Joan Jacobs and Irwin Jacobs, *Dead Sea Scrolls*, ed. Margaret Dykens, San Diego Natural History Museum (San Diego: San Diego State University Press, 2007), 64–65.

(11Q5Psa [Pss 124:8–127:1]) replaced the four consonant name of God (*YHWH*) with the ancient Paleo-Hebrew letters in order to preserve the ancient name while the rest of the text was written in the square Aramaic script.[38]

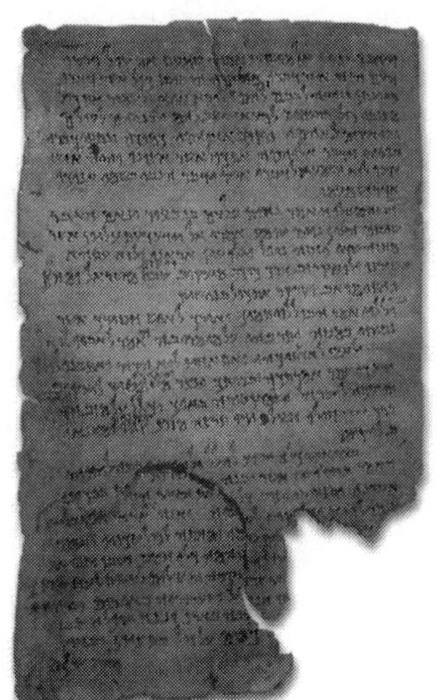

29. Dead Sea Scroll Messianic Testimony (4Q175). God's Name, Yahweh is represented by four dots.

Amman Museum, Jordan

Until their discovery it was believed that such perishable materials as parchment and papyrus could not have survived for two millennia. Since the discovery of the initial scrolls several others were discovered in eleven other caves north and south of Qumran along the west scarp of the Jordan River Valley, the most recent in 2017. This historic event is likely the greatest archaeological discovery of the twentieth century.[39]

Mishnaic Hebrew

Mishnaic Hebrew I, also known as Tannaitic, or Early Rabbinic Hebrew (first–fourth cent. AD), was used during the Roman Period after 70 AD and the destruction of the Temple, and has been identified as the spoken language of that time. Mishnaic Hebrew II, also known as Amoraic Hebrew or Late Rabbinic Hebrew, was the literary version.

For over 600 years, Jewish Pharisees recorded their writings into a compilation of some six thousand pages called the *Talmud* (Heb. "instruction"), that formed the authoratative body of Jewish tradition, comprising Jewish civil and ceremonial law. The *Jerusalem Talmud* (Palestinian), compiled at the end of the fourth or early fifth cent. AD, was combined with the *Babylonian Talmud,* which in its turn was compiled at the end of the fifth century. The heart of the *Talmud* was the *Mishnah* (Heb. pl. *Mishnayot*; "study by repetition" or "(oral) instruction"), the first major written redaction of Jewish oral traditions (oral law) and the first work of rabbinic literature (Rabbi Judah the Patriarch, third cent. AD), comprising sayings of Rabbi Judah the Patriarch (third cent. AD), and while originally written in Mishnaic Hebrew, the Talmud comments on the Mishnah's use of Aramaic. It is composed of six major sections, divided into sixty-three tractates. These documents deal with laws pertaining to the Sabbath, temple rituals, marriage, civil and criminal law. Over time additional comments and sayings called *Gemarah* (mid fourth to fifth cent. AD) were added to the *Mishnah* in Aramaic to form the *Talmud* (Heb. "translation" or "interpretation").[40]

This large volume of work is useful for understanding religious Jewish thought during the first century, although care must be exercised in using them. Perhaps Jesus refers to the *Mishnah* in speaking of the Jewish writings as "heavy burdens" (Matt 23:4).

The *Targums* were compiled using the Aramaic translation of the OT along with paraphrases, word studies, discussions of grammar and Jewish commentary. Collected over a five hundred year period, it is difficult to date individual passages. Fragments were found at Qumran among the Dead Sea Scrolls.

Midrash is another Jewish body of work that comments on the OT. They contain homilies,

---

[38] Ibid., 24–25.

[39] Keith N. Schoville, "Top Ten Archaeological Discoveries of the Twentieth Century Relating to the Biblical World," *Stone Campbell Journal* 4, no. 1 (2001): 29.

[40] An English translation is available online at www.come-and-hear.com/talmud.

commentaries, and notes. It is dated to the third cent. AD after the completion of the NT.

The *Tosefta* (Heb. "supplement") is another large collection of writings, written in Mishnaic Hebrew, that are similar to the *Mishnah* but not as authoritative for Jews.

Mishnaic Hebrew is also evident in some of the DSS's, particularly the Copper Scroll, and the Bar Kokhba Letters (AD 132–135). The shift from Aramaic to Hebrew during the Bar Kokhba revolt is explained by Yadin: "the earlier documents (DSS) are written in Aramaic while the later ones are in Hebrew. Possibly the change was made by a special decree of Bar-Kokhba who wanted to restore Hebrew as the official language of the state."[41]

While Rabbinical Hebrew was replaced with Aramaic as the spoken language, it survived in the form of a liturgical and literary language, evident in the Gemara text.[42] Aramaic had a profound impact on the development of Mishnaic Hebrew.[43]

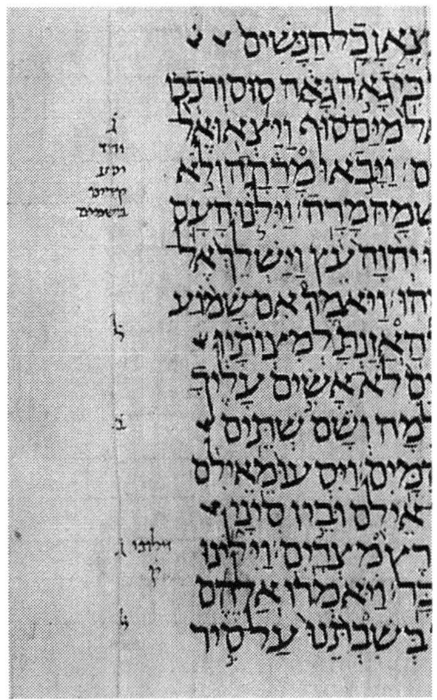

30. Codex Leningradensis, Text sample of Hebrew calligraphy.

Wikimedia Commons

Masoretic Text (MT)

This is the traditional (accepted) Hebrew text of the Bible (ca. AD 1000) composed by the Masoretes, a group of scribes in Tiberias who developed a vowel system (critical apparatus) so the text could read with confidence. There are no vowels in the early forms of Hebrew, with vowels only being added later by the *Masoretes* (המסורה from Heb. *Masora*, "tradition") scribes.[44] The complex work of adding vowel points (Heb. *niqqud*) and cantillation marks, called *Masora*, to the manuscripts (*Codex Orientales* [AD 820–850]; *Cairo Geniza* collection [AD 870]; *Codex Cairensis* [AD 896]; *Codex Babylonicus Petropolitanus* [AD 916]; *Codex Leningradensis* B19A [AD 1008; see Fig. 25]; *Aleppo Codex* [AD 1040–1050]),[45] was carried out by two independent schools (the Babylonian and Palestinian). The most famous group were led by the Palestinian families of Moses ben Asher (AD 895), and Moses ben Naphtali (AD 890–940), working from Tiberias.[46] Until that time the only way to determine the exact pronunciation and meaning of the words was by their context. Thus the Masoretes became famous for developing and standardizing the vowel notation (diacritic) system used for the pronunciation of Hebrew. The Masoretes also added a series of critical notes to ensure the accuracy of the text. According to Dotan they also "counted the letters and the words of the text; they discussed grammatical

[41] Yigael Yadin, *Bar-Kokhba: The Rediscovery of the Legendary Hero of the Last Jewish Revolt Against Imperial Rome* (London: Littlehampton, 1971), 181.

[42] Sáenz-Badillos, *A History of the Hebrew Language*, 170–71.

[43] Moshe Bar-Asher, "Mishnaic Hebrew: An Introductory Survey," in *The Literature of the Sages: Second Part: Midrash, and Targum; Liturgy, Poetry, Mysticism; Contracts, Inscriptions, Ancient Science and the Languages of Rabbinic Literature*, ed. Shmuel Safrai *et al.*, Compendia Rerum Ludaicarum Ad Novum Testamentum (Minneapolis, MN: Fortress, 2006), 567–96; Kutscher, *A History of the Hebrew Language*, 110–11.

[44] F. F. Bruce, Philip W. Comfort, and James I. Packer, *The Origin of the Bible* (Wheaton, IL: Tyndale, 2003), 158.

[45] The Russian National Library in Saint Petersburg, Russia houses the largest collection of Hebrew OT manuscripts in their Second Firkovitch Collection.

[46] Hayim Tawil and Bernard Schneider, *Crown of Aleppo: The Mystery of the Oldest Hebrew Bible Codex* (Philadelphia, PA: Jewish Publication Society, 2010).

rules, vowels, and accents."[47] The Masoretic apparatus was designed to protect the copies from error. The oldest dated Masoretic manuscript is ascribed to Moses Ben Asher and is known as the *Codex Cairensis* (AD 896) and is the basis for the Hebrew Bible today.[48]

History of Aramaic

Aramaic originated in Aram (modern Syria) and became the international language of the Persians. It belongs to the Northwest group of Semitic languages of the ancient Near East. Other similar languages are Canaanite (Hebrew, Phoenician, Moabite, and Edomite) and Ugaritic.[49]

When Abraham moved to Haran from Ur he settled in Aramean territory (Genesis 12:1–4; Acts 7:2). Abraham's father Terah and his family would have spoken Aramaic. Rebekah, Leah and Rachel would have spoken Aramaic even though they lived in Canaan after Abraham's move to Palestine.

Hebrew is similar in vocabulary and pronunciation to Aramaic and those who have mastered Hebrew find Aramaic easy to learn. But there are sufficient differences to make the two languages distinct in their look and sound.

Portions of the OT books of Ezra (Ch. 4–7) and Daniel (Ch. 2–7) are written in Aramaic along with Gen 31:47b and Jer 10:11b. Parts of Daniel were written in Aramaic because this was the language of the Persian Empire, where he was living and working as a high ranking political attaché. The correspondence of Ezra was of international interest and thus was written in the diplomatic language of the local rulers.

Along with Greek and Hebrew, Aramaic was also commonly used as a language in Israel in the first cent. AD. By then the OT was completely translated into Aramaic and available to Jesus and the disciples although they mostly used the Septuagint. The NT Aramaic dialect was sometimes called Hebrew (John 5:2; 19:13, 17, 20; 20:16; Acts 21:40; 22:2).

The Targum (Ezra 4:7) is the Aramaic translation of the OT and also the collection of Aramaic commentaries on the OT text.[50] It has varying degrees of accuracy with the translation of the Hebrew text. While the Targum assists in our understanding of Jewish interpretation, they are not a reliable witness to the Hebrew text.

History of Greek

The Greek language was popularized by Alexander the Great (336 BC) and remained in use until about AD 500. The NT was written in common marketplace Greek called *Koine* or Hellenistic Greek. It was the first cent. vernacular rather than the more sophisticated classical Greek of the philosophers.[51]

God gave his revelation of his son in the common expressive language of the people. For example, there are four words for love, which narrow the meaning to either: godly love (Gr.

---

[47] David Bridger and Samuel Wolk, *The New Jewish Encyclopedia* (Springfield, NJ: Behrman, 1962), 309.

[48] Aron Dotan, "Ben-Asher, Moses," ed. Fred Skolnik and Michael Berenbaum, *EJ* (New York: MacMillan, 2006), 3:321.

[49] Klaus Beyer, *Aramaic Language: Its Distribution and Subdivisions* (Göttingen: Vandenhoeck & Ruprecht, 1986); Joseph A. Fitzmyer, *The Semitic Background of the New Testament* (Grand Rapids: Eerdmans, 1997), 57–84; R. Buth, "Aramaic Language," ed. Stanley E. Porter and Craig A. Evans, *DNTB* (Downers Grove, IL: InterVarsity, 2000), 86–89; F. W. Dobbs-Allsopp, "Aramaic," ed. David Noel Freedman, Allen C. Myers, and Astrid B. Beck, *EDB* (Grand Rapids: Eerdmans, 2000), 84–85.

[50] Yehuda Komlosh, "Targum," ed. Fred Skolnik and Michael Berenbaum, *Encyclopaedia Judaica* (New York: MacMillan, 2006), 19:513.

[51] Matthew S. Demoss, *Pocket Dictionary for the Study of New Testament Greek* (Downers Grove, IL: InterVarsity, 2001), 77.

agape), sexual love (Gr. *eros*), brotherly love (Gr. *philios*), or the affection parents have for children, vassals for rulers, or the love of dogs for their masters (Gr. *storge*).

There are several unique characteristics of Greek, which include:

- The Greek alphabet contains 24 letters compared with 26 in English.
- Capitals are only used to describe proper names.
- Sentences begin with lower case.
- Sentences do not have spaces between the words.
- The question mark is a semi-colon [; = ?].

The Septuagint (LXX)

The *Septuagint* is the Greek translation of the Hebrew OT. The term *Septuagint* comes from the Latin word *septuaginta* meaning "seventy," and is based on the tradition that about 70 Jewish translators were involved in this work. The abbreviation for the Septuagint is thus LXX, the Roman numeral for seventy.[52]

One of the negative influences, which came from the spread of Hellenism, was that the Hebrew Scriptures were no longer understandable in the synagogues. Thus, the Septuagint was the first translation of the Bible (280–200 BC) and was the Bible predominately used by Jesus and the NT writers.[53]

31. The library of Celsus in Ephesus (modern Selçuk, Turkey). It was built in honour of Roman Senator Tiberius Julius Celsus Polemaeanus and completed by his son in 135 AD. The library held 12,000 scrolls but was destroyed by an earthquake with all of its contents in 262 AD.

Origin of the Septuagint

There are four ancient historical accounts of the origin of the Septuagint (*Ep. Arist.* 1–82; Aristobulus in Eusebius *Praep. Ev.* 13.12.1–2; Philo *Mos.* 2.26–44; Josephus *Ant.* 12.2.1–16 §§11–118; *Ag. Ap.* 2.4 §§45–47). One of the stories of the creation of the Septuagint is told in the *Letter of Aristeas* (*ca.* second cent. BC). Aristeas was reportedly an eyewitness to the events, that Demetrius of Phaleron (director of the Alexandrian Library?) was directed by Ptolemy II Philadelphus (285–246 BC) to collect all the books in existence for the library at Alexandria, Egypt. Noticing that the Jewish Scriptures were not found in Greek, he sent word to the Jews at the temple in Jerusalem to convince the high priest to send seventy-two Jewish scholars to translate the OT into Greek. The work was completed in seventy-two days on the isle of Pharos.[54]

---

[52] Natalio Fernández Marcos and Wilfred G. E. Watson, *The Septuagint in Context: Introduction to the Greek Version of the Bible* (Leiden: Brill, 2000); Jennifer Mary Dines and Michael Anthony Knibb, *The Septuagint* (New York: T&T Clark, 2004); Moisés Silva and Karen Jobes, *Invitation to the Septuagint* (Grand Rapids: Baker Academic & Brazos, 2005).

[53] Mogens Müller, *The First Bible of the Church: A Plea for the Septuagint*, JSOTSup 206 (Sheffield: Sheffield Acaemic Press, 2009).

[54] R. James H. Shutt, "Letter of Aristeas," ed. David Noel Freedman *et al.*, *ABD* (New York: Doubleday, 1996), 1:380–382; Stanley E. Porter, "Septuagint/Greek Old Testament," ed. Stanley E. Porter and Craig A. Evans, *DNTB* (Downers Grove, IL: InterVarsity, 2000), 1099–1106.

Although the technology for binding books was not developed until the first cent. BC, the Septuagint was never a complete Bible as we know it today until the early centuries of the Christian Church.

Western writers, up to this time, wrote longer works contained in scrolls. Scrolls were created by hand-stitching individual sheets together to form a single volume. The documents were classified and then rolled up to be stored in the library in small square storage boxes on shelves or racks. If there was room, then several scrolls would be stored together. A large document like the Hebrew Bible was too large to store as one scroll so it was broken down into smaller scrolls for storage and handling. As the OT books were translated into Greek and collected into one volume, the deuterocanonical writings were likely associated with the original Hebrew Bible as they were stored together. This is likely how the deuterocanonical books came to be included in the Septuagint volume.

The Septuagint is invaluable to the study of the Greek of the NT period in both the Jewish and Christian communities. Richard Longnecker argues for the multilingual context of first cent. Palestine exemplified in Jesus' use of the Septuagint: "it may be that in his applications of the OT, Jesus, who normally spoke in Aramaic but could also use Greek and Mishnaic Hebrew to some extent, at times engaged himself in textual selection among the various Aramaic, Hebrew and Greek versions then current, and some of the septuagintal features in the text-forms attributed to him actually arise from him."[55]

The LXX provides additional light on the original Hebrew Bible. For example Jewish scholars argue that the Hebrew word *almah* in Isaiah 7:14 should be translated "young woman" and not "virgin", but the translators of the Septuagint understood Isaiah as speaking about a virgin since they used the Greek word *parthenos* to translate the Hebrew word *almah. Parthenos* means virgin in Greek. In rebuttal Jewish scholars replied that other Greek translations, (i.e., Aquila, Symmachus, and Theodotion)[56] used the Greek word *neanis* which was translated as "young woman" in Isaiah 7:14. However, these Jewish scholars, who lived after the birth of Jesus, had a motive to weaken the prophecy of the virgin birth and thus used a different word. The Jewish scholars who translated the OT 300 years before Jesus' birth did not have any such agenda and simply translated the term as they understood Isaiah, which is confirmed by the discovery of the *Isaiah Scroll* in the DSS.

ORAL TRADITION

The tools of writing developed out of oral communication and changed forever the way in which people communicate. Before writing had come into existence, the only communication form was through spoken words. In early civilizations, people did not have the option of writing important information down; they would store it in their minds and pass it on by telling other people. Susan Niditch describes the process as: "They work the land, live in villages led by elders, and continue to tell stories, preserve custom and law, and cite proverbs orally."[57] Eventually people did acquire the ability and tools to write, yet even when they had gained the knowledge, the form of the communication remained the same. Writing was structured after the form of oral speech. Niditch goes on to explain that: "Those versed in oral tradition might create

[55] Richard N. Longenecker, *Biblical Exegesis in the Apostolic Period*, 2nd ed. (Grand Rapids: Eerdmans, 1975), 65–66.

[56] Dines and Knibb, *The Septuagint*, 84–90; Henry Wace, *A Dictionary of Christian Biography: And Literature to the End of the Sixth Century A.D. With an Account of the Principal Sects and Heresies* (Peabody, MA: Hendrickson, 1994), 22.

[57] Susan Niditch, *Oral World and Written Word: Ancient Israelite Literature*, Library of Ancient Israel (Louisville, KY: Westminster/Knox, 1996), 3.

oral-sounding works in literature. . . . An oral performance may be written down later from memory – people's memories in traditional cultures in which people are not used to printed or written texts are sometimes extraordinary."[58]

Often the ancient people would have to store vast amounts of information in their memory, because they did not have the modern convenience of physical storage devices. They either remembered the information or it was lost forever.

Spodek describes the results: "Over the millennia it grew into a rich literature, including chronological lists of kings, religious inscriptions, spells to protect the dead, autobiographies, stories, wisdom texts of moral instruction, love poems, hymns to gods, prayers, and mathematical, astronomical, and medical texts."[59]

Within Greco-Roman culture it was customary for educated boys to copy and memorize large sections of "the epics of Homer, the tragedies of Euripides, the comedies of Menander and the speeches of Demosthenes."[60] But by far, the most important work to be written down and memorized was the Bible. The process began with the skill of a scribe.

PROFESSIONAL SCRIBES

Strictly speaking a scribe means anyone who can write (Heb. *sôpēr* from *sāpar*, "to count, tell"; *pi'el*, "to recount").[61] In the biblical world, most people had no need to read or write, although more could read than could write.[62] Most people could go to a scribe sitting at the city gate and for a small fee have their message written down.[63]

32. Relief of a group of Egyptian scribes (*ca.* 2300 BC).

The tomb of Mereruka, Saqqara, Egypt

OT Scribes

The term scribe (Heb. *sôpēr)* developed into a technical term for a skilled professional who wrote (Ezek 9:2) or received dictation as a copying secretary or an *amanuensis* (Jer 36:4, 32) for letters or to copy legal records (Jer 32:12; 36:26). Baruch, Jeremiah's scribe, describes his occupation as: "He [Jeremiah] dictated all these words to me, while I wrote them with ink on the scroll" (Jer 36:18; see also 8:8).

In the ancient Near East, scribes had training in multiple languages, international law, and wisdom literature and its interpretation (Sir 39:1–8). While the earliest discovered examples of writing come from the nineth cent. BC, the Ten Commandments were written (Exod 19:10–25) considerably earlier (conservative view) and kept in the Ark of the Covenant for posterity (Deut 10:4–5).[64] In an oral culture a written record would provide authority, accuracy and accessibility.

---

[58] Ibid., 4–5.

[59] Howard Spodek, *World's History: Combined Volume*, 4th ed. (Upper Saddle River, NJ: Prentice Hall, 2010), 59.

[60] James S. Jeffers, *The Greco-Roman World of the New Testament Era: Exploring the Background of Early Christianity* (Downers Grove, IL: InterVarsity, 1999), 254.

[61] Joe Bailey Wells, "The Scribes," in *ZHB*, ed. David Alexander and Pat Alexander, 3rd ed. (Grand Rapids: Zondervan, 1999), 64–65; Donald J. Wiseman, "Scribe," ed. I. Howard Marshall *et al.*, *NBD* (Downers Grove, IL: InterVarsity, 1996), 1068.

[62] Millard, "The Practice of Writing in Ancient Israel," 98–111.

[63] Niditch, *Oral World and Written Word: Ancient Israelite Literature*, 58.

[64] A. S Diamond, *The Earliest Hebrew Scribes* (New York: Jewish Book Council, 1960).

The royal or chief scribe (2 Chr 24:11) acted as the "Secretary of State" and often advised the King but ranked under the Chronicler, who kept the state records (2 Sam 8:16; 1 Kgs 4:3). During war the scribes took on military duties, compiling the list of those called out for war (Judg 5:14). The profession was connected to the temple, but separated from the priesthood until at least the period of the Exile (2 Kgs 12:10; Jer 36:12–21). The Levites were scribes employed for the rebuilding of the temple (2 Chr 34:13). The role of the scribe developed into preachers, judges, copyists, preservers, and interpreters of the law (Ezra 7:6) in the post-exilic period. By the second cent. BC most of the scribes were priests who interpreted the law (1 Macc 7:12) similar to the NT model.

33. Qumran benches used by scribes to work on.
Old Amman Museum, Jordan

NT Scribes

In the NT they were called *Scribes* (Gr. *grammateis)* or more accurately lawyers (Gr. *nomikoi),* teachers of the law (Gr. *nomodidaskaloi),* or judges in the Sanhedrin (Matt 16:12; 22:35; 26:3; Mark 14:43, 53; Luke 22:66; Acts 4:5; Josephus *Ant.* 18.16f.).

In the NT their duties included developing the Jewish synagogue service, preserving the law (Heb. *torah*) by claiming their oral tradition was more important than the Mosaic law (Mark 7:5ff), and teaching the law to their disciples (1 Macc 7:12), frequently in the temple (Luke 2:46; John 18:20). According to Feinberg, Scribes were unpaid for their services in the Sanhedrin and "therefore obliged to earn their living by other means if they had no private wealth."[65] Scribes were part of the Pharisee's movement, siding with Paul against the Sadducees on the matter of the resurrection (Acts 23:9).[66]

Scribes' Toolbox

The scribe was well educated and carried tools of the trade. The typical scribe would wear a writing case on their belt called an "inkhorn" or "writing case" (Ezek 9:2). They would also carry reed-pens (Jer 8:8), a small knife for making corrections and cutting papyrus (Jer 36:23); and, optionally a stylus with a frayed reed tip or cut stem for forming the cuneiform script.

Messages written by OT scribes on stone would first mark the text in ink on the stone to be engraved. Then a sculptor or mason would engrave the writing into the stone, evident from some Assyrian scribes who left behind the ink marks.[67] Prior to the Persian period, when Aramaic dominated, no space was placed between words, but after the mid nineth cent. there is evidence of "clear mark of separation between words."[68]

The precision of ancient scribes is illustrated by Millard:

> In a recently published papyrus fragment from Elephantine, dated 484 B.C., the name of king Xerxes Ahasuerus) is seen for the first time written in Aramaic with prosthetic *alep* as in the Old Testament and

[65] Charles Lee Feinberg, "Scribes," ed. I. Howard Marshall *et al.*, *New Bible Dictionary* (Downers Grove, IL: InterVarsity, 1996), 1068.

[66] Asher Finkel, *The Pharisees and the Teacher of Nazareth: A Study of Their Background, Their Halachic and Midrashic Teachings, the Similarities and Differences*, Arbeiten Zur Geschichte Des Spa¨tjudentums Und Urchristentums 4 (Leiden: Brill, 1964).

[67] Samuel M. Paley, *King of the World: Ashur-Nasir-Pal II of Assyria* (New York: Brooklyn Museum, 1976), 117, 123 n.24.

[68] Alan R. Millard, "In Praise of Ancient Scribes," *Biblical Archaeologist* 45, no. 3 (1982): 147.

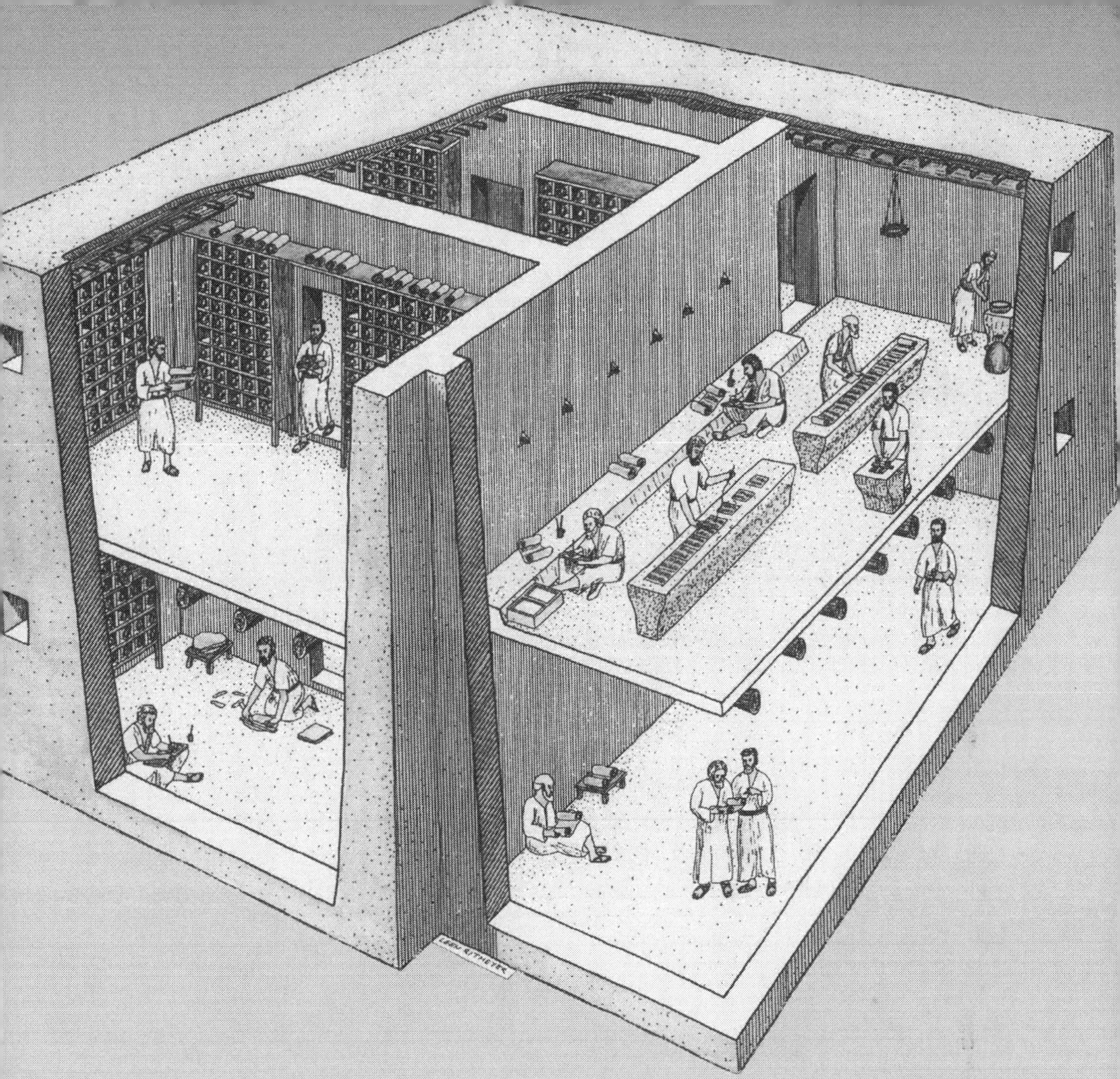

34. Qumran Scriptorium. According to the Dead Sea Scrolls, ten men were continually employed in the Qumran Library. Here we see the process of producing the scrolls from the cutting of individual pages and drawing lines on them, the copying from other scrolls, and the assemblage and mending of scrolls on long tables. A special room was set aside for the storing of the scrolls in individual boxes.

in Akkadian. From the same age there also survives a seal now in the British Museum. According to its Aramaic inscription, this cylinder seal belonged to a Persian, Parshandatha son of Artadatha. Where an identical name is read in Esth 9:7, the likelihood that the Jewish scribes correctly preserved a good Persian name seems high.[69]

When the NT documents were published, numerous professional copies were simultaneously made by scribes.[70] In the *scriptorium* at Qumran the ruins of a narrow masonry

[69] Ibid., 151; "The Persian Names in Esther and the Reliability of the Hebrew Text," *JBL* 96, no. 4 (December 1, 1977): 481–88.

[70] Emanuel Tov, "The Copying of a Biblical Scroll," in *Hebrew Bible, Greek Bible and Qumran: Collected Essays*, ed. Emanuel Tov, Texts and Studies in Ancient Judaism 121 (Tübingen: Siebeck, 2008), 107–27.

table were discovered together with long benches attached to the walls (see Fig. 33 and 34).[71] Also, four or five inkwells (ceramic and bronze) were discovered (see Fig. 36), two of which contained carbon based dried ink (Jer 36:18). The carbon was bound together with vegetable gum, oil or honey. Some of the Dead Sea Scrolls were damaged from acids in the ink that may have leached from the metal inkwells. Sometimes red ink was used, produced from red ochre or iron oxide and gum.[72]

36. Bronze inkwell from Qumran.

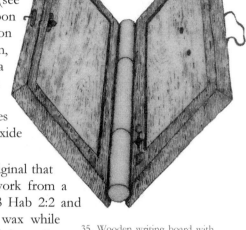

Each scribe would make a single copy from an original that was read aloud.[73] It was common for the scribe to work from a desk,[74] holding a wooden board (Ezek 37:16; Isa 30:8 Hab 2:2 and Luke 1:63; see Fig. 35) or stone covered with bees wax while impressing letters into the wax with a sharp stylus.[75] If the scribe made a mistake it was easy to either smooth out the wax or heat the tablet to 50°C. We derive our expression "a clean slate" (Lat. *tabula rasa*) from this practice. In 2016, over 400 tablets were found at an excavation in London, 87 of which have been deciphered.[76] At a later time the message was transferred from the wax board to papyrus or parchment (Heb. *klaf* leather sheets) and sewn together into a scroll. This makes the discovery of the original autographs of the Bible likely impossible since they were possibly first written in wax.

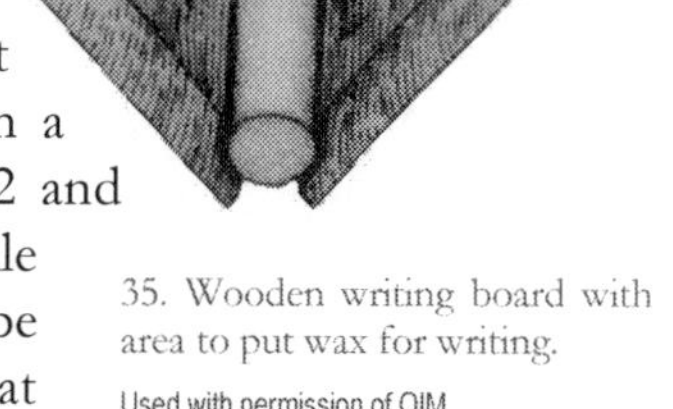

35. Wooden writing board with area to put wax for writing.
Used with permission of OIM

A well preserved wooden writing board was discovered in the wreck of a merchant ship off the coast of Turkey (Uluburun) dating to 1300 BC.[77] Bienkowski and Millard also describe the discovery of an ancient wax book: "Wax-covered tablets could also make books. A high-class set of twelve ivory leaves, with gold hinges at alternate edges, was prepared for Sargon II of Assyria and recovered from a well at Nimrud. Enough was remained to reveal that the book had apparently contained over 7,500 lines of an encyclopedia of omens."[78]

37. Ostracon bearing the name "ben Yair" which could be short for Eleazar ben Ya'ir, the leader of the Zealots.

Occasionally broken pieces of pottery (*ostracon*) were used to write short notes or letters (e.g Lachish letters). Ostraca were sometimes used

[71] Stephen Goranson, "Qumran: A Hub of Scribal Activity," *BAR* 20, no. 5 (1994): 36–39.

[72] Stephen Goranson, "An inkwell from Qumran," *Michmanim* 6 (1992): 37–40; Yoram Nir-El and Magen Broshi, "The Black Ink of the Qumran Scrolls," *Dead Sea Discoveries* 3, no. 2 (1996): 157–67.

[73] Millard, "In Praise of Ancient Scribes," 143–53.

[74] Bruce M. Metzger, "When Did Scribes Begin to Use Writing Desks?," in *New Testament Tools and Studies* (Leiden: Brill, 1960), 123–37.

[75] André LeMaire, "Writing and Writing Materials," ed. David Noel Freedman *et al.*, *ABD* (New York: Doubleday, 1996), 1002.

[76] Staff, "UK's Oldest Hand-Written Document at Roman London Dig," *BBC News*, June 1, 2016.

[77] Robert Payton, "The Ulu Burun Writing-Board Set," *Anatolian Studies* 41 (1991): 99–106.

[78] Piotr Bienkowski and Alan R. Millard, eds., *Dictionary of the Ancient Near East* (Philadelphia, PA: University of Pennsylvania Press, 2000), 56–57.

in placing a vote, as in the ballots discovered at Masada with names perhaps identifying the order or role in the resulting suicide (see Fig. 37).[79]

KINDS OF MANUSCRIPTS

Manuscripts (MSS) were produced by hand either on papyrus (Lat. via Gr. *papuros;* see Fig. 33) produced from the Egyptian bulrush (see Fig. 38) or parchment (Lat. *pergamenum*; French *parchemin,* Dutch *perkament*; Spanish *pergamino*), produced from thin untanned sheep, goat or calf skin (Herodotus *Hist.* 5.58). Vellum (Lat. *vitulus* "calf skin") is a type of fine parchment, but only made from calf skin.[80]

38. Papyrus plant harvested from the Nile River in Egypt prepared to make papyrus. The stem is triangular in shape, like a pyramid.

Papyrus, found as early as 3100 BC, was used for manuscripts,[81] and was manufactured from the pith of the bulrush plant, which grew almost exclusively on the marshy banks of the Nile River in Egypt (Job 8:11; Pliny *Nat.* 13.11; see Fig. 38).[82] In moist conditions Papyrus has a life of only a century or two; however, in the dry desert conditions of the Dead Sea such documents have survived for nearly 2000 years. Scrolls were formed by sewing sheets of parchment or papyrus together with a linen thread (see Jer 36:1–32, Ezek 3:1–3).

Manuscripts written on both sides are called *palimpsest* and one was found from the seventh cent. BC near Qumran[83] and 160 are known from St. Catherine's Monsatery in Sinai Egypt. The Dead Sea Scrolls were written primarily on tanned leather,[84] not on the fine processed leather parchment, produced in Pergamum in the fourth cent. AD. The Latin word for scrolls, *volvere* ("to roll"), is where the English word *volume* originated.

Uncial

Uncial is a script written entirely in capital letters (third to eighth cent. AD), but which can also be used as a type of manuscript that is all written in capital letters, such as the *Codex Sinaiticus.*

Minuscule

Minuscule (not spelled miniscule) refers to manuscripts that use lowercase letters. Minuscule manuscripts had their origins in the seventh century. The earliest Greek miniscule are the *Uspenski Gospels* (MS461 AD 835).[85] The ancient Greeks did not capitalize sentences, so writing

---

[79] Yigael Yadin, Y. Hevrah, and Y. Meshorer, *Masada: The Aramaic and Hebrew Ostraca and Jar Inscriptions: The Coins of Masada* (Jerusalem: Israel Exploration Society, 1989); Ehud Netzer, "The Last Days and Hours at Masada," *BAR* 17, no. 6 (1991): 20–32; Allen R. Millard, *Reading and Writing in the Time of Jesus* (New York: Continuum International, 2004), 97.

[80] Marion Kite and Roy Thomson, eds., *Conservation of Leather and Related Materials*, Conservation and Museology (Boston, MA: Butterworth-Heinemann, 2005), 201.

[81] Raymond P. Dougherty, "Writing upon Parchment and Papyrus among the Babylonians and the Assyrians," *Journal of the American Oriental Society* 48 (January 1, 1928): 109–35.

[82] LeMaire, "Writing and Writing Materials," 6:999–1006.

[83] Ibid., 1003.

[84] Philip J. King and Lawrence E. Stager, *Life in Biblical Israel* (Louisville, KY: Westminster/Knox, 2001), 309.

[85] Bruce M. Metzger, *Manuscripts of the Greek Bible: An Introduction to Greek Palaeography* (Oxford: Oxford University Press, 1981), 102.

in minuscule was not a problem for scribes.

IMPORTANT BIBLICAL MANUSCRIPTS

The study of ancient documents is called paleography. Biblical manuscripts were produced in the form of either scrolls or books (Latin *codex* meaning "block of wood;" plural *codices*). The apostles and prophets wrote God's message on parchments, which no longer exist. However, there are over 7000 NT manuscripts and between 30–35,000 Latin copies. Compare this with Plato, who died (348/347 BC) over 2300 years ago, but only one copy of his work has survived.

Of the notable discoveries the following stand out: the Dead Sea Scrolls; *Nag Hammadi* library (see Fig. 117); *Oxyrhynchus Papyri*; NT Papyri; and the Codex *Sinaiticus*. From the thousands of manuscripts that these discoveries have brought to light, translators are now able to provide more accurate translations of the text by correcting uncertain words through the discipline of Textual (lower) Criticism.[86] Following are several groups of manuscripts which stand out for their important to biblical research.

OT Pseudepigrapha

The term *Pseudepigrapha* means "false writings" and commonly refers to numerous works of Jewish religious literature dealing with people and events from the OT. They were written between 200 BC and AD 200. While most have been lost, *4 Ezra* (AD 120) mentions the existence of at least seventy (14:45–46), while portions of at least fifty still survive with some of them being quoted by the NT. None of them were accepted as part of the Hebrew OT, the Protestant or Catholic OT, or the Catholic Apocrypha. Some of these works include: *3 and 4 Maccabees, Assumption of Moses, Ethiopic Book of Enoch (1 En.), Slavonic Book of Enoch (2 En.), Book of Jubilees, Greek Apocalypse of Baruch (3 Bar.), Letter of Aristeas, Life of Adam and Eve, Martyrdom and Ascension of Isaiah, Psalms of Solomon, Sibylline Oracles, Syriac Apocalypse of Baruch (2 Bar.),* and *Testaments of the Twelve Patriarchs.*[87]

Oxyrhynchus Papyri

Oxyrhynchus in Egypt was the location for the discovery of 100,000 papyrus fragments comprising 3,875 individual documents. The *Oxyrhynchus Papyri*,[88] written in Greek and Latin, were uncovered between 1897 and 1907 (see Fig. 34). They are kept by the Egypt Exploration Society, in the Sackler Library, Oxford. Since 1898, seventy-one volumes have been published with an estimated forty more volumes to follow (one per year). While they contain numerous types of documents (legal, letters, bills, wills, etc.), of interest to biblical scholars are early

---

[86] Kurt Aland and Barbara Aland, *The Text of the New Testament an Introduction to the Critical Editions and to the Theory and Practice of Modern Textual Criticism*, trans. Erroll F. Rhodes, 2nd ed. (Grand Rapids: Eerdmans, 1995); Keith Elliott and Ian Moir, *Manuscripts and the Text of the New Testament: An Introduction for English Readers* (Edinburgh: T&T Clark, 1996); Emanuel Tov, *Textual Criticism of the Hebrew Bible* (Minneapolis, MN: Augsburg Fortress, 2001); Philip Comfort, *Encountering the Manuscripts: An Introduction to New Testament Paleography & Textual Criticism* (Nashville, TN: Broadman & Holman Academic, 2005).

[87] James H. Charlesworth, *The Old Testament Pseudepigrapha: Apocalyptic Literature and Testaments*, vol. 1, 2 vols. (Peabody, MA: Hendrickson, 1983); *The Old Testament Pseudepigrapha: Expansions of the Old Testament and Legends, Wisdom and Philosophical Literature, Prayers, Psalms, and Odes, Fragments of Lost Judeo-Hellenistic Works*, vol. 2, 2 vols., Anchor Bible Reference Library (New York: Doubleday, 1985); Michael E. Stone, ed., *Jewish Writings of the Second Temple Period: Apocrypha, Pseudepigrapha, Qumran Sectarian Writings, Philo, Josephus*, The Literature of the Jewish People of the Second Temple and the Talmud 2 (Leiden: Brill Academic, 1984); John Joseph Collins, *The Apocalyptic Imagination: An Introduction to Jewish Apocalyptic Literature*, 2nd ed., The Biblical Resource Series (Grand Rapids: Eerdmans, 1998); James R. Davila, *The Provenance of the Pseudepigrapha* (Leiden: Brill, 2005).

[88] Bernard Pyne Grenfell and Arthur Surridge Hunt, *The Oxyrhynchus Papyri*, 75 vols. (London: Egypt Exploration Society, 2009). See www.papyrology.ox.ac.uk/POxy for the online manuscripts.

fragments dating from the first half of the second to seventh cent. AD (Roman and Byzantine period), including the Gospels (𝔓[77], *P.Oxy.* 2683, Matt 23:30–39; 𝔓[104], *P.Oxy.* 4404, Matt 21:34–37, 43; and 𝔓[109], *P.Oxy.* 4448, John 21:18–20), Romans (𝔓[10], *P.Oxy.* 209, Rom 1; 𝔓[113] *P.Oxy.* 4497, Rom 2; 𝔓[27] *P.Oxy.* 1355, Rom 8–9), and Revelation (𝔓[115], *P.Oxy.* 4499, Rev 2–3, 5–6, 8–15; 𝔓[24], *P.Oxy.* 1230, Rev 5–6) along with non-canonical gospels, *Didache*, (*P.Oxy.* 1782), *The Shepherd of Hermas* (*P.Oxy.* 1172, 3527, 4705), and a work of Irenaeus (*P.Oxy.* 405).[89] The importance to Christian scholarship cannot be overstated, as many of the documents are much older than previously discovered texts.

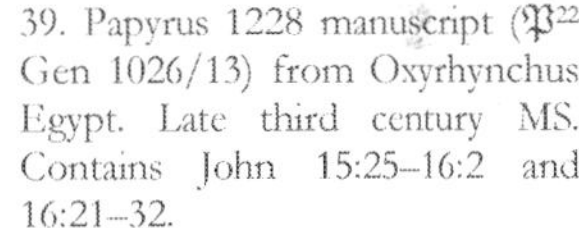

39. Papyrus 1228 manuscript (𝔓[22] Gen 1026/13) from Oxyrhynchus Egypt. Late third century MS. Contains John 15:25–16:2 and 16:21–32.

The NT Papyri

The NT Papyri are a series of over one hundred and twenty fragments mostly discovered in Egypt between 1895 and 1897.[90] In 1900 only 9 papyri manuscripts were known, but by 2008 there were 124 papyri. According to Daniel B. Wallace, director of The Center for the Study of New Testament Manuscripts in 2012:

> seven New Testament papyri had recently been discovered—six of them probably from the second century and one of them probably from the first. These fragments will be published in about a year. These manuscripts now increase our holdings as follows: we have as many as eighteen New Testament manuscripts (all fragmentary, more or less) from the second century and one from the first. Altogether, about 33% of all New Testament verses are found in these manuscripts. But the most interesting thing is the first-century fragment...if this Mark fragment is confirmed as from the first century, what a thrill it will be to have a manuscript that is dated within the lifetime of many of the original followers of Jesus! Not only this, but this manuscript would have been written before the New Testament was completed.[91]

These papyri are identified by the gothic letter 𝔓 with the number of the papyri in superscript. Other important manuscripts include:

- The *Rylands Papyri* (see Fig. 40) is an extensive collection of over 2,000 Greek manuscripts, 500 Coptic papyri, and around 800 Arabic papyri. The most famous Greek fragment is 𝔓[52] (Gr.P.457), known as St. John's fragment, which is generally accepted as the earliest (early second cent. AD) extant piece of the NT (see Fig. 35). However, a

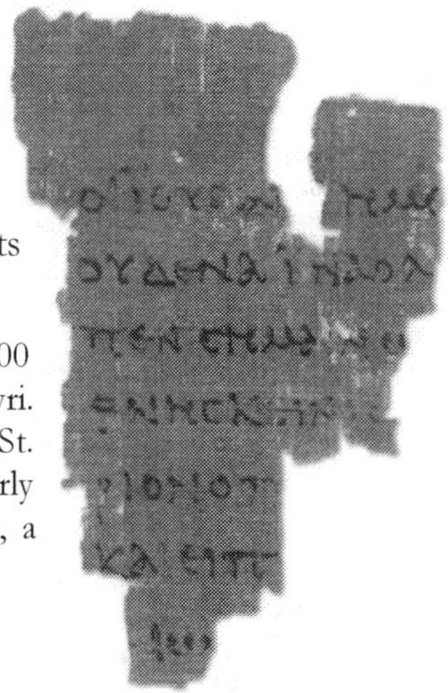

40. The *recto* of Rylands Papyrus 𝔓[52] (Gr.P.457) of John 18:31-33. Papyrologist Bernard Grenfell (1920), as preserved at the John Rylands Library.

---

[89] Roger S. Bagnall, *Early Christian Books in Egypt* (Princeton, NJ: Princeton University Press, 2009); AnneMarie Luijendijk, *Greetings in the Lord: Early Christians and the Oxyrhynchus Papyri* (Cambridge, MA: Harvard University Press, 2009).

[90] For a list of significant NT Manuscript Papyri see Geisler and Holden, *Popular Handbook of Archaeology and the Bible*, 111–22, 373–82.

[91] Daniel B. Wallace, "Earliest Manuscript of the New Testament Discovered?," *The Center for the Study of New Testament Manuscripts*, February 10, 2012, http://www.csntm.org/.

recent manuscript has come to light in 2012, which may predate it, along with the early dating of the *Magdalen Papyrus* (𝔓^{64}). The 𝔓^{52} fragment contains a small Greek fragment of papyri with John 18:31–33, on one side and verses 37–38 on the back (*verso*). It is the passage where Jesus was discussing the nature of truth with Pilate. The use of the Hadrianic script dates the fragment between AD 117 and 138.[92] The papyrus fragment was part of a larger codex, and one of the earliest surviving examples of a literary codex. This fact has lead many paleographers to conclude that NT codices did exist in the first cent. AD and supports the early date for the writing of John's Gospel.[93] It is conserved with the other *Rylands Papyri* at the John Rylands University Library, Manchester.[94]

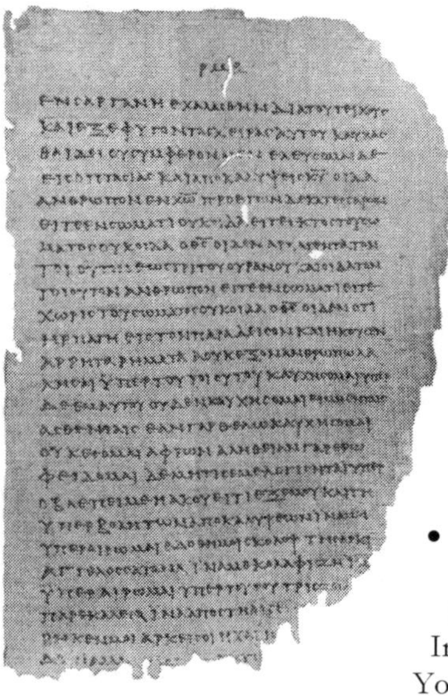

41. *Folio* from 𝔓^{46} a third cent. Papyrus codex of the Epistles of Paul containing 2 Corinthians 11:33–12:9.

P. Chester Beatty II; Ann Arbor, University of Michigan / Wikimedia Commons

- *Chester Beatty Papyri*: A total of eleven manuscripts (86 leaves), seven OT, three NT (Gregory-Aland no. 𝔓^{45}, 𝔓^{46}, and 𝔓^{47}), and portions of the *Book of Enoch* (fourth cent. AD, Dublin, Ireland 1930–31) dating to approximately AD 200 (see Fig. 41).[95] Young Kyu Kim claims that 𝔓^{46} and Qumran fragment 7Q5 should be dated to the mid first cent. AD,[96] while most scholars prefer the *ca.* AD 200 date.[97] However, if Kim's dating is correct, this would mean that there is an almost complete copy of Paul's letters written before the end of the first-century.[98] Even acceptance of the later date of AD 200 is significant, as it places a collection of Pauline writing in circulation very early.
- The *Magdalen Papyrus* (𝔓^{64}) consists of three small fragments of a papyrus of the gospel of Matthew discovered in Luxor, Egypt in 1901. Roberts dates the document to the late AD 200's.[99] Based on comparisons with other known papyri from the first-cent. Thiede concluded that 𝔓^{64} should be dated as early as 70–100 AD.[100] Several scholars have challenged Thiede's conclusions.[101]

---

[92] Philip W. Comfort and David P. Barrett, eds., *The Text of the Earliest New Testament Greek Manuscripts*, Corrected and Enlarged ed. (Wheaton, IL: Tyndale, 2001), 365–68, BibleWorks. v.8.; Christopher M. Tuckett, "𝔓^{52} and Nomina Sacra," *New Testament Studies* 47, no. 4 (October 2001): 544–48; Larry W. Hurtado, "𝔓^{52} (P.Rylands Gr 457) and the Nomina Sacra; Method and Probability," *TynBul* 54, no. 1 (2003): 443–74; Don Barker, "The Dating of New Testament Papyri," *New Testament Studies* 57, no. 4 (2011): 571–82; Stanley E. Porter, "Recent Efforts to Reconstruct Early Christianity on the Basis of Its Payrological Evidence," in *Christian Origins and Greco-Roman Culture: Social and Literary Contexts for the New Testament*, ed. Stanley E. Porter and Andrew W. Pitts (Leiden: Brill, 2013), 71–84.

[93] Brent Nongbri, "The Use and Abuse of 𝔓^{52}: Papyrological Pitfalls in the Dating of the Fourth Gospel," *HTR* 98, no. 1 (January 2005): 31.

[94] Colin H. Roberts, *An Unpublished Fragment of the Fourth Gospel, in the John Rylands Library* (Manchester: Manchester University Press, 1935).

[95] Frederic G. Kenyon, *The Chester Beatty Biblical Papyri, Fasciculus III Supplement, Pauline Epistles* (London: Walker, 1937).

[96] Young Kyu Kim, "Palaeographic Dating Of P46 To The Later First Century," *Biblica* 69 (1988): 248–57.

[97] S. R. Pickering, "The Dating of the Chester Beatty-Michigan Codex of the Pauline Epistles (P46)," in *Ancient History in a Modern University: Volume II (Early Christianity, Late Antiquity And Beyond)*, ed. T. W. Hillard *et al.*, Ancient History Documentary Research Centre, Macquarie University, NSW Australia (Eerdmans, 1998), 216–27.

[98] Philip W. Comfort and David P. Barrett, *The Complete Text of the Earliest New Testament Manuscripts* (Grand Rapids: Baker Books, 1999).

[99] Colin H. Roberts, "An Early Papyrus of the First Gospel," *HTR* 46 (1953): 233.

[100] Carsten P. Thiede, "Papyrus Magdalen Greek 17 (Gregory-Aland P64): A Reappraisal," *TynBul* 46 (1995): 29–42; Carsten P. Thiede, "Papyrus Magdalen Greek 17 (Gregory-Aland P64): A Reappraisal," *Zeitschrift Für Papyrologie Und Epigraphik* 105 (1995): 13–20; Matthew D'Ancona and Carsten Thiede, *The Jesus Papyrus* (New York: Doubleday, 2000).

[101] J. K. Elliott, "Review of the Jesus Papyrus by Carsten Peter Thiede; Matthew d'Ancona; Gospel Truth? New Light on Jesus and the Gospels by Graham Stanton," *NovT* 38, no. 4 (1996): 393–99; Peter M. Head, "The Date Of The Magdalen Papyrus Of

- *Martin Bodmer Papyri* (Bibliotheca Bodmeriana, Geneva 1955–56).[102]

Nag Hammadi Library

This collection of fifty-two Gnostic papyri (1,200 pages), written in Coptic, was discovered in a sealed jar by a local farmer at Jabal al-Tarif near *Nag Hammadi* in Egypt in December 1945 (see Fig. 117). Of the thirteen leather-bound papyrus codices, one was burned but not destroyed by the farmer's wife.[103]

While they date to the fourth cent. AD, they are based on earlier Greek manuscripts from the first to third cent. AD.[104] They are important for understanding the religious beliefs of the Gnostics, some of whom Paul dealt with in his NT letters (Col 2:8–23; 1 Tim 1:4; 2 Tim 2:16–19; Titus 1:10–16, etc.). Today they are stored in the Coptic Museum of Cairo[105] and are available online.[106] They deal with a reinterpretation of the biblical accounts of creation and include various visions that pertain to Gnostic beliefs as proposed by Marcion, Cerinthus, and Basilides.[107]

The most controversial document found among the papyri is the Gospel of Thomas, which contains a list of 114 sayings (Gr. *logia*) attributed to Jesus, but dates to *ca.* AD 140–170.[108] B. P. Grenfell and A. S. Hunt in the 1890's identified a number of fragments (*P.Oxy.* 1, *P.Oxy.* 654, and *P.Oxy.* 655) among the Oxyrhynchus Papyri without any title, which they called "Saying of Our Lord," "New Sayings of Jesus," and a "Fragment of a Lost Gospel" that have since been identified by Henri-Charles Puech as part of the Gospel of Thomas.[109] See also the Gospel of Judas in *Chapter Six: The Gospels* (see Fig. 117).

Some of the sayings are characterized by a series of questions that the disciples purportedly asked Jesus between the period of his resurrection and the ascension, but do not mention his messianic nature, crucifixion or resurrection.[110] While some similarities with the gospels have been pointed out,[111] the work is not accepted as canonical by the majority of scholars[112] and is seen as reliant on details found in the Gospels, not the reverse. While Yamauchi acknowledges the non-Christian nature of many of the tractates, based on their later date he argues that they

---

Matthew (P. Magd. Gr. 17 = P64): A Response To C. P. Thiede," *TynBul* 46 (1995): 251–85; D. C. Parker, "Was Matthew Written Before 50 CE? The Magdalen Papyrus Of Matthew," *ExpTim* 107 (1996): 40–43.

[102] James Neville Birdsall, *The Bodmer Papyrus of the Gospel of John* (Wheaton, IL: Tyndale, 1960).

[103] James M. Robinson, "The Discovery of the Nag Hammadi Codices," *BA* 42, no. 4 (October 1, 1979): 206–24; Christoph Markschies, *Gnosis: An Introduction* (New York: T&T Clark, 2003), 48.

[104] Marvin Meyer, *The Gnostic Discoveries: The Impact of the Nag Hammadi Library* (New York: HarperCollins, 2005); Marvin Meyer and James M. Robinson, eds., *The Nag Hammadi Scriptures: The Revised and Updated Translation of Sacred Gnostic Texts Complete in One Volume* (New York: HarperCollins, 2009).

[105] Birger A. Pearson, "Nag Hammadi Codices," ed. David Noel Freedman, *ABD* (New York: Doubleday, 1996), 4:984–93.

[106] www.nag-hammadi.com.

[107] James M. Robinson, ed., *The Nag Hammadi Library: A Translation of the Gnostic Scriptures* (London: HarperCollins, 1990); Meyer and Robinson, *Nag Hammadi Scriptures*.

[108] April D. DeConick, *The Original Gospel of Thomas in Translation: With a Commentary and New English Translation of the Complete Gospel*, The Library of New Testament Studies (New York: Bloomsbury, 2006); Darrell L Bock, *The Missing Gospels: Unearthing the Truth Behind Alternative Christianities* (Nashville, TN: Nelson, 2006); Craig A. Evans, *Fabricating Jesus: How Modern Scholars Distort the Gospels* (Downers Grove, IL: InterVarsity, 2006), 52–78; Christopher W. Skinner, *What Are They Saying About the Gospel of Thomas?* (New York: Paulist, 2012).

[109] Stephen J. Patterson, Hans-Gebhard Bethge, and James M. Robinson, *The Fifth Gospel: The Gospel of Thomas Comes of Age* (New York: Bloomsbury Academic, 1998), 34 n.2.

[110] Alister E. McGrath, *Christian Theology: An Introduction* (Hoboken, NJ: Wiley-Blackwell, 2006), 12.

[111] Christopher Tuckett, "Thomas and the Synoptics," *NovT* 30, no. 2 (April 1, 1988): 132–57.

[112] Helmut Koester, *Ancient Christian Gospels: Their History and Development*, 2nd ed. (New York: T&T Clark, 1992), 84–86; Christopher W. Skinner, *What Are They Saying About the Gospel of Thomas?* (New York: Paulist, 2012).

"do not therefore establish a case for a pre-Christian Gnosticism."[113]

NEW TESTAMENT CODICES

First century Christians appear to prefer their Bibles in the form of a codex (bound book) than a scroll. Virtually all manuscripts from the third and fourth cent. AD are found as codices. Some of the important codex manuscripts include Codex Alexandrianus (no. A or 02); Codex Vaticanus (no. B or 03); Codex Ephraemi Rescriptus (no. C or 04); Codex Bezae Cantabrigiensis (no. D or 05); Codex Claromontanus (no. D or 06); Codex Washingtonianus (no. W or 032); and Codex Koridethi (theta Θ or 038).[114]

42. St. Catherine Greek Orthodox Monastery in front of Jebel Musa, Egypt, the traditional location of Mount Sinai.

Codex Sinaiticus (א alpha)

Codex Sinaiticus[115] (01) was discovered in 1844 by Constantine von Tischendorf (1815–1874) in the Greek Orthodox monastery of St. Catherine in the Sinai Peninsula, Egypt (see Fig. 42). Being a Greek copy, it is one of the most important hand-written four-column uncial manuscripts, as originally it contained the complete Old and New Testaments, the epistle of *Barnabas*, and portions of *The Shepherd of Hermas* and dates to the fourth century. Sections of the *Codex Sinaiticus* can be found in libraries in Russia, Great Britain, and Egypt.[116] New work is being done on 160 palimpsest manuscripts from the Monastery. A new process called multispectral imaging allows scholars to read the text hidden underneath the visible writing, that include classical, Christian and Jewish texts dating from the fifth cent. until the twelfth cent. AD.[117] These could rank among the Dead Sea Scrolls and Nag Hammadi texts as some of the most important manuscripts ever discovered.

READING THE MANUSCRIPTS

Textual (lower) criticism is a branch of literary criticism that is concerned with the texts of the Bible and seeks to determine, as close as possible, the original reading of the text. Do modern NT English translations accurately reflect the original Greek text? Which texts are reliable? Advances in textual criticism and new manuscripts have contributed to the accuracy of translations.

Because of God's immediate inspiration, the apostle's parchments were preserved from errors. However, the copies of these manuscripts were made by uninspired scribes who could

---

[113] Edwin M. Yamauchi, "Pre-Christian Gnosticism in the Nag Hammadi Texts?," *Church History* 48, no. 2 (June 1, 1979): 141.

[114] Aland and Aland, *The Text of the New Testament*, 40–158; Bruce M. Metzger and Bart D. Ehrman, *The Text of the New Testament: Its Transmission, Corruption, and Restoration*, 4th ed. (Oxford: Oxford University Press, 2005), 36–66.

[115] *Codex Sinaiticus: Facsimile Prints*, Greek Edition, Ancient Greek Edition (Peabody, MA: Hendrickson, 2011). The complete manuscript can also be found at www.codexsinaiticus.org.

[116] Aland and Aland, *The Text of the New Testament*, 11–13, 107.

[117] Jo Marchant, "Archaeologists Are Only Just Beginning to Reveal the Secrets Hidden in These Ancient Manuscripts," *Smithsonian Magazine*, December 11, 2017, https://www.smithsonianmag.com/history/archaeologoists-only-just-beginning-reveal-secrets-hidden-ancient-manuscripts-180967455.

make mistakes when transcribing the text. Thus, the copies may have scribal imperfections such as:

- Incorrect punctuation.
- Misspelled words leading to misreading.
- Addition or exclusion of a word.
- Inclusion of marginal interpretive notes.
- Document damage leading to conjecture over missing content.
- Scribal changes made to soften offensive content.

These anomalies would be copied over and over again with each new copy. It would seem that the text was doomed to progressive corruption; however, the text was providentially preserved through the survival of many early copies of the original manuscripts, providing a large pool against which copies can be compared with one another. It's true that each may have erred in a small way but they did not all err at the same place. So by the majority testimony of the early copies, the error would always be witnessed against.

We do not have the original manuscripts, but we do in essence have the original text. By God's singular care and providence, he has ensured copies were available in such numbers that they have preserved the Bible from error, mistake or corruption, allowing us to use it authoritatively. This is not meant to imply that the thousands of ancient manuscripts now discovered are identical in every detail, but regardless of their age they agree in a truly remarkable way.

There are two different approaches to textual criticism. One follows the principles set down by Westcott and Hort, who use an eclectic approach with weight given to the older manuscripts (Alexandrian) as the basis for their Greek NT. The favoured two manuscripts in their NT are the *Vaticanus* and the *Sinaiticus*. Westcott and Hort, whose *New Testament in the Original Greek* (1881) is the basis for most modern translations, states: "our belief that even among the numerous unquestionably spurious readings of the New Testament there are no signs of deliberate falsification of the text for dogmatic purposes."[118]

Philip Comfort testifies to the value of the text of Westcott and Hort that it: "is extremely reliable. . . . Of course, the manuscript discoveries of the past one hundred years have changed things, but it is remarkable how often they have affirmed the decisions of Westcott and Hort."[119]

The second approach is based on the *Textus Receptus* (Latin "received text"), a newer Greek text used by Luther, Tyndale and the KJV. The *Textus Receptus* departs from the Westcot and Hort Greek NT in over 6,000 readings.

Now even though there are so many different manuscripts to compare, only four hundred or so affect the reading of the text, with within that number only fifty having any significance, and that only of a minor nature, affecting spelling and punctuation. And perhaps most importantly, there is no essential teaching of the NT affected by any of them. So after all is compared, what is left is a reliable text.

[118] Brooke Foss Westcott and Fenton J. A. Hort, *The New Testament in the Original Greek* (New York: Macmillan, 1964), 282.
[119] Comfort, *Encountering the Manuscripts*, 100.

Chart 2: Bronze Age Discoveries

GENESIS: CREATION – PATRIARCHS (EB & MB: 3600–1550 BC)					
Discovery	**Image**	**Place and Discoverer**	**Origin Date /Year Found**	**Biblical Passage**	**Significance**
Ebla Tablets		Paolo Matthiae	2300 BC 1976	Genesis	Historical context of Syria in third mill. and biblical names
Ziggurat of Ur		Leonard Woolley	*ca.* 2100– 2050 BC 1924	Gen 11:1–9	Tower of Babel
Sumerian King List	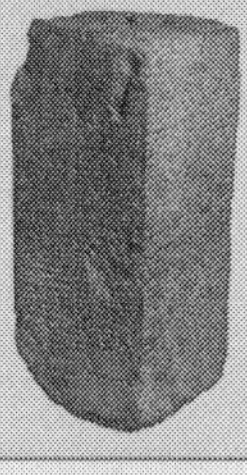	Herbert Weld-Blundell, Hermann Hilprecht	*ca.* 2100–1800 BC 1922	Gen 5–9	Geneologies and flood
Beni-Hasan Tomb Painting		Percy Newberry	1900 BC 1902	Gen 12:10; 37:28	Illustrates Semites from Canaan entering Egypt as in patriarchal period
Mari Tablets	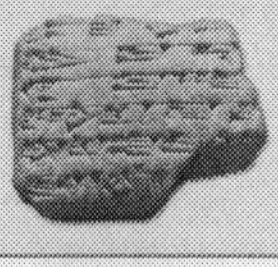	André Parrot	eighteenth cent. BC 1933	Genesis	Historical context of the earlier patriarchs and prophetic texts
Code of Hammurabi		Gustave Jéquier Jacques de Morgan	1725 BC 1901	Exod 20 Leviticus	Illustrates ANE law
Epic of Gilgamesh		Hormuzd Rassam George Smith	1600 BC 1853	Gen 1–9	Creation and the flood
Eridu Genesis or *Ziusudra Epic*		Arno Peobel	*ca.* 1600 BC 1893–1896	Gen 1–11	Creation, earliest cities, and the flood

Discovery	Image	Place and Discoverer	Origin Date /Year Found	Biblical Passage	Significance
Atrahasis Epic		A. Henry Layard George Smith A. R. Millard W. G. Lambert	1646–1626 BC 1872 1876 1965	Gen 1–9	ANE parallel to creation and the flood of Genesis
Ḫattuša Tablets		Ḫattuša near Boğhazköy, Turkey by Hugo Winckler	sixteenth cent. BC 1906	Genesis	Hittite history and treaties
Nuzi Tablets		Edward Chiera Richard Starr	1500–1350 BC 1925–1941	Gen 15–31	Customs and practices in mid-second mill. BC the time of the patriarchs
Amarna Tablets		Tel el-Amarna, Egypt by peasant woman	1400 BC 1887	Genesis	Confirms the Hebrews in Mesopotamia in second mill. BC
Enuma Elish		Nineveh (Iraq) by A. Henry Layard	eleventh cent. seventh cent. BC 1848–1876	Gen 1–2	Parallels to Genesis creation accounts

Genesis

Jewish and Christian tradition holds that Genesis was written by Moses, but despite such esteemed authorship, Genesis is still subject to perhaps the most criticism of any section of the Bible. There is little doubt that much of the content sounds mythical, especially considering the mystical descriptions of the creation of the world, the great flood of Noah, the confusion of languages at the tower of Babel, and the destruction of Sodom and Gomorrah. But is there any evidence that shows otherwise?

43. The larger and lesser mountains of Ararat, Turkey 16,854 feet (5,137 m). This is the traditional location for the resting of Noah's ark.

Creation Account (Gen 1–3)

When the biblical account is compared with the Babylonian epic tablets (i.e., *Epic of Gilgamesh*; *Eridu Genesis*; *Atrahasis Epic*; and *Enuma Elish*) it appears more natural and historic than the other ancient Near Eastern creation and flood myths, which are filled with heavenly feuds and amoral behaviour.

Development of Civilization (Gen 4)

Following the creation of Adam and Eve in the image of God, humanity began developing their creativity through various practices.

- Introduction of agriculture (Gen 4:2).
- Building of cities (Gen 4:17).
- Practice of polygamy (Gen 4:19).
- Animal domestication and raising livestock (Gen 4:20; Sheep and goats nineth millennium BC; cattle and pigs introduced, seventh millennium BC).
- Musical instruments (Gen 4:21; Egypt, fourth millennium BC; Ur, third millennium BC).
- Ancient metal technology (Gen 4:22; Copper alloys like bronze and use of Iron before the Iron Age, third millennium BC).

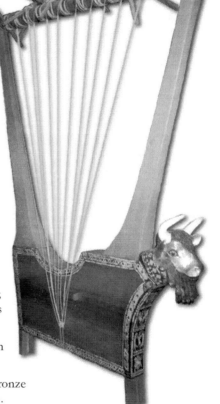

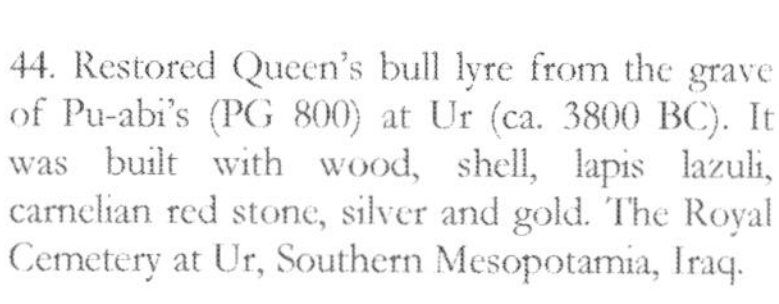

44. Restored Queen's bull lyre from the grave of Pu-abi's (PG 800) at Ur (ca. 3800 BC). It was built with wood, shell, lapis lazuli, carnelian red stone, silver and gold. The Royal Cemetery at Ur, Southern Mesopotamia, Iraq.

Genealogies (Gen 5, 11)

Genesis begins with an unusual genealogy. Ten patriarchs prior to the flood are listed in Genesis 5 with extremely long lifespans. With the exception of

"Enoch [who] walked with God [365 yrs], and he was not [LXX found], for God took him" (Gen 5:24), nine of the patriarchs lived close to 1,000 years. The longevity of the antediluvian period was extraordinarily high and comparatively uniform for one-and-a-half millennia. Following the catastrophe of the flood, the lifespan of humanity was drastically reduced in an exceptionally short period of time. Over the next 1,500 years, the ages humans lived to gradually reduced to their most recent historical values (see Table 1).[1]

The account recorded in Genesis 5 and 11 demonstrates the pattern of a sigmoid curve.[2] The pattern typifies phenomena that are initially stable but go through a period of rapid and significant change to stabilize at a different rate. López concludes that:

> This orderly pattern and sharp regularity of the lifespan data with time does not support the contention that Old Testament longevity values are wilfully assigned random figures or represent obscure mythological remnants of a dim past.[3]

Preflood Characters and Their Age

Adam 930	Mahalalel 895
Seth 912	Enoch 365
Enosh 905	Methuselah 969
Jared 962	Lamech 777
Kenan 910	Noah 950
Flood	
Abraham 175	70 yrs (Ps 90:10)
Moses 120	

Table 1. Pre-flood and post-flood patriarchs with a comparison of their ages.

While this biblical pattern may at first appear strange, it is also paralleled in the Sumerian King List (Weld-Blundell Prism *ca.* 1800 BC).

Sumerian King List

The Sumerian King List or Weld-Blundell prism, as it exists today, is a reconstruction of 20 fragments with an additional nearly complete copy of the Sumerian King List surviving as a cuneiform clay prism and published in 1939 by the renowned Danish Sumerologist Thorkild Jacobson (see Fig. 46).[4] The first fragment was discovered in the temple library at Nippur, Iraq, in 1922 and was purchased on the antiquities market shortly after World War I.

This ancient Mesopotamian genealogy dates to *ca.* 2100–1800 BC and is the oldest (one hundred years before Abraham) known outline of world history. It is a list of ten kings of the land once known as Sumer from before the flood with extremely long reigns. This list was inscribed during the reign of Damiqilishu of Isin (1816–1794 BC) only a few years before Hammurabi of Babylon captured the land of Sumer in the first half of the eighteenth cent. BC and added it as a province

45. Sumerian statue from ancient Mesopotamia (*ca.* 2900–2500 BC). Believed to be self portraits, they were presented to temples as votive gifts to honour the gods and represent their donors.

Used with permission of Oriental Institute Museum

[1] Psalm 90:10 states that during the United Monarchy the average man lived 70 years.

[2] D. J. Finney, *Probit Analysis. A Statistical Treatment of the Sigmoid Response Curve* (Cambridge: Cambridge University Press, 1947), 185; Raúl Erlando López, "Temporal Changes in the Ageing of Biblical Patriarchs," *Journal of Creation* 14, no. 3 (2000): 109–17.

[3] López, "Temporal Changes," 117.

[4] Thorkild Jacobsen, *The Sumerian King List*, Assyriological Studies (Chicago, IL: University of Chicago Press, 1939); Samuel Noah Kramer, *The Sumerians: Their History, Culture, and Character* (Chicago, IL: University Of Chicago Press, 1971), Appendix E; Pritchard, *ANE Texts*, 265–66.

Sumerian King List

CITY	KING	RULED YR.
Eridu	Alulim	28,800
	Alagar	36,000
Bad-tibira	En-men-lu-Anna	43,200
	En-men-gal-Anna	28,800
	Dumu-zi	36,000
Larak	En-sipa-zi-Anna	28,800
Sippar	En-men-dur-Anna	21,000
Shuruppak	Ubar-Tutu	18,600
FLOOD "The flood swept over [the land]. After the flood had swept over [the land] and kingship had descended from heaven [for a second time], Kish became the seat of Kingship."		
	Jucur	1,200
	Kullassina-bel	960
	Nanjiclicma	670
	En-Tarah-ana	420
	Babum	300
	Puannum	840
	Kalibum	960

Table 2. List of the Sumerian kings listed in the Weld-Blundell prism and the years they ruled.

to his new Babylonian empire.[5] The list recounts:

> After the kingship descended from heaven, the kingship was in Eridug. In Eridug, Alulim became king; he ruled for 28,800 years. Alaljar ruled for 36,000 years. 2 kings; they ruled for 64,800 years. . . Then the flood swept over. After the flood had swept over, and the kingship had descended from heaven, the kingship was in Kic. In Kic, Jucur became king; he ruled for 1,200 years. Kullassina-bel ruled for 960 years. Nanjiclicma ruled for 670 years. En-tarah-ana ruled for 420 years . . . , 3 months, and 3 1/2 days. Babum . . . . ruled for 300 years. Puannum ruled for 840 years. Kalibum ruled for 960 years.[6]

Prior to the flood, ten Sumerian kings ruled with superhuman lengths of reign (total 241,000 years). Following the flood the rule of the Sumerian kings is greatly reduced (under 1000 years). While the superhuman lengths can be explained by the Sumerian's sexagesimal[7] (base 60)[8] number system,[9] the "long-flood-short" pattern follows a sigmoid curve that is identical to the biblical pattern.

There is justifiable scepticism over the unreasonably long lifespans for not only the Sumerian kings, but also the biblical patriarchs. Carol A. Hill observes that:

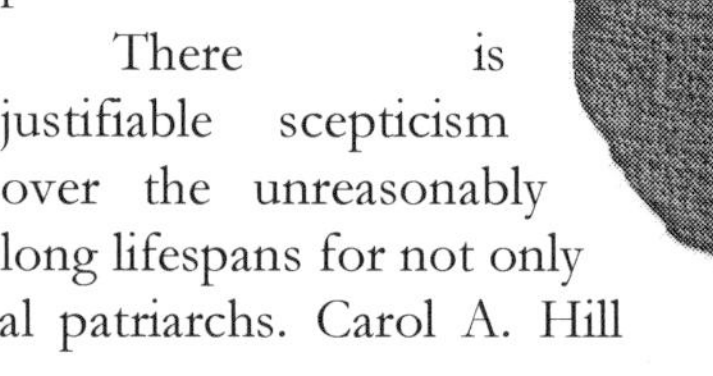

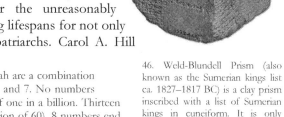

46. Weld-Blundell Prism (also known as the Sumerian kings list ca. 1827–1817 BC) is a clay prism inscribed with a list of Sumerian kings in cuneiform. It is only about 10 cm tall but it is inscribed on all sides.

> All age-numbers (30 in all) from Adam to Noah are a combination of the sacred numbers 60 (years and months) and 7. No numbers end in 1, 3, 4, 6, or 8—a chance probability of one in a billion. Thirteen numbers end in 0 (some multiple or combination of 60), 8 numbers end in 5 (5 years = 60 months), 3 numbers end in 7, 5 numbers end in 2 (5yrs + 7 yrs = 12), and 1 number ends in 9 (5yrs + 7yrs + 7yrs = 19). All of this cannot be coincidental. The Mesopotamians were using sacred

[5] Alan K. Bowman, Edward Champlin, and Andrew Lintott, eds., *The Cambridge Ancient History: The Augustan Empire, 44 BC-AD 70*, vol. 10 (Cambridge: Cambridge University Press, 1996), 200–201.

[6] The ETCSL project, Faculty of Oriental Studies, University of Oxford (2006), n.p. http://etcsl.orinst.ox.ac.uk/section2/tr211.htm.

[7] Hill, "Making Sense of the Numbers of Genesis," 241; Jöran Friberg, "Numbers and Measures in the Earliest Written Records," *Scientific American* 250, no. 2 (1984): 117.

[8] "When the kingdom durations of the antediluvian section are expressed in an early sexagesimal numerical system, all durations except two are expressed as multiples of 602. A simple tally of the ciphers used yields six 10 x 602 signs, six 602 signs and six 60 signs." Raúl Erlando López, "The Antediluvian Patriarchs and the Sumerian King List," *Journal of Creation* 12, no. 3 (1998): 347.

[9] Graham Flegg, *Numbers: Their History and Meaning* (Mineola, NY: Dover, 2002), 55.

numbers, not real numbers. Therefore, these numbers were not meant to be (and should not be) interpreted as real numbers.[10]

Those who do not take the numbers literally as Greco-Roman hard numbers, see them as a Semitic convention that represents an honorific representation.[11] In the ancient Near East numbers were often used to portray importance or status with the gods. Walton has demonstrated that when the ages of the individuals in Genesis are converted to the sexagesimal system "we get 241,200, the exact total of the Sumerian King List."[12]

The genealogies were selective to convey a specific theme; the same as in the NT's Gospel of Matthew, chapter 1. The names were not meant to calculate the genealogies or the age of the earth, as Bishop Ussher did (dating Creation and Adam to 4004 BC).[13] It is clear from archaeological remains that Jericho and other cities were inhabited as far back as 9000 BC.[14]

THE FLOOD AND NOAH

The fascination with the search for Noah's ark has at times reached what some call "ark fever." Archaeologists and explorers, both professional and amateur, have been searching for hundreds of years for the ark, but with little-to-no success for their efforts. The exact location still remains a mystery.

The importance of discovering Noah's ark is highlighted by Dr. Melville Bell Grosvenor, the fifty-fifth editor of *National Geographic*, who predicts: "If the ark of Noah is discovered it will be the greatest archaeological find in human history, the greatest event since the resurrection of Christ, and it would alter all the currents of scientific thought."[15]

There have been many reported sightings of the ark with, some claiming to have walked on and entered it,[16] but no empirical evidence has ever been produced to verify the claims. While there are contradictory reports, they all claim that the ark was spotted on Mount Ararat (*Agri-Dagh* [Ağri Daği] or "Mount of pain"), located in eastern Turkey on the border with Armenia (who call it Mount Masis) and Iran.

While most of the searches have been conducted on Mount Ararat, the Bible only states that the ark "came to rest on the mountains of Ararat" (Gen 8:4). The Hebrew *har* indicates a mountain range believed to be the mountain range of the ancient kingdom of Urartu in eastern Turkey between the river Araxes and Lake Van, rather than a specific mountain. The tallest mountain peak in this mountain range is Mount Ararat and thus, many argue, the best candidate for the landing place for the vessel of a world-wide flood, is within its glacier.[17] Others point out that a moving glacier would have destroyed any wooden vessel a long time ago. Still others argue

---

[10] Hill, "Making Sense of the Numbers of Genesis," 245.

[11] Fouts, "A Defense of the Hyperbolic Interpretation of Large Numbers in the Old Testament," 377–87; Hill, "Making Sense of the Numbers of Genesis," 239–51.

[12] Walton does not include Adam and Noah in the calculation because their equivalents are not included in the Sumerian King List. John H Walton, *Ancient Israelite Literature in Its Cultural Context: A Survey of Parallels between Biblical and Ancient Near Eastern Texts*, 2nd ed., Library of Biblical Interpretation (Grand Rapids: Zondervan, 1990), 129; "The Antediluvian Section of the Sumerian King List and Genesis 5," *BA* 44, no. 4 (October 1, 1981): 207–208.

[13] James Barr, "Why the World Was Created in 4004 BC: Archbishop Ussher and Biblical Chronology," *Bulletin of the John Rylands University Library of Manchester* 67 (85 1984): 575–608.

[14] Charles Gates, *Ancient Cities: The Archaeology of Urban Life in the Ancient Near East and Egypt, Greece, and Rome* (New York: Routledge, 2003), 18.

[15] Melville is quoted by Robert Cornuke, *Ark Fever: Legend Chaser* (Wheaton, IL: Tyndale, 2005), ix.

[16] Fernand Navarra, *Noah's Ark: I Touched it*, ed. Dave Balsiger (Needham, MA: Logos International, 1974).

[17] Cevat Başaran, Vedat Keleş, and Rex Geissler, "Mount Ararat Archaeological Survey," *Bible and Spade* 21, no. 1 (2008): 70–96.

that the mountain was not in existence during the time of the flood but was formed later by volcanic activity. Thus, some researchers look elsewhere for the ark such as in Iran (Mount Suleiman) and Turkey (Mount Çudi[18] and Durupinar).

47. Durupinar clay formation near Dogubayazit Turkey, which some claim is Noah's ark.

Durupinar

This clay formation, that looks like the hull of a ship, is located at Doğubayazit, Turkey, about 15 miles southwest of Mount Ararat (see Fig. 47). The formation is named after the Turkish scientist Captain Ilhan Durupinar, who in 1959 noticed it from satellite images. This unusual formation was ignored for twenty years until 1984, when Ron Wyatt convinced Col. Jim Irwin, Dr. John Morris and Marvin Steffins to examine the site.[19] However, geologists demonstrated that it is a clay formation resulting from the spring runoff around a lava flow and merely an anomaly of nature.[20] There was no evidence of petrified wood in the area, although the Turkish government have built a Noah's ark visitor centre at the site to promote tourism.

48. The crater at Takht-e Soleymān with the remains of a Zoroastrian fire temple built during the Sassanid period.

Wikimedia Commons

Mount Suleiman

The site of Mount Suleiman (Takht-e Soleymān, "Throne of Solomon"), is a mountain (13,120 ft, 4000 m) located 55 miles NW of Tehran, Iran (see Fig. 48). During a trip to Iran in June 2006, Bob Cornuke, the self-appointed president of the Bible Archaeology Search and Exploration Institute (BASE) reported finding an "unusual object" that he described as "dark rock with an uncanny beam-like appearance in several places,"[21] that is of the approximate dimensions of Noah's Ark. Cornuke believes that this object was what Ed Davis (an "ark witness") saw in 1943.[22] However, according to carbon-14 dating, one of the petrified samples of wood was only 500 years old.[23] Other samples

[18] Bill Crouse and Gordon Franz, "Mount Cudi: The True Mountain of Noah's Ark," *Bible and Spade* 19 (2006): 99–112.

[19] Staff "Noah's Ark? Boat like Form Is Seen near Ararat," *Life Magazine*, September 5, 1960, 112–14; Mary Nell Wyatt, *The Boat-Shaped Object on Doomsday Mountain: Is This the Remains of Noah's Ark* (Cornersville, TN: Wyatt Archaeological Research, 2004).

[20] L. D. Collins and David Fasold, "Bogus 'Noah's Ark' from Turkey Exposed as a Common Geologic Structure," *Journal of Geoscience Education* 44 (1996): 439–44; Avci Murat, "The Formation and Mechanisms of the Great Telçeker Earthflow Which Also Crept Noah's Ark at Mount Ararat" (presented at the Mount Ararat and Noah's Ark Symposium, Dogubeyazit, Turkey, 2005); Murat Avci, "'Noah's Ark': Its Relationship to the Telçeker Earthflow, Mount Ararat, Eastern Turkey," *Bulletin of Engineering Geology and the Environment* 66 (August 1, 2007): 377–80.

[21] http://www.baseinstitute.org/noah.html.

[22] Robert Cornuke and David Halbrook, *In Search of the Lost Mountains of Noah: The Discovery of the Real Mt. Ararat* (Nashville, TN: Broadman & Holman, 2001); Cornuke, *Ark Fever: Legend Chaser*, 226.

[23] http://www.baseinstitute.org/pages/noahs_ark/17.

49. Mount Ararat in modern day Turkey, where some believe Noah's ark came to rest.

have been identified by geologists as volcanic or metamorphic rock.[24]

Mount Ararat

Mount Ararat is 16,854 feet (5,137 m) high (see chapter photo). Many believe from the weight of evidence that the ark is above or in the Ahora Gorge on the northeast side of Mount Ararat. A portion of the glacier (Western Plateau) was examined using Ground Penetrating Radar (GPR) by the Willis Expedition in 1988 and the Aaron/Garbe/Corbin Expedition in 1989, with no indication of the ark.[25]

In 2006 a group of Christians from Hong Kong, funded by Media Evangelism Ltd., calling themselves Noah's Ark Ministries International, claimed to have found the ark under layers of rock and ice. They report that the cavity of the ark forms what looks like a cave. However, they have refused to share their samples with other organizations, like ArcImaging, who would like to perform tests on the samples. However, in February 2008 photos of geologic thin-sections of the "wood" were examined by creationary geologists Dr. Don Patton and Dr. Don Shockey, who concur that this is likely volcanic tuff and not petrified wood.

J. Randall Price of Liberty University was also working with the Chinese/Turkish team, and based on his experience and eyewitness testimony, doubts the claim, and as such embarked on his own expedition in 2009–2013, using heavy equipment to dig in a particular location in the ice.[26] Price performed a GPR scan of a section of the ice cap, took core samples to bedrock but

---

[24] http://www.noahsarksearch.com/iran.htm.

[25] For further information on ark research consult the following websites: www.noahsarksearch.com, and www.arcimaging .com.

[26] http://www.worldofthebible.com/news.htm; Brent Baum, *Finding Noah Movie*, 2015.

found no wood but intends to carry out further probes of the glacier if the political conditions permit.[27]

Eyewitness Accounts

The main reason that ark explorers have sought to climb Mount Ararat in Turkey is over 60 alleged eyewitnesses, who claim to have walked on, been inside and brought back pieces of wood, allegedly from the ark. Ancient historians such as Berossus (290 BC), Hieronymus (*ca.* AD 347–420), Nicholas of Damascus (64 BC–AD ?), and Josephus (*Ant.* 3.5–6) have recorded Mount Ararat as the location for sightings of the ark. Recent alleged eyewitness sightings from 1856 to 1974 are all documented in *The Explorers of Ararat.*[28] Of the eyewitnesses, some are reliable WWII and other military veterans, who did not know each other. Rex Geissler has spoken with 24 alleged eyewitnesses. However, while there are many drawings, paintings, and testimonies, there are no legible photos. But why did the alleged eyewitnesses see a boat, when the explorers over the past 50 years did not? One possible explanation is the phenomena of meltbacks of the ice during warm summers.

Quotes from Antiquity

Epic of Gilgamesh – Table XI

A portion of the text of the Epic of Gilgamesh reads as follows:

What I had I loaded thereon, the whole harvest of life
I caused to embark within the vessel; all my family and my relations,
The beasts of the field, the cattle of the field, the craftsmen, I made them all embark.
I entered the vessel and closed the door. . .
When the yound dawn gleamed forth,
From the foundations of heaven a black cloud arose. . .
All that is bright is turned to darkness,
The brother seeth his brother no more,
The folk of the skies can no longer recognize each other
The gods feared the flood,
They fled, they climbed into the heavens of Anu,
The gods crouched like a dog on the wall, they lay down. .
For six days and nights
Wind and flood marched on, the hurricane subdued the land.
When the seventh day dawned, the hurricane was abated, the flood
Which was waged war like an army;
The sea was stilled, the ill wind was calmed, the flood ceased.
I beheld the sea, its voice was silent,
And all mankind was turned into mud!
As high as the roofs reached the swamp! . . .
I beheld the world, the horizon of sea;
Twelve measures away an island emerged;
Unto Mount Nitsir came the vessel,
Mount Nitsir held the vessel and let it not budge. . .
When the seventh day came,
I sent forth a dove, I released it;
It went , the dove, it came back,
As there was no place, it came back,
I sent forth a swallow, I released it;
It went, the swallow, it came back,
As there was not place, it came back.
I sent forth a crow, I released it;
It went, the crow, and behold the subsidence of the waters;
It eats, it splashes about, it caws, it comes not back.

C. W. Ceram, *Gods, Graves & Scholars: The Story of Archaeology*, trans. E. B. Garside and Sophie Wilkins, 2nd Revised Edition (New York, NY: Vintage, 1986), 314–15.

Ancient Flood Texts[29]

- Gilgamesh Epic (Mesopotamian)[30]

[27] Personal conversations with Dr. Price.

[28] B. J. Corban, *The Explorers of Ararat and the Search for Noah's Ark*, ed. Rex Geissler (Long Beach, CA: Great Commission Illustrated Books, 1999).

[29] John Warwick Montgomery has provided a detailed chart of all the global accounts of the flood indicating their common elements. John Warwick Montgomery, *The Quest for Noah's Ark: A Treasury of Documented Accounts from Ancient Times to the Present Day of Sightings of the Ark*, 2nd ed. (Ada, MI: Bethany Fellowship, 1974); Arthur C. Custance, *The Flood, Local or Global?*, The Doorway Papers 9 (Grand Rapids: Zondervan, 1985).

[30] George E. Smith, *Assyrian Discoveries: An Account of Explorations and Discoveries on the Site on Nineveh, During 1878 and 1874* (New York: Scribner, Armstrong & Co., 1875), 13; Alexander Heidel, *Gilgamesh Epic and Old Testament Parallels*, 2nd ed. (Chicago, IL: University Of Chicago Press, 1970); Pritchard, *ANE Texts*, 72–99; Tikva Frymer-Kensky, "What the Babylonian Flood Stories Can and Cannot Teach Us About the Genesis Flood," *BAR* 4, no. 4 (December 1978): 32–41; Andrew R. George, *The Babylonian Gilgamesh Epic: Introduction, Critical Edition and Cuneiform Texts HELP*, vol. 1, 2 vols. (Oxford: Oxford University Press, 2003); Stephen Mitchell, *Gilgamesh: A New English Version* (New York: Free Press, 2006); Stephanie Dalley, *Myths from Mesopotamia: Creation, the Flood, Gilgamesh, and Others*, Revised, Oxford World's Classics (Oxford: Oxford University Press, 2009), 39–153.

- Atrahasis Epic (Mesopotamian)[31]
- Ziusudra Epic (Sumerian)[32]
- Ras Shamra Epic (Ugarit)[33]

Epic of Gilgamesh 1600 BC

The similarities between the Babylonian text and the Hebrew story are striking with around 20 items in common. There appears to be a connection, leaving several possibilities:

- Genesis was copied from an earlier Babylonian account, or
- The Gilgamesh account was copied from an earlier Hebrew story, or
- Both were copied from a common source that was earlier than both of them.

First, it is relevant to point out several areas of common detail between the Genesis and Gilgamesh stories:

- The Genesis account describes how humanity had become sinful and disobedient and deserved the judgment of God. In the Gilgamesh account, humanity had become too noisy because of their numbers.
- The gods (or God) decides to destroy the earth with a worldwide flood that will drown all humanity, and land animals and birds.

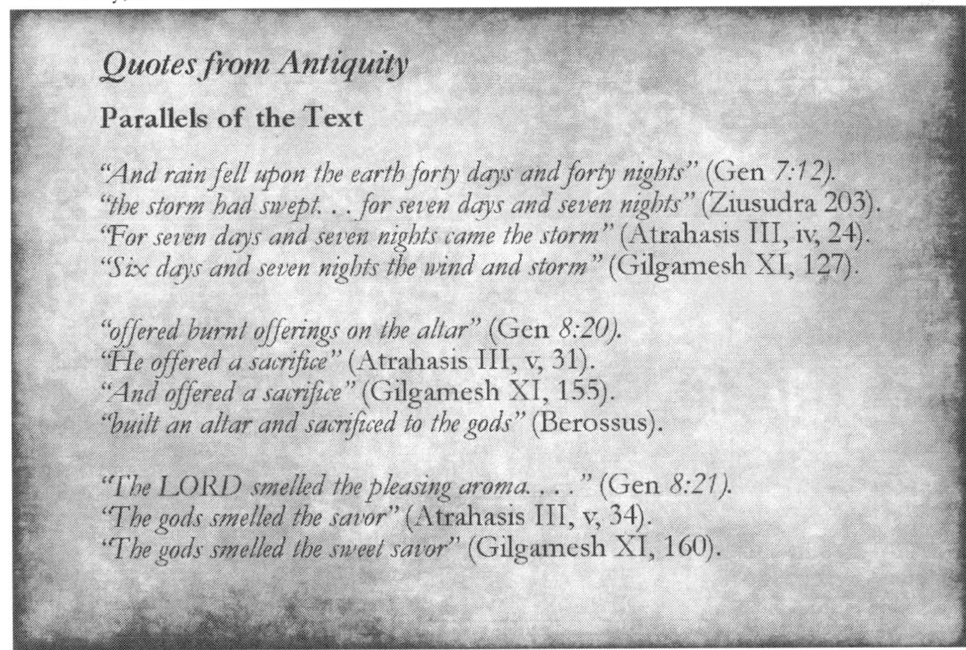

Quotes from Antiquity

Parallels of the Text

"And rain fell upon the earth forty days and forty nights" (Gen *7:12).*
"the storm had swept. . . for seven days and seven nights" (Ziusudra 203).
"For seven days and seven nights came the storm" (Atrahasis III, iv, 24).
"Six days and seven nights the wind and storm" (Gilgamesh XI, 127).

"offered burnt offerings on the altar" (Gen *8:20).*
"He offered a sacrifice" (Atrahasis III, v, 31).
"And offered a sacrifice" (Gilgamesh XI, 155).
"built an altar and sacrificed to the gods" (Berossus).

"The LORD smelled the pleasing aroma. . . " (Gen *8:21).*
"The gods smelled the savor" (Atrahasis III, v, 34).
"The gods smelled the sweet savor" (Gilgamesh XI, 160).

- The gods (or God) knew of only one righteous man, Ut-Napishtim or Noah.

---

[31] Isaac M. Kikawada, "The Double Creation of Mankind in Enki and Ninmah, Atrahasis I 1–351, and Genesis 1–2," *Iraq* 45 (1983): 43–45; Wilfred G. Lambert, Alan R. Millard, and Miguel Civil, *Atra-Hasis: The Babylonian Story of the Flood* (Winona Lake, IN: Eisenbrauns, 1999); Dalley, *Myths from Mesopotamia*, 1–38.

[32] Robert M. Best, *Noah's Ark and the Ziusudra Epic: Sumerian Origins of the Flood Myth* (Winona Lake, IN: Eisenbrauns, 1999); Thorkild Jacobsen, "The Eridu Genesis," *JBL* 100, no. 4 (December 1, 1981): 513–29.

[33] Stan Rummel, *Ras Shamra Parallels: The Texts From Ugarit and the Hebrew Bible* (Rome: Pontificium Institutum Biblicum, 1981).

- The gods (or God) instructed the hero to build a wooden ark.
- The ark would be sealed with pitch and contain various internal compartments.
- It would have a single window and door.
- The ark was built and occupied by the hero, members of his family, and a sample of all the animals.
- The rain covered the land and mountains with water.
- The ark landed on a mountain in the ancient Near East.
- The hero sent out various types of birds at different times to find dry land. The first two birds returned to the ark. The third bird found dry land and did not return to the ark.
- The survivors left the ark, and offered an animal as a sacrifice.
- The gods (or God) smelled the aroma of the sacrifice.
- Noah, or Ut-Napishtim, was blessed.
- The Babylonian gods were sorry for the destruction that they had created. Yahweh promised never to destroy the earth with a flood again.

However, while there are many commonalities between the Genesis and Gilgamesh stories there are also significant differences:

- Yahweh spoke directly to Noah while Ut-Napishtim received his instructions indirectly through a dream.
- Noah's ark was a sea worthy rectangular boat (450 x 75 ft.), three stories high. The Babylonian ark was an unfloatable square boat with six stories.
- While Noah only included his family, Ut-Napishtim invited a pilot and additional workmen.
- Noah's ark landed on Mount Ararat; Ut-Napishtim landed on Mount Nisir; these locations are only a few hundred miles apart in Turkey and Iran.
- The rain in the Hebrew flood lasted for forty days and nights and also came from beneath the earth while the Bablylonian flood only lasted six days.
- Noah sent out a raven and two doves while Ut-Napishtim sent a dove, swallow and raven.

On the issue of the possible dependence of the Genesis account on other ancient Near Eastern texts, the similarities between the two accounts could be explained by all of the texts attempting to describe the same worldwide flood. After Lambert and Millard suggest "one possible explanation" of a westward migration of the flood traditions during the Amarna Period (*ca.* 1400 BC), they conclude that "the question is very complex."[34]

As Sasson points out, today a more responsible handling of the two accounts is used by scholars.

> While scholars still compare the flood accounts in the GE [Gilgamesh Epic] and in Genesis, there is an appreciation that both have adapted traditional narratives to suit their own contexts. Moreover, scholars now generally avoid making judgmental contrasts among the accounts (e.g., which one has a better blueprint for a seaworthy ark or communicates a more spiritual description of the deity).[35]

[34] Wilfred G. Lambert, Alan R. Millard, and Miguel Civil, *Atra-hasis: The Babylonian Story of the Flood* (Winona Lake, IN: Eisenbrauns, 1999), 24.

[35] Jack M. Sasson, "Gilgamesh Epic," ed. David Noel Freedman *et al.*, *ABD* (New York: Doubleday, 1996), 2:1027.

TOWER OF BABEL (GEN 10–11)

According to the Bible, brick-building technology began early in the history of civilization (4000 BC)[36] at Shinar (Sumer Gen 11:3), likely under the direction of Nimrod (Gilgamesh?;[37] Gen 10:9–10). This technology was very different from the "boulder and chink" method used in Palestine. The Babylonian Epic of Creation called the *Enuma Elish* (Akkadian *Enûma Eliš*) describes the use of brick technology in the construction of Babylon (tablet 6, lines 60–62; see *ANET*, 68–69). Walton describes the technology of baking bricks as an ancient trade developed toward the end of the fourth millennium, and the resulting product, using bitumen as a mastic, proved waterproof and as sturdy as stone. Since it was an expensive process, it was used only for important public buildings.[38]

The tower of Babel was such a building. The term "tower of Babel" does not appear in the biblical text, but they built a city with a tower and later the text explains that "Therefore its [city] name was called Babel [That is, Babylon[39]; with a play on the Hebrew verb *bālal* meaning "to mix, confuse"], because there the LORD confused the language of all the earth. And from there the LORD dispersed them over the face of all the earth" (Gen 11:9). Most scholars suggest that the tower of Babel was a ziggurat.[40]

Ziggurat of Ur

50. The reconstructed facade of the Neo-Sumerian Ziggurat of Ur, near Nasiriyah, Iraq.

© Hardnfast / Wikimedia Commons

The Babylonian ziggurat (Akk. *ziqqurratu*), located at the city of Ur III, dedicated to Marduk at Esagila, was called *Etemenanki* (Sumerian "temple of the foundation of heaven and earth"). This man-made brick structure (62.5 m by 43 m at the base), built by Ur-Nammu, rose to three stories and was accessible via a prominent staircase (see Fig. 42). It contained a temple at its top, built to house and worship the gods of heaven (Akk. *Ningal, Nanna,* or *Sin*).[41] No priest resided in the structure as its only purpose was for the gods.[42] It was rebuilt by Nabopolassar and Nebuchadnezzar II in the sixth century BC (Herodotus *Hist.* 1.181:2–5; *Jub.* 10:20–21; Josephus *Ant.* 1.115–117; *3 Bar.* 3:5–8).

Alexander the Great attempted to rebuild the decaying ruins by moving the structure brick by brick. Unfortunately, he died before completing the project and all that remains today is the base.

---

[36] The Egyptians used bricks as early as 10,000 BC. The Early Egyptian *mastaba* (Arabic "bench") was the standard type of tomb in pre-dynastic (5500 - 3100 BC) and early dynastic (2920 - 2770 BC) Egypt for the Pharaoh. C. L. R. Williams, "A Model of the Mastaba-Tomb of Userkaf-Ankh," *The Metropolitan Museum of Art Bulletin* 8, no. 6 (1913): 125–30. The step pyramid at Saqqara, Egypt was built of brick for Pharaoh Djoser in 2630 BC.

[37] David P. Livingston, "Nimrod: Who Was He? Was He Godly or Evil?," *Bible and Spade* 14, no. 3 (2001): 67–72.

[38] John H. Walton, Victor H. Matthews, and Mark W. Chavalas, *The IVP Bible Background Commentary: Old Testament* (Downers Grove, IL: InterVarsity, 2000), 33.

[39] The ancient ruins of the city of Babylon are near Hillah, Babil Governorate, Iraq.

[40] Dale S. DeWitt, "The Historical Background of Gen 11:1–9: Babel or Ur?," *Journal of the Evangelical Theological Society* 22, no. 1 (n.d.): 15–26.

[41] Jean-cl. Margueron, "Ur (place)," ed. David Noel Freedman *et al.*, trans. Stephen Rosoff, *ABD* (New York: Doubleday, 1996), 6:766.

[42] Larry L. Walker, "Babel," in *ZPEB*, 1:470.

Stephen Harris and other OT scholars argue that Etemenanki influenced the biblical story of the Tower of Babel during the Babylonian captivity of the Hebrews.[43] Other scholars prefer the Ezida ziggurat in Borsippa (Birs Nimrud), although this option is less likely.[44]

A Sumerian tablet titled *Enmerkar and the Lord of Aratta* (2000 BC)[45] provides a compelling parallel with the Tower of Babel account in Genesis and provides the following background: "In those days of yore, when the destinies were determined, the great princes allowed Unug Kulaba's E-ana to lift its head high. Plenty, and carp floods-(fish aplenty, barley abundance), and the rain which brings forth dappled barley were then increased in Unug Kulaba. Before the land of Dilmun yet existed, the E-ana of Unug Kulaba was well founded."[46]

E-ana (Sumerian "Temple of Ana" or "house of Ana") was a brick temple or ziggurat in Uruk. The tablet also provides an account of a time when humankind spoke one language. The Sumerian version of the *Babel of Tongues* states that during the "Golden Age" nothing threatened the people: "There was no fear, no terror. . . In those days . . . the land Martu, resting in security, the whole universe, the people in unison (?), to Enlil in one tongue. . . . Enki, the Lord of wisdom. . . . Changed the speech in their mouths, (brought?) contention into it. Into the speech of man that (until then) has been one."[47]

Although there are no other parallels with the Tower of Babel account, the confusion of language by deity is an ancient theme. In the Sumerian text, the confusion of language was the result of rivalry between the gods Enki and Enlil and had nothing to do with a tower. In Genesis 11:1–9 the issue was between God and the people over the building of a tower.

ABRAHAM AND UR (GEN 12–25)

According to Genesis 11:31, the city of Ur in Chaldea was the place where Terah's family, including Abraham, lived and from where they left for Haran. While little more is mentioned in the Bible about this important city, it is usually identified with Tell Muqayyar ("Mount of Pitch" 30°56´N; 46°08´E) in modern day Iraq. Ur was occupied from about 5000 BC (Ubeid period) to 300 BC, although burned by the Elamites in 2004 BC. Abram was born just after its destruction in about 1952 BC.[48]

Excavation of Ur

Discovered in 1625 by Pietro della Valle, Tell Muqayyar was first excavated by Sir W. K. Loftus in 1849. Sir Henry C. Rawlinson identified the tell with the city of Ur based on an inscribed brick discovered in 1855. While several archaeologists showed interest, in 1918–1919 it was the famous Sir Charles Leondard Woolley who directed the joint excavation between the University

[43] Stephen L. Harris and Robert Platzner, *The Old Testament: An Introduction to the Hebrew Bible* (New York: McGraw-Hill, 2002), 37.

[44] W. Allinger-Csollich, "Birs Nimrud I. Die Baukörper Der Ziqqurat von Borsippa. Ein Vorbericht," *Baghdader Mitteilungen* 22 (1991): 383–499.

[45] Samuel Noah Kramer, "Man's Golden Age: A Sumerian Parallel to Genesis 11:1," *Journal of the American Oriental Society* 63 (1943): 191–94.

[46] Samuel Noah Kramer, *Enmerkar and the Lord of Aratta: A Sumerian Epic Tale of Iraq and Iran* (Philadelphia, PA: University Museum, University of Pennsylvania, 1952), 1.

[47] Samuel Noah Kramer, "The 'Babel of Tongues': A Sumerian Version," *Journal of the American Oriental Society* 88, no. 1 (1968): 111.

[48] Margueron, "Ur (place)," 766–67.

of Pennsylvania and the British Museum, from 1922 to 1934.[49] Unfortunately no research has been completed since that time, apart from a partial restoration of the ziggurat.

Several important structures were excavated, including temples, a cemetery (known as the royal tombs), and two storied residential houses complete with drainage systems. The largest structure is the ziggurat (see the description above under the tower of Babel) at the center of the city that was dedicated to the Moon god Nanna.

The royal library, containing important tablets, was discovered revealing a commercial system based on written contracts, money, and receipts. Perhaps some of the most spectacular objects came from the burial shaft of the royal tombs of Meskalamdug and the queen Puabi (2600–2500 BC). Her identity is confirmed from an inscription on a cylinder seal found close to her body. In the tomb were found royal chariots with some 80 servants who, no doubt, were executed to accompany the king and queen into the afterlife. Woolley uncovered a total of some 1,800 graves, prompting him to coin the title "The Great Death Pit".[50]

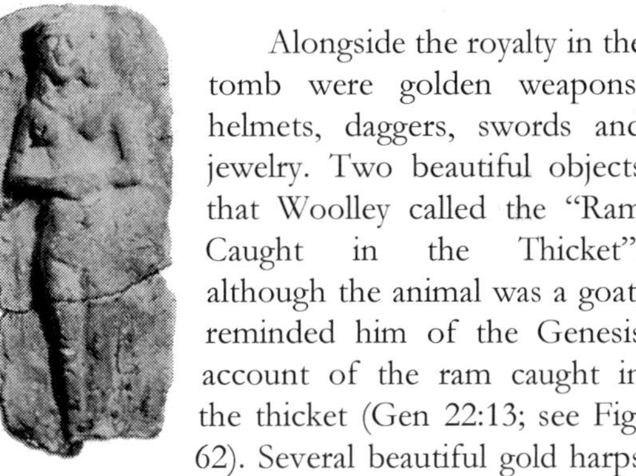

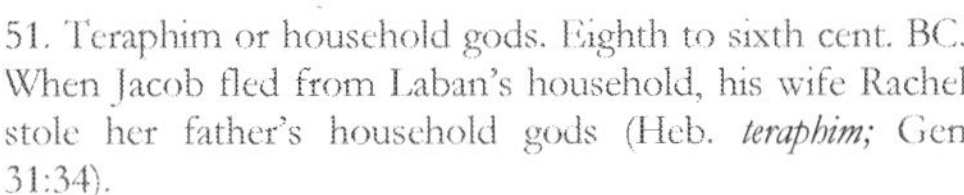

51. Teraphim or household gods. Eighth to sixth cent. BC. When Jacob fled from Laban's household, his wife Rachel stole her father's household gods (Heb. *teraphim;* Gen 31:34).

Alongside the royalty in the tomb were golden weapons, helmets, daggers, swords and jewelry. Two beautiful objects that Woolley called the "Ram Caught in the Thicket", although the animal was a goat, reminded him of the Genesis account of the ram caught in the thicket (Gen 22:13; see Fig. 62). Several beautiful gold harps and eleven silver lyres decorated with mother-of-pearl, carnelian, lapis lazuli, and shells were also uncovered along with the famous "standard of Ur."[51]

Woolley only excavated a very limited area of the site and focused on the religious buildings, larger structures and two smaller domestic dwellings. Therefore, there is some question as to the full picture of the city and the condition of life in this southern Mesopotamian city (modern Iraq).[52] Although there was no direct link to Abraham discovered, Woolley used the Bible stories about Abraham to create interest back in England and to fundraise. However, what is not in doubt is the rich culture and well developed society which these discoveries portray and out of which Abraham migrated.

Today the objects from the royal tombs are housed in the British Museum in London, the

[49] C. Leonard Woolley and Peter R. S. Moorey, *Ur "of the Chaldees,"* Revised and Updated (Ithaca, NY: Cornell University Press, 1982); C. L. Woolley and E. A. Speiser, *Excavations at Ur: The Pottery of Tell Billa* (London: Museum, 1933); C. Leonard Woolley and M. E. L. Mallowan, *Ur Excavations*, 9 vols. (Oxford: Oxford University Press, 1927).

[50] C. Leonard Woolley, *Discovering the Royal Tombs at Ur: Joint Expedition of the British Museum and of the Museum of the University of Pennsylvania to Mesopotamia* (New York: Macmillan, 1969), 124; Peter R. S. Moorey, "What Do We Know About the People Buried in the Royal Cemetery?," *Expedition* 20, no. 1 (1977): 24–40; "Where Did They Bury the Kings of the IIIrd Dynasty of Ur?," *Iraq* 46, no. 1 (1984): 1–18; Susan Pollock, "Chronology of the Royal Cemetery of Ur," *Iraq* 47 (1985): 129–47.

[51] Richard L. Zettler and Lee Horne, eds., *Treasures from the Royal Tombs of Ur* (Philadelphia, PA: University of Pennsylvania Museum of Archaeology and Anthropology, 1998), 43–174.

[52] Margueron, "Ur (place)," 766–67.

University Museum in Philadelphia, and the Iraq National Museum in Baghdad.

UNDERSTANDING ABRAHAM

Several ancient documents have shed light on the conduct and family practices of Abraham. These discoveries do not prove the truthfulness of the biblical accounts, but they do support the biblical data and help to understand the ancient customs and practices during Abraham's time.

Nuzi Tablets

The first discovery which sheds light on Abraham and his time period is the Nuzi tablets[53] discovered sometime between 1925 to 1931 (see Fig. 52).[54] About 20,000 Akkadian cuneiform clay tablets were found in Nuzu just east of ancient Asshur (modern Iraq).[55] They describe life in northern Mesopotamia in around 1500–1350 BC (mid-second mill. BC); a period a little after the lives of the patriarchs.[56]

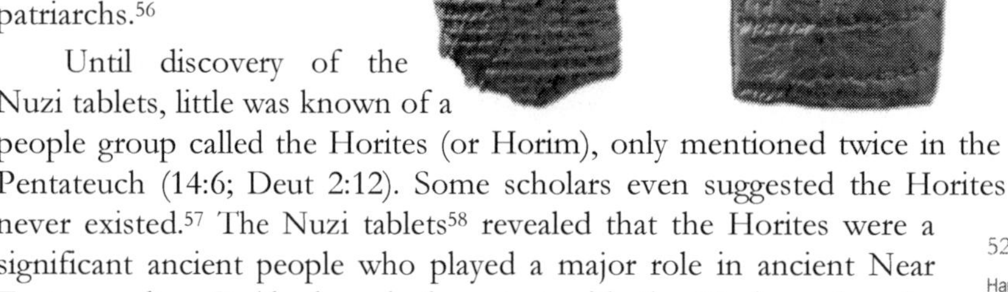

52. Three Nuzi tablets.

Harvard Semitic Museum. © Ferrell Jenkins / BiblicalStudies.info

Until discovery of the Nuzi tablets, little was known of a people group called the Horites (or Horim), only mentioned twice in the Pentateuch (14:6; Deut 2:12). Some scholars even suggested the Horites never existed.[57] The Nuzi tablets[58] revealed that the Horites were a significant ancient people who played a major role in ancient Near Eastern culture.[59] Abraham had contact with the Horites when he lived in Haran (25:21–25).

AN HEIR BY ADOPTION AND PROXY

Adoption tablets discovered at Nuzu shed light on adoption regulations in the ANE. According to Nuzi law, if a man was childless he could adopt a son to become heir and carry the family name (see also Hammurabi Code, §§191).[60] However, the law clearly stated that if a natural son

---

[53] M. A. Morrison, "Nuzi," ed. David Noel Freedman, *ABD* (New York: Doubleday, 1996), 4:1156–62; Diana L. Stein, "Nuzi," in *OEANE*, ed. Eric M. Meyers, vol. 4 (Oxford: Oxford University Press, 1997), 4:171–75.

[54] Ernest René Lacheman et al., eds., *Studies on the Civilization and Culture of Nuzi and the Hurrians*, 11 vols. (Winona Lake, IN: Eisenbrauns, 1989).

[55] Pfeiffer, ed., *Wycliffe Dictionary of Biblical Archaeology*, 422.

[56] Cyrus H. Gordon, "Biblical Customs and the Nuzu Tablets," *BAR* 2 (1964): 21–33; E. A. Speiser, *Genesis: Introduction, Translation, and Notes*, AB 1 (New York: Doubleday, 1964), 120; William F. Albright, "From the Patriarchs to Moses. I. From Abraham to Joseph," *BA* 36 (1973): 5–33; Alan R. Millard, "Abraham (person)," ed. David Noel Freedman et al., *ABD* (New York: Doubleday, 1996), 1:38; Kenneth A. Kitchen, "The Patriarchal Age: Myth or History?," *BAR* 21, no. 2 (1995): 48–57, 89–95; E. A. Speiser, "The Wife-Sister Motif in the Patriarchal Narratives," in *Biblical and Other Studies*, ed. Amnon Altman (Cambridge, MA: Harvard University Press, 1963), 15–28; J. Paradise, "A Daughter and Her Father's Property at Nuzi," *JCS* 32 (1980): 189–207; M. J. Selman, "Comparative Customs and the Patriarchal Age," in *Essays on the Patriarchal Narratives*, ed. Alan R. Millard and Donald J. Wiseman, 2nd ed. (, IL: InterVarsity, 1983), 91–139.

[57] Francis William Newman, *A History of the Hebrew Monarchy: From the Administration of Samuel to the Babylonish Captivity* (London: Chapman, 1853), 179 n. 2.

[58] Ernest René Lacheman et al., eds., *Studies on the Civilization and Culture of Nuzi and the Hurrians*, 11 vols. (Winona Lake, IN: Eisenbrauns, 1989); Richard F. S. Starr et al., *Nuzi: Report on the Excavation at Yorgan Tepa near Kirkuk, Iraq, Conducted by Harvard University in Conjunction with the American Schools of Oriental Research and the University Museum of Philadelphia, 1927-1931*, vol. 1 (Cambridge, MA: Harvard University Press, 1939).

[59] M. A. Morrison, "Nuzi," In *ABD* (1996): 4:1156–62.

[60] *CoS* 2:348.

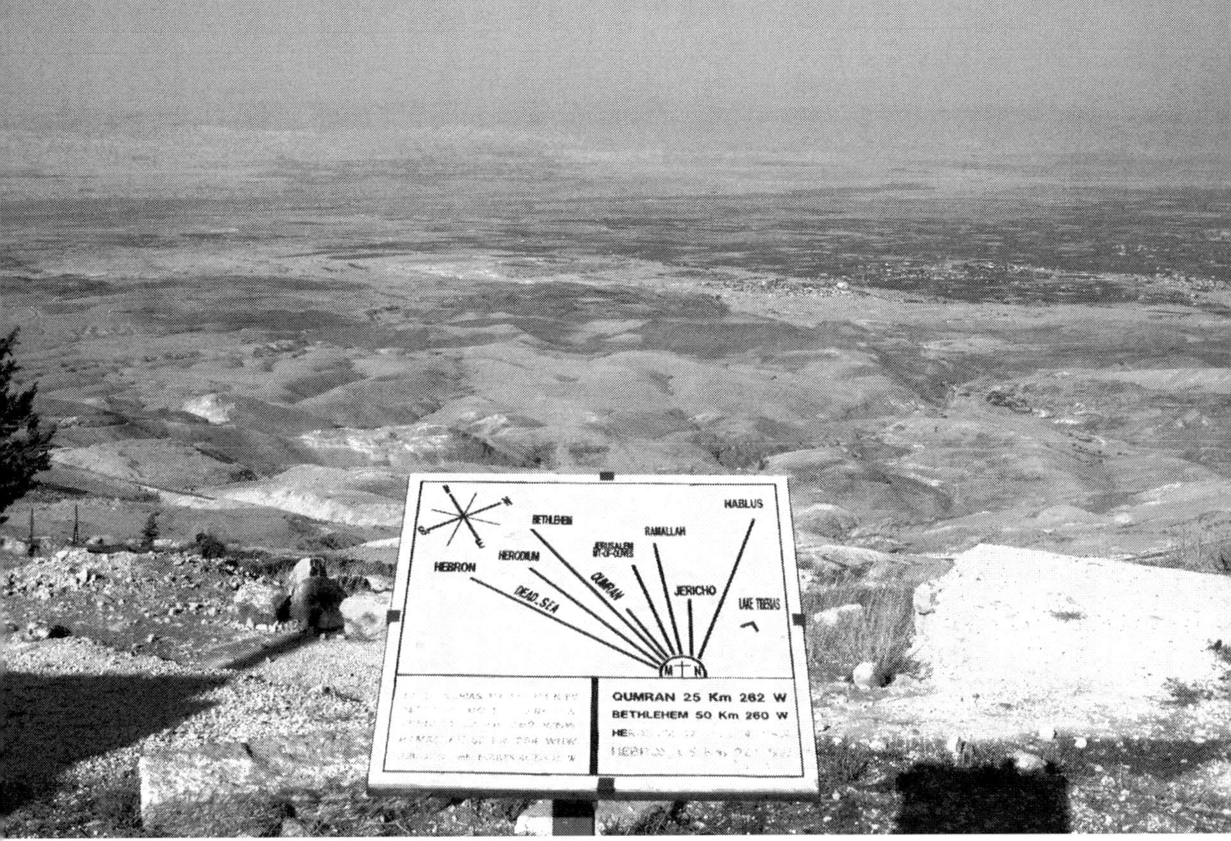

53. View of Israel from Mt. Nebo. The plaque indicates the location of various sites on the opposite side of the Jordan River . The southern Dead Sea area and Bâb edh-Dhrâ' are not visible from this location on top of Mt. Nebo.

were born to the couple, then all legal rights acquired by the adopted son were null and void. Eleazer of Damascus was Abraham's adopted son (15:2), but the birth of Isaac nullified his legal rights.[61]

Another means to provide an heir was to take a slave–wife, sometimes called an "heir by proxy".[62] Ishmael would then, according to custom, be the legal heir. But God would make void the customs of the time by providing a miraculous promised child (16:1–3).

Also, Nuzi law stated that after a son was born the previous heir was not to be expelled. This may explain part of Abraham's reluctance to expel Hagar and Ishmael at Sarah's request. In the end, the expulsion was by God's command, showing that Abraham did not blindly adopt all cultural laws.[63]

Separation of Abraham and Lot

The story of the separation of Abraham and Lot is found in Genesis 13:5–13 and resulted from a quarrel between their herdsmen over lack of real estate for their animals. From their location between Bethel and Ai, on the Israeli side of the Jordan, Abraham grants Lot the first choice of land for his flocks and "Lot looked around and saw that the whole plain [Heb. *kikkār*] of the Jordan toward Zoar [east] was well watered, like the garden of the Lord, like the land of Egypt.

---

[61] E. A. Speiser, "The Wife–Sister Motif in the Patriarchal Narratives," in *Biblical and Other Studies*, ed. Amnon Altman (Cambridge, MA: Harvard University Press, 1963), 15–28.

[62] See Hammurabi Code, §§144–46, 148; Mari text see *ANET*, 3rd ed./ Supp. 545 §13; Laqipum/Hatala text 543 §4; Lipit-Ishtar §28. Kitchen, *Reliability of the OT*, 234–28.

[63] Cyrus H. Gordon, "Biblical Customs and the Nuzu Tablets," *BAR* 2 (1964): 21–33.

(This was before the Lord destroyed Sodom and Gomorrah)" (Gen 13:10–11).

The plain of Jordan just in front of Jericho would have been visible from this mountainous location. The term *plain* is the unique Hebrew word *kikkār* which usually means a "round loaf of bread" (1 Sam 2:36; Prov 6:26; Exod 29:23; Jer 37:21; 1 Chr 16:3; 1 Sam 10:3, Jud 8:5) or a "circular disk for payment" (2 Sam 12:30, 1 Kgs 20:39, 2 Kgs 5:5; 1 Chr 29:7; 2 Kgs 9:14). Thus, from its shape it is used as a circular or oval geographical district/territory, used especially of the Jordan Valley north of the Dead Sea (Gen 13:10; 13:11; 1 Kgs 7:46; 2 Chr 4:17; Gen 19:17; 19:25; Deut 34:3; 2 Sam 18:23; Gen 19:28; 13:12; 19:29) or a district of Jerusalem (Neh 3:22, 12:28).[64]

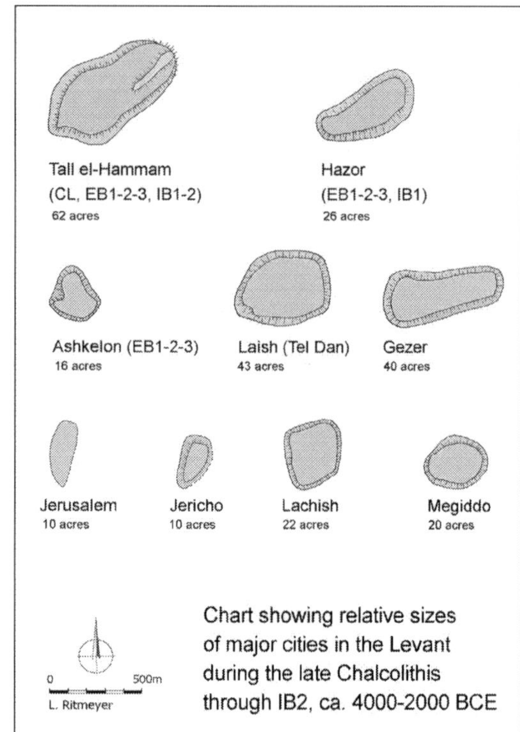

54. Chart showing the relative sizes of major cities in the Levant during the late Chalcolithic through to the IB2 period, *ca.* 4000–2000 BC. Bâb edh-Dhrâʿ at this time was 9–10 acres, the size of Jerusalem and Jericho.

SODOM AND GOMORRAH

Sodom and Gomorrah were a part of a larger agricultural confederation of cities known as the Cities of the Plain (Pentapolis) and included Sodom, Gomorrah, Zoar, Admah, and Zeboim (Gen 10:10–19; 13:12, 13; Deut 29:23). The cities of Sodom and Gomorrah were destroyed by God for their sin (Gen 19:24) and have long been associated with God's judgment of sin (Ezek 16:49–50; Isa 1:9–10; 3:9; 13:19–22; Jer 23:14; 49:17–18; 50:39–40; Lam 4:6; Amos 4:1–11; Zeph 2:9; Matt 10:14–15; 11:20–24; Luke 10:1–12; 17:28–30; Jude 1:7; *1 En.* 10:3; 34:1). Sodom is also mentioned outside the biblical text by other ancient authors (Philo *Abr.* 140f; 227, 228; *Somn.* 2:192, *Congr.* 92; 109; Josephus *Ant.* 1.170–206; 1QapGen XXI, 5ff [22:25]; etc.). But is there archaeological evidence of their existence? Recent excavations have provided two possible sites, Bâb edh-Dhrâʿ and Tall el-Ḥammâm.

Criteria for Locating Sodom

The location of the Cities of the Plain can be determined by the clues in the biblical text. The Bible states that the Jordan Valley (*kikkār*) was visible from between Bethel and Ai (Gen 13:3–4; 10–11) and that Lot travelled east settling among the cities of the valley, and eventually moved his tent to Sodom. While the exact location of Bethel (modern Beitin[65] or al-Bireh[66]) and Ai

[64] Briggs, Driver, and Brown, *The Brown-Driver-Briggs Hebrew and English Lexicon: With an Appendix Containing Biblical Aramaic*, 503.

[65] William F. Albright, "The Site of Bethel and Its Identification," in *The Excavation of Bethel (1934-1960)*, ed. James Leon Kelso and William F. Albright, AASOR 39 (Cambridge, MA: American Schools of Oriental Research, 1968), 1–3; Michael Avi-Yonah and Ephraim Stern, eds., "Beth-El," in *EAEHL*, 4 vols. (Upper Saddle River, NJ: Prentice Hall, 1978); Nadav Na'aman, "Bethel and Beth-Aven: The Location of the Early Israelite Sanctuaries," *Zion* 50 (1985): 25–25; Harold Brodsky, "Bethel (Place)," ed. David

(modern et-Tell, Khirbet Nisya or Khirbet el-Maqatir)[67] are debated, they are roughly 11–12 miles (19.31 km) north of Jerusalem on the other side of the Central Benjamin plateau, some 2,788 ft. (890 m) above sea level.

The destroyed cities of the Pentapolis are repeatedly mentioned located in "the plain" or "valley" (Gen 13:12; Heb. *kikkār*), also called "the land of the valley" (Gen 19:28) and "Jordan Valley" (Gen 13:10f). This distinctive Hebrew term (*kikkār*) is central to the arguments around the location of the city of Sodom.

The phrase, "Cities of the Plain", in Genesis 13:12 and 19:29 is formed in what is known in Hebrew as the "construct state". This means that the word "cities" has a very close association with the word "plain" (Heb. *kikkār).*

The etymology of the root word indicates that *kikkār* refers to something round, as in a "round loaf of bread" (1 Sam 2:36; Prov 6:26; Exod 29:23; Jer 37:21; 1 Chr 16:3; 1 Sam 10:3, Jud 8:5) or a "circular disk for payment" (2 Sam 12:30, 1 Kgs 20:39, 2 Kgs 5:5; 1 Chr 29:7; 2 Kgs 9:14).[68]

Other references to the *kikkār* place it between Zarethan (*Tell es-Saidiyeh,*[69] Josh 3:16; 1 Kgs 7:46; 2 Chr 4:17) and Succoth (*Tell Deir 'Alla;*[70] Josh 13:27) in the Jordan Valley near the Jabbok River, east of the Jordan River (1 Kgs 7:46; 2 Chr 4:17; 2 Sam 18:23. See Map 1). This would place the *kikkār* in the northern region between the Sea of Galilee and the Dead Sea (see Fig. 53 and 56).

The other Hebrew term used to describe the area is *kullahh mashgeh* which literally means to be "completely and totally irrigated". It was this area which was "well watered" like the garden of God and the Nile (Gen 13:10).

Following the destruction of four of the cities (Gen 19:23–25), Lot's wife was turned into a pillar of salt (Gen 19:26). The mention of salt may be an allusion to the salt curse and the destruction of a city and its vegetation in the ANE (Deut 29:21–23; Judg 9:45).[71] Ancient people would recognize the mention of salt as God speaking in terms of the ANE curse.[72] Tests of the soil from Tall el-Hammam at the end of the MB destruction level have revealed a toxic level of salt that would have prevented anything from growing in the region for several generations.[73]

Therefore, the criteria required to locate the Cities of the Plain are: located on the eastern side of the round alluvial, well watered, plain (*kikkār*) of the Jordan Valley; visible from the

---

Noel Freedman *et al.*, *ABD* (New York: Doubleday, 1996), 1:710–12; Robert T. Anderson, "Bethel (Place)," in *EDB*, ed. David Noel Freedman, Allen C. Myers, and Astrid B. Beck (Grand Rapids: Eerdmans, 2000), 170.

[66] David P. Livingston, "The Location of Biblical Bethel and Ai Reconsidered," *Westminster Theological Journal* 33, no. 1 (1970): 20–44; "One Last Word on Bethel and Ai," *BAR* 15, no. 1 (1989): 11.

[67] See Chapter Four under Joshua and the Conquest – Ai for a discussion of the location of Ai.

[68] George L. Robinson, "Jordan," in *Dictionary of the Bible, One Vol.*, ed. James Hastings and John A. Selbie (New York: Scribner's Sons, 1909), 761; R. Laird Harris, Gleason L. Archer, Jr., and Bruce K. Waltke, eds., "כִּכָּר," in *TWOT* (Chicago, IL: Moody, 1980), 503, no. 4673; Charles A. Briggs, Samuel R. Driver, and Francis Brown, "כִּכָּר," in *BDB* (Oxford: Clarendon, 1997), no. 1046c.

[69] Jonathan N. Tubb, "Sa'idryeh. Tell Es-," in *OEANE*, ed. Eric M. Meyers, vol. 4 (Oxford: Oxford University Press, 1997), 452.

[70] Hendricus J. Franken, "Deir 'Alla, Tell," in *OEANE*, ed. Eric M. Meyers, vol. 2 (Oxford: Oxford University Press, 1997), 138.

[71] David E. Graves, "Sodom And Salt in Their Ancient Near Eastern Cultural Context," *NEASB* 61 (2016): 15–32

[72] F. Charles Fensham, "Salt as a Curse in the Old Testament and the Ancient Near East," *Biblical Archaeologist* 25, no. 1 (February 1962): 48–50; James E. Latham, *The Religious Symbolism of Salt*, Theologie Historique 64 (Paris: Beauchesne, 1982), 81–82.

[73] Phillip J. Silvia, "The Middle Bronze Age Civilization-Ending Destruction of the Middle Ghor" (Trinity Southwest University, 2016), 111–13.

region around Bethel and Ai; destroyed during the time of the patriarchs (MBA); [74] and having evidence of a fiery destruction. See the chart below for additional criteria and a comparison of how the "Southern Sodom Theory" (SST) and the "Northern Sodom Theory" (NST) candidates meet this criteria.

Search for the Cities of the Plain

The search for the Cities of the Plain begins with some critical scholars saying they were merely non-existent unhistorical legends[75] and "purely mythical tale[s]" [76] from out of the past.[77] However, the historicity of the Cities of the Plain is not only verified by Jesus' treatment of the cities of Sodom and Gomorrah (Matt 10:1–15, 11:20–24; cf. Luke 10:1–12, 17:28–30) as historical, but also in their listing in Genesis 10 among other historically recognized cities such as: Babylon, Akkad, Nineveh, Sidon and Gaza. There is no reason to treat them as anything but historical and therefore remains of their destruction should be evident.[78]

While some fringe scholars have argued, on the basis of volcanic activity (fire and brimstone), that Sodom should be sought in Arabia[79] or Iraq,[80] the biblical text clearly places it around the Dead Sea region (Gen 13:11–12; 14:3).

With the discovery of the Ebla (Tell Mardikh) tablets in 1974 by Giovanni Pettinato and Paolo Matthiae,[81] Pettinato and Shea reported (1976) the tablets listed the Pentapolis (five cities) in the same order as Genesis.[82] However, many scholars today doubt these readings[83] and consider them to have "no bearing on … Sodom and Gomorra [*sic* Gomorrah]."[84] But if the Cities of the Plain are mentioned trading with Ebla in the EB period, Biblical archaeologists agree that Sodom was in existence in the EB period (Gen 10). The real qustion is when was it destroyed (Gen 19).

---

[74] Kitchen, *Reliability of the OT*, 352–53; John E. Goldingay, "The Patriarchs in Scripture and History," in *Essays on the Patriarchal Narratives*, ed. Donald J. Wiseman and Alan R. Millard (Winona Lake, IN: Eisenbrauns, 1983), 11–42; Alan R. Millard, "Methods of Studying the Patriarchal Narratives as Ancient Texts," in *Essays on the Patriarchal Narratives*, ed. Donald J. Wiseman and Alan R. Millard (Winona Lake, IN: Eisenbrauns, 1983), 43–58; Nahum M Sarna, "The Patriarchs Genesis 12-36," in *Genesis: World of Myths and Patriarchs*, ed. Ada Feyerick, Cyrus Herzl Gordon, and Nahum M Sarna (New York: New York University Press, 1996), 117–66.

[75] Martin Noth, *A History of Pentateuchal Traditions* (Upper Saddle River, NJ: Prentice-Hall, 1972), 191; *The History of Israel* (New York: Harper, 1960), 121; James Maxwell Miller and John Haralson Hayes, *A History of Ancient Israel and Judah* (Louisville, KY: Westminster/Knox, 1986), 60; M. J. Mulder, "Sodom and Gomorrah," ed. David Noel Freedman *et al.*, *ABD* (New York: Doubleday, 1996), 6:99, 102; Philip R. Davies, *Memories of Ancient Israel: An Introduction to Biblical History--Ancient and Modern* (Louisville, KY: Westminster/Knox, 2008), 64.

[76] Theodor Herzl Gaster and James G. Frazer, *Myth, Legend, and Custom in the Old Testament: A Comparative Study with Chapters from Sir James G. Frazer's Folklore in the Old Testament* (New York: Harper & Row, 1975), 161.

[77] Walter E. Rast, "Bab Edh-Dhra' (ABD)," ed. David Noel Freedman *et al.*, *ABD* (New York: Doubleday, 1996), 1:561.

[78] Bryant G. Wood, "The Discovery of the Sin Cities of Sodom and Gomorrah," *Bible and Spade* 12, no. 3 (1999): 67.

[79] Eduard Meyer and Bernhard Luther, *Die Israeliten und ihre Nachbarstämme: Alttestamentliche Untersuchungen* (Halle: Max Niemeyer, 1906), 71.

[80] Charles R Pellegrino, *Return to Sodom and Gomorrah: Bible Stories from Archaeologists* (New York: Avon Books, 1995), 180.

[81] Clifford A. Wilson, *Ebla Tablets: Secrets of a Forgotten City: Revelations of Tell Mardikh*, Third, Enlarged and Updated (San Diego, CA: Creation-Life, 1981).

[82] Hershel Shanks, "BAR Interviews Giovanni Pettinato: Original Ebla Epigrapher Attempts to Set the Record Straight," *BAR* 6, no. 5 (1980): 46–52; William H. Shea, "Two Palestinian Segments from the Eblaite Geographical Atlas," in *Word of the Lord Shall Go Forth: Essays in Honor of David Noel Freedman in Celebration of His Sixtieth Birthday*, ed. Carol L. Meyers and M. O'Connor, American Schools of Oriental Research (Winona Lake, IN: Eisenbrauns, 1983), 589–612.

[83] David Noel Freedman, "The Real Story of the Ebla Tablets: Ebla and the Cities of the Plain," *BA* 41 (1978): 143–64; Alfonso Archi, "Ebla Texts," in *OEANE*, ed. Eric M. Meyers, vol. 2, 5 vols. (Oxford: Oxford University Press, 1997), 184–86; "The Epigraphic Evidence from Ebla and the Old Testament"; Robert D. Biggs, "The Ebla Tablets: An Interim Perspective," *BA* 43, no. 2 (1980): 76–86.

[84] Sadly, Pettinato and Matthiae have taken opposite sides over this issue, ending their working relationship. Mark W. Chavalas and K. Lawson Younger, eds., *Mesopotamia and the Bible: Comparative Explorations* (Grand Rapids: Baker Academic, 2002), 41.

55. Western fortifications of Bâb edh-Dhrâʿ overlooking the southern Jordan Valley. Although destroyed in the EB period, some have suggested that this is biblical Sodom.

During the nineteenth century, several explorers travelled through the strange and unique landscape of the Dead Sea region and spoke of seeing the Cities of the Plain.[85] At the southwestern end of the Dead Sea there is a salt formation (mountain), which the locals call Jebel Usdum,[86] which in Arabic means "Mount of Sodom." Local Byzantine tradition has identified Zoar with eṣ-Ṣafi 24 km (15 miles) south of the Lisan[87] and placed the Cities of the Plain in this southern region of the Dead Sea, known as the Southern Sodom Theory (SST). Some, like Albright, placed the Pentapolis under the southern end of the Dead Sea (inundation theory).[88] Some, based on the geography of the biblical text, placed them at the northern end of the Dead Sea, in the Jordan Valley (Heb. *kikkār*). This view is called the Northern Sodom Theory (NST).

---

[85] The southern location was argued by the likes of Thomas Fuller (1650), Peter Graham (1836), William F. Lynch (1849), Louis Félix de Saulcy (1851), Samuel Wolcott (1868), Georg H. Ewald (1869), Charles Clermont-Ganneau (1846–1923), Sir Charles Warren (1899), William F. Albright (1891–1971), and James Penrose Harland (1943). The northern location has been argued by Charles W. Wilson (1869), Edward Henry Palmer (1871), Henry Baker Tristram (1873), Selah Merrill (1876, 1881), William F. Birch (1879), Claude Reignier Conder (1879-1883), William M. Thomson (1882-85), George Grove (1884), John Cunningham Geikie (1887), E. Power (1930), and Père Alexis Mallon (1929-1934). For a list of their sources see Graves, *Key Facts for the Location of Sodom*, 57–59

[86] Graves, *Key Facts for the Location of Sodom*, 139. See Fact 58: *Jebel Usdum is not Sodom or Lot's Wife.*

[87] Konstantinos D. Politis, "Death at the Dead Sea," *BAR* 38, no. 2 (2013): 45; Anthony D. Saldarini, "Babatha's Story," *BAR* 24, no. 2 (1998): 29; Naphtali Lewis, Jonas C. Greenfield, and Yigael Yadin, eds., *The Documents from the Bar Kokhba Period in the Cave of Letters, Greek Papyri*, Judaean Desert Series 2 (Jerusalem: Israel Exploration Society, 1989); Ada Yardeni *et al.*, eds., *The Documents from the Bar Kokhba Period in the Cave of Letters: Hebrew, Aramaic and Nabatean-Aramaic Papyri.* (Jerusalem: Israel Exploration Society, 2002), 1–4, 6–10; Avraham Negev, "Zoar," in *AEHL*, 3rd ed. (New York: Prentice Hall Press, 1996), op. cit.; Michael C. Astour, "Zoar (Place)," ed. David Noel Freedman *et al.*, *ABD* (New York: Doubleday, 1996), 6:1107.

[88] Georg Heinrich Ewald, *History of Israel: Introduction and Preliminary History*, ed. and trans. Russell Martineau, 2nd ed., vol. 1 (London: Longmans, Green, & Company, 1869), 313–14; Max Blanckenhorn, *Entstehung und Geschichte des Toten Meeres: Beitraeg zur Geologie Palaestinas*, Zeitschrift des deutschen Palästina-Vereins 19 (Leipzig: Baedeker, 1896), 51–59; James Penrose Harland, "Sodom and Gomorrah Part II: The Destruction of the Cities of the Plain," *BA* 6, no. 3 (1943): 41–42; William Foxwell Albright, *The Archaeology of Palestine and the Bible*, The Richards Lectures Delivered at the University of Virginia (New York: Flavell, 1935), 135–36; David Neev and Kenneth O. Emery, *The Dead Sea: Depositional Processes and Environments of Evaporites*, Ministry of Development: Geological Survey 41 (Jerusalem: Geological Survey of Israel, 1967), 30.

Southern Theory

In 1924 William F. Albright led an archaeological expedition to locate the Cities of the Plain, but after an investigation of the area, could not locate any suitable sites. It was suggested that they were swallowed up by the Dead Sea[89] and undiscoverable.[90] This theory was further corroborated by Ralph Baney's discovery in 1960 of small trees in the upright growth position beneath the southern basin of the Dead Sea, although ancient structures were not found.[91] Also, in 2011, a Russian exploration group used submarines to explore and photograph the bottom of the Dead Sea, but found no evidence of ancient ruins.[92] Albright did, however, find the ruins of a fortified site, named Bâb edh-Dhrâʿ (BeD; see Fig. 55), overlooking the deep ravine of Wadi Kerak, which he dated to the EBA (3150–2200 BC).[93] Taking into consideration the lack of occupational debris and seven fallen limestone monoliths, found a short distance east of Bâb edh-Dhrâʿ,[94] Albright concluded that this was not one of the Cities of the Plain but a place of pilgrimage where annual cultic feasts were celebrated.

Between 1965 and 1967 Bâb edh-Dhrâʿ was excavated under the direction of Paul Lapp. Extensive work was done at a large cemetery south of the city that contained a minimum of 20,000 EB 1 shaft tombs used by pastoral nomads from the region, estimating the dead at over half a million, although most of the tombs were from a much earlier period than the 2350 BC destruction.[95] He also uncovered a large destruction level at the end of the EBA 3. Unfortunately, Paul Lapp died unexpectedly in 1970, and so the task of further research fell to R. Thomas Schaub and Walter E. Rast.[96]

Rast and Schaub identified that in "approximately 2350 B.C., the EB 3 city suffered some sort of trauma, leaving it in ruins," [97] abandoned and "suffered exposure to fire."[98] Following its

---

[89] William F. Albright, "The Jordan Valley in the Bronze Age," *AASOR* 6 (1926): 57–58.

[90] Albright, "The Jordan Valley in the Bronze Age"; Albright, *The Archaeology of Palestine*, 135–36; Paul W. Lapp, "Bab Edh-Dhraʿ, Perizzites and Emim," in *Jerusalem Through the Ages: The Twenty-Fifth Archaeological Convention* (Jerusalem: Israel Exploration Society, 1968), 25; Joseph P. Free and Howard F. Vos, *Archaeology and Bible History* (Grand Rapids: Zondervan, 1992), 57; David Neev and Kenneth O. Emery, *The Destruction of Sodom, Gomorrah and Jericho: Geological, Climatological and Archaeological Backgrounds* (Oxford: Oxford University Press, 1995), 30.

[91] Ralph E. Baney, *Search for Sodom and Gomorrah*, 2nd ed. (Kansas City, MO: CAM Press, 1962), 178.

[92] David Lev, "Russia Decides to Search for Sodom and Gomorrah-in Jordan," *Arutz Sheva 7: Israel National News*, December 14, 2010, http://www.israelnationalnews.com/News/News.aspx/141132; Collins and Scott, *Discovering the City of Sodom*, 101; Todd Bolen, "Search for Sodom under Dead Sea," *BiblePlaces*, December 14, 2010, http://blog.bibleplaces.com/2010/12/search-for-sodom-under-dead-sea.html. See also the seismic survey of the Israelis side of the Dead Sea. John Kendrick Hall and David Neev, *Final Report No. 1[-2] on the Dead Sea Geophysical Survey, 19 July - 1 August 1974: Seismic Results and Intepretation* (Jerusalem: Ministry of Commerce & Industry, Geological Survey of Israel, 1975), 1–21.

[93] William F. Albright, J. L. Kelso, and J. P. Thorley, "Early Bronze Age Pottery from Bab-Ed-Dra in Moab," *BASOR* 95 (1944): 1–13.

[94] Albright, "The Jordan Valley in the Bronze Age," 58.

[95] Paul W. Lapp, "Bab Edh-Dhraʿ (RB 1966)," *RB* 73 (1966): 556–61; "Bab Edh-Dhraʿ Tomb A 76 and Early Bronze I in Palestine," *BASOR* 189 (1968): 12–41; "Bab Edh-Dhraʿ (RB 1968)," *RB* 75 (1968): 86–93, pls. 3–6a; Donald J Ortner and Bruno Frohlich, *The Early Bronze Age I Tombs and Burials of Bāb Edh-Dhrāʿ, Jordan*, Reports of the Expedition to the Dead Sea Plain, Jordan 3 (Lanham, MD: AltaMira, 2008).

[96] Walter E. Rast, "The Southeastern Dead Sea Valley Expedition, 1979," *BA* 43, no. 1 (1980): 60–61; Walter E. Rast and R. Thomas Schaub, "Expedition to the Southeastern Dead Sea Plain, Jordan, 1979," *American Schools of Oriental Research Newsletter*, no. 8 (1980): 12–17; *Bab Edh-Dhraʿ: Excavations in the Cemetery Directed by Paul W Lapp, 1965-1967*, Reports of the Expedition to the Dead Sea Plain, Jordan 1 (Winona Lake, IN: Eisenbrauns, 1989).

[97] Rast, "Bab Edh-Dhraʿ (ABD)," 1:560.

[98] Walter E. Rast, "Bab Edh-Dhraʿ and the Origin of the Sodom Saga," in *Archaeology and Biblical Interpretation: Essays in Memory of D. Glenn Rose*, ed. Leo G. Perdue, Lawrence E. Toombs, and Gary L. Johnson (Atlanta, Ga.: John Knox, 1987), 194; R. Thomas Schaub and Walter E. Rast, *The Southeastern Dead Sea Plain Expedition: An Interim Report of the 1977 Season*, AASOR 46 (Boston, MA: American Schools of Oriental Research, 1979), 16–18; Walter E. Rast and R. Thomas Schaub, "Survey of the Southeastern Plain of the Dead Sea, 1973," *ADAJ* 19 (1974): 8.

56. View from Tall Habbassa overlooking Tall el-Ḥammâm and the Middle Bronze age city-state area around the Tall. Jericho is directly across the Jordan Valley and Tall Kefrein is visible to the right below the arrow.

destruction, Bâb edh-Dhrâʿ was rebuilt in EB 4 (2350–2100 BC).[99]

In late May, 1973, not far to the south of Bâb edh-Dhrâʿ, they discovered four other sites; Numeira, eṣ-Ṣafi, Feifa, and Khirbet Khanazir[100] which, they claimed at the time, had a similar footprint.[101] It has since been verified that eṣ-Ṣafi, Feifa, and Khirbet Khanazir (believed by some to me the remaining cities of the plain) have no occupational evidence dating to the Bronze Age and were merely cemeteries.[102] While all five have a large cemetery, only two of them, Bâb edh-Dhrâʿ and Numeira, are known to have been inhabited with EBA occupational architecture in the southern region of the Dead Sea between *ca.* 3300 and 900 BC. What were thought to be walls at Khanazir, identified by Rast and Schaub

---

[99] R. Thomas Schaub, "Bab Edh-Dhraʿ (OEANE)," in *OEANE*, ed. Eric M. Meyers, vol. 1 (Oxford: Oxford University Press, 1997), 249; Walter E. Rast, "Bronze Age Cities along the Dead Sea," *Archaeology* 40, no. 1 (1987): 48.

[100] Eric H. Cline, *From Eden to Exile: Unraveling Mysteries of the Bible* (Tampa, Fla.: National Geographic, 2007), 59.

[101] Walter E. Rast, "Settlement at Numeira," in *The Southeastern Dead Sea Plain Expedition: An Interim Report of the 1977 Season*, AASOR 46 (Cambridge: American Schools of Oriental Research, 1979), 35–44; Walter E. Rast and R. Thomas Schaub, "The Dead Sea Expedition: Bab Edh-Dhraʿ and Numeira, May 24-July 10, 1981," *American Schools of Oriental Research Newsletter*, no. 4 (1982): 4–12.

[102] R. Thomas Schaub, "Southeast Dead Sea Plain," in *OEANE*, ed. Eric M. Meyers, vol. 5 (Oxford: Oxford University Press, 1997), 62–63; Bert de Vries, ed., "Archaeology in Jordan, 1991," *AJA* 95, no. 2 (1991): 262; Rast and Schaub, "Survey of the Southeastern Plain of the Dead Sea, 1973," 10; Meredith S. Chesson and R. Thomas Schaub, "Death and Dying on the Dead Sea Plain: Fifa, Al- Khanazir and Bab Adh-Dhra` Cemeteries," in *Crossing Jordan: North American Contributions to the Archaeology of Jordan*, ed. Thomas Evan Levy et al. (London: Equinox, 2007), 253, 258; Burton MacDonald, "EB IV Tombs at Khirbet Khanazir: Types, Construction, and Relation to Other EB IV Tombs in Syria-Palestine," *Studies in the History and Archaeology of Jordan* 5 (1995): 129–34.

in 1973,[103] were later revealed to be Early Bronze 4 (2300–2200 BC) shaft tombs.[104]

In addition, while Bâb edh-Dhrâ' and Numeira were reported to have been destroyed at the same time,[105] it has since been shown, from improved C-14 dating, that they were destroyed at different times.[106] Bâb edh-Dhrâ' was destroyed by a massive EB3 destruction that took place around 2350 BC[107] or 2300 BC,[108] while Numeira came to an end around 2600 BC, 300 years earlier.[109] If Bâb edh-Dhrâ' is Sodom, as Bryant Wood and others claim,[110] there is no evidence of any of the other Cities of the Plain.

The southern theory proponents, represented by Wood, maintain an early date of 2166–1991 BC (MB I-Intermediate Bronze) for the existence of the Patriarchs, which does not correspond to the destruction of Bâb edh-Dhrâ' in 2350 BC. For those like Albright, Kitchen, and Collins, who take a later Middle Bronze Age date for the Patriarchs (1950–1540 BC), this also rules out the southern location. There seems little doubt that Sodom did exist as early as the EB Age as it is mentioned in Genesis 10 and the Ebla tables. The question is when was Sodom destroyed? If one accepts the Middle Bronze date for the Patriarchs (accpeted my all evangelical archaeologists) then this must rule out Bâb edh-Dhrâ' as a candicate for biblical Sodom.

As Eric Cline recently admitted in his chapter on Sodom and Gomorrah, after assessing the current state of the "southern" evidence:

> [There] is no longer any particular reason to insist that Bab edh-Dhra and Numeira are definitely Sodom and Gomorrah, especially if we wish to have Abraham both as an eyewitness and living in the Middle Bronze Age....Perhaps it would be wise to untether Sodom and Gomorrah from Bab edh-Dhra and Numeira and search elsewhere for them. But where?[111]

Northern Theory

New ongoing research begun in 1996 by Dr. Steven Collins, of Trinity Southwest University, has reevaluated the evidence for BeD being Sodom,[112] and found that it had significant difficulties.[113] Based on the geography of the text (Gen 13:3),[114] Collins' quest for the location of Sodom let him to the northeastern end of the Dead Sea (Jordan *kikkār*), as was argued by many archaeologists prior to Albright.[115] He identified Tall el-Ḥammâm (TeH), the largest MB Age site

---

[103] Rast and Schaub, "Survey of the Southeastern Plain of the Dead Sea, 1973," 12–14.

[104] Rast, "Bab Edh-Dhra' (ABD)," 560; Schaub, "Southeast Dead Sea Plain," 62.

[105] Walter E. Rast *et al.*, "Preliminary Report of the 1979 Expedition to the Dead Sea Plain, Jordan," *BASOR* 240 (1980): 47.

[106] Cline, *From Eden to Exile*, 60.

[107] Rast, "Bronze Age Cities along the Dead Sea," 47; "Bab Edh-Dhra' (ABD)," 1:560; "Bab Edh-Dhra' and the Origin of the Sodom Saga," 194.

[108] Schaub, "Bab Edh-Dhra' (OEANE)," 1:249.

[109] Meredith S. Chesson and R. Thomas Schaub, "Life in the Earliest Walled Towns on the Dead Sea Plain: Numayra and Bab Edh-Dhra'," in *Crossing Jordan: North American Contributions to the Archaeology of Jordan*, ed. Thomas Evan Levy et al. (London: Equinox, 2007), 247.

[110] Wood, "Discovery of the Sin Cities," 1999, 68.

[111] Cline, *From Eden to Exile*, 59–60.

[112] Collins and Scott, *Discovering the City of Sodom*, 13–22; 87–99.

[113] Ibid., 90.

[114] Steven Collins, "The Geography of the Cities of the Plain," *Biblical Research Bulletin* 2, no. 1 (2002): 1–17; "A Chronology for the Cities of the Plain," *BRB* 2, no. 8 (2002): 1–9; "The Architecture of Sodom," *BRB* 2, no. 14 (2002): 1–9; "Explorations on the Eastern Jordan Disk," *BRB* 2, no. 18 (2002): 1–28.

[115] Henry Baker Tristram, *The Land of Moab: Travels and Discoveries on the East Side of the Dead Sea and the Jordan* (New York: Harper & Brothers, 1873), 326–33; William M. Thomson, *The Land and the Book: Southern Palestine and Jerusalem*, vol. 1 (New York: Harper & Brothers, 1880), 371–76; *The Land and the Book: Lebanon, Damascus, and Beyond Jordan*, vol. 3 (New York: Harper & Brothers, 1886), 668–70.

in the Jordan Valley north of the Dead Sea (see Fig. 56 and Map 9),[116] as the most promising site for Sodom from among the possible candidates.[117] Collins began excavations of the upper Tall in several locations in January 2005.[118]

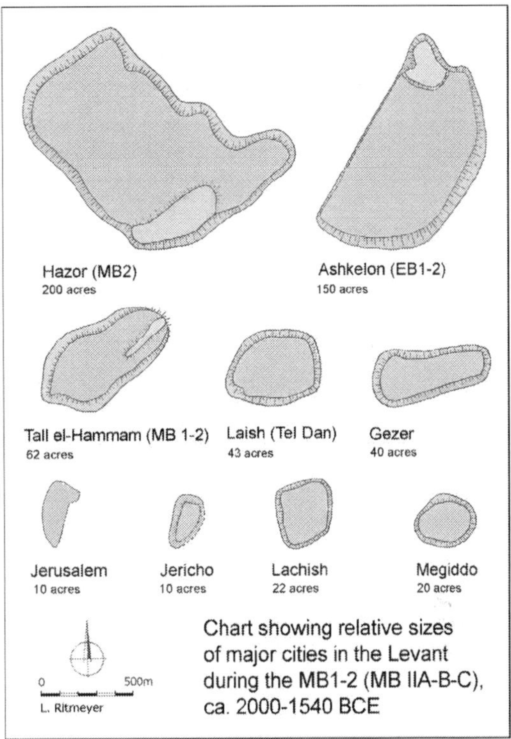

57. Chart showing relative sizes of major cities in the Levant during the MB1-2 (MB IIA-B-C), *ca.* 2000–1540 BC. During the MB Age, Bâb edh-Dhrâ' did not exist.

Used with permission © Ritmeyer Archaeological Design

Preliminary reports, even as late as 2013, identified the terminal destruction of TeH in the MBA at *ca.* 1600 BC (see Fig. 9).[119] However later in 2013, following eight seasons of excavations and reading over 40,000 separate vessels,[120] Collins published that "our refined date-range for Tall el-Ḥammâm's destruction is 1750–1650 BCE, [MB IIB] not 1600" (see Chart 14 and 15).[121] In 2017 Carbon-14 testing was perfomed on several samples from the MB destruction layer and returned dates of ca. 1773–1627 BC (ca. 3722–3576 cal BP), confirming the ceramic analysis.[122]

Archaeological evidence has indicated that TeH was occupied from the Chalcolithic period until it was destroyed in the Middle Bronze Age (1750–1650 BC),[123] but based on the absence of Late Bronze Age (1550–1000 BC) pottery,[124] it was not occupied again for over five centuries until the Iron Age (1000–586 BC; see Fig. 12, 14 and Chart 9).[125]

---

[116] Collins, Hamdan, and Byers, "Tall el-Hammam: Preliminary Report, Season Four, 2009," 386; Collins *et al.*, "Tall el-Hammam, Season Eight, 2013," 4.

[117] The possible sites included Tall Nimrin, Tall el-Musṭāḥ, Tall Bleibel, Tall Ghannam, Tall Ghrubba, Tall Kefrein, Khirbet Kafrayn, Tall el-Ḥammâm, Tall er-Ramêh, Tall Iktanu, Tall eahl es-Sarabet, Tulaylat al-Ghassul, Khirbet Sweimeh, and Tall el-Azeimeh (see Map 1). Rami G. Khouri, *Antiquities of the Jordan Rift Valley* (Manchester, MI: Solipsist, 1988), 68–86.

[118] Steven Collins, "2005-2006 Season Summary," *Digging the Past: Voice of the Tall el-Hammam Excavation Project, Jordan*, 2006.

[119] Steven Collins, "Where Is Sodom? The Case for Tall el-Hammam," *BAR* 39, no. 2 (2013): 70; Merrill, "Texts, Talls, and Old Testament Chronology," 1.

[120] Collins and Scott, *Discovering the City of Sodom*, 33.

[121] Collins, "Tall el-Hammam Is Still Sodom," 9; "Tall el-Hammam Is Sodom," 8; John Moore, "Dr. John Moore and Dr. Steven Collins Reflect on TeHEP's First Nine Years," *Update: Tall el-Hammam Excavation Project, The Official Newsletter of TeHEP*, April 11, 2014, 1; Collins and Scott, *Discovering the City of Sodom*, 226.

[122] Personal correspondence with Steven Collins, Nov 6, 2017.

[123] Collins, "Tall el-Hammam Is Still Sodom," 9; "Tall el-Hammam Is Sodom," 8; Moore, "Dr. John Moore and Dr. Steven Collins Reflect on TeHEP's First Nine Years," 1; Collins and Scott, *Discovering the City of Sodom*, 226.

[124] Collins *et al.*, "Tall el-Hammam, Season Eight, 2013," 4, 13. Although no residential structures have been identified at TeH, as of 2018 there is a small LB structure on the acropolis that has been confirmed by pottery and Carbon-14 that dates to ca. 1431–1283 BC. Moses and Joshua would have encountered this structure when they arrived on the Plains of Moab, camping "by the Jordan from Beth-jeshimoth as far as Abel-shittim in the plains of Moab" (Num 33:49).

[125] Ibid., 13.

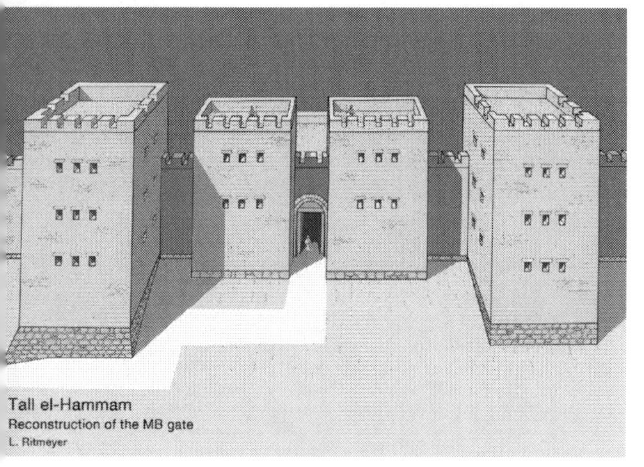

58. Reconstruction of the TeH MB gate complex discovered in 2012 and drawn by Leen Ritmeyer from the archaeological data provided by archaeologists. This is believed by Collins and others to be the gate of Sodom where Lot sat. A pillared chamber sat behind the two small towers.

Used with permission © Ritmeyer Archaeological Design

Late Bronze Gap in the Jordan Valley

This Late Bronze gap of 550 years is not unique to TeH, but characteristic of all the sites in the entire *kikkār* region including, Tall Iktanu, Tall Kefrein (al-Kefrayn), Tall Nimrin, Tall el-Musṭāḥ, Tall Bleibel (Bulaybil), etc. (see Map 1).[126] In 1993 Flanagan, McCreery, and Yassine coined the phrase "a Late Bronze gap"[127] speculating that "the 500 year gap of occupation from ca. 1500 to 1000 B.C. [LB/Iron Age I in the Jordan valley and Tall Nimrin] must be due to significant sociopolitical and/or environmental phenomena that remain to be explained."[128]

The Bible also provides an explanation for the Late Bronze gap in the Jordan valley north of the Dead Sea. The catastrophic destruction of the Pentapolis (Gen 19) would have affected the entire Jordan valley and prevented settlers from repopulating the area. Superstition of a cursed land would only keep shepherds, with hungry flocks of sheep and goats, off the land for perhaps a generation or two, but does not seem to be a reasonable explanation for the absence of 500 years. Something else must have happened to prevent farmers from using the region for agriculture.

Some have considered the destruction of the Cities of the Plain as described in the Bible the result of a cosmic airburst (3.7KYrBP),[129] which would have spread salt throughout the region of the Jordan Valley. If God had used such a cataclysmic event to bring about the destruction of the Pentapolis, this would have certainly left the region sterile, preventing the growth of vegetation.[130]

Whatever the direct cause, recent research has documented that the soil in the region north of the Dead Sea reveals evidence of saline levels that are above normal following the MB destruction. Geochemical analysis conducted by Allen West at the Activation Laboratories Ltd. in Ancaster, Ontario, Canada of the salt and sulphate content of the soil samples collected at various levels at Tall el-Hammam indicated that the soil above the MB destruction layer had an abnormal rise in the level of salt and sulphates.[131] The salt was typical of Dead Sea salt in

---

[126] Collins, Hamdan, and Byers, "Tall el-Hammam: Preliminary Report, Season Four, 2009," 385–414; Graves, *Key Facts for the Location of Sodom*, 115–17.

[127] James W. Flanagan, David W. McCreery, and Khair N. Yassine, "Tell Nimrin: Preliminary Report on the 1993 Season," *ADAJ* 38 (1994): 207.

[128] Ibid. 219; James W. Flanagan, David W. McCreery, and Khair N. Yassine, "Tall Nimrin: Preliminary Report on the 1995 Excavation and Geological Survey," *ADAJ* 40 (1996): 286.

[129] Phillip J. Silvia, "The Middle Bronze Age Civilization-Ending Destruction of the Middle Ghor," Albuquerque, N.M. (Ph.D. diss., Trinity Southwest University, 2015); Phillip J. Silvia and Steven Collins, "The Civilization-Ending 3.7KYrBP Kikkar Event: Archaeological Data, Sample Analyses, and Biblical Implications," in *Annual Meeting of the Near East Archaeological Society: Atlanta, Ga.* (Albuquerque, N.M.: TSU Press, 2015), 1–6.

[130] Jeffrey Goodman, *The Comets Of God: New Scientific Evidence for God: Recent Archeological, Geological and Astronomical Discoveries That Shine New Light on the Bible and Its Prophecies* (Tuscon, Ariz.: Archeological Research Books, LLC, 2010), 101–53.

[131] Silvia, "MBA Civilization-Ending Destruction," 111–13.

composition, and at these levels (above 300 ppm) would have made the soil toxic and unable to support the growth of vegetation or been conducive for agriculture. The soil would require a lengthy washing with water to purge the salt from the soil. As Silvia reports:

> The concentration of salts exceeded 600 ppm in the ash layer and 450 ppm in the soil layers immediately above and below the ash. Salt concentrations above 300 ppm are toxic to most plants used for human consumption. Therefore, it can be safely assumed that such a high concentration of salt was not present in the soil prior to the destruction event. Had it been otherwise, it would not have been possible to grow sufficient crops to sustain the population.[132]

Silvia speculates that the area may have been affected by an airburst and explains:

> The explosive force of a meteoritic airburst can accomplish the same scale of soil destruction and removal in a matter of seconds. If an airburst occurs close to a body of salt water, the vapor plume raised by the detonation can deposit a significant volume of salt brine over a very large area and poison the remaining soil for a long time. In semiarid regions, such as the Middle Ghor, the recovery time to regenerate usable soil is pushed to the longer end of the scale because of insufficient precipitation to flush the salt from the soil.[133]

Some may argue that the levels of the Dead Sea rose at one time in the past to cover Tall el-Hammam, but as Silvia points out:

> The highest level of the Dead Sea recorded in the walls of the Great Rift Valley is 185 m below mean sea level (bmsl) and is dated to about 18,000 YBP [years before present]…. Since then, the level of the Dead Sea has fluctuated between 350 and 400 m bmsl, and its current level is near its historic Byzantine Era (ca. 600 CE) low…. The highest point on Upper Tall el-Hammam is 124 m bmsl, and the highest point of Lower Tall el-Hammam is 154 m bmsl. No part of Tall el-Hammam has ever been inundated by the waters of the (now) Dead Sea. [134]

59. Human remains in the Middle Bronze Age (time of Abraham and Lot) destruction layer at Tall el-Ḥammâm of the city and not in a formal burial.

Courtesy of Michael C. Luddeni

Evidence of Destruction

The destruction level of TeH is significant and Collins reported in 2013 that:

> Across Tall el-Ḥammâm, archaeologists found widespread evidence of an intense conflagration that left the Middle Bronze Age city in ruins. They found scorched foundations and floors buried under nearly 3 feet of dark grey ash, as well as dozens of pottery sherds covered with a frothy, "melted" surface; the glassy appearance indicates that they were briefly exposed to temperatures well in excess of 2,000 degrees Fahrenheit, the approximate heat of volcanic magma. Such evidence suggests the city and its environs were catastrophically destroyed in a sudden and extreme conflagration.[135]

Trinitite Klinkers

Thus far, the TeH excavation has uncovered a total of five pieces of super-heated vitrified pottery (klinkers, see Fig. 60) from the MB destruction layer (ca. 1750 BC)[136] and desert glass at Tall Mwais, within five miles of TeH. Collins stated in *BAR* that: "It marks one of the most

---

[132] Ibid. 155.
[133] Ibid. 141–42.
[134] Ibid. 155.
[135] Collins, "Where Is Sodom?," 41.
[136] The *terminus ad quem* for Hammam's MB2 destruction is at 1750+/-50 BC (carbon-14 at 1773–1627 cal BC).

60. The 4.5-inch-long klinker of melted pottery (large piece to the left in the photo) that was discovered in the MB layer at TeH. To the right for conparison are two smaller pieces of trinitite from ground zero at Trinity New Mexico.

Courtesy of Michael C. Luddeni

violent, enormous destruction events imaginable. We have pieces of pottery melted into glass, some bubbled like lava, found across the site. . . . We have even documented pieces of desert glass (impact glass) strewn across the eastern Kikkar, created at temperatures exceeding 6,000 degrees Celsius."[137]

Something turned the pieces of pottery into glass, but only on one side. The material was blind tested at the U.S. Geological Survey Laboratory, on the campus of New Mexico Tech, and scientifically identified as "trinitite."[138] It derived its name from Trinity, New Mexico, where the first nuclear tests were conducted, the heat of which produced this same type of material.[139]

Dr. Dumbar, who tested the material at the laboratory, commented on the temperature necessary to create such a result. He reports:

> It would have to be at least two thousand degrees Fahrenheit at the zircon location. . . . Actually, the external air temperature would've had to be a lot higher than that, because ceramic material isn't a good conductor of heat, but it reached to the depth of the zircon to the tune of two thousand degrees. . . . An intensely burning room could only get to about sixteen hundred, maybe eighteen hundred degrees for a while, but not for long.[140]

Trinitite has unique characteristics different from obsidian (volcanic glass) and fulgurite (lightning glass), which scientists can distinquish. Dr. Dumbar, described the sample as "visually, materially and chemically"[141] the same as trinitite. The extreme heat required to melt pottery and produce trinitite indicates that there was an unusual phenomena that took place at and around TeH.

Does Zoar Help Identify Sodom?

There are several possible locations for the site of Zoar. Three sites on the north end of the Dead Sea (Tall Ikatanu, Serâbît el-Mushaqqar and a "port" on the Arnon River).[142] The southern location has traditionally been identified as the site on the Wadi Hesa near modern eṣ-Ṣafi, as identified on the sixth cent. AD Madaba Map in the church in Madaba, Jordan.[143] This beautiful pilgrams mosaic depicts the region of the Holy Land during the sixth cent. AD and places Zoar south of the Dead Sea at this location. However, early surveys of the area reported no

[137] Collins, "Tall el-Hammam Is Sodom," 4; Collins and Scott, *Discovering the City of Sodom*, 213.

[138] Collins and Scott, *Discovering the City of Sodom*, 207.

[139] Collins, "Where Is Sodom?, 71 n. 8, 9.

[140] Collins and Scott, *Discovering the City of Sodom*, 208–09.

[141] Ibid., 213.

[142] David E. Graves, *The Location of Sodom: Key Facts for Navigating the Maze of Arguments for the Location of the Cities of the Plain* (Toronto: Electronic Christian Media, 2016), 99–104.

[143] David E. Graves and D. Scott Stripling, "Identification of Tall el-Hammam on the Madaba Map," *BS* 20, no. 2 (2007): 35–45.

archaeological evidence uncovered at this site earlier than the Hellenistic Period.[144] R. Thomas Schaub, who excavated BeD, states that the sixth cent. AD Zoar on the Madaba map (Byzantine tradition) is not the same as the Middle Bronze Age Zoar as listed in Genesis.[145] However, if the Map was used by pilgrims they were interested in holy sites and the Cities of the Plain (point out Zoar). Since the city of Zoar was spared from destruction its location should be sought elsewhere. Interestingly there are two sites on the north end of the Dead Sea depicted on the Madabe map that are missing the tesserae depicting their names. Scholars have long speculated, based on the tesserae images and general location on the map, about the identification of these sites. While xcholars are still not unanious about the identification on the Madaba Map most cite Livias (Tall el-Ḥammâm)[146] and Abila (Tall el-Kafrayn).[147] But of what significance are these two sites to Chrisitan pilgrims? Since Zoar is named it is possible that these two sites were identified as Sodom and Gomorrah on the north end of the Dead Sea.

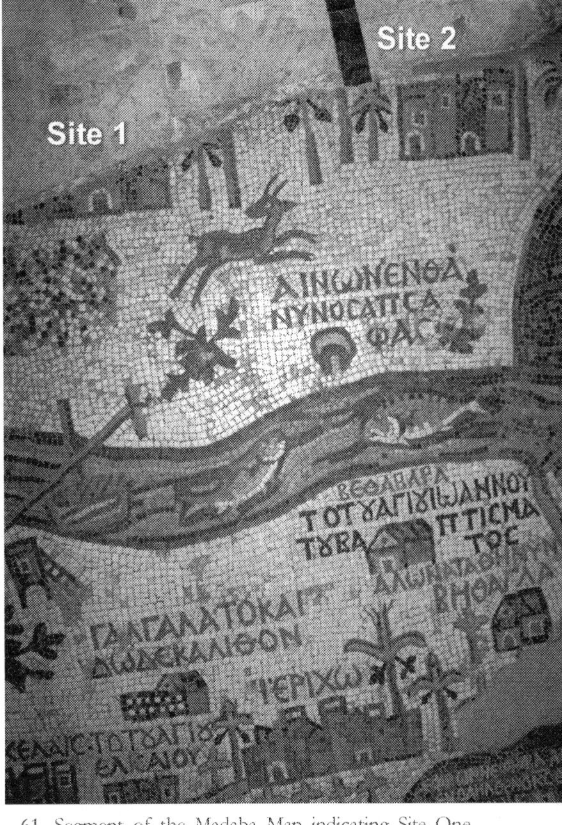

61. Segment of the Madaba Map indicating Site One (Tall el-Kafrayn) and Two (Tall el-Ḥammâm). The Jordan River is pictured in the centre with the site of Jericho identified at the bottom. (IEPIXω).

Conclusion

While there is still debate over the Northern and Southern theories,[148] given the geographical characteristics of the northern end of the Dead Sea and recent discoveries at TeH, it would be foolish to ignore it as a promising candidate for one of the Cities of the Plain (see Chart 3).

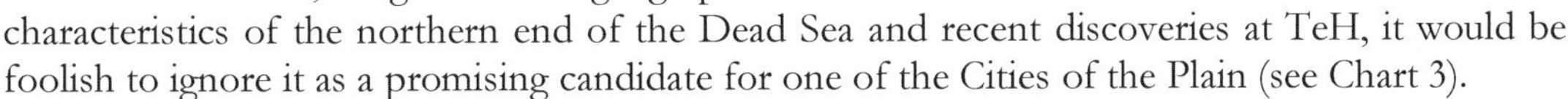

As Dr. William J. Fulco, the National Endowment of the Humanities Professor of Ancient Mediterranean Studies at Loyola Marymount University, states:

---

[144] Edward H. Palmer, *The Desert of the Exodus: Journeys on Foot in the Wilderness of the Forty Years' of Wanderings Undertaken in Connexion with the Ordance Survey of Sinai and the Palestine Exploration Fund*, vol. 1 (Cambridge: Deighton, Bell & Co., 1871), 1:29; Albright, "The Jordan Valley in the Bronze Age," 57; Alexis Mallon, "Voyage D'exploration Au Sud-Est de La Mer Morte," *Biblica* 10 (1929): 438; Konstantinos D. Politis *et al.*, "Survey and Excavations in the Ghawr as-Safi 2004," *ADAJ* 49 (2005): 314–18; "Survey and Excavations in the Ghawr as-Safi 2006–07," *ADAJ* 51 (2007): 199–210; David F. Graf, "Zoora Rises from the Grave: New Funerary Stelae from Palaestina Tertia," *Journal of Roman Archaeology* 22 (2009): 752–58; Konstantinos D. Politis, Adamantios Sampson, and Margaret O'Hea, "Ghawr As-Safi Survey and Excavations 2008-2009," *ADAJ* 53 (2009): 303–304.

[145] Schaub, "Southeast Dead Sea Plain," 5:64; Nahum M Sarna, *Genesis: The Traditional Hebrew Text with the New JPS Translation*, JPS Torah Commentary (Philadelphia: Jewish Publication Society, 1989), 388–89; Steven Collins, "Rethinking the Location of Zoar: An Exercise in Biblical Geography," *BRB* 4, no. 1 (2006): 1–5.

[146] David E. Graves and D. Scott Stripling, "Is Tall El-Hammam on the Madaba Map?," in *NEAS* (San Diego: NEAS, 2007), 1–20; "Identification of Tall El-Hammam on the Madaba Map," *BS* 20, no. 2 (2007): 35–45.

[147] David E. Graves and D. Scott Stripling, "Re-Examination of the Location for the Ancient City of Livias," Levant 43, no. 2 (2011): 179

[148] Wood, "Locating Sodom: A Critique of the Northern Proposal"; Steven Collins, "A Response to Bryant G. Wood's Critique of Collins' Northern Sodom Theory," *Biblical Research Bulletin* 7, no. 7 (2007): 1–36; Clyde E. Billington, "Tall el-Hammam Is Not Sodom," *Artifax*, Spring 2012, 1–3; Collins, "Tall el-Hammam Is Sodom."

Among the several sites or collection of sites that have been proposed for the notorious Cities of the Plain, which includes Sodom as its nucleus, Collins' proposal of Tall el-Hammam as this very place is convincing indeed. The evidence that the Tall al-Hammam Excavation Project (TeHEP) has brought to light and which Prof. Collins marshals to demonstrate the correlation between Tall Hammam and the biblical narrative must now enter the discussion as by far the strongest candidate for the site of Sodom.[149]

62. One of two statues of a he-goat, often called the "Ram caught in a Thicket" (Ur, ca. 2600–2350 BC). Daniel's vision in chapter 8 represents the he-goat as "the king of Greece" (8:21).

British Museum (ME 122200). © Jack1956 / Wikimedia Commons

[149] Collins and Scott, *Discovering the City of Sodom*, Preface. See also Holden and Geisler, *The Popular Handbook of Archaeology and the Bible*, 214-20, 383-87 and Graves, David E. "My Journey to Locate the Genesis Pentapolis North of the Dead Sea." In *Kikkar Dialogues*, edited by Steven Collins, 100–128. Albuquerque, N.M.: Trinity Southwest University Press, 2014.

CHART 3: CRITERIA FOR THE IDENTIFICATION OF SODOM FOR THE SST AND NST

Criteria for the Identification of Sodom for the SST and NST			
Criteria	**Scripture**	**BeD**	**TeH**
East of Canaan boundary	Gen 12:4–5	Yes	Yes
Large city listed first in pentapolis	Gen 14:2	10 acres	62 acres
Time of the patriarchs (MBA)	Gen 13	No EB3	Yes MB2
Well watered	Gen 13:10	No[1]	Yes[2]
Located on the *kikkar* (Jordan Valley)	Gen 13:11	No	Yes
Visible from Bethel and Ai	Gen 13:3–12	No	Yes
Distinct from the battlefield (Kedorlaomer)	Gen 14:1–8	No	Yes
Fortified city	Gen 19:1	Yes	Yes
Near Zoar[3]	Gen 19:23	Yes	Yes
Fiery destruction	Gen 19:24	Yes EB3	Yes MB2
Human remains in the destruction	Gen 19:25	No[4]	Yes
Large cemetery	Gen 19:25	Yes	Yes[5]
On a geological fault line[6]	Gen 19:25	Yes	Yes
Evidence of four destroyed Cities of the Plain	Gen 19:25	No[7]	Yes
Visible from Hebron	Gen 19:28	Yes	Yes
A wasteland in Late Bronze age	Num 21:20; 22:1	Yes	Yes
Visible from Mount Nebo	Deut 34:3	No	Yes
Abandoned forever	Jer 50:39–40	No EB4	No IA2
Returned to former state	Ezek 16:53–55	No only small EB4	Yes IA2

[1] Water supplied by wadi's that only flow during the rainy season and dry the rest of the year.

[2] Water supplied by several hotspring on the site providing water year round.

[3] Both BeD and TeH have possible locations for Zoar, but no one really knows for sure where Zoar is located, and over the years scholars have proposed several locations, though no clear archaeological evidence has ever emerged to positively identify it.

[4] Bodies were only identified in the cemetery.

[5] Large dolmen fields (Al Rawda Field) next to TeH that served as family memorials for the deceased.

[6] Some have suggested that Sodom was destroyed by an earthquake since it was located on a fault line. However, this is a moot criteria as both sites are located on the same fault line.

[7] Numeira and Bâb edh-Dhrâʿ were destroyed at different times, about 250 years apart. Feifa and Khirbet Khanazir, proposed for the other Cities of the Plain, do not have Early Bronze 3 domestic occupation, as they were both only cemeteries during this period.

Chart 4: Late Bronze Age Discoveries

EXODUS – CONQUEST (LB: 1550–1200 BC)					
Discovery	**Image**	**Place and Discoverer**	**Origin Date /Year Found**	**Biblical Passage**	**Significance**
1,000 Egyptian Execration Texts		Semna, Uronarti, Elephantine, Thebes, Balat, Abydos, Helwan, Saqqara, and Giza, Mirgissa, Egypt	2686–2160 BC *ca.* 1550–1069 BC MB1 to MB2B Various dates	Various	Mention of biblical cities (i.e., Dan, Ashkelon, Jerusalem, Hazor, etc.)
Ras Shamra or Ugarit Tablets		Ras Shamra (Syria) by Claude Schaeffer	fourteenth to twelfth cent. BC 1929–1937	Conquest	A NW Semitic cognate similar to biblical Hebrew and pagan religious practices of child sacrifice. It was possible for Moses to write in 1440 to 1400 BC
Merenptah Stele		Thebes, Egypt by Flinders Petrie	1210–1207 BC 1896	Judges 10:6	Egyptian mention of the name "Israel"
Two inscribed Phoenician columns	N/A	Algeria, North Africa by Moses of Khoren and Procopius of Caesarea	In the city of Tigisis (Tangiers) in Numidia. AD 370–86 sixth cent.	Conquest of Canaan	Phoenicians who settled in North Africa were driven out of Canaan by Joshua
Merenptah's Battle Reliefs Karnak Temple		Karnak Temple Luxor, Egypt identified by Frank Yurco	*ca.* 1212–1202 BC 1976–1977	Joshua 15:9; 18:15	Merenptah attacking an enemy, possibly Israel
Ipuwer Papyrus		Purchased in Egypt by Swedish consul to Egypt, Giovanni Anastasi	Thirteenth cent. BC P Leiden I 344/ 1928	Exod 7–11	Plagues in Egypt and the Exodus

Discovery	Image	Place and Discoverer	Origin Date /Year Found	Biblical Passage	Significance
Destruction of Mankind Papyrus		Walls of chambers in the tombs of Tutankhamun, Seti I, Ramesses II and Ramesses III and identified by Edouard Naville	ca. 1300 BC 1876	Exod 3:14	Parallels with the Exodus story "I am that I am."
Tale of Two Brothers Papyrus		Tomb of Seti II, Papyrus D'Orbiney in the British Museum	1200 to 1194 BC 1857	Exodus	Parallels with the Exodus story

The Exodus and Conquest

63. Jordan Valley seen from the Jordanian side. Tall el-Hammam (Abel-shittim) is visible in the center, where Israel camped before entering the promised land.

The archaeological evidence for Israel's 400–430 year stay in Egypt (Exod 12:40–41; Gal 3:15, 17; Acts 13:16–21) and the Exodus is universally acknowledged to be lacking. As a result of the meager archaeological evidence, skeptics have challenged the historical reliability of the biblical narratives. Based on this argument from silence (see *The Fallacy of Negative Proof*) John Van Seters and Thomas Thompson go as far as to consider the biblical accounts as legends and myths.[1] Hoffmeier observed the impact of the minimalist attack and that "once on the slippery slope of historical minimalism, these biblical scholars moved from Genesis to Exodus and marched on Joshua and Judges, and soon even the courts of David and Solomon were under siege."[2]

Lack of Evidence for the Patriarchs

However, there are several reasons for the lack of evidence for the Exodus and Conquest:

1). Due to our limited knowledge of this period of history (second millennium BC).[3] There are few written sources from this period to verify the names of the patriarchs, as much of the information was transmitted through oral tradition.[4]

2). Due to looking in the wrong era. Perhaps archaeologists have misidentified the period in which the patriarchs lived (MBA) and they miss the evidence because they are looking in the wrong strata (EBA). Bab edh-Dhra is a good example of this mistake (see "Sodom and Gomorrah").[5] Preconceived ideas and data interpretation are a major reason why some do not see the patriarchs in the archaeological records.

64. Partial reconstruction of an Iron Age four-roomed house from Tall Umayri, Jordan. There are three rooms in the front, with one at the back. Wattle and daub (sticks and twigs) are used to form the roof. A mudbrick floor is placed on top of the roof to form another living area.

3). Due to the desert environment the Exodus passed through that destroyed much of the evidence. Deserts are ever changing due to erosion and looting, hindering the recovery of archaeological evidence. Satellite imagery is

---

[1] Seters, *Abraham in History and Tradition*; Thompson, *Historicity of the Patriarchal Narratives*.

[2] James K. Hoffmeier, "The Evangelical Contribution to Understanding the (Early) History of Ancient Israel in Recent Scholarship," *Bulletin for Biblical Research* 7 (1997): 78.

[3] John J. Bimson, "Archaeological Data and the Dating of the Patriarchs," in *Essays on the Patriarchal Narratives*, ed. Alan R. Millard and Donald J. Wiseman (Downers Grove, IL: InterVarsity, 1980), 60.

[4] Kenneth A. Kitchen, "The Patriarchs Revisited: A Reply to Dr. Ronald S. Hendel," *NEASB* 43 (1998): 49–58.

[5] Bimson, "Archaeological Data," 62; William G. Dever, "The Patriarchal Period," in *Israelite and Judaean History*, ed. John H. Hayes and J. Maxwell Miller (Philadelphia, PA: Westminster, 1977), 102.

assisting to identify some ancient evidence.[6]

4). Due to their nomadic lifestyle, which included the efficient use of their resources. The patriarchs nomadic travel patterns during the Exodus prevented the establishment of permanent structures that can be excavated.[7]

5). Due to looking in the wrong place. For example, some archaeologists believe that et-Tell has been incorrectly identified as Joshua's Ai (see "Ai").[8]

6). Due to the large area of most sites, only a portion of the site is excavated, leaving many areas yet unexplored (see "Limitations of Archaeology, #3").[9]

7). Due to resettlement or looting. Successive occupation of a site often results in the removal of previous structures to build their own settlement. For example, the LBA structures at Jericho, that are sparse, are thought to have been robbed out by later populations to construct their own settlement.[10] Looting is a serious problem in both ancient and modern times.

8). Need to look harder. Although it is often stated that Egypt would not have recorded such an embarrassing event as the Exodus,[11] the fact remains that such a major event, that caused so much destruction (Exod 7:20–21; 9:6; 10:7, 15; 12:30), would not likely have eluded all Egyptian records.[12] A diligent search of Egyptian records which mention the Exodus has until very recently never been conducted.[13] Most Hieroglyphic Egyptian documents have been discovered purely by accident and none of them have been systematically compiled for research purposes.[14]

ISRAEL IN EGYPT: POSSIBLE EVIDENCE

Following Jacob and his family's migration to Egypt in "the land of Rameses" (Gen 47:11, 27), the Israelite slaves built the city of Rameses (Exod 1:11). Rameses was also the point of departure during the Exodus (Exod 12:37). Rameses is an important city during the period of Israel's Egyptian exile.

Hyksos and Rameses

Although the location of Rameses was disputed for many years, in 1966 Manfred Beitak of the Austrian Archaeological Institute, Cairo, and Irene Forstner-Muller began excavations in the northern Nile Delta region of Egypt at a site called Avaris (Tell el-Dabʿa, modern village of Ezbet Helmi),[15] which was the capital of Egypt under the Canaanite Hyksos.[16] Avaris was later

---

[6] Sarah H. Parcak, *Satellite Remote Sensing for Archaeology* (New York: Routledge, 2009), 165–69.

[7] Price, *The Stones Cry Out*, 132.

[8] Bryant G. Wood, "The Search for Joshua's Ai: Excavations at Kh. El-Maqatir," *BS* 12, no. 1 (1999): 21–32; "The Search for Joshua's Ai," in *Critical Issues in Early Israelite History*, ed. Richard S. Hess, Gerald A. Klingbeil, and Paul J. Ray Jr., Bulletin for Biblical Research Supplement 3 (Winona Lake, IN: Eisenbrauns, 2008), 205–40; "Researching Ai," *BS* 22, no. 3 (2009): 75–78.

[9] Bimson, "Archaeological Data," 69; Yamauchi, *The Stones and the Scriptures*, 146–58.

[10] Mazar, *Archaeology of the Land of the Bible*, 1:331.

[11] Charles F. Aling, *Egypt and Bible History: From Earliest Times to 1000 BC*, Baker Studies in Biblical Archaeology (Grand Rapids: Baker, 1981), 103.

[12] Geisler and Holden, *Popular Handbook of Archaeology and the Bible*, 221–22.

[13] Brad C. Sparks, *Egyptian Text Parallels to the Exodus*, Forthcoming.

[14] Kenton L. Sparks, *Ancient Texts for the Study of the Hebrew Bible: A Guide to the Background Literature* (Grand Rapids: Hendrickson, 2005).

[15] Manfred Bietak, ed., *Tell El-Dabʿa* (Vienna: Austrian Academy of Sciences, 1975); Manfred Bietak, *Avaris and Piramesse: Archaeological Exploration in the Eastern Nile Delta*, Proceedings of the British Academy 65 (Oxford: Oxford University Press, 1981); Donald B. Redford and J. M. Weinstein, "Hyksos: Archaeology," ed. David Noel Freedman *et al.*, *ABD* (New York: Doubleday, 1996), 344–45; Manfred Bietak, *Avaris, the Capital of the Hyksos: Recent Excavations at Tell El-Dabʿa* (London: British Museum Press, 1996); John S. Holladay, "The Eastern Nile Delta During the Hyksos and Pre-Hyksos Periods: Toward a Systemic/Socioeconomic

65. A sandy mudbrick wall of a rectangular hut (Stratum H, Areas F/I) of the Asiatic settlement at Tell el-Dab'a (Avaris or Rameses) that dates to 1973–1944 BC. The mudbricks were made without the use of straw.

called Pi-Ramesses following Ramesses II's (13th cent. BC) moving of the capital from Thebes to the Nile Delta region. Tell el-Dab'a was the centre of an international trading network that included Tell el-Maskhuta (Pithom; Exod 1:11), operated by the Hyksos.[17]

Asiatic Residences

Bietak revealed evidence of Asiatic Semites living in Avaris as early as the late 12th Dynasty (Amenemhat I, 1973–1944 BC according to K. Kitchen's chronology). Their residential houses at Avaris were four-roomed (typical Syro-Palestinian style; see Fig. 64) and made from sandy mudbrick[18] constructed with no straw (see Fig. 65). Straw was usually used to provide strength and to aid the drying of mudbricks, enabling faster production and higher levels of quality. The biblical account (Exod 5) states that as a punishment to Israel, Pharaoh decreed that the Israelites in captivity would produce mudbricks without being given straw (Exod 5:7–9). While this does not prove that the Israelites were in Egypt, it does indicate that mudbricks were made without straw in Egypt.

Hyksos Palace and Empty Sarcophagus

There was also evidence of an early Hyksos palace (13th Dynasty) at Tell el-Dab'a and an associated monumental sarcophagus, with a broken colossal statue of Asiatic descent identified by the hairstyle, skin color and the Egyptian word "foreigner" (throwstick hieroglyph) written on its shoulder. While there were skeletons in adjacent tombs, this tomb was missing the body.[19] While in antiquity tombs were routinely plundered, they did not take the bodies. David Rohl and others have suggested that this may have been the house and tomb of Joseph, since Joseph commanded his bones to be taken to Canaan (Gen 50:25–26; Exod 13:19), although there is no

Understanding," in *The Hyksos - New Historical and Archaeological Perspectives*, ed. Eliezer D. Oren (Philadelphia, PA: University of Pennsylvania Museum, 1997), 183–252; Manfred Bietak and Irene Forstner-Müller, "The Topography of New Kingdom Avaris and Per Ramesses," in *Ramesside Studies in Honour of K. A. Kitchen*, ed. Mark Collier and Steven R. Snape (London: Rutherford, 2011), 23–50.

[16] The Hyksos were an ethnically mixed group of Western Asiatic Semite (originating in the Levant i.e. Canaan or Syria) people who overthrew the Egyptian Thirteenth Dynasty and formed the Fifteenth and Sixteenth Dynasties in Egypt (*ca.* 1663–1555 BC). They were known for having introduced new tools of warfare into Egypt, including the composite bow and the horse-drawn chariot. Redford and Weinstein, "Hyksos: Archaeology," 3:344–45; Donald B. Redford, "Hyksos: History," ed. David Noel Freedman *et al.*, *ABD* (New York: Doubleday, 1996), 3:341–45; Holladay, "The Eastern Nile Delta During the Hyksos and Pre-Hyksos Periods: Toward a Systemic/Socioeconomic Understanding," 183–252.

[17] John S. Holladay, "The Eastern Nile Delta during the Hyksos and Pre-Hyksos Periods: Towards a Systemic/Socio-Economic Understanding," in *The Hyksos: New Historical and Archaeological Perspectives*, ed. Eliezer D. Oren (Philadelphia, PA: University of Pennsylvania Museum Publication, 1997), 209; "Maskhuta, Tell El-," in *OEANE*, ed. Eric M. Meyers, vol. 3 (Oxford: Oxford University Press, 1997), 3:432–37.

[18] Manfred Bietak, *Avaris and Piramesse: Archaeological Exploration in the Eastern Nile Delta*, Proceedings of the British Academy 65 (Oxford: Oxford University Press, 1981), 237; "Egypt and Canaan during the Middle Bronze Age," *BASOR*, no. 281 (1991): 32, 39.

[19] Manfred Bietak, *Avaris, the Capital of the Hyksos: Recent Excavations at Tell El-Dab'a* (London: British Museum Press, 1996), 20–21.

direct evidence (i.e., Joseph's name) to indicate this.[20]

A Plague and Abrupt End

There is also evidence of a plague in the late Middle Kingdom (1715 BC) (see Exod 5–11) uncovered in an archaeological investigation by Bietak of a nearby cemetery.[21] As Bietak and Forstner-Müller suggest:

> The palace district was probably abandoned after the reign of Amenophis II [=Amenhotep II, 1453–1419 BC][22]...The reason for the abandonment of this district, and, presumably, the entire city adjoining the district on the south is an unsolved puzzle at this time. Its solution would be of the greatest importance to historians. The suggestion that the peaceful foreign policy of the late reign of Amenophis II and Thutmosis IV made this militarily important settlement unnecessary is not convincing. A plague, such as the one documented for Avaris in the late Middle Kingdom, and associated with Avaris in later tradition, appears to be the most likely solution of this problem, although it cannot be proven at this time.[23]

For some unexplained reason the work on the palace came to an abrupt end and was abandoned. Workers left their tools in place, which would be consistent with the sudden release of slaves and the Exodus.[24]

Although the archaeological evidence is fraught with dating issues when correlating the evidence with the text, the physical evidence does appear to correlate with the Exodus account. Any one of these discoveries would not prove that Israel was in Egypt or that the Exodus happened, but collectively they certainly corroborate the biblical accounts.

Possible Egyptian References to the Exodus

Brad C. Sparks claims that some 90 Egyptian papyri[25] demonstrate similar parallels to the Exodus, including the *Admonitions of Ipuwer* (*ca.* 1543–1064 BC),[26] *Tale of Two Brothers* (Tomb of Seti II, who ruled from 1200 to 1194, BC),[27] El Arish Stele (305–31 BC),[28] *Speos Artemidos* Inscription (Queen Hatshepsut and Seti I, 1490–1460 BC; see Fig. 66),[29] Tempest Stela (*ca.* 1550 BC),[30] and *Demotic Chronicle* (*ca.* 1550 BC.).[31] This implies that the event of the Exodus may still

---

[20] Rohl, *Pharaohs and Kings*, 360–67; Bryant G. Wood, "The Sons of Jacob New Evidence for the Presence of the Israelites in Egypt," *Bible and Spade* 10, no. 3 (1997): 56–58; Gary A. Byers, "Israel in Egypt," *Bible and Spade* 18, no. 1 (2005): 4.

[21] Bietak, *Avaris, the Capital of the Hyksos: Recent Excavations at Tell El-Dab'a*; Manfred Bietak and Irene Forstner-Müller, "Ausgrabung eines Palastbezirkes der Tuthmosidenzeit bei 'Ezbet Helmi/Tell el-Dab'a: Vorbericht für Herbst 2004 und Frühjahr 2005," *Ägypten und Levante / Egypt and the Levant* 15 (2005): 95.

[22] William H. Shea, "Amenhotep II as Pharaoh of the Exodus," *Bible and Spade* 16 (2003): 41–51.

[23] Bietak and Forstner-Müller, "Ausgrabung eines Palastbezirkes," 93, 95.

[24] Geisler and Holden, *Popular Handbook of Archaeology and the Bible*, 229.

[25] Brad C. Sparks, "Egyptian Text Parallels to the Exodus: The Egyptology Literature," in *Out of Egypt: Israel's Exodus Between Text and Memory, History and Imagination Conference*, ed. Thomas E. Levy (presented at the Qualcomm Institute, University of California, San Diego, 2013), https://www.youtube .com/watch?v=F-Aomm4O794.

[26] Papyrus Leiden 334. Miriam Lichtheim, *Ancient Egyptian Literature: The Old and Middle Kingdoms*, 2nd ed., vol. 1 (Berkeley, CA: University of California Press, 2006), 150; Roland Enmarch, *Dialogue of Ipuwer and the Lord of All* (Oxford: Griffith Institute, 2005); Ronald Enmarch, "The Reception of a Middle Egyptian Poem: The Dialogue of Ipuwer and the Lord of All in the Ramesside Period and beyond," in *Ramesside Studies in Honour of K. A. Kitchen*, ed. Mark Collier and Steven R. Snape (Bolton: Rutherford, 2011), 173–75; *Contra* William H. Stiebing, *Out of the Desert?: Archaeology and the Exodus/Conquest Narratives* (Buffalo, N.Y: Prometheus, 1989).

[27] P. D'Orbiney, P. Brit. Mus. 10183. Miriam Lichtheim, *Ancient Egyptian Literature: The New Kingdom*, 2nd ed., vol. 2 (Berkeley, CA: University of California Press, 2006), 203.

[28] Barbara J. Sivertsen, *The Parting of the Sea: How Volcanoes, Earthquakes, and Plagues Shaped the Story of Exodus* (Princeton, NJ: Princeton University Press, 2011), 125–29.

[29] Hans Goedicke, "Hatshepsut's Temple Inscription at Speo Artemidos," *BAR* 7, no. 5 (1981): 42; Hershel Shanks, "The Exodus and the Crossing of the Red Sea, According to Hans Goedicke," *BAR* 7, no. 5 (1981): 42–50; Alan H. Gardiner, "Davies's Copy of the Great Speos Artemidos Inscription," *JEA* 32 (1946): 43–56; Sivertsen, *The Parting of the Sea*, 8–9.

[30] Ellen N. Davis, "A Storm in Egypt during the Reign of Ahmose," in *Thera and the Aegean World III*, ed. David A. Hardy and A. C. Renfrew, vol. 3, Proceedings of the Third International Congress, Santorini, Greece, 3–9 September 1989 (London: The Thera

66. Mortuary Temple (Gr. *Speos Artemidos*) of Queen Hatshepsut and Seti I.

have been part of the Egyptian living memory in either the fifteenth or thirteenth cent. BC. Kitchen suggested that *Ipuwer* and the Exodus account were possibly referring to the same kind of natural phenomenon.[32]

The Destruction of Mankind

The Destruction of Mankind (also called *The Book of the Cow of Heaven*) Papyrus, inscribed on the tomb walls of Seti I, Ramesses II, and Ramesses III, describes Hathor's divine punishment of Egyptians with the foreigners, who survive the suffering, separated from Ra to live on the back of Nut, the heavenly cow.[33] The parallels with the Exodus story are striking and Erik Hornung, in his German translation, finds a "startling" name for Ra that has Exodus parallels. "Evidently [it] means "I am I" or "I am that I am" [Egyptian root *Yawi*]. Since in the given context it must mean: "... as whom I have proven to be" ..., the phrase indeed recalls the Old Testament: see Exodus 3:14 "I am that I am" .... What is here of interest is of course the early [ancient] theology [surrounding] God's name YHWH, but not its origin and actual etymology [Trans. Brad Sparks]."[34]

Griffiths confirms Hornung's translation of *The Destruction of Mankind* text, declaring:

> since the meaning *I am I* seems the only one possible. Here it is rendered *Ich bin, der ich bin*, with a startling invocation by Fecht (p. 125) of Exodus 3:14 (I AM THAT I AM, or I WILL BE WHAT I WILL BE). The Hebrew is concerned with the meaning of the name Yahweh; the Egyptian context, as Fecht shows, relates to the sun-god's claim: he is what he has shown himself to be – the successful queller of men's mutiny, and so able to say in the following verse, *I will not allow them to make (a revolt).*[35]

Sparks reports that in addition to the "I am that I am" texts, he also discovered further parallels from the tomb painting of Seti I, 1300 BC. "Checking the tomb of Seti I for example, I discovered 'similar content' documents with color pictures of the Exodus - the parting of the Red Sea and the mass drowning of the Egyptian army."[36]

Foundation, 1990), 3:232–35; Donald B. Redford, "Textual Sources for the Hyksos Period," in *The Hyksos: New Historical and Archaeological Perspectives*, ed. Eliezer D. Oren (Philadelphia, PA: University of Pennsylvania Museum, 1997), 16; Hoffmeier, *Israel in Egypt*, 150–51; Kenneth A. Kitchen, "Ancient Egyptian Chronology for Aegeanists," *Mediterranean Archaeology and Archaeometry* 2, no. 2 (2002): 11; Nadine Moeller and Robert K. Ritner, "The Ahmose 'Tempest Stela', Thera and Comparative Chronology," *Journal of Near Eastern Studies* 73, no. 1 (April 1, 2014): 2.

[31] Papyrus CPJ 520. Jan Assmann, *The Mind of Egypt: History and Meaning in the Time of the Pharaohs* (Cambridge, MA: Harvard University Press, 2003), 406. The dates of these documents would indicate an early date (1445 BC) for the Exodus, although some texts are even earlier than this.

[32] Kitchen, *Reliability of the OT*, 250–52.

[33] Erik Hornung, *Der ägyptische Mythos von der Himmelskuh: Eine Atiologie des Unvollkommenen*, Orbis biblicus et orientalis 46 (Göttingen: Vandenhoeck & Ruprecht, 1982); E. A. Wallis Budge, *Legends of the Gods The Egyptian Texts, Edited with Translations* (London: Kegan Paul, Trench and Trubner & Co. Ltd., 1912).

[34] Seti I, KV 17, chamber Je, line 49. Hornung, *Der ägyptische Mythos von der Himmelskuh*, 63 n.121, 125 n.aa.

[35] J. Gwyn Griffiths, "Review of Der Ägyptische Mythos von Der Himmelskuh. Eine Ätiologie Des Unvollkommenen by Erik Hornung," *The Journal of Egyptian Archaeology* 74 (January 1, 1988): 276.

[36] Sparks, "The Egyptology Literature"; Erik Hornung, *The Tomb of Pharaoh Seti I* (Zürich: Artemis & Winkler, 1991).

Berlin Statue Pedestal Relief

For many years the Merenptah (also Merneptah) Stele (*ca.* 1208 BC) has been accepted as the monument with the oldest extra-biblical reference to "Israel"[37] and the only mention of Israel in Egypt.[38] It indicates that Israel, as a people-group, were in Egypt as early as the 13th cent. BC (Merenptah reigned from 1213 to 1203 BC).[39]

In 2001, a new hieroglyphic inscription, on a broken granite statue pedestal (*ca.* 18 inches high by 15.5 inches wide), was spotted in a storeroom of the Egyptian Museum in Berlin by University of Munich Egyptologist Manfred Görg, on which he identified another possible reading of Israel (see Fig. 55).[40] While the relief had been acquired from an antiquities dealer in 1913 by Ludwig Borchardt and listed in previous topographical studies, the readings of the three fragmentary name rings had not received adequate consideration. Following a careful examination of the pedestal by Görg and two colleagues, Peter van der Veen and Christoffer Theis, they suggested that the three name rings should be translated as Ashkelon, Canaan, and Israel.[41]

67. Drawing of the Berlin relief (ca. 1400 BC) which Borg, van der Veen and Theis translate as the name *Israel* and the bound Asiatic prisoner of West Semitic origin carried away captive. The shaded area, to the right, is the missing section that has been easily restored from the complete section.

Egyptian Museum, Berlin

Egyptian pharaohs often boasted of their conquests and etched them in their tombs and temples. The Merenptah stele records the exaggerated boast: "Israel is laid waste (and) his seed is not."[42] They would list the names of the people, cities, countries or territories they had conquered in a name ring (oval ring) in hieroglyphics, similar to a cartouche (name of the pharaoh), with the picture of the conquered people above it.[43]

[37] Kitchen has strongly argued that Israel in the Merenptah Stele was a people group rather than a formal nation. Kenneth A. Kitchen, "The Victories of Merenptah, and the Nature of Their Record," *JSOT* 28, no. 3 (March 1, 2004): 272.

[38] Frank J. Yurco, "Merenptah's Canaanite Campaign," *Journal of the American Research Center in Egypt* 23 (January 1, 1986): 189–215; John J. Bimson, "Merenptah's Israel and Recent Theories of Israelite Origins," *Journal for the Study of the Old Testament*, no. 49 (1991): 3–29; Michael G. Hasel, "Israel in the Merneptah Stela," *BASOR*, no. 296 (November 1, 1994): 45–61; Kenneth A. Kitchen, *Ramesside Inscriptions—Translated and Annotated, Translations, Vol. IV: Merenptah and the Late Nineteenth Dynasty*, vol. 4 (Oxford: Wiley-Blackwell, 2003), 4:10–15.

[39] Kitchen, *Reliability of the OT*, 241ff; Hoffmeier, *Israel in Egypt*, 135ff; Richard S. Hess, "Early Israel in Canaan: A Survey of Recent Evidence and Interpretations," *PEQ* 125, no. 2 (1993): 125–42; "The Jericho and Ai of the Book of Joshua," in *Critical Issues in Early Israelite History*, ed. Richard S. Hess, Gerald A. Klingbeil, and Paul J. Ray Jr., Bulletin for Biblical Research Supplement 3 (Winona Lake, Ind: Eisenbrauns, 2008), 33–46.

[40] Published in German. Manfred Görg, "Israel in Hieroglyphen," *Biblische Notizen* 106 (2001): 21–27; "Israel in Hieroglyphen," in *Mythos und Mythologie: Studien zur Religionsgeschichte und Theologie*, Agypten Und Altes Testament 70 (Wiesbaden: Harrassowitz, 2011), 251–58.

[41] Manfred Görg, Peter van der Veen, and Christoffer Theis, "Israel in Canaan (Long) Before Pharaoh Merenptah? A Fresh Look at Berlin Statue Pedestal Relief 21687," *Journal of Ancient Egyptian Interconnections* 2, no. 4 (2010): 15–25.

[42] Yurco, "Merenptah's Canaanite Campaign," 189.

[43] For a photograph of the Berlin Statue Pedestal Relief, see Price and House, *Zondervan Handbook of Biblical Archaeology*, 91.

While a portion of the third name ring on the right side of the relief was chipped off, it is easily reconstructed with confidence and the picture of the conquered people over each name ring is of a West Semite, easily identified by their long hair, pointed beards and headbands.[44]

Spelling

The center of the controversy revolves around the spelling of the name "Israel".[45] The Merenptah Stele uses an "s" in the name, while the Berlin Relief uses an "sh".[46] James Hoffmeier, an Egyptologist from Trinity Evangelical Divinity School, and Israeli paleographer Shmuel Ahituv, deny that it reads *Israel*.[47] But as Görg, Veen, and Theis suggest:

> the reading of "Israel" on the Berlin pedestal relief is at least possible for two main reasons. First, since there exists linguistic evidence that the original name "Israel" could have been written with š (for instance, based on the verb *yšr*), the Egyptian use of *š* (instead of *ś* as on Merenptah's Israel Stele) does not preclude the possibility that the name was originally written with *ś* in West Semitic. Second, and more significantly, the geographical proximity of *ʾI-šr-il/Y-šr-il* to Ashkelon and Canaan makes the identification with Israel likely. No known location (especially so near to those two familiar geographical entities) has a name so reminiscent of the biblical name "Israel."[48]

It is also not uncommon for the scribes to spell the same word in different ways, as there was no consistent spelling for toponyms.[49] The Merenptah Stele also strengthens this argument as the two nations beside the reference to Israel are Ashkelon and Canaan. As Görg, Veen and Theis point out: "their geographical nearness suggests the identification with the same topographical entity within central Palestine."[50]

Dating

The date of the relief is another difficult question, as there is no indication on the slab of its date. Scholars resort to the form of the hieroglyphs (paleography) and the spelling of the names (orthography) to determine the age, since these change over time. However, there is still not unanimity on the date, with ranges being suggested from as early as Amenhotep II (*ca.* 1453–1419 or 1427–1401 BC),[51] or Amenhotep III (1386 to 1349 BC),[52] to as late as Ramesses II (1279 to 1213 BC).[53]

Implications

If Görg, Veen, and Theis' reading of the slab and theory are correct, then: "this would indeed suggest that Proto-Israelites had migrated to Canaan sometime nearer the middle of the second

---

[44] Hershel Shanks, "When Did Israel Begin? New Hieroglyphic Inscription May Date Israel's Ethogenesis 200 Years Earlier than You Thought," in *Ancient Israel in Egypt and the Exodus*, ed. Dorothy Resig (Washington, DC: Biblical Archaeology Society, 2012), 34.

[45] For the debate over the origin of the name Israel see: Othniel Margalith, "On the Origin and Antiquity of the Name 'Israel,'" *ZAW* 102, no. 2 (1990): 225–37; Leonid Kogan *et al.*, eds., "The Etymology of Israel (with an Appendix on Non-Hebrew Semitic Names among Hebrews in the Old Testament)," in *Babel Und Bibel 3: Annual of Ancient Near Eastern, Old Testament, and Semitic Studies*, Papers of the Institute of Oriental and Classical Studies 14 (Winona Lake, IN: Eisenbrauns, 2006), 237–55.

[46] Görg, Veen, and Theis, "Israel in Canaan (Long) Before Pharaoh Merenptah?," 17–20.

[47] Hoffmeier, "What Is the Biblical Date for the Exodus?," 241; Shanks, "When Did Israel Begin?," 2012, 35.

[48] Görg, Veen, and Theis, "Israel in Canaan (Long) Before Pharaoh Merenptah?," 20.

[49] Shanks, "When Did Israel Begin?," 2012, 35.

[50] Görg, Veen, and Theis, "Israel in Canaan (Long) Before Pharaoh Merenptah?," 19.

[51] Manfred Görg, *Untersuchungen zur hieroglyphischen Wiedergabe palästinischer Ortsnamen*, Bonner Orientalische Studien NS 29 (Bonn: Selbstverlag des Orientalischen Seminars der Universität, 1974), 47ff.

[52] Following a personal conversation with Shanks, Israeli Egyptologist, Raphael Giveon and Shmuel Ahituv, it is believed that they hold this view. Görg, Veen, and Theis, "Israel in Canaan (Long) Before Pharaoh Merenptah?," 20; Hershel Shanks, "When Did Israel Begin? New Hieroglyphic Inscription May Date Israel's Ethogenesis 200 Years Earlier than You Thought," *BAR* 38, no. 1 (2012): 36; Raphael Giveon, "Three Fragments from Egyptian Geographical Lists," *Eretz Israel* 15 (1981): 137.

[53] Görg, Veen, and Theis, "Israel in Canaan (Long) Before Pharaoh Merenptah?," 20. Görg concluded that the names were copied from an earlier inscription around the time of Amenhotep II.

68. Top of *Jebel Musa* (Mount Sinai) at sunrise.

millennium BCE."[54] This is good news for those who hold to an early date for the Exodus and conquest, as Wood points out: "it would place Israel in Canaan at about the time of the biblical date for the Conquest."[55] For the debate over the ethnogenesis of Israel between two evangelicals, see the exchange between Bryant Wood and James Hoffmeier.[56]

Mount Sinai

The Israelites arrived at Mount Sinai (also called Mount Horeb) three months after leaving Egypt (Exod 19:1). It was here that God gave Moses the Ten Commandments and established his covenant with the people of Israel (Exod 19:16–20). Unfortunately the exact location of Mount Sinai is uncertain.[57] Locations have ranged from the area of Kadesh Barnea, northern Sinai Peninsula[58] (*Gebel Khashm et-Tarif*,[59] *Jebel Magharah*,[60] *Jebel Sin Bisher*[61]), NW Arabia (Midian), Saudi

---

[54] Ibid., 20–21.

[55] Bryant G. Wood, "Extra-Biblical Evidence for the Conquest," *Bible and Spade* 18, no. 4 (2005): 98. Görg, Veen, and Theis do not attempt to connect their discovery with Israel's conquest of Canaan.

[56] Hoffmeier, "The Evangelical Contribution to Understanding the (Early) History of Ancient Israel in Recent Scholarship"; "What Is the Biblical Date for the Exodus?," 225–47; Bryant G. Wood, "The Biblical Date for the Exodus Is 1446 BC: A Response to James Hoffmeier," *JETS* 50, no. 2 (2007): 249–58; "The Rise and Fall of the 13th-Century Exodus-Conquest Theory," *JETS* 48, no. 3 (2005): 475–89; "Pharaoh Merenptah Meets Israel," *Bible and Spade* 18, no. 3 (2005): 65–82; "Recent Research on the Date and Setting of the Exodus," *Bible and Spade* 21, no. 4 (2008): 97–108; "New Evidence Supporting the Early (Biblical) Date of the Exodus and Conquest," *Associates For Biblical Research*, November 11, 2011, 1–5.

[57] Ze'ev Meshel, *Sinai: Excavations and Studies*, Bar International (Oxford: Archaeopress, 2000); James K. Hoffmeier, "Sinai," ed. Avraham Negev and Shimon Gibson, *Archaeological Encyclopedia of the Holy Land* (New York: Continuum International, 2001), 4:1384–1403; *Ancient Israel in Sinai: The Evidence for the Authenticity of the Wilderness Tradition*, Illustrated edition (Oxford: Oxford University Press, USA, 2005); H. G. Andersen, "Sinai, Mount," in *ZPEB*, 5:526–29.

[58] Eliezer D. Oren, "The 'Ways of Horus' in North Sinai," in *Egypt, Israel, Sinai: Archaeological and Historical Relationships in the Biblical Period*, ed. Anson F. Rainey (Tel Aviv University, 1987), 69–119.

[59] Bryant G. Wood, "In Search of Mt. Sinai," *Associates for Biblical Research Electronic Newsletter* 7, no. 6 (2007): 1–3; Bryant G. Wood, "What Do Mt. Horeb, the Mountain of God, Mt. Paran and Mt. Seir Have to Do with Mt. Sinai?," *Associates for Biblical*

Arabia (*Jevel al-Lawz*),[62] to the traditional location in the southern Sinai peninsula, of *Jebel Musa* (mountain of Moses; see Fig. 42, 68).

The guiding clue for the location of Mount Sinai according to the book of Exodus is within a three day's journey into the wilderness from Goshen (3:18; 5:3; 8:27), arguing for a location somewhere in the northern region of the Sinai Peninsula[63] rather than in the southern traditional location.

According to Deuteronomy "it is eleven days' journey from Horeb [Mt Sinai] by the way of Mount Seir to Kadesh-barnea" (1:2). Davies calculated, based on actual journeys, that a person traveling on camelback could average *ca.* 32.17 km (20 miles) per day or less, while a donkey or camel caravan could average about 26–37 km (16–23 miles) per day.[64] In the fifteenth cent. BC the Egyptian Pharaoh Thutmosis III (1480–1426 BC) lead his army from Egypt to Gaza averaging 25 km (15 miles) per day, though it decreased to 11 km (7 miles) per day when he reached the rugged coastline of Canaan.[65] Based on these estimates, it would place Mount Sinai approximately 100 km (60 miles) from Kadesh Barnea in the northern Sinai.

Bryant Wood argued that the traditional location of Mount Sinai (Horeb or *Jebel Musa*), held since the fourth cent., is too far south of Kadesh Barnea to be the Mount of Moses based on Davies' calculations. Wood preferred *Gebel Khashm et-Tarif*, located *ca.* 35 km (22 miles) WNW of the northern end of the Gulf of Aqaba/Elat, rather than *Jevel al-Lawz* or *Jebel Musa*, which both are 241 km (150 miles) from Kadesh Barnea and too far to be reached in 11 days (see Map 4).[66] Following Wood's inspection of the area around *Gebel Khashm et-Tarif*, the physical and geographic features better fit the biblical text.

ENCAMPMENT PRIOR TO ENTERING THE PROMISED LAND

Abel-Shittim (Heb. meaning "Accacias of Mourning"),[67] which is the location of Israel's encampment prior to entering the Promised Land (Num 25:1, Deut 34:9; Josh 2:1; 3:1), is identified by most scholars as the Late Bronze Age area around Tall el-Ḥammâm (see Fig. 53 and

---

Research Electronic Newsletter 7, no. 5 (June 2007): 1–3; Uzi Avner, "Ancient Cult Sites in the Negev and Sinai Deserts," *Tel Aviv* 11 (1984): 115–31.

[60] Bromiley, *The International Standard Bible Encyclopedia*, 2:240.

[61] Menashe Har-El, *The Sinai Journeys: The Route of the Exodus* (San Diego: Ridgefield, 1981).

[62] Robert Cornuke and David Halbrook, *In Search of the Mountain of God: The Discovery of the Real Mt. Sinai* (Nashville, TN: Broadman & Holman, 2000); Gordon Franz, "Is Mount Sinai in Saudi Arabia?," *Bible and Spade* 13, no. 4 (2000): 101–12; "Mt. Sinai Is Not at Jebel El-Lawz in Saudi Arabia," in *ETS/NEAS Meetings* (presented at the ETS/NEAS, Broadmoor Hotel, Colorado Springs, Colo., 2001), 1–10.

[63] David Faiman, "From Horeb to Kadesh in Eleven Days," *The Jewish Bible Quarterly* 22 (1994): 91–102.

[64] Graham I. Davies, *The Way of the Wilderness a Geographical Study of the Wilderness Itineraries in the Old Testament*, The Society for Old Testament Study Monographs 5 (Cambridge: Cambridge University Press, 1979), 95–96.

[65] Pritchard, *ANE Texts*, 235 n. 16, 18.

[66] Bryant G. Wood, "Thoughts on Jebel Al-Lawz as the Location of Mount Sinai," *Associates for Biblical Research Electronic Newsletter* 6, no. 4 (May 17, 2006): 2.

[67] Selah Merrill, "Modern Researches in Palestine," *Journal of the American Geographical Society of New York* 9 (1877): 117; "Modern Researches in Palestine," *PEFSt.* 11, no. 1 (1879): 144; Thomson, *Land and the Book: Lebanon, Damascus, and Beyond Jordan*, 3:3:669; Nelson Glueck, *Explorations in Eastern Palestine IV. Part 1*, AASOR 25-28 (New Haven, CT: ASOR, 1945), 378; "Some Ancient Towns in the Plains of Moab," *BASOR* 91 (1943): 15; J. Maxwell Miller and Gene M. Tucker, *The Book of Joshua*, The Cambridge Bible Commentary of the English Bible (Cambridge, MA: Cambridge University Press, 1974), 199; R. K. Harrison, "Shittim," ed. Edward M. Blaiklock, *NIDBA* (Grand Rapids: Zondervan, 1983), 413; Khouri, *Antiquities of the Jordan Rift Valley*, 76; Burton MacDonald, *East of the Jordan: Territories and Sites of the Hebrew Scriptures*, ed. Victor H. Matthews, ASOR Books 6 (Boston, MA: American Schools of Oriental Research, 2000), 90; Walter C. Kaiser, Jr. and Duane Garrett, eds., *NIV Archaeological Study Bible: An Illustrated Walk Through Biblical History and Culture* (Grand Rapids: Zondervan, 2006), 233.

56). However, only recently has the site been excavated.[68] It is significant that no Late Bronze occupation was discovered at TeH.[69] Collins reports that after eight seasons of excavation at TeH and thousands of sherds "Late Bronze Age sherds are extremely rare in the area, and there is no discernable LBA architecture thus far (the only LBA sherds from around the site were found in a tomb)."[70]

One might conclude from the "Late Bronze Gap,"[71] as it is called, that Moses and the Israelites were never in the region. However, in the Late Bronze Age, Moses described the area around Abel-Shittim, below Mount Pisgah (beside Mount Nebo), as a desert, wasteland, and as uninhabited (Num 21:20; 22:1), and nomadic tent dwellers would not have built permanent structures that would have survived. What have survived are several LBA shaft tombs identified from the pottery remains.[72] Also among the items uncovered in the area is a "highly detailed steatite seal [scarab] of Hyksos [Egyptian Amenhotep III] design from the second half of the Middle Bronze Age."[73] One wonders if it was brought during the Exodus from Egypt among the belongings of the Israelites.

The absence of evidence in this case is significant. While Moses described the area around Abel-Shittim as uninhabited in the LBA (Num 21:20; 22:1), the Israelite presence at Abel-shittim is corroborated by the identification of LBA tombs containing Egyptian possessions.[74]

JOSHUA AND THE CONQUEST

The conquest of Canaan is highly debated by scholars and often misunderstood by Bible students. When assessing archaeological evidence, Albright looked for the following markers to identify *Israelites:* "the room was the 'Four-roomed house',[75] the jar was the collared-rim pithos, and the water storage method was the plaster-lined cistern."[76] However, since these markers have been found in earlier periods, caution needs to be exercised, and today some scholars no longer consider them as reliable identification markers for recognizing Israelite settlements. The absence of pig bones (pigs were considered unclean), although no longer definitive, has also been used in the past to identify Israelite settlements. Dever states:

> One animal species is conspicuously absent in our Iron Age villages: the pig. Although not nearly as common as sheep and goats at Bronze Age sites, pigs are well attested then. They are also common at Iron I coastal sites that are known to be Philistine. But recent statistical analysis of animal bones retrieved from our Iron I Israelites sites show that pig bones typically constitute only a fraction of 1% or are entirely absent. A number of scholars who are otherwise skeptical about determining ethnic identity

[68] Kay Prag, "The Excavations at Tell Al-Hammam," *Syria* 70, no. 1–2 (1990): 271–73; "Preliminary Report on the Excavations at Tell Iktanu and Tall el-Hammam, Jordan 1990," *Levant* 23 (1991): 55–66; "Tell Iktanu and Tell Al-Hammam. Excavations in Jordan," *Manchester Archaeological Bulletin* 7 (1992): 15–19; Collins *et al.*, "Tall el-Hammam, Season Eight, 2013."

[69] Collins, Hamdan, and Byers, "Tall el-Hammam: Preliminary Report, Season Four, 2009," 388; Collins and Scott, *Discovering the City of Sodom*, 95, 98, 144, 157–58.

[70] Collins *et al.*, "Tall el-Hammam, Season Eight, 2013," 4.

[71] James W. Flanagan, David W. McCreery, and Khair N. Yassine, "Tell Nimrin: Preliminary Report on the 1993 Season," *ADAJ* 38 (1994): 207, 219; James W. Flanagan, David W. McCreery, and Khair N. Yassine, "Tall Nimrin: Preliminary Report on the 1995 Excavation and Geological Survey," *ADAJ* 40 (1996): 286.

[72] Collins *et al.*, "Tall el-Hammam, Season Eight, 2013," 4.

[73] Collins and Scott, *Discovering the City of Sodom*, 33, 175.

[74] Collins, "Tall el-Hammam Is Sodom," 8.

[75] Yigael Shiloh, "The Four-Room House: Its Situation and Function in the Israelite City," *IEJ* 20, no. 3/4 (1970): 180–90; Avraham Faust, "The Rural Community in Ancient Israel during Iron Age II," *BASOR* 317 (2000): 17–39; Larry G. Herr and D. R. Clark, "Excavating the Tribe of Reuben: A Four Room House Provides a Clue to Where the Oldest Israelite Tribe Settled," *BAR* 27, no. 2 (2001): 36–47, 64–66; Avraham Faust and Shlomo Bunimovitz, "The Four Room House: Embodying Iron Age Israelite Society," *NEA* 66, no. 1/2 (2003): 29–30.

[76] Hess, "Early Israel in Canaan," 129.

> from material culture remains in this case acknowledge the obvious: that here we seem to have at least one ethnic trait of later, biblical Israel that can safely be projected back to its earliest days.[77]

However, the moat distinctive markers are regional, and not ethnic or cultural.

Conquest Theories

Scholars have suggested several theories, all of which appear to have some biblical support,[78] to reconcile the archaeological footprint and the biblical account of the conquest of Canaan.[79]

The Conquest Theory

The "Conquest Theory" believes that there were no warlike conquest as there is little evidence of fortified village occupations in Palestine in the period of the conquest (12th cent. BC). An exception is the 13th cent. BC destruction layer at Hazor (see below).[80]

The Peaceful Infiltration Theory

The "Peaceful Infiltration Theory" believes that a mixed group of semi-nomadic clans immigrated from Egypt into the hill country and gradually took over the Canaanite culture and replaced (biblical term "destroyed") the local inhabitants.[81]

The Peasant Revolt Theory

The "Peasant" or "Peaceful Revolt Theory" argues that Israel comprised the lower class in Canaanite society. This lower class revolted against their urban-based oppressors, fighting back against the hardships they were enduring, such as drought, excessive taxation to pay for defence and infrastructure, and tribute payments to Egypt.[82]

The Peaceful Withdrawal Theory

The "Peaceful Withdrawal" or "Transition Theory" argues that Israel emerged as a nation gradually on the basis of the social and technological changes evident in the archaeological

---

[77] William G. Dever, *Who Were the Early Israelites and Where Did They Come From?* (Grand Rapids: Eerdmans, 2003), 108; *Contra* Brian Hess, "Pig Lovers and Pig Haters: Patterns of Palestinian Pork Production," *Journal of Ethnobiology* 10 (1982): 195–225; Brian Hesse and Paula Wapnish, "Can Pig Remains Be Used for Ethnic Diagnosis in the Ancient Near East?," in *The Archaeology of Israel: Constructing the Past, Interpreting the Present*, ed. Neil Asher Silberman and David B. Small, JSOTSup 237 (Sheffield: T&T Clark, 1997), 238–70; Israel Finkelstein *et al.*, "Pig Husbandry in Iron Age Israel and Judah New Insights Regarding the Origin of the 'Taboo,'" *ZDPV* 129 (2013): 1–20.

[78] For a survey of the various theories see: Manfred Weippert, *Settlement of the Israelite Tribes in Palestine*, trans. J. D. Martin, Study in Bible Theology 21 (London: SCM, 1971), 5–62; George W. Ramsey, *The Quest for the Historical Israel* (Atlanta, Ga.: Knox, 1981), 65–98; Stiebing, Jr., *Out of the Desert?*, 149–65.

[79] Hess, "Early Israel in Canaan," 127–29; Koenraad van Bekkum, "From Conquest to Coexistence: Ideology and Antiquarian Intent in the Historiography of Israel's Settlement in Canaan" (Ph. D. diss., Theologische Universiteit Van De Gereformeerde Kerken, 2010), 7–8.

[80] Yigael Yadin, "Biblical Archaeology Today: The Archaeological Aspect," in *Biblical Archaeology Today: Proceedings of the International Congress on Biblical Archaeology Jerusalem, April 1984*, ed. J. Amitai (Jerusalem: Biblical Archaeology Society, 1985), 21–27.

[81] Gnues identifies four subviews within the "Peaceful Infiltration Theory": "peaceful withdrawal, internal nomadism, peaceful transition or transformation, and peaceful amalgamation or synthesis." Gnues, *No Other Gods*, 61. A. Alt, "The Settlement of the Israelites in Palestine," in *Essays on Old Testament History and Religion*, ed. A. Alt (Sheffield: University of Sheffield, 1989), 133–69; Volkmar Fritz, "Conquest or Settlement? The Early Iron Age in Palestine," *BA* 50 (1987): 84–100; Anson F. Rainey, "Rainey's Challenge," *BAR* 17, no. 6 (1991): 56–60, 93; Robert Karl Gnuse, *No Other Gods: Emergent Monotheism in Israel*, JSOTSup 241 (A&C Black, 1997), 25–61; "BTB Review of Current Scholarship: Israelite Settlement of Canaan: A Peaceful Internal Process - Part 1," *BTB* 21, no. 2 (1991): 56–66; "BTB Review of Current Scholarship: Israelite Settlement of Canaan: A Peaceful Internal Process - Part 2," *BTB* 21, no. 3 (1991): 109–17.

[82] N. K. Gottwald, *The Tribes of Yahweh: A Sociology of the Religion of Liberated Israel 1250-1050 B. C. E.* (New York: Knoll, 1979), 210–19, 389–587. *Contra* Alan J. Hauser, "Israel's Conquest of Palestine: A Peasants' Rebellion," *JSOT*, no. 7 (1978): 2–19.

records during the transition between the LBA and the IA.[83]

The Climate Change Theory

The "Imagination" or "Climate Change Theory" argues that the Bronze Age drought (1250 to 1200 BC) caused a decline in population in the ANE resulting in a "cultural collapse." Israel emerged from the surviving hill-country groups that came together to form the Israelite nation.[84]

Joshua indicates that Israel did not settle the entire Promised Land (Josh 13:1–7, 29–31; 17:5–6; 11–18). Monson points out:

> one of the complicating factors in understanding the so-called Israelite conquest is the commonly held belief that the Israelites entered rapidly into Cisjordan (the land west of the Jordan River), destroyed the majority of Canaanite cities, possessed the cities, built or rebuilt them, and settled down in place of the former population. This view, however, is derived from a misunderstanding of the vocabulary associated with city assaults in Joshua 6–11 [take, seize, smite, survive, wipe out, destroy, burn, possess, and settle] . . . Whereas cities in Transjordan are "Possessed" and "settled," all but three of the cities in Cisjordan are "taken," "seized," "wiped out," or such, but they were not "burned with fire".[85]

Israel did not destroy all the cities they conquered. Only three cities are singled out to be placed under the ban (Heb. *ḥāram, ḥērem*)[86] and burned: Jericho (Josh 2–6), Ai (Josh 8), and Hazor (Josh 11:13).

As Hoffmeier reminds us:

> When Joshua is viewed as a piece of Near Eastern military writing, and its literary character is properly understood, the idea of a group of tribes coming to Canaan, using some military force, partially taking a number of cities and areas over a period of some years, destroying (burning) just three cities, and coexisting alongside the Canaanites and other ethnic groups for a period of time before the beginnings of monarchy, does not require a blind faith.[87]

Jericho (Joshua 2–3)

DeVries summarizes the belief of the majority of scholars today,[88] regarding the evidence for the destruction of Jericho (Tell es-Sulṭân; see Map 1), when he states: "Jericho could be called "the big disappointment of biblical archaeology" because excavations at the site have failed to

[83] John Strange, "The Transition from the Bronze Age to the Iron Age in the Eastern Mediterranean and the Emergence of the Israelite State," *Scandinavian Journal of the Old Testament* 1, no. 1 (1987): 1–19; Israel Finkelstein, "The Emergence of Israel: A Phase in the Cyclic History of Canaan in the Third and Second Millennia BCE," in *From Nomadism to Monarchy: Archaeological and Historical Aspects of Early Israel*, ed. Israel Finkelstein and Nadav Na'aman (Jerusalem: Israel Exploration Society, 1994), 150–78; Joseph A. Callaway, "A New Perspective on the Hill Country Settlement of Canaan in Iron Age I," in *Palestine in the Bronze and Iron Ages: Papers in Honour of Olga Tufnell*, ed. Jonathan N. Tubb (London: Institute of Archaeology, 2008), 31–49.

[84] William H. Stiebing, Jr., "The End of the Mycenean Age," *BA* 43, no. 1 (1980): 7–21; *Out of the Desert?*, 189–97; "Climate and Collapse: Did the Weather Make Israel's Emergence Possible?," *Bible Review* 10, no. 4 (1994): 18–27, 54; William G. Dever, "'Will the Real Israel Please Stand up?' Part I: Archaeology and the Religions of Ancient Israel," *BASOR*, no. 297 (1995): 65.

[85] John M. Monson, "Enter Joshua: The 'Mother of Current Debates' in Biblical Archaeology," in *Do Historical Matters Matter to Faith?: A Critical Appraisal of Modern and Postmodern Approaches to Scripture*, ed. James K. Hoffmeier and Graham A. Magary (Wheaton, IL: Crossway Books, 2012), 434–35.

[86] BDB defines *ḥērem* as "ban, devote, exterminate [as]. . . most often of devoting to destruction cities of Canaanites and other neighbours of Isr., exterminating inhabitants, and destroying or appropriating their possessions." Charles A. Briggs, Samuel R. Driver, and Francis Brown, *Hebrew-Aramaic and English Lexicon of the Old Testament. Complete and Unabridged* (Peabody, MA: Hendrickson, 1996), 355–56.

[87] Hoffmeier, *Israel in Egypt*, 43–44.

[88] Kathleen M. Kenyon and Thomas A. Holland, *Excavations at Jericho, Vol. II (only): The Tombs excavated in 1955-8.* (British School of Archaeology in Jerusalem, 1965); H. J. Franken, "Tell Es-Sultan and Old Testament Jericho," *Oudtestamentische Studiën* 14 (1965): 190, 200; James F. Strange, "The Book of Joshua: A Hasmonean Manifesto?," in *History and Traditions of Early Israel: Studies Presented to Eduard Nielsen*, ed. André LeMaire and Benedikt Otzen, VTSup 50 (Leiden: Brill Academic, 1993), 141; Holland, "Jericho," 3:724–26; Michael D. Coogan *et al.*, eds., *The New Oxford Annotated Bible with Apocrypha: New Revised Standard Version*, 4th ed. (Oxford: Oxford University Press, 2010), 327.

produce the kind of evidence described in the biblical account of the conquest of Jericho in Joshua 6."[89]

As a result of five excavation campaigns at Jericho over the various years,[90] there is agreement on several issues. 1). The city was surrounded by a double stone wall topped with mudbrick distinguishing an upper and lower city.[91] 2). Significant quantities of grain was recovered from several of the storage rooms.[92] 3). Jericho was destroyed by a violent fire indicated by a thick (*ca.* 1 m) layer of char, and the stone revetment wall collapsed (see Fig. 70).[93]

The controversy revolves around the issue of when the destruction occurred. John Garstang (worked between 1930 and 1936) stated that it was in the LB period (1400 BC),[94] while Kathleen Kenyon (worked between1952 and 1958) argued that Garstang made an error, and dated it to the MB period (1550 BC).[95] The recent excavation by the University of Rome confirms Kenyon's assessment of a MB destruction[96] with a small LB occupation on the top of the tall (see Fig. 70).[97]

In 1990, Bryant Wood re-evaluated the data from the earlier excavations of Kenyon, and challenged her date of 1550 BC for the destruction of the city, based on his reading of her low grade imitations of Cypriot *"bichrome"* pottery (see Fig. 69).[98] Wood realigned the MB pottery dates to match *ca.* 1400 BC (LBA), aligning them with an early date for the Exodus and Conquest.

Wood identified several flaws in Kenyon's methodology. 1). First, she based her conclusions on the *absence* of Cypriot bichrome pottery (see Fig. 69).[99] 2). Second, she drew her conclusions from a very small area of the tell (two 26 by 26 foot [8 meter]

69. Philistine bichrome-ware jugs from Jericho excavated Kathleen Kenyon.

Courtesy of Ashmolean Museum, Drapers Gallery, Oxford England

[89] LaMoine F. DeVries, *Cities of the Biblical World: An Introduction to the Archaeology, Geography, and History of Biblical Sites* (Eugene, OR: Wipf & Stock, 2006), 189.

[90] Thomas A. Holland, "Jericho (Place)," ed. David Noel Freedman *et al.*, *ABD* (New York: Doubleday, 1996), 3:724–26.

[91] Kathleen M. Kenyon and Thomas A. Holland, *Excavations at Jericho*, vol. 3 (Jerusalem: British School of Archaeology in Jerusalem, 1982), 3:110.

[92] Kathleen M. Kenyon, *Digging up Jericho: The Results of the Jericho Excavations, 1952-1956* (London: Praeger & Benn, 1957), 230.

[93] Holland speculates that it may have come to an end by disease or a violent earthquake. Nigro favours the earthquake explanation. John Garstang and J. B. E. Garstang, *The Story of Jericho*, New revised edition (London: Marshall, Morgan & Scott, 1948), 136; Kathleen M. Kenyon and Thomas A. Holland, *Excavations at Jericho*, vol. 3 (Jerusalem: British School of Archaeology in Jerusalem, 1982), 3: pl. 236; Kathleen M. Kenyon, "Jericho," in *NEAEHL*, ed. Ephraim Stern, Ayelet Levinson-Gilboa, and Joseph Aviram, vol. 2 (New York: MacMillan, 1993), 2:679–80; Lorenzo Nigro and Hamdan Taha, eds., *Tell Es-Sultan/Jericho in the Context of the Jordan Valley: Site Management, Conservation, and Sustainable Development*, Studies on the Archaeology of Palestine & Transjordan 2 (Rome: University of Rome, "La Sapienza," 2006), 25, 34; Holland, "Jericho (Place)," 3:736.

[94] John Garstang, *The Foundations of Bible History: Joshua, Judges* (Grand Rapids: Kregel, 1978), 146; Garstang and Garstang, *The Story of Jericho*, 133–53, 167.

[95] Kenyon, *Digging up Jericho*, 261–62; "Jericho," 2:680.

[96] Nigro and Taha, *Tell Es-Sultan/ Jericho in the Context of the Jordan Valley*, 34.

[97] Ibid., 25.

[98] Wood, "Did the Israelites Conquer Jericho? A New Look at the Archaeological Evidence," 44–58; "Dating Jericho's Destruction: Bienkowski Is Wrong on All Counts," *BAR* 16, no. 5 (1990): 45, 47–49, 68–69; "From Ramesses to Shiloh: Archaeological Discoveries Bearing on the exodus–Judges Period," in *Giving the Sense: Understanding and Using Old Testament Historical Texts*, ed. David M. Howard, Jr. and Michael A. Grisanti (Grand Rapids: Kregel Academic & Professional, 2004), 256–82.

[99] Kathleen M. Kenyon, "The Middle and Late Bronze Age Strata at Megiddo," *Levant* 1, no. 1 (1969): 50–51; *Palestine in the Time of the Eighteenth Dynasty: Volume 2, Part 1: The Middle East and the Aegean Region, c.1800–1380 BC*, 3rd ed., Cambridge Ancient History 69 (Cambridge, MA: Cambridge University Press, 1973), 2.1:528–29; *Archaeology in the Holy Land*, 5th ed. (Nashville, TN: Nelson, 1979), 162–220.

squares).[100] 3). Third, she failured to publish her finds and research. While she did publish a popular work on Jericho in 1957 called *Digging Up Jericho* and two massive volumes in 1960 and 1964, her four final volumes were published posthumously (1981–1983) by Kenyon's editor Thomas A. Holland, who compiled and reworked her excavation reports.[101]

70. Tell es-Sulṭân, the site of biblical Jericho. ① Trench I excavated by Kathleen Kenyon (Area C, MB2 1800–1650 BC). ② 5 m. high Cyclopean Wall destroyed in ca. 1550 BC (Area A, MB2 1650–1550 BC). ③ Houses built outside Building A1 against the eastern side of the tower (Area A, MB2 1800–1650 BC).

Wood's views were met with criticism from several knowledgeable archaeologists.[102] In reply, Wood admitted that the difference between LBA and the MBA pottery styles are difficult to distinguish:

> it is important to recognize that the pottery of the Late Bronze I period is *very similar* to that of the final phase of the Middle Bronze period. In fact, the material culture of the Late Bronze I period is *simply a continuation* of that of the Middle Bronze period. As a result, many Middle Bronze forms *continue* into Late Bronze I. There are *subtle* differences in a number of types, however, and several new forms are introduced. With *careful study* of the pottery evidence, therefore, it is possible to distinguish the Late Bronze I period from the terminal phase of the Middle Bronze period [Emphasis added].[103]

Wood also acknowledged that: "It remains for me to publish a critique of Kenyon's theories and an in-depth study of the pottery from the various expeditions, to demonstrate that Kenyon's conclusions were incorrect and that Garstang's analysis is the correct interpretation for the dating of the destruction of Jericho."[104]

Since the 1950's and Kenyon's excavation, little was done at Jericho (Tell es-Sulṭân next to

---

[100] Michael A. Grisanti, "Recent Archaeological Discoveries That Lend Credence to the Historicity of the Scriptures," *Journal of Evangelical Theological Society* 56, no. 3 (2013): 480.

[101] Holland, "Jericho," 223. Ironically Wood is guilty of the same flaw (see his statement below).

[102] Piotr Bienkowski, *Jericho in the Late Bronze Age*, Ancient Near East (Warminster, Wiltshire: Aris & Phillips, 1986), Chapter 7; "Jericho Was Destroyed in the Middle Bronze Age, Not the Late Bronze Age," *BAR* 16, no. 5 (1990): 45, 46, 69; Geisler and Holden, *Popular Handbook of Archaeology and the Bible*, 235–37.

[103] Wood, "Dating Jericho's Destruction: Bienkowski Is Wrong on All Counts," 47.

[104] Bryant G. Wood, "Researching Jericho," *BS* 22, no. 3 (2009): 82.

71. The author holding a large mudbrick from the site of OT Jericho.

the modern city of Ariha) until the joint work of the Palestinian Department of Antiquities and Cultural Heritage and the Italian-Palestinian Expedition (1997–2000, 2009–2018) from the University of Rome, "La Sapienza". While the work carried out was primarily focused on restoration of the site and reconciling the previous work of Garstang and Kenyon in the EB and MB strata, they did identify Late Bronze age (Period V 1650–1550 BC) occupation in Area G, on the acropolis. In 2006, Nigro reported the location of these LB structures:

> One is the Spring Hill, on the top of which, in Area G, a major sustaining wall (W.633) was identified, presumably terracing the acropolis with public buildings, and at the bottom of which, in Area D, cleaning works brought to light a huge mud-brick wall (W.7; [see Fig. 71]), just in front of the Spring, cut by the modern road. LBA buildings (the so-called Middle Building and a house to the north-east) excavated by Garstang.[105]

However, Nigro goes on to explain the reason for the lack of evidence:

> A few materials and some tombs are known from period V, the Late Bronze Age [1550–1200 BC], even though not a single pottery fragment from this period was found on the *tell* by the Italian-Palestinian Expedition. Iron Age materials were found in Area B58, while in Areas G and F on the summit of the Spring Hill and on the northern plateau intensive razing of later periods had removed all strata down to the Middle or even to the Early Bronze Age.[106]

Archaeological Evidence

Wood and others have pointed out several parallels between the Biblical account of Jericho's destruction and the archaeological evidence.

- Jericho was strongly fortified (Josh 2:5, 7, 15; 6:5, 20). Holland described that excavations revealed the "remains of three successive and massive plastered ramparts which surrounded"[107] the city. The gateway was uncovered in 1998 by the University of Rome (see Fig. 71).[108]
- The fortification walls collapsed at the time the city was destroyed, possibly by earthquake activity (Josh 6:20; see Fig. 70).
- The destruction occurred at harvest time, in the spring (month of Adar, i.e., February/March), as indicated by the large quantities of grain stored in the city (Josh 2:6; 3:15; 5:10). Both Garstang and Kenyon found several grain filled storage jars that were burned. Kenyon reported over six bushels of grain excavated in one season alone (see Fig. 72).[109]
- The siege of Jericho was short, as the grain stored in the city was not consumed (Josh 6:1, 15, 20). Since it would normally take several months or even years to subdue a well-supplied city, as is illustrated from Masada, which took the Romans three years to capture, the storage jars at Jericho filled with charred grain indicate they did not have time to consume the grain, suggesting a shorter siege as described in the biblical narrative.

---

[105] Nigro and Taha, *Tell Es-Sultan/ Jericho in the Context of the Jordan Valley*, 25.
[106] Ibid., 35.
[107] Holland, "Jericho (Place)," 3:734.
[108] Agence France-Presse, "Jericho's Ancient Gates Found," *The New York Times*, November 28, 1998, 3.
[109] Kenyon, *Digging up Jericho*, 230.

72. Grain storage jars are still visible here in one of Kenyon's balks in Jericho.

© Todd Bolen / BiblePlaces.com

- Contrary to what was customary, the grain was not plundered to feed their armies, or taken by the citizens, but in accordance with God's command, Joshua burned it all (Josh 6:1, 17–18). This discovery is unique in archaeology, given the high value of grain in ancient culture. It would be like taking a bank and burning the money.
- The city walls were leveled as part of the destruction (Josh 6:20; see Fig. 70).[110]
- The city was massively destroyed by fire (Josh 6:24). The east side of the tell was excavated and they found a layer of burned ash and debris about one metre thick. Kenyon described the destruction in her own words:

> The destruction was complete. Walls and floors were blackened or reddened by fire, and every room was filled with fallen bricks, timbers, and household utensils; in most rooms the fallen debris was heavily burnt, but the collapse of the walls of the eastern rooms seems to have taken place before they were affected by the fire.[111]

- Jericho layed abandoned for a period of time following its destruction, in accordance with Joshua's curse (Josh 6:26).

As Amihai Mazar points out:

> At Jericho, no remains of the Late Bronze fortification were found; this was taken as evidence against the historical value of the narrative in the Book of Joshua. The finds at Jericho, however, show that there was a settlement there during the Late Bronze Age, though most of its remains were eroded or removed by human activity. Perhaps, as at other sites, the massive Middle Bronze fortifications were reutilized in the Late Bronze Age. The Late Bronze Age settlement at Jericho was followed by an occupation gap in Iron Age I. Thus, in the case of Jericho, the archaeological data cannot serve as decisive evidence to deny a historical nucleus in the Book of Joshua concerning the conquest of this city.[112]

While the date of the destruction of the city continues to be debated, there is no doubt that the city met with a violent end and scholars should at least be open to the possibility that the destruction involved the army of Israel as they entered into the Promised Land.

Ai (Joshua 7–8)

The second city that Joshua conquered and burned was Ai (see Fig. 73). The site of et-Tell has long been identified as the city of Ai (see Map 1).[113] However, no archaeological occupation during the period of the conquest (LBA from 2400–1230 BC, whether one accepts the early [*ca.* 1446 BC] or late date [*ca.* 1260 BC]) has been identified by Joseph Callaway, the most recent excavator of et-Tell (1964–1970).[114] Callaway concludes that: " 'Ai is simply an embarrassment to

---

[110] Holland, "Jericho (Place)," 3:736.

[111] Kenyon and Holland, *Excavations at Jericho*, 3:3:370.

[112] Mazar, *Archaeology of the Land of the Bible*, 1:1:331.

[113] Edward Robinson, *Later Biblical Researches in Palestine, and in the Adjacent Regions: A Journal of Travels in the Year 1852* (Boston, MA: Crocker and Brewster, 1856), 635; Charles W. Wilson, "On the Site of Ai and the Position of the Altar Which Abram Built Between Bethel and Ai," *PEFSt.* 1, no. 4 (1869): 123–26; William F. Albright, *The Biblical Period from Abraham to Ezra* (New York: Harper & Row, 1963), 29; Michael Avi-Yonah and Ephraim Stern, eds., "Ai; Hai," in *EAEHL*, 4 vols. (Upper Saddle River, NJ: Prentice Hall, 1978); Joseph A. Callaway, "Ai," in *NEAEHL*, ed. Ephraim Stern, Ayelet Levinson-Gilboa, and Joseph Aviram, vol. 1, 4 vols. (New York: MacMillan, 1993), 39–45; "Ai (Place)," ed. David Noel Freedman *et al.*, *ABD* (New York: Doubleday, 1996), 1:125–30.

[114] Hess, "The Jericho and Ai of the Book of Joshua," 33–34.

73. Burnt gate at Khirbet el-Maqatir (Ai?) from the time of Joshua (LB *ca.* 1400 BC). The Bible states that Joshua burned the gate.
Courtesy of Michael C. Luddeni

every view of the conquest that takes the biblical and archaeological evidence seriously."[115] This has led many scholars to conclude that the biblical account (Josh 7–8) of the conquest of Ai is not historically credible.[116]

However, others have considered the possibility that et-Tell has been misinterpreted[117] or Joshua's Ai misidentified.[118] Several archaeologists have proposed that Joshua's Ai was related to sites in the neighbourhood of et-Tell. David Livingston excavated at Khirbet Nisya (1979–2002),[119] while Bryant Wood (1995–2013) and Scott Stripling (2014–2017) have excavated the site of Khirbet el-Maqatir,[120] as possible candidates.[121]

---

[115] Joseph A. Callaway, "New Evidence on the Conquest of ‹Ai," *JBL* 87, no. 3 (September 1, 1968): 312; "Excavating Ai (Et-Tell): 1964-1972," *BA* 39 (1976): 18–31; "Was My Excavation of Ai Worthwhile?," *BAR* 11, no. 2 (1985): 68–69; "Ai," 1:39–45; "Ai (Place)," 125–130.

[116] Amihai Mazar, "The Iron Age I Period," in *The Archaeology of Ancient Israel*, ed. Amnon Ben-Tor, trans. R. Greenberg (New Haven, CT: Yale University Press, 1994), 283; Miller, "Archaeology and the Israelite Conquest of Canaan," 89.

[117] Merling, "Relationship Between Archaeology and Bible," 34–41; Monson, "Enter Joshua," 442–52.

[118] Wood believes that et-Tel is the Ai of Abraham's time, and "both Beitin and Khirbet Nisya were occupied during the Iron Age II and Persian periods and are close to el-Bira/Bethel, so it is possible that one of these sites was the Ai of Ezra and Nehemiah." Wood, "The Search for Joshua's Ai," 2008, 239.

[119] Livingston challenged the location of Bethel, from which Ai is measured, with modern Beitin and opted instead for El-Bireh, which is 12 Roman miles from Jerusalem, instead of Beitin which is 14 Roman miles. David P. Livingston, "Excavation Report for Khirbet Nisya," *BS* 12, no. 3 (1999): 95–96; "The Location of Biblical Bethel and Ai Reconsidered," 20–44; "Locating Biblical Ai Correctly," *Ancient Days*, 2003, http://davelivingston .com/ai15.htm; David P. Livingston, "Further Considerations on the Location of Bethel at El-Bireh," *PEQ* 126, no. 2 (1994): 154–59; David Livingston, *Khirbet Nisya: The Search for Biblical Ai, 1979-2002* (Manheim, PA: Masthof, 2012).

[120] Khirbet el-Maqatir lies fifteen km north of Jerusalem, on the east side of Highway 60, and 3.7 km east of El-Bireh, 1.6 km southeast of Beitin and ca. 1 km west of et-Tell. Wood, "The Search for Joshua's Ai," 1999, 21–32; "The Search for Joshua's Ai," 2008, 205–40; "Excavations at Kh. El-Maqatir 1995–2000, 2009–2013: A Border Fortress in the Highlands of Canaan and a Proposed New Location for the Ai of Joshua 7-8," *The Bible and Interpretation*, 2014, 1–16; "Khirbet El-Maqatir, 1995-1998," *IEJ* 50, no. 1–2 (2000): 123–30; "Khirbet El-Maqatir, 1999," *IEJ* 50, no. 3–4 (2000): 249–54; "Khirbet El-Maqatir, 2000," *IEJ* 51, no. 2 (2001): 246–52; Bryant G. Wood and D. Scott Stripling, *Joshua's Ai at Khirbet El-Maqatir: History of a Biblical Site* (Houston, Tex.:

In Wood's estimation, et-Tell does not meet the topographical or archaeological features necessary to match the geography of Joshua 7 and 8,[122] with Khirbet el-Maqatir lending itself to better fit the features described. The geography of Khirbet el-Maqatir matches the biblical criteria catalogued by Wood: adjacent to Beth-aven (Josh 7:2); East of Bethel (Josh 7:2); an ambush site between Bethel and Ai (Josh 8:9, 12); a militarily significant hill north of Ai (Josh 8:11); a shallow valley north of Ai (Josh 8:13–14); smaller than Gibeon (Josh 10:2); and in the vicinity of Bethel (Josh 12:9).[123]

Archaeological Evidence

The archaeological remains also support the identification of Khirbet el-Maqatir.

- Fiftteenth cent. BC pottery and a rare Egyptian scarab,[124] uncovered in a sealed locus, have been found at Khirbet el-Maqatir, which indicate that the fortress was occupied in the LBA (*ca.* 1500–1400 BC), the time of the early date for the conquest (see Fig. 62). The LBA 1 fortress was identified from pottery found on the "flagstone pavement just inside the gate" (Square Q17).[125] Briggs reports that the pottery was "suited to a small military outpost, including large, commercial-grade pithoi for storage of grains, water and olive oil, and common ware for cooking and table service."[126]
- At the time of the conquest of Canaan, biblical Ai was a fortified settlement (Josh 7:5, 8:29). The LBA 1 site of Khirbet el-Maqatir was strongly fortified with 4-meter-thick walls. The fortification of the site was also evident from 3 gate socket stones, along with the recovery of over 100 slingstones.[127]
- The gate of the fortified city of Ai was on the north side of the city wall (Josh 8:11) confirmed by the foundations of a LBA 1 chambered gate on the north side of Khirbet el-Maqatir (see Fig. 61).[128]

74. The scarab is of a rare type made in the early eighteenth dynasty (Amenhotep II, *ca.* 1485–1418 BC) like others from the reigns of Amenhotep II and Thutmose III (1506-1452). In addition to the pottery, it provides an independent date for the fortress at Khirbet el-Maqatir.

Houston Baptist University Press, 2014); D. Scott Stripling *et al.*, "Renewed Excavations at Khirbet El-Maqatir: Highlights of the 2009–2011 Seasons," in *Collected Studies of the Staff Office of Archaeology of Judea and Samaria*, Judea and Samaria Publication 13 (Jerusalem: Israel Antiquities Authority, 2014), Forthcoming.

[121] Briggs presents a survey of the proposed sites for Ai and argues that Khirbe el-Maqatir is the best candidate according to the critieria set out in the biblical text. Peter Briggs, "Testing the Factuality of the Conquest of Ai Narrative in the Book of Joshua," in *Beyond the Jordan: Studies in Honor of W. Harold Mare*, ed. Glenn A. Carnagey Sr, Glenn Carnagey Jr, and Keith N. Schoville (Eugene, Ore.: Wipf & Stock, 2005), 157–96.

[122] Wood, "The Search for Joshua's Ai," 1999, 210–12; Wood, "From Ramesses to Shiloh," 264–70.

[123] Wood, "The Search for Joshua's Ai," 2008, 231–37.

[124] An earlier Hyksos scarb (MB 3, ca. 1668–1560 BC) was recovered in the 2014 season. Gordon Govier, "Biblical Archaeology's Top Ten Discoveries of 2013," *Christianity Today*, December 31, 2013, http://www.christianitytoday.com/ct/2013/december-web-only/biblical-archaeologys-top-ten-discoveries-of-2013.html.

[125] Wood, "The Search for Joshua's Ai," 2008, 231–32.

[126] Briggs, "Testing the Factuality of the Conquest of Ai Narrative in the Book of Joshua," 190.

[127] Wood, "The Search for Joshua's Ai," 2008, 230; Briggs, "Testing the Factuality of the Conquest of Ai Narrative in the Book of Joshua," 161–62.

[128] A sealed loci adjacent to the gate foundation stones dated to LB 1. Briggs, "Testing the Factuality of the Conquest of Ai Narrative in the Book of Joshua," 188; Wood, "From Ramesses to Shiloh," 268.

75. The chambered gate of Hazor in the upper Galilee, Israel.

- At the time of the conquest, Ai was destroyed by fire (Josh 8:19, 28). Wood reports: "Abundant evidence for destruction by fire has been found at Khirbet el-Maqatir in the form of ash, refired pottery, burned building stones, and calcined bedrock."[129]

Khirbet el-Maqatir is certainly a small site, but the arguments overcoming et-Tell's small size could also be applied to Khirbet el-Maqatir.[130] While the excavations at Khirbet el-Maqatir have not proven that it is Joshua's Ai, its destruction in the LB 1 period, the time of the conquest along with the other evidence, made it a strong candidate for being Joshua's Ai.

Hazor (Joshua 11)

According to Joshua, the last city to be placed under the ban (see glossary) and burned was Hazor (Josh 11:10–11). The evidence of this destruction in the thirteenth century has been uncovered by Yigael Yadin (1955–1958 and 1968–1969),[131] and Amnon Ben-Tor, who have both excavated Hazor (see Map 2, 3, 5 and Fig. 75).[132] They have uncovered evidence of a destruction layer from the time of the conquest (thirteenth cent. BC).[133] Monson describes the destruction:

> Hazor's archaeological excavations have yielded Late Bronze Age finds that correlate with the book of Joshua very well. The site has destruction layers that fit both the early and late dates of the exodus/conquest, but because Hazor suffered a particularly massive conflagration in the thirteenth century BC, Ben-Tor contends that the Israelites were most likely the people who ransacked this large

---

[129] Wood, "The Search for Joshua's Ai," 2008, 231.

[130] Monson, "Enter Joshua," 437–38.

[131] Yigael Yadin, "The Fourth Season of Excavations at Hazor," *BA* 22, no. 1 (1959): 1–20; *Hazor: The Rediscovery of a Great Citadel of the Bible* (New York: Random House, 1975).

[132] Amnon Ben-Tor, "Who Destroyed Canaanite Hazor?," *BAR* 39, no. 4 (2013): 26–36, 58–60.

[133] Amnon Ben-Tor, "The Fall of Canaanite Hazor–The 'Who' and 'When' Questions," in *Mediterranean Peoples in Transition, 13th to 10th Centuries BC*, ed. Ephraim Stern, Seymour Gitin, and Amihai Mazar (Jerusalem: Israel Exploration Society, 1998), 456–67.

city, the "head of all those kingdoms." He reaches this conclusion through a process of elimination.[134]

In 2010, a newly discovered piece of Akkadian law code, similar to Hammurabi's law code, was uncovered at Hazor dating to the eighteenth or seventeenth centuries BC. Since the early 1950's, over "19 cuneiform documents have been found—the largest collection of such documents unearthed in Israel in one site."[135] It indicates that Hazor was a leading administrative centre for scribal work.

Recently, in 2013, a unique find was discovered at Hazor, near the entrance to the city palace, of an Egyptian Sphinx statue-base with a hieroglyphic inscription between the two front paws. The inscription bears the name of the Egyptian king Menkaure (fourteenth Dynasty *ca.* 2500 BC), who built the third and smallest pyramid of Giza about 1,000 years pior to the Exodus. While some 17 other Egyptian statues have been discovered at Hazor,[136] this is the first discovery of any statue of this Pharaoh anywhere in the world. As Ngo points out "this is the only piece of royal sphinx sculpture ever found in the Levant."[137] What is also of interest is that the statue was found in the thirteenth cent. BC destruction layer. According to Amnon Ben-Tor and Sharon Zuckerman, who excavated the site, they: "believe it is unlikely that King Menkaure sent the sphinx to Hazor, since there is no record of a relationship between Egypt and the southern Levant during his reign. The statue may have been brought to Hazor as plunder by the Hyksos, a dynasty of kings from Canaan who ruled Lower Egypt in the late seventeenth and early sixteenth centuries, or perhaps slightly later as a gift from a New Kingdom Egyptian ruler."[138] In either case it demonstrates a close connection with Egypt.

CONCLUSION

Although scholars have claimed for years that there is no evidence for the Exodus and Conquest, and therefore that the events described in the Bible could not have happened, the recent excavations and discoveries listed here and elsewhere, indicate that the biblical accounts of the Exodus and Conquest are historically reliable.

---

[134] Monson, "Enter Joshua," 436.

[135] Asaf Shtull-Trauring, "'Hammurabi-like' Cuneiform Discovered at Tel Hazor," *Haaretz*, July 27, 2010, http://www.haaretz.com/print-edition /news/hammurabi-like-cuneiform-discovered-at-tel-hazor-1.304266.

[136] Ben-Tor indicates that there is "abundant evidence that the statues were buried [5] and mutilated [11] . . . In all cases of mutilation, the heads and hands of the statues were the primary targets. . . . The fate of the statue of Dagon in his Temple at Ashdod in 1 Sam 5:4 . . . The account of the struggle between the god of Israel and the god of the Philistines was composed much later than the period of the Hazor statues and was religiously motivated. It does, however, echo practices common in much earlier times." Amnon Ben-Tor, "The Sad Fate of Statues and the Mutilated Statues of Hazor," in *Confronting the Past: Archaeological and Historical Essays on Ancient Israel in Honor of William G. Dever*, ed. Seymour Gitin, J. Edward Wright, and J. P. Dessel (Winona Lake, IN: Eisenbrauns, 2006), 3–16.

[137] Robin Ngo, "Rare Egyptian Sphinx Fragment Discovered at Hazor," *Bible History Daily: Biblical Archaeology Society*, July 12, 2013.

[138] Ibid.

CHART 5: IRON AGE AND PERSIAN DISCOVERIES

KINGS AND PROPHETS (IA & PERSIAN: 1200–332 BC)					
Discovery	**Image**	**Place and Discoverer**	**Origin date / Year Found**	**Biblical Passage**	**Significance**
Altar of Jeroboam I		Tel Dan, Israel by Avraham Biran	931 BC 1975	1 Kgs 12:25–31	Golden calf altar of Jeroboam I at Tel Dan. under Tiglath-Pileser III mentions child sacrifice
Sheshonq I Inscription		Precint of Amun-Ra, Karnak Temple, Luxor, Egypt by Jean-François Champollion	920–925 BC 1825	1 Kgs 11:40; 14:25; 2 Chr 12:1–12	Invasion of Judah and Israel with mention of Rehoboam and Sheshonq (Shishak) I
Gezer Calender		Gezer by R. A. S. Macalister	Tenth cent. BC	1 Kgs 14:31	Agricultural practices of Israel and mentions the name Abijah (one of the Kings of Judah)
Kurkh stele Monolith Inscription		Kurkh (modern Üçtepe, Diyarbakir Turkey) by John Taylor	879–853 BC 1861	1 Kgs 20:1–34	Victory of Shalmaneser III at the battle of Qarqar over "Ahab of Israel"
Mesha Stele		Dibon, Jordan by Frederick Augustus Klein	850 BC 1868	1 Kgs 16:28–33; 21:1–21; 1 Sam 16:13; 2 Sam 5:3–7	Moabite-Israelite relations, mentions King Ahab and King David

Discovery	Image	Place and Discoverer	Origin date / Year Found	Biblical Passage	Significance
Black Obelisk		Kalhu (modern Iraq) by A. Henry Layard	840 BC 1846	2 Kgs 8–10; 17:3–6	King Jehu paying tribute to Shalmaneser III
Tel Dan Stele		Tel Dan, Israel by Avraham Biran	841 BC 1993	2 Kgs 8:7–13; 8:28–29; 13:1–3	Mention of "house of David" and Ben-Hadad II, Hazael, Joram, Ahab, Ahaziah, Jehoram, and Jehu
Deir 'Alla Inscription (or Balaam Inscription)		Deir 'Alla, Jordan by H. J. Franken	840–760 BC 1967	Num 22:5	Warning from biblical seer, Balaam son of Beor
Jehoash Inscription		Purchased from a Palestinian antiquities dealer by Oded Golan (possible forgery)	800 BC 2003	2 Kgs 12	How Jehoash undertook repairs to the Temple
Pomegranate Inscription		Antiquities market (possible forgery)	eighth cent. BC 1979	1 Kgs 6:1–9	Oldest mention of Solomon's Temple
Incirli stele of Tiglathpileser III		Incirli in the Karamanmarash Valley (Turkey) by Elizabeth Carter	800–600 BC 1993	1 Chr 5:26; 2 Chr 26; 2 Kgs 15:19–29	Menahem of Israel and Pul were taken into captivity by the Assyrians

Discovery	Image	Place and Discoverer	Origin date / Year Found	Biblical Passage	Significance
Seal of Shema		Megiddo, Israel by Gottlieb Schumacher	782–745 BC 1904	1 Kgs 12–14	King Jeroboam II
Annals of Sargon II or Nimrud Prism		Dur-Sharruken (modern Khorsabad, Iraq) by Paul-Emile Botta and Eugène Flandin	738–720 BC 1842–1844	2 Kgs 17:6 27, 29; Isa 39:1	Israelites were taken into captivity by King Merodach-baladan
Ahaz Bulla		Antiquities market by Robert Deutsch	732–716 BC 1995	Isa 14:28	Fingerprint and name of King Ahaz
Winged Bull of Sargon II		Dur-Sharruken (modern Khorsabad, Iraq) by Paul-Emile Botta	722–705 BC 1843	Isa 20:1–6	Sargon's capture of Samaria
Shebna Inscription		Shiloam (Silwan) Kidron Valley, Jerusalem by Charles Clermont-Ganneau	715–687 BC 1870	Isa 22:15–19	Shebna, Steward of King Hezekiah
Hezekiah Bulla		Antiquities market by Nahman Avigad	728–699 BC 1986	2 Kgs 18:1–3	Hezekiah, King of Judah
Hezekiah's Tunnel	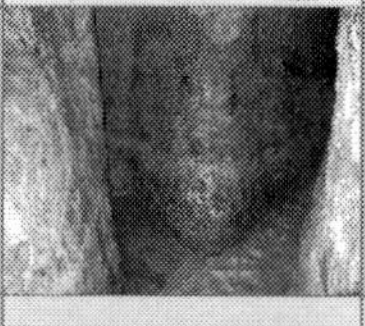	Siloam (Silwan) Kidron Valley, Jerusalem by Edward Robinson	711 BC 1838	2 Kgs 20:20; 2 Chr 32:2–6	Supplied water from Gihon Spring to the Pool of Siloam
Ekron Royal Dedicatory Inscription		Tel Miqne by Steve Oritz	705–701 BC 1996	1 Sam 21:10–15; 1 Kgs 2:39–40; 2 Kgs 18–19; Zeph 2:4	Mentions Ekron, King Achish and King Padi the Philistine king of Gath
Azekah Inscription		Libary of Ashurbanipal by Henry Rawlinson /Nadav Na'aman	705–681 BC 1903/1974	2 Kgs 18–19; 2 Chr 32	Assyrian attack of Azekah and mentions King Hezekiah

Discovery	Image	Place and Discoverer	Origin date / Year Found	Biblical Passage	Significance
Siloam Inscription		Siloam (Silwan) Kidron Valley, Jerusalem by Jacob (Eliyahu) Spafford	701 BC 1880	2 Kgs 20:20	Description of the completion of Hezekiah's tunnel in Hebrew language
Lachish Reliefs		The Southwest Palace of Sennacherib in Nineveh (modern Iraq) by A. Henry Layard	700–681 BC 1847	Isa 36:1–2	Siege of Lachish
Three Shekel or Moussaieff Ostraca		Purchased by Shlomo Moussaieff from the Jerusalem antiquities dealer Oded Golan	640-609 BC ninth to seventh cent. BC 2012	1 Kings 9:10	Mentions the house of Yahweh the earliest mention of Solomon's temple
Bethlehem Bulla		City of David Excavations by Eli Shukron	eighth to seventh cent. BC 2012	Micah 5:2	Earliest mention of Bethlehem
Sennacherib (Taylor) Prism		British Museum Prism, Nineveh, Iraq by John Taylor Oriental Institute Prism, Baghdad antiques dealer by James Henry Breasted	686 BC 1830	2 Kgs 18:13–19:35; 2 Chr 32:9	Describes siege of Jerusalem
Babylonian Chronicles		Babylon (British Museum) translated by Theophilus Pinches, Sidney Smith, and Donald Wiseman	626–594 BC 1887, 1924, 1956	2 Kgs 24:10–14	Extrabiblical account of the capture of Jerusalem (597 BC)

Discovery	Image	Place and Discoverer	Origin date / Year Found	Biblical Passage	Significance
Nebuchadnezzar's Brick		Babylon and Nineveh by Claudius James Rich and Robert Koldeway	604–561 BC 1899–1914	Dan 4:30	Nebuchadnezzar II building campaign and Nabopolassar, king of Babylon
House of Yahweh Ostracon		Tel Arad temple by Yohanan Aharoni	seventh to sixth cent. BC (before 586 BC) 1962	1 Kings 9:10	Mentions the 'House of Yahweh' second oldest reference to Solomon's temple
Jehoiachin Ration Record		Babylon by Robert Koldeway	595–570 BC 1899–1914	2 Kgs 24, 25:27–30	Jehoiachin taken captive to Babylon by Nebuchadnezzar II
Lachish Ostraca Letters		Guardroom of the city gate at Tel ed-Duweir (Lachish) by James L. Starkey	588 BC 1935	Isa 36:1–2; Jer 34"6–7	Babylonian seige conditions on Jerusalem
Sarsekim Tablet		Archive from a large sun-worship temple at Sippar by Hormuzd Rassam and Michael Jursa	586 BC 1880 2007	Jer 39:3–4	Mentions Sarsekim, Nebuchadnezzar's chief officer during the siege of Jerusalem
Bulla of Berachyahu ben Neriah		Purchased by an antiquities dealer and taken to Nahman Avigad	sixth cent. BC 1975	Jer 32:1–16	Mention of Baruch, the Son of Neriah, Jeremiah's scribe
Esarhaddon Chronicle		Babylon (British Museum) Claudius Rich? translated by Theophilus Pinches	*ca.* 550–400 BC 1811 1887	2 Kgs 19:37; Isa 37:38	Mention of King Esarhaddon

Discovery	Image	Place and Discoverer	Origin date / Year Found	Biblical Passage	Significance
Nabonidus Cylinder		Four from Sippar and Ur by John Taylor	540 BC 1854	Dan 5	Mention of Nabonidus and Balshazzar
Nabonidus Chronicle		Babylon? Antiquities dealers Spartali & Co. first mentioned by Sir Henry Rawlinson	556–539 BC 1882	Dan 5–8	Mention of Nabonidus and Balshazzar
Cyrus Cylinder		Temple of Marduk, Babylon by Hormuzd Rassam	*ca.* 539–530 BC 1879	2 Chr 36:22–23; Isa 44:28; Ezra 5:13–17	Decree of Cyrus which benefitted Judah
Behistun Relief Inscription		Mount Behistun in the Kermanshah Province of Iran by Robert Sherley and Henry Rawlinson	522–486 BC 1598 1835	Ezra 4:5, 24; Neh 12:22	Mention of King Darius I and Persian script
Persepolis Relief		Persepolis, Iran by Ernst Herzfeld, Erich Schmidt	515 BC 1930	Neh 2:1	Darius's son Xerxes I with cupbearer
Silver Bowl of Artaxerxes I		Hamadan? translated by E. Herzfeld	465–425 BC 1935	Esther 1:1–2	Ahasuerus (Xerxes I), Artaxerxes I & Darius I
Elephantine Papyri		Elephantine and Syene (Aswan), Egypt by Charles Edwin Wilbour	407 BC 1880–1896 1907–1908	2 Kgs 25:26; Neh 2:17–19; 12:23	Sanballat I, governor of Samaria, and Johanan ben Eliashib mentioned in Nehemiah
Famine Stele		Sehel Island, Egypt by C. E. Wilbour and deciphered by egyptologists: Brugsch (1891), Pleyte (1891), Morgan (1894), Sethe (1901), Barguet (1953) and Lichtheim (1973)	332–31 BC 1889	Gen 41	7 year famine

Discovery	Image	Place and Discoverer	Origin date / Year Found	Biblical Passage	Significance
Rosetta Stone		Rosetta Egypt by Pierre-François Bouchard	196 BC 1799	N/A	Unlocked Egyptian Hieroglyphs
The Prayer of Nabonidus (4Q242)		Dead Sea Scroll Cave 4 translated by J. T. Milik	75–50 BC 1956	Jer 29:10–12; Dan 9:2	Babylonian captivity
Uzziah Epitaph		Russian Orthodox manastery, Mount of Olives by Eleazer Sukenik	ca. 150 BC–AD 50 1931	2 Kgs 15:1–27; Josephus *Ant.* 9.10.4	Reburial ephetah of King Uziah of Judah

United and Divided Monarchy

76. Aerial view of Tel Shiloh (Tell-Seilûn) looking south. The ark of the covenant was located here for 369 years.

© Courtesy of Greg Gulbrandsen

The existence of King David and King Solomon in the period of the united monarchy (Iron Age 2, tenth cent. BC), is the next area to be critically debated by archaeologists.[1] The W. F. Albright and G. E. Wright era (1980's) saw most scholars embracing David and Solomon as OT historical figures.[2] But this is no longer the case. Today some minimalist scholars argue, on the basis of the lack of supporting archaeological evidence,[3] that the united monarchy (David and Solomon), and its capital Jerusalem, never existed in the tenth cent. BC and were fabricated as pure fiction.[4] David Ussishkin goes so far as to state: "I am afraid that evidence regarding the magnificent Solomonic capital [Jerusalem] was not discovered because it is nonexistent, not because it is still hidden in the ground."[5]

United Monarchy

With the discovery of the Tel Dan stele in 1993,[6] the extreme minimalist view of Ussishkin and others was challenged, since the phrase "house of David"[7] (Heb. *bytdwd*), was identified as part of the inscription.[8] David's reign has now also been identified on line 31 of the Mesha Stele (see Chart 5).[9] Amihai Mazar described the implications of this discovery: "It means that about 140 years after the presumed end of David's reign, in the region David was well-known as founder of

[1] Steven M. Ortiz, "The Archaeology of David and Solomon: Method or Madness?," in *Do Historical Matters Matter to Faith?: A Critical Appraisal of Modern and Postmodern Approaches to Scripture*, ed. James K. Hoffmeier and Graham A. Magary (Wheaton, IL: Crossway Books, 2012), 497–516.

[2] Knoppers, "The Vanishing Solomon," 19–20.

[3] McCarter states "no archaeological discovery can securely be linked to him [David]." P. Kyle McCarter Jr, "The Historical David," *Interpretation* 40, no. 2 (1986): 117; Margreet L. Steiner, "It's Not There: Archaeology Proves a Negative," *BAR* 24, no. 4 (1998): 26–33, 62–63. This is certainly correct in so far as no archaeological evidence can be directly connected to the historical David.

[4] Lemche, *The Israelites in History and Tradition*; Thompson, *The Mythic Past*; Garbini, *Myth and History in the Bible*.

[5] David Ussishkin, "Solomon's Jerusalem: The Text and the Facts on the Ground," in *Jerusalem in Bible and Archaeology: The First Temple Period*, ed. Andrew G. Vaughn and Ann E. Killebrew (Atlanta, Ga.: SBL, 2003), 112.

[6] While this inscription was widely debated, Grabbe maintains that "it is now widely regarded (a) as genuine and (b) as referring to the Davidic dynasty and the Aramaic kingdom of Damascus." Grabbe, *Ahab Agonistes*, 333.

[7] Kitchen also points out the possible mention of the "highland/heights of David" in the Sheshonq Relief. Kenneth A. Kitchen, "A Possible Mention of David in the Late Tenth Century BCE, and Deity *Dod as Dead as the Dodo," *JSOT*, no. 76 (1997): 39–41.

[8] Anson Rainey has commented that "[Philip] Davies and his 'deconstructionists' [Thomas L. Thompson] can safely be ignored by everyone seriously interested in Biblical and ancient Near Eastern studies." Rainey, "The 'House of David' and the House of the Deconstructionists," 47; Avraham Biran and Joseph Naveh, "An Aramaic Stele Fragment from Tel Dan," *IEJ* 43, no. 2/3 (January 1, 1993): 81–98; "The Tel Dan Inscription: A New Fragment," *IEJ* 45, no. 1 (January 1, 1995): 1–18; Millard, "The Tell Dan Stele," 2:161–62; George Athas, *The Tel Dan Inscription: A Reappraisal and a New Introduction*, JSOTSup 360 (New York: Bloomsbury, 2006); Hallvard Hagelia, *Tel Dan Inscription: A Critical Investigation of Recent Research on Its Palaeography & Philology*, Studia Semitica Upsaliensia 22 (Uppsala: Uppsala Universitet, 2006).

[9] LeMaire, "'House of David' Restored in Moabite Inscription," 30–37; Rainey, "The 'House of David' and the House of the Deconstructionists," 47; Eveline J. Van Der Steen and Klaas A. D. Smelik, "King Mesha and the Tribe of Dibon," *JSOT* 32, no. 2 (n.d.): 139–62.

77. From left to right Abigail Leavitt; Dr. David Graves and Dr. Scott Stripling standing in the Byzantine church on the summit of Tel Shiloh that was build over the proposed location (option 2) for the tabernacle. We are standing in what would have been the location of the Holy of holies of the Israealite tabernacle.

Courtesy of Michael C. Luddeni

the dynasty that ruled a kingdom centered in Jerusalem."[10]

In spite of these significant discoveries some scholars insisted that the inscription only proved that Judah existed and they continued to deny that David was an historical figure.[11]

Some, like Israel Finkelstein, from Tel Aviv University, while not denying David and Solomon as historical figures, challenged their biblical portrayal. For Finkelstein, David is not a powerful king ruling a large kingdom, but instead little more than a tribal chief, ruling over a small tribe of bandits.[12] Amihai Mazar explains how Finkelstein arrived at this popular view:

> Israel Finkelstein has suggested lowering the chronology of archaeological assemblages in Israel that were traditionally attributed to the twelfth to tenth centuries by seventy-five to one hundred years. This wholesale lowering of dates results in the removal of archaeological assemblages from the tenth century that have served for about half a century of scholarship as the bases for the archaeological portrait or paradigm of Solomon's kingdom. This suggested "low Chronology"[13] supposedly supports the replacement of this paradigm by a new one, . . . according to which the kingdom of David and Solomon

[10] Amihai Mazar, "Archaeology and the Biblical Narrative: The Case of the United Monarchy," in *One God - One Cult - One Nation: Archaeological and Biblical Perspectives*, ed. Reinhard Gregor Kratz and Hermann Spieckermann, BZAW 405 (Berlin: De Gruyter, 2011), 30.

[11] Niels Peter Lemche, *The Old Testament between Theology and History: A Critical Survey* (Louisville, KY: Westminster/Knox, 2008), 115.

[12] Israel Finkelstein and Neil Asher Silberman, *David and Solomon: In Search of the Bible's Sacred Kings and the Roots of the Western Tradition* (New York: Free Press, 2007), 50–53.

[13] Israel Finkelstein, "The Date of the Philistine Settlement in Canaan," *Tel Aviv* 22 (1995): 213–39; "The Archaeology of the United Monarchy: An Alternative View," *Levant* 28, no. 1 (January 1996): 177–87.

either did not exist or comprised at best a small local entity.[14]

The popular deconstruction of the biblical view of David and Solomon, involving low chronology, has led to a heated debate.[15] However, there is evidence of the prominence of the City of David in the tenth to nineth cent. BC (Iron 2A) that has been verified by several recent discoveries.

Shiloh – Tell-Seilûn

Following the Israelite conquest of the promised land of Canaan, God directed Joshua to set up the tent of meeting (or tabernacle) at Shiloh (Tell-Seilûn; שִׁילֹה "place of peace"; Lat. *Silo*), 20 miles (32 km) north of Jerusalem (see Fig. 76). Amorites were in control of this region at the time of the conquest (Num 13:29 [highlands]; Josh 7:7 [Ai]; 2 Sam 21:2 [Gibeon]). The apportioning of the tribal allotments of the land was also carried out at Shiloh (Josh 18), but the focus of the site was during the period of the Judges when it was the central worship site for the nation of Israel for 369 years and where the Israelites annually came to sacrifice and worship. Hannah left her son Anna at Shiloh to be raised by the priest (1 Sam 3:3).

During the MB3 period the Amorites constructed a massive fortification system that enclosed 4.25 acres (17 dunams), similar to Khirbet el-Maqatir, Jericho, Shechem, and Gezer at this time. The MB III city then suffered destruction but was quickly rebuilt as a cultic center in the Late Bronze Age, evident from the pottery, bone deposits in a pit, and cultic vessels along with the discovery of a rock-hewn altar found (2002) near Shiloh (not dateable)[16] and another discovered in 2013 in secondary usage in a Byzantine Wall.[17] While Finkelstein identified these cultic remains as an Israelite cleanup of the Amorites,[18] they may well be evidence of an Israelite sacrificial practice at the site. A high percentage of sheep and goats with a low percentage of cattle was found in the Late Bronze stratum which by the Iron Age had increased with the importance of cattle herding. Also, of note is the high percentage of young sheep and goats, common animals used for sacrifice.[19] In the Iron Age IB (ca. 1050 BC) a more severe destruction is recorded likely by the Philistines (1 Sam 4). The Iron Age II was only a small settlement (1 Kgs 11:29 and 12:15; Jer 41:5).[20]

Following the Babylonian captivity, the site was again resettled in the Early Hellenistic

---

[14] Amihai Mazar, "The Search for David and Solomon: An Archaeological Perspective," in *The Quest for the Historical Israel*, ed. Israel Finkelstein and Brian B. Schmidt, Archaeology and Biblical Studies 17 (Atlanta, Ga.: Society of Biblical Literature, 2007), 119–20; Seters, *The Biblical Saga of King David*, xii.

[15] On the debate over the high and low chronology see: Israel Finkelstein, "Philistine Chronology: High, Middle or Low?," in *Mediterranean Peoples in Transition, 13th to 10th Centuries BC*, ed. Ephraim Stern, Seymour Gitin, and Amihai Mazar (Jerusalem: Israel Exploration Society, 1998), 140–47; "Hazor and the North in the Iron Age: A Low Chronology Perspective," *BASOR* 314 (1999): 55–70; Amnon Ben-Tor, "Hazor and the Chronology of Northern Israel: A Reply to Israel Finkelstein," *BASOR* 317 (2000): 9–16; Ernst Axel Knauf, "The Low Chronology and How Not to Deal with It," *BN* 101 (2000): 56–63; "Low and Lower? New Data on Early Iron Age Chronology from Beth Shean, Tel Rehov and Dor," *BN* 112 (2002): 21–27; Amihai Mazar, "The Debate over the Chronology of the Iron Age in the Southern Levant," in *The Bible and Radiocarbon Dating: Archaeology, Text and Science*, ed. Thomas E. Levy and Thomas Higham (London: Routledge, 2014), 15–30; Lester L. Grabbe, *Ancient Israel: What Do We Know and How Do We Know It?* (New York: Bloomsbury, 2008), 12–16; Amihai Mazar, "The Spade and the Text: The Interaction between Archaeology and Israelite History Relating to the Tenth-Ninth Centuries BCE," in *Understanding the History of Ancient Israel*, ed. H. G. M. Williamson, Proceedings of the British Academy 143 (Oxford: Oxford University Press, 2007), 143–71.

[16] Yoel Elitzur and Doron Nir-Zevi, "A Rock-Hewn Altar Near Shiloh," *PEQ* 135, no. 1 (2003): 30–36.

[17] D. Scott Stripling, "The Israelite Tabernacle at Shiloh," *BS* 29, no. 3 (2016): 91.

[18] Israel Finkelstein et al., eds., *Shiloh: The Archaeology of a Biblical Site*, Monograph Series of the Institute of Archaeology 10 (Tel Aviv, Israel: Institute of Archaeology of Tel Aviv University, 1993).

[19] Shlomo Hellwing, Moshe Sade, and Vered Kishon, "Faunal Remains," in *Shiloh: The Archaeology of a Biblical Site*, ed. Israel Finkelstein et al., Monograph Series of the Institute of Archaeology 10 (Tel Aviv, Israel: Institute of Archaeology of Tel Aviv University, 1993), 323.

[20] D. Scott Stripling, "The Israelite Tabernacle at Shiloh," *BS* 29, no. 3 (2016): 88–94.

Period (ca. 332–167 BC); Late Hellenistic (ca. 167–63 BC), Early Roman (ca. 63 BC–AD 136) periods, Byzantine era (ca. AD 325–636) and continued through the Early Islamic Age (ca. AD 636–1099) and on into the Middle Ages where it came to an end.

While early references by Eusebius and Jerome (Eusebius On. 156:28–31)[21] and early explorers (i.e., Edward Robinson, Charles Wilson, Conder and Kitchner) have described the site, it was first excavated in 1922 by the Danish archaeologist Aage Schmidt, with the help of W. F. Albright[22] and later by Hans Kjaer (1926–1932) who died during the 1932 season.[23] The site was then carried on under the leadership of Nelson Glueck who closed the dig. Excavations resumed in 1963 under the direction of Svend Holm-Nielsen and published the finding in 1969.[24] Israel Finkelstein, then of Bar-Ilan University, excavated at Shiloh from 1981 to 1984 publishing his work in 1993.[25] Following Finkelstein excavations both Ze'ev Yeivin of the IAA and Hananya Hizmi, Staff Officer of the Civil Administration of Judea and Samaria, carried out limited excavations on the summit and southern approach.[26]

In 2017, the Associates for Biblical Research and the Civil Administration of Judea and Samaria, under the direction of Scott Stripling, conducted Season One of a planned multi-year expedition. The author was a square supervisor on this excavation, working on the northern city wall (AG28). The ABR excavation was one of the first digs in Israel to go 100% digital in the field. Supervisors record data on PDF forms on their iPads (designed by the author), which were backed up daily to their database. Each locus was methodically metal detected and resulted in astounding metallic discoveries. In the first season at Shiloh 240 coins (100 from Area H1) were recovered, plus other metal objects like an MB axe and dagger. Also, it was one of the first excavations outside of Jerusalem to wet-sift the soil from each square. Various small items were recovered including a scarab, beads, coins, and other small objects overlooked by the volunteers in the squares. A drone fly over was regularly done to get an overview of the site (see Fig. 76).

78. The author applying a special mortar mixture to the Canaanite wall with a morter gun to conserve the wall.

Courtesy of Leen Ritmeyer

A new process was designed by the author, Phil Silvia, Greg Gulbrandsen, led by Leen Ritmeyer to stabilize the walls and conserve the site for future generations (see Fig. 19, 78 and *Chapter One: Excavation Methods: Conservation*).[27]

[21] Herbert Donner, *The Mosaic Map of Madaba. An Introductory Guide*, Palaestina Antiqua 7 (Kampen: Kok Pharos, 1992), 47.

[22] William F. Albright, "The Danish Excavations at Shiloh." *BASOR* 9 (Feb 1923), 10–11.

[23] Hans Andersen Kjaer, "The Danish Excavation of Shiloh," *PEQ* 59, no. 4 (October 1927): 202–13; "The Excavatin of Shiloh 1929: Preliminary Report," *JPOS* 10 (1930): 87–174; "Shiloh a Summary Report of the Second Danish Expedition, 1929," *PEQ* 63, no. 2 (1931): 71–88.

[24] Marie-Louise Buhl and Svend Holm-Nielson, eds., *Shiloh, The Pre-Hellenistic Remains: The Danish Excavations at Tell Sailûn, Palestine, in 1926, 1929, 1932 and 1963* (Copenhagen: National Museum of Denmark and Aarhus University Press, 1969).

[25] Finkelstein et al., eds., *Shiloh*.

[26] Hananya Hizmi and Reut Livyatan-ben-Arie, "The Excavations at the Northern Platform of Tel Shiloh the 2012-2013 Seasons [Translated from Hebrew]," ed. D. Scott Stripling and David E. Graves, trans. Hillel Richman, *NEASB* 62 (2017): 35–52.

[27] https://www.ritmeyer.com/2017/07/12/conservation-program-at-tel-shiloh/; http://smyrnaean.blogspot.ca/ 2017/07/ preservation-of-shiloh-walls-2017.html

An unresolved question is: where was the tabernacle located at the site of Shiloh? Various proposals have been put forth and represented by the four options in Figure 79.

Option 1: The northern location was proposed as early as Charles Wilson[28] and still popular with many archaeologists.[29] Today the spot is partially covered with a covered shelter for tourists.

Option 2: The location on the summit of Shiloh is supported by Kjaer and Finkelstein.[30] The proposed location is under the remains of a Byzantine Church (see Fig. 77) south of the new Seer's Tower observation site.

Option 3: The location on the south side of the tel is proposed by Avi-Yonah[31] and Garfinkel.[32] Byzantine tradition favoured this site as witnessed by four Byzantine Churches built there. In 2006 a mosaic inscription was excavated in one of the churches that read "Lord Jesus Christ, have mercy on Seilun [Shiloh] and its inhabitants, Amen."[33]

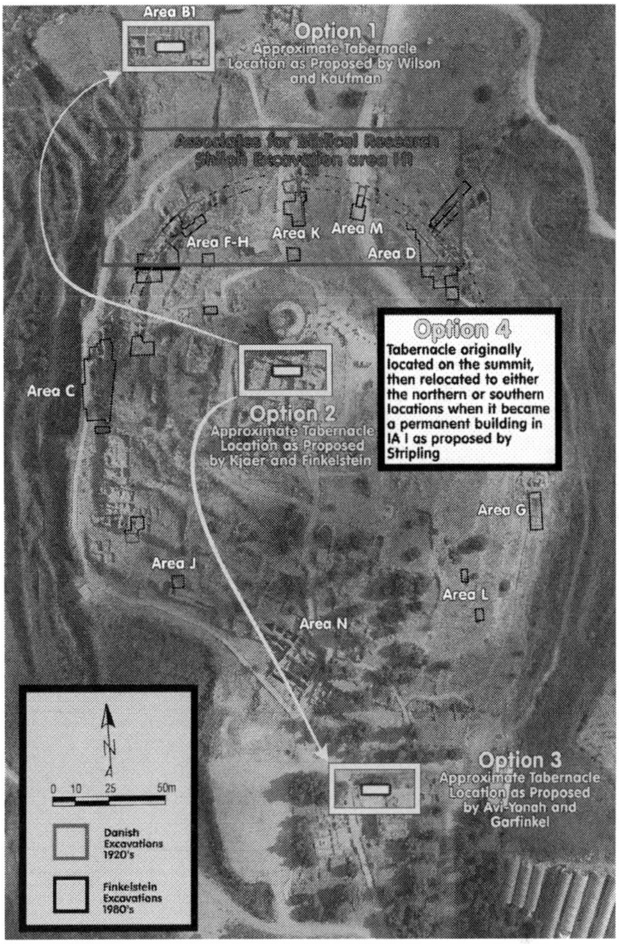

79. Possible locations for the tabernacle at Shiloh in yellow and the 2017 excavations by ABR in pink. The Danish and Finkelstein excavations are marked in red and black respectively.

Used with permission. Photo by Barry Kramer, graphics by Jerry Taylor and Steven Rudd

Option 4: This proposal is proposed by Dr. Scott Stripling and published in his article of 2016. Although the tabernacle was originally set up on the summit, it was moved either north or south of this location when there was a permanent building with a fieldstone fence and door (1 Sam 3:15).[34]

It is still impossible to determine with certainty the exact location of the tabernacle at

[28] Charles W. Wilson, "Shiloh." *PEFSt* 5–6 (1873), 38; Claude R. Conder and Horatio H. Kitchner, *The Survey of Western Palestine Memoirs 2, Sheets VII–XVI, Samaria* (London: Palestine Exploration Fund, 1882), 368.

[29] Asher S. Kaufman, "Fixing the Site of the Tabernacle at Shiloh." *BAR* 14.6 (Nov–Dec 1988), pp. 46–52; J. Price and House, *Zondervan Handbook of Biblical Archaeology*, 115–17.

[30] Israel Finkelstein, "Shiloh Yields Some, But Not All, of Its Secrets: Location of Tabernacle Still Uncertain," *BAR* 12, no. 1 (1986): 22–41.

[31] Gibson, Shimon and Michael Avi-Yonah, "Shiloh." *EJ*, 478.

[32] Garfinkel stated this view at the 23rd Judea and Samaria Studies Conference on June 13, 2013 at Ariel University Center of Samaria, West Bank.

[33] The church, excavated by Evgeny Aharonovic on behalf of the Staff Officer of the Civil Administration of Judea and Samaria, has not been published.

[34] Stripling, "The Israelite Tabernacle at Shiloh," 88–94.

Shiloh what all agree is that this is the site of Shiloh and that the tabernacle was located there.

80. Identification of the archaeological sites around the Temple Mount.
Berthold Werner/Wikimedia Commons/ Labels by D. E. Graves

Jerusalem – Large Stone Structure (David's Palace?)

In 2005, on the eastern slope, east of the Temple Mount in Jerusalem, Eilat Mazar uncovered the remains of a fine monumental palatial structure[35] known as a Large Stone Structure ("Fortress of Zion"), supported by a Stepped Stone Structure (built between the LB2 and IA1.[36] Possibly the Millo of 1 Kgs 9:15–24; 2 Chr 32:4–5. See Figs. 81 and 64),[37] dating to the time of David and Solomon (nineth to eighth cent. BC).[38]

---

[35] Eilat Mazar, "Did I Find King David's Palace?," *BAR* 32, no. 1 (2006): 16–27.

[36] Jane M. Cahill, "Jerusalem at the Time of the United Monarchy. The Archaeological Evidence," in *Jerusalem in Bible and Archaeology: The First Temple Period*, ed. Andrew G. Vaughn and Ann E. Killebrew, SBL Symposium Series 18 (Atlanta, Ga.: SBL, 2003), 32–54, especially 52.

[37] A portion of the Jebusite Wall was partially excavated by MacAliser and Duncan in the 1920's. Robert A. S. MacAlister and J. G. Duncan, *Excavations on the Hill of Ophel, Jerusalem 1923-1925*, PEF Annual 4 (London: Palestine Exploration Fund, 1926); Eilat Mazar, *The Palace of King David Excavations at the Summit of the City of David: Preliminary Report of Seasons 2005-2007* (Jerusalem, Israel: Shoham Academic Research and Publication, 2009), 67; Nadav Na'aman, "The Interchange Between Bible and Archaeology: The Case of David's Palace and the Millo," *BAR* 40, no. 1 (n.d.): 57–61.

[38] Based on the pottery in a sealed locus, uncovered by all three excavations (Kenyon, Shiloh, and E. Mazar), Amihai Mazar confirms that the Stepped Stone Structure and the Large Stone Structure are joined together and were constructed in the Iron Age I. Mazar, "Archaeology and the Biblical Narrative," 41.

81. The City of David Excavations. ① The "Large Stone Structure" that E. Mazar believes is David's Palace. ② The "Stepped Stone Structure" or Millo. ③ The House of Ahiel. This four-roomed house was built into and over the Millo around 650 BC in the days of young Josiah and Jeremiah. The staircase to the left provided access to the home's flat roof. Cahill states that "construction of the monumental stepped rampart in the City of David at the dawn of the Iron Age set the stage for Jerusalem's future development as capital of the united monarchy." Cahill, "Jerusalem at the Time of the United Monarchy," 54.

Archaeological Evidence

Mazar believes this to be the remains of the palace of David, which dates to the early tenth cent. BC,[39] although she has taken strong criticism for her claim.[40] Mazar's evidence consists of the following:[41]

1) The monumental size of the structure compared with other contemporary buildings

[39] Eilat Mazar, "Excavate King David's Palace," *BAR* 23, no. 1 (1997): 50–57, 74; "Did I Find King David's Palace?," 16; *Preliminary Report on The City of David Excavations 2005 at the Visitors Center Area* (Jerusalem, Israel: Shalem Press, 2008); *The Palace of King David Excavations*.

[40] Israel Finkelstein *et al.*, "Has King David's Palace in Jerusalem Been Found?," *Tel Aviv* 34, no. 2 (2007): 142–64; Margreet L. Steiner, "The 'Palace of David' Reconsidered in the Light of Earlier Excavations: Did Eilat Mazar Find King David's Palace? I Would Say Not," *The Bible and Interpretation*, September 2009, http://www.bibleinterp.com /articles/palace_2468.shtml; Todd Bolen, "Identifying King David's Palace: Mazar's Flawed Reading of the Biblical Text," *The Bible and Interpretation*, September 2010, http://www.bibleinterp .com/opeds/ident357928.shtml; Avraham Faust, "Did Eilat Mazar Find David's Palace?," *BAR* 38, no. 5 (2012): 47–52, 70.

[41] Mazar, *The Palace of King David Excavations*, 54–56.

demonstrates that it had a significant royal or public usage.[42]

2) The structure is located outside the Jebusite city walls.

3) The occupational strata of the Large Stone Structure and the Stepped Stone Structure, based on pottery and radiocarbon dating, dates both structures to the Iron 2A (tenth to nineth cent. BC).[43]

4) A fine black-on-red Cypriot juglet (Iron 2A) and several ivory inlays demonstrate a Phoenician connection and luxurious lifestyle.[44]

5) The discovery of several bullae inscriptions also supports the use of the building by royalty. Among the names on some 51 seals (bullae) recovered so far, are the names of two ministers of King Zedekiah's court, the last king of Judah and Hezekiah, King of Judah (see Fig. 99). "Yehuchal [English Jucal] Ben Shelamayahu, son of Shovi" (587/6 BC, discovered in 2010) and "Gedaliah Ben Pashchur" (587/6 BC, discovered in 2008 see Fig. 98) who were two of the four officials who plotted to kill the prophet Jeremiah (Jer 37:3; 38:1). Another bullae with the name, "Gemaryahu ben Shafan," is also mentioned in the Bible as being King Jehoiakim's scribe, towards the end of the First Temple period (Jer 36:10).[45]

6) The discovery in 2012 of the earliest alphabetic text (see Fig. 82) ever identified in Jerusalem also supports the administrative use of the structure.[46] It was discovered on the broken shoulder of a IA2A pithos ceramic jar (tenth cent. BC). While Mazar claims that the letters *m, q, p, h, n,* possibly *l,* and *n* "do not yield any intelligible combination"[47] of known words, Gershon Galil and Doug Petrovich suggest that it read: "[In the firs]t [(regnal) year]: pseudo-[wi]ne from [the garden of ...]".[48] Based on the paleo-Hebrew script (i.e., the formation of the two *yods*)[49] and date, imply that it was produced during "Regnal Year I of an unnamed Israelite king soon after Jerusalem had fallen into Israelite hands,[50] in turn implying that at

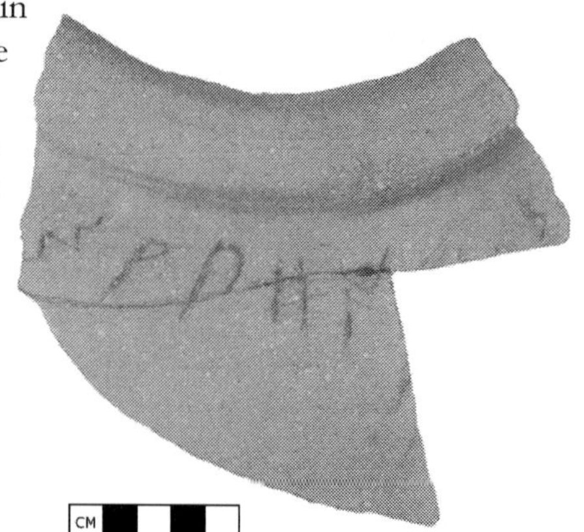

82. The Ophel Pithos Inscription from the "Large Stone Structure" excavation, in Jerusalem, discovered in 2012. The writing dates to the time of King David.

---

[42] A. Mazar points out that the "magnitude and uniqueness of the combined 'Stepped Structure' and the 'Large Stone Structure' are unparalleled anywhere in the Levant between the twelfth and ninth centuries B.C.E." Mazar, "Archaeology and the Biblical Narrative," 45.

[43] Faust suggests that the Large Stone Structure was constructed before the time of David and later adopted as David's fortress or palace. Either way, the structure is still present in the IA 2 and demonstrates that Jerusalem was a prominent city during David's reign. Mazar, "Divided Monarchy," 165; Faust, "Did Eilat Mazar Find David's Palace?," 51–52.

[44] Mazar, "Did I Find King David's Palace?," 16–27.

[45] Yair Shoham, "Hebrew Bullae," in *Excavations at the City of David 1978–1985, Directed by Yigal Shiloh: Inscriptions*, ed. Donald T. Ariel, vol. 6, Qedem 41 (Jerusalem: Hebrew University of Jerusalem, 2000), 33; Lawrence J. Mykytiuk, *Identifying Biblical Persons in Northwest Semitic Inscriptions of 1200-539 B.C.E.* (Atlanta, Ga.: SBL, 2004), 139–147; Mazar, *The Palace of King David Excavations*, 54–56; "Did Eilat Mazar Find David's Palace?," 16–27.

[46] Douglas Petrovich, "The Ophel Pithos Inscription: Its Dating, Language, Translation, And Script," *PEQ* 147, no. 2 (June 2015): 130–45; Original image http://phys.org/news/2013-07-inscription-david-solomon-temple-mount.html.

[47] Ibid.

[48] Petrovich, "The Ophel Pithos Inscription," 133.

[49] Yosef Garfinkel, "Christopher Rollston's Methodology of Caution," *BAR* 38, no. 5 (2012): 58–59; Petrovich, "The Ophel Pithos Inscription," 142.

[50] Mazar speculates that the author was "a descendant of the pre-Israelite inhabitants of Jerusalem (a 'Jebusite'?)." Eilat Mazar, David Ben-Shlomo, and Shmuel Ahituv, "An Inscribed Pithos from the Ophel, Jerusalem," *IEJ* 63, no. 1 (2013): 47. However, Petrovich argues that this was during the reign of Solomon.

least Judah already was governed by a strong, cental authority under monarchical rule."[51]

Jerusalem – Gihon Spring Rock–Cut Pool

Just south of the Gihon Spring in Jerusalem during the Iron 2 period a large *ca.* 15 X 10m pool was backfilled with *ca.* 3 m of fill in order to build a house, allowing the retaining walls to be used for the structure of the house. The fill was wet sifted in 2006, under the direction of Ronny Reich and Eli Shukron, who reported the recovery of late nineth cent. to early eighth cent. BC pottery,[52] 7,392 fish bones, 92% of which were from the Mediterranean Sea, and over 130 seal bullae impressions.[53]

83. The remains of a tenth cent. BC foundation wall that is part of the Large Stone Structure that Israeli archaeologist Eilat Mazar believes is part of David's palace.

Reich concludes that: "The large group of seals and bullae from Jerusalem seem to point to the existence of some administrative or commercial center which existed in the vicinity of the rock-cut "pool" in the late 9th century B.C.E. . . . [they] may be related to the political relations between the kingdom of Judah and the kingdom of Israel in the second half of the 9th century B.C.E."[54]

The high concentration of Mediterranean fish bones found at the site along with document seals also indicates that bureaucratic records were likely being kept of the fish that were being imported into Jerusalem (through "the Gate of Fish." Neh 3:3) in the IA 2, the time of King David.[55]

Amihai Mazar concludes that "they [Bullae seals] indicate the existence of a central administration and organized commerce, as should be expected in an established state."[56] Reich also points out that: "The removal of the icons from the seals is just an additional manifestation of Josianic religious reform, similar to the huge quantities of terra cotta figurines, which are found dumped on the eastern slopes of the city."[57]

---

[51] Ibid.

[52] It is to be noted that the finds were not found *in situ* and that the debris for the fill were taken from locations around the City of David. Therefore, as Singer-Avitz points out "this assemblage should rather be assigned a longer period of time – in both the Iron Age IIA and Iron Age IIB periods, in the 9th as well as the 8th centuries B.C.E." Ronny Reich, Eli Shukron, and Omri Lernau, "Recent Discoveries in the City of David, Jerusalem," *IEJ* 57 (2007): 154–56; Lily Singer-Avitz, "The Date of the Pottery from the Rock-Cut Pool Near the Gihon Spring in the City of David, Jerusalem," *ZDPV* 128 (2012): 10–14; Israel Finkelstein, "The Finds from the Rock-Cut Pool in Jerusalem and the Date of the Siloam Tunnel: An Alternative Interpretation," *Semitica et Classica* 6 (2013): 279–84.

[53] Ronny Reich, Eli Shukron, and Omri Lernau, "The Iron Age II Finds from the Rock-Cut 'Pool' near the Spring in Jerusalem: A Preliminary Report," in *Israel in Transition: From Late Bronze II to Iron IIA: (c. 1250-850 BCE): The Archaeology*, ed. Lester L. Grabbe, vol. 1, The Library of Hebrew Bible/Old Testament Studies 491 (New York: T&T Clark, 2008), 138–43; Ronny Reich and Eli Shukron, "The Excavations at the Gihon Spring and Warren's Shaft System in the City of David," in *Ancient Jerusalem Revealed*, ed. Hillel Geva (Jerusalem, Israel: Israel Exploration Society, 1994), 237–39; "Jerusalem, City of David," in *Hadashot Arkheologiyot: Excavations and Surveys in Israel*, ed. Zvi Ed Gal, 115 (Jerusalem, Israel: Israel Antiquities Authority, 2003), 51–53.

[54] Reich, Shukron, and Lernau, "The Iron Age II Finds from the Rock-Cut 'Pool' near the Spring in Jerusalem: A Preliminary Report," 142.

[55] Ibid., 140–41; Omri Lernau and H. Lernau, "Fish Remains," in *Excavations at the City of David 1978-1985 Directed by Yigal Shiloh*, ed. Donald T. Ariel and Alon De Groot, vol. 3, Qedem 33 (Jerusalem, Israel: Hebrew University, 1992), 131–48.

[56] Mazar, "Divided Monarchy," 165.

[57] Reich, Shukron, and Lernau, "The Iron Age II Finds from the Rock-Cut 'Pool' near the Spring in Jerusalem: A Preliminary Report," 143.

84. The main Tel Lachish gate with the siege ramp leading up to the gate.

Evidence that relates to the United Monarchy is also present outside of the city of Jerusalem.

Lachish – Six Chambered Gate-shrine

The Lachish six chambered gate-shrine was discovered from First Temple period (715 BC) by Sa'ar Ganor in 2016. The northern part of the gate was originally uncovered by the British expedition under the direction of James L. Starkey (1932–1938)[58] and then more work was done by the Tel Aviv University team headed by D. Ussishkin (1973–1994). The current excavation was engaged in completely exposing the gate (see Fig. 84). Finds also included oil lamps, seal impressions on jars and arrowheads from the First Temple period. It revealed a cultic shrine built behind it with some unusual finds. The horns were cut off the altar and a toilet was deposited in the holy of holies as a symbolic desecration (2 Kgs 10:27).

The discovery illustrates King Hezekiah's religious reforms in Judah.[59] Hezekiah "removed the high places and broke the pillars and cut down the Asherah. And he broke in pieces the bronze serpent that Moses had made, for until those days the people of Israel had made offerings to it" (2 Kgs 18:4, see also 18:22; 2 Chr 29:3).

Gath – Tell eṣ-Ṣafi

Aren Maeir of Bar-Ilan University has been excavating the Philistine site of Tell eṣ-Ṣafi (Tel Zafit; Gath, Goliath's hometown; 1 Sam 17:4; 52; 21:9) since 1996 (see Map 1).[60] As Maeir reports: "recent finds from the excavations at Tell es-Safi, Israel (identified as biblical Gath of the Philistines), uncovered a destruction level and a siege [earliest man-made trench] system dated to the late 9th cent. BCE, apparent evidence of the conquest of Gath by Hazael of Aram (2 Kings 12:18)."[61]

The identification of Gath of the Philistines is based on the large size of the city, with IA 1 and 2 Philistine remains, the destruction of dwellings with nineth cent. BC material remains such as pottery, jewelry, weapons and cultic objects, and the dramatic decrease of the size of the

---

[58] The earlier city gate on the North side of the Tall (588/6 BC) was where Starkey discovered the famous Lachish letters found in the guardroom.

[59] https://archaeologynewsnetwork.blogspot.ca/2016/09/first-temple-period-gate-shrine.html#j3IlAwMQPOvtU5gt.97.

[60] Aren M. Maeir, ed., *Tell Es-Safi / Gath I: The 1996 - 2005 Seasons: Part 1: Text*, Ägypten Und Altes Testament 69 (Wiesbaden: Harrassowitz, 2012).

[61] Aren M. Maeir, "The Historical Background and Dating of Amos VI 2: An Archaeological Perspective from Tell Es-Safi/Gath," *Vetus Testamentum* 54, no. 3 (July 1, 2004): 334.

settlement after its destruction in early eighth cent. BC.[62] In 2015 Maeir discovered the Philistine monumental city gate.

The Gath Ostracon

During the 2005 excavation season at Tell eṣ-Ṣafi, an important inscription on a body sherd (3.7 x 6.8 x 0.5 cm) of a ceramic bowl was uncovered below the late nineth cent. BC destruction level dating to the IA 2A period (the time period of Goliath in the Bible).[63] According to Maeir it is the oldest Philistine inscription ever discovered (see Fig. 85).

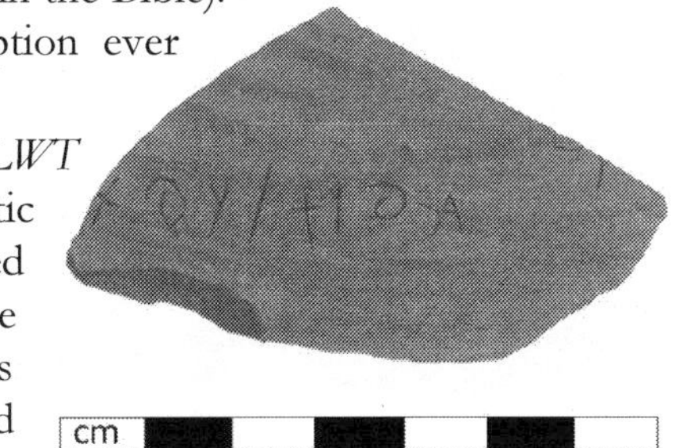

85. Drawing of the Gath (Tell eṣ-Ṣafi) Ostracon with two non-Semitic names *ALWT* and *WLT* written in Semitic "Proto-Canaanaite" script, that are both etymologically similar to the biblical name of Goliath.

The inscription has two non-Semitic names, *ALWT* (Heb. אלות) and *WLT* (Heb. ולת), written in a Semitic "Proto-Canaanite" script. Maeir and others have pointed out that both names are etymologically similar to the non-Semitic name Goliath (Heb. גלית, *Golyat*), who was the well-known Philistine champion from Gath as stated in the Bible (1 Sam 17:4; 52; 21:9).[64] Cross and Stager have challenged Maeir, arguing that his "reading violates method in paleographical typology and is linguistically cavalier,"[65] although Maeir categorically denies the claim.[66]

Maeir does not claim that the two names on the inscription are directly connected to Goliath, nor does he state that this is proof of Goliath's existence. What the inscription on this ostracon does indicate is 1) the Philistines were writing, using the proto-Canaanite (Semitic) alphabet during the nineth cent. BC (IA 2A), the time of David and Goliath, and 2) they were using similar names to Goliath in his hometown during his day.[67] These facts indicate that the biblical story of David and Goliath is completely plausible and supports the arguments that the biblical accounts were written at an early date instead of much later.

Sha'araîm – Khirbet Qeiyafa

Khirbet Qeiyafa (שעריים Sha'araîm "two gates")[68] is located in the Elah Valley on the border

---

[62] Ibid., 321–22; Aren M. Maeir and Carl S. Ehrlich, "Excavating Philistine Gath: Have We Found Goliath's Hometown?," *BAR* 27, no. 6 (2001): 22–31.

[63] Aren M. Maeir *et al.*, "A Late Iron Age I/Early Iron Age II Old Canaanite Inscription from Tell Es-Safi/Gath, Israel: Palaeography, Dating, and Historical-Cultural Significance," *BASOR*, no. 351 (August 1, 2008): 39–71; Aren M. Maeir, "A New Interpretation of the Term `Opalim (עפלים) in Light of Recent Archaeological Finds from Philistia," *JSOT* 32, no. 1 (2007): 23–40; Maeir and Ehrlich, "Excavating Philistine Gath," 22–31; Mariona Vernet Pons, "The Etymology of Goliath in the Light of Carian PN Wljat/Wliat: A New Proposal," *Kadmos* 51 (May 2012): 143–64.

[64] Maeir *et al.*, "A Late Iron Age I/Early Iron Age II Old Canaanite Inscription," 58.

[65] Frank Moore Cross and Lawrence E. Stager, "Cypro-Minoan Inscriptions Found in Ashkelon," *IEJ* 56, no. 2 (January 1, 2006): 151.

[66] Maeir *et al.*, "A Late Iron Age I/Early Iron Age II Old Canaanite Inscription," 39–71.

[67] In 1996 Dothan and Gitin discovered a seventh cent. BC inscription, at the Philistine site of Ekron, that contained the names of two kings, Achish and Padi. Similar names (different individuals) are found in 1 Samuel 21:11; 27:2, where David joins Achish, the king of Gath in his flight from Saul. Padi is mentioned on the Taylor Prism (701 BC). This demonstrates a continuity of Philistine names in their culture. Seymour Gitin, Trude Dothan, and Joseph Naveh, "A Royal Dedicatory Inscription from Ekron," *IEJ* 47, no. 1/2 (January 1, 1997): 1–16.

[68] There is debate over whether it is connected with Naṭa'im (the city of the kings' potters, 1 Chr 4:23) or Sha'araîm ("two gates"; Josh 15:36; 1 Sam 17:52), although this debate does not alter the arguments for it being a Judahite fortress. Yosef Garfinkel

86. Aerial photograph of the Judahite fortress of Khirbet Qeiyafa.
Photo by Avram Graicer / Wikimedia Commons

between Judah and Philistia, about 17 miles (27 km) southwest of Jerusalem (see Map 1 and Fig. 86). Although it was uncovered initially in the nineteenth cent. by Victor Guerin, in 2005 Iron Age pottery was identified from a surface survey carried out by Saar Ganor. In 2007 Yosef Garfinkel and Saar Ganor began excavations there for the Hebrew University of Jerusalem.[69] Then, according to Hawkins and Buchanan, "by 2008, the site had become internationally known because of its substantial fortifications and occupational evidence dating to the late eleventh or early tenth century BCE. This made it the only known fortified city in the territory of Judah dating to the time of David."[70] In addition it contains only one period of occupation, the Iron Age built on bedrock which assists in the analysis of the finds.

Archaeological Evidence

The archaeological evidence for the urbanization of Khirbet Qeiyafa as a Judahite fortress on the border with Philistia is presented by the director of the excavation, Yosef Garfinkel, in a rebuttal to Philip Davies,[71] and is outlined as follows:

1. Its strategic location controlled the entrance to the Elah Valley, a known trade and transportation route between Jerusalem and Hebron. This region was never occupied by the Philistines.[72]

2. The new 2.3 hectares settlement is built on bedrock and was important in the late eleventh to early tenth cent. BC.

3. Its megalithic ashlars (4–8 ton stones) and 4 m wide casemate wall fortification construction is unknown in LBA Philistine or Canaanite cities, where they used mudbrick.[73] Only the five largest Philistine cities were fortified.

4. Its two uniquely identical four-chambered gates, on the west and south side of the city, indicate that it was strongly fortified and it is not a typical Philistine construction.[74]

---

and Saar Ganor, "Khirbet Qeiyafa: Shaaraim," *The Journal of Hebrew Scriptures* 8, no. 22 (2010): 2–10; Levin, "The Identification of Khirbet Qeiyafa," 73–86.

[69] For a full discussion, see Yosef Garfinkel and Saar Ganor, "Site Location and Setting and History of Research," in *Khirbet Qeiyafa: Excavation Report 2007-2008*, ed. Yosef Garfinkel and Saar Ganor, vol. 1 (Jerusalem, Israel: Israel Exploration Society, 2010), 28–32; Yigal Levin, "The Identification of Khirbet Qeiyafa: A New Suggestion," *BASOR*, no. 367 (2012): 73–86.

[70] Ralph K. Hawkins and Shane Buchanan, "The Khirbet Qeiyafa Inscription and 11th-10th Century BCE Israel," *Stone-Campbell Journal* 14, no. 2 (2011): 221.

[71] Yosef Garfinkel, "A Minimalist Disputes His Demise: A Response to Philip Davies," *Bible History Daily: Biblical Archaeology Society*, June 13, 2012, http://www.biblicalarchaeology.org/uncategorized/a-minimalist-disputes-his-demise-a-response-to-philip-davies/.

[72] Galil, "The Hebrew Inscription from Khirbet Qeiyafa/Neta'im," 194.

[73] Michael G. Hasel, "New Excavations at Khirbet Qeiyafa and the Early History of Judah," in *Do Historical Matters Matter to Faith?: A Critical Appraisal of Modern and Postmodern Approaches to Scripture*, ed. James K. Hoffmeier and Graham A. Magary (Wheaton, IL: Crossway Books, 2012), 488.

[74] Levin, "The Identification of Khirbet Qeiyafa," 75; Garfinkel, "Minimalist Disputes His Demise."

These first four points indicate that Khirbet Qeiyafa was built specifically as a fortress during the rise of the Kingdom of Judah and not as a small nomad community, as the minimalists suggest.[75]

5. Its tenth cent. BC urban planning that consisted of dwellings abutting the casemate city walls, is identical to other IA2 Judahite cities of Tell en-Nasbeh, Beth-shemesh, Tell Beit Mirsim, and Beersheva.[76] The northern Israelite sites of Hazor and Gezer have freestanding walls with no dwellings abutting the city walls.

87. Cultic Shrine from Khirbet Qeiyafa with features similar to the later Solomonic Temple. Courtesy of Casey Olson. Used by permission

6. The simple red-slip burnished pottery was locally-made with fingerprint stamped handles (some 520), and is unique to the region.

7. Their diet and food preparation, that indicated "thousands of animal bones were found at the site, including goats, sheep and cattle. No pig bones were discovered. Almost every house contained a baking tray."[77] While Israelites did not normally consume pigs, pigs were consumed as part of the diet at nearby Philistine Gath.[78]

8. A 70-letter inscription on an ostracon found at Khirbet Qeiyafa, that according to epigraphist Haggai Misgav, was written in ancient Hebrew[79] (see Fig. 88 and details below).

9. The presence of cultic ritual paraphernalia and shrines such as "stone altars, a basalt altar, pottery libation vessels, a bench, a drainage installation for liquids that joined a channel in the next structure, a seal and a scarab. . . . [but] no human or animal figurines."[80] One shrine contained architectural features similar to the later Solomonic Temple (see Fig. 87).

10. The late eleventh and early tenth cent. BC (1051 to 925 BC) dating of the site was based

[75] James W. Flanagan, "Chiefs in Israel," *JSOT* 20 (1981): 47–73; Frank S. Frick, *The Formation of the State in Ancient Israel: A Survey of Models and Theories*, Social World of Biblical Antiquity Series 4 (Sheffield: Sheffield Academic, 1985); Gosta W. Ahlstrom, *The History of Ancient Palestine*, ed. Diana Edelman (Minneapolis, MN: Augsburg Fortress, 1993), 436.

[76] Mazar, "Archaeology and the Biblical Narrative," 49; Shiloh, "The Four-Room House: Its Situation and Function in the Israelite City," 180–90; "Elements in the Development of Town Planning in the Israelite City," *IEJ* 28 (1978): 36–51; Ze'ev Herzog, *Archaeology of the City: Urban Planning in Ancient Israel and Its Social Implications* (Tel Aviv: Tel Aviv University, Institute of Archaeology, 1997).

[77] The consumption of pigs at Israelite sites is known to occur but these are sites that have been destroyed by the Assyrians and Babylonians. The practice is indicative of a moral lapse as addressed by the prophets Isaiah and Jeremiah. Ron Kehati, "The Faunal Assemblage," in *Khirbet Qeiyafa: Excavation Report 2007-2008*, ed. Yosef Garfinkel and Saar Ganor, vol. 1 (Jerusalem, Israel: Israel Exploration Society, 2010), 201–98.

[78] Justin S. E. Lev-Tov, "Pigs, Philistines, and the Ancient Animal Economy of Ekron from Late Bronze to Iron Age II" (Ph.D. diss., University of Tennessee, 2000); Brian Hesse and Paula Wapnish, "Can Pig Remains Be Used for Ethnic Diagnosis in the Ancient Near East?," in *The Archaeology of Israel: Constructing the Past, Interpreting the Present*, ed. Neil Asher Silberman and David B. Small, JSOTSup 237 (Sheffield: T&T Clark, 1997), 238–70.

[79] Maintained by Émile Puech, Gershon Galil, Alan Millard, Haggai Misgav, Yosef Garfunkel, and Saar Ganor, but refuted by, the minimalists, Israel Finkelstein, Alexander Fantalkin, and Philip Davies.

[80] Garfinkel, "Minimalist Disputes His Demise."

on the pottery (*ca.* 20,000 potsherds), ostracon script, and the carbon-14 readings of olive pits.[81]

11. The site was suddenly destroyed by an unknown enemy and abandoned until the late Persian period.[82]

All of these arguments support Garfinkel's belief that this was a Judahite fortress on the Philistine border.

Khirbet Qeiyafa Ostracon

The Khirbet Qeiyafa ostracon, discovered in 2008, is a five line inscription written in faded ink on a piece of pottery (see Fig. 88). The ostracon was found *in situ* on the floor of a house west of the north gate and according to Hasel, the assistant director of the excavation, based on pottery and carbon-14 dating it "is securely dated to the early tenth century BC"[83] (*ca.* 1000 BC).

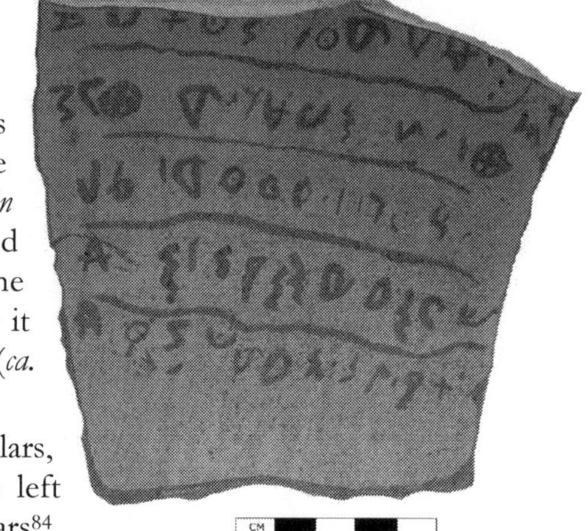

88. Colorized drawing of the Khirbet Qeiyafa Ostracon from the infrared photo of the ostracon by Clara Amit, Israel Antiquities Authority. It is believed to contain the names of David and Goliath (ca. 16.5 x 15 cm).

It is interpreted differently by various scholars, debating whether it should be read from right to left (Hebrew) or left to right (non-Semitic). Most scholars[84] agree with Haggai Misgav, who first published the inscription in Hebrew in 2009, that the language of the ostracon is Hebrew (proto-Canaanite),[85] while the alphabetic script is either Canaanite, Moabite, Phoenician, or Hebrew. Misgav claims that it is the earliest Hebrew inscription to date.[86] Misgav proposed that:

> The inscription begins with several words of command which may be judicial or ethical in content. . . . The end of the inscription contains words which may relate to the area of politics or government. It is difficult to extract more meaning from this text at the present stage. We can determine, however, that the text has continuity of meaning, and is not merely a list of unconnected words.[87]

Garfinkel based his identification on a three-letter verb from the inscription meaning "to do," a word, he argues, existed only in Hebrew.[88] Professor Aren Maeir, of Bar-Ilan University reported in the news that it is "one of the most important texts, without a doubt, in the corpus of Hebrew inscriptions."[89] However, its place as being the oldest Hebrew inscription is much debated.[90]

In 2009, Gershon Galil provided another translation of the ostracon which reads as:

---

[81] Yosef Garfinkel and Saar Ganor, eds., *Khirbet Qeiyafa: Excavation Report 2007-2008*, vol. 1 (Jerusalem, Israel: Israel Exploration Society, 2010), 1–14; Hershel Shanks, "Newly Discovered: A Fortified City from King David's Time Answers—and Questions—at Khirbet Qeiyafa," *BAR* 35, no. 1 (2009): 40.

[82] Garfinkel and Ganor, *Khirbet Qeiyafa*, 1:4.

[83] Hasel, "New Excavations at Khirbet Qeiyafa," 494.

[84] *Contra* Finkelstein and Fantalkin, "Khirbet Qeiyafa," 38–63.

[85] Misgav, Garfinkel, and Ganor, "The Ostracon," 245–46.

[86] Haggai Misgav, Yosef Garfinkel, and Saar Ganor, "The Khirbet Qeiyafa Ostracon," in *New Studies in the Archaeology of Jerusalem and Its Region*, ed. David Amit, Gary D. Stiebel, and Orit Peleg-Barkat, vol. 3 (Jerusalem, Israel: Israel Antiquities Authority, 2009), 111–23; "The Ostracon," 255.

[87] Misgav, Garfinkel, and Ganor, "The Ostracon," 255, 256.

[88] Ibid., 254.

[89] "'Oldest Hebrew Script' Is Found," *BBC*, October 30, 2008, sec. Middle East, 1, http://news.bbc.co.uk/2/hi/middle_east/7700037.stm; Shanks, "Oldest Hebrew Inscription Discovered," 1.

[90] Christopher A. Rollston, "What's the Oldest Hebrew Inscription?," *BAR* 38, no. 3 (June 2012): 32–40, 66–68.

1. Do not do [it], but worship [... Lord].
2. Judge the slave and the widow / judge the orph[an]
3. and the stranger. Plead for the infant / plead for the poor and
4. the widow. Avenge (the pauper's vengeance) at the king's hands.
5. Protect the needy and the slave / suppo[rt] the stranger.[91]

His translation was strongly criticized on the basis that several of the letters are either faded or missing from the ostracon.[92] Also, Hawkins and Buchanan report that the Khirbet Qeiyafa Expedition have charged Galil with unethical practices, claiming that some of his translations belong to other scholars and point out that: "Several words that reinforce Galil's argument—including אביון (*'bywn*), 'needy,' 'poor'; יתום (*ytwm*), 'orphan'; and אמנלה (*'blmnh*), 'widow'—are complete reconstructions and do not appear as such in the legible parts of the ostracon."[93]

Aaron Demsky read the text vertically, from top to bottom, and suggested that the tablet was a scribal writing exercise with a list of words.[94]

The renown epigraphist, Émile Puech, from the Sorbonne University in Paris, read the inscription from left to right, and rejected Demsky's theory.[95] Puech translated it as an administration text as follows:

1. Do not oppress, and serve God: I: . . . despoiled him/her.
2. The judge and the widow wept; he had the power
3. over the resident alien and the child, he eliminated them together.
4. The men and the chiefs/officers had established a king.
5. He marked 60 [?] servants among the communities/habitations/generations. [96]

Brian Edric Colless, a New Zealand Hebrew Scholar from Massey University, has proposed the following translation of the text, where he identified both Goliath and David in the script.[97] Dr. Colless' translation reads:

1. The cursing (*'lt*) of the Anak (giant) (*'nq*) against (*b*) the servant (*'bd*) of God (*'l*).
2. The servant of God (*'bd 'l*) has judged (*shpt.*) the (dead) man (*mt*) | | Yah has judged (*shpt. YH*)
3. Goliath (*glyt*) | [is dead (*mt*)] | David (*dwd*) is the master (*b'l*), he has prevailed (or: evermore) (*ns.h.*).
4. I rise up (*'qm*) and (*w*) together (*yh.d*) we raise up (*nrm*) a/the king (*mlk*).
5. I raise up (*'rm*) the people (*'m*) of my servant (*'bdy*) for his righteousness (*ls.dqtw*).[98]

Colless admits that his translation work is an ongoing project and deciphering the obscure and faded letters is difficult.

What is clear is that the scholarly epigraphers are struggling to determine the precise language and translation of the ancient script. Perhaps Millard's opinion is the safest at this

---

[91] Galil, "The Hebrew Inscription from Khirbet Qeiyafa/Neta'im," 196.

[92] The ostracon has been scanned with a sophiticated imaging system that has highlighted the faded letters. Sony George et al., "Spectral Image Analysis and Visualisation of the Khirbet Qeiyafa Ostracon," in *Image and Signal Processing: 6th International Conference, ICISP 2014, Cherbourg, France, June 30 - July 2, 2014 ; Proceedings*, ed. Abderrahim Elmoataz et al., Lecture Notes in Computer Science Image Processing, Computer Vision, Pattern Recognition 8509 (Cham: Springer, 2014), 272–279..

[93] See "Open Letter to Prof. Gershon Galil, Haifa University," at http://qeiyafa.huji.ac.il/galil.asp. Hawkins and Buchanan, "The Khirbet Qeiyafa Inscription and 11th-10th Century BCE Israel," 223.

[94] Millard suggests that the inscription might be a list of words in Canaanite and Hebrew. Demsky, "An Iron Age IIA Alphabetic Writing Exercise from Khirbet Qeiyafa," 186; Alan R. Millard, "The Ostracon from the Days of David Found at Khirbet Qeiyafa," *TynBul* 62, no. 1 (2011): 11.

[95] Émile Puech, "L'ostracon de Khirbet Qeyafa et Les Débuts de La Royauté En Israël," *RB* 17 (2010): 162.

[96] 1. N'opprime pas, et sers Di'eu'. : | : Le/la spoliait 2. le juge et la veuve pleurait: il avait pouvoir 3. sur l'étranger résident et sur l'enfant, il les supprimait ensemble. 4. Les hommes et les chefs/officiers ont établit un roi. 5. Il a marqué soixante serviteurs parmi les communautés / habitations / générations. Gerard Leval, "Ancient Inscription Refers to Birth of Israelite Monarchy," *BAR* 38, no. 3 (June 2012): 41; Puech, "L'ostracon de Khirbet Qeyafa et Les Débuts de La Royauté En Israël," 162–84.

[97] Brian Edric Colless, "The Lost Link: The Alphabet in the Hands of the Early Israelites," *ASOR Blog*, 2013, http://asorblog.org/the-lost-link-the-alphabet-in-the-hands-of-the-early-israelites.

[98] Brian Edric Colless, "Interpreting the Qeiyafa Ostracon," *Collesseum*, 2013, https://sites.google.com/site/collesseum/qeiyafa-ostracon-1.

point:

> The Khirbet Qeiyafa ostracon reveals nothing directly about the kingdom of David and Solomon! Since there is no proof the text is written in Hebrew rather than Canaanite, we cannot say it is an Israelite product. . . . Despite the negative attitudes some people take, I see no good reason to doubt the existence of a kingdom ruled by David from Jerusalem and happily associate the Khirbet Qeiyafa ostracon with that time, without supposing it tells us more than that someone wrote something in a local language on a potsherd in a small town in the countryside, or sent it to one. If someone could do that, there is good reason to believe others could write more and more extensively on perishable surfaces in larger places, even in Jerusalem.[99]

While Kathleen Kenyon stated (1987) that "no extra-Biblical inscription, either from Palestine or from a neighbouring country, has yet been found to contain a reference to them (David and Solomon),"[100] if Garfinkel's assessment of the Khirbet Qeiyafa ostracon is accurate, then this supports the view that Israelites, at the time of David, were able to record their own written history.[101]

89. Restored Esh-Baal inscription, Khirbet Qeiyafa. Photo by Casey Oldon. Israel Museum, Jerusalem

Esh-baal Inscription

In 2012 another inscription was discovered at Khirbet Qeiyafa by Yosef Garfinkel and Saar Ganor of biblical significance. The well crafted inscription on the shoulder of a storage Jar contains the Esh-baal, son of Beda, the same as that of King Saul's son (see Fig. 89; 1 Chr 8:33; 9:39; cf. 2 Sam 2:8–15; 3:7). Enough of the storage jar was recovered to painstakingly piece the amphora together indicating that it was a tenth cent. BC inscription, the time of the Davidic Kingdom. This is only one of four inscriptions that list the names from the early kingdom of Judah.[102]

Tel Reḥōv and Apiculture

Tel Reḥōv is a large site (10.2 hectares or 25.2 acres) situated in the Beth-shean Valley 116 m (380.6 ft) below sea level (see Map 5). While several cities of this name are mentioned in the OT (western Galilee, Josh 19:28–30; Syria, 2 Sam 10:6, 8), this location in the Beth-shean Valley is not mentioned in the Bible. However, it is mentioned in Egyptian sources, and it is listed as one of Pharaoh Shoshenq I's (biblical Shishak) conquered cities (*ca.* 925 BC).[103] Tēl Reḥōv was excavated under the direction of Amihai Mazar, for the Hebrew University, between 1997 and

[99] Millard, "Ostracon from the Days of David," 12, 13.

[100] Kathleen Kenyon, *The Bible and Recent Archaeology*, ed. Peter R. S. Moorey, Rev Sub (Louisville, KY: Westminster/Knox, 1987), 85.

[101] Rollston, "Khirbet Qeiyafa Ostracon."

[102] Yosef Garfinkel et al., "The ʾIšbaʿal Inscription from Khirbet Qeiyafa," *BASOR* 373 (2015): 217–33. http://qeiyafa.huji.ac.il/eshbaal.asp.

[103] Amihai Mazar, "Rehov, Tel," in *NEAEHL*, ed. Ephraim Stern, Ayelet Levinson-Gilboa, and Joseph Aviram, vol. 5 (Jerusalem: The Israel Exploration Society, 2008), 2013.

90. One of the beehives from the Tel Rehov apiary.
Eretz Israel exhibition. Photo courtesy of Ferrell Jenkins

2011.[104]

The IA 2A strata of the excavation demonstrated a thriving, well ordered, unfortified city with small piazzas, industrial areas and sacred enclosures.[105] Mazar reports on the history of the site:

> From all the evidence, it seems clear that during the tenth century B.C.E., the time of the United Monarchy, Rehov was a well-planned, thriving city of about 25 acres, with a material culture that resembles other sites throughout the country that are dated to the tenth century B.C.E., according to the traditional chronology. Sometime in the late tenth century, the city was destroyed, either by an enemy (Pharaoh Shishak?) or by nature (earthquake?). Yet it was soon rebuilt on a similar plan, only to be destroyed by violent fire, probably after King Ahab's reign in the mid-ninth century B.C.E. Following this destruction, the lower city was abandoned.[106]

Inscriptions

Some ten inscriptions have been recovered from the IA 2A strata at the site. One in particular, Mazar reports, from "inside the [sacred] room a red ink inscription, possibly mentioning the name 'Elisha,' [ʿlšʿ] was found."[107]

Apiary

An unusual[108] find came to light for Mazar and Panitz-Cohen, at Tēl Reḥōv in 2005, when they uncovered a large commercial apiary in Area C, stratum V, estimated to have originally contained over 100–200 beehives from "the United Monarchy and/or during the initial period of the Northern Kingdom of Israel, prior to the Omride Dynasty."[109] Inscriptional evidence found on

---

[104] Amihai Mazar, "Rehob," in *The Oxford Encyclopedia of the Bible and Archaeology*, ed. Daniel M Master et al. (New York: Oxford University Press, 2013), 223; "The 1997-1998 Excavations at Tel Rehov: Preliminary Report," *IEJ* 49 (1999): 1–42; "Tel Rehov, 1998-2001," *Excavations and Surveys in Israel* 114 (2002): 38–40.

[105] Mazar, "Rehob," 223.

[106] Amihai Mazar and John Camp, "Will Tel Rehov Save the United Monarchy?," *BAR* 26, no. 2 (2000): 51.

[107] Mazar, "Rehob," 224, 226; Amihai Mazar and Shmuel Ahituv, "The Inscriptions from Tel Re□ov and Their Contribution to Study of Script and Writing during the Iron Age IIA," in *"See, I Will Bring a Scroll Recounting What Befell Me" (Ps 40:8): Epigraphy and Daily Life from the Bible to the Talmud. Dedicated to the Memory of Professor Hanan Eshel*, ed. Esther Eshel and Yigal Levin, Journal of Ancient Judaism. Supplements 12 (Göttingen: Vandehoeck & Rupprecht, 2013), 39–68.

[108] As Mazar et al. declared they are: "the only beehives excavated so far in the ancient Near East." Amihai Mazar *et al.*, "The Iron Age Beehives at Tel Rehov in the Jordan Valley: Archaeological and Analytical Aspect," *Antiquity* 82 (2008): 636.

[109] Amihai Mazar and Nava Panitz-Cohen, "It Is the Land of Honey: Beekeeping in Iron Age IIA Tel Rehov - Culture, Cult and Economy," *NEA* 70, no. 4 (2007): 218; Mazar *et al.*, "Iron Age Beehives at Tel Rehov," 629–39.

pottery near the apiary revealed possible biblical connections. Mazar described that:

> Among the finds in the area of the apiary was a pottery jar carrying the inscription ***lnmš*** ("belonging to Nimshi"). This name was found also in an inscription from stratum IV and in nearby Tel 'Amal. This name appears in the Bible as that of Jehu's father and once as the name of his grandfather, perhaps indicating a family name [1 Kgs 19:16; 2 Kgs 9:2, 14, 20; 2 Chr 22:7]. It may be surmised that this is the same family mentioned in the three inscriptions and that the Nimshi family was an important one centered at Tel Rehob and its vicinity. Perhaps it was even influential enough to construct such an apiary inside the crowded city.[110]

Mazar and Panitz-Cohen further elaborated on the administrative and economic implications for the Israelite Monarchy debate and reasoned that:

> If there indeed were at least one hundred active hives, then we can reconstruct the presence of over one million bees. It seems most likely that only a strong central authority could have established and conducted such a well-planned industrial apiary in the center of the densely settled town. This has implications for our understanding of the social and economic urban system during the period of the Israelite Monarchy and the ability of the central authority to carry out broad-scale economic and administrative policies such as would have been required to set up and maintain this apiary.[111]

While the apiary and inscriptions at Tēl Reḥōv do not prove there was a strong centralized government in Jerusalem, they do support the picture of the Israelite Monarchy presented in the Old Testament.

Ziklag – Tel Zayit Abecedary

During the 2005 season of excavations at Tel Zayit (Libnah, Josh 10:32, 2 Kgs 19:8 or Ziklag, 1 Sam 27:6),[112] in the lowlands of Judah (see Map 1), archaeologists uncovered one of the earliest alphabets (22 letters), called an abecedary, in the tenth cent. BC destruction layer.[113] Tappy *et al.*, state that: "The Tel Zayit Abecedary represents the linear alphebetic script of central and southern Canaan at the beginning of the first millennium B. C. E., a transitional script that developed from the Phoenician tradition of the early Iron Age and anticipated the distinctive features of the mature Hebrew national script."[114]

The implications of the discovery of several abecedaries are well summarized by Rendsburg:

> If a lowly outpost in the Judaean Shephelah [Khirbet Qeiyafa] attests to writing (limited or otherwise) during the period of David and Solomon, then one may assume, with all due caution, that the capital city of Jerusalem would have possessed, ***qal wa-homer***, scribes and priests linked to palace and temple capable of producing (significant) literary and administrative texts. . . . taken together, the Tel Zayit abecedary, the Khirbet Qeiyafa inscription [see Fig. 88], and the Gezer calendar (also from the 10th century [see Fig. 24]) demonstrate that writing was well-established in 10th-century Israel.[115]

Not only has this and other abecedaries, such as the Izbet Sartah Abecedary (1200–1000 BC; see Fig 91),[116] had an important role to play in the evidence for writing in this early period, but it has also been suggested that the reversal of the later (Hebrew) order of the letters *ayin* (o) and *pe* (p) in the early abecedaries may help in providing an early date for the composition of the

---

110 Mazar, "Rehob," 225.

111 Mazar and Panitz-Cohen, "It Is the Land of Honey," 211–12.

112 It has been identified with the biblical cities of Libnah (Joshua 10:32, 2 Kings 19:8) or Ziklag (1 Samuel 27:6).

113 Ron E. Tappy *et al.*, "An Abecedary of the Mid-Tenth Century B.C.E. from the Judaean Shephelah," *BASOR* 344 (2006): 5–46; Ron E. Tappy and P. Kyle McCarter Jr., eds., *Literate Culture and Tenth-Century Canaan: The Tel Zayit Abecedary in Context* (Winona Lake, IN: Eisenbrauns, 2008).

114 Tappy *et al.*, "Abecedary of the Mid-Tenth Century B.C.E.," 5.

115 Rendsburg, "Review of Literate Culture and Tenth-Century Canaan," 91.

116 Moshe Kochavi, "An Ostracon of the Period of the Judges from 'Izbet Sartah," *Tel Aviv* 4 (1977): 1–13; Joseph Naveh, "Some Considerations on the Ostracon from 'Izbet Sartah," *IEJ* 28, no. 1/2 (1978): 31–35.

acrostic Psalms, which list this unusual early *pe/ayin* order in the alphabet, possibly used until the end of the First Temple Period (*ca.* 586 BC).[117]

91. Colorized drawing of Izbet Sartah Abecedary (1200–1000 BC). The Proto-Canaanite alphabet read from left to right. It was discovered in 1976 at what is believed to be the biblical city of Ebenezer (1 Sam 4). This demonstrates writing during the period of the Judges.

The sheer volume and variety of material on which inscriptions are found from this early period, including several abecedary inscriptions listing the alphabet, demonstrate that reading and writing was present during the period of the Israelite monarchy. Hess points out that this also "argues against the view that only priests, government officials, and professional scribes could read or write,"[118] although Rollston and Byrne are more cautious in their conclusions about what the Tel Zayit Abecedary can tell us about the extent of literacy in ancient Israel. Rollston states that "this abecedary serves as further evidence demonstrating that there was indeed *some* literacy in this region during this chronological horizon,"[119] but criticizes Hess for making more of the evidence than is warranted. Rollston argues that it is: "not methodologically tenable to attempt to draw conclusions about the rough percentage of people who were literate, . . . nor can conclusions be drawn about the non-elite social status of writers and readers at Zayit."[120]

But as this abecedary and others indicate, there is certainly no doubt that some were semiliterate and literate during the Israelite monarchy. As Rendsburg concludes: "Taken together, the Tel Zayit abecedary, the Khirbet Qeiyafa inscription, and the Gezer calendar (also from the 10th century [see Fig. 24]) demonstrate that writing was well-established in 10th-century Israel [time of David and Solomon] certainly sufficiently so for some or many of the works later incorporated into the Hebrew Bible to have been composed at this time."[121]

---

117 Michell First, "Can Archaeology Help Date the Psalms?," *BAR* 38, no. 4 (2012): n.p.

118 Richard S. Hess, "Writing about Writing: Abecedaries and Evidence for Literacy in Ancient Israel," *VT* 56, no. 3 (2006): 345 n.10; "Literacy in Iron Age Israel," in *Windows into Old Testament History: Evidence, Argument, and the Crisis of Biblical Israel*, ed. V. Philips Long, David W. Baker, and Gordon J. Wenham (Grand Rapids, Mich: Eerdmans, 2002), 82–102.

119 Christopher A. Rollston, "The Phoenician Script of the Tel Zayit Abecedary and Putative Evidence for Israelite Literacy," in *Literate Culture and Tenth-Century Canaan: The Tel Zayit Abecedary in Context*, ed. Ron E. Tappy and P. Kyle McCarter Jr. (Winona Lake, IN: Eisenbrauns, 2008), 63; Ryan Byrne, "The Refuge of Scribalism in Iron I Palestine," *BASOR* 345 (2007): 1–31; Seth L. Sanders, "Writing and Early Iron Age Israel: Before National Scripts, beyond Nations and States," in *Literate Culture and Tenth-Century Canaan: The Tel Zayit Abecedary in Context*, ed. Ron E. Tappy and P. Kyle McCarter Jr. (Winona Lake, IN: Eisenbrauns, 2008), 97–112.

120 Rollston, "The Phoenician Script of the Tel Zayit Abecedary," 63.

121 Rendsburg, "Review of Literate Culture and Tenth-Century Canaan," 91.

Solomonic Site – Tall el-Ḥammâm

92. Iron age oil lamp from the time of Solomon (*ca.* 750 BC). The fuel usually comprised olive oil or fish oil to provide light for homes.

Excavations at Tall el-Ḥammâm (2005–present) on the eastern side of the Jordan Valley reveal a major IA 2 city (1000–900 BC; see Map 1). It is believed that this was abandoned by the Ammonites (1 Kgs 9:20; 2 Chr 8:7) and is possibly one of Solomon's administrative centers. An IA 2 four-roomed house, characteristic of the Israelites,[122] was excavated by the author in 2004 (see Sodom and Gomorrah above and Fig. 14, 15, 16, 17 and 56). Collins, the excavation director, describes the IA city as:

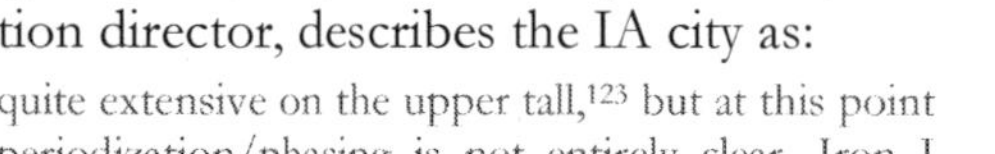

> quite extensive on the upper tall,[123] but at this point periodization/phasing is not entirely clear. Iron I pottery is infrequent at this point, but present (such as the IA1b pilgrim flask found in Field UB). The IA2b–c monumental gateway in Field UB[124] has an earlier phase dating to IA2a ([1000–900 BC] perhaps late IA1b), with the terminal phase dating to IA2c, perhaps IA3. The principal Iron Age city at Tall el-Hammam seems to have been built during IA2a–b. IA3 (Persian Period [539–332 BC]) sherds are present-but-infrequent at this point.[125]

This supports the Bible's description of the significant expansion in the territory of Solomon's kingdom.

Edomite Copper Mines

While the Bible does not mention King Solomon's mines,[126] it does speak of his great wealth and large quantities of precious metals (2 Chr 9:13–28). The question of where all his wealth came from, while partly answered in the gifts of the Queen of Sheba (2 Chr 9:9) and gold from Ophir (2 Chr 8:17–18; 9:10), has led some archaeologists to speculate that the Edomite copper industry, in southern Jordan, was controlled by King David and his son King Solomon. Nelson Glueck claimed in the 1930's that he had found the famed mines in Faynan/Edom.[127] However, minimalists have argued that Edom was a fringe settlement of nomads and did not achieve nationhood until the seventh cent. BC with the help of the Assyrians.[128] Thus, according to minimalists, such as Finkelstein and Silberman, the conflict with Israel and the Edomites, as depicted in the Bible (1 Sam 14:47; 2 Sam 8:13–15; 1 Kgs 11:14), is purely fictional. Their views about Edom also extend to the identity of Israel and Judah, whom they claim did not have a fighting army or a king ruling over them.[129]

Most archeologists had accepted the challenge of Glueck's dating of the Edomite mines, and most agreed that they were under Egyptian/Assyrian control in the 12th–11th cent. BC and

---

[122] Shiloh, "The Four-Room House: Its Situation and Function in the Israelite City," 180–90; Faust, "The Rural Community in Ancient Israel during Iron Age II," 17–39; Herr and Clark, "Excavating the Tribe of Reuben: A Four Room House Provides a Clue to Where the Oldest Israelite Tribe Settled," 36–47, 64–66; Faust and Bunimovitz, "The Four Room House," 29–30.

[123] The upper tall IA occupation covers approximately 12 ha. Collins *et al.*, "Tall el-Hammam, Season Eight, 2013," 4 n.6.

[124] The extensive IA 2 site is surrounded by a 3+m thick fortification casemate wall. Ibid., 5.

[125] Ibid., 13.

[126] King Solomon's mines was made legendary by the popular nineteenth cent. book by the same title by Sir H. Rider Haggard.

[127] Nelson Glueck, *The Other Side of the Jordan* (New Haven, CT: ASOR, 1970), 50–88; "On the Trail of King Solomon's Mines," *National Geographic* 85, no. 2 (1944): 233–56.

[128] Finkelstein and Silberman, *The Bible Unearthed*, 68.

[129] Ibid.

not under Solomon's rule.[130] However, new evidence and dating of the copper mines located approximately 56 km (35 miles) south of the Dead Sea in Edomite territory have challenged this view and place the operation of the mines in the twelvth to nineth cent. BC, supporting the possibility that the mines were under King Solomon's control.[131]

Khirbet en-Nahas

In 2002, Thomas Levy and Mohammad Najjar conducted an excavation in the region south of the Dead Sea called Khirbet en-Nahas (see Map 2 and 4), at what is believed to be the largest copper mine (*ca.* 25 acres) dating to the IA (1200–586 BC).[132] Their work has produced supporting evidence that Edom was a "complex society"[133] at the beginning of the IA, capable of doing battle with David (2 Sam 8), and not simply a nomadic pastoral group of Bedouin as had been suggested in the past.[134] Levy and Najjar conclude that: "the Biblical references to the Edomites, especially their conflicts with David and subsequent Judahite kings, garner a new plausibility."[135]

Khirbet Hamra Ifdan

Another site, close by in the Faynan copper ore resource zone, also supports the view that King Solomon may have controlled these mines. A rare scarab seal (see Fig. 93) or amulet was found that provides support for the military campaign of Pharaoh Sheshonq I (945–924 BC; *ca.* known in the Bible as Shishak, 1 Kgs 14:25; 2 Chr 12:1–12; see Chart 5),[136] who controlled the region after Solomon's death in *ca.* 931 BC and even invaded Jerusalem (*ca.* 925 BC; 2 Chr 12).[137] Thomas E. Levy, the director of the excavations at Khirbet Hamra Ifdan (see Map 2 and 4), states: "The scarab from Khirbat [*sic.* Khirbet] Hamra Ifdan contributes to understanding of what Kenneth Kitchen describes as the 'flying

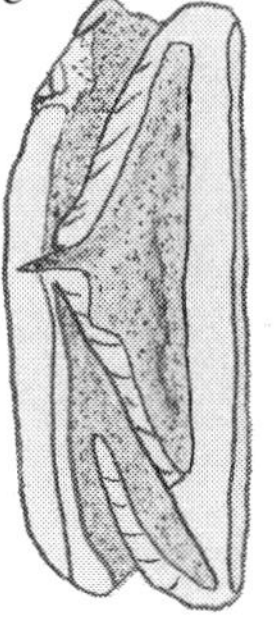

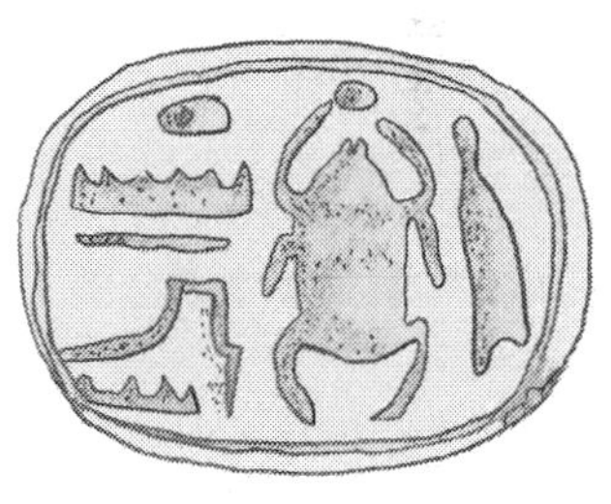

93. Drawing of the Sheshonq I scarab discovered at Khirbet Hamra Ifdan, Jordan. The hieroglyphs on the scarab read: "bright is the manifestation of Re, chosen of Amun/Re," and corresponds to the throne name of Sheshonq I, who ruled from 943 to 924 BC.

---

[130] Yohanan Aharoni, "Iron Age Pottery of the Timnaʿ and ʿAmram Area," *PEQ* 94 (1962): 66–67; Beno Rothenberg, "Notes and News," *PEQ* 98 (1966): 3–7; Yigael Yadin, "More on Solomon's Mines (Hebrew)," *Haaretz*, 1966.

[131] Fafafi, a Jordanian archaeologist at Yarmouk University in Iribid, argues that "There is no mention outside of the Biblical narratives, either, nor in other written documents, either local or foreign (Egyptian), that the area to the south of the Wadi Hesa, including Wadi Faynan, fell under the domination of the David or Solomon." Zeidan A. Kafafi, "New Insights on the Copper Mines of Wadi Faynan/Jordan," *PEQ* 146, no. 4 (2014): 277. However, is not the Biblical narrative sufficiently reliable to be accepted as a valid primary source?

[132] Thomas E. Levy, Mohammad Najjar, and Erez Ben-Yosef, eds., *New Insights into the Iron Age Archaeology of Edom, Southern Jordan: Surveys, Excavations and Research from the Edom Lowlands Regional Archaeology Project (ELRAP)*, Monumenta Archaeologica (Los Angeles, Calf.: The Cotsen Institute of Archaeology, 2014); Thomas E. Levy *et al.*, "Reassessing the Chronology of Biblical Edom: New Excavations and 14C Dates from Khirbat En-Nahas (Jordan)," *Antiquity* 78, no. 302 (2004): 874–76; Thomas E. Levy and Mohammad Najjar, "Edom & Copper: The Emergence of Ancient Israel's Rival," *BAR* 32, no. 4 (2004): 24–35, 70.

[133] Levy and Najjar, "Edom & Copper," 24.

[134] Robert Draper, "David and Solomon, Kings of Controversy," *National Geographic* 12 (December 2010): 85–87.

[135] Levy and Najjar, "Edom & Copper," 35.

[136] Kitchen, *The Third Intermediate Period in Egypt*, 588; *Contra* Rupert L. Chapman III, "Putting Sheshonq I in His Place," *PEQ* 141, no. 1 (2009): 4–17.

[137] Tiffany Fox, "A Scarab from a Biblical Pharaoh," *Artifax* 29, no. 4 (August 2004): 4–5.

column'[138] of Sheshonq I's forces during their Asiatic campaign when they made their way across the northern Negev, to the southern end of the Dead Sea and then south through the Wadi Arabah."[139]

Levy also comments on the implications for the discovery of the Egyptian items in the destruction level and states: "the discovery of Egyptian artifacts in the basal level of the 9th c. BCE building in Area M may be associated with the Pharaoh Sheshonq I's military campaign in the Negev and Arabah valley that occurred shortly after the death of Solomon."[140]

The termination date was also confirmed by carbon-14 dating and corresponds to the military activity of Sheshonq I in Iron Age 2A (ca. 931 BC).

94. Timna Park the location of many ancient copper mines, Negev, Israel. Was this the region that Job described in 28:1–11?

Photo by Little Savage/Wikimedia Commons

Timna Valley Site

Copper mines have also been excavated at Timna by Erez Ben-Yosef of Tel Aviv University (2008; 2009–2017; see Map 2 and 4), identified to the time of Solomon (tenth century BC) based on carbon-14 dating of eleven olive pits[141] and more recently (2017) by the analysis of donkey dung.[142] Among the discoveries were copper tools used in the mining process and high quality colored (red and blue) woven textiles indicating an upper class that had access to expensive textiles.[143]

Of particular interest was the 2017 analysis and dating of the remains of the livestock pen from Site 34 (*Giv'at Ha'avadim*, Slaves' Hill). Donkey dung samples, that included undecayed seeds and pollen spores which determined the animal's diet, could be analyzed yielding a significant surprise. The animals were feed high quality foods (hay and grape pomace) imported from the Mediterranean region at a distance of more than 65 miles (100 km) away. Ben-Yosef stated that: "until we started the project in 2013, this was considered to be a late Bronze Age site related to the New Kingdom of Egypt in the 13th and early 12th centuries BC,"[144] but the carbon dating indicate that the site was used during the time of David and Solomon (tenth cent. BC (1006-917 BC).[145]

---

138 Kitchen, *Reliability of the OT*, 296.

139 Thomas E. Levy, Stefan Münger, and Mohammad Najjar, "A Newly Discovered Scarab of Sheshonq I: Recent Iron Age Explorations in Southern Jordan," *Antiquity*, 2014, http://journal.antiquity.ac.uk/projgall/levy341.

140 Thomas E. Levy *et al.*, "High-Precision Radiocarbon Dating and Historical Biblical Archaeology in Southern Jordan," *Antiquity* 105 (2008): 16465.

141 Erez Ben-Yosef *et al.*, "A New Chronological Framework for Iron Age Copper Production at Timna (Israel)," *BASOR* 367 (August 2012): 31–71.

142 Erez Ben-Yosef, Dafna Langgut, and Lidar Sapir-Hen, "Beyond Smelting: New Insights on Iron Age (10th c. BCE) Metalworkers Community from Excavations at a Gatehouse and Associated Livestock Pens in Timna, Israel," *Journal of Archaeological Science: Reports* 11 (February 2017): 411–26.

143 Daniel Weiss, "Conspicuous Consumption," *Archaology*, October 16, 2017, https://www.archaeology.org/issues/275-1711/from-the-trenches/6002-trenches-israel-dyed-textiles.

144 Michelle Z. Donahue, "Found: Fresh Clues to Mystery of King Solomon's Mines," *National Geographic*, April 2, 2017, https://news.nationalgeographic.com/2017/03/king-solomon-mines-bible-timna-dung.

145 Ben-Yosef, Langgut, and Sapir-Hen, "Beyond Smelting," 418.

Levy summarizes the implications of the dating of these Edomite mining sites:

> The new radiocarbon dates push back by 2 centuries the accepted IA chronology of Edom. Data from Khirbat en-Nahas, and the nearby site of Rujm Hamra Ifdan, demonstrate the centrality of industrial-scale metal production during those centuries traditionally linked closely to political events in Edom's 10th century BCE neighbor ancient Israel. Consequently, the rise of IA Edom is linked to the power vacuum created by the collapse of Late Bronze Age (LB, *ca.* 1300 BCE) civilizations and the disintegration of the LB Cypriot copper monopoly that dominated the eastern Mediterranean.[146]

These discoveries of sizable copper mines in Edomite territory can now be directly linked to the territory in the north under the control of King David and Solomon's reign in the tenth cent. BC.

NORTHERN KINGDOM – ISRAEL

The status of the Northern Kingdom of Israel as a well-established state in the nineth to eighth cent. BC (*ca.* 922–721 BC) is accepted by most scholars due to the mention of king Ahab in the Kurkh stele monolithic inscription of Shalmaneser III (853 BC) that mentions Ahab's large number of chariots in the battle against the Assyrians at the battle of Qarqar. Inscriptional evidence is also found in the Mesha Stele that mentions King Ahab's conquest of northern Moab, in the Tel Dan inscription that likely mentions Jehoram, the last king of the Omride dynasty, and on the Black Obelisk of Shalmaneser III (see Fig. 71), that mentions King Jehu having surrendered to the Assyrian king.[147]

95. One of the panel's of the Black Obelisk depicts the Israelite King Jehu bringing tribute to King Shalmaneser III in around 841 BC.

Used with permission of Oriental Institute Museum

Mazar also reports on the archaeological evidence for the existence of Israel in the nineth and eighth cent. BC:

> Excavations at a number of other major cities in the Northern Kingdom like Dan, Hazor, Kinneret, Megiddo, Yoqne'am, Taanack, Beth-shean, Reḥōv, Dothan, Tell el-Far'ah (Tirzah), Shechem, Dor, and Gezer as well as surface surveys in the Galilee and Samaria hills and excavations in village sites, farms and citadels, reveal a flourishing kingdom with a complex and dense hierarchical settlement system, immense population growth, expanding international trade relations, a flourishing artistic tradition and the increasing use of writing during the ninth and eighth centuries.[148]

Thus, scholars largely accept the existence of the Northern Kingdom of Israel.

---

[146] Levy *et al.*, "High-Precision Radiocarbon Dating," 16460.

[147] Brad E. Kelle, "What's in a Name? Neo-Assyrian Designations for the Northern Kingdom and Their Implications for Israelite History and Biblical Interpretation," *JBL* 121, no. 4 (Winter 2002): 636–66; Albert Kirk Grayson, *Assyrian Rulers of the Early First Millennium BC I (858-745 BC)*, vol. 1, The Royal Inscriptions of Mesopotamia: Assyrian Periods 2 (Toronto, Can.: University of Toronto Press, 1991).

[148] Amihai Mazar, "The Divided Monarchy: Comments on Some Archaeological Issues," in *The Quest for the Historical Israel*, ed. Israel Finkelstein and Brian B. Schmidt, Archaeology and Biblical Studies 17 (Atlanta, Ga.: SBL, 2007), 163.

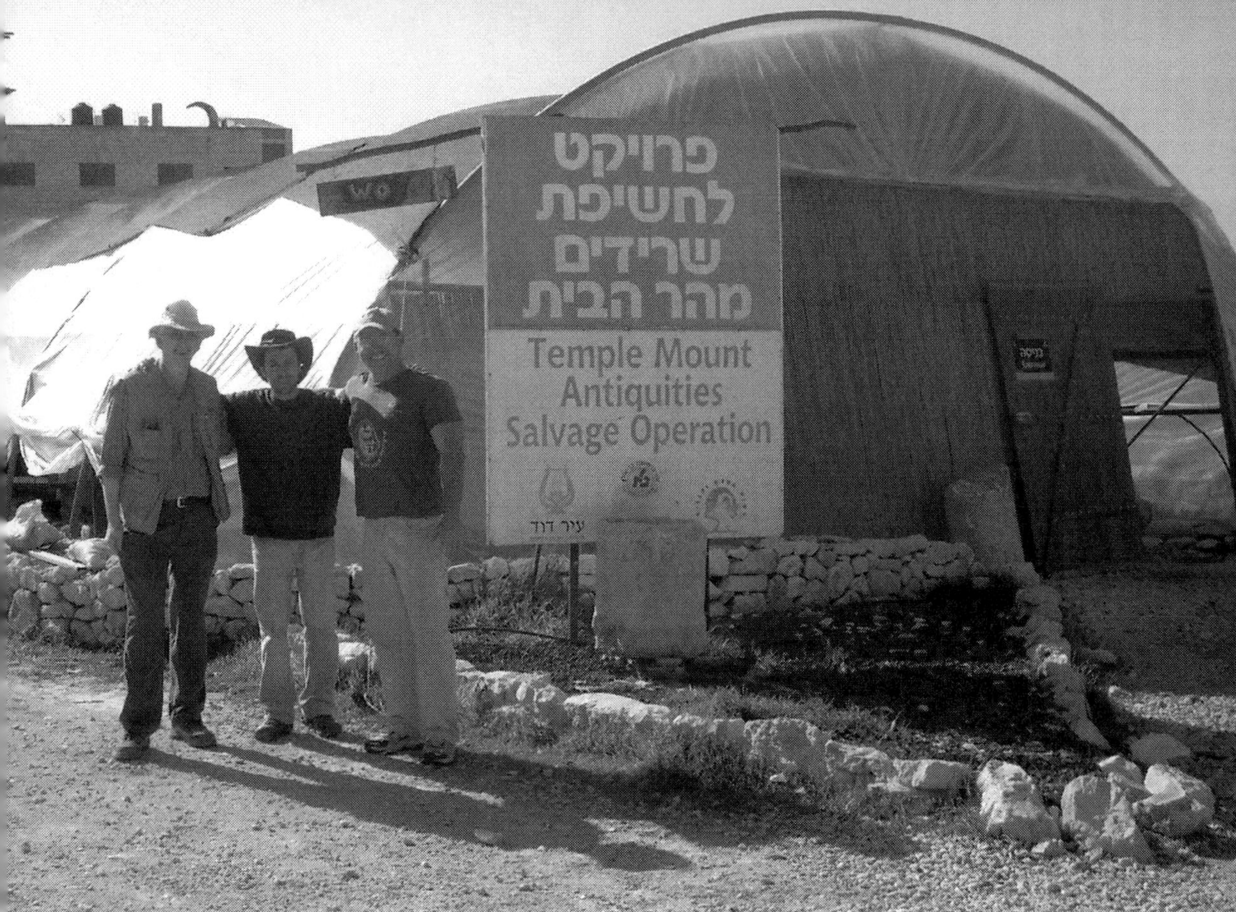

96. The Temple Mount Antiquities Salvage Operation. Left to right Dr. David E. Graves, Zachi Dvira and Dr. Scott Stripling, 2009.

SOUTHERN KINGDOM – JUDAH

There is growing archaeological evidence to support the biblical period of the southern kingdom that spans from Iron Age 1 to Iron Age 2.[149] Mazar describes the issues surrounding the confusion in the debate:

> Unlike its northern sister, Judah did not suffer from any severe military attacks until Sennacherib's invasion in 701 B.C.E., and Jerusalem was not noticeably affected even by that invasion. The lack of destruction layers and the durability of massive stone buildings in the Judean hills and the Shephelah indicate that the same stone buildings were in use for a long period of time. There is also considerable longevity in the pottery production in Judah: the changes were gradual, covering a long period of time. This longevity of the material culture in Judah has blinded the eyes of archaeologists who wish to define in detail the development of Judean material culture in the ninth century as opposed to that of the previous or later centuries. It appears that cities and towns that were founded in the late-tenth or ninth century when Sennacherib destroyed many of them. This can be demonstrated in Jerusalem, Beth-shemesh, Lachish, Tell Beit Mirsim, and other sites where only few occupation strata are attributed to these centuries.[150]

Jerusalem – Temple Mount Salvage Operation

During the archaeologically unsupervised construction at Solomon's Stables (1996–1999) and the replacement of an electrical cable at the el-Marwani Mosque underneath the al-Aqsa Mosque compound (July 2007) under the supervision of the Jerusalem Islamic *Waqf* which oversees the Mosques, some 400 truckloads of archaeologically rich topsoil were removed from the Temple

[149] Mazar, "Divided Monarchy," 164–66.
[150] Ibid., 164.

Mount and dumped in the Kidron Valley. Although this soil was disturbed from its original location (unprovenanced), Gabriel Barkay and Zachi Dvira (Zweig) proposed that it should be sifted to reclaim the valuable artifacts that may be lost forever if discarded.

97. Frankie Snyder holding two of the reconstructed tiles that origianally were used in the porticos of the Jewish Temple built by King Herod.

Courtesy of Hillel Richman and Frankie Snyder

The dirt and debris was moved to a location just below the Hebrew University's campus on Mount Scopus. The Temple Mount Sifting Project (formerly known as the Temple Mount Salvage Operation),[151] with the help of many volunteers including the author (see Fig. 96), began dry/wet sifting the piles of dirt in 2005 under the direction of Barkay and Zweig. Barkay explained that:

> since the layering of soil — its stratigraphy, a key element to dating artifacts — is no longer intact, they assume a reverse stratigraphy: The trucks dumped the uppermost layers of soil first, then heaped deeper layers atop it. . . . Barkay made regular reference to biblical and post-biblical characters in corresponding the items to time periods: clay figurines smashed during the time of the just kings of Judah, seal impressions with the names of priests mentioned in the book of Jeremiah and coins minted during the rein of King Antiochus IV Epiphanes, who fought the Maccabees.[152]

Since 1999 many *opus sectile* tiles in various colors, shapes and sizes have been recovered from the sifting of the soil. In 2016, Frankie Snyder, a project team member with an academic background in mathematics and Judaic studies, was able to recreate the geometric patterns of the stone tile floors of the porticos of the Jewish Temple built by King Herod (see Fig. 97). She has been able to recreate seven different Herodian floor tile designs and two Crusader patterns so far. For the first time we can look down at the floors of the courtyard of the Jewish Temple.

Z.R.

98. Seal impression from the Temple Mount with a partial inscription that reads "Belonging to Ga'alyahu son of *Immer*." *Immer* was the priestly family which controlled the Temple area during Solomon's day and who beat and imprisoned the prophet Jeremiah (Jer 20:1).

Courtesy of Zachi Dvira

While over 6,000 coins,[153] numerous seals (one made of stone), fragments of pottery and glass vessels, metal objects, bones, worked stones, *opus sectile* and mosaic tesserae stones,

---

[151] http://templemount.wordpress.com/

[152] Ilan Ben Zion, "Temple Mount Archaeological Project Yields Treasure, Unearths Conflict," *The Times of Israel*, June 6, 2014, n.p., http://www.timesofisrael.com/temple-mount-project-yields-treasure-but-unearths-conflict/.

[153] Among the noteable coins are some of the earliest Judean [Yehud] coins from the Persian period, and bronze and silver shekel coins from the First Jewish Revolt (AD 66–70).

one burned stamp seal[154] stands out.[155] The sixth cent. BC partially inscribed seal impression (bulla) contains the priestly name of *Immer* (see Fig. 98).[156] The Bible mentions the priestly family of *Immer* (Ezra 2:37, 59; 10:20; Neh 3:29; 7:40, 61; 11:13; 1 Chr 9:12; 24:14) and Pashur Ben Immer (Jer 20:1; 38:1), who had administrative control over Solomon's Temple (seventh–sixth cent. BC), and who "beat Jeremiah the prophet, and put him in the stocks that were in the upper Benjamin Gate of the house of the LORD" (Jer 20:2).[157]

Barkay stated in his second progress report that: "The letters preserved on the middle register are "ליהו" "...*lyhw*" while the bottom register reads "אמר..." "...)*mr*". In light of another published seal, it may be possible to complete the writing as "[לגא]ליהו.[בן]אמר" (Belonging to Ga'alyahu son of Immer [*Ha-Cohen*])"[158] or "Gedalyahu ben Pashur," meaning "Belonging to Gedaliah, son of Pashur [=the priest]" (see Fig. 98).

While these artifacts have been disturbed from their original location (not found *in situ)*, leading to some items not being identified, they do tell their own story about those who walked on the Temple Mount throughout history.

Jerusalem – Hezekiah Bulla

During the Ophel excavations in 2015, at the foot of the southern wall of the Temple Mount in Jerusalem, Eliat Mazar, from the Hebrew University in Jerusalem, discovered a small bulla that read "Belonging to Hezekiah [son of] Ahaz king of Judah" (r. 727–698 BC). The bulla was found wet-sifting the material excavated earlier in 2009 and came from the ancient dump near the Silwan neighborhood. The seal is believed to have been discarded as rubbish from a royal building. The bulla features a two-winged sun, with wings turned downward, flanked by two *ankh* symbols symbolizing life. The seal would have been used by the king of Judah to seal papyrus documents. Mazar reported that "it's very reasonable to assume we are talking about an impression made by the King himself, using his own ring."[159] This seal is especially important because other known Hezekiah seals were acquired from antiquity dealers (see Fig. 13), while this one was recovered from an excavation by archaeologists. The location and provenance of the seal is known, while the others are not.

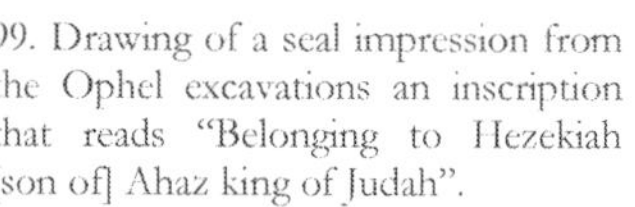

99. Drawing of a seal impression from the Ophel excavations an inscription that reads "Belonging to Hezekiah [son of] Ahaz king of Judah".

---

[154] Over 34 names from the OT have been identified from seal impressions. See the chart in Geisler and Holden, *Popular Handbook of Archaeology and the Bible*, 261–64; Yigal Shiloh and David Tarler, "Bullae from the City of David: A Hoard of Seal Impressions from the Israelite Period," *BA* 49, no. 4 (1986): 196–209; Lawrence J. Mykytiuk, *Identifying Biblical Persons in Northwest Semitic Inscriptions of 1200-539 B.C.E.* (Society of Biblical Lit, 2004); Meir Lubetski and Edith Lubetski, eds., *New Inscriptions and Seals Relating to the Biblical World* (Atlanta, Ga.: SBL, 2012).

[155] Zachi Dvira Zweig, "Sifting by Volunteers Reveals Hidden Story," *Esra Magazine*, May 2013, n.p., http://www.esra-magazine.com/blog/post/temple-mount-archaeology.

[156] Ibid.; Gabriel Barkay, *2nd Progress Report on the Temple Mount Antiquities Salvage Operation: A Hebrew Bulla from the Temple Mount* (The Temple Mount Sifting Project, August 11, 2005), 1–9; Franz and Hernandez, "The Most Important Discovery Was the People," 7–8.

[157] For a treatment of previous inscriptions and discoveries see Philip J. King, *Jeremiah: An Archaeological Companion* (Louisville, KY: Westminster/John Knox, 1993).

[158] Barkay, *2nd Progress Report on the Temple Mount Antiquities Salvage Operation*, 2.

[159] Will Heilpern, "Biblical King's Seal Discovered in Dump Site," *CNN*, December 4, 2015, https://www.cnn.com/2015/12/03/middleeast/king-hezekiah-royal-seal.

Other biblically important bullae have been discovered by Dr. Mazar's team unearthed with the names of Yehukhal (English Jucal) ben Shelemyahu (2005) and Gedaliah ben Pashur (2008 see Fig. 98), both names mentioned in Jeremiah 38:1.[160] And in 2018, Mazar published the slightly damaged bullae that "[belonging] to Isaiah *nvy*", possibly the biblical prophet during Hezekiah's reign.[161] Part of the Hebrew word for "prophet" (*Navi[a]*) is visible.

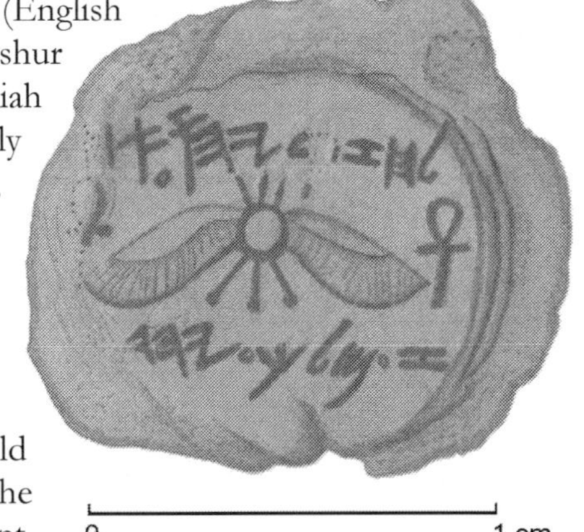

100. Drawing of a seal impression from the Temple Mount with a partial inscription that reads "Lematanyahu Ben Ho..." "Belonging to Matanyahu Ben Ho..." Matanyahu was mentioned in 1 Chr 1:25.

Jerusalem – Matanyahu Seal

During excavation in 2012 of the 2,000-year-old drainage channel beneath Robinson's Arch in the Archaeological Garden adjacent to the Temple Mount, The Israel Antiquities Authority (IAA), uncovered a Hebrew seal dating back to the First Temple period (between the end of the eight century BC and 586 BC; see Fig. 100).[162] According to a statement released by IAA, the seal "is made of a semi-precious stone and is engraved with the name of its owner: 'Lematanyahu Ben Ho...' ('למתניהובןהו...' meaning: 'Belonging to Matanyahu Ben Ho...'). The rest of the inscription is erased."[163] A similar seal bearing the name "Netanyahu Son of Yaush" in ancient Hebrew script was discovered at the site in March 2008.

According to Eli Shukron, excavation director on behalf of the Israel Antiquities Authority,

> the name Matanyahu, like the name Netanyahu, means giving to God. These names are mentioned several times in the Bible. They are typical of the names in the Kingdom of Judah in latter part of the First Temple period – from the end of the eighth century BCE until the destruction of the Temple in 586 BCE. To find a seal from the First Temple period at the foot of the Temple Mount walls is rare and very exciting. This is a tangible greeting of sorts from a man named Matanyahu who lived here more than 2,700 years ago. We also found pottery sherds characteristic of the period on the floor in the ancient building beneath the base of the drainage channel, as well as stone collapse and evidence of a fire.

The biblical significance is that the name Matanyahu is mentioned in the period of the Kingdom of Judah in the later part of the First Temple Period (1 Chr 1:25).

Jerusalem – Governor of the City Seal

Another important discovery recently unearthed (December 2017) from the Western Wall Plaza in Jerusalem is a rare, well-preserved burnt lump of clay (דוקט *ducat* "small coin") dating to the First Temple period (sixth to seventh cent. BC) with the Hebrew inscription "governor of the

---

[160] IMFA Staff, "Unique Biblical Discovery at City of David Excavation Site," *Israel Ministry of Foreign Affairs,* August 18, 2008.

[161] Megan Sauter, "Isaiah's Signature Uncovered in Jerusalem Evidence of the Prophet Isaiah?," *Bible History Daily: Biblical Archaeology Society,* February 22, 2018. https://www.biblicalarchaeology.org/daily/people-cultures-in-the-bible/people-in-the-bible/prophet-isaiah-signature-jerusalem.

[162] Matti Friedman, "Ancient Seal Found in Jerusalem the Times of Israel," *The Times of Israel,* May 1, 2012, http://www.timesofisrael.com/ancient-seal-found-in-jerusalem.

[163] BAR Staff, "First Temple Period 'Matanyahu' Seal Discovered in Jerusalem," *Bible History Daily,* May 2, 2012, https://www.biblicalarchaeology.org/daily/biblical-sites-places/temple-at-jerusalem/first-temple-period-matanyahu-seal-discovered-in-jerusalem.

city" (see Fig. 101). The upper part of the seal depicts two figures facing each other, and the lower part contains the inscription in ancient Hebrew script. Dr. Shlomit Weksler-Bdolah, excavator of the site on behalf of the IAA states: "The Bible mentions two governors of Jerusalem [2 Kgs 23:8; 2 Chr 34:8], and this finding thus reveals that such a position was actually held by someone in the city some 2,700 years ago."[164]

101. Drawing of a seal impression from the Temple Mount with a partial inscription that reads "Governor of the City". Two governors of Jerusalem are mentioned in the Bible.

CONCLUSION

Sanders in evaluating the inscription evidence from the tenth cent. BC concluded that these inscriptions: "challenge both the somewhat idealized reconstruction of a bureaucratized Solomonic state and the somewhat preconceived dismissal of complex culture in 10th–century Israel."[165]

Thus, the "Kingdom of David" might best be understood as an "ethnic entity that would become a nation."[166] However, the evidence is clear that Israel was more than a band of pastoral nomads, and King David was more than a tribal chieftain.

Although archaeology is indeed limited in what it can prove, and certainly cannot prove that the United Monarchy, described in the biblical narrative, occurred precisely as described in the Bible, the archaeological evidence laid out in this chapter indicates that the biblical account of David and Solomon is historically plausible. The monumental structures in Jerusalem and the inscriptional material found in surrounding sites, from the IA occupation, argue for a centralized literate authority in Jerusalem at the time of David and Solomon. This is a cautionary reminder for critical scholars, who place so much weight on negative evidence, to be cautious about making unsupported claims, since there is much more evidence available apparent from the discoveries listed in this chapter. As Grisanti cautions: "archaeology should limit the sweeping statements often made by critical scholars by which biblical narrative descriptions of various people or events are viewed as purely legendary. In many cases, the sweeping statements made with great academic authority are actually based on what has not been found or the slimmest thread of evidence."[167]

The recent archaeological discoveries presented here and in other new excavations harmonize with the biblical narrative and indicate that the text and the turf are not in conflict.

---

[164] Daniel K. Eisenbud, "Seal from First Temple Period Found at Kotel Supports Biblical Accounts," *The Jerusalem Post*, January 1, 2018, http://www.jpost.com/Israel-News/Seal-from-First-Temple-Period-found-at-kotel-supports-Biblical-accounts-522533; Editor, "Governor of Jerusalem's Seal," *Artifax* 33, no. 1 (Winter 2018): 4.

[165] Sanders, "Writing and Early Iron Age Israel: Before National Scripts, beyond Nations and States," 104.

[166] Shlomo Bunimovitz and Zvi Lederman, "The Iron Age Fortifications of Tel Beth Shemesh: A 1990–2000 Perspective," *IEJ* 51, no. 2 (January 1, 2001): 147.

[167] Grisanti, "Recent Archaeological Discoveries," 496.

CHART 6: ROMAN PERIOD DISCOVERIES I

GOSPELS (ROMAN PERIOD: 63 BC–33 AD)					
Discovery	**Image**	**Place and Discoverer**	**Origin Date /Year Found**	**Biblical Passage**	**Significance**
Alexamenos Graffiti		Palantine Hill, Rome	early third century AD 1857	Matt 1:23; John 5:17-18, 23; 10:30-33; 20:28	Early attitudes to Chritianity and worhipping Jesus as God
Herod the Great Ostraca		Masada by Ehud Netzer and G. Stibel	37-4 BC 1996	Matt 2:1–9; Luke 1:5; Mark 6:14	Identification of Herod as the King of Judea
Statue of Augustus		Villa of Livia, Prima Porta	10 BC-AD 14 1863	Luke 2:10	Identification of Emperor Augustus
Lysanias Inscription (lost) Abila Inscripiton (illustrated here)		Doric temple Hill of Nebi Abel, Damascus by Richard Pocock[1]	AD 14–29 1745	Luke 3:1; Josephus *J.W.* 2.12.8	Lysanias the tetrarch of Abilene
Portrait of Tiberius		Ephesus Museum	AD 14–37	Luke 3:1; Matt 22:15–22;Mark 12:13–17; Luke 20:20–26	Identification of Emperor Tiberius

[1] Richard Pococke, *A Description of the Easst and Some Other Countries*, vol. 2, Part 1 (London: Bowyer, 1745), 116; John Pinkerton, *A General Collection of the Best and Most Interesting Voyages and Travels in All Parts of the World*, vol. 10 (London: Longman, Hurst, Rees, Orme, & Brown, 1811), 497; August Böeckh et al., *Corpus Inscriptionum Graecarum*, 4 vols. (Berolini, Italy: Officina academica, 1877), §§4521, 4523.

Discovery	Image	Place and Discoverer	Origin Date /Year Found	Biblical Passage	Significance
Jacob's Well		Greek Orthodox St. Photini (Samarian) Church at Bir Ya'qub, Nablus, West Bank.	AD 384	John 4:6–30	Meeting of Jesus and the Samarian Woman
Kinneret Boat		Sea of Galilee by Moshe and Yuval Lufan of Kibbutz Ginosar	AD 30–70 1986	Matt 4:21; John 21:3	Fishing practices and style of Jesus' disciples fishing boat
Second Temple Stone Inscription		Temple Mount Jerusalem by Benjamin Mazar	second cent. BC–AD 70 1968	Matt 4:5; Josephus *J.W.* 4.582	Trumpeting location at the Temple
St. Philip's Martyrium Hierapolis		Hierapolis, Turkey by Francesco D'Andria	fourth or fifth cent. AD 2011	John 1:43	Philip was one of the original twelve disciples of Jesus and was martyred
Capernaum Synagogue		Capernaum, Israel by Charles Wilson	first cent., fourth–fifth cent. AD 1866	Matt 4:13; Mark 2:1; Luke 4:31; John 6:59	Jesus performed miracles there
Peter's House		Capernaum, Israel by Stanislao Loffreda and Virgilio	first cent., fourth–fifth cent. AD 1921/1968	Mark 1:29–34	Apostle Peter's house below Byzantine church
Pool of Bethesda		Near the Church of St. Anne, Jerusalem by Conrad Schick	second cent. BC–AD 70 1888	John 5:2	Ritual healing site or *miqveh*
Pilate Inscription		Caesarea Martima, Israel by Antonio Frova	AD 26–36 1961	John 18:33–40	Confirms historicity of Pontius Pilate and his title

Discovery	Image	Place and Discoverer	Origin Date /Year Found	Biblical Passage	Significance
James Ossuary		Purchased by Oded Golan in Jerusalem	AD 63 1970s	Matt 10:1–4	Identification of James the brother of Jesus
Judaea Capta Bronze Sestertius coin		N/A	AD 69–79	Matt 24:1–2; Mark 13:1–4	Depiction of Jews mourning over the destruction of Jerusalem.
Vespasian-Titus Inscription		Temple Mount excavations by Benjamin Mazar	AD 73–79 1970	Matt 24:1–2; Mark 13:1–4	Names of Vespasian, Titus and Silva that fulfils Jesus' prophesy of the destruction of Jerusalem
Arch of Titus		Roman Forum, Rome Italy	AD 81/ N/A	Matt 24; Mark 13:1–4	Destruction of the Temple AD 70.
Caiaphas Ossuary		South of Jerusalem by Zvi Greenhut	AD 42–43 1990	Matt 26:57–67; John 11:49–53; 18:14	High priest at Jesus' trial
Burnt House with Menorah		Upper city of Jerusalem by Nahman Aviagd	1969, 1983	Matt 26:57–67; John 11: 49–53; 18:14	earliest depiction of the Menorah in the Temple and destruction of Jerusalem
Gabbatha		Aelia Capitolina, Jerusalem	First cent. AD	Matt 27:27; John 19:13	Location "lithostrotos" of Jesus' trial by Pilate
Yehohanan heel bone		Giv'at ha-Mivtar near Mount Scopus Jerusalem by Vassilios Tzaferis	7 BC–AD 70 1968	Matt 27; Mark 15; Luke 23; John 19	Verification of crucificion in the first century

Discovery	Image	Place and Discoverer	Origin Date /Year Found	Biblical Passage	Significance
Herod's family tomb		Jerusalem by Conrad Schick	first cent. AD	Matt 27:59-60	Example of a sealed tomb with a rolling stone, similar to Jesus' tomb
Nazareth Inscription		Nazareth, Israel then sent to Paris and purchased by Wilhelm Fröhner	1878	Matt 28:11–15	Roman reaction to the Jewish response to the resurrection of Jesus

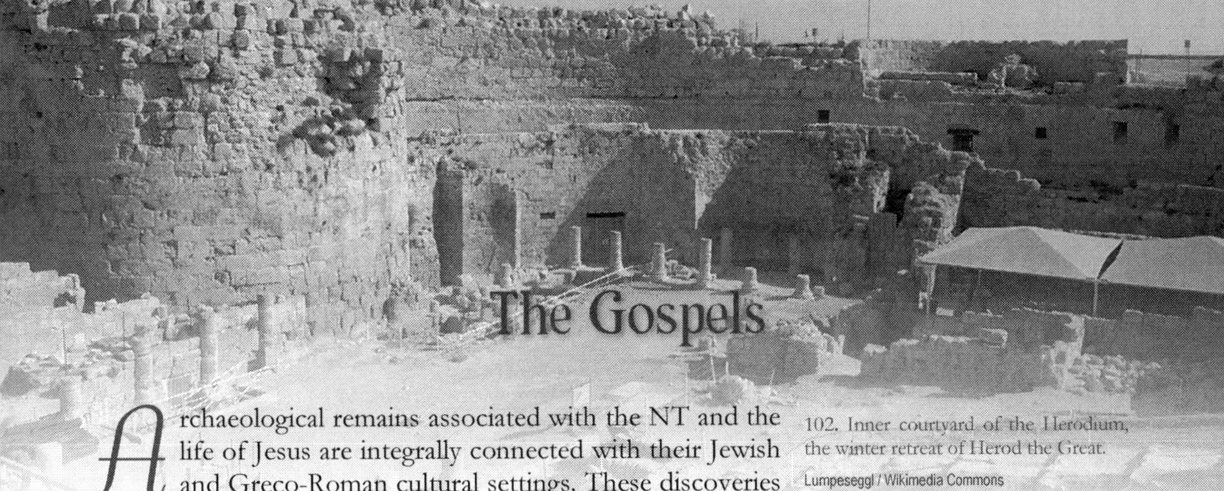

The Gospels

102. Inner courtyard of the Herodium, the winter retreat of Herod the Great.
Lumpeseggl / Wikimedia Commons

Archaeological remains associated with the NT and the life of Jesus are integrally connected with their Jewish and Greco-Roman cultural settings. These discoveries fall into several different categories.

First, there are the discoveries of ancient manuscripts that have greatly increased our understanding of the historical background of the NT period. These include the Egyptian *Nag Hammadi* texts which shed light on Gnostic heretical ideas,[1] and the Dead Sea Scrolls, discovered at Qumran, which contribute to our understanding of first cent. Jewish views of the Messiah and life inside the Essene community.[2] In addition there are hundreds of early Greek NT texts which help scholars in textual analysis of the NT. In 1900 only 9 papyri manuscripts were known, but by 2008 there were 124 papyri.[3]

Second, there are the numerous inscriptions that confirm the historical existence of people and places mentioned in the NT. Inscriptions mentioning Herod the Great[4] (Matt 2:1–23), Quirinius[5] (Luke 2:2), Pontius Pilate[6] (John 18:33–40), Sergius Paulus[7] (Acts 13:6–7), Emperor Claudius (Acts 18:2), Gallio[8] (Acts 18:12), Nero[9] (Acts 25:11–12; 26:32; Rev 13:18), and

---

[1] Available online at www.nag-hammadi.com Birger A. Pearson, "Nag Hammadi Codices," ed. David Noel Freedman, *ABD* (London: Doubleday & Company, 1996), 4:984–93.

[2] Roland de Vaux, *Archaeology and the Dead Sea Scrolls*, Schweich Lectures of the British Academy, 1959 (Oxford: Oxford University Press, 1973); William Sanford La Sor, *Dead Sea Scrolls and the New Testament* (Grand Rapids: Eerdmans, 1983); James H. Charlesworth, ed., *Jesus and the Dead Sea Scrolls* (New Haven, CT: Yale University Press, 1992); Peter W. Flint and James C. VanderKam, eds., *The Dead Sea Scrolls After Fifty Years: A Comprehensive Assessment*, vol. 2 (Leiden: Brill, 1999); F. F. Bruce and J. Julius Scott, Jr., "Dead Sea Scrolls," ed. Walter A. Elwell, *EDT*, Baker Reference Library (Grand Rapids: Baker Academic, 2001); Martin G. Abegg, Jr., Peter Flint, and Eugene Ulrich, *The Dead Sea Scrolls Bible: The Oldest Known Bible Translated for the First Time into English (QBE)* (New York: HarperCollins, 2002); James C. VanderKam and Peter W. Flint, *The Meaning of the Dead Sea Scrolls: Their Significance for Understanding the Bible, Judaism, Jesus, and Christianity* (San Francisco, Calf.: Harper, 2002).

[3] Daniel B. Wallace, "Earliest Manuscript of the New Testament Discovered?," *The Center for the Study of New Testament Manuscripts*, February 10, 2012, http://www.csntm.org/.

[4] Piotr Berdowski, "Garum Of Herod The Great (Latin-Greek Inscription On The Amphora From Masada)," *Analecta Archaeologica Ressoviensia* 1 (2006): 239–57.

[5] Victor Ehrenberg, Arnold H. M. Jones, and David L. Stockton, eds., *Documents Illustrating the Reigns of Augustus and Tiberius*, 2nd ed. (Oxford: Clarendon, 1976), 73.

[6] Robert J. Bull, "Caesarea Maritima: The Search for Herod's City," *BAR* 8, no. 3 (1982): 24–40; "Pontius Pilate Inscription," *BAR* 8, no. 5 (1982).

[7] G. Lafaye, R. Cagnat, and J. Toutain, eds., *Inscriptiones Graecae Ad Res Romanas Pertinentes* (Paris: Leroux, 1901), 930, 935; Bastian Van Elderen, "Some Archaeological Observations on Paul's First Missionary Journey," in *Apostolic History and The Gospel Biblical and Historical Essays Presented to F. F. Bruce on His 60th Birthday*, ed. W. Ward Gasque (Exeter: Paternoster, 1970), 155; Thomas W. Martin, "Paulus, Sergius (Person)," ed. David Noel Freedman *et al.*, *ABD* (New York: Doubleday, 1996), 205; William M. Ramsay, *The Bearing of Recent Discovery on the Trustworthiness of the New Testament*, Classic Reprint 1911 (Charleston, SC: Forgotten Books, 2012), 150–72.

[8] E. Mary Smallwood, *Documents Illustrating the Principates of Gaius Claudius and Nero* (Bristol: Bristol Classical, 1983), 105.

[9] Kevin Killan Carroll, *The Parthenon Inscription*, ed. Kent J. Rigsby, Greek, Roman, and Byzantine Studies Monographs 9 (Durham, N.C.: Duke University, 1982); Henry A. Sanders, "The Number of the Beast in Revelation," *JBL*, 95-99, 37, no. 1 (1918): 95–96.

103. Yad Avshalom (Absalom's Tomb) in the Kidron Valley.

© Ariel Horowit / Wikimedia Commons

Erastus[10] (Rom 16:23) have confirmed the historicity of the biblical text.

Third, there are the excavations of cities and monuments described in the NT that confirm the accuracy of the geography and history of the NT narrative. Cities such as Jerusalem,[11] Capernaum,[12] and Caesarea Philippi[13] just to mention a few (also see Chapter Seven), corroborate the accuracy of the biblical writers.

Although there are many sites that have not been excavated, there is a vast archaeological landscape to consider. While the discoveries are numerous they cannot all be considered here. However, there are significant discoveries which are worth mentioning, particularly in the last 20 years.

ABSALOM'S TOMB INSCRIPTION

In 2003, in the Kidron Valley just outside of Jerusalem, archaeologists Fr. Émile Puech, a professor at the École Biblique in Jerusalem, and Joe Zias of the Israel Antiquities Authority, discovered two inscriptions, one horizontal and one vertical, on the south side of Absalom's Tomb (also connected with the High Priest Zechariah. See Fig. 73).[14] This burial monument (*Nefesh*) was mentioned by Josephus (*Ant.* 7.10.3). The inscription contains 47 letters and is 1.2 meters long and 10 cms high. Using an old method called a squeeze, they made a silicon impression from which they formed a polyester mold. Using this easy to read replica they deciphered both texts and discovered that one was the oldest NT passage ever identified. The horizontal inscription read: "This is the tomb of Zacharias, martyr, very pious priest, father of John."[15]

The second vertical inscription which dates to the fourth cent. AD is a close paraphrase of

---

[10] John Harvey Kent, *The Inscriptions, 1926 to 1950: Corinth*, vol. 8, Part 3 (Athens: American School of Classical Studies at Athens, 1966); Andrew D. Clarke, "Another Corinthian Erastus Inscription," *TynBul* 42 (1991): 146–51; Steven J. Friesen, "The Wrong Erastus: Ideology, Archaeology, and Exegesis," in *Corinth in Context: Comparative Studies on Religion and Society*, ed. Steven J. Friesen, Daniel N. Schowalter, and James Walters (Leiden: Brill, 2010), 231–56.

[11] Nahman Avigad, *Discovering Jerusalem* (Nashville, TN: Nelson, 1983); Hillel Geva, "The History of Archaeology Research in Jerusalem," in *NEAEHL*, ed. Ephraim Stern, Ayelet Levinson-Gilboa, and Joseph Aviram, vol. 2, 4 vols. (New York: MacMillan, 1993), 801–4; Hillel Geva, ed., *Ancient Jerusalem Revealed* (Jerusalem, Israel: Israel Exploration Society, 1994); Andrew G. Vaughn and Ann E. Killebrew, eds., *Jerusalem in Bible and Archaeology: The First Temple Period*, SBL Symposium Series 18 (Atlanta, Ga.: SBL, 2003); Galyn Wiemers, *Jerusalem: History, Archaeology and Apologetic Proof of Scripture* (Waukee, Iowa: Last Hope Books, 2010); Craig A. Evans, ed., *The World of Jesus and the Early Church: Identity and Interpretation in Early Communities of Faith* (Peabody, MA: Hendrickson, 2011); Craig A. Evans, *Jesus and His World: The Archaeological Evidence* (London: SPCK, 2012).

[12] Stanislao Loffreda, "Capernaum-Jesus' Own City," *BS* 10, no. 1 (1981): 1–17; James F. Strange and Hershel Shanks, "Synagogue Where Jesus Preached Found at Capernaum," *BAR* 9, no. 6 (1983): 24–31.

[13] John Wilson, *Caesarea Philippi: Banias, The Lost City of Pan* (New York: Tauris, 2004).

[14] Émile Puech and Joseph Zias, "Le Tombeau de Zacharie et Siméon Au Monument Funéraire Dit d'Absalom Dans La Vallée de Josaphat," *RB* 110 (2003): 321–35.

[15] Shimon Gibson, "Absalom, Monument of," ed. Fred Skolnik and Michael Berenbaum, *Encyclopaedia Judaica* (New York: MacMillan, 2006), 1:332.

Luke 2:25 and a memorial to Simeon, who in his old age saw the long awaited and prophesied Christ child, and it reads: "The tomb of Simeon who was a very just man (διχαιοτατος [Gr. *dikaiotatos*]) and a very devoted (ευσηβηστατος [Gr. *eusebestatos*]) old (person) and waiting for the consolation of the people."[16]

The biblical text reads: "Now there was a man in Jerusalem, whose name was Simeon, and this man was righteous and devout, waiting for the consolation of Israel, and the Holy Spirit was upon him" (Luke 2:25).

Ehrman and Holmes explain the implications of this discovery: "This seems to offer good evidence that the reading εὐσηβής [Gr. *Eusebes*] (also found in [*Codex Sinaiticus*] א K Γ 565 700 1424 and others) was known in Jerusalem in the fourth century, even though this is not strictly a citation of the Lukan text."[17]

Parker cautions that: "It is certainly interesting that an inscription from Jerusalem should support the reading of a manuscript which scholars have often argued was written in Caesarea, but it would be folly to build any theory out of such a tiny scrap of evidence."[18]

Although the Absalom monument is a Jewish holy place, the inscription based on Luke indicates that it was also a Christian shrine in the fourth century.

Herod the Great

Herod lived from 73 BC until his death at Jericho in 4 BC. He was the Roman puppet king of Judea (Josephus *Ant.* 14.9.2). Herod was not a true Jew but an Idumaean (Edomite) from the Nabatean area around modern Petra, Jordan (Josephus *J.W.* 1.6.2; see Fig. 74). He had ten sons with ten different wives (Josephus *J.W.* 1.28.4). He married Malthace (a Samaritan) who was Herod Antipas' mother.

He is famous for several significant events such as building the Temple in Jerusalem in 22 BC (Josephus *Ant.* 15.11.1; *J.W.* 1.21.1) and for the massacre of the innocents (Matt 2). According to Matthew, he gave orders to kill all boys of the age of two and under in Bethlehem and its vicinity. While some have treated this event as a myth[19] it is certainly not out of character for him since Herod was paranoid of rivals and he is known for many atrocities, including killing one of his wives and two of his sons (Josephus *Ant.* 15.222–236; 15.365–372;

104. Al Khazneh or The Treasury at Petra, Jordan which was the Nabataean capital, and the center of their caravan trade.

[16] Bart D. Ehrman and Michael W. Holmes, eds., *The Text of the New Testament in Contemporary Research: Essays on the Status Quaestionis. Second Edition* (Leiden: Brill, 2012), 445.

[17] Ibid.; Émile Puech, "Le Tombeau de Siméon et Zacharie Dans La Vallée de Josaphat," *RB* 111 (2004): 570; D. C. Parker, *An Introduction to the New Testament Manuscripts and Their Texts* (Cambridge: Cambridge University Press, 2008), 128–29.

[18] Parker, *Introduction to the NT Manuscripts*, 129.

[19] Tom Mueller, "Herod: The Holy Land's Visionary Builder," *National Geographic*, 2008, 42; Michael Grant, *Herod the Great* (New York: American Heritage, 1971), 12.

105. Looking inside the dome of the Herodium. The pillared hall to the left is a reception room which later became a synagogue. In the center are the living quarters with the bath complex to the far right.

16.392–394; 17.182–187; *J.W.* 1.550–51).[20] Augustus is reported to have said that: "It is better to be Herod's pig (Gr. *hus*) than his son (Gr. *huios*)" (Macrobius *Satur.* 2.4.11). As France points out, given the political climate, the execution of a small number of children in a small town would not draw the attention of any but God.[21]

Upon his death his kingdom was divided among three of his sons. Archelaus would rule as king over Herod's entire kingdom (Josephus *Ant.* 17.8.1), while Antipas and Philip would rule as Tetrarchs over Galilee (Luke 3:1–3) and Perea (Transjordan), also over Gaulanitis, Trachonitis, Batanaea, and Panias (Josephus *Ant.* 17:20, *J.W.* 1.562).

Herod's Tomb

Matthew mentioned the death of King Herod in chapter 2 verse 19. Ehud Netzer searched for Herod the Great's (74/73–4 BC)[22] tomb or mausoleum at the Herodium (Lat. *Herodium;* הרודיון, Herodion; Ἡρώδειον *Herodeion;* see Map 1), one of Herod's winter retreats, since 1972 until his death in 2010. Netzer had long believed that the tomb was there, based on Josephus' testimony (*J.W.* 5.33.1–2). But on May 7, 2007, an Israeli team of archaeologists from Hebrew University,

[20] Richard Thomas France, "Herod and the Children of Bethlehem," *NovT* 31, no. 2 (1979): 98–120; Paul Maier, "Herod and the Infants of Bethlehem," in *Chronos Kairos Christos II*, ed. E. Jerry Vardaman (Macon, Ga.: Mercer University Press, 1998), 169–89.

[21] France, "Herod and the Children of Bethlehem," 114–19.

[22] It was under Herod's reign that Jesus and his parents escaped to Egypt until they received word of Herod's death (Matt 2:1-18).

under the direction of Netzer, discovered Herod's tomb near an large pool described by Josephus just outside the hill of the Herodium.[23]

Archaeologists discovered the tomb with a smashed extravagant limestone sarcophagus, but with no evidence of a body.[24] However, while most scholars agree with Netzer's identification, without an inscription or a body, Patrich, Arubas and others have unsuccessfully challenge his identification, claiming that the tomb was too modest for Herod.[25] Roi Porat, who replaced Netzer as the director of the excavations at Herodium after Netzer's untimely death at the site in 2010, stands by Netzer's identification.[26]

In 2013 the Israel Museum displayed the restored sarcophagus as part of the "Herod the Great—The King's Final Journey" exhibit.[27] A replica of Herod's Tomb has been errected at the Herodium (see Fig. 106).[28]

106. Reconstructed tomb of King Herod located on the original site at the Herodium, Israel.

Photo courtesy of Glen Ruffle

KHIRBET QUMRAN

Khirbet Qumran, on the northwestern side of the Dead Sea (see Map 1), is famous for the discovery of the Dead Sea Scrolls (DSS), however there has been significant archaeological work carried out at the site apart from the DSS, that also relates to the NT.

Qumran and the Essenes

While there is debate[29] over the connection between the Qumran community and the DSS (e.g., were they a group of Sadducees;[30] were the scrolls relocated from the Jewish Temple Library in

[23] Amiram Barkat and Haaretz Staff, "Archeologist: King Herod's Tomb Desecrated, but Discovery 'High Point,'" *Haaretz*, May 7, 2007, http://www.haaretz.com/news/archeologist-king-herod-s-tomb-desecrated-but-discovery-high-point-1.219914.

[24] Ehud Netzer, *Architecture of Herod, the Great Builder* (Grand Rapids: Baker Academic, 2008), 179–202.

[25] Joseph Patrich and Benjamin Arubas, "'Herod's Tomb' Reexamined: Guidelines for a Discussion and Conclusions," in *New Studies in the Archaeology of Jerusalem and Its Region*, ed. Gary D. Stiebel *et al.*, vol. 7, Collected Papers (Jerusalem, Israel: Hebrew University, 2013), 287–300; Hershel Shanks, "Was Herod's Tomb Really Found?," *BAR* 40, no. 3 (2014).

[26] Hasson, "Archaeological Stunner: Not Herod's Tomb after All?"

[27] Suzanne F. Singer, "Herod the Great—The King's Final Journey," *BAR* 39, no. 2 (2013): 14. For a video of the display see https://www.youtube .com/watch?v=Nux49aWNO54#t=101.

[28] Roi Porat, Rachel Chachy-Laureys, and Yakov Kalman, "The Continuation of the Activity of the Herodium Expedition for the Promotion of Research and Development of Herod," *The Institute of Archaeology: The Hebrew University of Jerusalem*, 1-11, July 2013.

[29] Lena Cansdale, *Qumran and the Essenes: A Re-Evaluation of the Evidence*, Texte Und Studien Zum Antiken Judentum 60 (Tübingen: Siebeck, 1997), 191–97.

[30] Lawrence H. Schiffman, *Reclaiming the Dead Sea Scrolls: The History of Judaism, The Background of Christianity, The Lost Library of Qumran*, Anchor Bible Reference Library (New York: Doubleday, 1995).

108. Scriptorium room at Qumran.

Jerusalem;[31] or was Qumran a Hasmonean fort and pottery factory?[32]) most scholars accept Eleazar Sukenik, and Dominican Father Roland de Vaux's view[33] that Qumran is the settlement of the Essenes, the people who placed the Dead Sea Scrolls in the Qumran caves (see Fig. 27).

The archaeological remains at Khirbet Qumran have revealed several connections with the scrolls and the Essene community. There are a number of convincing reasons why the Essene sect may have occupied the Qumran site, but the two main reasons rest with their location and their similar practices.

Josephus (*Vita* 1.2; *J.W.* 2.8, 2–13; *Ant.* 18.1, 2, 5) and Pliny (*Nat.* 5.17) mention the settlement of the Essenes in the general vicinity of En Freshkha in the Judean Desert. They withdrew to the wilderness of Judea because of the prophecy in Isaiah "A voice cries: 'In the wilderness prepare the way of the Lord; make straight in the desert a highway for our God.'" (Isa 40:3). Jars were discovered from the rooms at Qumran identical to those stored several of the Caves where the scrolls were discovered. They date to the same period and provide a connection between the scrolls and the Qumran community.

A prominent find is the *scriptorium* or writing room, measuring 43 by 13 feet (13 m by 3.6 m; see Figs. 34 and 108). This could have been where many of the DSS were copied and worked on. If a mistake was made to a scroll, or they were worn out, then the scribe would place it in a special place called a *Geniza*. The caves where the DSS were discovered meet the criteria for Geniza Caves with cave four containing 15,000 fragments of an estimated 600 separate manuscripts.

107. Bronze Sestertius coin (AD 71) of Vespasian (AD 69-79). On the left is the laureate head of Vespasian with the words IMP CAES VESPASIAN AVG P M TR P P P COS III. The right depicts Vespasian, holding a spear and standing with his left foot on a helmet over a Jewess who is mourning over the destruction of Jerusalem. It reads IVDAEA CAPTA: Judea captured. In AD 69 Vespasian left his son Titus to suppress the Jewish revolt led by the Zealots, John of Gischala and Simon bar Giora. Titus finished the task in AD 70 by entering Jerusalem and plundering the temple. It is believed that the Romans attacked Qumran on the way to Masada but the Essenes hid the scrolls in the caves before they arrived.

Courtesy of CNG

The *Manual of Discipline* scroll spoke of practices and beliefs similar to the Essene sect described by Josephus (*Vita* 1.2; *J.W.* 2.8.4, 2–13; *Ant.* 18.1, 2, 5). According to Josephus, Pliny, and Philo, the Essenes were a monastic order without money or women (Josephus *J.W.*

---

[31] Karl Heinrich Rengstorf, *Hirbet Qumran Und Die Bibliothek Vom Toten Meer*, trans. J. R. Wilkie (Stuttgart, Germany: Kohlhammer, 1960); Norman Golb, *Who Wrote the Dead Sea Scrolls?: The Search for the Secret of Qumran* (New York: Scribner's Sons, 1995).

[32] Yizhar Hirschfeld, *Qumran in Context: Reassessing the Archaeological Evidence* (Grand Rapids: Baker Academic, 2004); Yitshak Magen and Yuval Peleg, *The Qumran Excavations 1993 - 2004: Preliminary Report*, 6 (Jerusalem: Israel Antiquities Authority, 2007); Birdsall, *The Bodmer Papyrus of the Gospel of John*.

[33] Eleazar Lipa Sukenik, *The Dead Sea Scrolls of the Hebrew University* (Jerusalem: Hebrew University Press Magnes, 1955), 37; Roland de Vaux, *Archaeology and the Dead Sea Scrolls*, Schweich Lectures of the British Academy, 1959 (Oxford: Oxford University Press, 1973), 127.

2.8.4; Philo *Good Person* 77; *Hypoth.* 11.14; Pliny *Nat.* 5.73) although Josephus was aware of one group of Essenes who practiced marriage (Josephus *J.W.* 2.8.13).[34] Other similar beliefs included voting, speaking, eating seated, bathing and baptism rites (Josephus *J.W.* 2.8.4; 2.8.7; 1QS 3:4, 9; v, 13).[35]

109. Numerous *mikva'ot* (ritual purity baths) lined with plaster were discovered at Qumran scattered throughout the site indicating that the Essenes practiced baptism by immersion. Fresh water (living water) was supplied from local springs. This *miqveh* is split down the middle with a 30 cm. (12 in.) crack as a result of an earthquake in 31 BC which destroyed Qumran.

Courtesy of John Bondarchuck

Qumran and Baptism

Most scholars agree that baptism by immersion was practiced at Qumran to enter into the eschatological community (1QS 3:4–9; 4:18–22; 6:14–23).[36] Qumran is filled with many reservoirs for collecting water, necessary because of the scarcity of water in this inhospitable region. However, a number of them, called *miqva'ot* (sing. *miqveh),* served as ritual baptisteries (see Fig. 78). These ritual bathing pools are also found in many locations throughout the ancient Near East including Herodian Jericho, Machaerus, Masada, and Jerusalem,[37] but as Werlin points out "Qumran boasts the highest density of *mikva'ot* per square foot of any site so far discovered" with over ten identified *miqveh.*[38]

The *miqveh* was designed to provide flowing or "living water" that remained in continual contact with natural or flowing water (*Sifra* Lev 11:36). According to ancient requirements, a *miqveh* must contain enough water to cover or immerse an average adult (5 feet tall). Rabbinical literature specified that the amount of water must equal 40 *seah* (60 gallons) or 5,760 eggs (1 *seah* equals 144 eggs, *Rab.* Num 18:17; *miqva'ot* in the sixth tractate in the order *T'harot* [Purities] of the *Mishnah*), which translate into 3 cubits long, 1 cubit wide, and 1 cubit deep for the size of the *miqveh* (*b. ʿErub.* 4b; *b. Yoma* 31a).[39]

Not only did individual members of the community participate in regular ritual purifications throughout the year but the entire community participated in a special ceremony at an annual convention during which each member was baptised and new members were also initiated into the sect by baptism.[40] The physical structure of the *mikva'ot* usually accommodated the practice

---

[34] Merrill C. Tenney, *New Testament Times: Understanding the World of the First Century* (Grand Rapids: Baker, 2004), 396.

[35] John J. Collins, "Essenes," ed. David Noel Freedman *et al.*, *ABD* (New York: Doubleday, 1996), 2:623–25.

[36] B. E. Thiering, "Inner and Outer Cleansing at Qumran as a Background to New Testament Baptism," *New Testament Studies* 26, no. 2 (1980): 266–77; Bryant G. Wood, "To Dip or Sprinkle? The Qumran Cisterns in Perspective," *BASOR* 256 (1984): 45–60; William Sanford La Sor, "Discovering What Jewish Mikva'ot Can Tell Us About Christian Baptism," *BAR* 13, no. 1 (1987): 52–59.

[37] McRay, *Archaeology and the NT*, 48.

[38] Steven H. Werlin, "Qumran," ed. Judith R. Baskin, *The Cambridge Dictionary of Judaism and Jewish Culture* (Cambridge: Cambridge University Press, 2011), 505.

[39] Eugene J. Lipman, ed., *The Mishnah; Oral Teachings of Judaism* (Berlin: Schocken, 1974), 318; Evyatar Marienberg, "Mikveh," ed. Judith R. Baskin, *The Cambridge Dictionary of Judaism and Jewish Culture* (Cambridge: Cambridge University Press, 2011), 434.

[40] Matthew Black, *The Scrolls and Christian Origins: Studies in the Jewish Background of the New Testament*, BJS 48 (Atlanta, Ga.: Scholars Press, 1983), 95–97.

of separating the bathers with a centre hand rail to segregate the unclean entering the water and the clean person exiting (*Mid.* 2:2; see Fig. 78).

John the Baptist and the Essenes

There seems to be strong circumstantial evidence to suggest that John the Baptizer may have once been a part of the Essene community at Qumran.[41] The similarities between John and this NT period sect are striking and involved:[42]

- Both practicing baptism (Mark 1:4; 1QS 3:8–9, 12; 5:13–14).
- Both anticipating the coming Messiah (4Q186).
- Both using Isaiah as a theme, quoting a "voice crying: in the wilderness make straight a highway for our God" (Mark 1:3; Isa 40:3–5; 1QS 8.14).
- Both having a diet of locust (5Q12 12.14f.) and honey (Matt 3:4; Mark 1:6).[43]
- John coming out of the Judean wilderness (Matt 3:1) where the Essenes were located at Qumran.
- Both sharing the same ascetic regiment (Matt 3:1–6; 1QS).
- Both criticizing Herod (Luke 3:1–3) which eventually led to John's beheading at Machaerus (Josephus *Ant.* 18.119) and the conquest of the Qumran community by the Romans.

It may be that John was raised as an orphan by the Essenes who were known to care for orphaned children (Josephus *J.W.* 2.120; 8.2–13) since his parents were old when he was born (Luke 1:5–25), but at some point may have left the Essenes over his different view of repentance and community[44] and become a disciple of Jesus. This is speculation, but seems reasonable given the common beliefs and practices.

HEROD ANTIPAS

Herod Antipas (*ca.* 20 BC – *ca.* AD 39) built/rebuilt three cities in his lifetime: Tiberias,[45] Sepphoris[46] and Livias[47] (Betharamphtha or Julias, Josephus *Ant.* 18.27, 36). He is known for having John the Baptist imprisoned and put to death (Matt 14:6–11; Mark 6:14–28) at Machaerus (Josephus *Ant.* 18.119).[48] Apart from being mentioned in Josephus he is attested to in

---

[41] Harold Henry Rowley, "The Baptism of John and the Qumran Sect," in *New Testament Essays*, ed. A. J. B. Higgins (Manchester, MI: Manchester University Press, 1959), 219–23; John A. T Robinson, "The Baptism of John and the Qumran Community," in *Twelve New Testament Studies*, Studies in Biblical Theology 34 (London: SCM, 1962), 11–17; Leonard F Badia, *The Qumran Baptism and John the Baptist's Baptism* (Lanham, MD: University Press of America, 1980); D. S. Dockery, "Baptism," ed. Joel B. Green, Scot McKnight, and I. Howard Marshall, *DJG* (Downers Grove, IL: InterVarsity, 1992).

[42] VanderKam, *The Dead Sea Scrolls Today*, 168–70.

[43] Abraham Rabinovich, "Operation Scroll: Recent Revelations about Qumran Promise to Shake up Dead Sea Scrolls Scholarship," *Jerusalem Post Magazine*, May 6, 1994, 6–10; Zdzislaw Jan Kapera, "Archaeological Interpretations of the Qumran Settlement: A Rapid Review of Hypotheses Fifty Years After the Discoveries at the Dead Sea," in *Mogilany 1989: Papers on the Dead Sea Scrolls Offered in Memory of Jean Carmignac:*, ed. Zdzislaw Jan Kapera, Qumranica Mogilanensia (Krakow: Enigma, 1993), 26 n. 40.

[44] LaSor argues that John was not a member of the Essenes based on his different views and teachings. William Sanford La Sor, *Dead Sea Scrolls and the New Testament* (Grand Rapids: Eerdmans, 1983), 152. The current opinion is that John was not a member of the Qumran community. John C. Hutchison, "Was John the Baptist an Essene from Qumran?," *BSac* 159 (2002): 187–200.

[45] Michael Avi-Yonah *et al.*, "Tiberias," in *EJ*, ed. Michael Berenbaum and Fred Skolnik, 2nd ed., vol. 18 (New York: Macmillan, 2007), 714–16.

[46] Carol L. Meyers and Eric M. Meyers, "Sepphoris," in *OEANE*, ed. Eric M. Meyers, vol. 5 (Oxford: Oxford University Press, 1997), 530; Eric M. Meyers, "Sepphoris," in *EJ*, ed. Michael Berenbaum and Fred Skolnik, 2nd d., vol. 18 (New York: Macmillan, 2007), 306–7.

[47] Graves and Stripling, "Re-Examination of the Location for the Ancient City of Livias," 178–200.

[48] Morten Horning Jensen, *Herod Antipas in Galilee: The Literary and Archaeological Sources on the Reign of Herod Antipas and Its Socio-Economic Impact on Galilee*, Wissenschaftliche Untersuchungen Zum Neuen Testament (Tübingen: Siebeck, 2006); "Herod Antipas in Galilee: Friend or Foe of the Historical Jesus?," *Journal for the Study of the Historical Jesus* 5, no. 1 (January 2007): 7–32.

rare coins from his era, which bear the inscription "Herod the tetrarch" (Gr. ΗΡωΔΌΥ ΤΕΤΡΆΡΧΌΥ) alongside a palm branch.[49]

Some scholars believe that Herod Antipas was living at Livias, an important administration centre,[50] when he arrested John (Matt 14:3) and had him transported to Machaerus where he was put to death (Josephus *Ant.* 18.119). Edersheim speculates that while Herod was building his capital, Tiberias, on the Galilean shores, and while Jesus was ministering in Galilee, that Herod was living in the south at Livias in Perea.[51] He argued that this was why Jesus and Herod did not come into contact with each other until Jesus was in Jerusalem in the south near Perea and Livias, which was on the Roman road that leads to Jerusalem.

110. Livia Drusilla, (58 BC-AD 29, Tiberius' mother). After her formal adoption into the Julian family in AD 14, she was deified by Claudius, subsequently acquiring the additional name Julia Augusta.

Ephesus Museum, Turkey.

While Herod Antipas posed as a Jewish leader, celebrating Passover and the Feast of Tabernacles (Heb. *Sukkoth*) in Jerusalem, his subjects were unconvinced and Jesus compared him to a fox, a ceremonially unclean animal (Luke 13:31–33). Herod desired to see Jesus (Luke 9:7–9), but they never met face to face until Jesus' trial in Jerusalem (Luke 23:5–12).

Livias (Tall el-Ḥammâm)

The traditional location for the Roman city of Livias, rebuilt and named by Herod Antipas in 13 AD, is Tall er-Ramêh in Jordan.[52] However, upon closer examination of the evidence from archaeology, cartography, and ancient texts, the area around Tall el-Ḥammâm is considered by Graves and Stripling as a stronger candidate (see Map 1 and Fig. 61).[53] The smaller and less significant site of Tall er-Ramêh could

111. Roman bath complex excavated in 2011–2012 from Tall el-Hammâm, Jordan. The site is believed to be the city of Livias and this structure originally may have been Herod Antipas' bath complex. The building this room was located in measures 35 x 40 meters (115 x 131 ft).

[49] Jensen, *Herod Antipas in Galilee*, 2006, 204.

[50] Harold W. Hoehner, *Herod Antipas: A Contemporary of Jesus Christ* (Grand Rapids: Zondervan Academie Books, 1980), 47–48; Jensen, *Herod Antipas in Galilee*, 2006, 10.

[51] Alfred Edersheim, *The Life and Times of Jesus the Messiah*, New updated ed. (Peabody, MA: Hendrickson, 1993), 450.

[52] Siméon Vailhé, "Livias," trans. Mario Anello, *CE* (New York: Appleton & Company, 1913), 315; Albright, "The Jordan Valley in the Bronze Age," 49; Glueck, *Explorations in Eastern Palestine*, 11; Kay Prag, "A Walk in the Wadi Hesban," *PEQ* 123, no. 1 (1991): 60–61.

[53] Graves and Stripling, "Re-Examination of the Location for the Ancient City of Livias," 178–200. In the EB and MB periods Tall el-Ḥammâm is also believed to be Sodom (see Chapter Three: Sodom and Gomorrah).

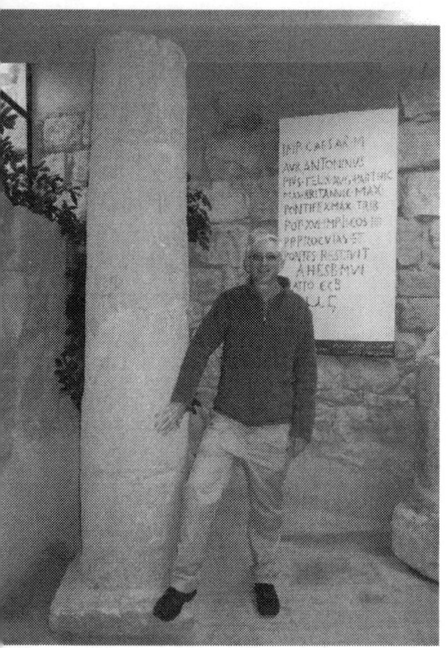

112. The author standing beside a Roman mile marker indicating 6 Roman miles to Livias. Mt. Nebo museum, Jordan.

not have been the regal city named after Emperor Augustus' wife, Livia (see Fig. 110), at least not all of it.

On the other hand, the region adjacent to Tall el-Ḥammâm is a good candidate, identified in the proper Roman period with significant monumental material remains. Remains include a 35 m by 40 m bath complex (see Fig. 111), aqueduct system, 5 cisterns, which could hold over 1 million liters of water, six defensive fortifications and two Roman defensive towers. Tall el-Ḥammâm is in the right place for it to be the Livias of the Madaba Map (see Fig. 61).[54] In addition, early Christian pilgrims' testimony of the thermal springs (*aquae calidae*) of Livias[55] validates the location of Livias as being in the same vicinity as Tall el-Ḥammâm (means "hill of the hot baths") which still has several active hot springs.

And finally, but most importantly, the Roman mile markers (see Fig. 112) and textual distances provide an indisputable indicator for the location of Livias at Tall el-Ḥammâm, which was 12 Roman miles east of Jericho (Theodosius *Top.* 19), 12 Roman miles west of Heshbon (Esbus, Eusebius *On.* 12; 18; 48; 136), and 5 Roman miles south of Tall Nimrin (Eusebius *On.* 44). When these coordinates are triangulated they intersect at Tall el-Ḥammâm and not Tall er-Ramêh.

During previous seasons at Tall el-Ḥammâm, the excavations of the Roman areas have supported the theory that the region around Tall el-Ḥammâm, which grew in the Early Roman period, is the administrative centre of Livias (see Fig. 111).[56]

Oil Lamps

In 2010, Graves and Stripling reported on the significant discovery which confirms that Tall el-Ḥammâm was located on the Roman road leading from Jerusaem to Heshbon, stating:

> A piece of a Byzantine oil lamp, with a Greek inscription, was uncovered along the SW wall of the large structure at TeH (see Fig. 113). The oil lamp was identical (5 of 7 Greek letters) to one published from the 2009 Temple Mount Salvage Operation in Jerusalem.[57] According to Alliata, these oil lamps are "recognized as a typical product of the Jerusalem area … considered to be ***eulogies*** or souvenirs that the

---

[54] Graves and Stripling, "Identification of Tall el-Hammam," 35–45.

[55] John Rufus, "Vita Petri Iberi," in *Petrus Der Iberer. Ein Characterbild Zur Kirchen- Und Sittengeschichte Des Fünften Jahrhundert*, trans. Richard Raabe (Leipzig: J. C. Hinrichs'sche Buchhandlung, 1895), l. 116 [R83]; Horn and Phenix Jr., *John Rufus*, 19; John Wilkinson, ed., *Egeria's Travels: Translated with Supporting Documents and Notes*, trans. John Wilkinson, 3rd ed. (Warminster: Aris & Phillips, 1999); John Wilkinson, *Jerusalem Pilgrims Before the Crusades* (Oxford: Aris & Phillips, 2002), 82, 165–66; Gregory of Tours, *Glory of the Martyrs [Liber in Gloria Martyrum]*, trans. Raymond Van Dam, Translated Texts for Historians Latin Series 3 (Liverpool: Liverpool University Press, 2004), 1–17; Egeria, *The Pilgrimage of Etheria*, 19, 23.

[56] Collins, "2005-2006 Season Summary"; Collins, Hamdan, and Byers, "Tall el-Hammam: Preliminary Report, Season Four, 2009"; Steven Collins *et al.*, *The Tall Al-Hammam Excavation Project End of Season Activity Report Season Two: 2006/2007 Excavation and Exploration* (Submitted to the Department of Antiquities of the Hashemite Kingdom of Jordan, 2007); Kobs, *The Tall Al-Hammam Excavation Project 2005–2013: Volume One: Seven Seasons of Ceramics, Eight Seasons of Artifacts.*

[57] Gordon Franz and Stephanie Hernandez, "The Most Important Discovery Was the People: An Interview with Dr. Gabriel Barkay," *Bible and Spade* 22, no. 1 (2009): 8.

pilgrims took back from Jerusalem to their home."[58] These *eulogae*, from the holy places in Jerusalem, have been found at Abila, Jerash, Amman, Heshbon, Madaba, Mount Nebo and as far south as Qorayat.[59]

Based on the absence of soot on the lamps, Hirschfeld and Solar following Antoninus Placentius's description of the ritual bathing practices at Hammat-Gader, suggest that the lepers used the lamps in some ritual healing ceremony carried out at the thermal springs (*aquae calidae*).[60] The complete Greek inscription reads "The Light of Christ Shines for All" (φῶς Χριστοῦ φένιπαῦιν) and dates to the 5th to 7th century AD.[61] The oil lamp establishes a Christian presence at TeH during the period of the construction of the Madaba Map (AD 542 and 570) and lends credibility to the structure being a bath house.[62]

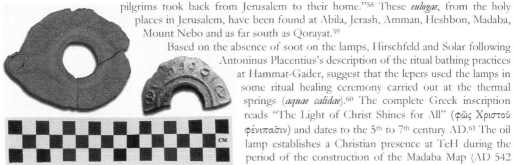

113. Oil lamp fragments from the 2009 Tall el-Ḥammâm excavation. Left: The top section of a pear shaped oil lamp with tongue handle that dates to the Umayyad period, eighth to eleventh cent. AD. Right: Byzantine oil lamp fragment with Greek letters that represent "The Light of Christ Shines for All" dating to the fifth to seventh cent. AD.

The discovery of the oil lamp manufactured in Jerusalem, along with all the other evidence, lends support to the theory that Tall el-Ḥammâm was on the Roman road from Jerusalem to Heshbon and is indeed part of Livias, Herod's capital of Perea.

EPHRAIM – KHIRBET EL-MAQATIR

The Associates for Biblical Research organization excavated at Khirbet el-Maqatir from 2007 to 2017. They believe that the MB level of the site is the biblical city of Ai (see Chapter Four: Ai). However, the Roman level is believed by Stripling to be the NT city of Ephraim,[63] where Jesus stayed for a period of time with his disciples (John 11:53–54; Josephus *J.W.* 4.9.551; Josephus listed Ephraim with Bethel).[64] Stripling reports that as of 2016 the numismatic finds at Khirbet el-Maqatir include some 1351 coins and states that the: "excavated coins are especially instructive, as the number spikes dramatically in the second cent. BC and abruptly ends in AD 69 with Year 3 Revolt coins."[65] Stripling also reports that: "a memorial church and monastery dating from the fourth century has been excavated on the western ridge of Khirbet el-Maqatir; unfortunately, the mosaics are badly damaged, and one cannot determine what biblical event(s)

[58] Eugenio Alliata, "The Pilgrimage Routes during the Byzantine Period in Transjordan," in *The Madaba Map Centenary: Travelling Through the Byzantine Umayyad Period. Proceedings of the International Conference Held in Amman 7–9 April 1997*, ed. Michele Piccirillo and Eugenio Alliata, Studium Biblicum Franciscannum Collectio Maior 40 (Jerusalem: Studium Biblicum Franciscannum, 1999), 123; Jodi Magness, *Jerusalem Ceramic Chronology: Circa 200-800 CE*, JSOT/ASOR Monographs 9 (Sheffield: Sheffield Academic, 1993), 176.

[59] Alliata, "Pilgrimage Routes," 123.

[60] Yizhar Hirschfeld and G. Solar, "The Roman Thermae at Hammat-Gader: Preliminary Report of Three Seasons of Excavations," *IEJ* 31, no. 3/4 (1981): 202, 206; Estee Dvorjetski, *Leisure, Pleasure, and Healing: Spa Culture and Medicine in Ancient Eastern Mediterranean*, Supplements to the Journal for the Study of Judaism 116 (Leiden: Brill, 2007), 230.

[61] Donald Michael Bailey, *Greek and Roman Pottery Lamps*, Rev. ed. (London: British Museum, 1972), 14a; Viviane Hoff, Catherine Metzger, and Christiane Lyon-Caen, *Catalogue Des Lampes En Terre Cuite Grecques et Chrétiennes*, Musée Du Louvre. Département Des Antiquités Grecques et Romaines (Paris: Ministère de la Culture et de la Communication, 1986), 172–76; Srdjan Djuric, *Ancient Lamps from the Mediterranean* (Toronto: Eika, 1995), c253; Henning Wetzel, *Antike Tonlampen* (Leipzig: Leipziger Universitätsverlag, 1997), 25; Stanislao Loffreda, *Light and Life: Ancient Christian Oil Lamps of the Holy Land*, Studium Biblicum (Jerusalem: Franciscan, 2001), 22–31; Noam Adler, *Oil Lamps of the Holy Land from the Adler Collection* (Jerusalem: Old City, 2005), 150–51.

[62] Graves and Stripling, "Re-Examination of the Location for the Ancient City of Livias," 196–97.

[63] D. Scott Stripling, "Have We Walked in the Footsteps of Jesus? Exciting New Possibilities at Khirbet El-Maqatir," *Bible and Spade* 27, no. 4 (2014): 88–94.

[64] The traditional location for Ephraim is Taybe. Yoel Elitzur, *Ancient Place Names in the Holy Land: Preservation and History* (Jerusalem, Israel: The Hebrew University Magnes Press, 2004), 270; Stripling, "Have We Walked in the Footsteps of Jesus?," 88–94.

[65] Ibid., 92.

114. Whole stone vessels from Khirbet el-Maqatir.
Courtesy of Tommy Chamberlin and Scott Stripling

115. Pool of Siloam, discovered in 2004. Currently over 20 steps have been excavated leading down into the pool.
Courtesy of Todd Bolen/BiblePlaces.com

they commemorate."[66]

Excavations at Khirbet el-Maqatir also yielded over 100 stone vessel fragments, including several whole vessels (see Fig. 114). Jesus' first miracle involved changing water to wine in a large stone jar (John 2). Stone vessels appear in the archaeological record around 100 BC. While archaeologists set forth various explanations for this change in material culture, most agree that it reflects a wave of ritual purity observance, rooted in Leviticus 11 and 15.

POOL OF SILOAM

The Pool of Siloam (Heb. *siloam* meaning "sent") was part of the water system of Jerusalem (lower pool, Isa 22:9; by the King's Garden, Neh 3:15). Hezekiah's tunnel,[67] brought water from the Gihon Spring to the Pool of Siloam, in the Silwan neighbourhood of East Jerusalem (see Fig. 115 and 116).

Until 2004 most scholars accepted a small narrow Byzantine pool, called the *Birkeh Silwan*, as the traditional site of the Pool of Siloam and associated it with the healing miracle of Jesus mentioned in John (John 9:1–11). A Byzantine church was built on the location by empress Aelia Eudocia (*ca.* AD 440), which is also depicted on the Madaba Map (AD 575).[68] A Moslem mosque now occupies the place where the church once stood. However, Bahat, in an article on this subject, concludes it by postulating: "There is no available proof that the Second Temple period Siloam Pool was situated at the present-day site, and it is more plausible that the pool was situated at the location of the nearby *Birket el-Hamra* ["the red pool"], where there is now a flourishing vegetable garden."[69]

---

[66] Ibid., 91.

[67] Built through 1,777 feet of solid rock by King Hezekiah in 711 BC and discovered in 1838 to supply fresh water for Jerusalem.

[68] W. Harold Mare, "Siloam, Pool of (Place)," ed. David Noel Freedman *et al.*, *ABD* (New York: Doubleday, 1996), 25; Avraham Negev, "Siloam," in *EAEHL*, ed. Michael Avi-Yonah and Ephraim Stern, 3rd ed., vol. 4, 4 vols. (New York: Prentice Hall, 1996).

[69] Dan Bahat, *The Atlas of Biblical Jerusalem* (Jerusalem: Carta, 1994), 33; Frederick Jones Bliss and A. C. Dickie, *Excavations at Jerusalem 1894-1897* (London: PEF, 1898), 140–54; John Wilkinson, "The Pool of Siloam," *Levant* 10, no. 1 (January 1978): 125.

116. A stepped pool was discovered at the mouth of the Central or Tyropoeon Valley which is located between the Western and Eastern Hills of Jerusalem. This large pool served as one of the water reservoirs of Jerusalem. The building with the double entrance at the top of the drawing probably had a religious function. It was perhaps in that building that the blind man, who was healed by Jesus, washed himself (John 9:11).

During 2004, repairs to a sewage line, less than 200 ft. (61 m) southeast of the *Birkeh Silwan*, caught the attention of archaeologists Ronny Reich and Eli Shukron, who were working nearby (see Fig. 115). They visited the *Birket el-Hamra* site and noticed the remains of the steps leading down to the pool and put a halt to the work to investigate.[70]

Over the next few weeks they discovered (20 ft (6 m) wide Herodian stones which lead from the pool (*miqveh*) to the street level and then up to the Temple. These stones confirm that this was likely the Pool of Siloam mentioned in John's gospel. Based on coins and pottery embedded in the cement, the structure was securely dated to the First Jewish Revolt against Rome (AD 66 to 70) and the time of Jesus. After the destruction of Jerusalem in AD 70 it was no longer used.[71]

While scholars debate the function of the pool, questioning whether it was a Jewish ritual pool called a *miqveh* (for example see Fig. 109) or a swimming pool,[72] what is not debated is that

---

[70] Hershel Shanks, "The Siloam Pool: Where Jesus Cured the Blind Man," *BAR* 31, no. 5 (2005): 18.

[71] Ronny Reich and Eli Shukron, "The Siloam Pool in the Wake of Recent Discoveries," in *New Studies on Jerusalem*, ed. Eyal Baruch, Ayelet Levy-Reifer, and Avraham Faust, 10 (Jerusalem, Israel: Bar-Ilan University, 2004), 137–39; Ronny Reich, "The Pool of Siloam," in *NEAEHL*, ed. Ephraim Stern, Ayelet Levinson-Gilboa, and Joseph Aviram, vol. 5 (Jerusalem: The Israel Exploration Society, 2008), 5:1807.

[72] Shimon Gibson, "The Pool of Bethesda in Jerusalem and Jewish Purification Practices of the Second Temple Period," *Proche-Orient Chrétiens* 55 (2005): 291; Yoel Elitzur, "The Siloam Pool-- 'Solomon's Pool-- Was a Swimming Pool'," *PEQ* 140, no. 1 (2008): 17–25; Hershel Shanks, "Ritual Bath or Swimming Pool?," *BAR* 34, no. 3 (2008): 18; James H. Charlesworth, "The Tale of Two Pools: Archaeology and the Book of John," *Near East Archaeological Society Bulletin* 56 (2011): 1–14.

the pool was used in Jesus' day, with this confirming the topographical accuracy of the Gospel of John.

It is yet undetermined whether the Pool from Hezekiah and Isaiah's time was located on the same site as the Herodian remains. While Reich and Shukron would like to further explore the site for IA pottery, the remainder of the site is under the adjacent garden of the Greek Orthodox church, who at present do not want to damage the gardens to allow further archaeological work.[73]

Commentators have pointed to the Byzantine Pool of Siloam (*Birkeh Silwan*) and claimed that the Herodian Pool of Siloam did not exist in Jesus' day. For these commentators, John invented the Herodian Pool of Siloam based on the meaning of Siloam, which is "sent", for rhetorical purposes, because Jesus was sent as the Light of the World to give sight to the blind (John 9:1–11). For some the miracle at the Pool of Siloam was merely a parable based on a play on words. But now, with the discovery of the *Birket el-Hamra*, there is no doubt that the symbolism, which is present in the text, is based on history and John's eyewitness account of the sites in Jerusalem.[74]

GOSPEL OF JUDAS

The Gnostic writings called the *Nag Hammadi* texts have been available since the mid 1940's (see *Chapter Two, Nag Hammadi Library*). However, one of the texts, called the *Gospel of Judas,* and known from the writings of Irenaeus (AD 180),[75] Epiphanius (*Pan.* 38.1.5), and Theodoret (*Com.* 1.15), was not among the *Nag Hammadi* texts. The codex came to public awareness at a press conference in 2006 by the National Geographic Society, which announced it to the world.

The discovery of the *Gospel of Judas* (Codex Tchacos[76]; see Fig. 117) is a story of intrigue and misfortune. To the best of our knowledge the leather bound book (codex), with papyrus pages written in Coptic, based on an earlier Greek text, was discovered in a cave somewhere in Egypt in the 1970's. Following a few years floating around Egyptian antiquities dealers, Stephen Emmel, a respected Coptic scholar, examined the fragments in Geneva in 1983 and determined that it was a legitimate fourth cent. document. While the carbon-14 dating has indicated a date of *ca.* AD 220–340, most of the members of the research team have settled on AD 300–320. Failing to obtain the asking price, the codex found its way to the United States, where it was placed in a safety deposit box, and subsequently in a freezer, where the manuscript sustained significant damage before it was recovered and partially restored (*ca.* 85%; 13 pages extant with 42 pages missing) by the National Geographic Society. It was announced to the world in March 2006 at a

---

[73] Shanks, "The Siloam Pool," 23; Charlesworth, "The Tale of Two Pools," 8.

[74] Urban C. von Wahlde, "The Pool of Siloam: The Importance of the New Discoveries For Our Understanding of Ritual Immersion in Late Second Temple Judaism and the Gospel of John," in *John, Jesus, and History: Aspects of Historicity in the Fourth Gospel,* ed. Paul N. Anderson, Felix Just, and Tom Thatcher (Atlanta, Ga.: SBL, 2009), 155–73; Charlesworth, "The Tale of Two Pools," 7–11.

[75] Irenaeus, writing against a Gnostic group called the Cainites (because they make heroes out of the biblical villains, such as Cain, who killed his brother), stated: "they produce a fictitious history of this kind, which they style the *Gospel of Judas*" (*Haer.* 1.31.1). Witherington is unconvinced that Irenaeus is talking about the same document, while Van Oort argues for the same document. Ben Witherington III, *What Have They Done with Jesus?: Beyond Strange Theories and Bad History–Why We Can Trust the Bible*, Reprint edition (New York: HarperOne, 2007), 7–8; Johannes van Oort, "Irenaeus's Knowledge of the Gospel of Judas: Real or False? An Analysis of the Evidence in Context," *HTS Teologiese Studies* 69, no. 1 (January 2013): 1–8.

[76] Named after the antiquities dealer, Frieda Nussberger-Tchacos.

press conference.[77]

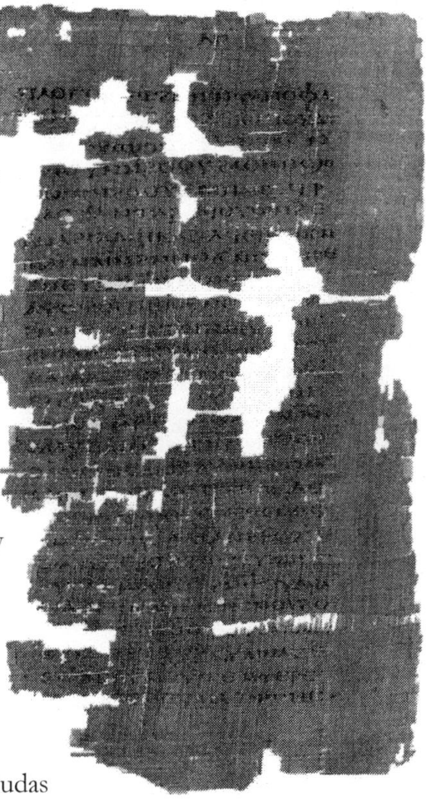

117. The first page of the *Gospel of Judas* (Page 33 of Codex Tchacos. Wikimedia Commons

The *Gospel of Judas* opens with these words: "the secret account of the revelation that Jesus spoke in conversation with Judas Iscariot" (p. 33, lines 1–3)[78] and ends with the words: "the Gospel of Judas" (p. 58, lines 28–29). Between these statements, Judas Iscariot, who betrayed Jesus (Matt 26:21–25; Mark 14:18–21; Luke 22:21–23; John 13:21–30), is portrayed as the greatest of the disciples of Jesus with the ability to understand Jesus' profound and mysterious teachings. While the other disciples are confounded by Jesus' teaching, it is Judas who truly comprehends that Jesus has come from "the immortal realm of Barbelo" (p. 35, line 18). As a result, Judas is privately tutored by Jesus and told that he will sacrifice the body of Jesus, thus becoming the greatest disciple and hero of the story. According to the *Gospel of Judas,* only Judas knew and understood the true gospel.

There is no doubt that this document is not from Judas, the disciple of Jesus, but rather a Gnostic pseudonymous document, falsely attributed to Judas and written to deceive the reader into thinking it was from the Judas of the Bible.

Craig Evans argues that: "the imaginative tale in Judas may in fact reflect an authentic tradition, in which it was remembered that Judas was an important disciple and that Jesus had given him a private assignment of some sort. This is what may be hinted at in Jn 13. The *Gospel of Judas* alerts us to this possibility, even if we judge its narrative to be wholly fictional."[79]

The value of this document is in presenting a copy of the kind of Gnostic teaching circulating in the first two centuries of Christianity.[80] Gathercole summarized the implications of the *Gospel of Judas* well when he stated:

> One should be extremely sceptical of claims that "it will open up new vistas for understanding Jesus".[81] It has very little that can be regarded as historically reliable: indeed nothing that is new in the ***Gospel of Judas*** can be said with any confidence to go back to historical bedrock. In addition, it is difficult to imagine a twentyfirst-century reader who would find its vision of a somewhat loveless Jesus detached from a body in any way theologically attractive.[82]

---

[77] Andrew Cockburn, "The Judas Gospel," *National Geographic* 209, no. 9 (2006): 78–95; Sandra Scham, "An Apology for Judas," *Archaeology* 59, no. 4 (2006): 50–51; Herbert Krosney and Bart D. Ehrman, *The Lost Gospel: The Quest for the Gospel of Judas Iscariot* (Washington, DC: National Geographic, 2007); Evans, *Fabricating Jesus*, 240–41.

[78] Rodolphe Kasser *et al., The Gospel of Judas* (Washington, DC: National Geographic, 2008).

[79] Evans, *Fabricating Jesus*, 271 n.9.

[80] James M. Robinson, *From the Nag Hammadi Codices to the Gospel of Mary and the Gospel of Judas*, Institute for Antiquity and Christianity Occasional Papers 48 (Claremont, Calf.: Institute for Antiquity & Christianity, 2006).

[81] Bart D. Ehrman, "Christianity Turned on Its Head: The Alternative Vision of the Gospel of Judas," in *The Gospel of Judas*, ed. Rodolphe Kasser et al. (Washington, DC: National Geographic, 2008), 80.

[82] Simon Gathercole, "The Gospel of Judas," *ExpTim* 118, no. 5 (February 2007): 215; N. T. Wright, *Judas and the Gospel of Jesus: Have We Missed the Truth about Christianity?* (Grand Rapids: Baker, 2006).

118. In 1955, during construction of the Dominus Flevit ("The Lord wept") Church, a burial chamber was discovered. Excavations uncovered a number of ossuaries (bone boxes) from the time of Jesus with numerous inscriptions of biblical names and geometric shapes.

OSSUARIES

In the Mediterranean climate bodies decomposed quickly. Therefore, the body was washed and wrapped in a clean cloth (shroud)[83] in preparation for burial (Matt 27:59; Luke 23:53; John 11:44; 19:40; Acts 5:6; 9:37).[84] Spices and perfume (Gr. *aromata*) were then added to the body to control the odour of decay (Josephus *Ant.* 15.61; 17.196–99; John 19:39–40). Thus, several women went to the tomb in order to anoint the body of Jesus with spices (Luke 24:1). The ladies were going to treat Jesus' body with something that would control the decaying flesh.

While the Egyptians embalmed their dead bodies, and the Romans and the Greeks cremated theirs (Dionysius *Thuc.* 2.34.5; Herodotus *Hist.* 9.85.2)[85], during the Second Temple period (between 530 BC and AD 70), the Jewish burial practices were different and carried out in two stages. First, the body was placed in a cave for a period of about one year (*b. Qidd.* 31b), where the flesh would decompose and fall off the bones (*m. Sanh.* 6:6). Then the bones were collected and placed in inscribed ossuaries (Limestone bone box, Lat. *ossilegium; b. Sem.* 3.2; 12.9), then placed in small niches in caves (see Fig. 118, 119, and 120). This two-stage practice was only popular during the Hellenistic and Roman periods.[86] The body of a crucified criminal was buried properly, but not in places of honor, such as the family tomb (*m. Sanh.* 6:5; *b. Sem.* 13.7).[87] Also, there was to be no mourning for the executed criminal (*m. Sanh.* 6:6).[88]

However, in fulfillment of Scripture (Isa 53:9), Jesus' body would not be treated with disgrace, but rather he would be buried with the wealthy. This was part of his exaltation.

The Talpiot Tomb

The Talpiot (or Talpiyot) Tomb is a cave tomb cut out of the rock and discovered in 1980 in the

---

[83] There is no archaeological evidence that the shroud of Turin is connected with the cloth used in Jesus' burial. Kenneth L. Feder, *Encyclopedia of Dubious Archaeology: From Atlantis to the Walam Olum* (Santa Barbara, CA: Greenwood, 2010), 241–43.

[84] Robert L. Kelly and David Hurst Thomas, *Archaeology* (Boston, MA: Cengage Learning, 2012), 133.

[85] Philip Sabin, Hans van Wees, and Michael Whitby, *The Cambridge History of Greek and Roman Warfare: Volume 1, Greece, The Hellenistic World and the Rise of Rome* (Cambridge: Cambridge University Press, 2007), 175.

[86] Craig A. Evans, *Jesus and the Ossuaries: What Burial Practices Reveal About the Beginning of Christianity* (Waco, Tex.: Baylor University Press, 2003), 28–29.

[87] Mordechai Aviam, "Regionalism of Tombs and Burial Customs in the Galilee During the Hellenistic, Roman and Byzantine Periods," in *Jews, Pagans and Christians in the Galilee: 25 Years of Archaeological Excavations and Surveys: Hellenistic to Byzantine Periods*, ed. Mordechai Aviam, Land of Galilee 1 (Rochester, NY: University of Rochester Press, 2004), 257–313; E. Regev, "Family Burial, Family Structure, and the Urbanization of Herodian Jerusalem," *PEQ* 136 (2004): 109–31.

[88] Craig A. Evans, "The Family Buried Together Stays Together: On the Burial of the Executed in Family Tombs," in *The World of Jesus and the Early Church: Identity and Interpretation in Early Communities of Faith*, ed. Craig A. Evans (Peabody, MA: Hendrickson, 2011), 89.

East Talpiot neighborhood, in the Old City of Jerusalem (see Fig. 118). Ten ossuaries (bone boxes) were discovered (No. 701–709)[89] and on six of them there were inscriptions. One of the inscriptions has been translated as "Yeshua bar Yehosef" ("Jesus, son of Joseph"), although the letters are not clear and scholars debate its authenticity.[90]

It was first mentioned in the media some sixteen years later in 1996 and published in a journal article later that year.[91] It was popularized in a TV program by journalist Simcha Jacobovici called *The Lost Tomb of Jesus* to promote his upcoming book called *The Jesus Family Tomb.*[92] They presented what they believed to be evidence to prove that this was the burial place of Jesus of Nazareth along with other key figures of the NT, like Mary and Martha. The claims, if true, would negate the resurrection and possibly nullify the Christian faith. Many archaeologists and language experts have disputed the claim.[93] As Heiser points out:

> The problems presented below must not be overlooked or minimized, for the Jesus tomb theory is only compelling if two items are true: (1) that the Jesus of the tomb's Jesus ossuary was in fact Jesus of Nazareth, and (2) the names of the people in the tomb are related to the Jesus of this tomb in the same way that people with those names were related to the Jesus of the New Testament. Both these items are inextricably linked. We can only embrace the Jesus tomb theory if its Jesus figure was Jesus of Nazareth, and that in turn can really only be established if the other people in the tomb are the people who knew Jesus of Nazareth. Hence the Jesus figure of the tomb only takes on the identity of Jesus of Nazareth if it can be established if the other people in the tomb were related to the Jesus figure they [*sic.* the] way the New Testament describes. The inscriptions must match the New Testament record to get Jesus in the tomb, so to speak. If they do not, there is no case.[94]

The names on the ossuaries read *Mariamenou [e] Mara* ("Mary, who is…"), *Yhwdh br Yshw'* ("Judah/Jude, son of Jesus"), *Mtyh* ("Matiyahu" or, "Matthew"), *Yshw' br Yhwsp* ("Jesus, son of Joseph"), *Ywsh* ("Joseph/Jose"), and *Mryh* ("Mary"). While these names are familiar to any reader of the NT, and our minds automatically gravitate to these stories, the names are very common in the first century.

119. The inscribed ossuary of the high priest, Joseph, son of Caiaphas (*Yosef Bar Kayafa*), found in Jerusalem in 1990 (Josephus *Ant.* 18.35; 18.95). Caiaphas was the leader of the Sanhedrin from AD 18–36 and played an integral role in Jesus' conflict with the Jewish leaders in the final week of his life (John 11:49–53; 18:14). Caiaphas presided over the evening trial in which Jesus confessed to being the Messiah and ultimately condemned him to death (Matt 26:57–68).

The Israel Museum, Jerusalem. Photo by Deror_avi / Wikimedia Commons

Ben Witherington shared some statistics gathered by Richard Backham (Professor of New Testament Studies and Bishop Wardlaw Professor at St Andrews): While there are limited numbers of archaeological discoveries, the number of occurrences of popular Jewish names is quite high (see Table 3).[95]

Peter Lampe, professor of New Testament

[89] L. Y. Rahmani, *A Catalogue of Jewish Ossuaries: In the Collections of the State of Israel* (Jerusalem: Israel Academy of Sciences and Humanities, 1994), 304.

[90] Michael S. Heiser, "Evidence Real and Imagined: Thinking Clearly About the 'Jesus Family Tomb,'" *Www.michaelsheiser.com*, 2008, 1–22.

[91] Amos Kloner, "A Tomb with Inscribed Ossuaries in East Talpiyot, Jerusalem," *Atiquot* 29 (1996): 15–22.

[92] Simcha Jacobovici and Charles Pellegrino, *The Jesus Family Tomb: The Evidence Behind the Discovery No One Wanted to Find* (San Francisco, Calf.: HarperOne, 2008).

[93] Gary R. Habermas, *The Secret of the Talpiot Tomb: Unraveling the Mystery of the Jesus Family Tomb* (Nashville, TN: Holman Reference, 2008), 23–66.

[94] Heiser, "Evidence Real and Imagined: Thinking Clearly About the 'Jesus Family Tomb,'" 6.

[95] Ben Witherington III, "The Jesus Tomb? 'Titanic' Talpiot Tomb Theory Sunk From the Start," Blog, *Ben Witherington*, (February 26, 2007), http://benwitherington .blogspot.ru/2007/02/jesus-tomb-titanic-talpiot-tomb-theory.html.

Popular First Cent. Names

Name	Total References	On Ossuaries
Simeon	243	59
Joseph	218	45
Eleazar	166	29
Judah	164	44
John	122	25
Jesus	99	22
Hananiah	82	18
Jonathan	71	14
Matthew	62	17
Menahem	42	4
Mary/Mariamne	70	42
Salome	58	41
Shelamzion	24	19
Martha	20	17

Table 3. A list of first cent. names indicating how popular these names were in the first century. Out of a total number of 2625 male names, Bauckham provides the top ten males and top four female names.

Studies at the University of Heidelberg, mentions that in the 120/130's AD in the port of Maoza near the southern end of the Dead Sea lived a Jewish family with the names of Jesus, Simon, Mariame, Jacobus and Judah (Papyri Babatha 17 from AD 128; 25–26 and 34 from AD 131).[96] However, none of these individuals had anything to do with the NT or the Talpiot tomb. A combination of such names was certainly common, as this small sampling of names indicates.

While there are additional arguments put forth on both sides, the general consensus of almost all scholars it that the names found on the ossuaries of the Talpiot tomb were not the NT individuals mentioned in the Bible.

In 1955, during the construction of the Dominus Flevit church on the Mount of Olives in Jerusalem, a necropolis (ancient city cemetery) was discovered with two periods of occupation. The earlier tombs were connected with the ossuaries (185–136 BC) and contained religious symbols, along with 43 inscriptions (in Hebrew, Aramaic and Greek) of common NT names such as Mary, Martha, Philo the Cyrene, Matthew, Joseph, and Jesus.[97]

The James Ossuary

This bone box (ossuary) was brought to the attention of the public in October 2002, through *BAR* editor Hershel Shanks, when the owner, Oded Golan, an Israeli antiquities collector, announced the discovery of the inscription at a press conference in Washington (see Fig. 90). The inscription was initially translated and published by the noted Semitic epigrapher André Lemaire in *BAR* magazine in December 2002.[98]

The Aramaic inscription transliterated reads: *Ya'akov bar Yosef akhui di Yeshua* which when translated into English reads: "Jacob (James), son of Joseph, brother of Jesus" (see Fig. 91).[99] Within months (2003) the Israeli Antiquities Authority declared the last part of the inscription "brother of Jesus" was a forgery[100] and charged Golan in December of 2004 with 44 counts of

[96] Peter Lampe, "MEXPI THC CHMEPON: A New Edition of Matthew 27:64b; 28:13 in Today's Pop Science and a Salty Breeze from the Dead Sea," in *Neutestamentliche Exegese Im Dialog: Hermeneutik - Wirkungsgeschichte - Matthäusevangelium*, ed. Peter Lampe, Moisés Mayordomo, and Migaku Sato, Festschrift Für Ulrich Luz Zum 70 (Geburtstag: Neukirchener Verlag, 2008), 355–66; Ross Shepard Kraemer, *Women's Religions in the Greco-Roman World: A Sourcebook* (Oxford: Oxford University Press, 2004), 143–52; Yigael Yadin, Jonas C. Greenfield, and Ada Yardeni, "Babatha's Ketubbah," *IEJ* 44, no. 1–2 (1994): 75–101; Yigael Yadin, "The Judean desert expeditions, 1962. Expedition D. Cave of letters," *Yedot* 26 (1962): 204–36; Lewis, Greenfield, and Yadin, *Documents from the Bar Kokhba.*

[97] Bellarmino Bagatti and Józef Tadeusz Milik, *Gli Scavi Del "Dominus Flevit": Monte Oliveto-Gerusalemme*, vol. 2 (Jerusalem: Tipografia dei PP. Francescani, 1958).

[98] André LeMaire, "Burial Box of James the Brother of Jesus: Earliest Archaeological Evidence of Jesus Found in Jerusalem," *BAR* 28, no. 6 (2002): 24–33, 70.

[99] Ibid., 24.

[100] Uzi Dahari, *Final Report of the Examining Committees For the Yehoash Inscription and James Ossuary* (Israeli Antiquities Authority, 2011).

deception, forgery, and fraud.[101] Much debate inside and outside of court ensued, with the court proceedings coming to a close in October 3, 2010 and Golan being acquitted of forgery charges on March 14, 2012.[102]

Holden summarizes the historical implications of the discovery: "It informs us that 1) James, Joseph, and Jesus had historical corroboration as individuals and a family in the first century; 2) early Christians, like James, may have been buried according to Jewish custom; 3) Aramaic was used by early Christians; and that 4) early Christianity emerged from its Jewish roots, making it extremely difficult to divorce Christianity from its Jewishness."[103]

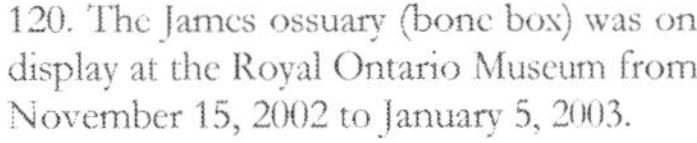

120. The James ossuary (bone box) was on display at the Royal Ontario Museum from November 15, 2002 to January 5, 2003.

While the inscription has been verified as legitimate by the Israeli courts, they did not answer the question as to whether the name Jesus, whose brother was James (mentioned on the ossuary) is the Jesus of the NT. This is another debate that is being fought outside the courts by archaeologists and epigraphers.[104]

121. Close-up of the Aramaic inscription on the James ossuary which was on display at the Royal Ontario Museum from November 15, 2002 to January 5, 2003.

GABRIEL'S REVELATION

This unusual stone slab is also known as the "Hazon Gabriel stone" or the "Jeselsohn stone", after Dr. David Jeselsohn who owns it. It is unusual because the Hebrew text is written in ink on a stone stele rather than on papyrus or leather. It was discovered near the Dead Sea in Jordan in the late 1990's (see Fig. 92) and dates to the first cent. BC or AD. It was first published in 2007 in an article by Ada Yardeni and Binyamin Elitzur.[105] The monolithic stele, of whitewashed limestone, is 30cm wide and 90cm high.

The text is similar to the eschatological writings of the Dead Sea Scrolls. It was discovered that the stele was prepared to accept two columns of writing with 43 lines of Hebrew on one

---

[101] Mattew Kalman, "Judge Mulls Verdict in Jesus Forgery Trial," *AOL News*, October 5, 2010, http://www.aolnews.com/2010/10/05/judge-considers-verdict-in-5-year-long-jesus-forgery-trial/.

[102] Hershel Shanks, "Breaking News: Golan and Deutsch Acquitted of All Forgery Charges: Forgery Allegations Dismissed by James Ossuary Trial Verdict," *Bible History Daily: Biblical Archaeology Society*, March 14, 2012, http://www.biblicalarchaeology.org/daily/breaking-news-golan-and-deutsch-acquitted-of-all-forgery-charges/.

[103] See the list of 22 expert witnesses and their opinions in Appendix C "Expert Witness Opinions Regarding the Authenticity of the James Ossuary" in Geisler and Holden pages 389–93. Geisler and Holden, *Popular Handbook of Archaeology and the Bible*, 315; Joseph M. Holden, "The James Ossuary: The Earliest Witness to Jesus and His Family?," *Bible Translation Magazine*, July 2012.

[104] LeMaire, "Burial Box of James the Brother of Jesus," 24–33, 70; James D. Tabor, *The Jesus Dynasty: The Hidden History of Jesus, His Royal Family, and the Birth of Christianity* (New York: Simon & Schuster, 2007); Ryan Byrne and Bernadette McNary-Zak, *Resurrecting the Brother of Jesus: The James Ossuary Controversy and the Quest for Religious Relics* (Raleigh, NC: The University of North Carolina Press, 2009); Hershel Shanks and Ben Witherington III, *The Brother of Jesus: The Dramatic Story and Meaning of the First Archaeological Link to Jesus and His Family*, Rev Upd (New York: HarperCollins, 2009); Holden, "The James Ossuary: The Earliest Witness to Jesus and His Family?"; Geisler and Holden, *Popular Handbook of Archaeology and the Bible*, 310–15.

[105] Ada Yardeni and Binyamin Elitzur, "Document: A First-Century BCE Prophetic Text Written on a Stone: First Publication, (in Hebrew)," *Cathedra* 123 (2007): 155–66.

side and 44 lines on the other.[106] Lines 77 through 87 are translated into English by Israel Knohl as:

122. A detail of the text written in Hebrew of the Gabriel Revelation Stone.

Israel Museum/Wikimedia Commons

> 77. Who am I? I am Gabriel .... [ ]
> 78. You will rescue them............. for two [ ] ...[ ]
> 79. from before of you the three si[g]ns three .. [ ]
> 80. In three days, [live], I Gabriel com[mand] yo[u],
> 81. prince of the princes, the dung of the rocky crevices [ ]... ..[ ]
> 82. to the visions (?) ... their tongue (?) [ ] ... those who love me
> 83. to me, from the three, the small one that I took, I Gabriel
> 84. Lord of Hosts God of Is[rael] [
> 85. then you will stand ...
> 86. ... /
> 87. ... world ?[107]

What is so significant is that Israel Knohl, of the Hebrew University of Jerusalem, believes that the text states that a man named Simon, who was killed by the Romans in 4 BC, would rise from the dead three day after his death. Knohl states:

> *The Gabriel Revelation* presumably expresses the messianic hope of Simon's follower; the stone on which the text was inscribed may well have been placed as a monument near the site of his death. Faced with the crisis of a failed revolt and the death of their messianic king, Simon's followers cultivated the belief of their messianic king, Simon's followers cultivated the belief that the slain leader was resurrected three days after his death by the Archangel Gabriel… The text, like other texts of its time (which survived only in later adaptations), presents a Messiah quite
>
> different from the conventional messianic view: not the heroic son of David, but the suffering son of Joseph, who will die in battle and be resurrected three days later.[108]

Knohl understands line 80 as directed at the Messianic figure and believes he is portrayed much differently from the messiahs of either Jews or Christians. This find has produced understandable controversy among scholars.

Some have suggested that the early Christians drew their idea of a risen Messiah from this stone.[109] However, Ben Witherington, of Asbury Theological Seminary in Kentucky argues that the word *Knohl* translates as "rise" can also be understood to mean "show up."[110] Witherington goes on to state:

> Most radical Jesus scholars have argued that the passion and resurrection predictions by Jesus found in the Gospels were not actually made by Jesus—they reflect the later notions and theologizing of the Evangelists.
>
> But now, if this stone is genuine there is no reason to argue this way. One can show that Jesus, just as well as the author of this stone, could have spoken about a dying and rising messiah. There is in any case a reference to a messiah who dies in the late first century A.D. document called *4 Ezra.*
>
> Long story short–this stone certainly does not demonstrate that the Gospel passion stories are created on the basis of this stone text, which appears to be a Dead Sea scroll text. For one thing, the text is hard to read at crucial junctures, and it is not absolutely clear it is talking about a risen messiah. BUT

---

[106] Ada Yardeni and Binyamin Elitzur, "A Hebrew Prophetic Text on Stone from the Early Herodian Period: A Preliminary Report," in *Hazon Gabriel: New Readings of the Gabriel Revelation*, ed. Matthias Henze (Atlanta, Ga.: Society of Biblical Literature, 2011), 12.

[107] Israel Knohl, "The Messiah Son of Joseph 'Gabriel's Revelation' and the Birth of a New Messianic Model," *BAR* 34, no. 5 (2008).

[108] Israel Knohl, *Messiahs and Resurrection in "The Gabriel Revelation"* (New York: Continuum International, 2009), Xiii.

[109] David Van Biema and Tim McGirk, "Was Jesus' Resurrection a Sequel?," *Time Magazine*, July 7, 2008.

[110] Ben Witherington III, "The Death and Resurrection of Messiah—Written in Stone," *Ben Witherington*, July 5, 2008, http://benwitherington .blogspot.com/2008/07/death-and-resurrection-of-messiah.html.

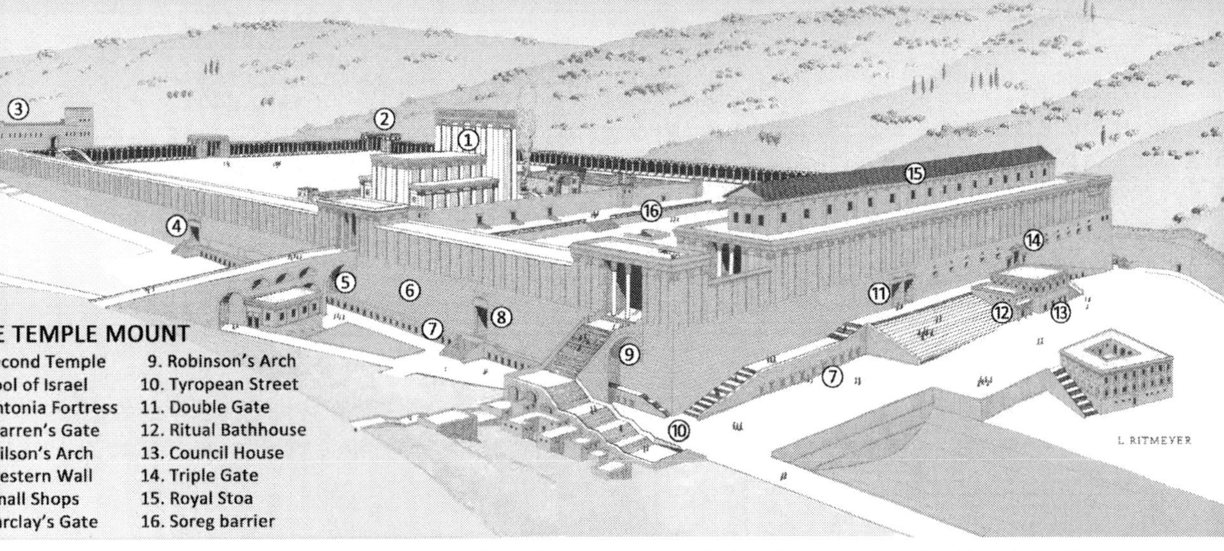

123. Jerusalem, Herod's Temple Mount at the time of Jesus. A reconstruction based on archaeological and historical evidence. This drawing illustrates the Herodian Temple Mount with associated structures and features, as seen from the southwest. This reconstruction is based directly on Leen Ritmeyer's own work at the Temple Mount.

Used by permission © Ritmeyer Archaeological Design. Labels and colorized by David E. Graves

what it does do is make plausible that Jesus could have said some of the things credited to him in Mk. 8.31, 9, 31, and 10.33–34.[111]

Soreg Inscriptions

The Gentile court of the Jewish Temple in Jerusalem had a 1.5 m (5 ft.) fence (Heb. *soreg*) or barricade (Fr. *balustrade*) wall which contained notices in Greek, Hebrew, and Latin warning foreigners not to enter (see Fig 123 no. 16).[112] This wall was erected in the Gentile court, which came between the beautiful *stoa basileia* and the sacred space of the Temple itself (*Mid.* 2:3; see Fig. 123 no. 16).[113] Josephus described it in two of his works as:

124. The Theodotus (priest and synagogue ruler) inscription, discovered by Raymond Weill in Jerusalem in 1913, describing the leader of a synagogue as archisynagogos (Mark 5:35).

Courtesy of Ferrell Jenkins, BiblicalStudies.info

> In the midst of which, and not far from it, was the second [enclosure], to be gone up to by a few steps: this was surrounded by a stone wall [*soreg*] for a partition, with an inscription, which forbade any foreigner to go in under pain of death. (*Ant.* 15.417 [Whiston])
>
> When you go through these [first] cloisters, to the second [court of the] temple, there was a partition made of stone [*soreg*] all around, whose height was three cubits: its construction was very elegant; upon it stood pillars, at equal distances from one another, declaring the law of purity, some in Greek, and some in Roman letters, that "no foreigner should go within that sanctuary;" for that second [court of the] temple was called "the Sanctuary." (*J.W.* 5.193–194 [Whiston])

One such inscription was discovered by Charles Simon Clermont-Ganneau in 1871 and is

[111] Ibid.

[112] C. S. Clermont-Ganneau, "The Discovery of a Tablet from Herod's Temple," *PEQ* 3 (1871): 132–33; Walter A. Elwell and Robert W. Yarbrough, *Readings from the First-Century World: Primary Sources for New Testament Study*, Encountering Biblical Studies (Grand Rapids: Baker Academic, 1998), 83.

[113] Stephen R. Llewelyn and Dionysia van Beek, "Reading the Temple Warning as a Greek Visitor," *Journal for the Study of Judaism* 42, no. 1 (2011): 1–22.

now displayed in the Archaeological Museum in Istanbul. It dates to before the destruction of the Temple in AD 70, and reads: "No foreigner is to enter within the balustrade around the temple and (its) enclosed area. Whoever is caught, will have himself to blame because the incurred (penalty is) death. (*CIJ* 2.1400 = *OGIS* II 598)"[114]

The sign was intended to keep foreigners/Gentiles (Gr. *allethne*) from entering the Temple area with the punishment being death for any who disobeyed (Num 1:51; 3:10, 38; 18:7; *Sifra* Num 116; *m. Sanh.* 9:6; *Mid.* 2:1ff; Philo *Legat.* 31.212; Josephus *J.W.* 6.124–126).[115]

In Acts 21:28, Paul was accused of allowing Gentiles into the Temple and defiling the holy place. This barricade may also have been the "the dividing wall of hostility" that Paul refers to when he stated: "For he himself is our peace, who has made us both one and has broken down in his flesh the dividing wall of hostility" (Eph 2:14).

[114] Stephen R. Llewelyn and J. R. Harrison, *New Documents Illustrating Early Christianity: A Review of the Greek and Other Inscriptions and Papyri Published Between 1988 and 1992*, ed. E. J. Bridge, vol. 10 (Grand Rapids: Eerdmans, 2012), 136.

[115] S. Zeitlin, "The Warning Inscription of the Temple," *JQR* 38, no. 1 (1947): 111–16; Elias J. Bickerman, "The Warning Inscriptions of Herod's Temple," *JQR* 37, no. 4 (1947): 387–405; Peretz Segal, "The Penalty of the Warning Inscription from the Temple of Jerusalem," *IEJ* 39, no. 1/2 (1989): 79–84; Leen Ritmeyer, *The Quest: Revealing the Temple Mount in Jerusalem* (Jerusalem: Carta, 2006), 346–47; Price, *Rose Guide to the Temple*, 78.

CHART 7: ROMAN PERIOD DISCOVERIES II

ACTS AND EPISTLES (ROMAN PERIOD: AD 33–70)					
Discovery	**Images**	**Location and Discoverer**	**Origin Date / Year Found**	**Biblical Passage**	**Significance**
Portrait of Emperor Claudius		Rome, Italy; National Archaeological Museum of Spain, Madrid, anonymous	41–54 AD	Acts 11:28–30; 18:1–2	Identifies Emperor Claudius
God-fearers Inscription		Miletus, Turkey by Theodor Wiegand and Hubert Knackfuss	1903–1905	Acts 13:16, 20:17–28	Identified a group in Miletus called God-fearers
Areopagus on Mars Hill, Athens		Athens, Greece	N/A	Acts 17:22	Benches carved into the rock, meeting place of Areopagus council
Synagogue Inscription, Corinth		Lechaion road near the Agora Corinth, Greece by Rufus Richardson	second to fourth cent. AD 1898	Acts 18:4	
Bema Seat		Corinth, Greece by Oscar Broneer	ca. 50 BC 1935–37	Acts 18:12–17	Paul's tribunal before Gallio
Tyrannus Inscription		Epheus, Turkey by William Ramsay *I.Eph.* 10B.40 *I.Eph.* 1012.4	AD 54–59 AD 92–93 1905	Acts 19:9	Mentions Tyrannus
Temple of Artemis		Ephesus, Turkey by John T. Wood	550 BC 1869	Acts 19:27	Worshipped all over Asia Minor

Discovery	Images	Location and Discoverer	Origin Date / Year Found	Biblical Passage	Significance
Theater of Ephesus		Ephesus, Turkey by John T. Wood	281, 58 BC 1863	Acts 19:23–41	Riots against Paul were here
Statue of Ephesian goddess Artemis		Ephesus, Turkey by John T. Wood	AD 150–200 ca. 1863	Acts 19:35	Image that Paul preached against
Diploma granting Roman Citizenship		Carnuntum, Austria	*CIL* XVI 26 = *CIL* III 854	Acts 22:23–29; 25:10–12	Protection of Roman Citizens by Roman law
Praetorian Guard		Puteoli, Italy	second cent. AD ca. 1800	Acts 28:16; Phil 1:13	The gospel reached the Praetorian guard
Mamertine Prison		Rome, Italy	640–616 BC restored in AD 21 ?	Acts 28:16, 30; 2 Tim 4:6–8	Possible prison of Peter and Paul

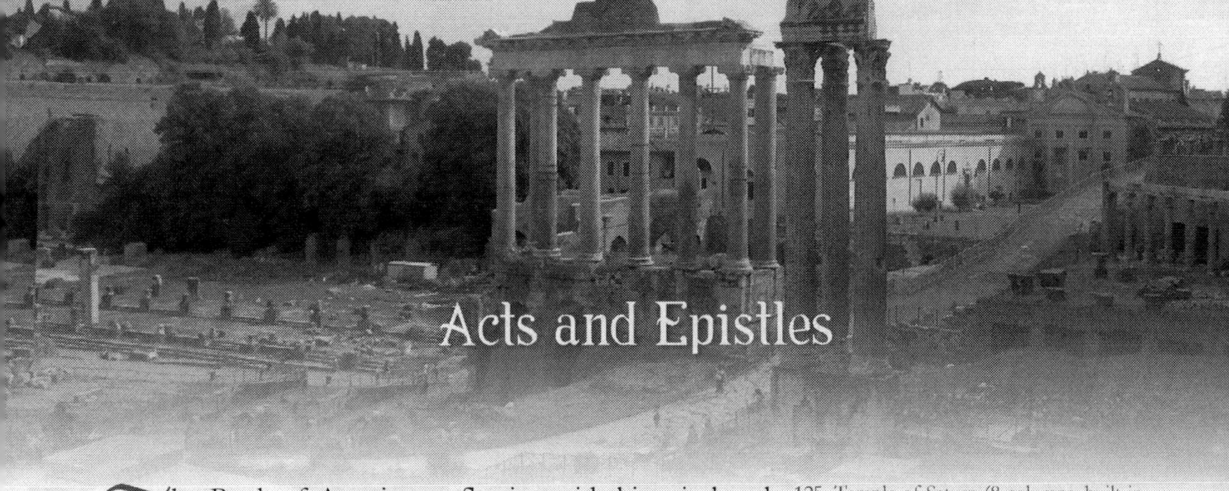

Acts and Epistles

125. Temple of Saturn (8 columns, built in 42 BC and reconstructed in 283 AD) and Temple of Vespasian dn Titus (3 columns built in 79 AD) at the Roman Forum seen from the Capitol, anient Roman ruins, Rome, Italy.

The Book of Acts is overflowing with historical and geographical details. Sir William Ramsay, Regius Professor of Humanity at the University of Aberdeen from 1886–1911, began his career as an historical skeptic, but after visiting Asia Minor in 1890[1] testified to the reliability of Luke and John's writings. He wrote of his trips: "I began with a mind unfavorable to it [the reliability of Acts] . . . but more recently I found myself often brought into contact with the Book of Acts as an authority for the topography, antiquities, and society of Asia Minor. It was gradually borne in upon me that in various details the narrative showed marvelous truth."[2]

The majority of the archaeology pertaining to the book of Acts deals with the cities that Paul visited on his missionary trips to Syria, Asia Minor (modern Turkey), Macedonia (modern Bulgaria and Greece), Greece, and Italy. While most of the cities Paul visited have been excavated, there still remains some that await excavation, like Colossae, Iconium, Lystra, and Derbe. For a detailed treatment of the cities found in the Book of Acts one may consult the older works on archaeology,[3] as well as the footnotes for the following cities:

Cities in Syria

Antioch on the Orontes[4]

Damascus[5]

---

[1] Elliott R. Ohannes, "William Mitchell Ramsay: An Intellectual Biography" (Ph.D., University of Washington, 2007), 96–115.

[2] William M. Ramsay, *St. Paul the Traveler and Roman Citizen*, ed. Mark W. Wilson, Reprinted from printing of 1897 (Grand Rapids: Baker, 1966), 8.

[3] Edward M. Blaiklock, *Cities of the New Testament* (New York: Revell, 1965); McRay, *Archaeology and the NT*, 225–350; Edwin M Yamauchi, *The Archaeology of New Testament Cities in Western Asia Minor* (Grand Rapids: Baker, 1980); Colin J. Hemer, "Seven Cities of Asia Minor," in *Major Cities of the Biblical World*, ed. R.K. Harrison (Nashville, TN: Nelson, 1985), 234–48; Colin J. Hemer and Conrad H. Gempf, eds., *The Book of Acts in the Setting of Hellenistic History*, WUNT 49 (Winona Lake, IN: Eisenbrauns, 1990); *New Testament Cities in Western Asia Minor: Light from Archaeology on Cities of Paul and the Seven Churches of Revelation* (Eugene, OR: Wipf & Stock, 2003); Roland H. Worth, Jr., *The Seven Cities of Apocalypse and Greco-Asian Culture* (New York: Paulist, 2002); *The Seven Cities of the Apocalypse and Roman Culture* (New York: Paulist, 2002); LaMoine F. DeVries, *Cities of the Biblical World: An Introduction to the Archaeology, Geography, and History of Biblical Sites* (Eugene, OR: Wipf & Stock, 2006); William M. Ramsay, *The Cities of St. Paul: Their Influence on His Life and Thought, The Cities of Eastern Asia Minor* (Whitefish, MT: Kessinger, 2004); *The Historical Geography of Asia Minor* (Cambridge, MA: Cambridge University Press, 2010); Mark W. Wilson, *Biblical Turkey: A Guide to Jewish and Christian Sites of Asia Minor* (Istanbul: Ege Yayinlari, 2010); Jack Finegan, *The Archeology of the New Testament: The Life of Jesus and the Beginning of the Early Church*, Revised (Princeton, NJ: Princeton University Press, 2014).

[4] Carl H. Kraeling, "The Jewish Community at Antioch," *JBL* 51, no. 2 (June 1, 1932): 130–60; Glanville Downey, "The Gate of the Cherubim at Antioch," *The Jewish Quarterly Review*, New Series, 29, no. 2 (October 1, 1938): 167–77; *A History Of Antioch In Syria: From Seleucus To The Arab Conquest* (Literary Licensing, LLC, 2012); Bruce M. Metzger, "Antioch-on-the-Orontes," *BA* 11, no. 4 (1948): 69–88; Jean Lassus, "Antioch on the Orontes," in *The Princeton Encyclopedia of Classical Sites*, ed. Richard Stillwell, William L. MacDonald, and Marian Holland McAllister (Princeton, NJ: Princeton University Press, 1976), 62; Ulrich Wickert, "Antioch," in *The Encyclopedia of Christianity*, ed. Erwin Fahlbusch *et al.*, vol. 1 (Grand Rapids: Eerdmans, 1998), 81–82.

[5] John McRay, "Damascus: The Greco-Roman Period," ed. David Noel Freedman *et al.*, *ABD* (New York: Doubleday, 1996), 7–8; Ellen Reeder Williams and Suzanne Heim, "Ebla to Damascus: Art and Archaeology of Ancient Syria," *BA* 48, no. 3 (1985):

126. The interior of the theater in Side Pamphylia.

CITIES IN EASTERN ASIA MINOR

Tarsus[6]
Antioch of Pisidia[7]
Iconium, Lystra and Derbe[8]
Perga[9]
Attaleia[10]
Side of Pamphylia[11]

CITIES IN WESTERN ASIA MINOR

Thyatira[12]
Philadelphia[13]
Laodicea[14]
Hierapolis and Colossae[15]
Ephesus[16]

140–47; Harvey Weiss, ed., *Ebla to Damascus: Art and Archaeology of Ancient Syria: An Exhibition from the Directorate-General of Antiquities and Museums, Syrian Arab Republic* (Washington, DC: Smithsonian Institution Traveling Exhibition Service, 1985); Ross Burns, *Damascus: A History*, Cities of the Ancient World (London: Routledge, 2005); Peter Walker, *In the Steps of Saint Paul: An Illustrated Guide to Paul's Journeys* (Oxford: Lion Books, 2014), 18–31.

[6] Hetty Goldman, *Excavations at Gözlü Kule, Tarsus*, 3 vols., Institute for Advanced Studies. Princeton (Princeton, NJ: Princeton University Press, 1956); W. Ward Gasque, "Tarsus (Place)," ed. David Noel Freedman *et al.*, *ABD* (New York: Doubleday, 1996); Ramsay, *The Cities of St. Paul*, 85–246; W. C. van Unnik, *Tarsus or Jerusalem: The City of Paul's Youth*, trans. George Ogg (Eugene, Ore.: Wipf & Stock, 2009); Walker, *In the Steps of Saint Paul*, 60–70.

[7] David M. Robinson, "Roman Sculptures from Colonia Caesarea (Pisidian Antioch)," *The Art Bulletin* 9, no. 1 (1926): 5–69; William M. Calder, "Studies in Early Christian Epigraphy: Two Episcopal Epitaphs from Laodicea Combusta," *JRS* 10 (1920): 42–59; William M. Ramsay, "Studies in the Roman Province Galatia: II. Dedications at the Sanctuary of Colonia Caesarea," *JRS* 8 (January 1, 1918): 107–45; "Studies in the Roman Province Galatia. VI.–Some Inscriptions of Colonia Caesarea Antiochea," *JRS* 14 (1924): 172–205; "Studies in the Roman Province Galatia. IX. Inscriptions of Antioch of Phrygia-towards-Pisidia (Colonia Caesarea).," *JRS* 16 (1926): 102–19; *The Cities of St. Paul*, 317–384; E. Kitzinger, "A Fourth Century Mosaic Floor in Pisidian Antioch," in *Mansel'e Armağan (Mélanges Mansel)*, ed. Arif Müfid Mansel (Ankara: Türk Tarih Kurumu Basimeri, 1974), 385–95; Stephen Mitchell, "Antioch (Place): Antioch of Pisidia," ed. David Noel Freedman *et al.*, *ABD* (New York: Doubleday, 1996), 265; Stephen Mitchell and Marc Waelkens, *Pisidian Antioch: The Site and Its Monuments* (Oxford: Classical Press of Wales, 1998).

[8] W. H. Buckler, William M. Calder, and C. W. M. Cox, "Asia Minor, 1924. I.--Monuments from Iconium, Lycaonia and Isauria," *JRS* 14 (January 1, 1924): 24–84; M. Ballance, "The Site of Derbe: A New Inscription," *AS* 7 (1957): 147–51; Bastian Van Elderen, "Some Archaeological Observations on Paul's First Missionary Journey," in *Apostolic History and The Gospel Biblical and Historical Essays Presented to F. F. Bruce on His 60th Birthday*, ed. W. Ward Gasque and Ralph P. Martin (Exeter: Paternoster, 1970), 150–61; Ramsay, *The Cities of St. Paul*, 317–422.

[9] Arif Müfid Mansel, *Excavations and Researches at Perge*, Türk Tarih Kurumu. Yayinlarindan 8 (Ankara: Türk Tarih Kurumu Basimevi, 1949); George E. Bean, *Turkey's Southern Shore - An Archaeological Guide* (London: Praeger, 1968); "Perge," in *The Princeton Encyclopedia of Classical Sites*, ed. Richard Stillwell, William L. MacDonald, and Marian Holland McAllister (Princeton, NJ: Princeton University Press, 1976), 692–93; S. Mitchell and A. W. McNicoll, "Archaeology in Western and Southern Asia Minor 1971-78," *Archaeological Reports*, no. 25 (1978): 59–90; W. Ward Gasque, "Perga (Place)," ed. David Noel Freedman *et al.*, *ABD* (New York: Doubleday, 1996), 228.

[10] A. H. M. Jones, *The Cities of the Eastern Roman Provinces*, 2nd ed., Oxford University Press Academic Monograph (Eugene, OR: Wipf & Stock, 2004), 130–47; J. D. Wineland, "Attalia (Place)," ed. David Noel Freedman *et al.*, *ABD* (New York: Doubleday, 1996), 523.

[11] Mitchell and McNicoll, "Archaeology in Western and Southern Asia Minor 1971-78," 88; Stephen Mitchell, "Archaeology in Asia Minor 1979-84," *Archaeological Reports*, no. 31 (1984): 103; Ekrem Akurgal, *Ancient Civilizations and Ruins of Turkey from Prehistoric Times until the End of the Roman Empire*, trans. John Whybrow and Mollie Emre, 2nd ed. (Istanbul: Mobil Oil Turk A. S., 1985), 336–41.

[12] See Chapter Eight–Revelation: Thyatira

[13] See Chapter Eight–Revelation: Philadelphia

[14] See Chapter Eight–Revelation: Laodicea

[15] Alan H. Cadwallader and Michael Trainor, eds., *Colossae in Space and Time: Linking to an Ancient City*, NTOA / SUNT (Göttingen: Vandenhoeck & Ruprecht, 2011).

Sardis[17]
Pergamum[18]
Smyrna[19]

CITIES IN MACEDONIA[20]

Samothrace[21]
Neapolis[22]
Philippi[23]
Amphipolis[24]
Thessalonica[25]
Dion[26]

CITIES IN CYPRUS

Salamis and Paphos[27]

CITIES IN GREECE

Athens[28]

127. The restored Temple A in Laodicea with 19 columns restored and raised. It was originally dedicated to Apollo. Two columns were discovered, each with three registers in wreaths. Column A was inscribed with the image and inscription of Artemis, two deer and relief of Laodicea with the Latin inscription LADICIA SACRUM (Laodicea Sacred), while Column B had Apollo, two griffins and Fortuna.

Photo by Rjdeadly/Wikimedia Commons

---

[16] See Chapter Eight–Revelation: Ephesus

[17] See Chapter Eight–Revelation: Sardis

[18] See Chapter Eight–Revelation: Pergamum

[19] See Chapter Eight–Revelation: Smyrna

[20] Paul E. Davies, "The Macedonian Scene of Paul's Journeys," *BA* 26, no. 3 (1963): 91–106.

[21] For a good bibliography see http://www.samothrace.emory.edu/resources/bibliography Karl Lehmann, *Samothrace: A Guide to the Excavations and the Museum*, ed. J. R. McCredie, 6th ed. (Thessaloniki: Institute of Fine Arts, New York University, 1998); Karl Lehmann, Phyllis Williams Lehmann, and J. R. McCredie, eds., *Samothrace*, 12 vols. (New York: Princeton University Press, 1998); Donald A. D. Thorsen, "Samothrace (Place)," ed. David Noel Freedman *et al.*, *ABD* (New York: Doubleday, 1992), 949.

[22] Dimitrios Lazarides, "Neapolis," in *PECS*, ed. Richard Stillwell, William L. MacDonald, and Marian Holland McAllister (Princeton, NJ: Princeton University Press, 1976), 614; Conrad H. Gempf, "Neapolis (Place)," ed. David Noel Freedman *et al.*, *ABD* (New York: Doubleday, 1992), 1052–53; McRay, *Archaeology and the NT*, 281–83.

[23] Georgios Gounaris and Emmanuela Gounari, *Philippi: Archaeological Guide*, trans. Sophia Tromara (Thessaloniki: Thessaloniki University Studio Press, 2004); Helmut Koester, *Philippi at the Time of Paul and after His Death*, ed. Charalambos Bakirtzis (Eugene, OR: Wipf & Stock, 2009); McRay, *Archaeology and the NT*, 283–88; Chaido Koukouli-Chrysanthaki, "Philippi," in *Brill's Companion to Ancient Macedon: Studies in the Archaeology and History of Macedon, 650 BC - 300 AD*, ed. Robin J. Fox and Robin Lane Fox (Leiden: Brill, 2011), 437–52.

[24] McRay, *Archaeology and the NT*, 288–92; Koukouli-Chrysanthaki, "Politarchs in a New Inscription from Amphipolis," 229–41; "Excavating Classical Amphipolis," in *Excavating Classical Culture: Recent Archaeological Discoveries in Greece*, ed. Maria Stamatopoulou and Marina Yeroulanou, Studies in Classical Archaeology, British Archaeological Reports British Series 1031 (Oxford: Archaeopress, 2002), 57–73; "Amphipolis," in *Brill's Companion to Ancient Macedon: Studies in the Archaeology and History of Macedon, 650 BC - 300 AD*, ed. Robin J. Fox and Robin Lane Fox (Leiden: Brill, 2011), 409–36; Elpida Kosmidou, "Greek Coins from the Eastern Cemetery of Amphipolis," *NumC* 166 (2006): 415–31.

[25] K. Rhomiopoulou, "New Inscriptions in the Archaeological Museum, Thessaloniki," in *Ancient Macedonian Studies in Honor of Charles F. Edson*, ed. Harry J. Dell (Belgrade, Serbia: Institute for Balkan Studies, 1981), 299–305; Holland L. Hendrix, "Thessalonica (Place)," ed. David Noel Freedman *et al.*, *ABD* (New York: Doubleday, 1996), 523–27; Karl Paul Donfried, *Paul, Thessalonica, and Early Christianity* (Grand Rapids: Eerdmans, 2002); P. Adam-Veleni, "Thessalonike," in *Brill's Companion to Ancient Macedon: Studies in the Archaeology and History of Macedon, 650 BC - 300 AD*, ed. Robin J. Fox and Robin Lane Fox (Leiden: Brill, 2011), 545–62.

[26] Dimitrios Pandermalis, *The Sacred City of the Macedonians at the Foothills of Mt. Olympus* (Athens: Archaoelogical Receipts Fund, 1987); *Dion, the Archaeological Site and the Museum* (Athens: Archaoelogical Receipts Fund, 1997).

[27] A. H. S. Megaw, "Archaeology in Cyprus, 1957," *AR* 4 (1957): 43–50; Vassos Karageorghis, *Salamis in Cyprus*, New Aspects of Antiquity (London: Thames & Hudson, 1970); *Excavating at Salamis in Cyprus, 1952-1974* (Athens: A.G. Leventis Foundation, 1999); Gloria S. Merker, "Some Recent Books on Cypriote Archaeology," *IEJ* 52, no. 1 (2002): 106–11.

[28] David W. Gill and Conrad H. Gempf, eds., *The Book of Acts in Its Graeco-Roman Setting*, vol. 2, BAFCS 2 (Grand Rapids: Eerdmans, 1994), 441–48.

Corinth[29]
Nicopolis[30]

CITIES IN ITALY

Rome[31]

Along with the excavation of cities, sometimes significant inscriptions are discovered that attest to the historical accuracy of Luke and Paul's writings. Following are several that are noteworthy.

SERGIUS PAULUS INSCRIPTIONS (ACTS 13)

During Paul's first missionary journey (*ca.* AD 46–48), he was introduced to the Roman proconsul who lived in Cyprus serving under Emperor Claudius.

From 22 BC to the time of Emperor Hadrian (AD 117 to 138), Cyprus was being administered as a senatorial province by a proconsul (Gr. *anthypatos*). While the proconsul is not attested in secular literature, except possibly by Pliny the Elder (*Nat.* 2.113),[32] his name is mentioned on ancient coins from Soli, Cyprus.[33] There are at least three inscriptions that have been uncovered mentioning a Proconsul by the name of 'Sergius Paulus' (Lat. *Paullus*); two in Cyprus and one in Rome.

Quotes from Antiquity

Luke's description of Sergius Paulus:

When they had gone through the whole island as far as Paphos, they came upon a certain magician, a Jewish false prophet named Bar-Jesus. He was with the proconsul, Sergius Paulus [Gr. *Sergios Paulos*], a man of intelligence, who summoned Barnabas and Saul and sought to hear the word of God. But Elymas the magician (for that is the meaning of his name) opposed them, seeking to turn the proconsul away from the faith. (Acts 13:6–8)

Inscription 1

In 1887 a boundary stone was discovered in Rome with the phrase "in the proconsulship of Paulus."[34] Sergius is listed as the curator of the channel and banks of the Tiber

[29] Victor Paul Furnish, "Corinth in Paul's Time—What Can Archaeology Tell Us?," *BAR* 14, no. 3 (1988): 14–27; Jerome Murphy-O'Connor, *St. Paul's Corinth: Text and Archaeology*, Good News Studies 6 (Minneapolis, MN: Liturgical, 2002); Steve Friesen, Daniel N. Schowalter, and James Walters, eds., *Corinth in Context: Comparative Studies on Religion and Society*, Supplement to Novum Testamentum 134 (Leiden: Brill, 2010).

[30] Colin Kraay, "The Coinage of Nicopolis," *NumC*, Seventh Series, 16, no. 136 (1976): 235–47; John M. Carter, "A New Fragment of Octavian's Inscription at Nicopolis," *ZPE* 24 (1977): 227–30; James H. Oliver, "Octavian's Inscription at Nicopolis," *The American Journal of Philology* 90, no. 2 (1969): 178–82; Andrew G. Poulter, Thomas Blagg, and Judith Butcher, *Nicopolis Ad Istrum: A Roman, Late Roman and Early Byzantine City: Excavations 1985-1992*, ed. J. Reynolds, Journal of Roman Studies Monograph 8 (London: Roman Society Publications, 1995); Andrew G. Poulter, *Nicopolis As Istrum: A Roman to Early Byzantine City: The Pottery and Glass*, vol. 1, Reports of the Research Committee of the Society of Antiquar (London: Bloomsbury, 1999); *Nicopolis Ad Istrum: A Late Roman and Early Byzantine City: The Finds and the Biological Remains*, vol. 3, Reports of the Research Committee of the Society of Antiquar 67 (Oxford: Society of Antiquaries of London, 2007).

[31] Leonardo B. Dal Maso, *Rome of the Caesars*, trans. Michael Hollingworth (Firenze, Italy: Bonechi Edizioni, 1983); Ross R. Holloway, *The Archaeology of Early Rome and Latium* (New York: Routledge, 1996); Jon C. Coulston and Hazel Dodge, eds., *Ancient Rome: The Archaeology of the Eternal City*, Monograph 54 (Oxford: Oxford University School of Archaeology, 2000); Amanda Claridge, *Rome*, 2nd ed., An Oxford Archaeological Guide (Oxford: Oxford University Press, 2010).

[32] Riesner, *Paul's Early Period*, 142.

[33] Edward M. Blaiklock, "Paulus, Sergius," in *ZPEB*, 4:747.

[34] G. Lafaye, R. Cagnat, and J. Toutain, eds., *Inscriptiones Graecae Ad Res Romanas Pertinentes* (Paris: Leroux, 1901), III.930; T. B. Mitford, "Notes on Some Published Inscriptions from Roman Cyprus," *Annual of British School at Athens* 42 (1947): 201–06.

river in AD 47 during the reign of Emperor Claudius. However, Martin and others believe that the date of the inscription is too late to be referring to the Paulus in Acts 13.[35] However, Unger states that the inscription "without any reasonable doubt refers to the Sergius Paulus whom Paul introduced to Christianity."[36] Ramsay also places this inscription at the time of Acts 13.[37]

Inscription 2

In 1912, William Ramsay and J. G. C. Anderson discovered an inscription near Pisidian Antioch, which is now housed in the Yalvac Museum, Pisidian Antioch. They claimed that "L[ucius] Sergius Paulus the younger, son of L[ucius]" was the son of the elder Sergius Paulus mentioned as the proconsul in Acts 13 (see Fig. 95).[38] However, Van Elderen raised the issue of there being no mention of Cyprus in the inscription and the date being placed in the reign of Claudius (AD 41–54), which he thinks is late for some Pauline scholars.[39]

128. Inscription (2) of Sergius Paulus, the proconsul in Paphos, Cyprus, housed in the Yalvac Museum, Pisidian Antioch. Some scholars suggest that: "L[ucius] Sergius Paulus the younger, son of L[ucius]" may be the son of the elder Sergius Paulus, the proconsul of Acts 13. The name of Sergius Paulus (*nomen*, name of tribe) was certainly known in Cyprus.

Courtesy of Mark Wilson

Inscription 3

A third inscription was discovered in 1877 in the city of Silo near Paphos (Acts 13:6), and translated as "Q. Sergius Paulus" (AD 54; *IGR* 3.935). It is considered by most to be the best possibility of identifying the proconsul of Acts 13.[40]

These inscriptions indicate that the name of Sergius Paulus (*nomen*, name of tribe) was certainly known in Cyprus and that the office of proconsul was appropriately used by Luke in referring to the government official in Cyprus.[41]

POLITARCH INSCRIPTIONS (ACTS 17)

According to Schuler "politarchs were the chief administrative and executive officers of their respective cities or communities."[42] Horsley adds that they were an: "annual magistracy attested predominantly in cities of Macedonia after Roman intervention in the second century B.C."[43] While the term *politarchas* was used once by Aelianus Tacticus (*Siege* 26.12), it was uncommon in texts outside the Bible until 1835, when an inscription listing seven Politarchs was discovered on

---

[35] Martin, "Paulus, Sergius (Person)," 205.

[36] Merrill F. Unger, "Archaeology and Paul's Tour of Cyprus, Part 1," *BSac* 117 (1960): 233.

[37] Ramsay, *St. Paul the Traveler: Updated*, 74.

[38] William M. Ramsay, *The Bearing of Recent Discovery on the Trustworthiness of the New Testament*, Classic Reprint 1911 (Charleston, SC: Forgotten Books, 2012), 150–72.

[39] Van Elderen, "Some Archaeological Observations on Paul's First Missionary Journey," 155.

[40] Van Elderen, "Some Archaeological Observations on Paul's First Missionary Journey," 155; Martin, "Paulus, Sergius (Person)," 5:205; Gabba, *Iscrizioni Greche E Latine per Lo Studio Della Bibba*, 71–73.

[41] Campbell, "Possible Inscriptional Attestation to Sergius Paulus," 1–29.

[42] Carl Schuler, "The Macedonian Politarch," *Classical Philology* 55 (1960): 91.

[43] G. H. R. Horsley, "Appendix: The Politarchs," in *The Book of Acts in Its Graeco-Roman Setting*, ed. David W. Gill and Conrad H. Gempf, vol. 2, BAFCS 2 (Grand Rapids: Eerdmans, 1994), 421.

an arch on Egnatia Street in Thessalonica. It dated to the first cent. (between AD 69 and 79), and read "in the time of the Politarchs..."[44]

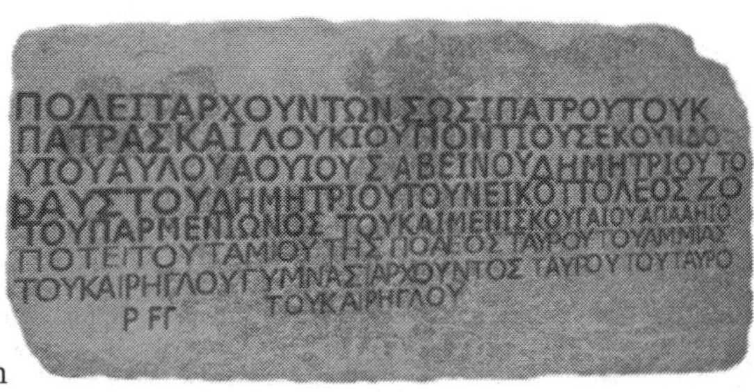

129. Reproduction and enhancement of the inscripiton mentioning city officals called "politarchs" in Thessalonica.

Drawing by David E. Graves. Original in the Brisih Museum

Some scholars had challenged the historicity of Luke's work arguing that no such office of Politarch (πολιτάρχης politarcho) existed in the first cent. in Thessalonica (Acts 17:6, 8), and that he misused the term for the governor (*archon*) in Thessalonica. To date, thirty-two inscriptions have been discovered, effectively silencing the critics.[45] Nineteen of these have come from Thessalonica[46] and three of these are from the first cent. AD (one from nearby Amphipolis[47]).[48] One of these inscriptions is now on display in the British Museum.[49]

The discovery of first cent. inscriptions from Thessalonica indicates that the office of politarchs existed in Thessalonica and that Luke knew the political context of the city.

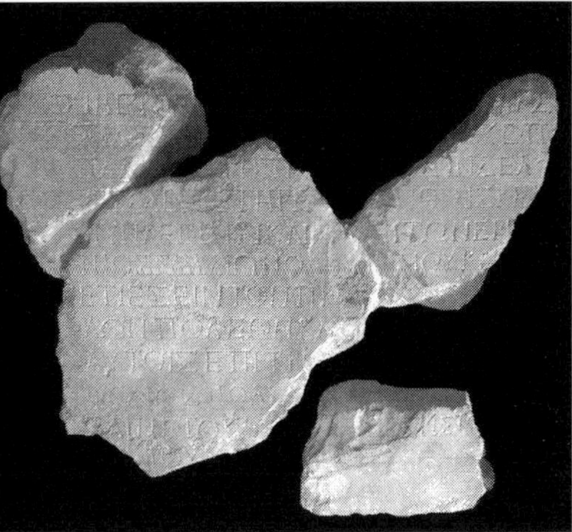

130. The Gallio inscription from the Temple of Apollo in Delphi, Greece.

Courtesy of Todd Bolen / BiblePlaces.com

GALLIO INSCRIPTION (ACTS 18)

The Biblical Context

The presence of Silas and Timothy with Paul in Corinth (Acts 18:5; 1 Thess 1:1) indicates that the letters of First (1 Thess 3:1–2, 6) and Second Thessalonians were written from Corinth. Following Paul's departure from Corinth, there is no further mention of Silas traveling with Paul. Because of the report from Timothy, Paul wrote to the Thessalonians and addressed several issues:

- He commended their zeal
- He encouraged them in persecution
- He defended himself against attacks
- He taught them about holiness
- He instructed them on the second coming
- He exhorted them to steadfastness and patience.

---

[44] McRay, *Archaeology and the NT*, 295; Geisler and Holden, *Popular Handbook of Archaeology and the Bible*, 356.

[45] Schuler, "The Macedonian Politarch," 96–98; Geisler and Holden, *Popular Handbook of Archaeology and the Bible*, 355.

[46] Geisler and Holden, *Popular Handbook of Archaeology and the Bible*, 355.

[47] Chaido Koukouli-Chrysanthaki, "Politarchs in a New Inscription from Amphipolis," in *Ancient Macedonian Studies in Honor of Charles F. Edson*, ed. Harry J. Dell (Belgrade, Serbia: Institute for Balkan Studies, 1981), 229–41.

[48] S. Pelekides, *Απο Οήν Πολιτεία Χαί Χοινωνία Τής Άρχαίας Θεσσαλονίχης* (Thessaloniki: Triantaphyllu, 1934), 25 no. 2; Ernest DeWitt Burton, "The Politarchs," *American Journal of Theology* 2 (1898): 604 no. 2; Werner Peek, ed., *Griechische Vers-Inschriften*, Grab-Epigramme 1 (Berlin: Hakkert, 1955), 91 no. 365.

[49] B. F. Cook, *Greek Inscriptions*, 3rd ed. (Berkeley, CA: University of California Press, 1987), 22–23.

Sometime later, when he learned they were still confused about the second coming, he wrote his second letter (AD 50–51).

> *Quotes from Antiquity*
>
> **Luke's description of Gallio:**
>
> But when Gallio was proconsul of Achaia, the Jews made a united attack on Paul and brought him before the tribunal, saying, "This man is persuading people to worship God contrary to the law." But when Paul was about to open his mouth, Gallio said to the Jews, "If it were a matter of wrongdoing or vicious crime, O Jews, I would have reason to accept your complaint. But since it is a matter of questions about words and names and your own law, see to it yourselves. I refuse to be a judge of these things." And he drove them from the tribunal. And they all seized Sosthenes, the ruler of the synagogue, and beat him in front of the tribunal. But Gallio paid no attention to any of this. (Acts 18:12–17)

Paul made his headquarters in the home of Titus Justus, next to the local synagogue. The first convert was the ruler of the synagogue, by the name of Crispus. While Paul baptised Crispus and Gaius, he did not baptise many "so that no one may say that you were baptized in my name" (1 Cor 1:14–15).

When the Jews complained to Gallio, the Roman Proconsul of Achaea (Gr. *Achaïa*), he dismissed their arguments as only a disagreement among Jews (AD 51).[50] Paul was thus given a free hand to continue his preaching unhindered in Corinth and stayed there eighteen months.

The Inscription

This Greek inscription is also sometimes called the Delphi Inscription because it was discovered at the Temple of Apollo in Delphi, Greece.[51] Nine fragments were uncovered in 1908 that date to the time of the Roman emperor Claudius (AD 41–54) and mention Lucius Junius Gallio Annaeus (Pliny *Nat.* 31.33), the proconsul (governor) of Corinth in either AD 51 or 52[52] of the newly constituted senatorial province of Achaea (see Fig. 96).[53]

Fitzmyer reconstructs the Greek inscription which begins:

> Tiber[ius Claudius Cae]sar Augustus Ge[rmanicus, invested with tribunician po]wer [for the 12th time, acclaimed Imperator for t]he 26th time, F[ather of the Fa]ther[land...]. For a l[ong time have I been not onl]y [well-disposed towards t]he ci[ty] of Delph[i, but also solicitous for its pro]sperity, and I have always guard[ed th]e cul[t of t]he [Pythian] Apol[lo. But] now [since] it is said to be desti[tu]te of [citi]zens, as [L. Jun]ius Gallio, my fri[end] an[d procon]sul, [recently reported to me, and being desirous that Delphi] should retain [inta]ct its for[mer rank, I] ord[er you (pl.) to in]vite well-born people also from [ot]her cities [to Delphi as new inhabitants....][54]

As Köstenberger points out: "This historical note is particularly helpful since Roman custom dictated that Roman officials in the senatorial provinces should hold office for only one year and the terms of proconsuls typically extended from July 1 to July 1 of the following year"

---

[50] Osvaldo Padilla, *The Speeches of Outsiders in Acts: Poetics, Theology and Historiography* (Cambridge: Cambridge University Press, 2008), 135–62.

[51] E. Mary Smallwood, *Documents Illustrating the Principates of Gaius Claudius and Nero* (Bristol: Bristol Classical, 1983), 105.

[52] Craig A. Evans and Stanley E. Porter, eds., *Dictionary of New Testament Background: A Compendium of Contemporary Biblical Scholarship* (Downers Grove, IL: InterVarsity, 2000), 206–207; Riesner, *Paul's Early Period*, 202–11.

[53] Gustav Adolf Deissmann, *St Paul: A Study in Social and Religious History*, trans. Lionel R. M. Strachan (Charleston, SC: BiblioBazaar, 2011), 238; Geisler and Holden, *Popular Handbook of Archaeology and the Bible*, 356–57.

[54] Raymond E. Brown, Joseph A. Fitzmyer, and Roland Murphy, eds., *New Jerome Biblical Commentary* (New York: Bloomsbury, 1995), 79.9; Hans Conzelmann, *Acts of the Apostles: A Commentary on the Acts of the Apostles*, Hermeneia: A Critical and Historical Commentary on the Bible (Philadelphia, PA: Fortress, 1987), 153–54.

131. The visible area of the synagogue in Miletus next to the colossal circular Harbor Monument (63 BC). Paul may have met the Ephesian elders here.

(Dio Cassius *Hist. Rom.* 57.14.5).[55]

Based on the mention of the twenty-sixth acclamation of Claudius in the letter, scholars agree that it was published in July of AD 52.[56] As Novak points out: "while the dates of the 25th and 26th acclamations are not know, they could not have occurred before late 51 C.E. and must have been prior to August 1, 52 C.E., when Claudius was acclaimed for the 27th time."[57]

The importance of this inscription is that both Gallio and Claudius are mentioned on this inscription and in the NT (Acts 18:1–4; 18–23). Since this inscription gives details that provide a secure date (AD 52)[58] it assists in determining the time of Paul's trip to Corinth in Acts 18:1–2 (AD 51) and Paul's trial before Gallio in Achaea (Acts 18:12–17; summer of AD 51).[59] Most dates used to indicate the time of Paul's missionary trips are derived from this date.

132. An inscription on a theatre seat in the Miletus theatre that states "Place of the Jews, who are also called God-fearing." The term Godfearer is mentioned in the NT (Acts 13:16; 26).

MILETUS INSCRIPTION (ACTS 20)

The Biblical Context

Paul stopped at the port of Miletus and called the Ephesian elders together to say goodbye and exhort them in the faith in what must have been a sorrowful departure (Acts 20:17–38; see Fig. 131). He stated: "I am going to Jerusalem, constrained by the Spirit, not knowing what will happen to me there, except that the Holy Spirit testifies to me in every city that imprisonment and afflictions await me" (Acts 20:22–23).

Paul departed, knowing that he would not see their faces again. Paul hinted at future persecution and possible imprisonment in his address to the Ephesian elders.[60] Despite knowing that he may face possible persecution in Jerusalem because of his Gentile ministry, he was determined to report to the Jerusalem church. It was

---

[55] Köstenberger, Kellum, and Quarles, *The Cradle, the Cross, and the Crown*, 400.

[56] Jewett, *A Chronology of Paul's Life*, 38–40; Jerome Murphy-O'Connor, *St. Paul's Corinth: Text and Archaeology*, Good News Studies 6 (Minneapolis, MN: Liturgical, 2002), 164; Deissmann, *St Paul*, 261–79.

[57] Ralph Martin Novak, *Christianity and the Roman Empire: Background Texts* (Harrisburg, PA: Trinity, 2001), 20.

[58] Steinmann, *From Abraham to Paul*, 305.

[59] *Contra* H. Dixon Slingerland, "Acts 18:1-18, the Gallio Inscription, and Absolute Pauline Chronology," *JBL* 110, no. 3 (1991): 439–49.

[60] Colin J. Hemer, "The Speeches of Acts: I. The Ephesian Elders at Miletus," *TB* 40, no. 1 (1989): 77–85; Charles K. Barrett, "Paul's Address to the Ephesian Elders," in *God's Christ and His Peopl E, Studies in Honour of Nils Alstrup Dahl*, ed. J. Jervell and W. A. Meeks (Oslo: Univer sitetsforlaget, 1977), 107–21.

here in Miletus that Paul left Trophimus because he was ill (2 Tim 4:20), although it is speculated that it may have been on another visit to the city.

The Inscription

In Paul's day there was a large theatre in Miletus that could seat some 15,000 people. On one of the seats in the fifth row from the bottom and in the second section from the west, is an inscription which translates "place of [those] Jews who [are] also [called] Godfearers (θεοσεβίον *theosebion*)" [Horst; see Fig. 132].[61] In the NT "those among you who fear God" (φοβούμενοι τὸν Θεόν *phoboumenoi ton Theon)* are usually understood as Gentiles (Acts 13:16, 26), who were equivalent to Jewish proselytes (converts), but uncircumcised.[62]

However, this inscription seems to indicate "reserved seating" rather than segregated seating for Jews and Gentiles.[63] It also indicates that there was a prominent Jewish population in Miletus. The term "god-fearer" is also found in synagogue inscriptions in Aphrodisias.[64]

CAESAREAN MOSAIC INSCRIPTION (ROM 13)

John McRay, the retired professor emeritus of NT and archaeology at Wheaton College Graduate School, states:

> While I was excavating at Caesarea on the coast of Israel in 1972, we uncovered a large mosaic inscription of the Greek text of Romans 13:3. A shorter one had been found in 1960 by an Israeli archaeologist, Abraham Negev. The two texts, dating to at least the fifth century, are part of a mosaic floor of a large public building (perhaps a praetorium or archives building) and are identical to that passage in the Greek New Testament. These are as old as some of our oldest manuscripts of the New Testament.[65]

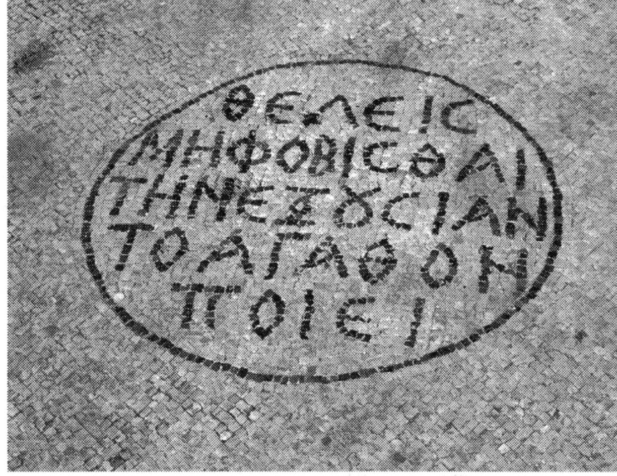

133. One of two mosaics at Caesarea Maritima quoting Romans 13:3. This is the shorter version. The original mosaic is on display at the Kibbutz Sdot Yam Museum.

Courtesy of Ferrell Jenkins, BiblicalStudies.info

The building has been identified as "a revenue office in a public building."[66] The sign located at the site of Caesarea Maritima identifies the building as "Byzantine government

---

[61] Pieter Willem van der Horst, *Ancient Jewish Epitaphs: An Introductory Survey of a Millennium of Jewish Funerary Epigraphy (300 BCE-700 CE)* (Leuven, Belgium: Peeters, 1991), 70.

[62] For an extended bibliography and current research on God-fearers, including inscriptions, see Feldman's work, chapter seven "sympathizers" ("God-fearers"). Louis H. Feldman, *Jewish Life and Thought Among Greeks and Romans: Primary Readings* (New York: Continuum International, 1996), 137–46.

[63] Gustav Adolf Deissmann, *Light from the Ancient East*, trans. Lionel R. M. Strachan (New York: Harper & Brothers, 1927), 451.

[64] Jerome Murphy-O'Connor, "Lots of God-Fearers? Theosebeis in the Aphrodisias Inscription," *RB* 99 (1992): 418–24.

[65] John McRay, "Archaeology and the Bible: How Archaeological Findings Have Enhanced the Credibility of the Bible," *4Truth.Net of the Southern Baptist Convention*, September 28, 2013, http://www.4truth.net/fourtruthpbbible.aspx?pageid=8589952738; Clayton Miles Lehmann and Kenneth G. Holum, *The Greek and Latin Inscriptions of Caesarea Maritima*, ed. Robert J. Bull and David Larrimore Holland, BASOR: Supplemental Studies. Issue 19. The Joint Expedition to Caesarea Maritima 5 (Missoula, MT: Scholars Press, 1975), 100–101 (and Pl. LCIV: nos. 88 and 89); Kenneth G. Holum, "Caesarea Palaestinae: Inscriptions of the Imperial Revenue Office," in *The Roman and Byzantine Near East: Some Recent Archaeological Research*, ed. John H. Humphrey, Journal of Roman Archaeology Supplement Series 14 (Ann Arbor, Mich.: Journal of Roman Archaeology, 1995), 333–345.

[66] Peter M. Head, "Additional Greek Witnesses to the New Testament," in *The Text of the New Testament in Contemporary Research: Essays on the Status Quaestionis. Second Edition*, ed. Bart D. Ehrman and Michael W. Holmes (Leiden: Brill, 2012), 445.

offices where clerks recorded tax revenues."[67]

The pair of Greek medallion mosaics (see Fig. 133) translate as: " 'Do you wish to have no reason to fear the authority? Then do what is good'—one stops here, the other continues to include—'and you will receive its approval.' "[68]

The context of this quote in Paul's letter to the Romans, reads as follows: "For rulers are not a terror to good conduct, but to bad. *Would you have no fear of the one who is in authority? Then do what is good, and you will receive his approval,* for he is God's servant for your good. But if you do wrong, be afraid, for he does not bear the sword in vain. For he is the servant of God, an avenger who carries out God's wrath on the wrongdoer" (Rom 13:3–4 emphasis added).

134. Erastus inscription which some claim refers to the Erastus mentioned by Paul in Romans 16:23.

Courtesy of Todd Bolen / BiblePlaces.com

ERASTUS INSCRIPTION (ROMANS 16)

The Biblical Context

While Paul was in Corinth, he wrote and sent greetings letters from some of the Corinthians to the Church in Rome. Among them was one named Erastus, whom Paul described as "the city treasurer" (Gr. *oikonomos*, Lat. *aedilis*, Rom 16:23).[69] The NIV translates *oikonomos* as "director of public works." Each city had yearly elected magistrates (*duovirs*) and a senate. The city managers (*aediles*) were also elected annually and managed public works in the city, including the financial income.[70] A person named Erastus is also mentioned in 2 Timothy 4:20 and Acts 19:22, and most scholars accept all these references as referring to the same person.[71] Fellows has gathered actual statistical data derived from the occurrence of inscriptions, and states: "restricting ourselves to the first cent., the frequency of the name can be estimated at 1 in 1100."[72]

The Inscription

In 1928–1929, archaeologists excavating in Corinth uncovered three slabs of hard white limestone[73] with an inscription that read: "ERASTVS PRO AEDILIT[AT]E S P[74] STRAVIT"

---

[67] Ferrell Jenkins, "Have No Fear of the Authorities," *Ferrell's Travel Blog: Commenting on Biblical Studies, Archaeology Travel and Photography*, September 10, 2010, https://ferrelljenkins .wordpress.com/2010/09/10/.

[68] Head, "Additional Greek Witnesses to the New Testament," 445.

[69] BDAG defines *oikonomos* as "public treasurer, treasurer." Bauer, Arndt, and Gingrich, *BDAG*, 698.

[70] Gary M. Burge, Lynn H. Cohick, and Gene L. Green, *The New Testament in Antiquity: A Survey of the New Testament within Its Cultural Context* (Grand Rapids: Zondervan, 2009), 298.

[71] G. A. Lee, "Erastus," ed. Geoffrey W. Bromiley, *ISBE2* (Grand Rapids: Eerdmans, February 1995), 126.

[72] Richard Fellows, "Erastus (Rom 16:23) Was Erastus (Acts 19:22)," *Paul and Co-Workers*, June 25, 2010, http://paulandco-workers.blogspot.pt/2010 /06/erastus-rom-1623-was-erastus-acts-1922.html.

[73] Steven J. Friesen, "The Wrong Erastus: Ideology, Archaeology, and Exegesis," in *Corinth in Context: Comparative Studies on Religion and Society*, ed. Steven J. Friesen, Daniel N. Schowalter, and James Walters (Leiden: Brill, 2010), 236 n. 18.

[74] S. P. is a standard abbreviation for *sua pecunia*, "with his own money." John Harvey Kent, *The Inscriptions, 1926 to 1950: Corinth*, vol. 8, Part 3 (Athens: American School of Classical Studies at Athens, 1966).

"[...]erastus,[75] in return for his aedileship, paved (this [road]) at his own expense" (see Fig. 134).[76] Erastus paid to have the street paved in return for an appointment as either the city engineer or chief of public works (Lat. *Aedile).*[77]

A common view is that this is the same Erastus that is mentioned in Romans. Murphy argues that: "Since the pavement was laid before the middle of the first century AD, this individual is identified with the Erastus who was city treasurer at the time of Paul and a Christian (Rom 16:23)."[78]

However, Friesen points out that the dating information is incorrect. Friesen argues: "Since 1929, many specialists have claimed that Paul's *oikonomos* [manager of a household] Erastus was identical to an aristocratic Erastus named in a Latin inscription from Corinth. In this chapter I argue that we can disentangle the inked Erastus from the inscribed one. They were two different individuals, one from the highest sector of elite society and the other from a lower level."[79]

While this is unlikely to be the same person mentioned by Paul it does indicate that Erastus was a well known name in Corinth. Paul's use of the name in his letter from Corinth certainly fits the cultural setting of the first century.[80]

135. Honorary inscription for T. Mucius Clemens, shortly after AD 70. Ciruclar stone inscription fragment on a round base for a statue of the governor. Translation "(Someone)... honored Marcus Paccius son of Publius...Silvanus Quintus Coredius Gallus Gargilius Antiquus, imperial governor with praetorian rank [of the province Syria Palaestina]." [Gera and Cotton, 2001, 497; *CIIP* 2: 2122]. Found near Dor.

Courtesy of *CIIP*. Displayed at the Center of Nautical and Regional Archaeology at Nahsholim

GOVERNOR GARGILIUS ANTIQUUS INSCRIPTION

In January 2016 an inscription was discovered that mentioned the name of another governor[81] (*praeses provinciae,* ἡγεμων, *hēgemōn*) of Judea.[82] But before examining the new discovery, a little background on Judea and who a Roman governor was and what they did.

From 63 BC until 6 AD, following the conquest of Judea by Pompey in 63 BC, Judea was initially ruled by descendants of the Hasmonaean house without

[75] Meggitt argues that the name should be [Ep]erastus and is found 15 times in Latin and 18 times in Greek. Justin J. Meggitt, "The Social Status of Erastus (Ro. 16:23)," *NovT* 38, no. 3 (1996): 140.

[76] Friesen, "The Wrong Erastus," 236; Andrew D. Clarke, *Secular and Christian Leadership in Corinth: A Socio-Historical and Exegetkal Study of 1 Corinthians 1-6* (Leiden: Brill, 1993), 49–54; Andrew D. Clarke, "Another Corinthian Erastus Inscription," *TB* 42 (1991): 146–51.

[77] This wording and practice is also present in the recent Megiddo church mosaic which reads: "Gaianus, also called Porphyrius, centurion, our brother, has made the pavement at his own expense as an act of liberality. Brutius has carried out the work." Edward Adams, "The Ancient Church at Megiddo: The Discovery and an Assessment of Its Significance," *ExpTim* 120 (2008): 64. Adams notes that "The word "centurion" (*hekatontarches*) is represented by the chi-rho symbol, an established abbreviation for the term."

[78] Murphy-O'Connor, *St. Paul's Corinth*, 34–35; David W. J. Gill, "Erastus the Aedile," *TynBul* 40 (1989): 293–301; Geisler and Holden, *Popular Handbook of Archaeology and the Bible*, 358.

[79] Friesen, "The Wrong Erastus," 231.

[80] Clarke, *Secular and Christian Leadership in Corinth*, 46–57.

[81] For a list of Latin terms used in ancient sources for Governor see Appendix G in Simon Corcoran, *The Empire of the Tetrarchs: Imperial Pronouncements and Government, AD 284-324* (Oxford, UK: Clarendon, 2000), 337–39.

[82] For more information on the Governors of Judea and the new inscriptions, see David E. Graves, "Fresh Light on the Governors of Judea," *BS* 30, no. 3 (2017): 58–68.

royal title and later by the Herodian dynasty. Pompey reduced the territory of Judea by annexing the Decapolis and all the coastal cities to the new province of Syria.[83] Although the province of Judea (*provincia Iudaea*) did not initially include Galilee, Gaulanitis [the Golan], nor Peraea or the Decapolis, it later came to include Judea proper, Idumaea, Samaria, the Peraea and the Galilee. Its capital was at Caesarea Maritima and not Jerusalem.[84] The governor lived at the capital of his province in a palace-fortress called the *praetorium* (Acts 23:35), which in the case of Judea province was located at Caesarea. There was also a *praetorium* in Jerusalem for when the governor was in residence there (Matt 27:27; Mark 15:16; John 18:28; 19:9). According to Josephus the Province of Judea, during the late Second Temple period was divided into five administrative districts (*conclaves*): Jerusalem, Gadara, Amathus, Jericho, and Sepphoris (*Ant.* 14.5.4).

Governors

A Roman governor (*praeses provinciae,* ἡγεμων, *hēgemōn*) or senator was an official appointed to be the chief administrator of Roman law in the province and included military and administrative duties.[85] In the Senatorial provinces (i.e., Italy, Macedonia, Asia, Africa) during the time of Augustus (r. 27 BC–AD 14), the provinces were governed by former *praetors* called proconsuls[86] who usually served for twelve months (Ulpian *Dig.* 1.16.1–16).[87] However, in the border Imperial provinces (i.e., Syria, Arabia, and, Judea), the "envoy of the emperor—acting praetor" (*legati Augusti pro praetore),* were divided into two further categories.

1). Those in the regions where legions were stationed, like Syria, were governed by *legates*, appointed by the Emperor and their office typically lasted thirty-six months.[88]

2). The smaller Imperial provinces like Judea [*Ioudaía/Iudaea*], where no legions were based, but governed with small auxiliary armies;[89] the governor was of lower "equestrian" rank (*Equites Romani*) called *prefects* (*equestrian praefecti).*[90] Later under Claudius (r. AD 41–54) governors in these provinces were fiscal officials, rather than soldiers and were designated *procurators* (Lat. *procurare*, "to take care of" as in "to manage or administer"; ἐπίτροπος, *epitropos*; Matt 27:2; cf. Luke 2:2). In late antiquity (Diocletian AD 284–305), provincial governors were known by the titles *consularis*, *corrector* and *praeses.*[91] The administration of the provinces was a supervisory role where the governor utilized the council of elders (τοπάρχης, *toparchiēs,* "leader of a district") and a diversity of advisors and staff *(comites* "companions").[92]

---

[83] Emil Schürer, *The History of the Jewish People in the Age of Jesus Christ (175 BC–AD 135)*, ed. G. Vermes, F. Miller, and M. Black, Rev (Edinburgh, UK: T&T Clark, 1979), 240.

[84] Shimon Applebaum, *Judaea in Hellenistic and Roman Times: Historical and Archaeological Essays*, ed. Jacob Neusner (Leiden: Brill Academic, 1989), 123.

[85] Fred K. Drogula, "The Office of the Provincial Governor under the Roman Republic and Empire [to AD 235]: Conception and Tradition" (University of Virginia, 2005); Daniëlle Slootjes, *The Governor and His Subjects in the Later Roman Empire* (Leiden: Brill, 2006).

[86] Ruth B. Edwards, "Rome," *DJG*, 712.

[87] Egypt was directly ruled by the Emperor, so the governor of Egypt held a unique role called *Praefectus Aegypti* (Ulpian *Dig.* 1.17.1).

[88] Edwards, 712.

[89] Jeffers, *The Greco-Roman World of the NT*, 134; Michael Speidel, "The Roman Army in Judaea under the Procurators," in *Roman Army Studies*, ed. Michael Speidel (Stuttgart: Gieben, 1992), 2:224–32.

[90] Edwards, "Rome," 712.

[91] Walter Eder, "Governor," *BrillPauly*, 2006. http://dx.doi.org/10.1163/1574-9347_bnp_e1121630 (accessed 24 January 2018).

[92] C. Gizewski and F. Tinnefeld, "Comes, comites," *BrillPauly*, 2006. http://dx.doi.org/10.1163/1574-9347_bnp_e303300 (accessed January 2018).

New Discovery of Gargilius Antiquus, AD 122–31

136. Roman-era 1900-year-old inscription that mentions "The city of Dor honors Marcus Paccius... Gargilius Antiquus governor of the province of Judea."

Courtesy of Haifa University Library Museum

In January of 2016, a new seven-line Greek dedicatory inscription, that is believed to be part of a statue base, was recovered from off the coast of Dor[93] by Haifa University underwater archaeologists, under the direction of Professor Assaf Yasur-Landau (see Fig. 136).[94]

The Greek inscription (not Latin) translated as: "The City of Dor honors Marcus Paccius, son of Publius, Silvanus Quintus Coredius Gallus Gargilius Antiquus, governor of the province of Judea, as well as [...] of the province of Syria, and patron of the city of Dor" [Dr. Gil Gambash].[95]

Gargilius Antiquus' anglicized name was Mark Paktsy Sylvan Quintus Coredo Gull Gargily Antiqua. However, this is not the first time that someone has been identified with the name Gargilius Antiquus, although his son and grandson also carried the same name (see below). The details in the inscriptions help to identify and date the corresponding Gargililus Antiquus.[96]

Gargililus was first mentioned in an inscribed circular stone discovered in 1948, by the East Gate of the ancient city of Dor, during the Israeli War of Independence (*CIIP* 2:2122=*SEG* 37.1477; 41.1547; 45.1946: see Fig. 135).[97]

Following the discovery of the new inscription there was some debate over where Gargilius Antiquus ruled, either in Syria or Syria-Palaestina.[98] Now the debate has been settled with the new discovery of the previously known Gargilius Antiquus, who was suspected of being the governor of Judea before the Bar Kochba Revolt, that was suppressed in *ca.* AD 135.[99]

What do we know of Gargilius Antiquus?

Gargilius Antiquus (father was Publius Gargilius Antiquus and a relative by the name of Quintus Gargilius Antiquus) was a Roman politician in the first half of the second cent. AD. He held the position of Praetorian governor of the province of Arabia Petraea in approximately AD 116–119

---

[93] Dor (Gr. *Dora*) is a coastal city, just 9 Roman miles (8.3 miles/ 13 km) north of Caesarea Maritima (Eusebius *On.* 78.9; 136.16). In the early 2nd century AD their status changed when it was annexed to the province of Phoenicia and in the late Roman period (AD 390) it became part of *Palaestina Prima.* Negev and Gibson, *AEHL*, 144–45.

[94] Philippe Bohstrom, "Divers Find Unexpected Roman Inscription from the Eve of Bar-Kochba Revolt," *Haaretz*, November 30, 2016, n.p., http://www.haaretz.com/jewish/archaeology/1.756193; Ilan Yavelberg and Ela Kehat, "Ancient Inscription Permits, for the First Time, the Definite Identification of Gargilius Antiques as the Roman Prefect during the Period before the Bar Kochba Revolt," University of Haifa, December 12, 2016, n.p., http://www.haifa.ac.il/index.php/en/home-page3/2025.

[95] Ibid.

[96] Staff. "Rare Find Reveals Previously Unknown Roman Ruler in Judea." *The Times of Israel* (blog), December 1, 2016. http://www.timesofisrael.com/rare-find-reveals-previously-unknown-roman-ruler-in-judea.

[97] Ephraim Stern and Ilan Sharon, "Tel Dor, 1986: Preliminary Report," *IEJ* 37, no. 4 (1987): 209; Ephraim Stern, Ilan Sharon, and Ayelet Gilboa, "Tel Dor 1987: Preliminary Report," *IEJ* 39, no. 1/2 (1989): 37. First published in Hebrew in *Qadmoniot.* Dov Gera and Hannah M. Cotton, "A Dedicatory Inscription to the Ruler of Syria [Hebrew]," *Qadmoniot* 22, no. 1/2 (1989): 42. It was also found listed in the Dor inspection file (1951), of the Israel Antiquities Authority (IAA).

[98] Dov Gera and Hannah M. Cotton, "A Dedication from Dor to a Governor of Syria," *IEJ* 41, no. 4 (1991): 258–66; Edward Dąbrowa, "M. Paccius Silvanus Quintus Coredius Gallus Gargilius Antiquus et son cursus honorum," in *Nunc de suebis dicendum est: studia archaeologica et historica Georgio Kolendo ab amicis et discipulis dicata*, ed. Aleksander Bursche and Jerzy Kolendo (Warsaw: Instytut Archeologii Uniwersytetu Warszawskiego, 1995), 99.

[99] Dąbrowa, "M. Paccius," 99–102.

and in May of AD 119 became the *consul suffectus*.[100] He was confirmed at Dor between 122 and 125.[101] He is believed to be the proconsul of Asia in ca. AD 134/5.[102] His position as the Governor of Judea, once suspected has now been confirmed.

What else is learned?

First, according to Prof. Yasur-Landau, of the University of Haifa, the inscription stone, "is the longest discovered in maritime excavations in Israel".[103] It consists of seven lines and the statue base measures 27.5 by 25.5 inches (70 by 65 centimeters) and weights over 1322 pounds (600 kilograms), and was encrusted by sea shells when it was discovered.[104]

Second, not only does this discovery confirm the identity of another governor of Judea, but it is also only the second time that Judea has been mentioned in an inscription outside of the Bible.[105] The other occurrence is in the inscription from Caesarea of Pontius Pilate.[106] Immediately following the Bar Kochba revolt, the Romans abolished the province of Judea obliterating any mention of its name.

The historical context of the two inscriptions mentioning Gargilius Antiquus is less clear. Certainly he is being honored on two sculptures and lauded as the prefect Antiquus. The reason for this is unclear. Do they celebrate two different events or do cities erect commemorative monuments without a special reason?

Dating

Werner Eck based on the first inscription convincingly argued that Gargilius Antiquus was not the governor of Syria. He argued:

> he could not have obtained the governorship of Syria, which was reserved for senior consulars, before 128 AD or later (i.e. at least ten years after the consulate). However, Poblicius Marcellus, consul in 120, is attested in Syria in March 129,[107] and his governorship there had started at the latest in summer 128, and continued till 134/5 AD. In other words, there was no room in Syria for Gargilius Antiquus of the inscription from Dor till 134/5, when he is attested in Asia.[108]

The new inscription mentions "the province of Judaea, as well as [...] of the province of Syria". Emperor Hadrian united the province of Judea with Syria to create a single province called Syria–Palestine just prior to AD 136, following the Bar Kokhba revolt (AD 132–136).[109] So this inscription must date to just before Judea joined Syria as a province. This recent discovery is the latest of the two inscriptions and may be the last mention of Judea as an independent province in an inscription that will ever be found, given the rare occurrence of the

---

[100] Werner Eck and Christmann Eckhard, "Gargilius," *BrillPauly*. http://dx.doi.org/10.1163/1574-9347_bnp_e419020 (accessed January 2018); Theodor Mommsen, *Corpus inscriptionum latinarum*, 20 vols. (Berlin: De Gruyter, 1974), 6:2384.

[101] Dąbrowa, "M. Paccius," 99–102; William David Davies, Louis Finkelstein, and Steven T. Katz, *The Cambridge History of Judaism: The Late Roman-Rabbinic Period*, vol. 4 (Cambridge University Press, 1984), 4:101.

[102] Werner Eck, "Jahres- Und Provinzialfasten Der Senatorischen Statthalter von 69/70 Bis 138/139, 1. Teil," *Chiron* 12 (1982): 361; "Jahres- Und Provinzialfasten Der Senatorischen Statthalter von 69/70 Bis 138/139. 2. Teil," *Chiron* 13 (1983): 148–76.

[103] Staff. "Rare Find Reveals Previously Unknown Roman Ruler in Judea." *The Times of Israel* (blog), December 1, 2016. http://www.timesofisrael.com/rare-find-reveals-previously-unknown-roman-ruler-in-judea.

[104] Ibid.

[105] Ibid.

[106] Alfred Merlin, ed., *L'Année Épigraphique* (Villejuif: Collège de France, 1963), 104.

[107] Werner Eck and Andreas Pangerl, "Syria Unter Domitian Und Hadrian: Neue Diplome Für Die Auxiliartruppen Der Provinz," *Chiron* 36 (2006): 221–47.

[108] Eck, *CIIP* 2:844.

[109] Emil Schürer, *The History of the Jewish People in the Age of Jesus Christ (175 BC–AD 135)*, ed. G. Vermes, F. Miller, and M. Black, Rev, 4 vols. (Edinburgh, UK: T&T Clark, 1979), 1:542–52.

name Judea on inscriptions.

This would indicate that Gargilius Antiquus' was the governor of Judea sometime before AD 135. This criterion has at least two time frames that work. First, based on the first inscription,[110] Werner Eck speculated that "Gargilius Antiquus could have followed Cossonius Gallus[111] as governor of Judaea, *ca.* 123/5".[112] But second, between Quintus Tineius Rufus who was governor from AD 130 to 132 and Caius Quinctius Certus Publius Marcellus who was governor in 134 there is room for Gargilius Antiquus to have been governor between AD 132–134 for a post of one to two years. This would also fit within the list of governors and match the existence of an independent Judea as mentioned in the inscription. Not only is there now another inscription confirming the governor of Judea, but it has provided the missing governor of Judea from AD 123–125 or 130–132.

MEGIDDO CHURCH INSCRIPTIONS

In 2005, during construction work at the Megiddo Prison, inmates came upon archaeological remains. Israeli archaeologist Yotam Tepper, of Tel-Aviv University, was called in to investigate and discovered the remains of a third cent. AD church with a large (54 sq m/580 sq ft) beautiful mosaic with several Greek inscriptions.[113]

137. Akeptous mosaic inscripton from one of the earliest Christian churches.

Megiddo, Israel

Over 100 coins were uncovered from the reigns of emperors Elagabalus (AD 218–222) and Severus Alexander (AD 222–235), with the latest coin dating to Diocletian's reign in the late third cent. (AD 284–305). The absence of any post- Diocletian coins means that the building was abandoned sometime in the fourth century.[114] Tepper places the date of the structure to sometime in the first half of the third cent. AD (*ca.* AD 230).[115] This could be the earliest Christian church yet discovered.

Among the geometrical patterns on the mosaic was a picture of two fish, which became an early Christian symbol based on the Greek word for fish (Gr. *ichthys*), that represented the first letter of each word in an acrostic for "Jesus Christ, God Son Saviour."[116]

The mosaic also contained three inscriptions. The first is a dedicatory inscription mentioning the benefactor of the mosaic. It reads: "Gaianus, also called Porphyrius, centurion, our brother, has made the pavement at his own expense as an act of liberality. Brutius has

---

110 Eck, *CIIP* 2:2122.

111 Eck, *CIIP* 2:1227.

112 cf. Dąbrowa, "M. Paccius," 99–102; Eck, *CIIP* 2:844.

113 Yotam Tepper and Leah Di Segni, *A Christian Prayer Hall of the Third Century CE at Kefar ' Othnay (Legio): Excavations at the Megiddo Prison 2005* (Jerusalem: Israel Antiquities Authority, 2006), 31–42.

114 Andrew Lawler, "First Churches of the Jesus Cult," *Archaeology* 60, no. 5 (2007): 50.

115 Vassilios Tzaferis, "Inscribed to 'God Jesus Christ': Early Christian Prayer Hall Found in Megiddo Prison," *BAR* 33, no. 2 (2007): 38.

116 Everett Ferguson, *Encyclopedia of Early Christianity*, 2nd ed. (New York: Routledge, 2013), 431–32.

carried out the work" [Leah di Segni].[117]

A second memorial (Women) inscription mentioned four common Greek women's names. It translates: "Remember Primilla and Cyriaca and Dorothea, and moreover also Chreste."[118]

However, it was the third (Akeptous) inscription which caught the world's attention. This mosaic inscription reads: "The God-loving Akeptous has offered the table to God Jesus Christ as a memorial" [Leah di Segni; see Fig. 137].[119] This speaks, both of the deity of Jesus Christ, and the place of the communion table or Eucharist in the early Christian ceremony.

Significance

As Adam's points out, the importance of the discovery to the early Christian movement is directly linked to the date of the structure, which is contested.[120] Assuming a pre-313 AD date for the construction and use of the building as a church, there are several contributions that this discovery makes.

The first is to our understanding of the architecture of early Christianity. The Megiddo church is a unique public building (i.e., the Dura Europos church, was privately owned), with a room devoted to the use of a church, such as a house church (*domus ecclesia* cf. Acts 2:46; 5:42), and was not an exclusively-built basilica church (i.e., as the Aqaba church in southern Jordan).[121]

The second contribution is that it illuminates our understanding of "early Christian belief and worship" in the development of the Church. Adams states that the inscriptions could: "rank among the oldest epigraphic data for Christianity"[122] that mentions Jesus Christ. In addition, the Akeptous inscription, which states "God Jesus Christ," has been provided as proof against the 'Da Vinci Code' theory that states that Jesus was not considered as God before Constantine.[123]

While it is true that Christians were persecuted in the early centuries (first through fourth cent. AD) of the Church, especially under Nero, Decius, Diocletian and Galerius, Lawler points out that: "the evidence from Near Eastern digs, combined with new thinking about the Roman Empire, demonstrates that there were substantial periods when Christians were tolerated, accepted, and even embraced by their tormentors."[124]

The discovery of an early church at Megiddo illustrates the theory that there were times in the early church when there was tolerance for Christians and their churches.

SARCOPHAGUS OF ST. PAUL

In 2002 archaeologists began investigating a tomb (AD 390) that was buried under the altar in a crypt in the basilica of St Paul's Outside-the-Walls in Rome (see Fig. 138).[125] After three years

---

[117] Yotam Tepper and Leah Di Segni, *A Christian Prayer Hall of the Third Century CE at Kefar ' Othnay (Legio): Excavations at the Megiddo Prison 2005* (Jerusalem: Israel Antiquities Authority, 2006), 36–40; Edward Adams, "The Ancient Church at Megiddo: The Discovery and an Assessment of Its Significance," *ExpTim* 120, no. 2 (2008): 64.

[118] Tepper and Leah Di Segni, *A Christian Prayer Hall*, 41–42.

[119] Ibid., 34–42; Tzaferis, "Inscribed to 'God Jesus Christ': Early Christian Prayer Hall Found in Megiddo Prison," 39; Adams, "The Ancient Church at Megiddo," 65.

[120] Edward Adams, "The Ancient Church at Megiddo: The Discovery and an Assessment of Its Significance," *ExpTim* 120, no. 2 (2008): 66.

[121] Ibid., 67.

[122] Adams, "The Ancient Church at Megiddo," 66.

[123] Dan Brown, *The Da Vinci Code* (London: Bantam, 2003), 233.

[124] Andrew Lawler, "First Churches of the Jesus Cult," *Archaeology* 60, no. 5 (2007): 48.

[125] Christian Fraser, "St Paul's Tomb Unearthed in Rome," *BBC News, Rome*, December 7, 2006, sec. Europe, http://news.bbc.co.uk/2/hi/6219656.stm.

they removed two large slabs of marble to reveal a sarcophagus that contained a Latin inscription on the top that read: *Paulo Apostolo Mart[yri]* ("Paul Apostle Martyr").[126] It was not opened but archaeologists inserted a probe that revealed purple linen covered with gold flecks, incense, and some small bone fragments. The remains were radiocarbon (carbon-14) dated to the first or second cent. AD.[127]

138. Statue of St. Paul in front of the facade of the Basilica of Saint Paul Outside-the-Walls, Rome.

Photo by Berthold Werner / Wikimedia Commons

Father Scott Brodeur of the Pontifical Gregorian University states that "I think it's highly probable that the human remains that we have found in that sarcophagus are that of the Apostle of Paul."[128] Pope Benedict XVI also agreed and in 2009 stated that the scientific analysis "seems to confirm the unanimous and uncontested tradition that these are the mortal remains of the Apostle Paul."[129]

---

[126] Ottavio Bucarelli and Martín Maria Morales, eds., *Paolo apostolo martyri: l'apostolo San Paolo nella storia, nell'arte e nell'archeologia*, Miscellanea Historiae Pontificiae 69 (Rome: Gregorian and Biblical Press, 2009), 290; Angela Donati, *Pietro E Paolo La Storia Il Culto La Memoria Nei Primi Secoli*, Catalogo Della Monstra (Milan: Electa, 2000), 175.

[127] Katia Lopez Hodoyan, "The Mysteries Surrounding the Tomb of St. Paul," *Rome Reports TV News Agency*, February 5, 2012, http://www.romereports.com/palio/the-mysteries-surrounding-the-tomb-of-st-paul-english-5996.html.

[128] Ibid.

[129] Ibid.

CHART 8: ROMAN PERIOD DISCOVERIES III

REVELATION (ROMAN PERIOD: AD 70–90)					
Discovery	**Image**	**Discoverer**	**Origin Date /Year Found**	**Biblical Passage**	**Significance**
Coin of Domitian's deified infant son		N/A	AD 82–83 N/A	Rev 1:13, 16	Seven stars with Domitian's son sitting on the globe
Altar of Zeus, Pergamum		Pergamum, Turkey by Carl Humann	170–159 BC 1878–1886	Rev 2:12–17	Possible "Satan's Throne . . . where Satan lives"
Portrait of Nero		Palatine Hill, Antiquarium of the Palatine	AD 54–68	Rev 13:3; 17:8–11	Nero redivius and the antichrist
Pompeii Graffiti from the door of Ottavius Primo	VIIRVS HIC VBI STAT NIHIL · VIIRI	Pompeii, Italy "the number of her honorable name is 45" by Giuseppe Fiorelli	AD 79 1875	Rev 13:18	Use of Gematria for 666
Basilica of St. John		Ephesus, Turkey by John T. Wood	sixth cent. AD/ 1863	Rev 1–22	Tomb of John the apostle
Madaba Map		Madaba, Jordan by Monk Ananias and Athanasios Andreakis	542–570 AD 1884	N/A	Identification of biblical cities and geography

Revelation

139. Acropolis of Pergamum, with the Hellenistic theater (ca. 225–200 BC) carved vertically out of the side of the mountain with a capacity of ca. 10,000 citizens. Visible on the top are the pillars of the Temple of Trajan (second cent. AD).

Archaeology is no less important in understanding the historical context of the Book of Revelation than the other books in the Bible, but sadly this area is often neglected. Revelation is perhaps the least understood and most misrepresented book in the NT. The title for Revelation comes from the first sentence which, as in many other ancient books, provides the title for the work along with the content and the name of the author. The book begins with the phrase "The revelation (ἀποκάλυψις *apokalypsis*) of Jesus Christ" (Rev 1:1) and "John" is simply stated as the author. *Apocalypse*[1] means "to disclose," "unveiling" or "revealing,"[2] but for most readers the book tends to hide rather than reveal its message, as much of it is disputed by scholars. Therefore, archaeology has an important role to play in unlocking the enigma of this fascinating book.

The Occasion of Revelation

The letter of Revelation was written as an individual message, to seven real churches, in the Asia Minor cities of Ephesus, Smyrna, Pergamum, Thyatira, Sardis, Philadelphia, and Laodicea. The seven cities were located on what Ramsay considered a circular postal route.[3] Each church had their own set of problems and issues, and the message of Revelation sought to address, reprimand and provide encouragement to them. It was thus designed to be read aloud in each one of the seven churches.[4]

The letter of Revelation, which presents the triumph of Christ over evil, was meant to be a source of encouragement to these suffering churches, dealing with the crisis of persecution from Rome (see below under "External Problems"; Eusebius *Chron.* 19.551–52; *Hist. eccl.* 3.23.3–4) and the Jewish community (see below under "Internal Problems").[5]

---

[1] For the study of genre and apocalyptic literature and the book of Revelation see E. Frank Tupper, "The Revival of Apocalyptic in Biblical and Theological Studies," *RevExp* 72, no. 3 (1975): 279–303; Jan Lambrecht, "The Book of Revelation and Apocalyptic in the New Testament," in *L'Apocalypse Johannique et L' Apocalyptique Dans Le NouveauTestament*, ed. Jan lambrecht (Leuven: Leuven University Press, 1980), 18; David Hellholm and Kungl Vitterhets, *Apocalypticism in the Mediterranean World and the Near East: Proceedings of the International Colloquium on Apocalypticism, Uppsala, August 12-17, 1979* (Tübingen: Siebeck, 1989); David E. Aune, "The Apocalypse of John and the Problem of Genre," in *Early Christian Apocalypticism: Genre and Social Setting*, Semeia 36 (Atlanta, Ga.: Scholars Press, 1986), 65–69; John M. Court, *The Book of Revelation and the Johannine Apocalyptic Tradition* (Sheffield: Sheffield Academic, 2000).

[2] Richard J. Bauckham, "Apocalyptic," ed. Sinclair B. Ferguson, David F. Wright, and James I. Packer, *NDT* (Downers Grove, IL: InterVarsity, 1988), 34.

[3] William M. Ramsay, *The Letters to Seven Churches: Updated*, ed. Mark W. Wilson (Peabody, Mass.: Hendrickson, 1994), 183.

[4] David E. Graves, *Jesus Speaks to Seven of His Churches: A Commentary on the Messages to the Seven Churches in Revelation* (Toronto, Ont.: Electronic Christian Media, 2017), 43.

[5] Thompson and Yarbro Collins have argued that the message was *creating* the feeling of a "perceived crisis" rather than *responding* to one. Leonard L. Thompson, *The Book of Revelation: Apocalypse and Empire* (New York: Oxford University Press, USA, 1997), 27–28; Adela Yarbro Collins, *Crisis and Catharsis: The Power of the Apocalypse* (Louisville, Ky.: Westminster/Knox, 1984), 84.

140. Island of Patmos where John received his vision of Revelation.
Courtesy of Todd Bolen / BiblePlaces.com

The Location of Writing

John received his vision *(Apocalypse)* on the island of Patmos (in modern Greece; Rev 1:9; Origin *Comm. Apoc.* 10.3 see *Quotes from Antiquity*), located in the Aegean Sea southeast of Miletus (in modern Turkey; see Fig. 140). Eusebius, referencing Irenaeus, states that in the fourteenth year of Domitian's reign, during a persecution of Christian, "the apostle John is banished to Patmos and sees his Apocalypse" (*Chron.* 19.551–52; *Hist. eccl.* 3.23.3–4).

> ***Quotes from Antiquity***
>
> An old tradition based on Origen and recorded by Victorinus of Pettau (d. ca. AD 304), states that:
>
> When John saw this revelation, he was on the island of Patmos, having been condemned to the mines by Caesar Domitian. There, it seems, John wrote the Revelation, and when he had already become aged, he thought that he would be received into bliss after his suffering. However, when Domitian was killed, all of his decrees were null and void. John was, therefore, released from the mines, and afterward he disseminated the revelation that he had received from the Lord.
>
> (*Comm. Apoc.* 10.3 [Weinrich])

Presumably John was banished to Patmos because of his faith (1:9). Scholars speculate that the island was used by Rome as a place to exile criminals and political prisoners. This is based on Tacitus' mention of three other islands in the Aegean (Donusa, Gyarus and Amorgus) where the Romans exiled political prisoners (Tacitus *Ann.* 3.69).[6]

There is evidence of continual occupation during the time when John lived there, showing that the island was not deserted or just used as a Roman penal colony[7] (Pliny *Nat.* 4.12.69; Tacitus *Ann.* 4.30).[8] There is no evidence from ancient writers that Patmos ever had mines or quarries on it.[9] Tertullian (*Praescr.* 36; AD 220), Origen (*Comm. Matt.* 16.6 on Matt 20:22–23; AD 254), and Eusebius (AD 313) state that John was "exiled to an island" (*Hist. eccl.* 3.18.1), using language of banishment and condemnation for John's removal. However, the biblical text only states: "I, John, your brother and partner in the tribulation and the kingdom

[6] Henry Barclay Swete, *Commentary on Revelation*, reprint 1906 (Eugene, OR: Wipf & Stock, 1999), 12; Robert H. Charles, *A Critical and Exegetical Commentary on the Revelation of St John*, ICC (Edinburgh, UK: T&T Clark, 1963), 1:21; Ernst Lohmeyer, *Die Offenbarung Des Johannes*, HNT 16 (Tübingen: Siebeck, 1926), 15; Eduard Lohse, *Die Offenbarung Des Johannes*, Das Neue Testament Deutsch 11 (Göttingen: Vandenhoeck & Ruprecht, 1993), 19; Heinrich Kraft, *Die Offenbarung Des Johannes*, HNT 16a (Tübingen: Siebeck, 1974), 40.

[7] For more details on Roman law, see Adolf Berger, *Encyclopedic Dictionary of Roman Law*, Reprint of the 1953 edition, Transactions of the American Philosophical Society V. 43, Pt. 2. (The Lawbook Exchange, Ltd., 2002), 633; David E. Aune, *Revelation 1–5*, WBC 52A (Nashville: Nelson, 1997), 79.

[8] Otto F. A. Meinardus, *St. John of Patmos and the Seven Churches of the Apocalypse*, In the Footsteps of the Saints (New York: Caratzas, 1979), 13.

[9] Brian M. Rapske, "Exiles, Islands, and the Identity and Perspective of John in Revelation," in *Christian Origins and Greco-Roman Culture: Social and Literary Contexts for the New Testament*, ed. Stanley E. Porter and Andrew W. Pitts, Texts and Editions for New Testament Study: Early Christianity in Its Hellenistic Context 1 (Leiden: Brill, 2012), 311–46.

and the patient endurance that are in Jesus, was on the island called Patmos on account of the word of God and the testimony (μαρτυρίαν, *martyrian*[10] meaning "witness") of Jesus (Rev 1:9)."[11]

Scholars note that the modern idea of martyrdom for this term *martyrian* did not develop until much later.[12] Perhaps, John was carrying out missionary (witnessing) activities on Patmos when he received his vision,[13] although scholars speculate that surely he would have chosen a larger and more populated island as a location to engage in evangelism.[14]

During the Hellenistic period, Patmos was part of Miletus, and along with two other islands, formed the "fortresses" of Miletus to protect its harbour on the Gulf of Latmique. By the second century BC these three islands were populated by a Milesian garrison.[15] A second century AD inscription mentions the presence of the cult of Artemis flourishing on the island, including the existence of a temple to Artemis which is now under the Christian basilica.[16] Between the seventh and eleventh century Patmos was deserted due to pirates. However, as mentioned earlier, the island was definitely not deserted or a Roman penal colony in John's day (Pliny *Nat.* 4.12.69; Tacitus *Ann.* 4.30).

In 1088, Emperor Alexios I Comnenos granted Christodoulos Latrenus, a Nicaean monk, permission to build the Monastery of St. John the Theologian on Patmos over the Christian basilica and the temple of Artemis (see Figs. 153). Near the Grotto or cave of the Apocalypse, which was supposedly the place where John received his vision, he built the Chapel of St. Anne, named either after the virgin Mary or the mother of Alexios I Comnenos.[17]

Today the monastery holds a collection of valuable manuscripts, including the sixth cent. AD Codex Purpureus Petropolitanus (a copy of the Gospel of Mark), and an eighth cent. AD book of Job. Also, the museum houses a fourth cent. BC marble inscription stating that "Orestes (son of Agamemnon and Clytemnestra) visited Patmos and established a temple to Artemis on the island, supposedly in the same location as the Monastery of St. John."[18]

THE RECIPIENTS OF REVELATION

John addresses his messages to individual churches he knew well with a preliminary message from Christ, before communicating a general message that each church was to read publicly (Rev 1:3, 22:181 Eusebius *Hist. eccl.* 7.25.9–10). The plural addresses in the refrain "let him hear what the Spirit says to the churches" (2:7, 11, 29; 3:6, 13, 22) are a strong indication that all the churches were to read the document. As Graves concludes, "John wrote his messages to the seven churches in Revelation using a prophetic oracle genre in the tradition of OT prophets."[19]

---

[10] Scholars note that the modern idea of martyrdom for this term *martyrian* did not develop until much later. Boudewijn Dehandschütter, "The Meaning of Witness in the Apocalypse," in *L'Apocalypse Johannique et L' Apocalyptique Dans Le Nouveau Testament*, ed. Jan Lambrecht (Gembloux, Belgium: Louvain University Press, 1980), 283–88.

[11] Perhaps, John was carrying out missionary (witnessing) activities on Patmos when he received his vision, although scholars speculate that surely he would have chosen a larger and more populated island as a location to engage in evangelism. Kistemaker, *Revelation*, 91; John R. Yeatts, *Revelation*, Believers Church Bible Commentary (Harrisonburg, VA: Herald, 2003), 40.

[12] Dehandschütter, "The Meaning of Witness in the Apocalypse."

[13] Rapske, "Exiles, Islands, and the Identity and Perspective of John in Revelation," 311.

[14] Kistemaker, *Revelation*, 91; Yeatts, *Revelation*, 40.

[15] H. D. Saffrey, "Relire l'Apocalypse À Patmos," *RB* 82 (1975): 388–91.

[16] Aune, *Rev 1–5*, 77; Saffrey, "Relire l'Apocalypse À Patmos," 399–407; Werner Peek, "Die Hydrophore Vera von Patmos," *Rheinisches Museum Für Philologie*, 1964, 315–25; Clyde E. Fant and Mitchell G. Reddish, *A Guide to Biblical Sites in Greece and Turkey* (Oxford: Oxford University Press, 2003), 93.

[17] Frank Leslie Cross and Elizabeth A. Livingstone, eds., *The Oxford Dictionary Of The Christian Church* (Oxford: Oxford University Press, 2005), 1024.

[18] Fant and Reddish, *Guide to Biblical Sites*, 98.

[19] Ibid., 123.

141. Restored Library of Celsus, Ephesus. The relief in the foreground is reminiscent of the elements of armor given in Ephesians 6:13–17, including the belt, breastplate, greaves for the feet, shield, helmet and sword. While the Library was only completed in 135 AD and was not present in Paul's day, the relief may have existed earlier, as it was not attached to the structure.

The book of Revelation is filled with vivid pictures, symbols and beautiful scenes of the throne room of God (Rev 4–5) contrasted with the evil of the many-horned beast (Rev 13) and the desperate calamity of the faithful witnesses (Rev 11). What do all these pictures mean? Can archaeology help in unraveling the mystery?

LOCAL REFERENCES[20]

It is believed there are several allusions to *local references* within the message to the seven churches (Rev 2–3), which refer to local geographical, historical or cultural references that are illustrated from archaeology, museum artifacts, coins (numismatics), and inscriptions (see Fig. 141).[21]

According to de Lassus, the presence of local references "increases the realism and impact of the message of the letters on their recipients."[22] For example, the warning about being lukewarm would have a deeper significance to Laodicea (Rev 3:16) than to another city, due to the unique qualities of the Laodicean water system (see Laodicea below).

However, one must not be too dogmatic about all associations, as it is impossible to know what was going through John's mind during the process of inspiration,[23] but as Beale points out "the ancient readers would have been more familiar with some of these than the modern interpreter."[24] As Malina reminds us: "The goal is to understand the document in terms that would have made sense to a first-century A.D. audience. Only such a historical approach can be considered fair and adequate to the prophet's concern about "anyone taking away from the utterances of the scroll of this prophecy" (Rev 21:19).[25]

This is precisely the role of archaeology in helping to provide a basic historical context in which to understand the passage, since God first intended his message to be read by first-century

---

[20] The majority of this section on local references and the next section on the seven churches were previously published in the *BS* magazine and reprinted here with permission. Graves, David E. "Jesus Speaks to Seven of His Churches, Part 1." *BS* 23, no. 2 (Spring 2010): 46–56. "Jesus Speaks to Seven of His Churches, Part 2." *BS* 23, no. 3 (Summer 2010): 66–74.

[21] Ramsay, *The Letters to Seven Churches*; Colin J. Hemer, *The Letters to the Seven Churches of Asia in Their Local Setting*, The Biblical Resource Series (Grand Rapids: Eerdmans, 2001); Charles H. Scobie, "Local References in the Letters to the Seven Churches," *New Testament Studies* 39, no. 4 (1993): 616–17; Peter Wood, "Local Knowledge of the Letters of the Apocalypse," *ExpTim* 73 (1962 1961): 263–4; Stanley E. Porter, "Why the Laodiceans Received Lukewarm Water (Rev 3:15–18)," *TynBul* 38 (1987): 143–9; Philip A. Harland, "Imperial Cults within Local Cultural Life: Associations in Roman Asia," *Ancient History Bulletin* 17, no. 1–2 (2003): 85–107.

[22] Alain-Marie de Lassus, "Le Septénaire Des Lettres de L'apocalypse de Jean: De La Correction Au Témoignage Militant" (Ph.D. diss., University of Strasbourg, 2005), 112.

[23] Hemer, *Letters to the Seven Churches*, 210.

[24] Gregory K. Beale, "Review of Colin J. Hemer, The Letters to the Seven Churches of Asia in Their Local Setting," *Trinity Journal* 7, no. 2 (1986): 110.

[25] Bruce J. Malina, *On the Genre and Message of Revelation: Star Visions and Sky Journeys* (Peabody, MA: Hendrickson, 1995), 10.

Christians.[26] As Johnson reasons, this:

> encourages us to understand Revelation in the context of the cultural and intellectual forces that were affecting the churches of first-century Asia: religious institutions, political structures, military conflicts, natural disasters, and even, perhaps, the symbolic vocabulary of Jewish apocalyptic literature or pagan myth. God is so much the sovereign of history that he can use every dimension of his people's experience to communicate his word.[27]

Archaeology helps to provide this first-century backdrop for understanding the message of Revelation.

THE CULTURAL BACKGROUND

Understanding the political, religious, and historical context of the Book of Revelation is essential to unraveling the message of the book. In this regard a variety of problems are addressed in John's messages to each church. They may be categorized into the problems from "without" and the problems from "within."

External Problems

Several problems affected the churches from the cultural surroundings.

142. Martyrdom of Polycarp. Painting on the ceiling of St. Polycarp Catholic Church, Smyrna (modern Izmir), Turkey.

Jewish persecution

Firstly, the Christians in Asia Minor were experiencing persecution from the side of the Jews. The Jews were granted an exemption from worshiping the emperor because of their distinctive religion, and for a period in the first cent. the Christians were permitted to participate in this exemption.[28] But the Jews became jealous and pointed out that the Christians were not Jews and worshiped a Messiah the Jews did not recognise, and began turning in the Christians to the Roman authorities. This led to pockets of persecution by the Romans.

The Roman authorities did not care who their citizens worshiped as long as they obeyed the Roman edicts and worshiped the imperial cult as well (Pliny *Ep.* 10.96). The general polytheistic populace had no problem in worshiping their own gods and offering sacrifices to Roma, however the Christians could not do this as they were exclusive in their worship, so they were punished for disobeying the Roman law (Pliny *Ep.* 10.96). The Jews were often instrumental in getting the Christians in trouble, as is evident from the martyrdom of two bishops of Smyrna: Polycarp (*Mart. Pol.* 1.13; 12.2; *FrgPol.* 64.23; see Fig. 142) and Pionius (AD 250; *Mart. Pionii* 2.1; 3.6; 4.2, 8; 13.1; 14.1).[29] Two churches, Smyrna and Philadelphia, speak of the Jewish elements in their cities as the "synagogue of Satan" (2:9; 3:9). The synagogue in Smyrna is also mentioned in the second cent. in the account of the martyrdom of Pionius (*Mart. Pionii* 13.1).

---

[26] Steven J. Friesen, "Revelation, Realia, and Religion: Archaeology in the Interpretations of the Apocalypse," *HTR* 88, no. 3 (1995): 297; Ramsay, *The Letters to Seven Churches*, xiii, 62–67, 289, 362; Grant R. Osborne, *Revelation*, BECNT (Grand Rapids: Baker Academic, 2002), 110; Worth, Jr., *Greco-Asian Culture*, 67; Robin Scroggs, "The Sociological Interpretation of the New Testament: The Present State of Research," *NTS* 26 (1980): 179.

[27] Dennis E. Johnson, *Triumph of the Lamb: A Commentary on Revelation* (Phillipsburg, NJ: P&R, 2001), 20–21.

[28] Jeffers, *The Greco-Roman World of the NT*, 102.

[29] Graves, *SMRVT*, 245–46.

While some scholars doubt Jewish involvement,[30] others point out that the Jews gathered wood on the Sabbath and ventured into the stadium to watch Polycarp burn (see Fig. 142), arguing for the viability of Jewish hostility.[31] While Aune, with others, questions the historical reliability of the account,[32] Lightfoot affirms that: "the story is told with a good deal of restraint, and may be judged to provide a generally reliable, and certainly very moving, account of Polycarp's martyrdom."[33]

Trade guilds

Secondly, there were trade guilds that focused on a particular trade or guild, like tanners, dyers (Thyatira; Acts 19:10), shoemakers, clothiers, bakers, potters, slave traders, and copper smiths, but which also participated in various religious ceremonies.[34] Although membership was voluntary and not directly connected to business activities, few could perform business activities without membership. Members typically participated in cultic rituals, which included offering imperial cult sacrifices to the guild god when they attended the guild meetings (see Figs. 143, 145).[35] While the Roman authorities were apathetic over religious practices and did not normally apply economic sanctions against their citizens,[36] trade guilds were different. Refusal to participate in their respective trade guild may have led to poverty and financial ruin (Rev 2:9).[37]

143. Round altar (*ara*) used in the Imperial Cult from the second or third cent. AD. Altars were usually decorated with the works of the most notable artists of the day. Most altars were erected outside in the open air and in sacred groves.

Side Museum, Turkey.

Imperial cult

Thirdly, the imperial cult created a problem for the early Christians.[38] This problem centerd on the worship of the

[30] Judith M. Lieu, "Accusations of Jewish Persecution in Early Christian Sources, with Particular Reference to Justin Martyr and the Martyrdom of Polycarp," in *Tolerance and Intolerance in Early Judaism and Christianity*, ed. Graham N. Stanton and Gedaliahu A. G Stroumsa (Cambridge, UK: Cambridge University Press, 1998), 285–6; Hebert Musurillo, ed., *The Acts of the Christian Martyrs*, trans. Hebert Musurillo (Oxford: Clarendon, 1972), 11 n. 16.

[31] E. J. Banks, "Smyrna," ed. Geoffrey W. Bromiley, *ISBE* (Grand Rapids: Eerdmans, 1995), 4:8183; William H. C. Frend, "The Persecutions: Some Links between Judaism and the Early Church," *JEH* 9 (1958): 157; Alan James Beagley, *The "Sitz Im Leben" of the Apocalypse With Particular Reference to the Role of the Church's Enemies* (Berlin: De Gruyter, 1987), 179– 80; Gregory K. Beale, *The Book of Revelation: A Commentary on the Greek Text*, NIGTC 12 (Grand Rapids, Mich.: Eerdmans, 1998), 25 nn. 127, 31 15.

[32] Aune, with others, believes that this entire account is "historically tendentious as well as strikingly anti-Jewish, consciously formulated in an attempt to replicate the Gospel narratives of the passion of Jesus." Aune, *Rev 1–5*, 162; Musurillo, *Acts of the Christian Martyrs*, xiv; Boudewijn Dehandschütter, "The Martyrium Polycarpi: A Century of Research," ed. Wolfgang Haase and Hildegard Temporini, *Aufstieg Und Niedergang Der Römischen Welt: Geschichte Und Kultur Roms Im Spiegel Der Neueren Forschung* 27, no. 2 (1993): 485–522.

[33] Joseph B. Lightfoot, *The Apostolic Fathers: Greek Texts and English Translations*, ed. Michael W. Holmes, trans. J. R. Harmer, 2nd ed. (Grand Rapids: Baker Academic, 1989), 133.

[34] David Magie, *Roman Rule in Asia Minor to the End of the Third Century After Christ*, ed. T. James Luce, Roman History (New York: Arno, 1975), 1:48; 2:812 n. 78; A. H. M. Jones, *The Greek City: From Alexander to Justinian* (Oxford: Clarendon, 1940), 83; Colin J. Hemer, "Unto the Angels of the Churches," *Buried History* 11 (1975): 110.

[35] David E. Aune, *Revelation 6–16*, WBC 52B (Dallas, Tex.: Word Books, 1998), 768.

[36] George B. Caird, *The Revelation of St. John the Divine*, HNTC (Peabody, Mass.: Hendrickson, 1987), 173.

[37] Aune, *Rev 1–5*, 161; Charles, *Revelation*, 1:56; Caird, *Revelation*, 35; Hemer, *Letters to the Seven Churches*, 68; Osborne, *Revelation*, 151–52.

[38] Allen Brent, *The Imperial Cult and the Development of Church Order: Concepts and Images of Authority in Paganism and Early Christianity Before the Age of Cyprian* (Leiden: Brill, 1999), 178–90.

Roman emperor (see Fig. 143) and Roma, the spirit of Rome ("sharp, double-edged sword"; "throne of Satan" Rev 2:13). This practice goes back to the Roman Senate deifying Julius Caesar upon his death. This flourished in the East of the Empire, where the worship of a hero or leader was encouraged, while initially in the West it was discouraged by the emperors. However, the practice of paying homage to an Emperor as god soon found widespread favour with the emperors as a means of unifying the empire and demonstrating loyalty to Rome. Those who sacrificed to the emperor received a certificate (Lat. *libellus;* see Fig. 146) to confirm their practice (see *Quotes from Antiquity*). Christians of course would not sacrifice to the Roman god Roma and thus were persecuted for their disobedience to Rome.

144. Priest who served in the temple of the Imperial Cult. This statue comes from Ephesus and dates from the second cent. AD. The priesthood of the emperor cult was usually held by the local aristocracy, providing them with political status and a means of social advancement.

Izmir Archaeological Museum

The imperial cult[39] was well-established in Asia minor and represented in all seven cities of Revelation, each with an imperial temple. Thompson reports that: "Five of the seven cities had imperial altars (all but Philadelphia and Laodicea), six had imperial temples (all but Thyatira),[40] and five had imperial priests (all but Philadelphia and Laodicea)."[41] Evidence of it exists in Smyrna (c. 23–26 AD; Tacitus *Ann.* 4.15), Pergamum (by the provincial council κοινόν, *koinon]*[42] of Asia in 29, BC), in Ephesus (where it dedicated the temple of *Sebastoi* in 89–90 AD), Thyatira (*I.Thyat.* 902; 980; *I.Sard.* 8.99); including a temple (*I.Thyat. 1098*), Philadelphia (*I.Phil.* 1428, 1434, 1472; 1484), and Laodicea[43]. Temples dedicated to the worship of Rome were common in the Roman Empire, but the temple of the *Sebastoi* (Gr. "venerable one") was more particular in that they only venerated the family of the emperor (the family of Vespasian, Titus and Domitian; see Fig. 150).[44] Nicolas of Damascus was Augustus' (63 BC–AD 14) chief orator and he had this to say about the emperors' deification:

> Because mankind addresses him thus [as *Sebastos*] in accordance with their estimation of his honour, they revere him with temples and sacrifices over islands and continents, organized in cities and provinces, matching the greatness of his virtue and repaying his benefactions towards them.[45]

---

[39]For a survey of research on the imperial cult and Revelation see Naylor's thorough article. Michael Naylor, "The Roman Imperial Cult and Revelation," *CBR* 8, no. 2 (2010): 207–39; Thompson, *Apocalypse and Empire*, 158–64.

[40] There was a temple dedicated by Xenon in Thyatira (*I.Thyat.* 1098).

[41] Thompson, *Apocalypse and Empire*, 159.

[42] Thompson, *Apocalypse and Empire*, 160.

[43] *BMC Phrygia* 307.181; 185; 308.187–188; 314.217, 221; 315.225; 316.226–227; *I.Laod.* 45.

[44] Joyce Reynolds, "New Evidence for the Imperial Cult in Julio-Claudian Aphrodisias," *ZPE* 43 (1981): 317–27; Geraldine Thommen, "The Sebasteion at Aphrodisias: An Imperial Cult to Honor Augustus and the Julio-Claudian Emperors," *Chronika* 2 (2012): 82–91.

[45] S. R. F. Price, *Rituals and Power: The Roman Imperial Cult in Asia Minor*, Reprint (Cambridge, UK: Cambridge University Press, 1985), 1; Felix Jacoby, ed., *Die Fragmente Der Griechischen Historiker*, trans. Felix Jacoby, Part 2 Zeitgeschichte: A: Universalgeschichte Und Hellenika (Leiden: Brill Academic, 2004), 90 F125.

145. Emperor Marcus Aurelius (AD 161–180) and members of the Imperial family offer sacrifice in gratitude for success against Germanic tribes. In the backgrounds stands the Temple of Jupiter on the Capitolium (this is the only extant portrayal of this Roman temple).

Bas-relief from the Arch of Marcus Aurelius, Capitoline Museum, Rome. Photo by Matthias Kabel / Wikimiedia Commons

Price documents priests of Augustus in 34 Asia Minor cities, priests of Tiberius in 11 cities, 35 cities using the title temple warden (νεωκόρος *neōkoros,* Acts 19:35), and at least 80 cities with priests servicing *Sebastoi* [46] The wealthy citizens of the city would "bid for the honor of becoming priests in the imperial cult" (Suetonius *Cal.* 22.3; see Fig. 144).[47] Friesen points out that:

> It has long been recognized that the worship of the emperors in some way constituted an important aspect of the relationships between the emperor and the cities of the Roman province of Asia. The importance of imperial cults in Asia is reflected in the city titles that permeate the epigraphic record. These titles tend to focus on the word νεωκόρος *(neōkoros),* which is often translated into English as 'temple warden,' because the term began as the titles for an official who had special responsibilities related to the precincts of a deity. During the Roman imperial period, however, *'neōkoros'* took on a specialized meaning. It became the technical term for a city where a provincial temple of the emperors was located. Thus, in the secondary literature the words *'neōkoros'* and *'neōkorate'* have become synonymous with provincial imperial cults.[48]

The book of Acts mentions several technical terms related to the imperial cult in Ephesus and the cult of Artemis: "And when the town clerk [γραμματεύς *grammateus,* Thucydides *Hist.* 7.10] had quieted the crowd, he said, "Men of Ephesus, who is there who does not know that the city of the Ephesians is temple keeper [νεωκόρος *neōkoros]* of the great Artemis, and of the sacred stone that fell from the sky?" (Acts 19:35–38).

Libellus

The *libelli* (pl. certificates of sacrifice; see Fig. 146)[49] were documents instituted in AD 249 by

[46] Price, *Rituals and Power,* 58, 66–67.

[47] Craig S. Keener, *Acts: An Exegetical Commentary: 15:1–23:35,* vol. 3 (Grand Rapids: Baker Academic, 2014), 3:2871.

[48] Steven J. Friesen, "The Cult of the Roman Emperors in Ephesos: Temple Wardens, City Titles, and the Interpretation of the Revelation of John," in *Ephesos Metropolis of Asia: An Interdisciplinary Approach to Its Archaeology, Religion, and Culture,* ed. Helmut Koester, HTR 41 (Valley Forge, PA: Trinity, 1995), 229.

[49] However, as Leadbetter points out, technically: "the libellus is not a certificate of sacrifice, meaning a document issued by the state upon the completion of a prescribed act, but rather a request from the sacrificer asking for confirmation of an act publicly performed." W. L. Leadbetter, "Libellus of the Decian Persecution," in *NewDocs* 2:181.

Emperor Decius (AD 249–251) to help unify the Roman Empire and return it to its old traditions.[50] Origen noted that the political problems being experienced in his day were due to the increased number of Christians (*Cels.* 3.15; see also Cyprian *Ep.* 55.9).[51] The Roman authorities required a *libelli* from Roman citizens to verify that they had offered a pagan sacrifice to the ancestral gods to demonstrate their allegiance to Rome.[52] As Potter points out, "failure to sacrifice could result in exile, the confiscation of property, prison, or death."[53] Nobbs describes the creation and relevance of the *libellus* and explains that it was to:

> show the solidarity of all Romans behind their ancestral gods and sacrifices, every household was obliged to appear on a fixed day, veiled and crowned, and submit a *libellus* (certificate) declaring participation in the sacrifice. The requirement to produce documentary witness to the act of sacrifice was novel. The obligation to retain a personal copy indicated that this proof of religious piety had ongoing significance and implications for the civil identity of those concerned.[54]

146. This papyrus document, found in Oxyrhynchus in Egypt, is a certificate of sacrifice (*libellus*) from the Decian persecution (AD 250).

Papyrology Room, Ashmolean Museum, Oxford (P.Oxy. 58.3929).

Four examples of *libelli* have been identified in the papyrus documents discovered at Oxyrhynchus, Egypt (P.Oxy. 4.658;[55] 12.1464;[56] 41.2990;[57] 58.3929[58] [see Fig. 146].[59] *Libelli* have also been discovered outside of Egypt, including at Carthage, Smyrna, Rome, and Spain.[60] A comparison of forty-six extant *libelli* texts indicates that there was a standard format used for all *libelli*.[61]

---

[50] J. B. Rives, "The Decree of Decius and the Religion of Empire," *JRS* 89 (1999): 135–54.

[51] G. E. M. de. Ste. Croix, "Aspects of the 'Great' Persecution," *HTR* 47, no. 2 (1954): 73–113; "Why Were the Early Christians Persecuted?," *Past and Present* 26 (1963): 1–38; "Christianity's Encounter with the Roman Imperial Government," in *The Crucible of Christianity: Judaism, Hellenism and The Historical Background to the Christian Faith*, ed. Arnold Toynbee (New York: Thames & Hudson, 1969), 345–46.

[52] Graeme Wilber Clarke, "The Persecution of Decius," in *The Letters of St. Cyprian*, ed. Graeme Wilber Clarke, vol. 1, Ancient Christian Writers 43 (New York: Newman, 1984), 103–14; Paul Keresztes, "The Decian Libelli and Contemporary Literature," *Latomus* 34, no. 3 (1975): 761–81; John R. Knipfing, "The Libelli of the Decian Persecution," *HTR* 16, no. 4 (1923): 345–90; W. L. Leadbetter, "Libellus of the Decian Persecution," in *NewDocs*, 2:180–84; Paul McKechnie, "Roman Law and the Laws of the Medes and Persians: Decius' and Valerian's Persecutions of Christianity," in *Thinking Like a Lawyer: Essays on Legal History and General History for John Crook on His Eightieth Birthday*, ed. J. A. Crook and Paul McKechnie, Mnemosyne, Bibliotheca Classica Batava Supplementum 231 (Leiden: Brill Academic, 2002), 253–69; Rives, "Decree of Decius," 135–54.

[53] David S. Potter, "Persecution of the Early Church," ed. David Noel Freedman et al., *ABD* (New York: Doubleday, 1996), 233.

[54] Alanna M. Nobbs, "Christians in a Pluralistic Society: Papyrus Evidence from the Roman Empire," *International Journal of New Perspectives in Christianity* 1, no. 1.7 (2009): 52.

[55] AD 250. Presently housed in the Beinecke Library, Yale University, New Haven, Connecticut.

[56] AD 250, June 27. Presently housed in the Department of Manuscripts, British Museum, London.

[57] AD third century. Presently housed in the Papyrology Rooms, Sackler Library, Oxford.

[58] AD 250, June 25–July 24. Presently housed in the Papyrology Room, Ashmolean Museum, Oxford.

[59] Olivier Joram Hekster and Nicholas Zair, *Rome and Its Empire: Ad 193–284* (Edinburgh, UK: Edinburgh University Press, 2008), 130; Knipfing, "The Libelli of the Decian Persecution," 386–87.

[60] Knipfing, "The Libelli of the Decian Persecution," 352, 354.

[61] AnneMarie Luijendijk, *Greetings in the Lord: Early Christians and the Oxyrhynchus Papyri* (Cambridge, Mass.: Harvard University Press, 2009), 167.

A Greek *libellus* (P.Oxy. 58.3929; see Fig. 146) from the Decian persecution (AD 250, June 25–July 24) translates into English as:

> [first hand] To the commissioners of sacrifices of the village of Thosbis, from Aurelius Amois styled as the son of his mother Taamois from the village of Thosbis. Always have I continued to sacrifice and pour libations to the gods, and since now too in your presence in accordance with the orders I sacrificed and poured a libation and tasted the sacrificial meats together with my mother Taamois and my sister Taharpaesis, I request that (you) subscribe to this fact for me. Year 1 of imperator Caesar Gaius Messius Quintus Traianus Decius, Pius Felix Augustus, Epeiph ... [second hand] 1, Aurelius Amois, have delivered [the petition]. 1, Aurelius ... ion, wrote on his behalf [On the back, along the fibers first hand?] Registration of Amoitas. mother Taarnois [Luijendijk].[62]

147. Silver Denarius coin (AD 82–83) of Domitian, which features his deified infant son, who was born in AD 73 and died young (Suetonius *Dom.* 3.1), seated on a globe surrounded by seven stars. The child has been identified as the empress Domitia Longinas' son (AD 82–96 left). DIVVS CAESAR IMP DOMITIANI: "The Deified Caesar, Son of the Emperor Domitian." The stars symbolize the child's divine status. The globe suggests that the Romans believed the earth was a sphere although Eratosthenes (276–194 BC) of Cyrene (modern Libya) was the first to discover that the earth is round. Did John have this coin in mind when he penned "and in the midst of the seven lampstands One like the Son of Man, clothed with a garment down to His feet ... He had in His right hand seven stars" (Rev 1:13, 16).

Courtesy of CNG

During the Valerian persecution, several official documents (AD 259–260; P.Oxy. 43.3119; 42.3035) mention the arrest of Christians, one of which is the oldest mention of the word "Christian" in a papyrus document.[63]

While not intentionally directed at Christians, having a *libellus* became proof that the person in possession was not a Christian, and thus exempted them from persecution. Cyprian, the bishop of Carthage in North Africa, addressed the question at length in his *Concerning the Lapsed* (*Laps.* 15–21), of what to do with Christians who either sacrificed (Lat. *sacrificati*) or bought certificates (Lat. *libellatici*). Should they be readmitted into the church? This led to a controversy, which Cyprian sought to address, but which was finally settled at the Council of Carthage (AD 251), where it was determined that repentant *libellatici* should have their church membership restored, but those who actually sacrificed must do penance for the rest of their lives. Several bishops died as a result of the Decian persecution, including Fabian, bishop of Rome (AD 250), the bishop of Alexandria, and the bishop of Jerusalem.

While these documents date later than the NT and the book of Revelation, they illustrate the result of the growing issues that were being created by the Christians in first cent. Rome.

Deification of Emperors

Evidence of the deification of emperors or the belief that emperors were transformed into gods (ἀποθέωσις, *apotheōsis*) is clearly supported by ancient texts and archaeology (see Fig. 148, 147).

Deification of Domitian

Domitian (Lat. *Titus Flavius Caesar Domitianus Augustus* AD 81–96), the son of Vespasian, succeeded his brother Titus in AD 81 and gradually acquired despotic powers, demanding that public worship should be given to him as Lord and God (Lat. *dominus et Deus*). Suetonius states

[62] Ibid., 165–66.

[63] J. E. G. Whitehorne, "P. Oxy. XLIII 3119: A Document of Valerian's Persecution?," *ZPE* 24, no. 1 (1977): 187–96; Lincoln H. Blumell, *Lettered Christians: Christians, Letters, and Late Antique Oxyrhynchus*, NTTS 39 (Leiden: Brill Academic, 2012), 252 n.61.

that Domitian requested his correspondence sent out in the name of "Our Lord and God" (Lat. *dominus et dues noster*) and that "the custom arose of henceforth addressing him in no other way even in writing or in conversation" (Suetonius *Dom.* 13.2 [Rolfe], see also Cassius *Hist. Rom.* 67.4.7; 67.13.4; see also Fig. 147).[64]

Deification of Anoninus Pius

A statue of Antoninus Pius (ca. AD 161), now displayed in the Vatican Museum (see Fig. 148) depicts the ἀποθέωσις (*apotheōsis*, "transformed into a god") of Antoninus Pius and his wife Faustina, as they are carried to heaven by the genius "eternity," a winged spirit that protected nature. The female figure saluting them (right side) personifies Rome, holding a shield depicting the legendary founders of Rome—Romulus and Remus—being suckled by a wolf. The nude figure (left side) is believed to be the personification of the Roman Field of Mars (Lat. *Campus Martius*), where imperial funerals took place.[65]

148. *Apotheōsis* of Antoninus Pius and Faustina. The basis of the Campo Marzio Colonna Antonina, relief on the front face of the pedestal of the Antoninus Pius' column, three-quarter view AD 161.

Rome, gardens of the Vatican Museums, Cortile delle Corazze.

Photo by Lalupa / Wikimedia Commons

Pliny the Younger

The first recorded mention of Christians in the Roman imperial record is in a letter written to Emperor Trajan (ca. AD 111; see Fig. 149) by Pliny the Younger, the governor of Bithynia, a province north of the seven churches of Revelation. In his letter, Pliny asks Trajan for "advice on how to handle cases where citizens have pressed charges against individuals suspected of being Christians" (Pliny *Ep.* 10.96–97, see *Quotes from Antiquity*).[66] It is also the first time that Christianity is officially recognized as a separate religion from Judaism and begins the persecution of Christians in the second and third centuries.

Pliny is presented with a number of Christians who have had charges laid against them, and is unsure whether he should prosecute them or not. It appears that this is a new dilemma for them both. He decided, in spite of the fact that they appeared harmless to him, to execute them if they did not recant their faith. Uncertain of the legality of his actions, he sought the advice of the emperor[67] (see *Quotes from Antiquity).*

What is clear from this exchange of letters is that although the growth of Christianity had spread throughout the cities and villages of Asia Minor, even affecting the sale of sacrifices for the temple and number of worshipers of the imperial cult, Trajan ordered that no official persecution of Christians be carried out by Pliny.

Price documents priests of Augustus in 34 Asia Minor cities, priests of Tiberus in 11 cities, 35 cities using the title temple warden (νεωκόρος *neōkoros* Acts 19:35), and at least 80 cities with priests servicing Sebastoi (see Fig. 110).[68] Friesen points out that:

---

[64] Contra, see Thompson, *Revelation*, 105.

[65] Lise Vogel, *The Column of Antoninus Pius* (Cambridge, Mass.: Harvard University Press, 1973), 32–55.

[66] J. Nelson Kraybill, Apocalypse and Allegiance: Worship, Politics, and Devotion in the Book of Revelation (Grand Rapids: Brazos Press, 2010), 75.

[67] Downing, "Pliny's Prosecutions of Christians."

[68] Price, *Rituals and Power*, 58, 66–67.

149. Marble Statue of Trajan (Imperator Marcus Ulpius Trajanus, AD 98–117) in armor.
Antalya Müzesi, Antalya Turkey

It has long been recognized that the worship of the emperors in some way constituted an important aspect of the relationships between the emperor and the cities of the Roman province of Asia. The importance of imperial cults in Asia is reflected in the city titles that permeate the epigraphic record. These titles tend to focus on the word *'neokoros,'* which is often translated into English as 'temple warden,' because the term began as the titles for an official who had special responsibilities related to the precincts of a deity. During the Roman imperial period, however, *'neokoros'* took on a specialized meaning. It became the technical term for a city where a provincial temple of the emperors was located. Thus, in the secondary literature the words *'neokoros'* and *'neokorate'* have become synonymous with provincial imperial cults.[69]

The book of Acts mentions several technical terms related to the imperial cult in Ephesus[70] and the cult of Artemis: "And when the town clerk [γραμματεύς *grammateus*] had quieted the crowd, he said, "Men of Ephesus, who is there who does not know that the city of the Ephesians is temple keeper [νεωκόρος *neōkoros*] of the great Artemis, and of the sacred stone that fell from the sky?" (Acts 19:35–38).

Internal Problems

Several internal issues were addressed in the seven messages. Various heresies (Nicolaitans Rev 2:6, 15) identified with OT figures (Balaam Rev 2:14; Jezebel Rev 2:20) had arisen in several churches. Closely connected with their teaching was the practice of eating food sacrificed to idols and sexual immorality (Rev 2:14; 20). John recorded these events by describing the Ephesian church as having forsaken their first love (Rev 2:4), while the Laodicean Church was lukewarm (Rev 3:16).

Quotes from Antiquity

Trajan replied:

You have followed the right course of action, my dear Secundus [i.e., Pliny], in your examination of the cases of those who have been charged with being Christians. For it is impossible to lay down a general rule in something like a fixed formula. They [the Christians] must not be hunted out; if they are brought before you and convicted, they must be punished, excepting, however, anyone who denies that he is a Christian and makes this fact clear, by offering prayers to our gods, he is to be pardoned as a result of his repentance, however suspect his past conduct may be. But pamphlets (*libelli*) circulated anonymously ought to have no part in any accusation. For they are the worst sort of precedent (*exemplum*) and are not in keeping with the spirit of our age.

(Pliny *Ep.* 10.97 [Radice])

---

[69] Steven J. Friesen, "The Cult of the Roman Emperors in Ephesos: Temple Wardens, City Titles, and the Interpretation of the Revelation of John," in *Ephesos Metropolis of Asia: An Interdisciplinary Approach to Its Archaeology, Religion, and Culture*, ed. Helmut Koester, HTS 41 (Valley Forge, PA: Trinity, 1995), 229.

[70] For a survey of research on the Imperial Cult and Revelation see Naylor's thorough article. Michael Naylor, "The Roman Imperial Cult and Revelation," *Currents in Biblical Research* 8, no. 2 (2010): 207–39.

John came to these troubled churches in the tradition of the OT prophets (Moses, Jeremiah, Ezekiel, and Daniel) to exhort (Gr. *paraenesis*) them to repentance and know God's covenant blessing. This was the classic prophetic message for times of persecution and suffering. To guard the message from the Roman authorities, John concealed his message using OT symbols and obscure cultural clues. This cryptic methodology (conceal/reveal Mark 4:10–12) is evident from the same parabolic formula (Rev 2:7, 11, 17, 29; 3:6, 13, 22) used by Jesus, where he taught in parables: "he who has ears to hear, let him hear" (Mark 4:9, 23; 4:11–12; Isa 6:9–10).[71]

150. Parts of a colossal statue from the Temple of Sebastoi. The head is over 1.18 m high. Originally identified as Emperor Domitian (AD 81–96), but has since been shown to be Emperor Titus.

Ephesus Museum, Selçuk, Turkey

[71] Beale, *The Book of Revelation*, 234, 236–39.

151. Map of the seven churches.

THE SEVEN CHURCHES OF ASIA MINOR

The seven churches to which the book of Revelation was written are real cities in Asia Minor with real problems. Ephesus, Smyrna, Pergamos, Thyatira, Sardis, Philadelphia and Laodicea are located on what Ramsay considered the postal route.[72] Jesus, speaking through John, has a different message for each of them. The message written down in Revelation was read aloud in each one of the Churches. Archaeology provides helpful insights into their message, revealed through their excavations, museum artifacts, coins (numismatics), and inscriptions. For an comprehensive treatment of the seven messages, see David E. Graves, *Jesus Speaks to Seven of His Churches: A Commentary on the Messages to the Seven Churches in Revelation* (Toronto, Ont.: Electronic Christian Media, 2017).

[72] Ramsay, *The Letters to Seven Churches*, 183.

152. The colonnaded Arcadian Way street leading to the harbour at the archeological excavations at Ephesus.

Photo by Ad Meskens/Wikimedia Commons

Ephesus (Rev 2:1–7)

As the fourth largest city in the Roman Empire, (after Rome, Antioch and Alexandria), Ephesus[73] (Ἔφέσος, modern *Selçuk*)[74] held a prominent place in Asia Minor (Strabo *Geogr.* 14.1.24; population 50,000–90,000).[75] Inscriptions testify that Ephesus was the "first and greatest metropolis in Asia,"[76] and in the first-century AD the residence for the Roman proconsul of Asia (see the wealthy residence Fig. 162).[77]

The Christian faith came to Ephesus in about AD 53 when Paul left Aquila and Priscilla there, heading for Antioch via Corinth (Acts 18:18–22). During Paul's second missionary journey, he stayed in Ephesus for two years (Acts 19:8, 10), and later Timothy ministered there (1 Tim 1:3).

The Temple of Artemis

The Temple of Artemis was built by Croesus, the rich King of Lydia in 550 BC over a period of 120 years. It was known as the Artemision (Aristides *Orat.* 23.25) and located just outside of Ephesus (modern Selçuk; see Figs. 155). It was considered one of the seven wonders of the ancient world.[78] The Artemision[79] was one of the largest Greek temples ever built and the first temple to be constructed out of marble.[80] Originally it measured 67 meters (220 ft.) wide by 130 meters (425 ft.) long and was 18 meters (60 ft.) high with some 127 columns (see Figs.

153. Recreation of the Temple of Artemis (Artemision), as it would have looked at Ephesus.

Miniatürk Park, Istanbul, Turkey. Photo by Magnus Manske / Wikimedia Commons

[73] John Turtle Wood, *Discoveries at Ephesus: Including the Sites and Remains of the Great Temple of Diana* (London: Longmans, Green & Company, 1877); Steven J. Friesen, "Ephesus: Key to a Vision in Revelation," *BAR* 19, no. 3 (1993): 24–37; Jerome Murphy-O'Connor, *St. Paul's Ephesus: Texts and Archaeology* (Minneapolis, MN: Liturgical, 2008); Mark D. Roberts, "Ancient Ephesus and the New Testament: How Our Knowledge of the Ancient City of Ephesus Enriches Our Knowledge of the New Testament," *Reflections on Christ, Church, and Culture*, 2011, http://www.patheos.com/blogs/markdroberts/series/ancient-ephesus-and-the-new-testament.

[74] For an extensive treatment of Ephesus, see Ludwig Bürchner, "Ephesos," in *Paulys Realencyclopädie Der Classischen Altertumswissenschaft*, ed. August Friedrich Pauly, Georg Wissowa, and S. Kroll, 5th ed., vol. 2 (Stuttgart, Germany: Metzler, 1905), 2773–2822; Ramsay, *Letters to Seven Churches*, 151–71; Josef Keil, *Zur Topographie Und Geschichte von Ephesos*, JÖAI 21–22 (Vienna: ÖAI, 1922), 21–22; George E. Bean, *Aegean Turkey: An Archaeological Guide* (New York: Praeger, 1966), 160–84; Hemer, *Letters to the Seven Churches*, 35–41; Worth, Jr., *Greco-Asian Culture*, 9–68; Richard Oster, *A Bibliography of Ancient Ephesus* (Dorst: Scarecrow, 1987).

[75] J. W. Hanson, "The Urban System of Roman Asia Minor and Wider Urban Connectivity," in *Settlement, Urbanization, and Population*, ed. Alan Bowman and Andrew Wilson, OSRE (Oxford: Oxford University Press, 2011), 258.

[76] Cecil J. Cadoux, *Ancient Smyrna: A History of the City from the Earliest Times to 224 A.D.* (Oxford: Basil Blackwell, 1938), 291.

[77] Aune, *Revelation 1-5*, 138.

[78] Pausanias *Descr.* 4.31.8; 7.5.4; Pliny *Nat.* 16.79; 36.21; Antipater of Sidon *Gr. Ant.* 9.58; Kai Brodersen, "Seven Wonders," in *OEAGR*, 6:289.

[79] Ulrike Muss, "The Artemision at Ephesos: From Paganism to Christianity," in *Mustafa Büyükkolancı'ya Armağan: Essays in Honour of Mustafa Büyükkolancı*, ed. Celal Şimşek, Bahadır Duman, and Erim Konakçi (Istanbul: Yayinlari, 2015), 413–22.

[80] Oster, "Ephesus (Place)," in *ABD* 2:545–46.

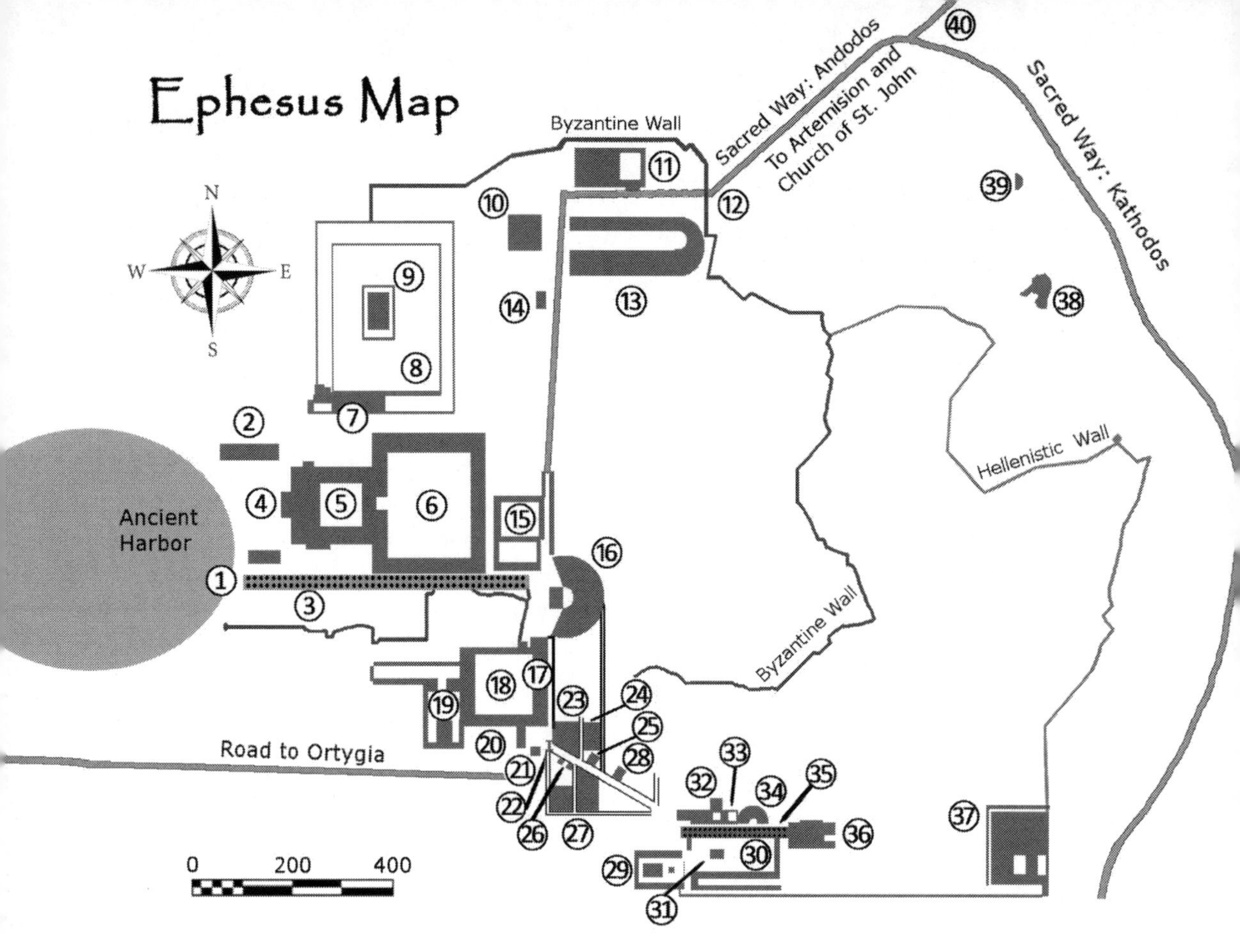

Ephesus Map

154. Urban plan of the city of Ephesus. 1). Harbour gate; 2). Warehouses; 3). Street of Arcadius; 4). Harbour baths; 5). Harbour gym; 6). Xystol of the Harbour gym; 7). Church of Mary; 8). Stoa of the Olympieion; 9). Temple of Hadrian Olympios; 10). Macellum; 11). Vedius gym; 12). North gate; 13). Stadium; 14). Fountain; 15). Theater Gym; 16). Theater; 17). Hall of Nero; 18). Commercial agora; 19). Sarapeion; 20). Library of Celsus; 21). Altar of Artemis; 22). Hadrian's gate; 23). Latrine; 24). Scholastikia baths; 25). Temple of Hadrian; 26). Heroon of Androklos and Arsinoë IV; 27). Slope Houses; 28). Fountain of Trajan; 29). Temple of Domitian [Flavian Sebastoi]; 30). State agora; 31). Temple of Divius Julius and Deo Roma [Temple of Isis?]; 32). Prytaneion; 33). Peristyle; 34). Odeon or Bouleuterion; 35). Baslike Stao; 36). Upper gym; 37). East gym; 38). Seven Sleepers; 39). Kybele Sanctuary; 40). Road to Artemision and Church of St. John.

153).[81] It was also the most important financial institution in Asia Minor, widely known as being a secure place to deposit money.[82]

In 356 BC the temple of Artemis was destroyed by arson. A man by the name of Herostratus, set fire to the wooden roof-beams, seeking fame. For this outrage, the Ephesians sentenced the perpetrator to death and forbade anyone from mentioning his name; but historian Theopompus later noted it (*Tim.Frag.* 137).[83] In Greek and Roman historical tradition, the temple's destruction coincided with the birth of Alexander

155. Ephesian coin struck under Nero (AD 54–68). Rev.: four column ionic temple in three-quarter view, likely the Temple of Artemis. It is inscribed with the first occurance of the term NEOKORΩN (*neokorōn*, "Keeper of the Temple") on a coin.

Courtesy of CNG (*RPC* 2626; Waddington 1620)

[81] Pliny *Nat.* 36.21.95ff; Vitruvius *Arch.* 3.2.7; 10.2.11–12.

[82] Dio Chrysostom *Rhod.* 31.54–55; Appian *Bell. civ.* 3.33; Plautus *Bacch.* 312; Aristides *Orat.* 42.522; *CIG* 2:2953b; Trebilco, "Asia," 325.

[83] Karl Müller, Theodor Müller, and Victor Langlois, *Fragmenta historicorum graecorum* (Paris: Ambrosio Firmin Didot, 1841).

the Great (around 20/21 July 356 BC).[84]

156. Tetradrachm coin mined in Ephesus (*ca.* 25–20 BC). Obv.: Head of Augustus (r. 27 BC–14 AD). AVGVSTVS Rev.: The altar of Artemis (Diana) with two deer, animals sacred to Ephesus, facing each other. Courtesy of CNG (*RPC* 1:2215).

The foundation of the temple's altar was discovered outside the temple in 1965.[85] According to the apocryphal work *Acts of John* (42), the temple was destroyed by John the apostle, though the final temple on this site was in fact destroyed by the Goths in AD 262 and never reconstructed.[86] All that remains today of the once magnificent Artemision is a single column from the fifth temple built on the site (see Fig. 157),[87] along with the great altar (see Fig. 156),[88] although many of the sculptured sections of the temple, excavated by Wood and Hogarth,[89] were shipped to the British Museum.[90]

157. This single, remaining column of the original 127, and this foundation, are all that remains of the Temple of Artemis in Ephesus, one of the seven wonders of the ancient world. Originally it measured 67 meters (220 ft.) wide by 130 meters (425 ft.) long and was 18 meters (60 ft.) high.

The temple of Artemis (see Fig. 153, 157) provided Ephesus the prestigious title of "temple-keeper or warden" (νεωκόρος *neokoros*, cf. Acts 19:35) of the goddess Artemis,[91] a designation usually reserved for temples to the imperial cult.[92] It was the first to be named νεωκόρον (*neōkorōn*, "temple-keeper"), a deduction made from the term appearing on their coins from the reign of Nero (AD 54–68), likely representing the temple of Artemis[93] and not the temples dedicated to the imperial cult.[94] However, under Elagabalus (AD 218–222), Ephesus was again made "four times *neōkoros*"[95] by including the temple of Artemis.[96] In the first-century, the Ephesian

[84] Plutarch remarked that Artemis was too preoccupied with Alexander's delivery to save her burning temple (*Alex.* 1.3.5).

[85] Oster, "Ephesus (Place)," 2:545.

[86] Ibid.

[87] W. R. Lethaby, "The Earlier Temple of Artemis at Ephesus," *JHS* 37 (1917): 1–16.

[88] Hemer, Letters to the Seven Churches, 138.

[89] For the details of the excavations of the temple of Artemis by John T. Wood and David G. Hogarth, see John Turtle Wood, *Discoveries at Ephesus: Including the Sites and Remains of the Great Temple of Diana* (London, UK: Longmans, Green & Company, 1877); David George Hogarth, *Excavations at Ephesus: The Archaic Artemisia* (London, UK: Longmans & Co., 1908); Steven J. Friesen, "Ephesus: Key to a Vision in Revelation," *BAR* 19, no. 3 (1993): 24–37; David E. Graves, *Biblical Archaeology: An Introduction with Recent Discoveries That Support the Reliability of the Bible*, vol. 1 (Toronto, Ont.: Electronic Christian Media, 2017), 210–14.

[90] W. R. Lethaby, *The Sculptures of the Later Temple of Artemis at Ephesus* (London, UK: The Society for the Promotion of Hellenic Studies, 1913).

[91] *SIG* 3.867; *I.Eph.* 2.212; *SEG* 37.886; and *CIG* 2972; "Temple-keeper of Artemis" Acts 19:35; Steven J. Friesen, *Twice Neokoros: Ephesus, Asia and the Cult of the Flavian Imperial Family* (Leiden: Brill Academic, 1993), 56–59.

[92] Ramsay, *The Letters to Seven Churches*, 168–69.

[93] Josef Keil, "Die Erste Neokorie von Ephesos," *NZ* 48 (1919): 125–30; Price, *Rituals and Power*, 65 n.47.

[94] *RPC* 2.433.

[95] Ramsay, *Letters: Updated*, 168.

[96] Hans Willer Laale, *Ephesus (Ephesos): An Abbreviated History from Androclus to Constantine XI* (Bloomington, IN: WestBow, 2011), 269; Barclay Vincent Head, *Catalogue of the Greek Coins of Ionia in the British Museum* (Bologna, Italy: Forni, 1964); Barbara Burrell, *Neokoroi: Greek Cities and Roman Emperors*, CCS 9 (Leiden: Brill, 2004), 59–85.

Christians had to live in a city with fourteen additional deities with temples.[97]

While the temple to Artemis is not mentioned in the Book of Revelation, it no doubt was the basis for perseverance and endurance of "hardship for my name" (Rev 2:3). This verse is illustrated in the incident in Acts over the Artemis statues (*I.Eph.* 3.961; 6.2212), and also in the account in Second Timothy of Alexander the coppersmith (2 Tim 4:14; *NewDocs* 4:7–10).[98] Demetrius, the silversmith (Acts 19:23–41), feared that Paul's preaching against idols would affect his business of producing miniature idols of Artemis.[99]

158. The "beautiful Artemis", the goddess of hunting, as portrayed in Cyrene (second cent. AD). She was originally holding a bow in her hand. In Ephesus, her statues show her with many breasts or eggs (see Fig. 159).

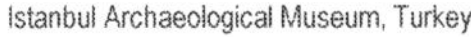

Istanbul Archaeological Museum, Turkey

159. Reproduction of the Ephesian Greek goddess Artemis (Roman goddess *Diana*) from the Prytanaeum (city hall) of Ephesus. This statue is known as "the Great Artemis" (inv. no. 712).

The Goddess Artemis

Artemis (Lat. *Diana*) was a popular mythical Greek goddess worshiped throughout the Roman Empire (Acts 19:27; Pausanias *Descr.* 4.31.8), but particularly in Asia Minor and Ephesus.[100] She is often depicted with a short skirt carrying a bow and arrow (Ovid *Metam.* 3.251) and accompanied with a hunting dog or deer (see Figs. 158). Homer describes Artemis "of the Wilds" (Ἀγροτέρα, *Agrotera,* "the huntress") and "Mistress of Animals" (Ἡ Πότνια Θηρῶν, *Ho Potnia Therōn*; *Il.* 21.470). In Greek mythology she was the daughter of Zeus and twin sister of Apollo (Hesiod *Theog.* 918–20).[101] She was the virgin goddess of the hunt, wild animals, childbirth, virginity, and thus associated with various animals such as lions, bulls, rams, deer and bees.[102]

---

[97] Mark W. Wilson, *Revelation*, Zondervan Illustrated Bible Backgrounds Commentary (Grand Rapids: Zondervan, 2007), 18; Paul R. Trebilco, *The Early Christians in Ephesus from Paul to Ignatius* (Grand Rapids: Eerdmans, 2007); Helmut Koester, ed., *Ephesos Metropolis of Asia: An Interdisciplinary Approach to Its Archaeology, Religion, and Culture*, HTS 41 (Cambridge, MA: Harvard Divinity School, 1995).

[98] G. H. R. Horsley, "The Inscriptions of Ephesos and the New Testament," *NovT* 34, no. 2 (1992): 142–45.

[99] Richard E. Oster, "The Ephesian Artemis as an Opponent of Early Christianity," *JAC* 19 (1976): 24–44; Rick Strelan, *Paul, Artemis, and the Jews in Ephesus* (Berlin: de Gruyter, 1996), 135–37.

[100] Lynn R. LiDonnici, "The Images of Artemis Ephesia and Greco-Roman Worship: A Reconsideration," *HTR* 85, no. 4 (October 1992): 389–415; Trebilco, "Asia," 332–36; Murphy-O'Connor, *St. Paul's Ephesus*, 120–31; C. L. Brinks, "'Great Is Artemis of the Ephesians': Acts 19:23–41 in Light of Goddess Worship in Ephesus," *CBQ* 71, no. 4 (2009): 776–94; Zynep Aktüre, "Reading into the Mysteries of Artemis Ephesia," in *Curating Architecture and the City*, ed. Sarah Chaplin and Alexandra Stara (New York: Routledge, 2009), 145–63; Morna D. Hooker, "Artemis of Ephesus," *JTS* 64, no. 1 (2013): 37–46.

[101] William K. C. Guthrie, *The Greeks and Their Gods*, Ariadne Series (Boston, Mass.: Beacon, 1950), 99ff.; Burkert, *Greek Religion*, 149–52.

[102] Fifty-five Ephesian Drachma coins (*ca.* 202–133 BC) represent the Artemesian priestess as a bee, with a stag standing under a tree on the obv., representing the sacred grove of Artemis. Christine Sourvinou-Inwood, "Artemis," *OCD*, 176–77; Marjatta Nielsen, "Diana Efesia Multimammia: The Metamorphoses of a Pagan Goddess from the Renaissance to the Age of Neo-Classicism," in *From Artemis to Diana: The Goddess of Man and Beast*, ed. Tobias Fischer-Hansen and Birte Poulsen, Acta Hyperborea 12 (Copenhagen: Museum Tusculanum, 2009), 455–96.

160. Ephesian Cistophoric Tetradrachm coin. Obv.: The bare head of Claudius (*ca.* AD 41–54). TI CLAVD CAES AVG. Rev.: DIAN EPHE. The cult statue of Artemis (Diana) of Ephesus within a tetrastyle temple set on a four-tiered base.

Courtesy of CNG (*RPC* I 2222; *BMC* 229; *RSC* 30)

During the excavations of the Prytaneion (city hall) in Ephesus, four cult statues of Artemis were excavated by Franz Miltner in 1956.[103] Two large marble statues of Artemis and two smaller copies were discovered.[104]

The Ephesian depiction of Artemis was unique,[105] with what appears to be multiple breasts (Felix *Oct.* 22.5; Jerome *Comm. in Ep. Paul*),[106] or, as variously identified by scholars, bulls' scrota,[107] pomegranates,[108] eggs,[109] ostrich eggs[110] or bee ova (see Fig. 159).[111] Until recently, most scholars suggested that whatever they are, they are linked to fertility in some way.[112] However, the general consensus now is that she retained her role as the virgin huntress and protector of young women, rather than becoming an Anatolian sex and fertility goddess.[113]

The "Great Artemis" statue (see Fig. 159) is depicted wearing a three-level headdress with the top level depicting the temple of Artemis (see Figs. 155, 160). Sadly, both of her arms are missing. She is wearing a long cloak of various animals, including bees and bulls. Bulls were often sacrificed to Artemis, leading some to suggest that this is connected to fertility symbolism.[114]

The "Beautiful Artemis" (inv. no. 718; see Fig. 158), dates to the second cent. AD. The headdress is missing on this statue, but she does retain both of her hands. She is situated between two deer and two beehives. The necklace is also encrusted with the signs of the Zodiac.[115] According to Eustathius, the Archbishop of Thessalonica, the incantations of the

---

[103] Peter Scherrer, ed., *Ephesus: The New Guide* (Turkey: Ege Yayinin, 2000), 86; Murphy-O'Connor, *St. Paul's Ephesus*, 191.

[104] The "Great Artemis" (inv. no. 712; see Figs. 159) was discovered fallen in the courtyard likely toppled by an earthquake in the fourth cent. or pushed over by Christians. The "Beautiful Artemis" (inv. no. 718) was found purposefully buried in a side room (no. 5) of the Prytaneion (see Fig. 158). The "Small Artemis," along with its copy, were discovered in the vestibule of the stoa and the courtyard of the Prytaneion. They have been dated to AD 150–200. Guy MacLean Rogers, *The Mysteries of Artemis of Ephesos: Cult, Polis, and Change in the Greaeco-Roman World* (New Haven, CT: Yale University Press, 2012), 180–83.

[105] Morna D. Hooker, "Artemis of Ephesus," *JTS* 64, no. 1 (2013): 37–46; Frederick E. Brenk, "Artemis of Ephesos: An Avant Garde Goddess," *Kernos* 11 (1998): 157–71; Aktüre, "Reading into the Mysteries," 145.

[106] Edward Falkener, *Ephesus, and the Temple of Diana* (London, UK: Day & Son, 1862), 290; Richard E. Oster, "Ephesus as a Religious Center Under the Principate, I: Paganism Before Constantine," *ANRW* 18, no. 3 (1990): 1725–26.

[107] Lilian Portefaix, "The Image of Artemis Ephesia–A Symbolic Configuration Related to Her Mysteries?," in *100 Jahre Österreichische Forschunge in Ephesos*, ed. Herwig Friesinger and Friedrich Krinzinger, Archäologische Forschungen 1 (Wien: VÖAW, 1999), 611–17.

[108] Yulia Ustinova, *The Supreme Gods of the Bosporan Kingdom: Celestial Aphrodite and the Most High God* (Leiden: Brill, 1999), 62; Bernard Saftner, *Punctuated Equilibrium Featuring The Proepistrephomeniad* (Bloomington, Ind.: Xlibris, 2008), 210.

[109] Finegan, *The Archeology of the New Testament*, 156.

[110] Christoph Briese, "Ostrich Eggs," in *BrillPauly*, vol. 10 (Leiden: Brill, 2007), 10:290.

[111] Stefan Karweise, "Ephesos," *RE Supp* 12 (1970): 323–26; Gerard Mussies, "Pagans, Jews, and Christians at Ephesus," in *Studies on the Hellenistic Background of the New Testament*, ed. Pieter Wilhelm van der Horst and Gerard Mussies, Utrechtse Theologische Reeks 10 (Utrecht: Theological Faculty Utrecht University, 1990), 117–94.

[112] Clinton E. Arnold, *Ephesians: Power and Magic: The Concept of Power in Ephesians in Light of Its Historical Setting*, SNTS 63 (Cambridge, Mass.: Cambridge University Press, 1989), 25.

[113] Ramsay, *Paul the Traveler: Updated*, 212; Craig S. Keener, *Acts: An Exegetical Commentary: 15:1-23:35*, vol. 3, 3 vols. (Grand Rapids: Baker Academic, 2014), 2875; Gerard Mussies, "Artemis," in *Dictionary of Deities and Demons in the Bible*, ed. Karel van der Toorn, Bob Becking, and Pieter Willem van der Horst, 2nd ed. (Grand Rapids: Eerdmans, 1999), 91–97.

[114] Nielsen, "Diana Efesia Multimammmia," 455–96.

[115] Rogers, *Mysteries of Artemis*, 180–83.

161. The theater in Ephesus with the colonnaded street, The Arcadian Way, leading down to the now silted harbour. Here for two hours the Ephesians gathered and chanted "Great is Diana (Artemis) of the Ephesians" (Acts 19:32–34).

mysterious "Ephesian letters" (Ἐφέσια Γράμματα, *Ephesia grammata*) were inscribed on the feet, girdle and crown of some of the statues of Artemis (*Hom. Od.* 19.247).[116] There seemed to be similar attributes with Cybele (or Tyche Τύχη; an Anatolian mother goddess), including being served in the temple by female slaves, young virgins, and eunuch priests (Strabo *Geogr.* 14.1.23).[117]

The Theater of Ephesus

The theater/stadium of Ephesus, the largest in Asia Minor (154 m in width), with a capacity of ca. 24,000 people,[118] was the site of the famous riot against the preaching of Paul, which had negatively affected the businesses of the craftsmen of Artemis, led by Demetrius the Silversmith (Acts 19:23–41; see Fig. 161).[119] An inscription mentioning the "place of the silversmiths" (ἀργυροκόπων, *argurokopōn I.Eph.* 2.547.1) has been located near the theater beside the commercial agora.[120]

The theater was an important institution during the Graeco-Roman period and was the location for much more than just plays. The city assembly regularly met here in the spring, during the month of Artemision,[121] and it was also used as a gathering place to hear imperial edicts read (*SIG* 3.883.26–27) and for civic festivals called *Artemisia*,[122] which were all accompanied by sacrifices and prayers to the gods (*SIG* 3.1003.15–17). A statue base bore the following inscription in honor of Artemis. It read: "Therefore, it is decreed that the entire month of Artemision be sacred for all its days, and that on the same (days) of the month, and throughout the year, feasts and the festival and the sacrifices of the Artemisia are to be conducted, inasmuch as the entire month is dedicated to the goddess [Artemis]" (*NewDocs* 4:75–76).

---

[116] Alberto Bernabé, "The Ephesia Grammata: Genesis of a Magical Formula," in *The Getty Hexameters: Poetry, Magic, and Mystery in Ancient Selinous*, ed. Christopher A. Faraone and Dirk Obbink (Oxford: Oxford University Press, 2013), 73–74; Strelan, *Paul, Artemis, and the Jews in Ephesus*, 88.

[117] LiDonnici, "Images of Artemis," 389–415.

[118] Horsley, "Inscriptions of Ephesos," 110 n.15; Margarete Bieber, *The History of the Greek and Roman Theater* (Princeton, NJ: Princeton University Press, 1961); Mary T. Boatwright, "Theaters in the Roman Empire," *BA* 53, no. 4 (1990): 184–92.

[119] Kreitzer concludes that: "These coins, which coincide remarkably well with recent attempts to establish Pauline chronology in relation to the Ephesian ministry, suggest that the Empress's syncretistic association with the goddess Artemis/Diana (as implied by the coins) could help explain the surge of popular fervour and support for the temple cultus which occurs in reaction to Paul's ministry in Ephesus." L. Joseph Kreitzer, "A Numismatic Clue to Acts 19:23–41: The Ephesian Cistophori of Claudius and Agrippina," *JSNT* 9, no. 30 (1987): 59–70.

[120] Erol Atalay, "Die Kurudağ-Höhle [Bei Ephesos] Mit Archäologischen Funden," *JÖAI* 52 (1980 1978): 40, no. 56a.

[121] *I.Eph.* 1.28.9–10; 1.29.19–20; Dio Chrysostom *Or.* 7.24; 40.6; Tacitus *Ann.* 2.80; Cicero *Flac.* 16; Josephus *Ant.* 14.150; Newton suggests the month of March, while Barclay records that the games were held in the month of May and Murphy-O'Connor states April. Charles Thomas Newton, *The Collection of Ancient Greek Inscriptions in the British Museum*, ed. E. L. Hicks, 5 vols. (Oxford: Clarendon, 1874), 145; Murphy-O'Connor, *St. Paul's Ephesus*, 175.

[122] *I.Eph.* 4.1452.3; 1457.4; Xenophon *Eph. Tale* 1.1–3.

162. The so-called "terrace houses" showing an example of wealthy family life in Ephesus during the Roman period. They were built according to the Hippodamian plan that transected each other at right angels and included clay pipe heating systems. There are six residential units on three terrances (used from first cent. BC to seventh cent. AD).

Photo by Ronan Reinart/Wikimedia Commons

Thus, it is not surprising that during the Acts 19 demonstration the masses congregated in the theater, where for two hours they chanted "Great is Diana (Artemis) of the Ephesians" (Acts 19:32–34).[123] During the festivals of Artemis, the statue of Artemis (see Fig. 159) was carried from the temple into the city, and set on nine pedestals in the theater, only to be returned to the temple after the festival.[124] It is possible that the statue of Artemis was present in the theater during the crowd's demonstration in Acts 19.

The theater was built in the first half of the third cent. BC, into the side of Mount Pion, and enlarged under Emperor Claudius (AD 41–54), with more renovations during Nero and Trajan. The Arcadian Way (Street), that leads to the harbour (see Fig. 161), was lined on both sides with shops and colonnades.

The Library of Celsus

The famous library of Celsus and Gate of Macaeus and Mithridates (see Figs. 31, 141) were only constructed in 135 AD and not present when John was in the city.[125]

The blessing promised to the overcomers "to eat of the tree of life, which is in the paradise

---

[123] Sherman E. Johnson, "The Apostle Paul and the Riot in Ephesus," *LTQ* 14 (1979): 179–88.

[124] *SIG* 3.1003.15–17; *I.Eph.* 2.202–208; 3.145; 4.1457; Xenophon *Eph. Tale* 1.2–3; Guy Maclean Rogers, *The Sacred Identity of Ephesos: Foundation Myths of a Roman City*, Routledge Revivals (New York: Routledge, 2014), 83–85.

[125] On the library of Celsus, see George W. Houston, *Inside Roman Libraries: Book Collections and Their Management in Antiquity* (Raleigh, NC: University of North Carolina Press, 2014), 189–94.

of God" (Rev 2:7), while clearly recalling the garden of Eden (Gen 2:9; 3:23–24; Ezek 31:2–9),[126] may also be understood against the background of the Artemision royal gardens (Gr. *paradeisos*) outside Ephesus. These sacred gardens were believed to be the traditional birthplace of Artemis, and were stocked with deer and edible fruit (Strabo *Geogr.* 14.1.5, 20).[127] The sacred groves are depicted on fifty-six Ephesian coins as a sacred palm tree (tree-shrine) with a stag on one side, and a bee depicting the Artemision priestess on the other (see Fig. 117).[128] Two inscriptions quoted by Hemer describe the foundations of the sacred temple of Artemis as a tree-shrine.[129]

Certainly, the Ephesian citizens would have recognized the relevance of the imagery of eating fruit from paradise's sacred groves, and the cultic worship of Artemis around the sacred tree. But as Beale reminds us: "What paganism promised only Christianity as the fulfillment of OT hope could deliver."[130] The Artemis "paradise" pales in comparison with the paradise granted the overcomer in the New Jerusalem (Rev 21:16–18; 22:2).

---

[126] Aune, *Revelation 1-5*, 152–54.

[127] Darice E. Birge, "Sacred Groves in the Ancient Greek World" (Ph.D. diss., University of California-Berkely, 1982), 27; Hemer, *Letters to the Seven Churches*, 50.

[128] Hemer, *Letters to the Seven Churches*, 46; M. Rakicic, "The Bees of Ephesos," *The Celator* 8, no. 12 (1994): 6–12.

[129] Hemer, *Letters to the Seven Churches*, 44–45.

[130] Beale, *The Book of Revelation*, 236.

163. The colonnaded western stoa of the commercial agora, Smyrna.

Smyrna (Rev 2:8–11)

Smyrna (modern *Izmir*) is a major seaport on the Aegean about forty miles north of Ephesus. It was a beautiful metropolis with purposely-symmetrical streets through which cool breezes off the Mediterranean cooled the citizens on hot summer nights. In Paul's day, it had a population of about 250,000 and developed into an important commercial centre.[131] Inscriptions and coins record Smyrna's distinction as the "first of Asia in beauty and size, and the most brilliant, and Metropolis [Capital] of Asia, and thrice Temple–Warden [*Neokoros*] of the Augusti, according to the decrees of the most sacred Senate, and ornament of Ionia" (*CIG* 2: no. 3202)[132]

The citizens of Smyrna would be familiar with this claim of primacy from the well-known rivalry with Ephesus and Pergamum to be "the first in Asia."[133] While Smyrna claimed to be the "first of Asia in beauty and size," Christ declares that He is the "first and the last" providing a superior foundation for security as the eternal savior.[134]

Smyrna's long-time alliance with Rome can be traced back to 195 BC when it became the first city to erect a temple to the goddess Roma, and Cicero celebrates Smyrna as "the city of our most faithful and most ancient ally" (Cicero *Phil.* 11.2.5 [Yonge]).[135] Smyrna's faithfulness to the Romans is also supported in their application before Tiberius in AD 26 to build and become the keeper (Gr. *neokoros*) of the second Imperial Cult temple in Asia (Tacitus *Ann.* 4:56). Unfortunately, no archaeological evidence for this temple has been discovered.[136] Several scholars draw similarities between the Christians' faithful loyalty to Christ and Smyrna's allegiance to Rome.[137] Christ now appeals to the Smyrnaean Christians to remain faithful just as Smyrna had been faithful to the

164. Silver Tetradrachm coin from Smyrna (*ca.* 155–145 BC) featuring Tyche/Cybele wearing a turreted crown, and with the obverse displaying the magistrate's monogram ZMUR/NAIWN within a laurel wreath

Courtesy o f CNG

---

[131] Cadoux, *Ancient Smyrna*, 23–170; Ekrem Akurgal, "Smyrna," ed. Richard Stillwell, William L. MacDonald, and Marian Holland, *Princeton Encyclopaedia of Classical Sites* (Princeton, NJ: Princeton University Press, 1976), 848; David S. Potter, "Smyrna," ed. David Noel Freedman, *ABD* (New York: Doubleday, 1996), 73–5; David E. Graves, "Local References in the Letter to Smyrna (Rev 2: 8–11), Part 2: Historical Background," *BS* 19, no. 1 (2006): 23–41.

[132] Dietrich O. A. Klose, *Die Münzprägung Von Smyrna in Der Römischen Kaiserzeit* (Berlin: de Gruyter, 1987), 40; Lafaye, Cagnat, and Toutain, *Inscriptiones Graecae Ad Res Romanas Pertinentes*, 4: no. 1420; Donald F. McCabe, *Smyrna Inscriptions: Texts and List*, ed. Tad Brennan and Neil Elliott R. (Princeton, NJ: Princeton Institute for Advanced Study, 1988), 150, 156, 171–72.

[133] William M. Ramsay, *Cities and Bishoprics of Phrygia* (Oxford: Oxford University Press, 1895), 2:632; Magie, *Roman Rule in Asia Minor*, 2:635–36.

[134] Graves, *Jesus Speaks to Seven of His Churches: A Commentary*, 158-160; "Local References in the Letter to Smyrna (Rev 2: 8–11), Part 3: Jewish Background," *BS* 19, no. 2 (2006): 23–31.

[135] Meinardus, *St. John of Patmos*, 62.

[136] Edwin M. Yamauchi, *New Testament Cities in Western Asia Minor: Light from Archaeology on Cities of Paul and the Seven Churches of Revelation* (Eugene, OR: Wipf & Stock, 2003), 55–62; Potter, "Smyrna," 6:73–75.

[137] Charles, *Revelation*, 1:55; Cadoux, *Ancient Smyrna*, 113–15; Hemer, *Letters to the Seven Churches*, 70.

Romans, even when other cities were not.

The Smyrnaean church would know suffering and persecution, although it was only to be for a short time, symbolically limited to ten days (Rev 2:10; see also Dan 1:12–15). This prophecy is partially fulfilled through two of Smyrna's martyred bishops; Polycarp (AD 155; *Mart. Pol.* 1.13; 12.2; *FrgPol.* 64.23) and Pionius (AD 250; *Mart. Pionii* 14.1). The Jews, identified as the "synagogue of Satan" (Rev 2:9; 3:9), played an integral role in the arrest and martyrdom of both bishops (*Mart. Pol.* 12.2; 13:1; 17:2; 18:1; *Mart. Pionii* 2.1; 3.6; 4.2, 8; 13.1; 14.1),[138] as well as in the early church (Acts 13:50; 17:13). Considering the Christians' belief in one God (Exod 20:3; 1 Cor 8:4), they could not worship Caesar as god, which resulted in persecution, and in some cases, martyrdom.

165. Bronze statue of a runner wearing the laurel wreath (crown) awarded to the winner. Found in the Aegean Sea off the coast of Cyme. Roman copy of a late Hellenistic statue dating to the second cent. AD.

Izmir Archaeological Museum, Turkey.

The Crown of Life

The blessing for the Smyrnaean overcomers who are "faithful, even to the point of death," is Christ's promise of "the crown of life" (Rev 2:10) and protection from the "second death" (Rev 2:11). The crown or wreath (Gr. *stephanos*) was a familiar symbol in the ancient culture of the Empire, and particularly to Smyrna's history.[139] The crown imagery is predominantly pictured on Smyrna's coins,[140] illustrated on the silver tetradrachm on which the Anatolian goddess Cybele is displayed wearing a turreted crown with the obverse displaying an oak wreath (see Fig. 118).[141] The beauty of Smyrna's structure was also described as resembling a crown by ancient writers (Aristides *Orat.* 15, 20–22, 41; Philostratus *Vit. Apoll.* 1.4.7; 1.8.24). The priests of the Imperial Cult wore their crowns (Lat. *coronatus*) with the image of Caesar Augustus on them (see Fig. 108 and 119). The municipal officer or priests of this cult were called *stephanephoros* (Gr. to wear a crown; Wis 4:2).

Ramsay suggests that the terms *coronatus* and *stephanephoros* should be understood as relating to the same role as that of cultic priest.[142] Arundell points out that these *stephanephori* wore crowns of laurel during their public ceremonies and were "attached to the temples of the emperors."[143] In the ancient mind the crown of life conjured up many types of images including glory or honor (Isa 28:5; Jer 13:18; Aeschines *Ctes.* 45; Lucian *Luct.* 19), accomplishment, and victory (Aeschines *Ctes.* 179, Philo *Prob.* 26). However, the "wreath of life" used metaphorically

[138] For a comprehensive treatment of the Crown of Life, see Graves, *Jesus Speaks to Seven of His Churches: A Commentary*, 211–19.

[139] Hemer, *Letters to the Seven Churches*, 55–60.

[140] Klose, *Die Münzprägung Von Smyrna in Der Römischen Kaiserzeit*, 24–26.

[141] Head, *Catalogue of the Greek Coins of Ionia*, Nos. 1–119; Joseph Grafton Milne, *The Silver Coinage of Smyrna* (London: Taylor & Walton, 1914), 275 2(b), pl. xvi; Hans von Aulock and Gerhard Kleiner, *Sylloge Nummorum Graecorum, Vol. 1: Pontus, Paphlagonia, Bithynia, Mysia, Troas, Aiolis, Lesbos, Ionia* (Berlin: Gebr. Mann, 1957), no. 2162.

[142] Ramsay, *Cities and Bishoprics of Phrygia*, 2:56–57.

[143] Francis Vyvian J. Arundell, *A Visit to the Seven Churches of Asia with an Excursion into Pisidia* (London: Rodwell, 1828), 2:375.

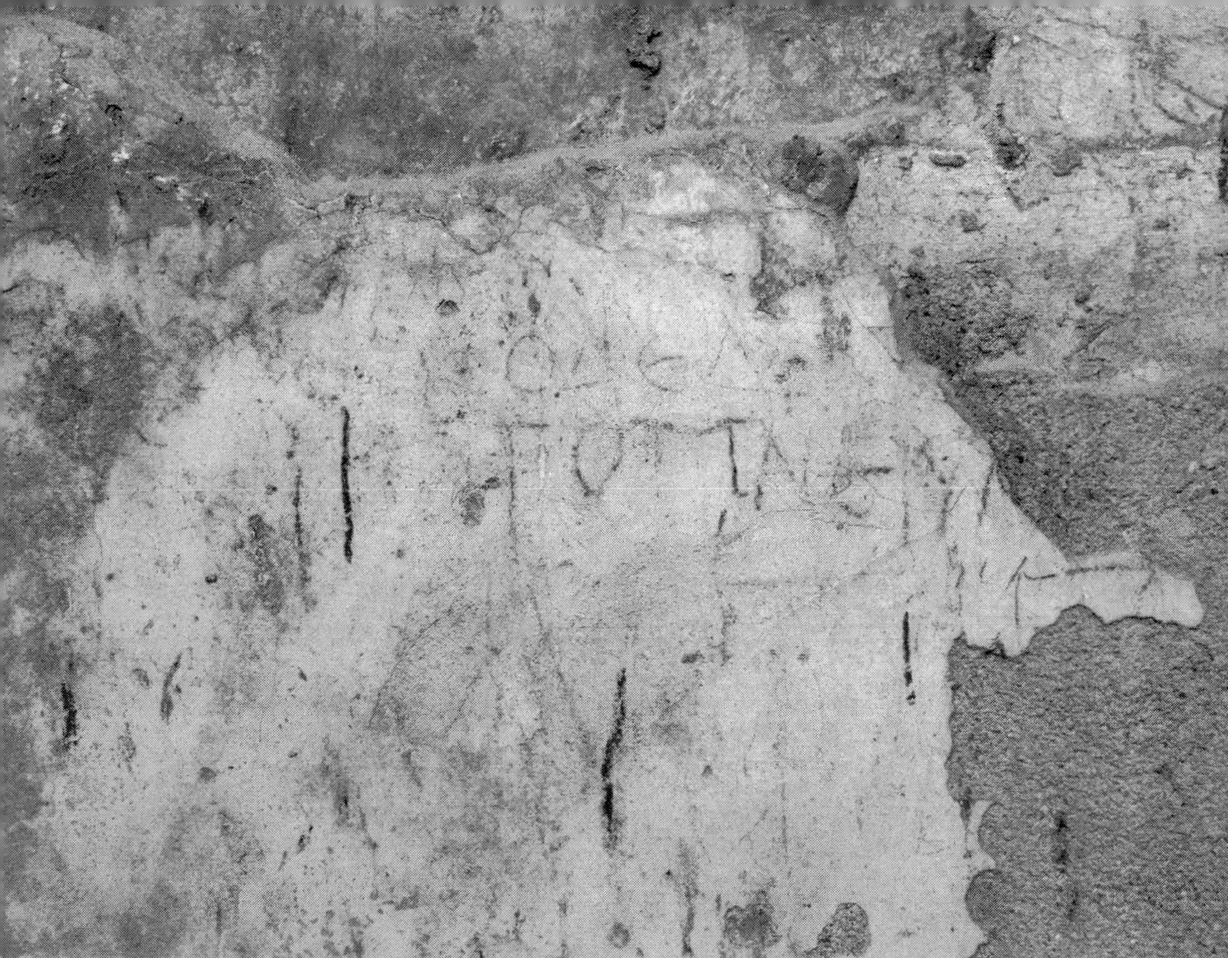

166. Perhaps the earliest Christian Graffiti to be discovered. The graffitio states: ὁ δεδωκ[ώς] τὸ πνεῦμ[α], *o dedok[os] to pneum[a]*: "the one who has given the Spirit. . ." (T20.1).

Courtesy of Mark Wilson, used by permission. Commercial agora, Smyrna (modern Izmir), Turkey.

for eternal life (Jas 1:12; *4 Macc.* 17:15) is likely drawn from the prize given in athletic contests[144] or the crown buried with the deceased, symbolic of their victories in life.[145] While athletes only receive a crown of flowers, Christ promises the overcomers an authentic crown of eternal life.

Agora Graffiti

Between 1932 and 1942, German and Turkish archaeologists excavated the agora under the direction of Numan, Kantar and Miltner.[146] Excavations were resumed in 2002 by the Izmir Archaeology Museum under the direction of the Museum's director, Mehmet Taslialan. Excavations in the northern and western portions of the civic basilica have revealed many sculptures and architectural pieces. A portion of the basilica and part of the west stoa are being

[144] Aune, *Revelation 1-5*, 175–76; William H. C. Frend, *Martyrdom and Persecution in the Early Church: A Study of a Conflict from the Maccabees to Donatus* (Oxford: Blackwell, 1965); Reinhold Merkelbach, "Der Griechische Wortchatz Und Die Christen," *ZPE* 18 (1975): 108–136; Zeph Stewart, "Greek Crowns and Christian Martyrs," in *Mémorial André-Jean Festugière: Antiquité Païenne et Chrétienne*, ed. E. Lucchesi and H. D. Saffrey (Geneva: Cramer, 1984), 119–24.

[145] Clement of Alexandria *Paed.* 2.8; Cicero *Flac.* 31, 75; *Odes Sol.* 1:17, 20; Apuleius *Metam.* 11.24; *Mart. Pol.* 17.1; *Ascen. Isa.* 9.6–18, 7.22; Josephus *Ant.* 14.153; Demosthenes *Cor.* 54–55, 84, 116; Erwin R. Goodenough, "The Crown of Victory in Judaism," *Art Bulletin* 28 (1946): 139–59.

[146] Bernard McDonagh, *Blue Guide: Turkey*, 3rd ed. (London: A & C Black, 2001), 178.

restored to a height of two stories.[147] According to Taslialan,

> The inscriptions on stone provide information about civic life and the Roman government of the Province of Asia, and very numerous graffiti, preserved on the plaster which covers the north wall and many of the pillars of the lower story of the Basilica, constitute a Greek counterpart to the Latin graffiti of Pompeii, unique in the Roman East. [148]

Thomas Derwbear, an inscription expert employed by the Smyrna excavation, states that "Smyrnian youth ornamented the walls with everything about their daily life. Gladiator figures describing a fight with lions, comedians on stage, and other graffiti about sport and health were found".[149] Some of the messages used isopsephism (ἴσος *isos* "equal" + ψῆφος *psēphos* "pebble, used for counting"; similar to Jewish *gematria*), the Greek practice of assigning values to letters in a name and then adding up the numbrers to give a single number, a common practice in antiquity to convey their messages of love, sex and religion.[150] The secret code is similar to that used in Revelation 13:18 for the number 666. Three female names, in the same building, are identified representing 616. One reads "I love a woman whose number is 616" (T22.1).[151] Others read "whose number is 731" (T24.2) and "1308" (T27.3).[152] Another inscription from the agora Basilica, that was an example of isopsephism from Smyrna, states: "equal in value: lord, 800; faith 800" (TP100.3 = *SIG* 3.973).[153]

Perhaps one of the earliest Christian graffiti's ever discovered was also uncovered during the excavaion of the agora. It reads ὁ δεδωκ[ὼς] τὸ πνεῦμ[α], *o dedōk[ōs] to pneum[a]*: "the one who has given the Spirit. . ." (T20.1) that is, the Lord (*kurios*) Jesus (see Fig. 166). The graffito would indicate to those who read it that there were Christians in the city of Smyrna.[154]

---

[147] Mehmet Taslialan, "New Excavations and Restorations in the Agora of Smyrna," in *Paper Presented at Institut Für Archäologie, Abt. Archäologie Des Mittelmeerraumes* (University of Berne, Institute of Archaeology, University of Berne, Institute of Archaeology, June 24, 2004), n.p.

[148] Ibid; Antonio Sogliano, "Isopsephia Pompeiana," *Rendiconti Della Reale Academia Dei Lincei* 10 (1901): 256–59.

[149] Thomas Derwbear, "Secret of Ancient Graffiti," *US Daily EU News*, July 22, 2003, n.p., www.turks.us/article.php?story = 20030722090305725.

[150] Dimitris K. Psychoyos, "The Forgotten Art of Isopsephy and the Magic Number KZ," *Semiotica* 154, no. 1–4 (2005): 157–224.

[151] Roger S. Bagnall, "Isopsephisms of Desire," in *Graffiti from the Basilica in the Agora of Smyrna*, ed. Roger S. Bagnall et al., Institute for the Study of the Ancient World (New York: New York University Press, 2016), 50, 226.

[152] Ibid. 48.

[153] Roger S. Bagnall, "Christianity," in *Graffiti from the Basilica in the Agora of Smyrna*, ed. Roger S. Bagnall et al., Institute for the Study of the Ancient World (New York: New York University Press, 2016), 46.

[154] Ibid, 45–46.

167. The Trajaneum (temple) in Pergamum was started under the Roman Emperor Trajan (98–117 AD) and enlarged and completed under Hadrian (117–138 AD). This temple for the worship of the emperor may have been similar to the temple to Tiberius which was built earlier in Smyrna. If one holds to a late date for the writing of Revelation, then this temple to the emperor Trajan was built shortly after the book was written. The temple was uncovered in the 1880's under the direction of the architect H. Stiller. It was abandoned, but received renewed interest in the 1960's from the Turkish Antiquities and the German Archaeological Institute.

Pergamum (Rev 2:12–17)

Follow the coastline north from Izmir for some forty miles, and one comes upon Pergamum (*Pergamos* or modern *Bergama;* see Fig. 120, 121, and 122),[155] with an estimated population in the first cent. of under 100,000,[156] celebrated as "the most famous place of Asia" (Pliny *Nat.* 5.126 [Rackham]). This was the site of many temples dedicated to such gods as Zeus, Dionysus, Athena, and Asclepius. The enormous structure around the altar of Zeus is no longer there as it was transported in its entirety to the Pergamum Museum in Berlin in 1910.[157]

The most prominent candidate for a local reference in Pergamum is the identification of "Satan's Throne . . . where Satan lives" (Rev 2:13). For Wood and Charles, "Satan's throne" is likened to the shape of the acropolis,[158] although Hemer believes this is just a scenic feature.[159] Friesen prefers representing Satan's throne with the "local hostility toward the Pergamene assembly"[160] and not to any physical structure. Some suggest that Pergamum was the capital of the province of Asia and that Satan was essentially the god of the Romans, and that they were in some way doing Satan's work.[161] However, the premise that Pergamum was the capital of Asia in the first century can be challenged, as this honor more likely belonged to Ephesus (under Augustus ca. 29 BC).[162]

The judge's bench (βῆμα, *bēma*),[163] where the proconsul sat, has been suggested as perhaps being the throne of Satan. The word "throne" (θρόνος, *thronos*) has occasionally been identified with a judge's bench (Plutarch *Praec. ger. publ.* 807b), and in the NT it is always a seat of office or state for a judge (Matt 19:28), or a king (Luke 1:32, 52), or Christ, or God.[164] Understood as a

---

[155] William M. Ramsay, "Pergamum," in *DBib5*, 3:750; Max Fränkel, Ernst Fabricius, and Carl Schuchhardt, *Die Inschriften von Pergamon*, vol. 8, Sonderausgabe Aus Den Altertümern von Pergamon (Berlin: Spemann, 1890); Edward M. Blaiklock, *Cities of the New Testament* (New York: Revell, 1965), 105; Steven J. Friesen, "Satan's Throne, Imperial Cults and the Social Settings of Revelation," *JSNT* 27, no. 3 (2005): 351–73.

[156] Graves, *Jesus Speaks to Seven of His Churches: A Commentary*, 231; Hanson, "Urban System" 258.

[157] Aune, *Revelation 1-5*, 194.

[158] Wood, "Local Knowledge," 264; Charles, *Revelation*, 1:61.

[159] Hemer, *Letters to the Seven Churches*, 84.

[160] Friesen, "Satan's Throne," 365.

[161] Sherman E. Johnson, "Asia Minor and Early Christianity," in *Judaism and Christianity in the Age of Constantine*, ed. Jacob Neusner, vol. 2 (Leiden: Brill, 1975), 93; Austin M. Farrer, *The Revelation of St. John the Divine: Commentary on the English Text* (Oxford: Clarendon, 1964), 73; George Aaron Barton, *Archaeology and the Bible* (Alexandria , Egypt: Library of Alexandria, 1933), 268; Bean, *Aegean Turkey*, 77. Bean contradicts himself by also claiming that "the most likely" explanation is the "temple of Rome and Augustus."

[162] Graves, *Jesus Speaks to Seven of His Churches: A Commentary*, 101; Trebilco, "Asia," 304; Friesen, "Satan's Throne," 361.

[163] Matt 27:19; John 19:13; Acts 18:12; 25:10.

[164] Matt 5:34; 25:31; see also Rev 4:2–11; 7:9–12; 20:11–12; 21:3–5; Henry Barclay Swete, *The Apocalypse of St. John*, 3rd ed. (London: MacMillan & Co., 1917), 34; Stephen S. Smalley, *The Revelation to John: A Commentary on the Greek Text of the Apocalypse* (Downers Grove, IL: InterVarsity Press, 2005), 68; Robert H. Mounce, *The Book of Revelation*, Revised, NICNT 17 (Grand Rapids: Eerdmans, 1997), 79.

subjective genitive, Pergamum was where "Satan was enthroned." As Aune explains:

> The Roman proconsul resided in Pergamon, and it was to Pergamon that Christians in the surrounding area were brought after being denounced by informers even at a later date (*Mart. Carp.* 1–23). The Province of Asia was divided into first nine, then eleven, regions; in the main city of each area (one of which was Pergamon), the ***conventus juridicus***, "judicial assembly," was convened by the proconsul or the legates and a court of provincial judges called the ***centumviri***. In a trial, the first state involved a hearing ***in iure***, i.e., before the jurisdictional magistrate (the ***praetor***), while the second stage of the trial was the ***iudicium centumvirale***, i.e., an appearance before a court selected from the ***centumviri*** (Philostratus *Vit. Soph.* 1.22).[165]

However, Pergamum was not the only region in Asia Minor with the responsibility of the *conventus juridicus* (see the trial of Polycarp in Smyrna; see Figs. 142; *Mart. Pol.* 1.13; *FrgPol.* 64.23) and this does not explain what was so special about Pergamum to set it apart from other cities to deserve this title of Satan's throne.

An Important Center of Graeco-Roman Religion

However, there are three more probable contenders from the surrounding culture: the altar of the temple of Zeus,[166] the cult of Asclepius,[167] and Asia Minor's centre for the Imperial Cult with temples to Augustus, Severus, and Trajan.[168] The least likely connection seems to be the altar of Zeus: the cult of Asclepius and epicenter of the Imperial Cult attracts the most scholarly attention.

Andrew of Caesarea, one of the oldest Greek patristic commentators on the book of Revelation, describes the city as "full of idols"[169] (κατείδωλος *kateidōlos*),[170] and the throne being representative of the immoral excesses displayed by Pergamum's citizens.[171] Some scholars suggest that Pergamum was somehow more pagan than other cities,[172] but this contradicts the common pagan and polytheistic culture of the first cent.[173] with a pervasive focus on the imperial cult throughout Asia Minor.[174] However, a case may be made for the combined concentration of pagan religious practices, considered satanic by Christians, that led to John's

---

[165] Aune, *Rev 1–5*, 183; Berger, *Encyclopedic Dictionary of Roman Law*, 386, 521.

[166] Deissmann, *Light from the Ancient East*, 85, 281 n. 3; J. Massyngberde Ford, *Revelation: Introduction, Translation and Commentary*, AYBC 38 (New York: Doubleday, 1985), 393; George R. Beasley-Murray, *Book of Revelation*, NCB (Grand Rapids: Eerdmans, 1983), 84; Edward M. Blaiklock, *The Archaeology of the New Testament* (Grand Rapids: Zondervan, 1970), 126–28.

[167] Edward M. Blaiklock, *Cities of the New Testament* (New York: Revell, 1965), 105; Andrew Tait, *The Messages to the Seven Churches of Asia Minor: An Exposition of the First Three Chapters of the Book of the Revelation* (London: Hodder & Stoughton, 1884), 228; Ramsay, *The Letters to Seven Churches*, 285–86.

[168] Hemer, *Letters to the Seven Churches*, 85, 87, 104; Aune, *Revelation 1-5*, 183–84; William Barclay, *Letters to the Seven Churches* (London: SCM, 1957), 44–45; Charles, *Revelation*, 1:61; Mounce, *Revelation*, 79.

[169] Eugenia Scarvelis Constantinou, "Andrew of Caesarea and the Apocalypse in the Ancient Church of the East: Studies and Translation" (Ph.D. diss., Université Laval, 2008), 36; Alan F. Johnson et al., *Hebrews - Revelation*, ed. Tremper Longman III and David E. Garland, Revised, EBC 13 (Grand Rapids: Zondervan, 2006), 619–20. Johnson describes Pergamum as "a center for worship of the pagan gods" and "a center of idolatry."

[170] For the background of the gods worshipped in Pergamum see "Famous for Her Religious Worship" above and also Worth, Jr., *Greco-Asian Culture*, 112–16. See pages 136–37 for his treatment of this view.

[171] Specific evidence is not provided by these authors. J. A Seiss, *The Apocalypse* (Colorado Springs, Colo.: Cook, 1906), 100–101; Tait, *Messages to the Seven Churches*, 229; John T. Hinds, *A Commentary on the Book of Revelation*, New Testament Commentaries (Gospel Advocate) (Nashville, TN: Gospel Advocate, 1974), 34.

[172] Richard C. H. Lenski, *The Interpretation of St. John's Revelation*, CNT (Minneapolis, MN: Augsburg Fortress, 1963), 104; Homer Hailey, *Revelation: An Introduction and Commentary* (Grand Rapids: Baker, 1979), 130; Jürgen Roloff, *The Revelation of John*, trans. John E. Alsup, CC (Minneapolis, MN: Fortress, 1993), 50–51.

[173] Paul in Rome, Acts 17:16, 22; Dio Cassius *Hist. Rom.* 51.20.7.

[174] Karen Louise Jolly, *Tradition and Diversity: Christianity in a World Context to 1500* (New York: Routledge, 2015), 27; Steven Muir, "Religion on the Road in Ancient Greece and Rome," in *Travel and Religion in Antiquity*, ed. Philip A. Harland, ESCJ 21 (Waterloo, Ont.: Wilfrid Laurier University Press, 2011), 29–48; Harland, "Imperial Cults within Local Cultural Life," 85–107; Naylor, "The Roman Imperial Cult and Revelation," 207–39; Duncan Fishwick, *The Imperial Cult in the Latin West*, Studies in the Ruler Cult of the Western Provinces of the Roman Empire, 2.1 (Leiden: Brill Academic, 2005).

comments (see conclusion).

The Great Altar of Zeus

Perhaps the most spectacular structure in Pergamum was to Zeus and Athena Nike (goddess of Victory; Ampelius *Lib. Mem.* 8.14). It has been called a temple and altar, but perhaps it is more accurate to describe it as a colonnaded court (see Fig. 168). Built around 170 BC by King Eumenes II of Greece, it became a prominent landmark in Asia Minor and the largest altar in antiquity. The base of the altar contained a frieze of the epic battle between the Giants and the Gigantomachy (Olympian gods).[175] Smoke from the altar would have continually marked the skyline, as Aune states, "sacrificial victims were burned twenty-four hours a day, seven days a week by a rotating group of priests,"[176] making this reminiscent of the smoke rising from the golden altar to the heavenly throne (Rev 8:3–4).

168. The Great Altar of Pergamum. Some of the details, researched by Otto Puchstein based on coins, may not be accurate.

Staatliche (formerly Pergamum) Museum, Berlin, Germany. Photo by Raimond Spekking/Wikimedia Commons

It was excavated between 1878 and 1886 by the German engineers, Carl Humann and Alexander Conze, who negotiated a deal with the Turkish officials to relocate the frieze fragments in 1910 to the Staatliche Museum in Berlin, where they remain today (see Fig. 168).[177] During the Second World War it was dismantled and housed in a bomb shelter that protected it from the allied bombing raids that heavily damaged the museum.[178] All that remains today at the site is the five-stepped base, with a large tree growing in the center (see Fig. 169). The remains were being looted by the local residents in Pergamos, who were using the stones as building materials and burning pieces of the marble for lime.

169. The remains of the Altar of Zeus. The structure around the altar is actually not a temple but an open air altar. The two trees mark the location of the altar, but the structure which surrounded it is now in the Staatliche (formerly Pergamum) Museum in Berlin (see Fig. 168).

According to Kosmetatou, little is actually known about the Great Altar:

---

[175] Evamaria Schmidt, *The Great Altar of Pergamon* (Boston, MA: Boston Book and Art Shop, 1965); Max Kunze and Volker Kästner, *Der Altar von Pergamon: Hellenistische Und Römische Architektur*, 2nd ed., Antikensammlung II: Fuhrer Durch Die Ausstellung Des Pergamon Museums (Berlin: Henschelverlag Kunst und Gesellschaft, 1990), 30.

[176] Aune, *Rev 1–5*, 180; Bruce M. Metzger, *Breaking the Code: Understanding the Book of Revelation* (Nashville, TN: Abingdon, 1999), 34.

[177] Aune, *Rev 1–5*, 194.

[178] Yamauchi, *NT Cities*, 36.

170. Asclepeion complex and the north stoa viewed from the theater, that could thirty-five hundred spectators.

We do not know to whom it was dedicated, when exactly it was built, its purpose or its impact on artistic developments of the period, while its reconstruction remains a matter of fierce debate among art and architectural historians. However, scholars agree that the popular Gigantomachy theme probably symbolized Attalid victories against the Galatians and functioned as a symbol of the struggle of good vs. evil and the forces of civilization vs. the "barbarians."[179]

However, the theory that it was a victory over the Gauls[180] is now rejected by most scholars,[181] and another frieze on the inside wall of the court depicted the account of Telephus, the son of Hercules who was hailed as the legendary founder of Pergamum.[182] Although one of the greatest works of Hellenistic art,[183] in antiquity it is only mentioned by Ampelius, who describes it as "a large marble altar, forty feet high with a great many sculptures, among which a

179 Elizabeth Kosmetatou, "The Attalids of Pergamon," in *A Companion to the Hellenistic World*, ed. Andrew Erskine, Blackwell Companions to the Ancient World (Oxford: Blackwell, 2003), 165; Brunilde Sismondo Ridgway, *Hellenistic Sculpture II: The Styles of Ca. 200–100 B.C.*, Wisconsin Studies in Classics (Madison, WI: University of Wisconsin Press, 2000), 19–102; Andrew Stewart, "Pergamo Ara Marmorea Magna: On the Date, Reconstruction, and Functions of the Great Altar of Pergamon," in *From Pergamon to Sperlonga: Sculpture and Context*, ed. Nancy T. de Grummond and Brunilde Sismondo Ridgway, Hellenistic Culture and Society (Berkeley, CA: University of California Press, 2001), 32–57.

180 Akurgal, *Ancient Civilizations*, 71.

181 Bernard Andreae, "Datierung Und Bedeutung Des Telephosfrieses Im Zusammenhang Mit Den Übrigen Stiftungen Der Ataliden von Pergamon," in *Der Pergamonaltar. Die Neue Präsentation Nach Restaurierung Des Telephosfrieses*, ed. Wolf-Dieter Heilmeyer (Tübingen: Wasmuth, 1997), 68.

182 Wilson, *Biblical Turkey*, 285; Fant and Reddish, *Guide to Biblical Sites*, 294.

183 Thomas Bertram Lonsdale Webster, *Hellenistic Poetry and Art* (London: Methuen, 1964), 189–91.

Battle of the Giants" (*Lib. Mem.* 8.14).

Prior to the archaeological work at Pergamum in the twentieth century, the common belief was that the shape of the altar of the temple of Zeus (see Fig. 169) was identified with "Satan's throne" (2:13),[184] since it was reconstructed and prominently on display in the Berlin museum (see Fig. 168).[185] In 1990, Thompson supported the notion, though provided no grounds for this,[186] though more recently Adela Yarbro Collins has revived the idea and included not only the altar, but also the temple of Athena and the temple of Zeus, perhaps wrongly assuming that "Satan's throne" must refer to a physical monument.[187]

However, this does not explain how local monuments in Pergamum would be the "adversarial mirror-image of the throne of God."[188] And while some commentators argue that the altar of Zeus resembles a throne, this is simply not the case, as ancient thrones looked very different from altars or the acropolis.[189] The Olympia in Greece also has open-air altars to Zeus,[190] so it seems unlikely that this one in Pergamum should be singled out as the throne of Satan.[191]

171. Column in the courtyard of the entrance (*propylon*) of the Asclepion, from the lower site of Pergamum, decorated with three symbols of health: snakes, olive branches, and the wheel of life. Snakes were worshiped in the cult of Asclepius, the god of healing.

The Asclepeion

The temple of Asclepius offers two options for an allusion to "Satan's throne": first, the Christian's aversion to calling the Greek god of healing, Asclepius, god-savior (θεός σωτήρ, *Theos sōtēr,* later called Zeus Asclepius, and second the Asclepeion emblem of the serpent (Plutarch *Mor.* 755f; Homer *Il.* 2.299–332; see Figs. 171, 174), associated by Christians as Satan (12:9; 14, 15; 20:2; see also Gen 3:1–4; 1 Cor 11:3). Both have lead commentators to connect them with Satan's throne.[192]

---

[184] While Blaiklock is tentative in his earlier work, he uses the stronger "must" to argue for the throne of Zeus in his *Archaeology of the NT*. Blaiklock, *Cities of the NT*, 105; Blaiklock, *Archaeology of the NT*, 126–28.

[185] Deissmann, *Light from the Ancient East*, 85, 280 nn.2, 281 3; Lohmeyer, *Offenbarung*, 25; Erwin Rohde, *Pergamon: Burgberg Und Altar* (Berlin: Henschelverlag, 1982), 60–62; Michael Avi-Yonah, ed., *Views of the Biblical World: The New Testament*, vol. 5 (Jerusalem: International, 1961), 271; Terence Kelshaw, *Send This Message to My Church: Christ's Words to the Seven Churches of Revelation* (Nashville, TN: Nelson, 1984), 93–94; Ford, *Revelation*, 393; Beasley-Murray, *Revelation*, 84.

[186] Thompson, *Apocalypse and Empire*, 173; Beasley-Murray, *Revelation*, 84; John E. Stambaugh and David L. Balch, *The New Testament in Its Social Environment*, LEC 2 (Philadelphia, PA: Westminster, 1986), 153.

[187] Adela Yarbro Collins, "Pergamon in Early Christian Literature," in *Pergamon-Citadel of the Gods*, ed. Helmut Koester, HTS 46 (Harrisburg, Pa.: Trinity Press International, 1998), 166–76.

[188] Ibid.

[189] Friesen, "Satan's Throne," 359 n.21.

[190] Frederick Norman Pryce et al., "Altar," in *OCD*, 66.

[191] Robert L. Thomas, *Revelation 1–7 Commentary* (Chicago, IL: Moody, 1992), 183.

[192] Schmitz *TDNT* 3:166; Wilhelm Bousset, *Die Offenbarung Johannis* (Göttingen: Vandenhoeck & Ruprecht, 1906), 211; Swete, *Apocalypse*, 34; Theodor Zahn, *Die Offenbarung Des Johannes*, KZNT 17 (Leipzig: Deichert, 1924), 253–63; Tait, *Messages to the Seven*

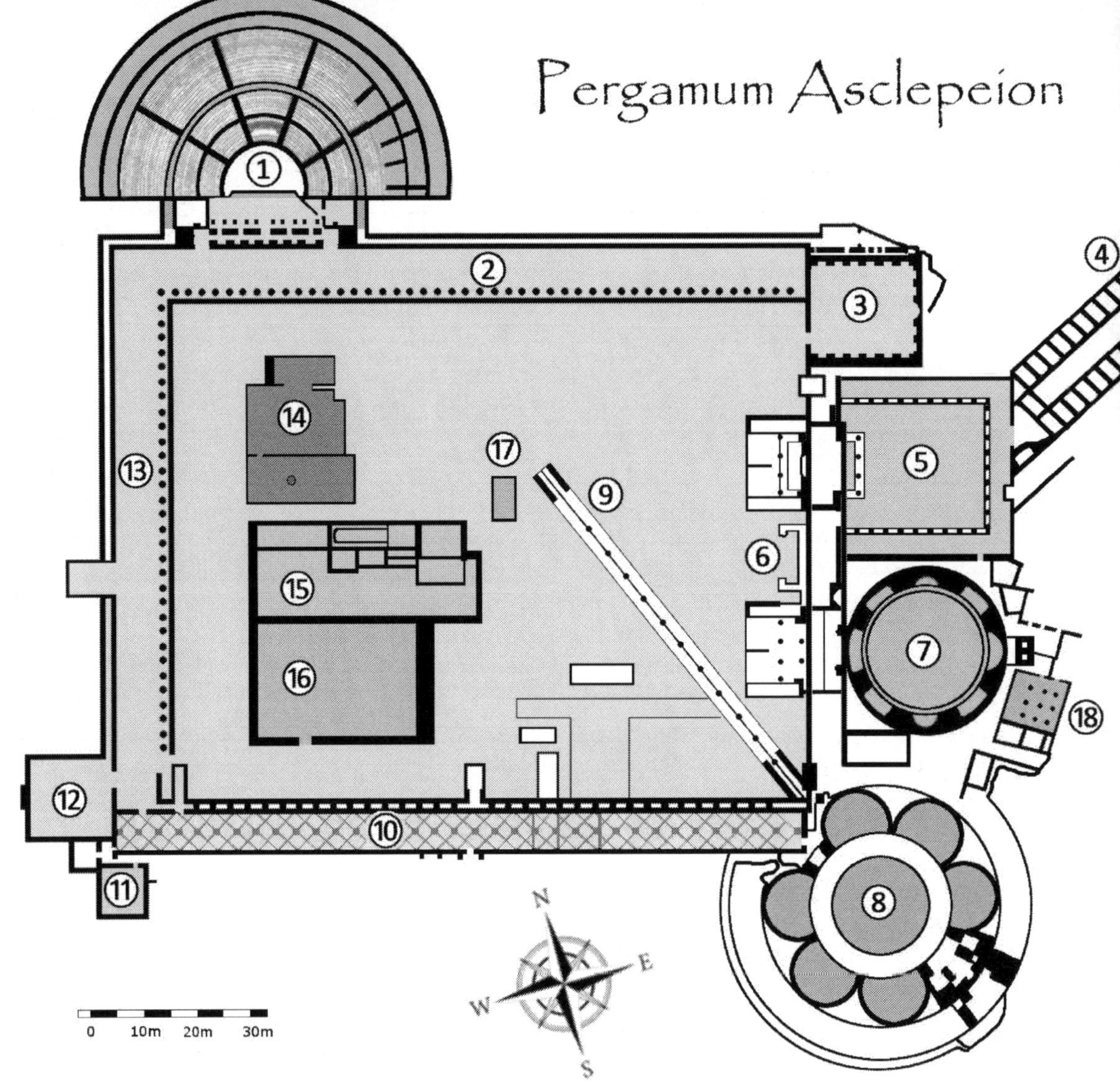

172. The Pergamum Asclepion, the sanctuary of *Asclepios Soter:* 1). Small theater; 2). North Stoa; 3). Small Library; 4). *Via Tecta*, Colonnaded Sacred Way leading to the Acropolis; 5). Propylaeum and Forecourt; 6). Cult niche; 7). Temple of Asclepius; 8). Treatment center; 9). Cryptopoticus, a vaulted underground tunnel; 10). South Stoa; 11). Latrines; 12). Southwest Hall; 13). West Stoa; 14). Hellenistic temple and Sacred Spring; 15 & 16). Incubation complex; 17). Pool; 18). Peristyle House.

Throughout the Graeco-Roman world numerous cities (i.e., Athens, Rome, Corinth, and Cos) had sanctuaries dedicated to the healing god, Asclepius (Ἀσκληπιός, *Asklēpiós;* see Fig. 174). The largest sanctuary was at Epidaurus,[193] Greece. This became the model for the sanctuary at Pergamum (Philostratus *Vit. Apoll.* 4.34), a major center for the cult of Asclepius.[194]

Pausanias states that the Asclepius Soter (savior) cult was introduced to Pergamum in ca.

Churches, 228; Kraft, *Offenbarung*, 64; Ramsay, *Letters: Updated*, 285–86; Esther Onstad, *Courage for Today, Hope for Tomorrow: A Study of the Revelation* (Minneapolis, MN: Augsburg, 1993), 19; Barclay, *Letters*, 42–43.

[193] Lynn R. LiDonnici, *The Epidaurian Miracle Inscriptions*, SFSHJ 36 (Atlanta, Ga.: Scholars Press, 1995); Angeliki Charitonidou, "Epidaurus: The Sanctuary of Asclepius," in *Temples and Sanctuaries of Ancient Greece*, ed. Evi Melas (London: Thames & Hudson, 1973), 89–99.

[194] Lucian *Icar.* 24; Polybius *Hist.* 32.15.1; Galen *Anat. Admin.* 1.2; Aristides *Orat.* 42.4; Statius *Silv.* 3.4.21–25; Philostratus *Vit. Apoll.* 4.34.

350 BC from gratitude by Archias who was cured in the sanctuary of Epidaurus, following a hunting accident (*Descr.* 2.26.7; Aristides *Orat.* 39.5).[195] It reached the height of its popularity in the second cent. AD with a new temple of Zeus Asclepius built as part of the complex by L. Cuspius Pactumenius Rufinus in AD 142 (Aristides *Orat.* 42.6; Galen *Anat. Admin.* 1.2).[196]

The Asclepeion[197] (360 ft. by 425 ft.; see Figs. 170, 172),[198] modeled after the Roman Pantheon,[199] was more like an ancient religious spa with a healing center (hospital) that included a large temple of Asclepius, three small temples (for Asclepius (see Fig. 174), Apollo, and Hygeia, three springs for drinking and bathing, a sacred pool, and an incubation or sleeping room to interpret dreams (Philostratus *Vit. Apoll.* 4.11).[200] They also often included a gymnasium (γυμνάσιον, *gumnasion*),[201] bath, library, and theater (see Fig. 139) as this one did.[202] Visitors to the sanctuary would provide an offering to Asclepius when they were cured, commonly a replica of the body part that was healed.[203] Science and religion were not separated disciplines in the ancient world and they were inseparable in Pergamum.

One of the most famous ancient physicians was Galen (Claudius Galenus, AD 129–ca. 216), who was born in Pergamum and began his medical training there at the early age of sixteen, but after completing his studies in Smyrna, Alexandria and Corinth, returned to Pergamum when he was twenty-eight in order to care for sick and injured gladiators. He was also the court physician for emperors Marcus Aurelius, Commodus, and Septimius Severus, spending several years in Rome.[204] His systematic medical work formed the basis of western medicine.[205]

Aelius Aristides (AD 117/129–189), a hypochondriac, also spent two years in the Asclepeion for treatment of his ailments and described his experience in his *Sacred Tales*.[206] Patients were examined at the main gate and if there was no treatment for their illness they were

---

[195] Emma Jeannette Levy Edelstein and Ludwig Edelstein, *Asclepius: A Collection and Interpretation of the Testimonies* (Baltimore, MD: Johns Hopkins Press, 1998), 2:249.

[196] Akurgal, *Ancient Civilizations*, 105; Behr, *Aelius Aristides and the Sacred Tales*, 27–28.

[197] On the archaeology of the Asclepeion see McRay, *Archaeology and the NT*, 270–72; Pfeiffer, *Wycliffe Dictionary of Biblical Archaeology*, 438–40; Machteld J. Mellink, "Archaeology in Asia Minor," *AJA* 81, no. 3 (1977): 289–321; Oskar Ziegenaus and Gioia De Luca, *Altertümer von Pergamon* (Leiden: de Gruyter, 1968); Jörg Schäfer, "Pergamon Mysia, Turkey," in *The Princeton Encyclopedia of Classical Sites*, ed. Richard Stillwell, William L. MacDonald, and Marian Holland McAllister (Princeton, N.J.: Princeton University Press, 1976), 688–91.

[198] McRay, *Archaeology and the NT*, 271.

[199] Alexia Petsalis-Diomidis, *Truly Beyond Wonders: Aelius Aristides and the Cult of Asklepios* (Oxford: Oxford University Press, 2010), 194.

[200] Oskar Ziegenaus and Gioia De Luca, *Das Asklepieion*, vol. 1–4, Altertümer von Pergamon 11 (Berlin: Deutsches Archäologisches Institut, 1968); Adolf Hoffmann, "The Roman Remodeling of the Asklepieion," in *Pergamon-Citadel of the Gods: Archaeological Record, Literary Description, and Religious Development*, ed. Helmut Koester (Harrisburg, PA: Trinity Press International, 1998), 41–61.

[201] Three gymnasium were present in Pergamum on three levels, each dedicated to a different group: Young men (*neoi*), adolescents (*epheboi*), and little boys (*paides*). Fikret K. Yegül, "The Bath-Gymnasium Complex in Asia Minor During the Imperial Roman Age" (Harvard University, 1975); Roger Chambers, "Greek Athletics and the Jews: 165 BC–AD 70" (Miami University, 1980).

[202] For other reconstructions of the Asclepeion, see Michael J. Vickers, *The Roman World*, 2nd ed., The Making of the Past (New York: Peter Bedrick Books, 1989), 124; Karl Kerényi, *Asklepios: Archetypal Image of the Physician's Existence* (Princeton, NJ: Princeton University Press, 1959), 45.

[203] Examples of these replica body parts are on display in the Bergama and Corinth museums. Gerald David Hart, *Asclepius: The God of Medicine* (New York: Royal Society of Medicine, 2000); Kerényi, *Asklepios*; Edelstein and Edelstein, *Asclepius*.

[204] Vivian Nutton, "The Chronology of Galen's Early Career," *CQ* 23, no. 1 (1973): 158–71; Mattern, *The Prince of Medicine*, 7–35.

[205] John G. Simmons, Doctors and Discoveries: Lives That Created Today's Medicine from Hippocrates to the Present (New York: Houghton Mifflin, 2002), 34–38.

[206] Ido Israelowich, *Society, Medicine and Religion in the Sacred Tales of Aelius Aristides* (Leiden: Brill, 2012); Christopher P. Jones, "Aelius Aristides and the Asklepieion," in *Pergamon-Citadel of the Gods: Archaeological Record, Literary Description, and Religious Development*, ed. Helmut Koester (Harrisburg, PA: Trinity Press International, 1998), 63–76.

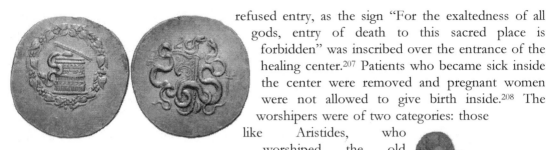

173. Cistophoric Tetradrachm coin from Pergamum (*ca.* 160–150 BC). Obv.: A basket used for housing sacred snakes (Lat. *cista mystica*); all within an ivy wreath. Rev.: A bow-case with serpents; and stylis

Courtesy of CNG (*BMC* 88)

refused entry, as the sign "For the exaltedness of all gods, entry of death to this sacred place is forbidden" was inscribed over the entrance of the healing center.[207] Patients who became sick inside the center were removed and pregnant women were not allowed to give birth inside.[208] The worshipers were of two categories: those like Aristides, who worshiped the old healing deity, and those who preferred to worship the imperial cult, as there was the statue of Hadrian in the cult niche on the western wall (given by Flavia Melitine).[209]

Treatments at the healing center ranged from incantations and magical potions to bloodletting, herbal medicine and ointments, but also included cold water and mud treatments, along with fasting, diet, and exercises one would expect to see at a typical modern-day spa.[210] Based on the presence of bronze and ivory surgical instruments in the Bergama Museum, it is believed that basic surgery was also performed there.[211]

Asclepius

Asclepius was pre-eminently the god of Pergamum (Philostratus *Vit. Apoll.* 4.34). Pausanias speaks of Asclepius (see Fig. 174), "sitting on a seat [θρόνος, *thronos*, throne] grasping a staff; the other hand he is holding above the head of the serpent" (*Descr.* 2.27.2 [Jones]). Asclepius's symbol was two serpents entwined around a staff: the *caduceus* (or *kerykeion*) portrayed on the columns of the Asclepius (see Fig. 171) and the Cistophoric coins (see Fig. 173).[212] The snake and staff are still the symbol of modern medicine.[213] Live snakes were used in the healing process in the cult of Asclepius and permitted to roam freely in the healing center (Plutarch *Mor.* 755f; Homer *Il.* 2.299–

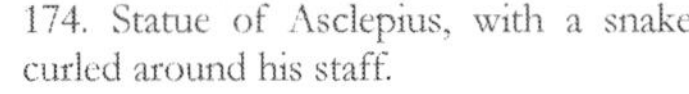

174. Statue of Asclepius, with a snake curled around his staff.

Museum of Epidaurus Theater. Photo by Michael F. Mehnert/Wikimedia Commons. background and shade by David E. Graves

[207] A. Atac, N. Aray, and R. V. Yildirim, "Asclepions in Turkey," *Balkan Military Medical Review* 9, no. 2 (2006): 83.

[208] Walter Addison Jayne, *Healing Gods of Ancient Civilizations* (New Haven, CT: Yale University Press, 1925), 176–85.

[209] Ido Israelowich, *Patients and Healers in the High Roman Empire* (Baltimore, MD: Johns Hopkins University Press, 2015), 114; McDonagh, *Blue Guide: Turkey*, 163.

[210] Jayne, *Healing Gods*, 283–84.

[211] Atac, Aray, and Yildirim, "Asclepions in Turkey," 83; Howard C. Kee, "Self-Definition in the Asclepius Cult," in *Jewish and Christian Self-Definition: Self-Definition in the Graeco-Roman World*, ed. Ben F. Meyer and E. P. Sander, vol. 3 (Philadelphia, PA: Fortress, 1982), 129. Kee argues that only natural/miraculous healing took place at Pergamum due to the absence of surgical instruments, which have been found at other Asclepeion centres in Rhodes and Cyrene.

[212] Ramsay, *Letters: Updated*, 208–11.

[213] Lura Nancy Pedrini and Duilio Thomas Pedrini, *Serpent Imagery and Symbolism: A Study of the Major English Romantic Poets* (New Haven, CT: College and University Press, 1966), 7.

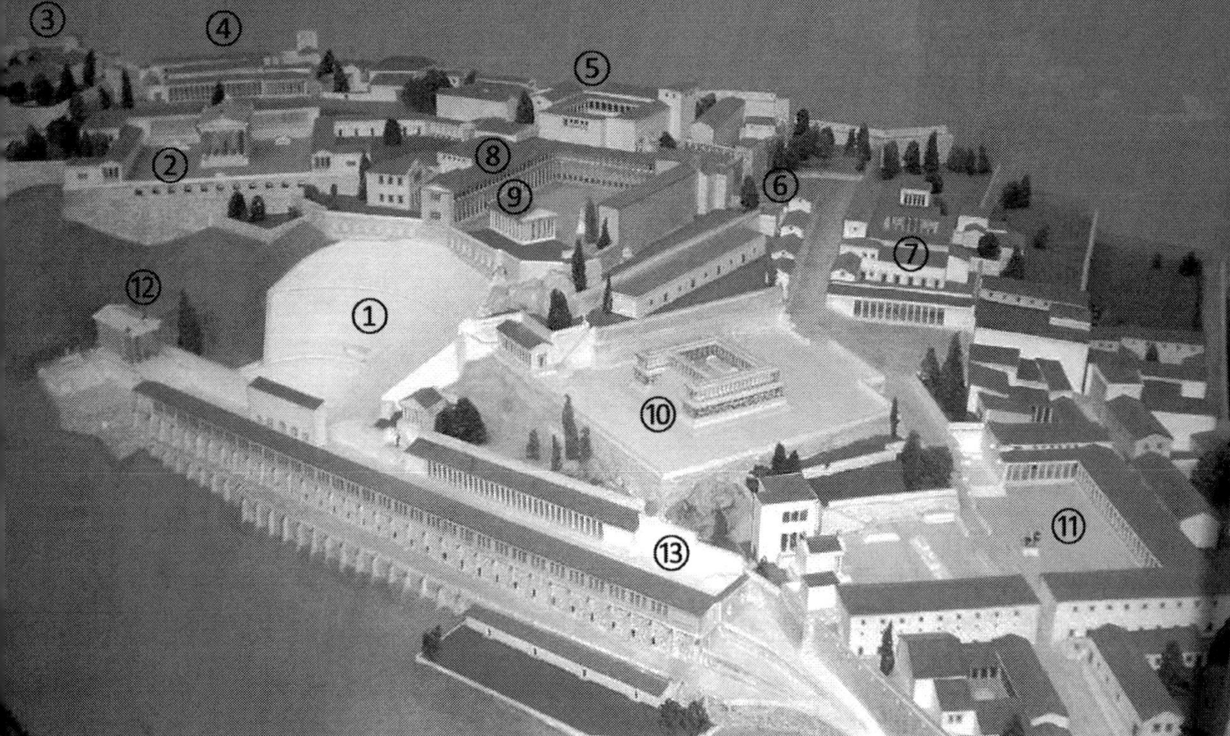

175. A model of the acropolis of the ancient Greek city of Pergamum, showing the situation in the second cent AD, by Hans Schleif (1902–1945). 1). Theater; 2). Trajaneium; 3). Arsenal Terrance; 4). Barraks; 5). Palace; 6). Citadel Gate; 7). Heroon; 8). Library; 9). Athena Temple; 10). Altar of Zeus; 11). Upper agora; 12). Dionysius Temple; 13). Stoa Terrace.

Wladyslaw Sojka with numbers by D. E. Graves / Wikimedia Commons

332).[214]

However, Barclay dismisses these connections, since Laodicea also had a similar connection with Asclepius and the phrase was not used for Laodicea.[215] Although Philostratus points out that Asclepius was pre-eminently the god of Pergamum (*Vit. Apoll.* 4.34), Zeus was worshiped throughout Greece, Macedonia, and Asia Minor (Acts 14:12), and the serpent appears in many other cults in the Roman period, including Dionysus, Demeter, Zeus and others.[216]

The Asclepeion only became prominent in the second cent. AD. Friesen argues that in the late first cent. AD it was hardly the sort of institution where John would have located the throne of Satan. But although the Asclepeion was rebuilt several times and a new temple added in the second cent. AD, it was still a prominent feature from its founding in 350 BC (Pausanias *Descr.* 2.26.7; Aristides *Orat.* 39.5). Also, Barclay reasons that: "the Christians would regard the place where men went to be healed—and often were—with pity rather than with indignation."[217]

The Imperial Cult

With Pergamum hosting imperial cult temples to Augustus, Severus and Trajaneium, many scholars maintain this view,[218] with Hemer noting the "growth of a 'polemical parallelism'

---

[214] See "The Use of Live Snakes in the Worship of Asclepius" in James A. Kelhoffer, *Miracle and Mission: The Authentication of Missionaries and Their Message in the Longer Ending of Mark*, WUNT 112 (Tübingen: Mohr Siebeck, 2000), 369–71; Martin Persson Nilsson, *Geschichte Der Griechischen Religion*, 2nd ed., Handbuch Der Altertumswissenschaft, 5.2 (Munich: Beck, 1955), 2:216–17.

[215] Barclay, *Letters*, 32; Isbon T. Beckwith, *The Apocalypse of John* (New York: MacMillan, 1919), 458. Beckwith points out the Asclepius cult at Epidauros.

[216] Steven J. Friesen, "Myth and Symbolic Resistance in Revelation 13," *JBL* 123 (2004): 218–313; "Satan's Throne," 361.

[217] Barclay, *Revelation*, 1:90; Donald D. Guthrie, *The Relevance of John's Apocalypse* (Exeter, UK: Paternoster, 1987), 76; Worth, Jr., *Greco-Asian Culture*, 135–36.

[218] Zahn, *Offenbarung*, 1:249; Ramsay, *Letters: Updated*, 294–96; Hemer, *Letters to the Seven Churches*, 85, 87, 104; Gordon Franz, "Propaganda, Power and the Perversion of Biblical Truths: Coins Illustrating the Book of Revelation," *BS* 19, no. 3 (2006): 80;

between Christ and Caesar."[219] The temple of Augustus,[220] built in 29 BC to the imperial cult,[221] was one of the first and most important temples built in the province of Asia,[222] with Tacitus stating that it was dedicated to "the divine Augustus and to the city of Rome" (*Ann.* 4.37; *Roma* = whore, Rev 17). But as Hemer reminds us, there was "a prolonged and bitter rivalry between Ephesus, Smyrna and Pergamum"[223] for prominence (πρώτη, *prōtē)* among the province of Asia (Dio Chrysostom *Or.* 34.48). However, Pergamum responded to the challenges around it by achieving the status of *neōkoros* three times and being first (πρώτη, *prōtē)* in each case. It won this status without the addition of an Artemis-cult, as was the case with Ephesus.[224] As Hemer points out: "there are many instructive indications on the coinage of the early years of Roman rule to suggest that Pergamum had a close, though perhaps not exclusive, connection with authority. . . [and] served as a precedent for the cult in other provinces (Tacitus *Ann.* 4.37)"[225]

As the initial capital of Asia under the Romans, Pergamum had a long history of allegiance to the Romans and like Smyrna and Ephesus, it was famed for its worship of the emperor (imperial cult)[226] and was granted the title *neōkoros* (νεωκόρος*)*, as the keeper of the temple (see *The Introduction: Imperial Cult*).[227] As Ramsay points out:

> Here was built the first Asian Temple of the divine Augustus [by the provincial council (κοινόν, *koinon*) of Asia in 29 BC], which for more than forty years was the one centre of the Imperial religion for the whole Province. A second Asian Temple had afterwards been built at Smyrna, and a third at Ephesus; but they were secondary to the original Augustan Temple at Pergamum.[228]

Three temples were dedicated to the imperial cult including Augustus, Trajan, and Severus,[229] granting Pergamum the distinction of three times *neōkoros* (τρίς νεωκόρος, "temple keeper").[230]

The Temple of Augustus

While the temple of Augustus has yet to be identified in excavations,[231] is only known from numismatic records, the ruins of the Trajaneium, not to be confused with the temple of Augustus, can still be seen on the acropolis of the upper city (see Fig. 59). Coins with Augustus's

---

Boring, *Revelation*, 91; Mounce, *Revelation*, 79; Charles, *Revelation*, 1:61; Martin Kiddle, *The Revelation of St. John*, vol. 17, MNTC (London: Hodder & Stoughton, 1952), 30; Swete, *Apocalypse*, 34; Osborne, *Revelation*, 141–43; Barclay, *Letters*, 44–45; Friesen, "Satan's Throne," 366; Brent, *The Imperial Cult*, 178–90; Otto Pfleiderer, *Primitive Christianity: Its Writings and Teachings in Their Historical Connections*, trans. W. Montgomery (London: Williams & Norgate, 1910), 415; Heinrich Schlier, *Principalities and Powers in the New Testament* (New York: Herder & Herder, 1961), 29.

[219] Hemer, *Letters to the Seven Churches*, 87.

[220] Not to be confused with the Trajaneium on the acropolis as Ford and Kraft have done. Ford, *Revelation*, 398; Kraft, *Offenbarung*, 64.

[221] For the background of the Imperial Cult see Graves, *Jesus Speaks to Seven of his Churches: A Commentary*, 57–63.

[222] Ramsay, *Letters: Updated*, 214–15; Ronald Mellor, *Thea Rhōme: The Worship of the Goddess Roma in the Greek World*, Hypomnemata 42 (Göttingen: Vandenhoeck & Ruprecht, 1975), 140–41.

[223] Hemer, *Letters to the Seven Churches*, 84.

[224] Ibid., 237–38 n.36.

[225] Ibid., 84–85.

[226] During the Hellenistic and Roman period, Attalus I and Eumenes II were deified and worshipped in the Heroon as part of the Imperial cult. Tevhit Kekec, *Pergamon* (Istanbul: Hitit Color, 1987), 30.

[227] For a comprehensive treatment of the Imperial Cult in Pergamum from numismatic and epigraphic remains, see chapter 1. Pergamon in Mysia (Augustus) in Burrell, *Neokoroi*, 17–37.

[228] Ramsay, *Letters: Updated*, 215.

[229] Hemer, *Letters to the Seven Churches*, 85, 87, 104; Franz, "Propaganda, Power and the Perversion," 80; Eugene M. Boring, *Revelation* (Louisville, Ky.: Westminster/Knox, 1989), 91; Ramsay, *Letters: Updated*, 215; Mounce, *Revelation*, 79; Charles, *Revelation*, 1:61; Kiddle, *Revelation*, 30; Swete, *Apocalypse*, 34; Osborne, *Revelation*, 141–43; Barclay, *Letters*, 44–45; Aune, *Rev 1–5*, 183–84; Friesen, "Satan's Throne," 366; Brent, *The Imperial Cult*, 178–90; Otto Pfleiderer, *Primitive Christianity: Its Writings and Teachings in Their Historical Connections*, trans. W. Montgomery (London, UK: Williams & Norgate, 1910), 415.

[230] Ramsay, *Letters: Updated*, 207.

[231] Wilson, *Biblical Turkey*, 284.

image on one side and the temple front on the other were minted by Augustus and his successor in the first century. On some of the coins the temple was represented with six columns (hexastyle), while more commonly it had four columns (tetrastyle).[232] Hadrian (r. AD 117–38) was later deified and worshiped in his own temple, which was also depicted on coins.[233]

The Trajaneium

The Trajaneium (Trajan temple, see Fig. 167, 176) in Pergamum was built of white marble and was started under the Roman Emperor Trajan (AD 98–117) but enlarged and completed under Hadrian (AD 117–138). Colossal statues of both emperors have been discovered in the ruins along with a statue of Zeus. who was also worshiped here. The temple extended 68 meters by 58 meters (223 by 190 ft.) with nine Corinthian columns on the two longer sides and six Corinthian columns on the two shorter sides.[234] According to Yamauchi, it was "the most splendid monument erected to Trajan anywhere in Asia."[235]

176. The partially restored Trajaneium in Pergamum.

This peristyle temple, for the worship of the emperor, may have been similar to the temple to Tiberius which was built earlier in Smyrna. If one holds to a late date for the writing of Revelation, then this temple to the emperor Trajan was built shortly after the book was written. The temple was uncovered in the 1880's under the direction of the architect H. Stiller. It was abandoned, but received renewed interest in the 1960's from the Turkish Antiquities and German Archaeological Institute (DAI), who partially reconstructed it (see Fig. 176). Next to the entrance is an inscription from the *dēmos* and *boulē* of Thyatira congratulating Pergamum on the privilege of "becoming the *neokoros* for two imperial cult temples."[236]

But while many scholars support this view, Aune points out that: "While Pergamon did function as one among many important centers for the imperial cult, there is no explicit evidence in 2:12–17 (or in Rev 2–3) to suggest that the imperial cult was a major problem for the Christians of Asia or for the author of the final edition of Revelation."[237]

Also, as Friesen points out, the imperial cult was everywhere in first-century culture, as "Emperors were worshiped in their own temples, at temples of other gods, in theaters, in gymnasia, in stoas, in basilicas, in judicial settings, in private homes and elsewhere."[238] And while Aune is correct that the evidence in Revelation is not explicit, and Freisen's claim is correct that

---

[232] Carol Humphrey Vivian Sutherland, *Coinage in Roman Imperial Policy, 31 B.C.–A.D. 68* (London: Methuen & Company, 1951), 43 (see plate II, coin 4); Magie, *Roman Rule in Asia Minor*, 2:1293 n.15; Warwick Wroth, *A Catalogue of the Greek Coins in the British Museum: Mysia*, ed. Reginald Stuart Poole (London: Quaritch, 1892), 137–38, nos. 236–37 and 252–53.

[233] Magie, *Roman Rule in Asia Minor*, 1:594; Akurgal, *Ancient Civilizations*, 82; Martin J. Price and Bluma L. Trell, *Coins and Their Cities: Architecture on the Ancient Coins of Greece, Rome, and Palestine* (Detroit, MI: Wayne State University Press, 1977), 16. Price and Trell provide a view of the temple from the coins of Pergamum.

[234] Fant and Reddish, *Guide to Biblical Sites*, 289.

[235] Yamauchi, *NT Cities*, 42.

[236] Wilson, *Biblical Turkey*, 285.

[237] Aune, *Rev 1–5*, 183; Friesen, "Satan's Throne," 366.

[238] Friesen, "Satan's Throne," 363; Steven J. Friesen, *Imperial Cults and the Apocalypse of John: Reading Revelation in the Ruins* (Oxford: Oxford University Press, 2001), 123–131.

"Pergamum was not the center of imperial cults in Asia,"[239] others have demonstrated the threat of the imperial cult to the Christian community and the polemics which followed in Pergamum were implicit and real.[240]

Conclusion

These suggestions cannot individually be connected with "Satan's throne", but in combination[241] they provide support for the use of this statement, understanding Pergamum as the Roman "seat of special authority"[242] and the "*Roman opposition* to early Christianity."[243] Friesen prefers to represent Satan's throne as the "local hostility toward the Pergamene assembly."[244] Certainly, the Christian's aversion to calling Zeus and Asclepius θεός Σωτήρ (*theos sōtēr*, God Savior), along with the serpent–the Christian symbol for Satan (Gen 3:1–4; Rev 12:9)–depicted on the structures and statues of the cult (see Figs. 173, 171, 174); combined with temples of the Imperial Cult to Augustus, Severus, and Trajan,[245] and the seat of the proconsul's power (Lat. *ius gladii*, right of the sword) being centerd in Pergamum; would altogether justify calling Pergamum the "throne of Satan." Pergamum was celebrated as the first (πρώτη, *prōtē*) *neōkoros* (temple keeper) on three separate occasions, setting it apart from other cities as an important center of the imperial cult and seat (βῆμα, *bēma*) of Roman rule. [246]

While some or all of these elements were present in other cities, it was the sheer scale and concentration of them here at Pergamum that justified John in identifying this place as Satan's throne, the very place where Satan lived.[247] While the proconsul carried the right of the sword (Lat. *ius gladii*), Christ wields the 'sharp two-edged sword' (Rev 2:13) of authority and would "fight against them with the sword" (Rev 2:16) of his mouth (Rev 1:16), if they did not repent. The suzerain knew that, from a Christian perspective, Pergamum was a concentrated center of demonic activity, and it was this activity that elicited John's harsh comment.[248] Christ praises their faithfulness to his name; faithfulness despite the martyrdom of Antipas (Rev 2:13), but rebukes them for allowing in false teachers (those compromising with the current culture). A Messianic banquet awaits the overcomers.

---

[239] Friesen, "Satan's Throne," 362.

[240] Price, *Rituals and Power*, 155–65, 221–22; Harland, "Imperial Cults within Local Cultural Life," 85–107; Friesen, *Imperial Cults*; "Satan's Throne," 351–73; Kraybill, *Imperial Cult and Commerce in John's Apocalypse*; *Apocalypse and Allegiance*; Naylor, "The Roman Imperial Cult and Revelation," 207–39; Beale, *The Book of Revelation*, 246–47; Kistemaker, *Revelation*, 129 n.41.

[241] Pfleiderer, *Primitive Christianity*, 415; Johnson, *Triumph of the Lamb*, 75–76.

[242] Barclay, *Letters*, 35.

[243] Aune, *Rev 1–5*, 184.

[244] Friesen, "Satan's Throne," 365.

[245] Hemer, *Letters to the Seven Churches*, 85, 87, 104; Aune, *Rev 1–5*, 183–84; Barclay, *Letters*, 44–45; Charles, *Revelation*, 1:61; Mounce, *Revelation*, 79.

[246] Collins, *Crisis and Catharsis*, 101–2; Charles, *Revelation*, 1:60–61; Hemer, *Letters to the Seven Churches*, 82–84; Ramsay, *Letters: Updated*, 289; Tait, *Messages to the Seven Churches*, 225–26; Farrer, *Revelation*, 73; William M. Ramsay, "Pergamus or Pergamum," in *DBib*, 3:750.

[247] Thomas, *Rev 1–7*, 179–80.

[248] Caird, *Revelation*, 37; Hugh Martin, *The Seven Letters* (Philadelphia, PA: Westminster, 1956), 69; Wood, "Local Knowledge," 264; Johnson, *Triumph of the Lamb*, 440.

177. Ruins of the Byzantine bascilica of Thyatira.
Photo by Klaus-Peter Simon/ Wikimedia Commons

Thyatira (Rev 2:18–29)

Thyatira[249] (modern *Akhişar*) is located between Pergamum and Sardis in Lydia or Mysia (Strabo *Geogr.* 13.4). During the first and second-century, Thyatira belonged to the region (Lat. *conventus*) of Pergamum[250] within the Roman province of Asia, with an approximate population of 25,000 citizens.[251] Hemer points out that: "the longest and most difficult of the seven letters is addressed to the least known, least important and least remarkable of the cities. The letter was not, I think, obscure to the church in Thyatira, the problem lies in our remoteness from the contemporary facts."[252] It is difficult for the modern reader to find local references in this message, although scholars have pointed out a few possibilities.

Trade Guilds

Trade guilds[253] flourished in Thyatira, especially from the textile industry, contributing to its economic growth as a manufacturing center.[254] There were textile guild associations in such trades as dyers (βαφεῖς, *bapheis*; Lat. *lanarii carminatores*[255]), linen weavers (λινουργοί, *linourgoi)*,[256] wool workers (λανάριοι; *lanarioi;* Lat. *lanarius*),[257] and clothes cleaners or fullers (γναφέις, *gnapheis*; Lat. *lanarii purgatories, SEG* 40.1045; *CIG* 3480).[258] Guilds involved in leather included, tanners (βυρσεῖς, *byrseis*),[259] leather cutters or shoemakers (σκυτοτόμοι, *skytotomoi*).[260] Other guild

---

[249] E. L. Hicks, "Inscriptions from Thyatira," *The Classical Review* 3, no. 3 (1889): 136–38; William M. Ramsay, *The Letters to Seven Churches of Asia and Their Place in the Plan of the Apocalypse* (London: Hodder & Stoughton, 1904), 324–35; Colin J. Hemer, *The Letters to the Seven Churches of Asia in Their Local Setting*, The Biblical Resource Series (Grand Rapids: Eerdmans, 2001), 106–128; Otto F. A. Meinardus, "The Christian Remains of the Seven Churches of the Apocalypse," *BA* 37, no. 3 (September 1, 1974): 76–78; Graves, *Jesus Speaks to Seven of his Churches: A Commentary*, 276–324.

[250] Jones, *The Greek City*, 83; Mounce, *Revelation*, 84.

[251] Graves, *Jesus Speaks to Seven of his Churches: A Commentary*, 279–81.

[252] Hemer, *Letters to the Seven Churches*, 106.

[253] For more details on trade guilds in Asia Minor, see *External Problems.*

[254] Flohr recently cautions making broad conclutions from small samples of inscritpions has stated that "the situation at Thyatira, where we have ten inscriptions of three occupational groups, is comparable: here, it is dyers rather than linen-workers that happen to be over-represented, but the evidence again is too haphazard to allow for any credible reconstruction of the city's textile economy." Miko Flohr, "Textiles, Trade and the Urban Economies of Roman Asia Minor," in *Wirtschaft Als Machtbasis: Beiträge Zur Rekonstruktion Vormoderner Wirtschaftssysteme in Anatolien*, ed. Katja Piesker, BYZAS 22 (Istanbul: Ege Yayinlari, 2016), 28.

[255] *I.Thyat.* 935; 945; 972; 989; *CIG* 3422, 3496, 3497. For the meaning of *lanarii*, see Suzanne Dixon, *Childhood, Class and Kin in the Roman World* (New York, N.Y.: Routledge, 2005), 216 n.12. and see "Working in Wool and Working for Status?" in Jonathan S. Perry, "Sub-Elites," in *A Companion to Roman Italy*, ed. Alison E. Cooley, Blackwell Companions to the Ancient World (New York, N.Y.: John Wiley & Sons, 2016), 498–512.

[256] *I.Thyat.* 933 = *IGR* 4.1226 = PHI 264363.

[257] *IGR* 4:1252 = *AGRW* 141 = PHI 264450; *I.Thyat.* 933; 1019; *CIG* 3504.

[258] Perry, "Sub-Elites," 498–512.

[259] *I.Thyat.* 986 = *CIG* 3499 = *IGR* 4.1216 = PHI 264416.

[260] *SEG* 41.1033 = PHI 277547; *I.Thyat.* 1002 = *AGRW* 131 = *IGR* 4.1169 = PHI 264433. Jones, *Cities of the Eastern Roman Provinces*, 83–84; Philip A. Harland, *Associations, Synagogues, and Congregations: Claiming a Place in Ancient Mediterranean Society*, 2nd ed. (Kitchener, Ont.: Harland, 2011), 86 n.45.

associations included coppersmiths ([χα]λκεῖς χαλκοτύποι, *chalkeis chalkotypoi*; *I.Thyat.* 936 = *IGR* 4.1259), blacksmiths (σιδηρουργός, *sidērourgos*),[261] potters (κεραμεῖς, *kerameis*),[262] and others.[263] While we may liken them to modern "trade unions," they were involved in both industry and religion. The city deity, Apollo Tyrimnaeus, the patron of the guilds, was celebrated with feasts and religious activities.[264] The purple dyers guilds were operated by an executive council (Lat. *proedria;* Hierapolis ἐργατηγοί, *ergatēgoi;* Thyatira ἐπιστάται, *epistatai; CIG* 3926),[265] who elected an annual president.[266]

Wilson reports on two inscriptions from Laodicea located on separate marble bases (AD 218–22) and states: "The inscriptions still show the prominence of trade guilds in the city. The last line of each indicates that one was sponsored by the fullers (ΟΙ ΓΝΑΦΕΙΣ; *oi gnapheis*), the other by the wool workers (ΟΙ ΛΑΝΑΡΙΟΙ; *oi lanarioi*)."[267]

It must be noted that the proliferation of guilds in Thyatira was like that of many other cities of the time and this city should not be singled out as a community where the trade associations pressured Christians to join, as some commentators have done,[268] as though this was exceptional for Thyatira.[269] This was an issue that Christians faced in many first-century cities in Asia Minor, since guilds have been documented in many cities. Elaborate guild halls have been uncovered at Ostia and Ephesus.[270] There is also inscriptional evidence of the presence of guilds in Phrygian Hierapolis (dyers *CIJ* 2.36);[271] Pergamum (dyers? *IGR* 4.425); Smyrna (silversmiths and goldsmith *CIG* 3154; *IGR* 4.1427); Ephesus (money changers *SEG* 4.541; dyers[272]); Philadelphia (wool workers, *IGR* 4. 1632); and Methylene (fullers *IG XII* 2.271; leather workers, *IG XII* 2.109).[273] However, for whatever reason, there does appear to be a large concentration of guilds in Thyatira. And as Keener points out "social pressures for Christians to accommodate the worship of Graeco-Roman deities would have come from various sources, not only from associations."[274]

The Roman province of Lydia and especially the city of Thyatira was famous for its

---

[261] Jean Pierre Waltzing, *Étude historique sur les corporations professionnelles chez les Romains depuis les origines jusqu'à la chute de l'Empire d'Occident*, vol. 3 (Louvain: Peeters, 1895), 3:59, no. 163.

[262] *I.Thyat.* 914 = *CIG* 3485 = *IGR* 4.1205 = PHI 264344), bakers (ἀρτοκόποι, *artokopoi*; *AGRW* 138 = *IGR* 4.1244 = *I.Thyat.* 966; *CIG* 3495.

[263] Craig R. Koester, *Revelation: A New Translation with Introduction and Commentary*, ed. John J. Collins, AYBC 38A (New Haven, Conn.: Yale University Press, 2014), 295–96.

[264] Hemer, *Letters to the Seven Churches*, 109.

[265] Ramsay, *Cities and Bishoprics*, 1:106.

[266] Jones, *Cities of the Eastern Roman Provinces*, 84.

[267] Wilson, *Biblical Turkey*, 321.

[268] Ramsay, *Letters: Updated*, 238; Charles, *Revelation*, 1:68; Mounce, *Revelation*, 87; Osborne, *Revelation*, 156–57; Leslie N. Pollard, "The Function of *loipos* in Contexts of Judgment and Salvation in the Book of Revelation" (Ph.D., Andrews University, 2007), 288–90; Pamela Thimmes, "Women Reading Women in the Apocalypse: Reading Scenario 1, the Letter to Thyatira (Rev. 2:18–29)," *CBR* 2, no. 1 (2003): 139.

[269] T. R. S. Broughton, "Roman Asia Minor," in *An Economic Survey of Ancient Rome: Africa, Syria, Greece, Asia Minor*, ed. Tenney Frank, vol. 4, 5 vols. (Baltimore, MD: John Hopkins University Press, 1975), 4:841–44; cf. 819, 824–25, 830; Harland, *Associations, Synagogues, and Congregations*, 39–40; Koester, *Revelation*, 295–96.

[270] Russell Meiggs, *Roman Ostia* (Oxford: Clarendon Press, 1973), 67–71.

[271] Philip A. Harland, "Acculturation and Identity in the Diaspora: A Jewish Family and 'Pagan' Guilds at Hierapolis," *JJS* 57, no. 2 (2006): 222–44.

[272] Elisabeth Trinkl, "Artifacts Related to Preparation of Wool and Textile Processing Found inside the Terrace Houses of Ephesus, Turkey," in *Ancient Textiles: Production, Craft and Society*, ed. Carole Gillis and Marie-Louise B. Nosch, Ancient Textile Series 1 (Oxford: Oxbow, 2007), 81–86.

[273] Hemer, "Unto the Angels of the Churches," 110; Broughton, "Roman Asia Minor," 2:841–44; J. Nelson Kraybill, *Imperial Cult and Commerce in John's Apocalypse*, JSNTSup 132 (Sheffield, UK: Sheffield Academic, 1999): 111 n.49; Magie, *Roman Rule in Asia Minor*, 1:48; 2:812 n. 78; Jones, *Cities of the Eastern Roman Provinces*, 83.

[274] Koester, *Revelation*, 295–96.

178. The two types of shellfish found in the western Mediterranean which produce small amounts of purple used for the dyeing of textiles (Pliny *Nat Hist.* 9.61). The *hexaplex trunculus* produces a red or violet purple (*left*), while the *haustellum brandaris* produces a blue purple (*right*).

Photos by (*left*) Dezidor and *right*) M. Violante/Wikimedia Commons

clothing industry (Homer *Il.* 4.141–42)[275] and essential to this was the dyeing process and the prominent role that the dyers guild played in city associations.[276] Calpino estimated that "of the 103 inscriptions that contain references to purple trade (πορφύρα *porphura*), twenty-nine percent 29% are from Asia Minor,"[277] and many of these were from Thyatira. Fifteen of the twenty-eight inscriptions from Thyatira are related to the trade of purple-dyers (πορφυροβαφεῖα *porphurobapheia*),[278] although no inscriptions from Thyatira mention πορφυροβαφεῖα (*porphurobapheia*), "purple dyers," but only βαφεῖς (*bapheis*, "dyers").[279] More than half of the inscriptions (32/53) from Thyatira and the area of Saittai pertain to the textile industry.[280]

Reimer rightly notes that Thyatira was known for more than purple goods (*purpurarii*), and likely produced a wide range of dyed products[281] in a variety of colours.[282]

Lydia, The Seller of Purple

The importance of the dyers guild is highlighted by the NT reference to Lydia,[283] one of Paul's

---

[275] Pliny the Elder claims it was invented in Sardis (*Nat.* 7.56.195).

[276] Harland, *Associations, Synagogues, and Congregations*, 121–29; Magie, *Roman Rule in Asia Minor*, 1:48; 2:812 n. 80; Trinkl, "Artifacts Related to Preparation of Wool and Textile Processing Found inside the Terrace Houses of Ephesus, Turkey," 81–86. There is also evidence of the dyers guild in Phrygian Hierapolis (*CIJ* 2.36) and Ephesus (see Trinkl).

[277] Teresa J. Calpino, "Lydia of Thyatira's Call," in *Women, Work and Leadership in Acts* (Tübingen: Mohr Siebeck, 2014), 199 n.81.

[278] Tullia Ritti, "Associazioni di mestiere a Hierapolis di Frigia," in *Viaggi e commerci nell'antichità*, ed. Bianca Maria Giannattasio (Geneva: Università di Genova, Facoltà di Lettere, 1995), 71–72.

[279] Deborah Ruscillo, "Reconstructing Murex Royal Purple and Biblical Blue in the Aegean," in *Archaeomalacology: Molluscs in Former Environments of Human Behaviour*, ed. Daniella Bar-Yosef Mayer (Oxford: Oxbow, 2005), 100.

[280] Ilias Arnaoutoglou, "Hierapolis and Its Professional Associations: A Comparative Analysis," in *Urban Craftsmen and Traders in the Roman World*, ed. Andrew Wilson and Miko Flohr (Oxford: Oxford University Press, 2016), 282.

[281] Ivoni Richter Reimer, *Women in the Acts of Apostles: A Feminist Liberation Perspective* (Minneapolis, MN: Fortress, 1995), 99–100.

[282] Reimer notes that *CIG* 3496 and 3497 do not specifically make mention of purple goods.

[283] Hemers suggested that her name is likely an ethnic cognomen, "The Lydian woman" (*TAM III* 661). Attested in the first century not only as a slave but also a women of high social prestige. i.e., Julia Lydia Laterane of Ephesus, high priestess and daughter of Asia (*SEG* 28) and Julia Lydia of Sardis. Louis Robert, "Documents d'Asie Mineure," *BCH* 101, no. 1 (1977): 43–132; Hemer, *The Book of Acts in the Setting of Hellenistic History*, 114 n.32.

179. Workers putting up clothes for drying. Roman fresco from the *fullonica* (dyer's shop) of Veranius Hypsaeus in Pompeii.

Museo Archeologico Nazionale. Photo by Wolfgang Rieger/Wikimedia Commons

first converts in Asia (Acts 16:14–15, 40), who lived in Philippi as a πορφυρόπωλις (*porphuropōlis*), widely translated as a seller of purple (πορφύρα, *porphura*; Lat. *purpurarius/a*) cloth, but who probably learned her textile business (*IGR* 4.1252; *CIG* 3496–8 [λανάριοι, *lanarii carminatores*,[284] dyers]) in Thyatira.[285] The textile industry contributed greatly to Thyatira's prosperity. Menippus of Thyatira, was also of the *collegia* of purple-dyers (πορφυροβάφ, *porphuropobaph*), selling purple goods in Thessalonica[286] but originally came from Thyatira (Acts 16:14–15, 40). It is known that women were involved in the purple dye trade from an inscription where the term "purple dealers" is in the feminine form (*CIG* 2519).

Porphyrology[287] has a long history, with much written[288] on the production of purple dye in ancient times.[289] It is not the intention to repeat it here.[290] The archaeological indicators of the purple-dye industry include purple stained containers, crushed murex shells in large quantities or in occupational strata, burnt organic matter, and various equipment such as vats, cisterns, crushing and perforating tools.[291] There may also be weaving instruments such as loom weights and spinning apparatus nearby. The archaeological and literary evidence indicate that the most prestigious purple dye, "Tyrian Purple", was derived from the Mollusk shellfish (see Fig. 178) which flourished along the Mediterranean coast (Pliny *Nat.* 35.26.45) [292] and was extracted in specialized workshops (Lat.

---

[284] Inscriptional references to λανάριοι (*lanrioi*) include *AE* (1993): 1028a; (1909): 11a; (1946): 210; (1971) 49; (1987): 443; (1995): 146; (2001): 865; (2010): 326; *CIL* 5.4501; 5.4504; 5.4505; 6.9489; 6.9490; 6.9491; 6.9492; 6.9493; 6.9494; 6.9669; 6.31898; 6.33869; 6.38869; 9.826; 9.2226; 10.5678; 11.741; 11.862; 11.1031; 11.5835; 11.6367; 12.4480; 12.4481; *I.Eph.* 4.1387; 2.454; 3.727; *TAM V* 1.85; 2.1019.

[285] Magie, *Roman Rule in Asia Minor*, 1:47–48; 2:812 n.79; Keener, *Acts: 15:1–23:35*, 3:3:2399–2407.

[286] *IG* X 2.1 291 = PHI 137473; Istanbul Museum cat. no. 271. Hemer claims "that this term is not known otherwise from Thyatira," but this inscription would qualify as another. Hemer, *Letters to the Seven Churches*, 109.

[287] Rabbi Isaac Herzog coined the term Porphyrology (the study of purple) in his 1913 doctoral dissertation on the subject of Hebrew Porphyrology. Isaac Herzog, "Semitic Porphyrology (The Dyeing of Purple in Ancient Israel) I: Tekhelet" (D. Litt. diss., University of London, 1919).

[288] Ehud Spanier, Nira Karmon, and Elisha Linder, "Bibliography Concerning Various Aspects of the Purple Dye," *Levantina* 37 (1982): 437–47.

[289] H. F. Heinisch, "Ancient Purple, an Historical Survey," *Fibre Engineering and Chemistry, Great Britain* 18, no. 6 (1957): 203–6; Lloyd B. Jensen, "Royal Purple of Tyre," *JNES* 22 (1963): 104–18.

[290] For an overview see Graves, *Jesus Speaks to Seven of His Churches: A Commentary*, 290–96; "What Is the Madder with Lydia's Purple? A Re-Examination of the Purpurarii in Thyatira and Philippi," *NEASB* 62 (2017): 3–29.

[291] Maria Emanuela Alberti, "Murex Shells as Raw Material: The Purple-Dye Industry and Its By-Products. Interpreting the Archaeological Record," *Kaskal* 5 (2008): 75–76.

[292] For a general list of Mediterranean coastal purple dye centres, see Liza Cleland, Glenys Davies, and Karen Stears, eds., *Colour in the Ancient Mediterranean World*, BARI 1267 (Oxford: John and Erica Hedges, 2004).

tinctoria),[293] before being sold to local craftsmen. It is also worth noting that several of the sites are inland from the coast.

Joshel suggests that most individuals both produced and sold purple goods from the same fullers' shop (*fullonica*[294]).[295] However, this is challenged by Hughes who provided new research, derived from inscriptional evidence, that the shops in Vicus (where Pubius Clodius Philonicus' wife Eurania was carrying out her business of *Purpuranii*) were not suitable for producing these goods.[296] She argued that the odor[297] and size of the location needed to carry out the dyeing process[298] making it impossible to have had the manufacturing shop located in Vicus. Also, Hughes demonstrated from an examination of the literary, epigraphic, and archaeological evidence of *purpurarii* in Rome, that "members of their *familia* could produce or sell a number of goods, other than textile, from their workshops,"[299] including foodstuffs, dye and pigments for paints (Pliny *Nat.* 36.26.45; Vitruvius *Arch.* 7.13.2–3).

Similarly, Lydia was probably selling a variety of purple goods in Philippi that were manufactured elsewhere. If she was producing the purple products in Philippi, then she would probably have owned a fairly large installation which was well ventilated,[300] although a small number of sites have demonstrated that the production of purple dye was "carried out on a small-scale by households."[301] This suggests that Lydia likely did not dye her goods in Philippi unless at home, but rather her purple cloth was doubtless imported from a dyeing facility, perhaps from Thessalonica near Philippi.[302] However, Philippi was only 7.75 miles (12.5 km) from the coast and she could easily have transported the murex shells, used to collect purple dye, overland,[303] so the use of murex dye did not require that the facility be close to the coast.[304]

Traditionally scholars have claimed that the textiles sold in Thyatira by *purpurarius*, such as Lydia, were made from the famous and expensive "Tyrian Purple" derived from several varieties of the *murex*[305] shellfish.[306] More recent commentators, led by William Ramsay and Colin Hemer,

[293] Graves, "What Is The Madder With Lydia's Purple?," 6–7.

[294] The Fullonica of Stephanus, or *Fullonica Stephani*, that is situated on the south side of the Via dell'Abbondanza is the only laundry (*fullonica*) in Pompeii. Only 103 Murex shell were discovered in Pompeii leading to a variety of opinions on the dyeing capabilities. See David S. Reese, "Marine Invertebrates, Freshwater Shells, and Land Snails: Evidence from Specimens Mosaics, Wall Paintings, Sculputure, Jewelry, and Roman Authors," in *The Natural History of Pompeii*, ed. Wilhelmina Feemster Jashemski and Frederick G. Meyer (Cambridge, UK: Cambridge University Press, 2002), 296–98.

[295] S. R. Joshel, *Work, Identity and Legal Status at Rome: A Study of the Occupational Inscriptions* (Norman, OK: University of Oklahoma Press, 1992), 71.

[296] Lisa Hughes, "Dyeing in Ancient Italy? Evidence for the Purpurarii," in *Ancient Textiles: Production, Craft and Society*, ed. Carole Gillis and Marie-Louise B. Nosch (Oxford: Oxbow Books, 2007), 89.

[297] Robert J. Forbes, *Studies in Ancient Technology* (Leiden: Brill, 1993), 4:119; B. Bartosiewicz, "'There's Something Rotten in the State . . .': Bad Smells in Antiquity," *European Journal of Archaeology* 6, no. 2 (2003): 175–95.

[298] J. P. Wild, *Textile Manufacture in the Northern Roman Provinces*, CamCS (Cambridge, UK: Cambridge University Press, 1970), 82.

[299] Hughes, "Dyeing in Ancient Italy," 82.

[300] Ibid., 88; S. G. Schmid, "Decline or Prosperity at Roman Eretria? Industry, Purple Dye Works, Public Buildings, and Gravestones," *JRA* 12 (1999): 275–78.

[301] Cornelia Becker, "Did the People in Ayios Mamas Produce Purple Dye during the Middle Bronze Age? Considerations on the Prehistoric Production of Purple-Dye in the Mediterranean," in *Animals and Man in the Past*, ed. Hijlke Buitenhuis and Wietschke Prummel (Groningen: Rijksuniversiteit, 2001), 123. For example the small scale facility at the Middle Bronze Age tell Ayios Mamas in Greece.

[302] Keener, *Background Commentary: NT*, 370.

[303] This is confirmed by a vessel from the hill of "El Molinete" in Carthago Nova, Spain that contained an early Roman jar with 3 kg of crushed shells including *murex trunculus*, *murex thais*, and *murex brandaris*. David S. Reese, "The Industrial Exploitation of Murex Shells: Purple-Dye and Lime Production at Sidi Khrebish, Benghazi (Berenice)," *Libyan Studies* 11 (1980): 86.

[304] Graves, "What Is The Madder With Lydia's Purple?," 1–47.

[305] The term "murex" is used here in a broad sense to indicate the molluscs that produce purple dye.

[306] Richard C. H. Lenski, *The Interpretation of the Acts of the Apostles*, CNT (Minneapolis, Minn.: Augsburg Fortress, 1961), 656–57; Keener, *Background Commentary: NT*, 370; F. F Bruce, *Paul, Apostle of the Heart Set Free* (Grand Rapids: Eerdmans, 2000), 220. Horsley assumes that the government has a monopoly over the "royal" purple. However, this was only introduced late in the Roman Empire

based on the research of French scholar Michel Clerc, have challenged this view,[307] as articulated by Ramsay's claim that

> the dyeing in Thyatira was performed in ancient times with madder-root, *[rubia peregrina L.* that also grew in the region of western Anatolia and used today in the region to dye carpets*]*. . . , [and that] the purple stuffs which the Thyatiran Lydia sold in Philippi (Acts 16:14) was dyed with what is, in modern times, called 'Turkey red'.[308]

Hemer also points to Strabo who testifies that "the water at Hierapolis is remarkably adapted also to the dyeing of wool, so that wool dyed with the roots [madder roots] rivals that dyed with the coccus [kermes] or with the marine purple [murex]. And the supply of water is so abundant that the city is full of natural baths" (*Geogr.* 13.4.14 [Jones]).[309]

The argument is also made that the "Tyrian Purple" dye could not have been used at Thyatira, because of the assumption that the dyeing facilities must be housed on the coast (Pliny *Nat.* 35.26.45) to take advantage of the marine supply of murex shellfish.[310] This old view is refuted by new research presented in an artilce by the author.[311]

Lydia Used Various Dyes

Graves argues that various textiles were dyed using different methods and dye combinations, depending on the color, quality and value. More expensive dyes, such as purple, allowed for more expensive clothes, while more economical dyes provided for less expensive textiles. The diverse purple dyed product line formulated from the various shades of purple provided a wide range of priced textiles to meet the demand in the local and general economy.[312] While it is possible that madder alone was used to dye textiles purple in Laodicea or Philippi, it is more likely that both madder and murex, along with other ingredients, were used to provide a wide selection of variously priced textiles, as trade routes ensured murex shellfish did reach inland.[313]

Thus, it is fair to argue that Lydia likely did not deal in just one type of dye or method, but used a combination of dyes to participate in the competitive market of her day. Given the everyday use of togas and tunics, with purple *clavi,* in Roman society, along with the more specialty groups, such as the Jewish and military community in Philippi that used purple garments, Lydia would have had a market for a wide price range of products to offer her customers. There seems little doubt that she would have either employed or purchased textiles,

---

(Horsley, "The Purple Trade and the Status of Lydia of Thyatira," *NewDocs* 2:28). Keener states in the *IVP Bible Background Commentary* (1993) that the dye was "procured from the murex shellfish near Tyre, but in Macedonia it could have been procured from the mollusks near Thessalonica" (1993: Acts 16:15). However, in the newer edition (1994) Keener adds "Thyatiran purple often came from the madder plant, not the more expensive Tyrian shellfish" (*IVP Bible Background Commentary* 1994:370). Keener holds to this updated view in his *Acts Commentary* (2013, 2:2396).

[307] Michel Armand Edgar Anatole Clerc, *De rebus Thyatirenorum commentatio epigraphica* (Paris: Picard, 1893), 93; Ramsay, *Letters: Updated*, 238–39; Hemer, "Unto the Angels of the Churches," 114; *Letters to the Seven Churches*, 109; Mounce, *Revelation*, 85 n.4; Bradley B. Blue, "Acts and the House Church," in *Graeco-Roman Setting*, ed. David W. J. Gill and Conrad H. Gempf, BAFCS 2 (Eugene, OR: Wipf & Stock, 2000), 186 n.258; Worth, Jr., *Greco-Asian Culture*, 289 n.44; Steven M. Baugh et al., *Zondervan Illustrated Bible Backgrounds Commentary Set*, ed. Clinton E. Arnold (Santa Rosa, CA: Zondervan, 2002), 27; Yamauchi, *NT Cities*, 54; Blaiklock, "Thyatira," in ZPEB 5:854; Eckhard J. Schnabel, *Acts*, ed. Clinton E. Arnold, ZECNT 5 (Grand Rapids, Mich.: Zondervan, 2012), 680; Keener, *Acts: 3:1–14:28*, 2:2:2396.

[308] Banks, "Thyatira," in *ISBE2* 2977–78; Ramsay, "Thyatira," in *DBib* 4:759. In his commentary on *CIG* 3496, Waltzing mentions Lydia's profession (Acts 16:14) and comments "La *teinture rouge* de Thyatire était renommée [the red dye of Thyatira was famous]" (emphasis added). Waltzing, *Étude historique*, 3:3:57.

[309] Hemer, *Letters to the Seven Churches*, 109.

[310] E. J. W. Barber, *Prehistoric Textiles: The Development of Cloth in the Neolithic and Bronze Ages with Special Reference to the Aegean* (Princeton, NJ: Princeton University Press, 1991), 228–29.

[311] Graves, "What Is The Madder With Lydia's Purple?," 1–47.

[312] Meyer Reinhold, *History of Purple as a Status Symbol in Antiquity*, 116 (Brussels: Latomus, 1970).

[313] Graves, "What Is The Madder With Lydia's Purple?", 1–47.

dyed from both madder as well as murex, to meet the demands of her clients. To insist that her products were only madder dyed seems to argue against the evidence.

It seems likely that Lydia was a wealthy woman who learned her trade in Thyatira, and moved to Philippi to carry on her business. She most likely not only dealt in purple textiles, made from madder root, but also from the murex shellfish, since there was a demand from many in Roman Society for a diverse quality purple cloth. The murex raw materials were available inland (Philippi is just 7.75 miles [12.5 km] from the coast) and less complicated to produce than madder dye.

180. This white stone pillar at Pergamum with names inscribed on it reminds us of Jesus' words: "And to the angel of the church in Pergamum write:... I will give him a white stone, with a new name written on the stone that no one knows except the one who receives it." (Rev 2:12, 17).

Other Possible Local References

In the second chapter of Revelation verse 18, Christ is identified from chapter one (Rev 1:15; compare Dan 10:6) with feet like burnished bronze, a reference which can possibly be identified as a copper-zinc produced by a special distillation process, familiar to the local bronze guild.[314] Caird believes that the bronze imagery of Christ is also contrasted with the depiction of Apollo Tyrimnaeus on their coins (*IGR* 4:1259).[315]

The church at Thyatira is reprimanded for tolerating "that woman Jezebel, who calls herself a prophetess and is teaching and seducing my servants to practice sexual immorality and to eat food sacrificed to idols" (Rev 2:20). This reference is identified with the practices of immorality and idolatry in the trade-guilds.[316] The parallel between Jezebel's seduction of Israel from her worship of Yahweh through syncretism with Baal (2 Kgs 9:22), and the first-century potential for syncretism with the Imperial Cult is striking.[317] Based on an inscription (*CIG* 2: no. 3509) Schürer identifies Jezebel as Sibyl Sambathe (a local femal prophetess), whose shrine was "before the city."[318] Ramsay remarks that this theory is "as yet a mere tantalising possibility"[319] while Charles and Beckwith reject it, because the sibylline priestess would not be a church member.[320] Hemer on the other hand, argues, "this view deserves consideration."[321] The immoral practices of the trade-guilds are

---

314 Kiddle, *Revelation*, 37; Caird, *Revelation*, 43.

315 Caird, *Revelation*, 43.

316 Ramsay, *The Letters to Seven Churches*, 346–49; Kiddle, *Revelation*, 17:39; Charles, *Revelation*, 1:70–71; Hemer, *Letters to the Seven Churches*, 128.

317 Caird, *Revelation*, 44–45.

318 Emil Schürer, *Die Prophetin Isabel in Thyatira, Offen. Joh., II, 20, 11.*, ed. A. V. Harnack, Theologische Abhandlungen: Carl von Weizsäcker Zu Seinem Siebzigsten Geburtstage (Freiburg, Germany: Mohr Siebeck, 1892), 39–58.

319 Ramsay, *The Letters to Seven Churches*, 323.

320 Charles, *Revelation*, 1:70; Beckwith, *Apocalypse*, 466.

321 Hemer, *Letters to the Seven Churches*, 117.

identified with some in the church of Thyatira who were committing adultery (Rev 2:22),[322] and as such were to experience death (spiritual and physical), like the Corinthian Christians who were also involved in immorality (1 Cor 11:30).

The bed (couch) of suffering (Rev 2:22; Exod 21:18) they were to experience for their immorality is contrasted with the bed of adultery and couch of the banquet hall. Jezebel's couch of pleasures would be turned into a bed of suffering if they did not repent.

The reference to the deep secrets (Rev 2:24) of Satan could very well be a veiled reference to the secret knowledge of the Gnostics, who believed in the liberty to sin in the body, holding that it would not affect their spiritual state (cf. 1 Cor 6:12–18).

The overcomers in Thyatira are promised authority to rule "over the nations" (cf. Ps 2:9), and given the "morning Star" (Rev 2:26–28; See also Num 24:17; *T. Levi* 18:3; *T. Jud.* 24:1; cf. 2 Pet 1:19). In the ancient mind the "morning star" carried regal connotations and was associated with the planet Venus, which was symbolized as the bull in the zodiac and proudly displayed on the Roman legion's standards.[323] There is a contrast between the Roman idea of "morning star" and the Messianic Jewish belief of a coming king.

---

[322] Barclay, *Letters*, 61; William Hendriksen, *More than Conquerors* (Grand Rapids: Baker, 1982), 71.
[323] Wilson, *Revelation*, 28.

Sardis (Rev 3:1–6)

181. The Bath-gymnasium complex at Sardis (second cent. AD), late section dates to the early third cent. AD.

Sardis (modern *Sart*) was the capital of the kingdom of Lydia (680–547 BC), and exercised its power for over 1,500 years through the Alexandrian, Persian, Seleusid, and Roman empires. In the first century it had a population of between 50,000 and 80,000 citizens[324] and was a major fortified city (over 115 hectares about 290 acres/1,150 dunams). Strategically located sixty miles east of Smyrna with an acropolis rising 1,500 feet on top of Mount Tmolus, it overlooked the fertile Hermus plain (see Fig. 125).[325] Due to its location, fertile soil, gold deposits and textile industry (Pliny *Nat.* 33.66; Philostratus *Vit. Apoll.* 6.37), Sardis became a wealthy and self-sufficient city.

Of all the seven cities, Sardis' acropolis was the best protected, having a vertical rock face on three sides which formed a naturally defensible citadel. Mitten points out that due to erosion, the acropolis is about one-third its original size[326] and several major structures lie outside the city walls.[327] The lower city included, among other buildings, the impressive gymnasium, temple of Artemis and large Beth Alpha Synagogue.

The main archaeological work at Sardis was carried out by the American Society for the Excavation of Sardis, under the direction of Howard Crosby Butler of Princeton University, in 1910–1914 and 1922; and by the Archaeological Exploration of Sardis, directed by George M. A. Hanfmann of Harvard University, from 1958 to the present.[328]

The Jewish synagogue

The synagogue (called Beth Alpha), discovered in 1961, was originally part of the north wing of the Palaestra, or Marble Hall, of the Bath Complex. However, in the late third cent. AD it was given to the Jewish community (*synodos;* Josephus *Ant.* 14.259–61), isolated from the Palaestra, and renovated as a large synagogue (see Figs. 184 no. 2, 182, 183).[329] Its importance is characterized by its large size (262 ft./80 m long), capable of holding a congregation of a thousand people, and prominent location on the main street.[330] The building went through at least four stages of renovation.[331]

---

[324] Graves, *Jesus Speaks to Seven of his Churches: A Commentary*, 333–35.

[325] Mounce, *Revelation*, 92; Aune, *Revelation 1-5*, 218.

[326] David Gordon Mitten, "A New Look at Ancient Sardis," *BA* 29, no. 3 (1966): 55.

[327] George M. A. Hanfmann and Jane C. Waldbaum, *A Survey of Sardis and the Major Monuments Outside the City Walls* (Cambridge, MA: Harvard University Press, 1975).

[328] George M. A. Hanfmann, Nelson Glueck, and Jane C. Waldbaum, *New Excavations at Sardis and Some Problems of Western Anatolian Archaeology* (High Wycomb: University Microfilms, 1975); for a bibliography, see George M. A. Hanfmann, William E. Mierse, and Clive Foss, eds., *Sardis from Prehistoric to Roman Times: Results of the Archaeological Exploration of Sardis, 1958-1975* (Cambridge, MA: Harvard University Press, 1983), xvii–xxxv.

[329] Yegül, *Bath-Gymnasium Complex*, 5.

[330] Lee I. Levine, "Synagogues," in *EDEJ*, 1264.

[331] Andrew R. Seager, "The Building History of the Sardis Synagogue," *AJA* 76 (1972): 425–35.

182. The *bema* of the third cent. AD synagogue in Sardis (modern Turkey), which was used as the reading platform in the synagogue. Some believe that the lion statues and the eagles carved on both sides of the altar (table) are evidence of syncretism to appease the Roman authorities.

Stage 1: Originally after the AD 17 earthquake the structure served as a dressing room or lecture hall with three rooms extended from the Gymnasium complex.[332]

Stage 2: Between AD 150–250[333] it was transformed into a civic basilica[334] and perhaps turned over to the Jewish community during this time in gratitude for their assistance in rebuilding the city following the earthquake of AD 17.[335]

Stage 3: The first use of the building as a Jewish synagogue (AD ca. 170–250).[336]

Stage 4: Renovations carried out in the eastern end of the building provided a colonnaded entrance court (Forecourt, 20 m. long) and porch, separated from the long assembly hall (Main Hall, 60 m. long; AD 350–400).[337]

The large table or altar was decorated with two large Roman eagles on each of its stone legs (second cent. BC–first cent. AD; see Fig. 182),[338] leading some to speculate that the Jews were involved in a kind of syncretism to appease the Roman authorities.[339] Two lion statues (5–fourth cent. BC), the symbol of the city and its goddess, were also located in the synagogue and may originally have been set beside a Cybele statue (or Tyche, Τύχη). Within the Jewish context, they would have symbolized the tribe of Judah (Gen 49:9). The central nave of the main hall was divided into two side aisles from two rows of pillars. On the western wall, there were two niches used as Torah shrines (*aediculae*) for the storage of the Torah scrolls.[340]

A Greek inscription refers to the Torah shrine as the *nomophulákion*, or "the place that protects the Torah."[341] The congregation stood or used wooden benches or sat on the floor. It

---

[332] On the date of construction, see Ibid.; Marcus Rautman, "Sardis in Late Antiquity," in *Archaeology and the Cities of Late Antiquity in Asia Minor*, ed. Ortwin Dally and Christopher Ratté (Ann Arbor, Mich.: Kelsey Museum of Archaeology, 2012), 1–26; Jodi Magness, "The Date of the Sardis Synagogue in Light of the Numismatic Evidence," *AJA* 109 (2005): 443–75.

[333] Only the synagogues of Masada and Delos are older. E. Mary Smallwood, *The Jews Under Roman Rule: From Pompey to Diocletian: A Study in Political Relations*, SJLA 20 (Leiden: Brill, 1981), 509 n.16.

[334] Fatih Cimok, *Guide To The Seven Churches* (Istanbul: Tuttle, 1999), 81.

[335] Shemuel Safrai, M. Stern, and David Flusser, *The Jewish People in the First Century: Historical Geography, Political History, Social, Cultural and Religious Life and Institutions* (Assen, Netherlands: Uitgeverij Van Gorcum, 1974), 479.

[336] Yegül, *Bath-Gymnasium Complex*, 5.

[337] George M. A. Hanfmann, Letters from Sardis (Cambridge, MA: Harvard University Press, 1972), 323; Andrew Ramage, Crawford H. Greenewalt, Jr., and Faruk Akca, "The Fourteenth Campaign at Sardis (1971)," *BASOR*, no. 206 (1972): 37–39; A. Thomas Kraabel, "Impact of the Discovery of the Sardis Synagogue," in *Sardis from Prehistoric to Roman Times: Results of the Archaeological Exploration of Sardis, 1958-1975*, ed. George M. A. Hanfmann, William E. Mierse, and Clive Foss (Cambridge, MA: Harvard University Press, 1983), 168.

[338] The altar eagles at synagogue in Sardis have been replaced by replicas to protect them from vandalism. The originals now stand outside flanking the doorway of the permanently closed Manisa Archaeological Museum as mere decorations.

[339] Mitten, "A New Look at Ancient Sardis," 51–52; Hemer, *Letters to the Seven Churches*, 137.

[340] Levine, "Synagogues," in *EDEJ*, 1265.

[341] Steven Fine, *Art and Judaism in the Greco-Roman World: Toward a New Jewish Archaeology*, Revised (Cambridge, UK: Cambridge University Press, 2010), 126.

was elaborately decorated with a beautiful mosaic floor[342] and marble panels (*skoutlōsis*) on the lower portion of the walls[343] and inlaid marble with geometric shapes on the upper portion, similar to the floor of the Herodian Second Temple complex in Jerusalem.[344] A menorah (*heptamyxion* "seven-branched lampstand") plaque, flanked by a *shofar* and *lulab* with a scrolled Torah, was carved into the main *aediculae* (see Fig. 183). The remains of some nineteen menorahs have been discovered etched on various materials.[345] Eighty-five Jewish dedicatory inscriptions in the mosaics and on the wall, two in Hebrew, have been recovered during excavations of the structure, indicating that the members of the Jewish community were wealthy. Eight men are identified as members of the city council.[346] A rare Hebrew inscription mentions the word "shalom."[347] In the center of the mosaic is the inscription mentioning "Samoe, *hiereus* [priest] and *sophodidaskalos* [wise teacher or teacher of wisdom]."[348] Another Greek inscription found near the synagogue entrance directed the Jews to "Find, open, read, observe" the commands (*phylaxon,* observe) of God.[349]

183. The Torah shrine (*aediculae*) that would have housed the copy of the Torah used in worship in the synagogue.

The synagogue held a prominent place within the city of Sardis with twenty-seven Byzantine shops (AD 400) constructed along the south-eastern wall of the synagogue on the main avenue of the city, which were also used in earlier periods.[350] Six of the shops were occupied by Jews, identified by menorahs etched in their walls, and ten were used by Christians, identified by crosses. Even though the Jewish people were enmeshed in the daily activities of Sardis they managed to maintain their own customs and religion.

The main archaeological work at Sardis has been carried out by the American Society for the Excavation of Sardis, under the direction of Howard Crosby Butler of Princeton University, in 1910–1914 and 1922; and by the Archaeological Exploration of Sardis, directed by George M.

---

342 On the resetting of the mosaic floor of the Synagogue see the report from Greenewalt. Ramage, Greenewalt, Jr., and Akca, "The Fourteenth Campaign at Sardis (1971)," 20–23.

343 Levine, "Synagogues," in *EDEJ*, 1264–65.

344 Daniel K. Eisenbud, "Archaeologists Restore Ancient Tiles from Second Temple in Jerusalem," *The Jerusalem Post*, September 6, 2016, 1, http://www.jpost.com/Israel-News/Archeologists-restore-tiles-from-Second-Temple-in-Jerusalem-467021. See also http://www.nrg.co.il/online/1/ART2/823/143.html.

345 George M. A. Hanfmann, G. F. Swift, and Crawford H. Greenewalt, Jr., "The Ninth Campaign at Sardis (1966)," *BASOR*, no. 187 (1966): 27; Yigal Shiloh, "Torah Scrolls and the Menorah Plaque from Sardis," *IEJ* 18, no. 1 (1968): 54–57; Steven Fine and Leonard Victor Rutgers, "New Light on Judaism in Asia Minor During Late Antiquity: Two Recently Identified Inscribed Menorahs," *JSQ* 3, no. 1 (1996): 12, 15.

346 Marianne Palmer Bonz, "Differing Approaches to Religious Benefaction: The Late Third-Cent. Acquisition of the Sardis Synagogue," *HTR* 86 (1993): 139–54; Hanfmann, *Letters from Sardis*, 119; Levine, "Synagogues," in *EDEJ*, 1265.

347 Frank Moore Cross, "The Hebrew Inscriptions from Sardis," *HTR* 95, no. 1 (2002): 8–10.

348 A. Thomas Kraabel, "The Diaspora Synagogue: Archaeological and Epigraphic Evidence since Sukenik," in *ANRW*, ed. Wolfgang Haase and Hildegard Temporini, 2.19 (Berlin: de Gruyter, 1979), 486; Louis H. Feldman, *Studies in Hellenistic Judaism* (Leiden: Brill, 1996), 588, 600; Levine, "Synagogues," in *EDEJ*, 1265.

349 Fine, *Art and Judaism*, 126.

350 J. Stephens Crawford, *The Byzantine Shops at Sardis*, AESM 9 (Cambridge, Mass.: Harvard University Press, 1990).

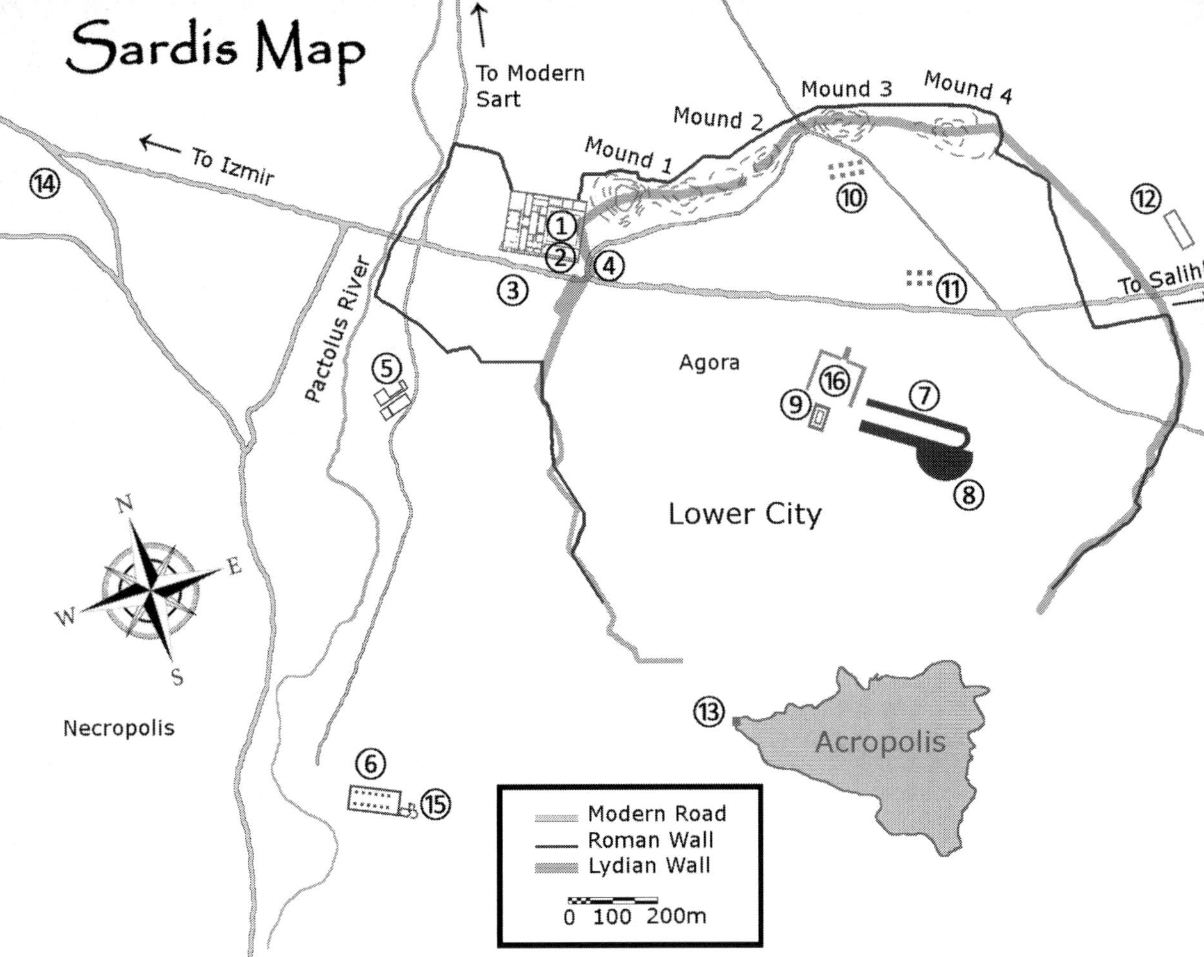

184. Urban plan of the city of Sardis. 1). Bath-Gymnasium; 2). Synagogue; 3). Byzantine Shops; 4). Lydian Gate; 5). Cybele Altar, Lydian Gold Refinery and Byzantine Churches; 6). Temple of Artemis; 7). Stadium; 8). Theater; 9). Temple of the Imperial Cult; 10). Temple?; 11). Temple?; 12). Bath; 13). Tower; 14). Sanctuary of Demeter; 15). Byzantine church; 16). Terrace.

A. Hanfmann of Harvard University and Cornell University, from 1958 to the present.[351]

The church at Sardis received the severest reprimand of the seven messages for accommodating its pagan surroundings. Caird refers to it as "a perfect model of inoffensive Christianity."[352] Christ, perceiving the true condition of their hearts, states that they had a reputation of being alive, but that in actual fact they were dead (Rev 3:1). The city was in fact already declining by the first-century. The possible allusion to the city's history would have a more powerful impact in Smyrna than in the other churches.

The Acropolis

The imperatives "be watchful" (Rev 3:2 KJV) and "I will come like a thief, and you will not know at what hour I will come against you" (Rev 3:3) are understood against the history of the acropolis, during which twice (Cyrus in 549 BC and Antiochus III in 195 BC), Sardis fell to its

[351] George M. A. Hanfmann and Jane C. Waldbaum, "New Excavations at Sardis and Some Problems of Western Anatolian Archaeology," in *Near Eastern Archaeology in the Twentieth Century: Essays in Honor of Nelson Glueck*, ed. James A. Sanders (Garden City, NY: Doubleday, 1970), 307–26; for a bibliography, see George M. A. Hanfmann, William E. Mierse, and Clive Foss, eds., *Sardis from Prehistoric to Roman Times: Results of the Archaeological Exploration of Sardis, 1958–1975* (Cambridge, MA: Harvard University Press, 1983), xvii–xxxv.

[352] Caird, *Revelation*, 48.

185. The Temple of Artemis in Sardis (330 BC). The scrolled (Ionic) capitals on the top of the columns add to the beauty of this temple. However, because these capitals were never fluted, it indicates the temple was never finished. The small red brick building in the foreground is a fourth cent. AD Byzantine church. The acropolis of the city is visible on the mountain in the distance. The only remains visible on the summit are Byzantine structures.

enemies as a result of a lack of vigilance by the defenders of Sardis.[353] In both cases, the wall to the city was breached while the city slept.

In 549 BC, Cyrus sent one of his soldiers up the vertical cliff to find an entry point, and in 195 BC, Lagoras of Crete led fifteen men up to the same spot to breach the wall and open the city gates from the inside. It became proverbial in the literature of the day to speak of Sardis' overconfidence, pride and arrogance (Lucian *Merc. Cond.* 13).[354] Mitten believes that the words could be understood against the history of four sudden earthquakes in twelve years (AD 17–29), with the words speaking of the suddenness of these events.[355] Sardis was hit by a major earthquake in AD 17 which destroyed most of the city (Tacitus *Ann.* 2.47; Pliny *Nat.* 2.86.200), but was rebuilt with financial aid from Tiberius and Claudius (Strabo *Geogr.* 13.4.8). There is little doubt that this warning of Christ's sudden coming to the Sardinian's in judgment (contrast with the second coming in 1 Thess 5:2 and 2 Pet 3:10), would have more relevance to Sardis than to other cities.

---

[353] Wood, "Local Knowledge," 264; Worth, Jr., *Greco-Asian Culture*, 184–88; Mounce, *Revelation*, 93; Caird, *Revelation*, 47.

[354] Mounce, *Revelation*, 94; T. Scott Daniels, *Seven Deadly Spirits: The Message of Revelation's Letters for Today's Church* (Grand Rapids: Baker Academic, 2009), 92.

[355] Mitten, "A New Look at Ancient Sardis," 61.

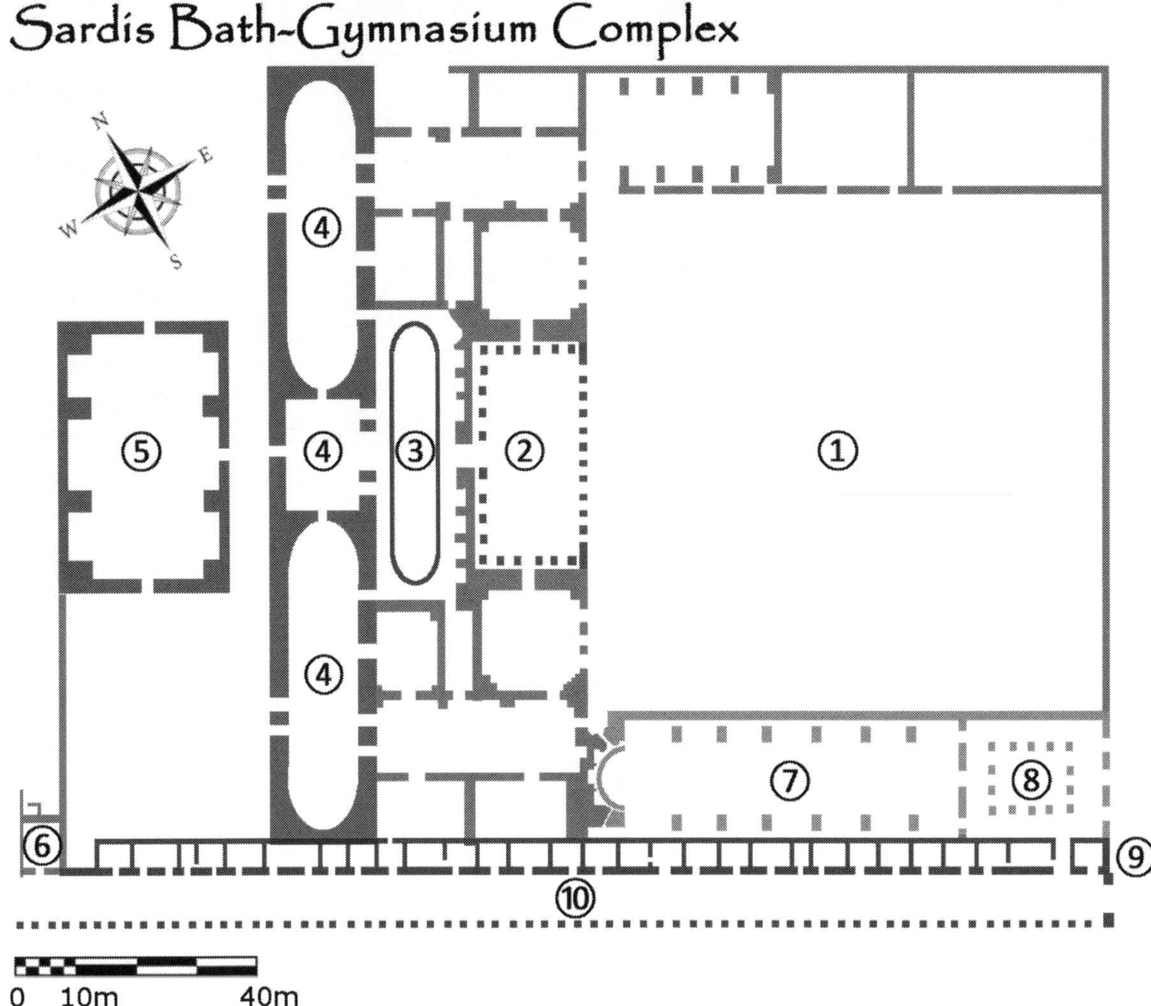

186. Floor plan of the Bath-Gymnasium Complex at Sardis. 1). Palaestra; 2). Marble courtyard; 3). Frigidarium; 4). Tepidarium; 5). Caldarium; 6). Latrine; 7). Synagogue; 8). Forecourt; 9). Twenty-seven Byzantine shops; 10). Marble road.

There were a few in Sardis who had not compromised or had "not soiled their garments, and they will walk with me in white, for they are worthy. The one who conquers will be clothed thus in white garments" (Rev 3:4–5). For a city preoccupied with the dying of cloth in their textile industry, and the woolen trade,[356] as was Laodicea (Rev 3:18), the obvious focus on clothing in verses 4 and 5 is curious. Hemer suggests that the reference to the textile industry is less clear here than in the Laodicea passage.[357] White garments were proper attire for worship,[358] feasts,[359] and the Gymnasium.[360] Some commentators see a specific reference to the practice of the wearing of white for baptismal candidates, or by the members of the Essene community.[361]

There is no doubt that white garments are used to depict moral purity (Dan 7:9; 10:5; Matt 17:2) while soiled garments represent defilement (Zec 3:1–3). In the apocryphal story "the

---

[356] James Moffatt, *The Revelation of St. John the Divine*, ed. W. Robertson Nicoll, Expositor's Greek Testament 5 (London: Hodder & Stoughton, 1910), 365; Ford, *Revelation*, 410; Johnson, *Triumph of the Lamb*, 54.

[357] Moffatt, *Revelation*, 365; Ford, *Revelation*, 410; Johnson, *Triumph of the Lamb*, 54.

[358] Ramsay, *The Letters to Seven Churches*, 386; Ford, *Revelation*, 409; Johnson, *Triumph of the Lamb*, 55.

[359] Blaiklock, *Cities of the New Testament*, 117; Meinardus, *St. John of Patmos*, 106; Ramsay, *The Letters to Seven Churches*, 386.

[360] Kelshaw, *Send This Message*, 133–34.

[361] Martin, *The Seven Letters*, 90–91; Adela Yarbro Collins, *The Apocalypse*, New Testament Message: A Biblical-Theological Commentary Series (Wilmington, Del.: Michael Glazier, Inc., 1979), 25; Guthrie, *The Relevance of John's Apocalypse*, 80.

Shepherd of Hermas," the faithful are also rewarded with white clothing (Herm. *Vis.* 4.2:1; *Sim.* 8.2:3).

To the overcomer from Sardis, three promises were given, including: 1) they will be dressed in white (cf. Rev 6:11; 7:9, 13–14); 2) their names will not be blotted from the book of life (cf. Rev 20:15; 21:27); and 3) they will be acknowledged by Christ before God (cf. Matt 10:32). Citizens in Greek cities had their names written in the public registry, while convicted criminals had their names blotted from the registry (Dio Chrysostom *Rhod.* 31.84; Xenophon *Hell.* 2.3.51). For the overcomer, citizenship in the heavenly city is secured and the final sentence in the heavenly courtroom will reflect our relationship with Christ (Rev 3:5).

187. Byzantine Church of St. John, Alaşehir, Turkey.

Photo by Simon Jenkins/Wikimedia Commons

Philadelphia (Rev 3:7–13)

Philadelphia[362] (modern *Alaşehir*) is about thirty miles east-south-east of Sardis on the eastern end of the fertile valley at the foot of the Tmolus mountains (Pliny *Nat.* 5.30; 14.9). This city is the newest of all the seven cities, founded sometime between 189–138 BC, possibly by Attalus II of Pergamum (159–138 BC). The name of the city means "brotherly love," coming from the love between Attalus II and his brother (Polybius *Hist.* 30:1–3; 31:1; 32:1). The population in the second cent. AD has been estimated—based on "analogies" with other parts of the Roman Empire—to be about 10,000[363] or a bit higher.[364] It is impossible to calculate the population based on area since the ancient city of Philadelphia has been encroached by the modern city of *Alaşehir.*[365] Due to the frequent earthquakes and tremors, the population always remained small, as many chose to live outside the city on agricultural farms (Strabo *Geogr.* 12.8.18; 13.4.10). The population was a mixture of Lydian and Mysian citizens along with Roman and Macedonian business people (*I.Phil.* 1423; 1455).

Earthquake Prone Area

Given the agricultural productivity (grapes; celebrated by the chief cult of the city, the cult of Dionysus), and strategic location as the "gateway to the east", the city prospered.[366] However, the downside was that the region was prone to seismic (volcanic and earthquake) activity which produced numerous cracks in the city walls and resulted in few residents actually living in the city for fear of devastation (Strabo *Geogr.* 12.8.18; 13.4.10). Their fear was justified because in AD 17 twelve cities, including Philadelphia, were leveled by a devastating earthquake (Tacitus *Ann.* 2.47; Pliny *Nat.* 2.86.200). With the help of Emperor Tiberius, the city was rebuilt; and in gratitude the city added Neocaesareia to its name, and later added the name Flavia (wife of Vespasian, AD 69–79), as is attested to on its coins.[367] Having lived in a city that had already undergone two name changes, notification that a third permanent name change would take place (Rev 3:12) would certainly have grabbed the attention of the Christians resident in Philadelphia.[368]

---

[362] Hemer, "Unto the Angels of the Churches," 4–27, 56–83, 110–35, 164–90; Franz, "Propaganda, Power and the Perversion," 73–87; William M. Ramsay, *The Letters to Seven Churches: Updated Edition*, ed. Mark W. Wilson (Peabody, MA: Hendrickson, 1994).

[363] J. C. Russell, *Late Ancient and Medieval Population*, APSP (Philadelphia, PA: American Philosophical Society, 1958), 80.

[364] Worth, Jr., *Greco-Asian Culture*, 194, 302 n.2.

[365] Hanson, "Urban System."

[366] Mounce, *Revelation*, 98.

[367] Ibid., 99.

[368] Aune, *Revelation 1-5*, 244.

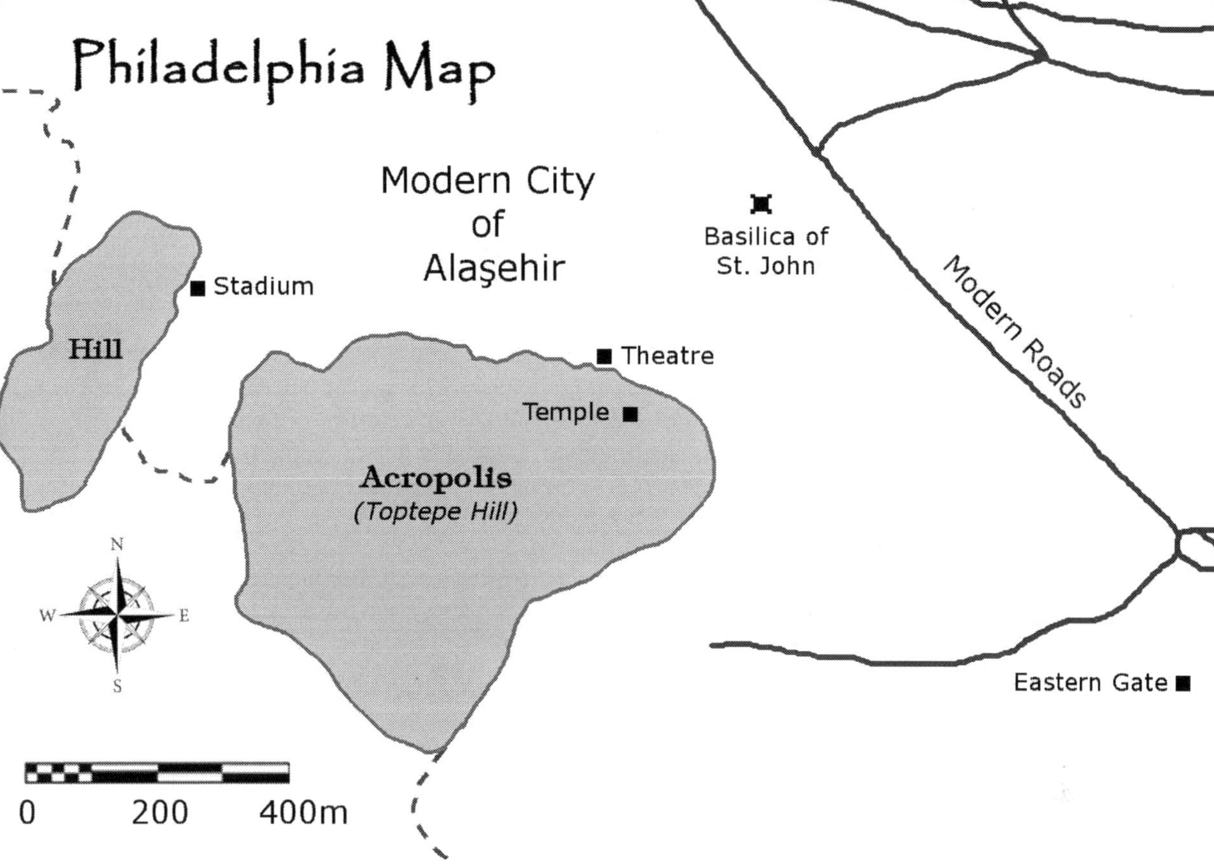

188. Urban plan of the city of Philadelphia (modern *Alaşehir*).

Since the ancient site is covered by the modern city of Philadelphia, it has never been excavated and few ancient artifacts remain.[369] The message in Revelation is the earliest mention of Christian churches, although literary references state that Ignatius of Antioch briefly stayed here while being escorted under guard to Rome in AD 110. Ignatius later wrote to the church in Philadelphia, referring to the church leadership and the influence of Judaizers (Ign. *Phld.* 6.1–3). In AD 155, eleven Philadelphian Christians were martyred along with Polycarp, bishop of Smyrna (*Mart. Pol.* 19.1).

A structural theme is prominent in the message to Philadelphia with references to doors, keys, temples, and pillars. These elements of a building's structure would be susceptible to earthquake damage and would register with the Philadelphian Christians.

The reference to the open door (Rev 3:8; cf. Col 4:3) may be a veiled reference to the closed door represented by the excommunication of Christians from Jewish synagogues (cf. John 9:22; 12:42; 16:2), formalized in the Jewish Council of Jamnia[370] in AD 90.[371] Rather than being an open door to evangelism, the reference is likely to contrast the Christians being kicked out of synagogues with the welcome they will receive into heaven, the door of which "no one is able to shut" (Rev 3:8). Together with Smyrna, Philadelphia is not reprimanded for their conduct, but praised throughout and warned of the coming suffering from the "synagogue of Satan." Because the Philadelphian church has endured patiently (Rev 3:10), they can be called overcomers, and as such are promised "a pillar in the temple of my God. Never shall he go out

[369] Ibid., 234.

[370] Jack P. Lewis, "Jamnia (Jabneh), Councel of," in *ABD*, 3:634–37.

[371] William Horbury, "The Benediction of the Minim and Early Jewish-Christian Controversy," *JTS* 33 (1982): 19–61; Wilson, *Revelation*, 32.

of it" (Rev 3:12). This may be an allusion to the temple pillars and the stability that was necessary for a city plagued by earthquakes to have.[372] Wilson, describing the ability of the temple to withstand earthquakes, states that: "their foundations were laid on beds of charcoal covered with fleeces, which caused the structure to 'float' on the soil like a raft. Each block was joined to another by metal cramps, so the platform was a unity."[373] This would make the temple the most secure building in the city (Pliny *Nat.* 36.95; cf. 1 Tim 3:15; Gal 2:9).

Several commentators understand the phrase "never shall he go out of it [the Temple]" (Rev 3:12) against the background of the city's evacuation following the earthquakes in AD 17 and 23 (Strabo *Geogr.* 12.8.18; 13.4.10).[374] As the Philadelphian Christians would no longer need to run from the city in fear of their lives, they would never need to leave the temple (Rev 21:22). Eternal security is certainly a comfort for believers living under constant fear of seismic destruction.

The promise to "write on him the name of my God, and the name of the city of my God, the new Jerusalem, which comes down from my God out of heaven, and my own new name." (Rev 3:12) may be understood against the background of inscribing names into pillars, evident at many sites.[375] It is noted that when the priests of the Imperial Cult retired, their names were etched into the temple pillars.[376] The practice is also evident in the Jewish synagogue in Capernaum, where the names of financial contributors were written on two pillars. While Hemer dismissed any direct connection because there was no temple of the Imperial Cult in Philadelphia until AD 213, he does acknowledge that the reference is plausible.[377] When Christ promises to write his name on the believer, making them a permanent resident of the New Jerusalem (cf. Gal 4:26; Phil 3:20), it would register with everyone familiar with the practice. The writing of names for commemorative purposes and to express ownership would have been a familiar practice.

---

[372] Kiddle, *Revelation*, 17:53.

[373] Wilson, *Revelation*, 33.

[374] Hemer, *Letters to the Seven Churches*, 171–73; Caird, *Revelation*, 55; Gerhard A. Krodel, *Revelation* (Minneapolis, MN: Augsburg Fortress, 1989), 135.

[375] Hemer, *Letters to the Seven Churches*, 268.

[376] Moffatt, *Revelation*, 369; Charles, *Revelation*, 1:91–92; Kiddle, *Revelation*, 17:53–54.

[377] Hemer, *Letters to the Seven Churches*, 166.

Laodicea (Rev 3:14–22)

Laodicea (Col 2:1; 4:13–16) is situated forty miles south-east of Philadelphia in the Lycus River Valley, six miles from Hierapolis (Col 4:13; see Fig. 192), and ten miles west of Colossae. In the second century its population would be between 25,000 and 50,000 people.[378] It was named after Antiochus II's wife, Laodice, and served as the capital and judicial centre of Cibyratic, a region (conventus) including twenty five districts (Cicero *Att.* 5.15.2). It held the reputation of being the wealthiest city in Phrygia in the Roman period, primarily due to its textile (black wool), and banking industries (Cicero *Fam.* 3.5.4).

189. The restored Temple A with 19 columns restored and raised. It was originally dedicated to Apollo. Laodicea,Turkey.

Photo by Klaus Walter//Wikimedia Commons

Since its location was determined by the trade routes, it suffered from an adequate supply of fresh water. It is believed this is the background to the reference in Revelation 3:15–16 "neither cold nor hot. Would that you were either cold or hot! So, because you are lukewarm, and neither hot nor cold, I will spit you out of my mouth."[379] Jesus compared the tepid waters near the city, which produced vomiting, to the lukewarm spiritual life of the Laodiceans, eliciting the imagery of Christ vomiting the Laodiceans out of his mouth.

The Water System

Laodicea was founded based on its trade routes and central roadways. However, it had a serious disadvantage: the city lacked an adequate fresh water supply,[380] with the Lycus river drying up in the summer.[381] The drinkable water at Laodicea came from the Karcı mountains, supplied through five miles (8 km) of aqueducts from the *Başpinar* [382] (Turkish "the head or main")

---

[378] Graves, *Jesus Speaks to Seven of His Churches: A Commentary*, 436–47.

[379] F. F. Bruce, "Colossian Problems, Part 1: Jews and Christians in the Lycus Valley," *BSac* 141 (1984): 3–15; Yamauchi, *NT Cities*, 141; Mounce, *Revelation*, 123; Sherman E. Johnson, "Laodicea and Its Neighbors," *BA* 13 (1950): 1–18; David Chilton, *The Days of Vengeance: An Exposition of the Book of Revelation* (Fort Worth: Dominion, 1987), 134; Beasley-Murray, *Revelation*, 105.

[380] Chandler records the testimony of a local landowner of *Eçirli* (Denizli see Hemer, *Letters to the Seven Churches*, 189–90, 277 n.49) who "expressed his regret, that no waters fit to drink could be discovered there." Richard Chandler, *Travels in Asia Minor, and Greece: Or An Account of a Tour Made at the Expense of the Society of Dilettanti*, 2 vols. (London, UK: Booker & Priestley, 1817), 270. Aqueducts were considered a real asset for cities in the ancient world and people believed the water they provided was safe to drink (Athenaeus *Deipn.* 2.42).

[381] M. J. S. Rudwick and E. M. B. Green, "The Laodicean Lukewarmness," *ExpTim* 69, no. 6 (1958): 177.

[382] William John Hamilton, *Researches in Asia Minor, Pontus and Armenia: With Some Account of Their Antiquities and Geology* (London, UK: Murray, 1842), 1:510; "Extracts from Notes Made on a Journey in Asia Minor in 1836 by W. I. [= J.] Hamilton," *JRGS* 7 (1837): 59–61. Hamilton described the location of the pure spring as a mile and a half on the road from Chonos (Honaz) to Denizli and confirmed that one of the three streams (*Ak Su*, white water) that merged in Khonas (Chonos) was highly petrified (Pliny *Nat.* 31.20.29; cf. Herodotus *Hist.* 7.30) and left travertine deposits similar to those at Hierapolis. Ramsay identified it with the sacred spring (*ayasma*) of mediaval legend. William M. Ramsay, *The Church of the Roman Empire Before AD 170*, 3rd ed. (London, UK: Hodder & Stoughton, 1894)., 469–71.

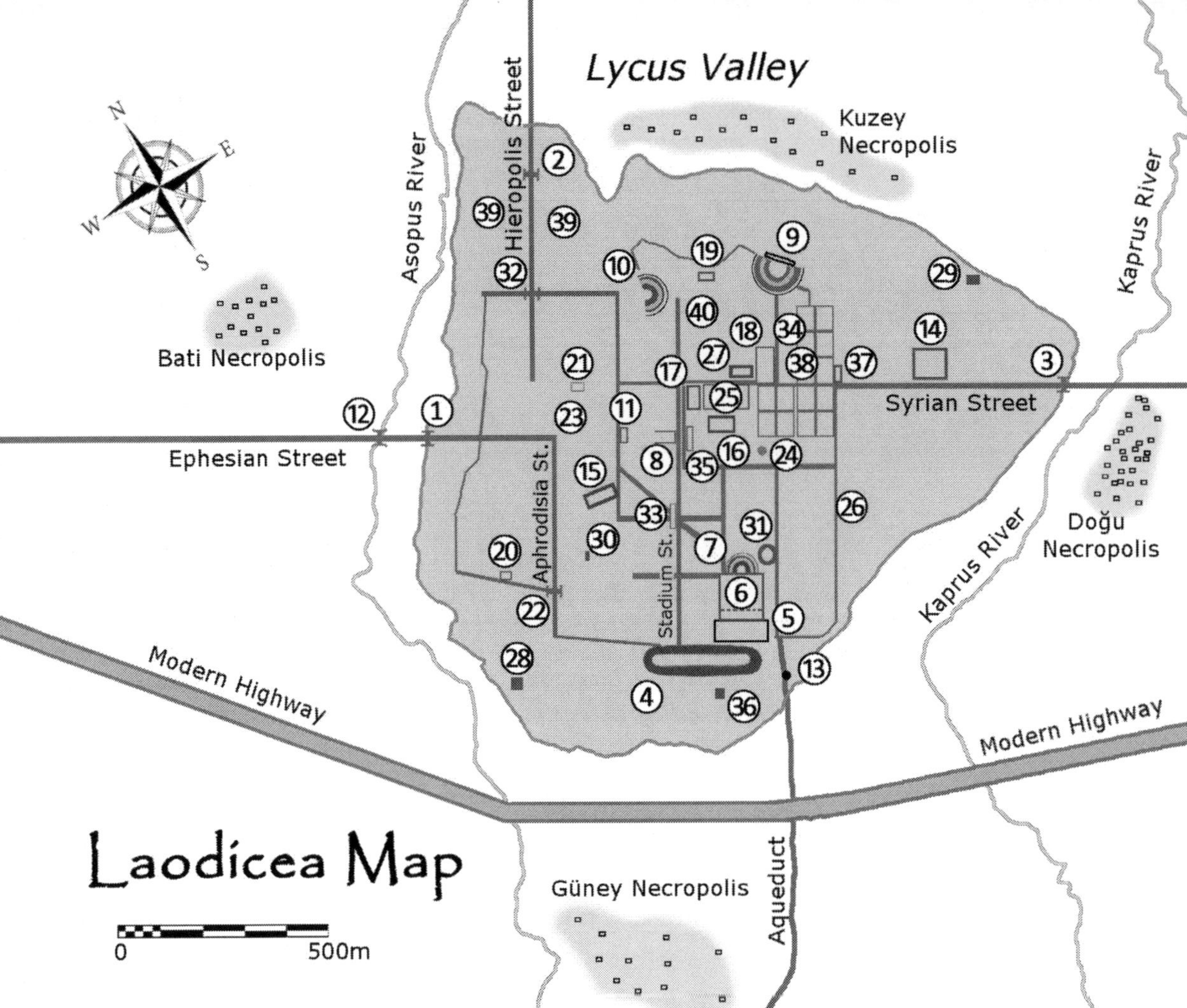

190. Urban plan of the city of Laodicea according to the latest discoveries by Pamukkale University, University of Venice and Denizli University. 1). Ephesus Gate; 2). Hierapolis Gate; 3). Syrian Gate and Byzantine Nymphaeum; 4). Stadium; 5). Gymnasium/Bath complex; 6). Civic agora; 7). Bouleuterion; 8). Ephesus Porticos; 9). N. Theater; 10). W. Theater; 11). Monumental passage; 12). Roman Bridge on Ephesian Street; 13). Water Tower I; 14). East Baths; 15). West Baths; 16). Central Baths; 17). Caracalla Nymphaeum; 18). Temple A; 19). North Church; 20). SW Church; 21). NW Church; 22). Aphrodisian Gate; 23). W agora, Temple and W. Nymphaeum; 24). Water Tower II; 25). Central agora; 26). Byzantine walls; 27). Nymphaeum A; 28). Roman villa; 29). N. Workshop; 30). SW Temple; 31). Round Pytaneion; 32). NW Byzantine Gate; 33). S. Nymphaeum; 34). Laodicea Church; 35). Nymphaeum B, latrine and water storage; 36). Stadium Church; 37). E. Byzantine Nymphaeum; 38). House A and street water distribution center; 39). Asopos I–II; 40). North state agora.

spring,[383] at Denizli in the south,[384] that was the source of the Kaprus river.[385]

However, even this water contained a high percentage of minerals, as is evident from the thick calcified buildup inside the clay pipes (see Figs. 191, 194). An inscription on a structure near the water tower possibly highlights the quality of the drinking water. The inscription stated "Hedychrous built me and named me 'Hedychrous'" (*I.Laod.* 13.1–4). According to Corsten the

[383] Celal Şimşek, "A Menorah with a Cross Carved on a Column of Nymphaeum A at Laodicea Ad Lycum," JRA 19 (2006): 343. Porter suggested that the cold water supplied to Laodicea came from the spring (Turk. *Bounar Bashi)* at Colossae, however the fresh water was known to be from the spring south at Denizli. Porter, "Why the Laodiceans Received Lukewarm Water," 147.

[384] George E. Bean, *Turkey Beyond the Maeander*, 2nd ed. (London, UK: Murray, 1989), 255–56; Finegan, *The Archeology of the New Testament*, 179; Hemer, *Letters to the Seven Churches*, 188; Fant and Reddish, *Guide to Biblical Sites*, 236–37.

[385] Ulrich R. Huttner, *Early Christianity in the Lycus Valley*, trans. David Green, AJEC: ECAM, 85.1 (Leiden: Brill, 2013), 156, 157 n.65. According to Ramsay "the water [for Laodicea] was brought from the upper springs of a branch of the Kadmos [Cadmus] which rises in Mount Salbakos near Denizli." (*Cities and Bishoprics*, 1:48).

name "Hedychrous" means "sweet complexioned", and was related to the pleasant drinking water provided in the first cent. AD.[386] The quality of the drinking water at Laodicea is also attested by an inscription from the fourth or fifth cent. AD, from one of the pumping stations that states: "To good fortune! We, the nymphs of the spring, have the sweet, clear water of the Aidiskos", likely the name of the supplying stream (*I.Laod.* 11.1–2 [Koester]).[387]

Porter argued that the water supply at Laodicea was from the hot springs in Hierapolis (see Fig. 192) because of the calcification from the hard water evident in the *terra-cotta* water pipes.[388] But Strabo reported:

> The changing of water into stone [cake] is said also to be the case with the rivers in Laodicea, although their water is potable [ποτίμων, *potimōn;* i.e., drinkable, fresh, or sweet]. The water at Hierapolis is remarkably adapted also to the dyeing of wool, so that wool dyed with the roots [madder] rivals that dyed with the coccus [kermes oak] or with the marine purple [murex]. And the supply of water is so abundant that the city is full of natural baths. (*Geogr.* 13.4.14 [Jones]; see also Vitruvius *Arch.* 8.3.1)[389]

A section of the aqueduct, which supplied the water, has been identified (see map Fig. 190 no. 13, 195), and dated to the time of Hiero (Strabo *Geogr.* 12.8.16)[390] in the first cent. BC.[391] The aqueduct was created by hewed stones, about 36 inches (91 cm) by 18 inches (46 cm) square, with a 12–inch (30 cm) hole carved out of the middle, each stacked together to form the aqueduct pipe. The stream flowed at a rate of 80–150 liters per second.[392] There is also an all-season stream known as *Baş Pınar Çay* at

191. Water distribution tower (*castellum aquae*), terminal 1 at Laodicea.

192. Hieropolis' (modern Pamukkale, Turkey) travertine terrace pools formed by the mineral laden hot springs. The water not only provided a medical eye salve but also water for the city of Laodicea across the valley.

[386] Thomas Corsten, *Die Inschriften von Laodikeia Am Lykos*, IGSK 49 (Bonn: Habelt, 1997), 48–49.

[387] Craig R. Koester, "The Message to Laodicea and the Problem of Its Local Context: A Study in the Imagery in Rev 3.14–22," *NTS* 49, no. 3 (2003), 410 n.6.

[388] Porter, "Why the Laodiceans Received Lukewarm Water," 147; Blaiklock, *Cities of the NT*, 124; Finegan, *The Archeology of the New Testament*, 2014, 182; Ford, *Revelation*, 418–19.

[389] E. J. Davis, *Anatolia: or The Journal of a Visit to Some of the Ancient Ruined Cities of Caria, Phrygia, Lycia and Pisidia* (London, UK: Grant & Co., 1874), 101.

[390] Ramsay, *Cities and Bishoprics*, 1:48; Hemer, *Letters to the Seven Churches*, 190.

[391] Hamilton, *Researches in Asia Minor, Pontus and Armenia*, 1:515–16; Şimşek and Büyükkolancı, "Die Aqueduct Und Das Wasserverteilungssystem," 137–46.

[392] Y. Ersel Tanriöver and N. Orhan Baykan, "The Water Supply Systems of Caria," in *Cura Aquarum In Ephesus: Proceedings of the Twelfth International Congress on the History of Water Management and Hydraulic Engineering in the Mediterranean Region* (Ephesus-Selçuck, October 2–10, 2004), Part 1, ed. Gilbert Wiplinger, BABesch Suppl. 12 (Leuven, Belgium: Peeters, 2006), 128.

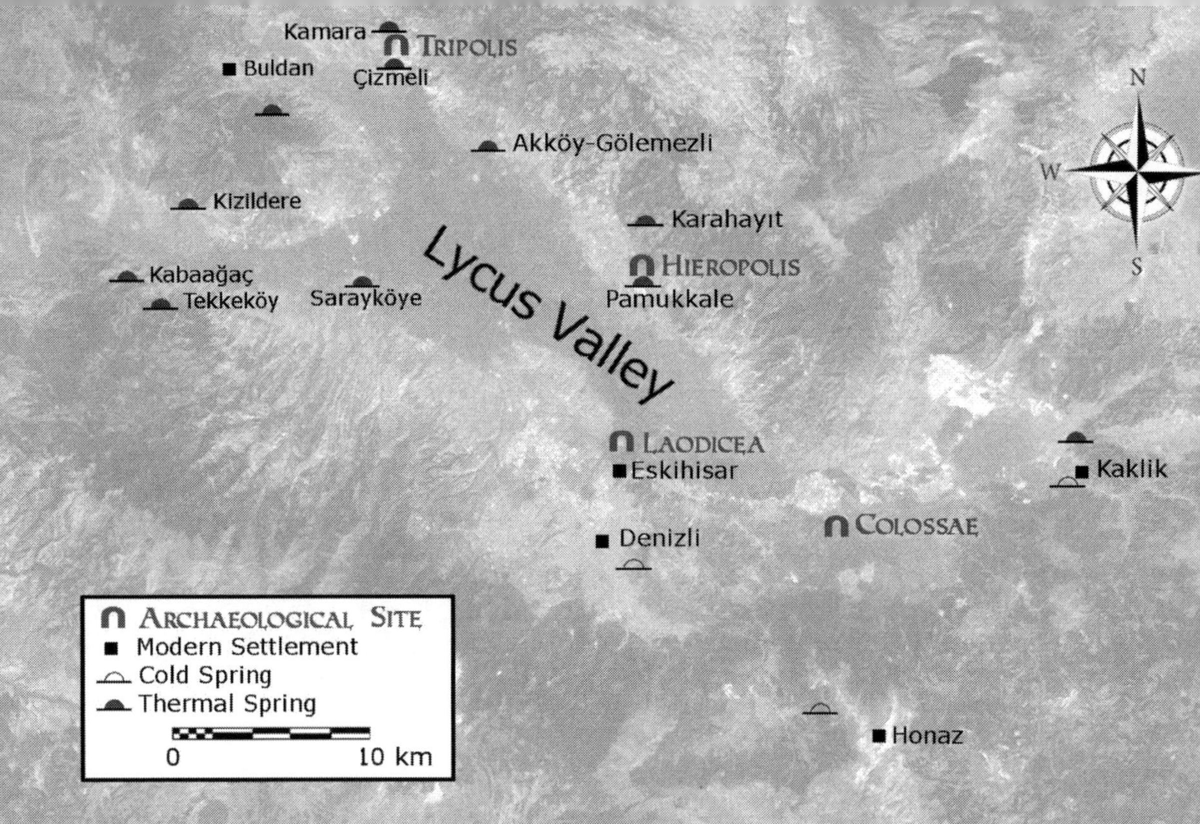

193. Map of the modern area around Laodicea, indicating the location of the archaeological sites, and the thermal (hot) and cold springs.

Eskihisar, a Turkish village just south of Laodicea. Hemer, based on discussions with a local Turkish water-engineer, claimed it was a "constant tepid temperature,"[393] but goes on to state that the "actual temperature cannot be deduced from the uncertain data."[394] Koester points out that "If Laodicea's water was lukewarm, the same would have been true at Ephesus, Smyrna, Pergamum, and Sardis"[395] since they also had several aqueducts.

The clay pipes supplied water by force of gravity to a clearing pool (*castellum aquae*) on the south side of Laodicea,[396] and from there it was distributed in four directions under pressure, to a central water station using a triple staining and inverted siphon system,[397] that supplied a fountain dedicated to Emperor Trajan.[398] The water of the fountain was closely managed, as evident from a recent discovery in 2011 of a Greek inscription uncovered by Celal Şimşek, director of the Laodicea excavations.[399] The inscription was prepared by Aulus Vicirius Martialis,[400] the proconsul of Asia (AD 113/114), who also intervened in a water dispute over

[393] Hemer, *Letters to the Seven Churches*, 277 n. 47.

[394] Ibid., 277 n. 48.

[395] Koester, "Message to Laodicea," 411.

[396] See map 34 no. 13. Water Tower I; map 34 no. 24. Water Tower II.

[397] Bruce, "Laodicea (Place)," in *ABD* 4:230; G. Weber, "Die Hochdruck Wasserleitung von Laodicea Ad Lycum," *JDAI* 19 (1904): 95–96. See the map pl. 3.

[398] See Laodicea map. 13. Water Tower I; 17. Caracalla's Nymphaeum; 24. Water Tower II; 27. Nymphaeum and Fountain of S. Severus.

[399] Şimşek and Büyükkolancı, "Die Aqueduct Und Das Wasserverteilungssystem," 137–46.

[400] John D. Grainger, *Nerva and the Roman Succession Crisis of AD 96–99*, Roman Imperial Biographies (New York: Routledge, 2003), xiii, 101. Not Matrialis as initially reported.

provisions in Ephesus.[401] The Laodicean inscription, dating to between AD 113 and 120, reads in part:

> Those who divide the water for his personal use, should pay 5,000 denarius to the empire treasury; it is forbidden to use the city water for free or grant it to private individuals; those who buy the water cannot violate the Vespasian Edict; those who damage water pipes should pay 5,000 denarius; protective roofs should be established for the water depots and water pipes in the city; the governor's office [will] appoint two citizens as curators every year to ensure the safety of the water resource; nobody who has farms close to the water channels can use this water for agriculture (*I.Eph.* 3217 a + b = *SEG* 31.953; 55.2001; [Şimşek].[402]

To help understand the severity of this penalty, the Gospel of Matthew (last quarter of the first cent. AD) reported that a denarius was equivalent to an average day's wage for an agricultural worker (Matt 20:2–13), thus 5,000 denarii were equal to about 13.7 years of work for a farmer. With inflation, in AD 301, the Diocletian Edict of Maximum Prices listed the daily wage for most experienced tradesmen, such as carpenter, baker, blacksmith, stone mason, wagon wright, tailor of silk and teacher as 50 denarii.[403] One pound of gold was 50,000 denarii.[404] During the republic (509–527 BC), professional legionary soldiers were paid 112.5 denarii per year (0.3/day), which was later doubled by Julius Caesar (early second cent. AD) to 225 denarii (0.6/day), although soldiers had to pay for their own food and arms (Tacitus *Ann.* 1.17; Suetonius *Jul.* 26.3).[405] During this period, based on a legionary's wage, 5,000 denarii were equal to about 22 years of work. Thus any Laodicean found tampering with the water system would be hit with severe penalties, indicating the extreme value of ancient water systems.

194. Closeup of the water distribution tower (*castellum aquae*), terminal 1 at Laodicea. Calcification is visible inside the terra-cotta water pipes, formed by the mineral laden ground water from the springs.

The thermal springs in the region are located on the opposite side of the Lycus valley at *Pamukkale* (at Hierapolis see Fig. 192, 82°–138° F. [28–59°C.][406] with 17 spring discharges; Ca-Mg-HCO_3_SO_4 type), Buldan (36–57°C.), *Kabaağaç*, *Kamara* (32–57°C.; Na-HCO_3 type), *Çizmeli*

[401] Sjef Van Tilborg, *Reading John in Ephesus*, NovTSup 83 (Leiden: Brill Academic, 1997), 108; Eck, "Jahres- Und Provinzialfasten. 1. Teil," 355; "Jahres- Und Provinzialfasten Der Senatorischen. 2. Teil," 154, 210.

[402] Celal Şimşek, "Ancient 'water Law' Unearthed in Laodicea," *Hürriyet Daily News*, September 13, 2011, n.p., http://www.hurriyetdailynews.com/ancient-water-law-unearthed-in-laodicea-.aspx?pageID = 238&nid = 87259.

[403] Elsa R. Graser, "A Text and Translation of the Edict of Diocletian," in *An Economic Survey of Ancient Rome: Rome and Italy of the Empire*, ed. Tenney Frank, vol. 5 (Baltimore, Md.: John Hopkins University Press, 1975), 5:338–45, § 7.1–14, 49, 64–66, 69.

[404] Ibid., 5:412, § 30.1.

[405] Pat Southern, *The Roman Army: A Social and Institutional History* (Oxford: Oxford University Press, 2007), 106–8.

[406] Ali Gökgöz, "Geochemistry of the Kizildere-Tekkehamambuldan-Pamukkale Geothermal Fields, Turkey," *Geothermal Training Programme The United Nations University Reports* 5 (1998): 119. Davies described the water in Hierapolis as "not wholesome, and good drinking water must be brought from a considerable distance; but after the water of the source has been thoroughly exposed to the air it loses its injurious properties, and though not palatable, may be drunk." Davis, *Anatolia*, 101.

195. Ground level aqueduct at Laodicea. Calcification is visible inside the terra-cotta water pipes, formed by the mineral laden ground water that flowed from the spring at Denizli.

Photo courtesy of Mark Wilson

(Yenice at Tripolis), *Akköy-Gölemezli* (4 springs), *Tekkeköy* (Roman baths), *Karahayıt* (42–54.4°C.; Ca-Mg-HCO_3-SO_4 type), *Kaklik*, and *Kizildere* (55–100°C, Na-SO_4-HCO_3 type),[407] but no thermal springs are identified to the south of Laodicea near Denizli.[408] The closest thermal spring on the southern side of the Lycus valley is *Sarayköy,* 12 miles (19 km) north-east of Laodicea. Akşit, a Turkish archaeologist born in Denizli, indicated that there are aqueducts at Hierapolis[409] that carried water to Laodicea,[410] however the archaeological reports from Hierapolis only identified two aqueducts, both drawing drinking water from the northern region above Hierapolis, and leading to a large settling tank (*castellum aquae*) in the east.[411]

The water from Hierapolis emerged with a heavy concentration of carbon dioxide ($CaCO_3$), that when mixed with water, formed a weak carbonic acid (H_2CO_3). When these elements are mixed together, they form calcium bicarbonate ($Ca(HCO_3)_2$) sometimes called "hard water", which, when some of the Carbon dioxide evaporated, left the white insoluble calcium carbonate limestone deposit that formed a formation 300 ft. (91 m) high, extending for almost a mile (1.6 km). They are visible on the slopes of Pamukkale from Laodicea and in the water pipes of the region.[412] Fresh water for Hierapolis had to be provided by an aqueduct to the north of the city. However, the ground water in the region still had mineral deposits that over time calcified. The subterranean network of springs extended some fifty miles under the mountains and surfaced at Hierapolis and other locations with a temperature range of 82°–138° F. (28°–59°C.) and a flow rate of ca. 5,547 gallons per minute (350 lit./sec.).[413]

---

[407] A. Ten Dam and C. Erentöz, "Kizildere Geothermal Field — Western Anatolia," *Geothermics* 2 (January 1, 1970): 124–29.

[408] Halil Kumsar et al., "Historical Earthquakes That Damaged Hierapolis and Laodikeia Antique Cities and Their Implications for Earthquake Potential of Denizli Basin in Western Turkey," *Bulletin of Engineering Geology and the Environment*, (September 10, 2015), 4, Fig. 2; Tanriöver and Baykan, "Die Aqueduct Und Das Wasserverteilungssystem," 127–32; Francesco D'Andria, Mustafa Büyükkolancı, and Lorenzo Campagna, "The Castellum Aquae of Hierapolis of Phrygia," in *Cura Aquarum In Ephesus: Proceedings of the Twelfth International Congress on the History of Water Management and Hydraulic Engineering in the Mediterranean Region (Ephesus-Selçuck, October 2–10, 2004), Part 1*, ed. Gilbert Wiplinger, BABesch Suppl. 12 (Leuven, Belgium: Peeters, 2006), 359–61; Gökgöz, "Geochemistry," 115–56.

[409] The source of the water is from Müştak, Kocapinar, Çaltılı, Karahayıt along an 18 km aqueduct. Tanriöver and Baykan, "Die Aqueduct Und Das Wasserverteilungssystem," 128.

[410] İlhan Akşit, *Pamukkale Hierapolis* (Istanbul: Akşit, 2003), 65.

[411] D'Andria, Büyükkolancı, and Campagna, "Die Aqueduct Und Das Wasserverteilungssystem," 359–60.

[412] Hemer, *Letters to the Seven Churches*, 277 n.48; Tarhan Toker, *Pamukkale (Hierapolis)* (Denizli, Turkey: Haber Gazetecilik, 1976), 6.

[413] Gökgöz, "Geochemistry," 127.

Why Hot or Cold but not Lukewarm?

The all-important question here is: why the suzerain prefers either hot or cold to lukewarm? While it is certainly understandable that the suzerain would want his subjects to be hot (ζεστός, *zestos*; i.e., spiritual fervour) toward him, it is not suitable that he should want them cold (ψυχρός, *psychros*). Aune points out that: "in OT wisdom literature, the images of the 'hot' (negative) and 'cold' (positive) person relate to the motif of self-control, for 'hot' is a pejorative metaphor for a lack of control (Prov 15:18), while "cold" is a positive metaphor for restraint (Prov 17:27; *m. Pir.* ʾ*Abot* 1:17)."[414] However, in the context of this message both hot and cold are positive images, while lukewarm is negative. Several explanations have been proposed for the meaning of "cold" in this context.

1. An unlikely view is that ψυχρός (*psychros*) pertains to a cold backslidden Christian.[415] However, this is similar to the lukewarm condition and not a possitive image.

2. A second view maintains that "cold" refers to an unbeliever who has never heard the gospel.[416] Lenski held that "cold=never converted, never touched by the gospel fire."[417] Tait maintains that while "numbered amongst the Lord's people, their hearts have never yet been touched by grace."[418] However, Christ is speaking to those in the church who would have heard the gospel, unless he preferred they had never heard which seems unlikely.

3. The traditional interpretation moralizes the term ψυχρός (*psychros*) representing an unbeliever who has rejected[419] or is "unwilling to listen to the gospel"[420] and demonstrating an "antagonism towards religious matters."[421] Aune suggests that "'cold' and 'hot' are figures of speech meaning 'against me' and 'for me' or 'hostile towards me' and 'friendly towards me'."[422] It conveys the notion of the degree of spiritual temperature of the Laodiceans,[423] however, this does not explain why the suzerain prefers either hot or cold to lukewarm, although it is possible to have some of these type of people in a church. Alford states that it:

> keeps its meaning of fervent, warm, and earnest in the life of faith and love, ψυχρός [*psychros*] cannot here mean "dead and cold," as we say of the listless and careless professor of religion: for this is just what these Laodiceans were, and what is expressed by χλιαρός [*chliaros*] below. So that we must, so to speak, go farther into coldness for χλιαρὸς [*chliaros*] and take it as meaning, not only entirely without the spark of spiritual life, but also and chiefly, by consequence, openly belonging to the world without, and having no part nor lot in Christ's church, and actively opposed to it.[424]

---

[414] Jay G. Williams, *Those Who Ponder Proverbs: Aphoristic Thinking and Biblical Literature* (Sheffield, U.K.: Almond, 1981), 29–30.
[415] Scott, *Revelation*, Rev. 3:15 op. cit.
[416] Trench, *Commentary on Seven Churches*, 258–63.
[417] Lenski, *Revelation*, 1963, 154.
[418] Tait, *Messages to the Seven Churches*, 406.
[419] Beasley-Murray, *Revelation*, *NCB*, 105; Charles, *Revelation*, 1:96; Swete, *Apocalypse*, 60; Kiddle, *Revelation*, 58; Thomas, *Rev 1–7*, 306–7.
[420] Krodel, *Revelation*, 142.
[421] Caird, *Revelation*, 57; Plumptre, *Seven Churches of Asia*, 198–202.
[422] Aune, *Rev 1–5*, 257.
[423] Swete, *Apocalypse*, 60–61; Aune, *Rev 1–5*, 257–58.
[424] Alford, *Revelation*, 4:588.

4. Recently, some have understood the adjectives "hot," "cold" (ψυχρός (*psychros*) and "lukewarm" as metaphors associated with the Laodicean water supply,[425] which they contrast to the positive medicinal properties of the hot springs from Hierapolis (see Fig. 192) and the cool, refreshing spring waters from Colossae (see chapter 16, *Water System*). This view does not see any moral connection to any religious state (i.e., backslidden, unbeliever, hypocrisy, etc.). Thus, the church in Laodicea "was providing neither refreshment for the spiritually weary nor healing for the spiritually sick. It was totally ineffective, and thus distasteful to its Lord."[426] According to this view, Laodicea is not rebuked for its lack of spiritual temperature but rather their ineffective[427] service.[428] This exegesis solves the problem of why the suzerain would prefer a *cold* church to one that was *lukewarm*.[429] As Smalley points out:

> this congregation is being chastised for the barrenness of its works, rather than the nature of its commitment: although it has to be said that the two (praxis [works] and faith) are inextricably related. . . . Despite the threatened judgment (vomiting), repentance is still possible (verses 18–20). As ever, condemnation can lead to commendation (Rev 3:21).[430]

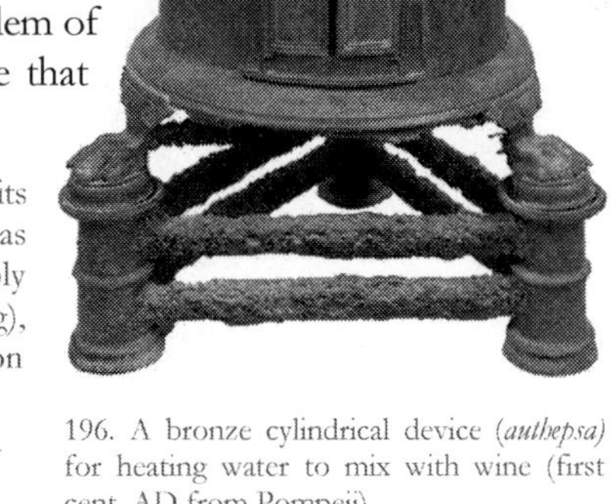

196. A bronze cylindrical device (*authepsa*) for heating water to mix with wine (first cent. AD from Pompeii).

The British Museum Exhibition. Photo courtsy of Mary Beard

However, while the water that supplied Laodicea by aqueduct, shared many of the same qualities as 192, it is known that the water for Laodicea came from springs near Denizli to the south (see Fig. 190), rather than the hot springs of Hierapolis to the north (see Fig. 192).

This view proposes that passion for Christ ought to lead to a healing for the spiritually sick (hot) and refreshment for the spiritually weary (cold). Christian service should flow with fresh water of service and not a lukewarm apathy for the needs of others.

5. In addition the city of Laodicea had several bath complexes, including the gymnasium/bath complex and the central baths. The central baths contained a *caldarium* (hot bath), *tepidarium* (lukewarm bath), *frigidarium* (cold bath). The notion of hot, cold, and lukewarm were well known bathing concept in the ancient world, although in this context the warm or lukewarm room did not have a negative connotation.

---

425 Bruce, "Colossian Problems, Part 1," 3–15; Yamauchi, *NT Cities*, 141; Mounce, *Revelation*, 123; Johnson, "Laodicea and Its Neighbors," 1–18; Chilton, *Days of Vengeance*, 134; Beasley-Murray, *Revelation, NCB*, 105.

426 Rudwick and Green, "The Laodicean Lukewarmness," 178.

427 Tyconius (*ca.* AD 370–390) suggested that the phrase "neither cold nor hot" means that "it is useless." Tyconius, *Turin Fragments of Tyconius*, 74–75.

428 Beckwith, *Apocalypse*, 489; Rudwick and Green, "The Laodicean Lukewarmness," 176–78; Wood, "Local Knowledge," 263–64; Mounce, *Revelation*, 125–26; Sweet, *Revelation*, 107; Hemer, *Letters to the Seven Churches*, 187–91; Osborne, *Revelation*, 205.

429 Contra. Thomas, *Rev 1–7*, 306–7. However, Koester takes exception to this idea and believes that "the imagery is clear without special knowledge of Laodicean topography" (*Revelation*, 415) and that John used "common expressions to address local issues." *Revelation*, 420.

430 Smalley, *Revelation*, 98.

6. Koester has recently reintroduced an earlier view proposed by Jeremy Taylor in the 1800's. Taylor wrote: "In feasts or sacrifices the ancients did use "*apponere frigidain*" [Lat. "add cold"] or "*calidam*" [Lat. "hot"]; sometimes they drank hot drink, sometimes they poured cold upon their gravies or in their wines, but no services of tables or altars were ever with lukewarm."[431] Koester envisions a banquet scene where guests are offered hot and cold drinks (Plato *Resp.* 2.437D) but not lukewarm. This preserves the positive sense of hot and cold metaphor, and negative sense of lukewarm. Refreshing drinks were made either from water heated in a *authepsa* (αὐθέψης, *authephēs* "self-boiler,"[432] or μιλιάριον, *miliarion*[433]), to an enjoyable temperature or chilled with snow or placing underground in a jar to cool (Athenaeus *Deipn.* 3.123a–d). The Romans also preferred a drink of heated wine and water (*caldum*),[434] as only barbarians drank their wine unmixed.[435] Koester goes on to describe that "even more desirable was wine that had been heated or chilled. Both Greeks and Romans chilled wine by placing it in a well or mixing it with snow and ice. A common method was to cool wine by pouring it through a strainer [*colum nivarium,* see Fig. 198] filled with snow".[436] A first cent. AD Bronze *authepsa* was discovered at Pompeii used for heating water (*calda*) to mix with wine (*caldum,* see Fig. 196). Coals were put inside a chamber in the bottom of the cylinder to heat the water, then the host could offer their guest either hot or cold water to mix with their wine (Martial *Epig.* 14.105).[437] Most cities in Asia would have had a *thermopolium* where hot drinks could be purchased at stands along the street, such as were discovered at Herculaneum (see Fig. 197) and Pompeii.

197. *Thermopolium* in Herculaneum.
Photo by Aldo Ardetti/Wikimedia Commons

The imagery of the banquet is further alluded to later in the message where the suzerain says "Behold, I stand at the door and knock. If anyone hears my voice and opens the door, I will come in to him and eat with him, and he with me." (3:20). The suzerain prefers either hot or cold service, but lukewarm (χλιαρὸς, *chliaros)* behavior makes him want to vomit (ἐμέσαι, *emesai).*

Other Possible Local References

In verse 17 we see their true spiritual condition. "You say 'I am rich,'" "have become wealthy"

[431] Jeremy Taylor and Reginald Heber, *The Whole Works of the Right Rev. Jeremy Taylor: With a Life of the Author and a Critical Examination of His Writings* (London, U.K.: Rivington, 1828), 186–87.

[432] William Smith and William Wayte, "Authepsa," in *DGRA*, 1:263. Cicero *Rosc. Amer.* 133; Seneca *Nat. quaest.* 3.24.2; Lucian *Lex.* 8; Heron of Alexandria *Pneum.* 2.34–5.

[433] Henry George Liddell and Robert Scott, *An Intermediate Greek-English Lexicon*, 9th ed. (Oxford, U.K.: Clarendon, 1889), 28451 op. cit.

[434] Plautus *Curc.* 292–93; *Rud.* 1013–14; Petronius *Sat.* 65; Lucian *Lex.* 8.

[435] Katherine M. D. Dunbabin, *The Roman Banquet: Images of Conviviality* (Cambridge, UK: Cambridge University Press, 2010), 20.

[436] Koester, *Revelation*, 343. Xenophon *Mem.* 2.1.30; Athenaeus *Deipn.* 3.124cd; Seneca *Ep. Mor.* 78.23; Martial *Epig.* 5.64.1–2; 14.103–4.

[437] Katherine M. D. Dunbabin, "Wine and Water at the Roman Convivium," *JRA* 6 (1993): 116–41; *Roman Banquet*, 178; Koester, "Message to Laodicea," 413–15.

198. Roman bronze wine-strainer found near Nijmegen in the River Waal. First cent. AD, made possibly in Campania

Allard Pierson Museum (Inv. No. APM 3422). Photo by Near EMPTiness/Wikimedia Commons

and "have need of nothing" (Rev 3:17). This is connected to the affluence of the city. The most striking example of her wealth is a statement by Tacitus, who wrote: "Laodicea, one of the famous Asiatic cities, was laid in ruins by an earthquake [AD 60], but recovered by its own resources [unlike Philadelphia], without assistance from ourselves" (*Ann.* 14.27.1 [Jackson]). Cicero cashed his treasury bill here, as it was a major banking centre (Cicero *Fam.* 3.5.4; *Att.* 5.15.2). Their monetary riches and self sufficiency are contrasted with their spiritual poverty. "For you say, I am rich, I have prospered, and I need nothing, not realizing that you are wretched, pitiable, poor, blind, and naked" (Rev 3:17). The reference to blindness is almost universally accepted to be connected to the eye salve produced from the Phrygian powder from Hierapolis, likely developed at the medical school (Strabo *Geogr.* 12.8.20) founded by Zeuxis at Laodicea.[438]

Their "nakedness" (Rev 3:17) is contrasted with the "white garments so that you may clothe yourself and the shame of your nakedness may not be seen" (Rev 3:18). This is further contrasted against Laodicea's dependence on its thriving textile industry, which was centered around the soft, jet-black wool from local sheep (Strabo *Geogr.* 12.8.16). In spite of the fact they have access to excellent wool, they are in fact naked, but to the overcomer is given the white garments of righteousness to hide their shame (Rev 3:3, 5; 4:4; 6:11; 7:9; 13–14; 19:14).

Only God can provide, by his grace, what we need in our salvation. Only Christ can clear our sight, cover our naked shame (Gen 3:7; 21; Rev 16:15), and make the poor rich (Matt 5:3; Luke 1:52–53; Jas 2:5). Each church is called to repentance because they have broken the covenant relationship and violated God's stipulations (seven of the ten commandments are mentioned). If they return to the Lord, they will know his blessing, but if they do not, then they will know his malediction (curse). Like the OT prophets, John calls the churches to repentance before they have to experience the consequences.

[438] Colin J. Hemer, "Seven Cities of Asia Minor," in *Major Cities of the Biblical World*, ed. R.K. Harrison (Nashville, TN: Nelson, 1985), 196–99; Ramsay, *Cities and Bishoprics of Phrygia*, 2:52; Rudwick and Green, "The Laodicean Lukewarmness," 176; Michael Wilcock, *The Message of Revelation: I Saw Heaven Opened*, Bible Speaks Today (Downers Grove, IL: InterVarsity, 1975), 56–57; Yamauchi, *NT Cities*, 145–46; Blaiklock, *Cities of the New Testament*, 125.

Conclusion

As with all books of the Bible, the meaning of the book of Revelation can be uncovered by the careful use of archaeology. Thus, from the ever-increasing collection of archaeological discoveries and artifacts now available from the past, what is abundantly clear is that both the OT and NT are historically reliable sources of information. We may not always fully understand what was written so very long ago, but from what archaeology can expose and shine a light on, we can rely on scriptural accuracy. Those who would dismiss the Bible as myth or fiction must now come to grips with this collection of archaeological data. When one picks up a Bible and begins to read its pages, one can do so with confidence that the history it contains is reliable.

MAP 1: PROPOSED SITES FOR THE THE CITIES OF THE PLAIN

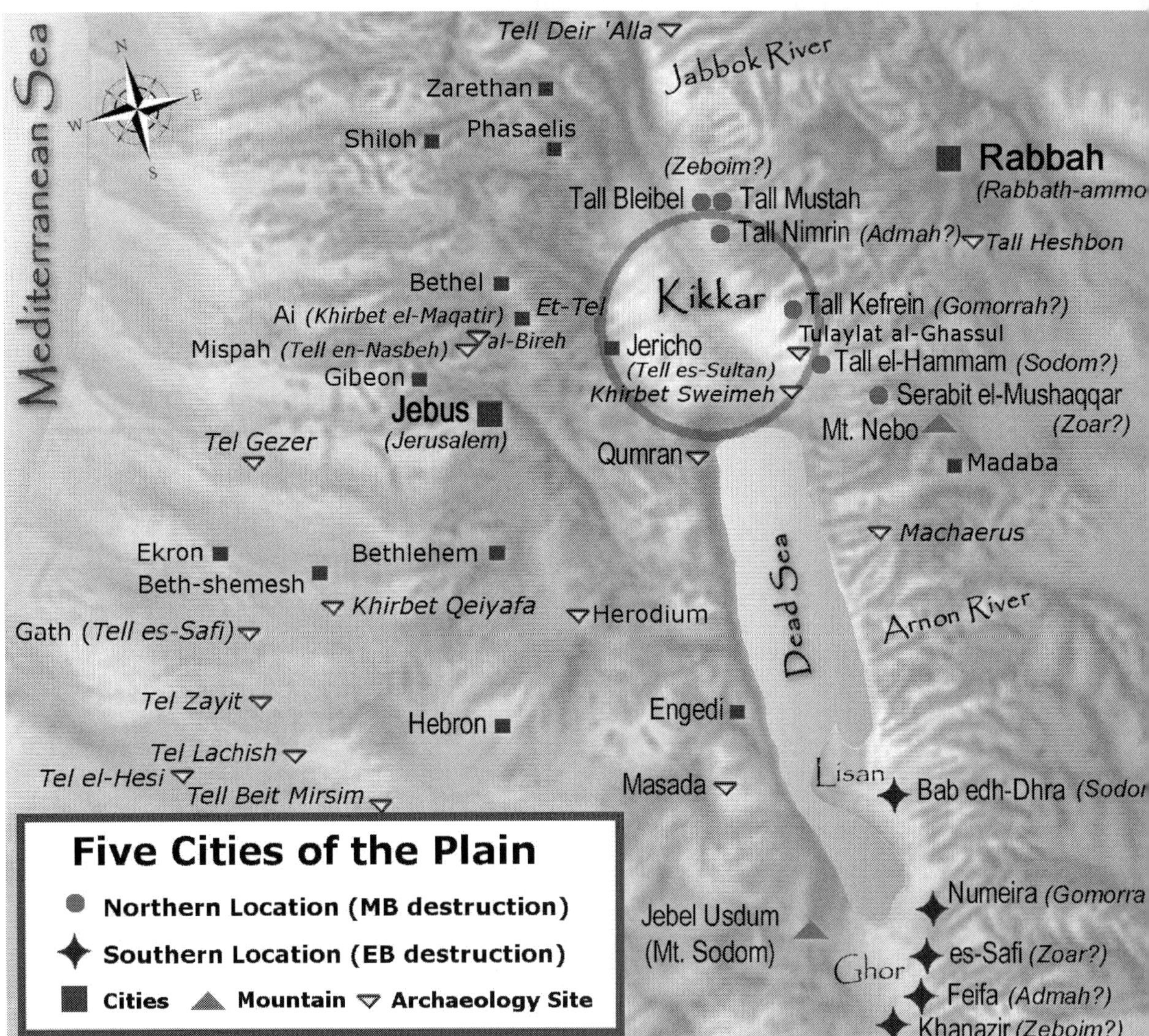

199. **MAP 1:** Proposed sites for the northern and southern location of the Cities of the Plain.

MAP 2: MIGRATION OF ABRAHAM FROM BABYLON

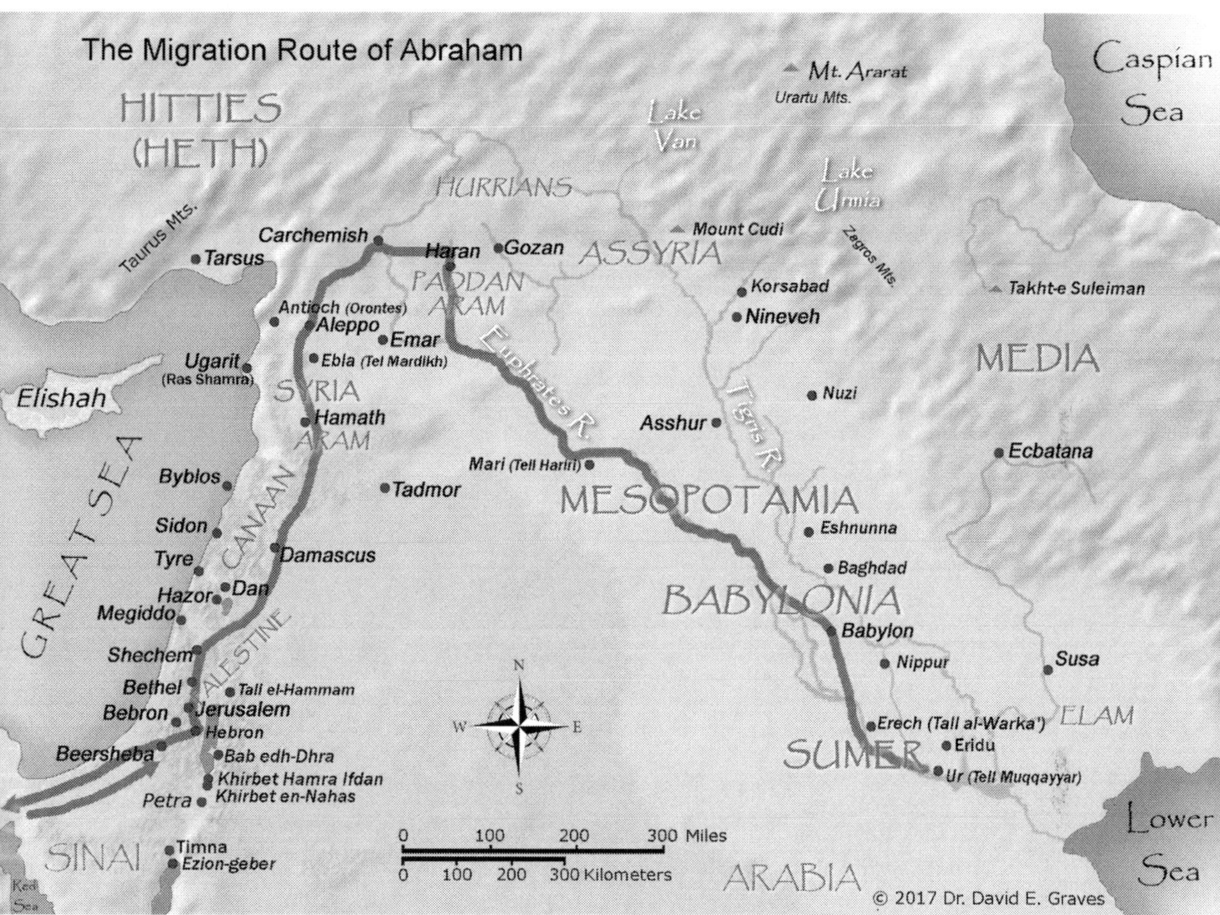

200. **MAP 2:** Migration of Abraham from Babylon.

MAP 3. TRIBAL ALLOTMENTS OF ISRAEL

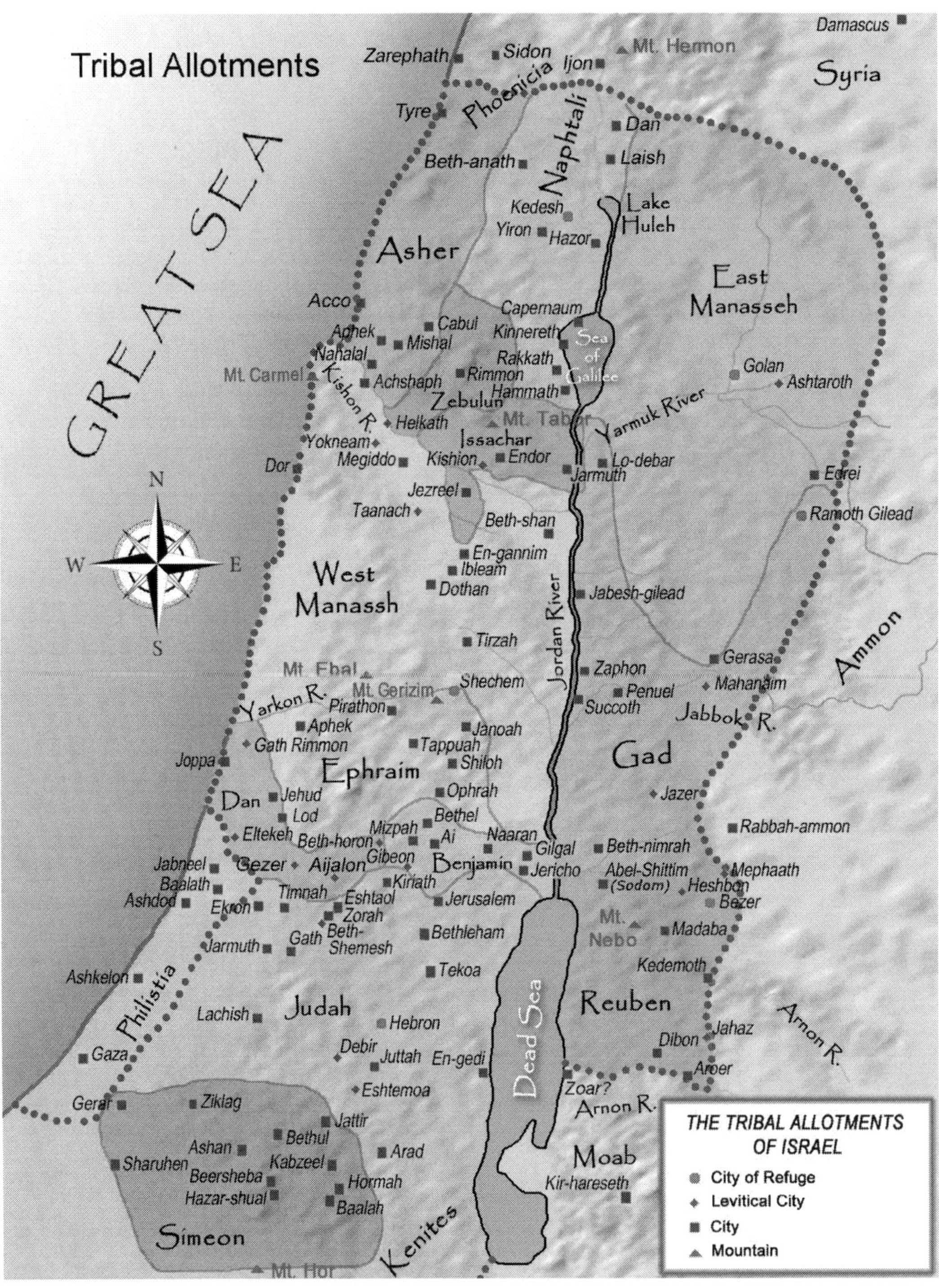

201. **MAP 3.** Map of the tribal allotments of Israel with Levitical cities and cities of refuge.

MAP 4: THE ROUTE OF THE EXODUS

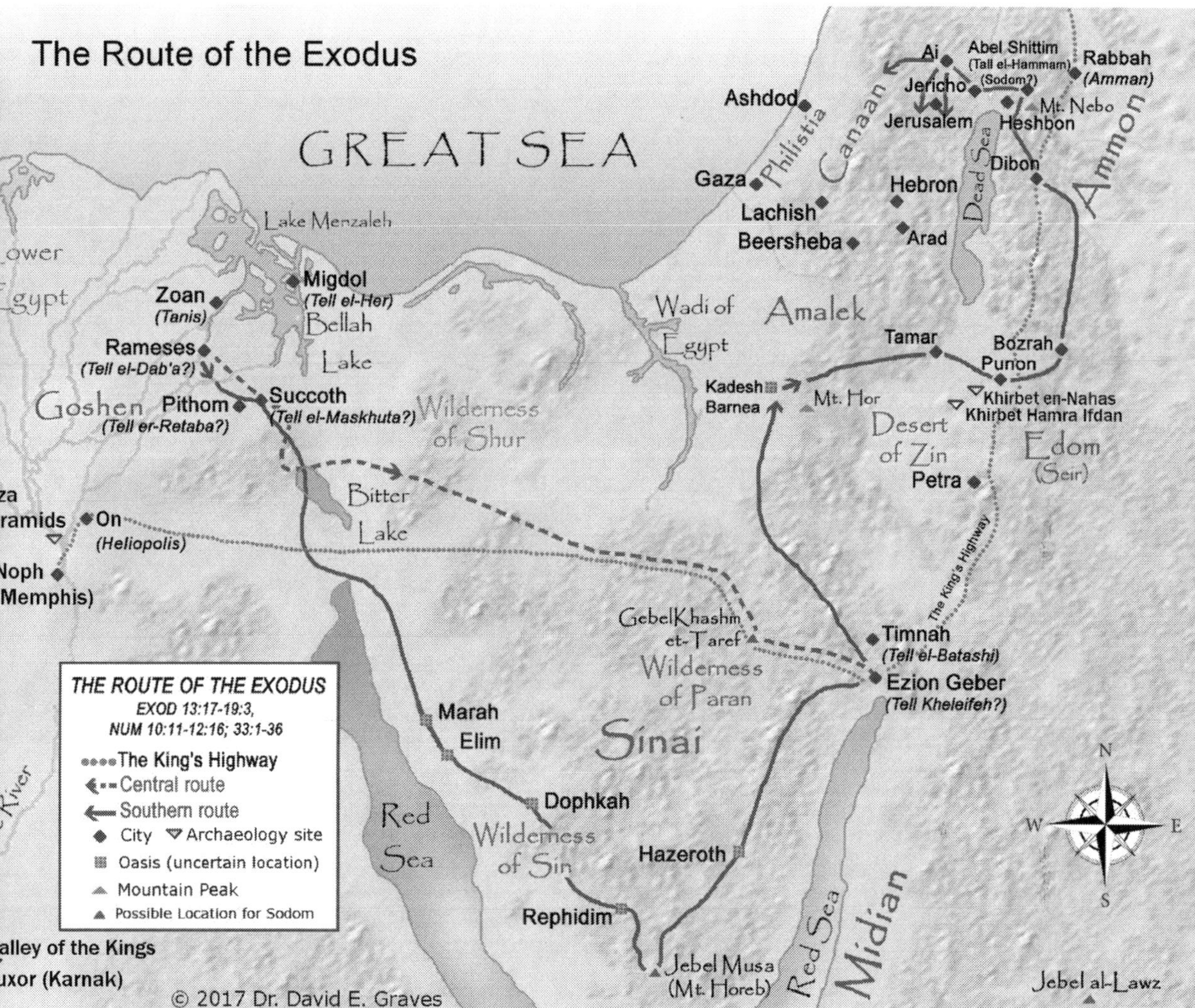

202. **MAP 4:** The route of the Exodus.

MAP 5: ISRAEL IN THE TIME OF JESUS

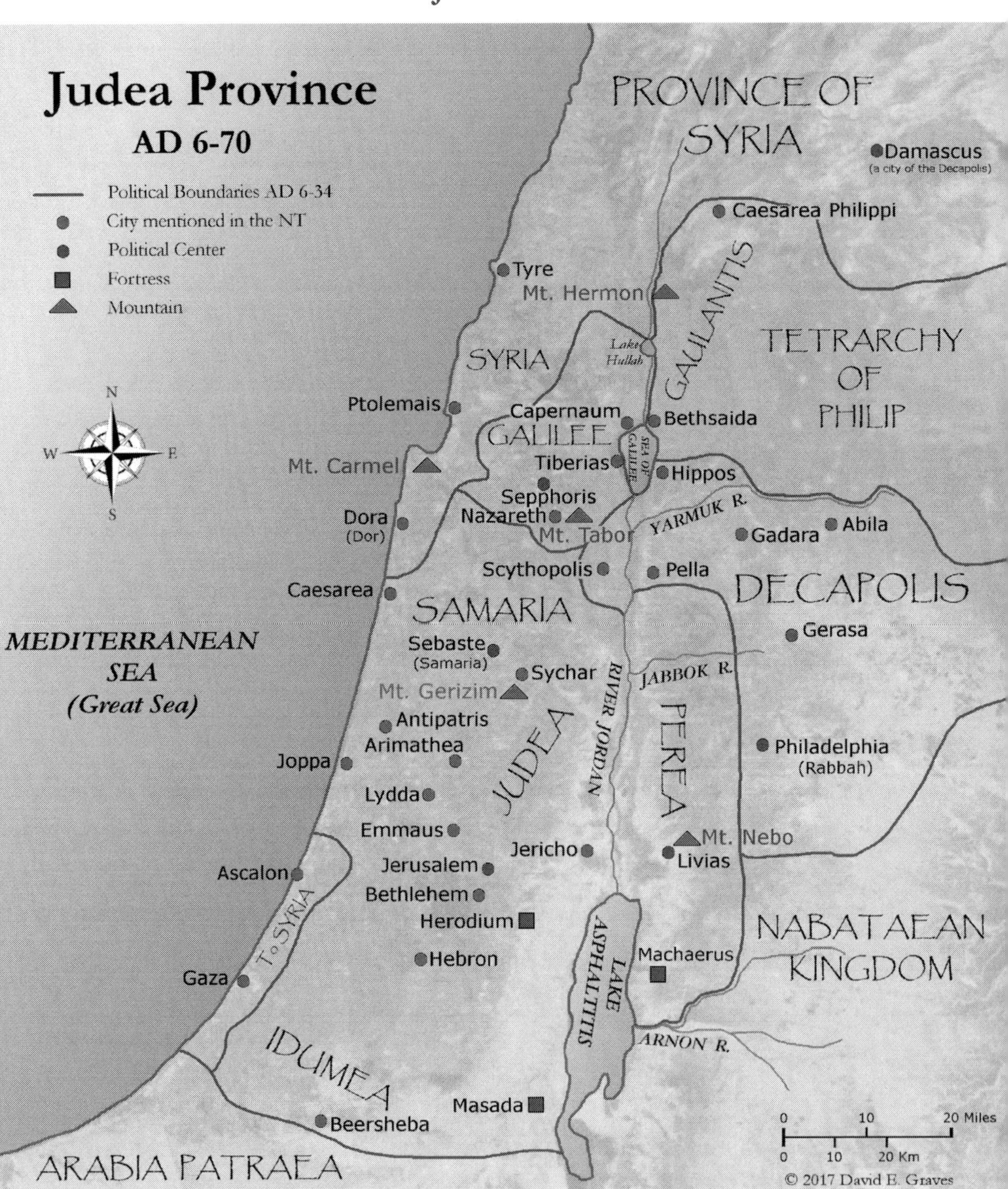

203. **MAP 5:** Israel in the time of Jesus.

MAP 6: THE FIRST MISSIONARY JOURNEY

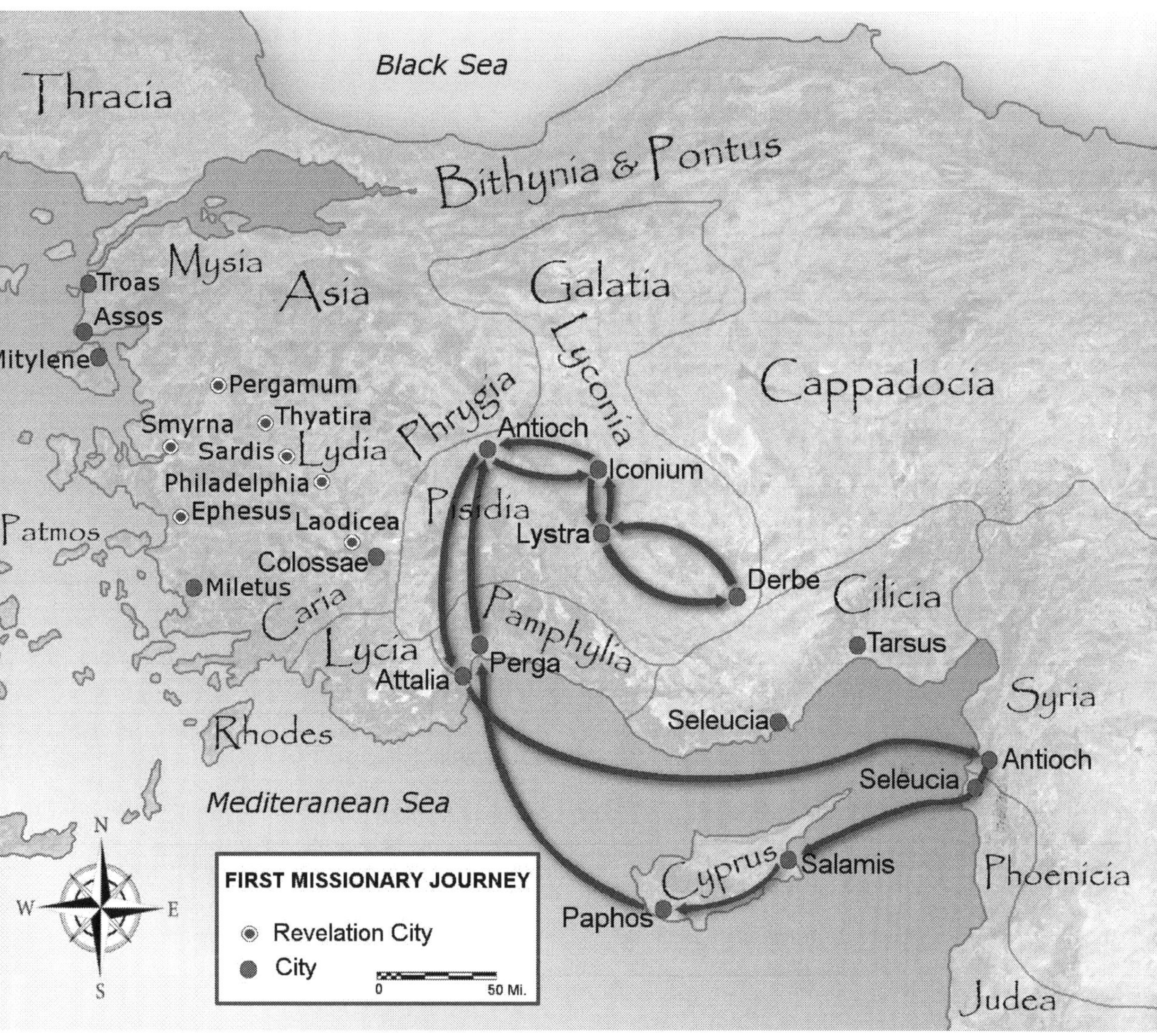

204. **MAP 6**: The First Missionary Journey.

MAP 7: THE SECOND MISSIONARY JOURNEY

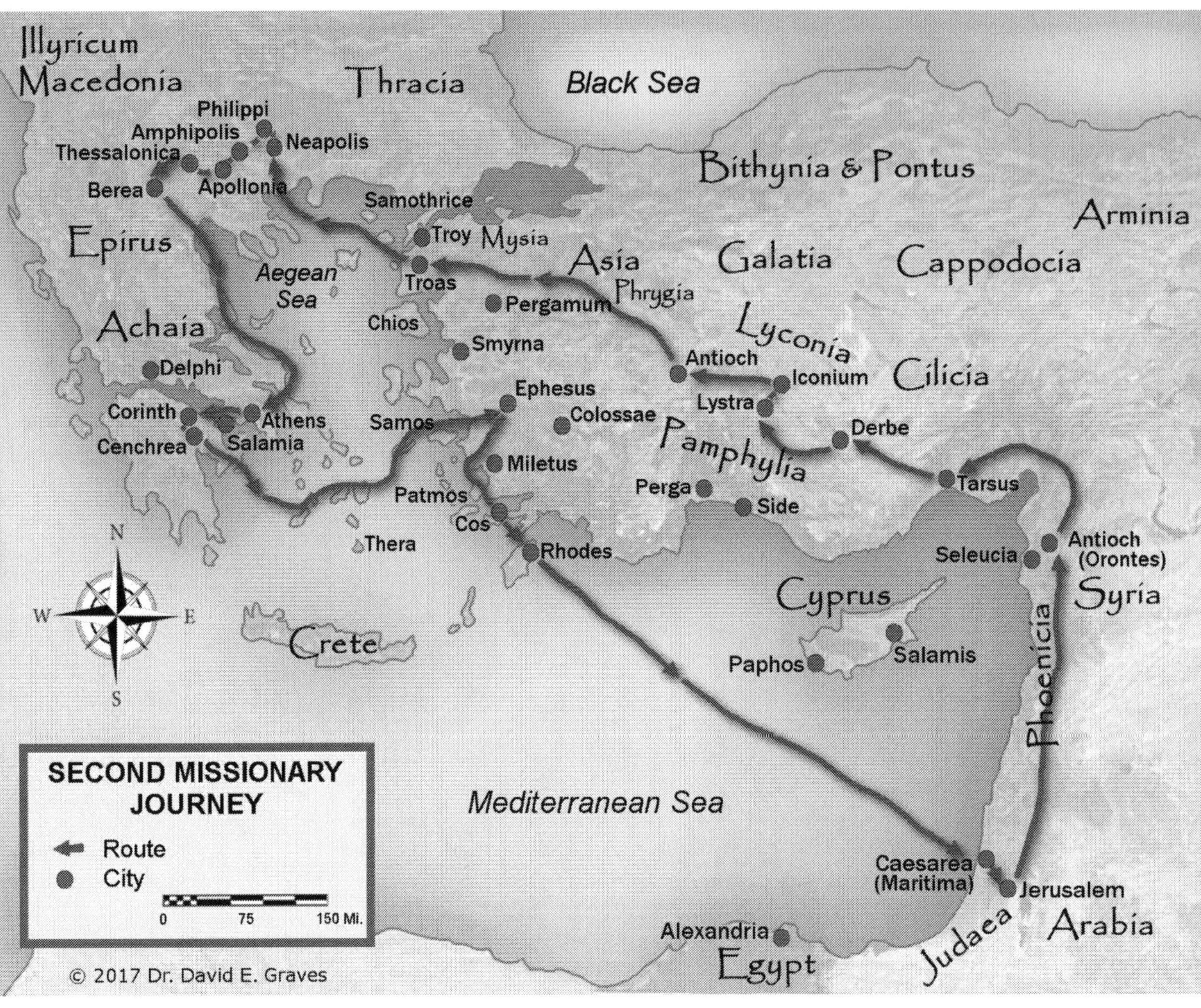

205. **MAP 7:** The Second Missionary Journey.

MAP 8: THE THIRD MISSIONARY JOURNEY AND TRIP TO ROME

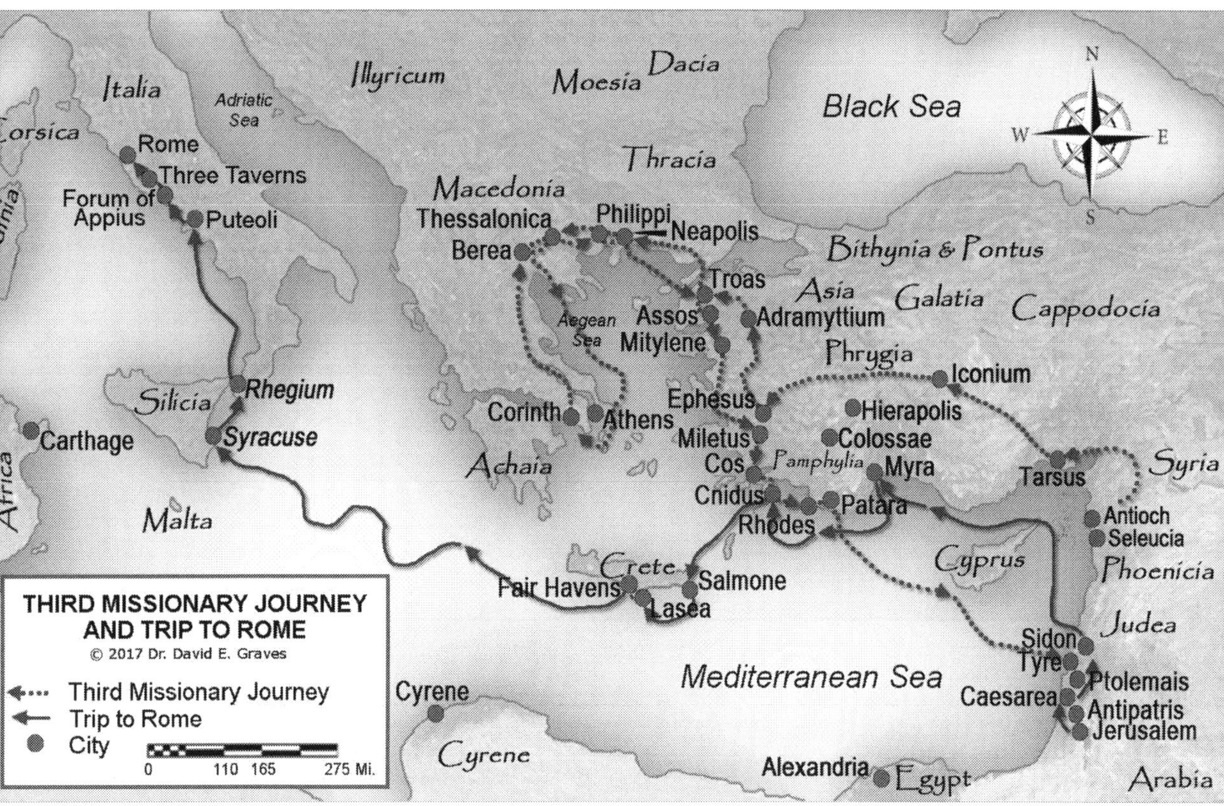

206. **MAP 8**: The Third Missionary Journey and trip to Rome.

MAP 9. SITE PLAN OF TALL EL-ḤAMMÂM

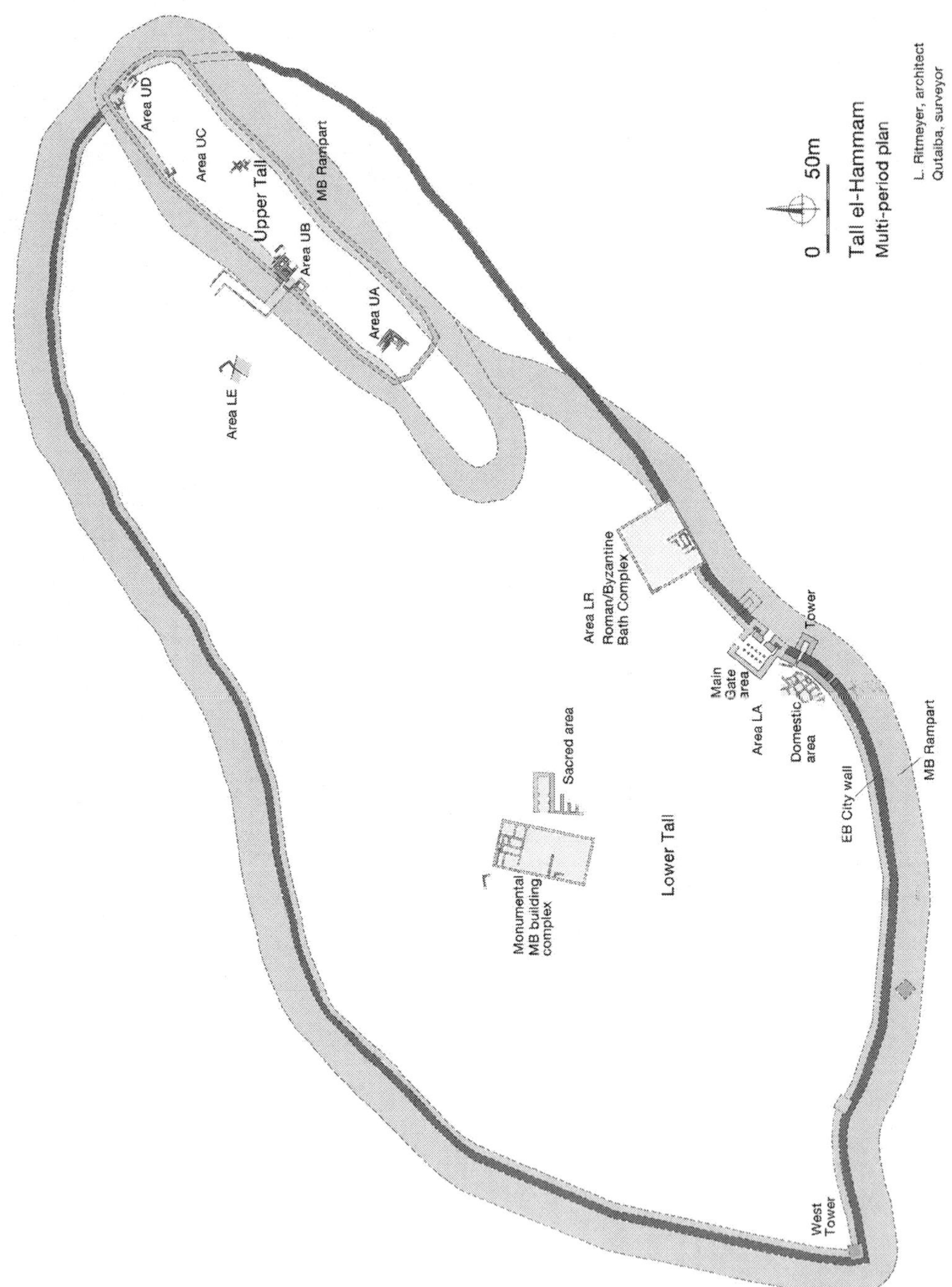

207. **MAP 9**. Multi-period site plan of Tall el-Ḥammâm showing excavation Fields. Courtesy of Leen Ritmeyer. Used with permission.

CHART 9: ARCHAEOLOGICAL PERIODS (NEW CHRONOLOGY)[1]

Period	Abbreviation	Historical Period	Dates
PREHISTORIC PERIOD			
Pre-Pottery Neolithic A, B	PPNA, PPNB	Post Creation	8500–6000 BC
Pottery Neolithic A, B	PNA, PNB	Ubaid Period (Sumer)	6000–4300 BC
Chalcolithic Period	Cal.	Ubaid Uruk Period (Sumer)	4300–3600 BC
BIBLICAL PERIOD			
Early Bronze Age 1	EB1	Uruk Period (Sumer) Writing	3600–3000 BC
Early Bronze Age 2	EB2	Dynastic Period (flood?)	3000–2700 BC
Early Bronze Age 3	EB3	Dynastic Period (flood?)	2700–2500 BC
Intermediate Bronze Age 1	IB1 (formerly EB IV or EB IVA)	Third Dynasty of Ur	2500–2200 BC
Intermediate Bronze Age 2	IB2 (formerly MB I or EB IVB) or)	Third Dynasty of Ur	2200-1950 BC
Middle Bronze Age 1	MB1 (formerly MB IIA)	Middle Kingdom Egypt	1950–1800 BC
Middle Bronze Age 2	MB 2 (formerly MB IIB)	Israel's Patriarchs	1800–1540 BC
Late Bronze Age 1	LB1	Mosaic Period /New Kingdom Egypt	1540–1400 BC
Late Bronze Age 2	LB2	Exodus & Conquest	1400–1200 BC
Iron Age 1	IA1	Judges	1200–1000 BC
Iron Age 2	IA2	United & Divided Monarchy / Babylonian Conquest	1000–586 BC
Persian Period	Pers.	Neo-Babylonian Period/	586–332 BC

[1] Regev *et al.*, "Chronology of the Early Bronze Age in the Southern Levant: New Analysis for a High Chronology," 525–66.

Period	Abbreviation	Historical Period	Dates
CLASSICAL PERIOD			
Hellenistic Period	Hell.	Alexander the Great	332–63 BC
Maccabean / Hasmonean Period	Macc.	Maccabean Revolt	165–63 AD
Early Roman Period	ER or E. Rom.	Herodian/ NT Period	63 BC–70 AD
Middle Roman Period	MR or M. Rom.	Yavne Period	70–135 AD
Late Roman Period	LR or L. Rom.	Mishnaic Period	135–200 AD
Late Roman Period	LR or L. Rom.	Talmudic Period	200–330 AD
Byzantine Period	Byz.	Eastern Roman Empire	330–638 AD
ISLAMIC PERIOD			
Umayyad Period	Umay.	Arab Caliphate Period	638–750 AD
Abbasid Period	Abb.	Arab Caliphate Period	750–969 AD
Fatimid Period	Fat.	Caliphate Egyptians	969–1171 AD
Kingdom of Jerusalem Period	Crus.	Crusader Period	1099–1187 AD
Ayyubid Period	Ayy.	Crusader Period	1187–1244 AD
Mamluk Period	Mam.	Crusader Period	1244–1517 AD
Ottoman Period	Ott.	Ottoman Empire	1517–1917 AD
MODERN PERIOD			
British Mandate Period	Brit. Man.	British Occupation and Arab states	1917–1948 AD
Israeli Period	Isr.	Modern Israel	1948–Present

CHART 10: COMPARATIVE ARCHAEOLOGICAL DATING

Period	Geisler[1]	ABD[2]	Collins[3]	Price[4]
Neolithic Age	8500–4600	8300–5000	6000–4500	8000–4300[5]
Chalcolithic Period	4600–3600	5000–3500	4500–3600	4300–3300[6]
Early Bronze 1	3600–2900	3500–3100	3600–3000	3300–2950
Early Bronze 2[7]	2900–2700	3100–2650	3000–2800	2950–2700
Early Bronze 3[8]	2700–2500	2650–2350[9]	2800–2500	2700–2176
Early Bronze 4	2500–2350	2400–2000[10]		2176–1973
Intermediate Bronze	2350–2000		2500–1950[11]	
Middle Bronze 1 (IIA)	2000–1800	2000–1800	1950–1800[12]	1973–1750
Middle Bronze 2 (IIB)	1800–1550	1800–1650	1800–1540[13]	1750–1615
Middle Bronze 3 (IIC)		1650–1500		1615–1483
Late Bronze 1	1550–1400	1500–1400	1540–1400	1483–1400
Late Bronze 2	1400–1200	1400–1200	1400–1200	1400–1290

---

[1] Geisler and Holden, *Popular Handbook of Archaeology and the Bible*, 191–92.

[2] William G. Dever *et al.*, "Palestine, Archaeology of," ed. David Noel Freedman *et al.*, *ABD* (New York: Doubleday, 1996), 5:99–119.

[3] Steven Collins et al., "Tall El-Hammam Season Ten, 2015: Excavation, Survey, Interpretations And Insights," *BRB* 15, no. 1 (2015): 26–27.

[4] Price and House, *Zondervan Handbook of Biblical Archaeology*, 41.

[5] Price, *The Stones Cry Out*, 350–51.

[6] Ibid.

[7] "The transition between EB II and EB III is not as clearly connected to Egyptian chronology due to the cessation of trade connections between the regions from the 2nd Dynasty onwards. Thus, the traditional correlation of later EB II with the 2nd Dynasty, or even the 3rd Dynasty, is based on virtually no material evidence." Regev *et al.*, "Chronology of the Early Bronze Age in the Southern Levant: New Analysis for a High Chronology," 526.

[8] "EB III is traditionally defined as coinciding with [Egyptian] dynasties 3–6. These correlations, however, have no secure material basis. The end of the period is conventionally placed around 2300 BC, during the reign of Pharaoh Pepi I, when there is evidence of Egyptian military intervention along the southern Coastal Plain of Israel. The date of Pepi's reign, however, is disputed and could be somewhat earlier." Ibid., 527.

[9] The end of EB III is given as 2350 BC in the *ABD* (William G. Dever *et al.*, "Palestine, Archaeology of," ed. David Noel Freedman *et al.*, *ABD* (New York: Doubleday, 1996), 5:110), 2200 BC in the *New Encyclopedia of Archaeological Excavations in the Holy Land* (Edited by Ephraim Stern, Ayelet Levinson-Gilboa, and Joseph Aviram, 4 vols. (New York: MacMillan, 1993), 4:1529), and 2300 BC in *The Oxford Encyclopedia of Archaeology in the Near East* (Edited by Eric M. Meyers, 5 vols. (Oxford: Oxford University Press, 1997), 413).

[10] According to Dever this was "Albright's 'Middle Bronze I,' Kenyon's 'Intermediate EB–MB'" William G. Dever *et al.*, "Palestine, Archaeology of," ed. David Noel Freedman *et al.*, *ABD* (New York: Doubleday, 1996), 5:111.

[11] 2500-2200 BC IB1, formerly EB IV; 2200-1950 BC IB2, formerly MB I.

[12] Formerly MB IIA

[13] Formerly MB IIB-C

COMPARATIVE ARCHAEOLOGICAL DATING (*cont.*)				
Period	**Geisler**	**ABD**	**Collins**	**Price**
Iron 1	1200–1000	1200–900	1200–1000	1177–925
Iron 2	1000–586	900–600	1000–539	925–587/6
Iron 3/Persian	586–332	586–332	539–332	586/7–330
Hellenistic	332–63	332–50	332–63	330–149
Hasmonean Period		50 BC–AD 150		167–37
Roman Period	63 BC–AD 324			149 BC–AD 637
Early Roman			63 BC–AD 135	

CHART 11: EGYPTIAN CHRONOLOGY

Period	Dynasty[1]	Kitchen[2]	Grimal[3]	Rhol[4]
Early Dynastic Archaic	1–2	3000–2700	3150–2700	2770–2554
Old Kingdom	3–8	2700–2160	2700–2190	2554–2044
1st Intermediate	9–10	2160–2010	2200–2040	2044–1944
Middle Kingdom	11–12	2106–1786	2040–1674	1944–1632
2nd Intermediate	13–17	1786–1550	1674–1553	1632–1203
New Kingdom	18–20	1550–1069	1553–1069	1202–827
3rd Intermediate	21–25	1069–656	1069–702	822–658
Late Period (Persian)	26–31	664–332	747–333	664–332
Greco-Roman		332–AD641	332–AD395	332–AD641

[1] Manetho, an Egyptian priest and historian, arranged Egyptian history into 30 dynasties in the 3rd century BC in his work *Aegyptiaka*. Manetho, *Manetho*.

[2] Kitchen, "The Chronology of Ancient Egypt," 206.

[3] Grimal, *A History of Ancient Egypt*, 389–95.

[4] Rohl, *A Test Of Time*, 159–74; *Pharaohs and Kings*; *From Eden to Exile*; *The Lords Of Avaris: Uncovering the Legendary Origins of Western Civilisation*.

CHART 12: CHRONOLOGY OF PAUL'S LIFE

Date *ca.* AD	Time of Year	Event
33–36		Paul's conversion in Damascus (Gal 1:12–17; Acts 9:1–25).
36–37		The visit to Arabia and Syria and the return to Damascus for three years (Gal 1:17–18; 2 Cor 11:23–33).
37		The first visit to Jerusalem for two weeks (Acts 9:26–30; Gal 1:18–19).
37–40		The death of Aretas IV Philopatris (Acts 9:25; 2 Cor 11:32).
37–43		Visit to Syria (Antioch Acts 11:26a) and Cilicia (Tarsus; Acts 9:30; Gal 1:21).
41	January	Caligula was assassinated.
41–54		Claudius Caesar's rule (Acts 11:28; Acts 18:2).
44		Paul's trip to Antioch (Acts 11:25–26) and the prophet Agabus predicts a great famine which "came to pass in the days of Claudius Caesar" (Acts 11:28).
		James the apostle beheaded and the imprisonment of Peter (Acts 12:1–2).
		The death of Herod Agrippa I (Acts 12:20–23).
45/46		Famine in Judea (Acts 11:28).
46		Second visit to Jerusalem for famine relief.
46–48		First missionary journey (Acts 13:2–14:28).
49		Apostolic conference at Antioch (Acts 15:1–2; Gal 2:12–14). Galatians written.
		Jews expelled from Rome.
50		After 14 years, Paul visits Jerusalem with Barnabas and Titus for a conference (Acts 15:2–29; Gal 2:1).
50–52		Paul's second missionary journey (Acts 15:40–18:23).
50	Spring	Berea, southern Greece and Athens. Paul's arrival in Corinth.
50–51	Autumn	Paul stayed in Corinth for about 1.5 years (Acts 18:1, 5, 11, 18) then sailed to Caesarea. 1 & 2 Thess were written from Caesarea.
51–52	July	Gallio governed Achaea (Acts 18:12–17).
51	Summer	Paul's trial before Gallio in Achaea (Acts 18:12–17).
52	Passover?	Paul visits Jerusalem for the feast (Acts 18:21–22).
52–60		Felix is Roman procurator in Palestine.
52–53	Winter	Paul spent several months in Antioch, Syria (Acts 18:23).
53–58	Spring	Paul's third missionary journey (Acts 18:23–21:17). Activity in the churches of Galatia, Asia, Macedonia, and Achaea with special emphasis on the collection of the offering for Jerusalem (Gal 2:10; 1 Cor 16:1–4; 2 Cor 8–9; Rom 15:25–32).
53	Autumn	Paul arrives in Ephesus where he writes 1 Corinthians.
54–68		Nero's reign.
55	Spring	Painful visit to Corinth; Paul sends severe letter ("Corinthians C") by the hand of Titus.

56	Summer	Paul leaves Ephesus after three years (Acts 20:31).
	Autumn	Paul in Troas.
	October	Paul leaves Troas for Macedonia, meets Titus, sends letter of reconciliation ("Corinthians D").
57	Spring	Paul arrives in Corinth where he likely wrote Romans.
	Passover	Paul in Philippi where he likely wrote 2 Corinthians.
	Pentecost	Paul's arrival in Jerusalem with an offering (1 Cor 16:3; Rom 15:25–32).
57–59		Paul was imprisoned by Felix in Caesarea for two years until Festus took over (Acts 23:23–26:32).
59–60	October	Festus took over from Felix as the Roman Procurator of Judea (Acts 24:27–25:1).
60–62		Porcius Festus became procurator of Judea (Acts 24:27; 25:12).
60		Shipwrecked on Malta (Acts 27:1–28:16).
60–62	Spring	Paul arrived in Rome and was imprisoned where he wrote Ephesians, Colossians, Philemon and Philippians.
62		James the Lord's brother stoned.
64	July	Fire in Rome.
63–67		Paul's trip to Spain and later journeys (Pastoral Epistles).
64/65		1 Timothy and Titus written from Philippi.
66		Jewish rebellion against Rome and Christians in Jerusalem flee.
67		2 Timothy written from Rome.
67–68		Paul beheaded; Peter crucified.

CHART 13: ARCHAEOLOGY AND LOCAL REFERENCES

There are local references mentioned in the seven oracles to the churches in Revelation. If two or three of these examples strike a chord of credibility, then a case for references to local and cultural settings has been made. The messages proclaimed to each church have relevance for today, but it must also be remembered that they were first given to the churches living in the first-century and they likely understood them better than we do.

METHODOLOGY

In the following chart, listing various options for local references, certain criteria were established for their consideration. *Unlikely* means there is very little possibility of a connection between the cultural context and the text, since it is unlikely that the first-century readers would have recognized the connection.[1] There would be a limited numbers of commentators taking this position and generally, strong reasons argue against it.

Possible means there is a good possibility that there is a connection, but for some reason it has been prevented from becoming a mainstream consideration. This would be due to the weight of the scholars opposed to it and the strength of their arguments.

The *Likely* indicates a strong likelihood of a connection due to the strength of the social-historical parallels with the text and likelihood of the first-century readers' recognition of the connection. In addition, based on the strength of scholarly support, the allusions are identified as Likely.

Certainly, one does not settle the issue of local reference by counting scholars; however, while this methodology is somewhat subjective, it does give a comparative analysis between the various weaknesses/strengths of the local references. This demonstrates that the approach to local reference is not an all-or-nothing proposition. It requires the examination of each allusion on its own merits. Although at times there can be a good deal of speculation (*Unlikely*) there are also some solid (*Likely*) connections with the local socio-historical setting.

[1] There is a significant difference between what the first-century readers actually understood and what the modern reader believes the first-century readers understood. Ramsey makes much of the difference between the twenth-century (European) and first-century (Asiatic) readers. Ramsay, *The Letters to the Seven Churches*, v–ix.

Ephesus	Unlikely	Possible	Likely
	2:1 *Holds the seven stars in his right hand* represents Ephesus as the leading city in Asia.[1] 2:6 The practice of the *Nicolaitans* is identified with the prostitution cult of the priestesses of Artemis.[2] 2:7 The church was a *paradise of God* and haven for repentant sinners, while the Artemis temple was an asylum for criminals.[3] 2:7 The *tree of life* is associated with the cross of Christ.[4]	2:1 Receives the first message as *Ephesus* is the most important city in Asia.[5] 2:2 *Deeds, hard work and perseverance* are pictured in "manifesting similar virtues in keeping the harbour" from silting up.[6] 2:4 *Giving up loving one another as they did at first* is recognized as a fault of the ordinary citizens (trade guild and commerce workers) of Ephesus according to Apollonius of Tyana.[7] 2:5 *Remove your lampstand from its place* is understood to mean that the primacy of the Ephesus ecclesiastical Holy See will be moved. It is now at the city of Magnesia ad Sipylum (modern Manisa, Turkey) only surpassed by Smyrna. Also, over time the citizens of Ephesus have relocated to Kirkindje.[8] 2:5 *Repent and do the things you did at first.* In a secular sense, this may have been a call to act now on the problem of the River Cayster silting as it had done in the past.[9] 2:5 The danger for both city and church was it "would be moved back under the	2:3 *You have persevered and have endured hardships* is exemplified by the persecution of Alexander the coppersmith (led by Jews - 2 Tim 4:14) and Demetrius the silversmith (led by Gentile - Acts 19:32–38).[13] 2:7 The *tree of life* is reminiscent of the sacred palm tree on Ephesian coins.[14] 2:7 *Tree of life* and *paradise of God* (Gen 3:23–24) had an analogue with the sacred groves of the temple of Artemis and the New Jerusalem (21:16–18).[15]

[1] Ramsay, *The Letters to Seven Churches*, 237–9.

[2] Alan F. Johnson, "Revelation," in *Hebrews—Revelation*, ed. Tremper Longman and David E Garland, Revised, EBC 13 (Grand Rapids: Zondervan, 2006), 614.

[3] Hemer, *Letters to the Seven Churches*, 50–52.

[4] Ibid., 42; J. Schneider, "Ξύλον," ed. Gerhard Kittel and Gerhard Friedrich, trans. Geoffrey W. Bromiley, *TDNT* (Grand Rapids: Eerdmans, 1985), 5:40; Richard Roberts, "The Tree of Life (Rev 2:7)," *ExpTim* 25 (1914): 332; Kraft, *Offenbarung*, 59; Osborne, *Revelation*, 124; Beale, *The Book of Revelation*, 235.

[5] Mounce, *Revelation*, 66.

[6] Worth, Jr., *Greco-Asian Culture*, 63; Chilton, *Days of Vengeance*, 96–97.

[7] Kiddle, *Revelation*, 17:23.

[8] Ramsay, *The Letters to Seven Churches*, 243–44. Hemer comments that where the city moved to is debatable and the this interpretation "may be open to some doubt." Hemer, *Letters to the Seven Churches*, 53, 37.

[9] Worth, Jr., *Greco-Asian Culture*, 63; Chilton, *Days of Vengeance*, 96–97. Oster indicates that documents from the second and fifth centuries AD indicate that the dredging was successful, revealing that the harbour was not silted up and at risk during the first century. Richard E. Oster, "Ephesus," ed. David Noel Freedman *et al.*, *ABD* (New York: Doubleday, 1996), 2:543.

	deadening power of the temple" of Artemis.[10] 2:6 The practice of the *Nicolaitans* is connected to the second cent. Gnostic sect of the same name (Irenaeus *Haer.* 1.26.3; 3.9.1).[11] 2:6 The practice of the *Nicolaitans* is identified with the Balaamites (Num 22–23) based on a similar etymology (2:14; Acts 15:20).[12]	

Smyrna	Unlikely	Possible	Likely
	2:8 The name *Smyrna* (myrrh) has coincidental connection to suffering from the NT use of myrrh in weeping, burial, and resurrection.[16] 2:8 *Who died and came to life* is compared to the resurrection of the Phoenix.[17] 2:9 *Synagogue of Satan* is partially justified by a reference to the reference to Rufina the Jewess, head of the synagogue, indicating that women were holding improper roles in the Synagogue.[18]	2:9 *Synagogue of Satan* is understood against the parallel in the assembly of Belial (1QHII:22) and the syncretistic worship of Zeus in the Jewish synagogues in Mysia and Delos.[22] 2:9 *Synagogue of Satan* is referring to a "hybrid Jewish-pagan cult."[23] 2:9 *Synagogue of Satan* is referring to a christian Gnostic group within the church.[24] 2:11 The Rabbinic phrase *second death* "perhaps answered	2:8 *The first and the last* is contrasted with Smyrna being the leading city of Asia, as prominently displayed on her coins.[26] 2:8 *Who died and came to life* is understood against the background of Smyrna's own destruction and restoration in 290 BC.[27] 2:9 *Synagogue of Satan* is understood against the backdrop of antagonism shown by local Jews, jealousy of Christian's exemption from participation in the imperial

[13] Tait, *Messages to the Seven Churches*, 136.

[14] While the obvious source of the tree of life imagery is the OT (Gen 2:9; 3:23–24; Ezek 31:2–9) and clearly a Jewish eschatological concept (*1 En.* 25:5; *3 En.* 23:18; *T. Levi* 18:11; *Apoc. Mos.* 28:4; *Apoc. El.* 5:6), Ramsay identified it with their Graeco-Asian roots. See Aune for a full development of the OT background. Aune, *Revelation 1-5*, 152–4. The *tree of life* motif was also known in other cultural contexts. Darice E. Birge, "Sacred Groves in the Ancient Greek World" (Ph.D. diss., University of California-Berkely, 1982), 27; Osborne, *Revelation*, 124; Ramsay, *The Letters to Seven Churches*, 246–9; Hemer, *The Letters to the Seven Churches*, 41–47; Franz, "Propaganda, Power and the Perversion," 80; Ford, *Revelation*, 388; Earl F Palmer, *1, 2, 3 John; Revelation* (Atlantia, Ga.: Nelson, 1982), 130; Worth, Jr., *Greco-Asian*, 68.

[15] Colin J. Hemer, "Seven Cities of Asia Minor," in *Major Cities of the Biblical World*, ed. R.K. Harrison (Nashville, TN: Nelson, 1985), 238; Hemer, *Letters to the Seven Churches*, 42, 44–45, 51; Franz, "Propaganda, Power and the Perversion," 80; Gerhard A. Krodel, *Revelation* (Minneapolis, MN: Augsburg Fortress, 1989), 109–110. Certainly, the Smyrnaean citizens would have known the Artemision royal gardens but the primary OT allusion in Genesis 2:9 is predominant.

[10] Hemer, *Letters to the Seven Churches*, 53.

[11] For a survey of the interpretations of the Nicolaitans see Henry Alford, *Hebrews-Revelation*, ed. Everett F. Harrison, GTCEC 4 (Chicago, IL: Moody, 1968), 4:563–4; Tait, *Messages to the Seven Churches*, 157–8.

[12] Tait, *Messages to the Seven Churches*, 159–60; Barclay, *Letters*, 23–24; Beale, *The Book of Revelation*, 251.

[16] Hemer, *Letters to the Seven Churches*, 58–59, 76; Thomas, *Rev 1–7*, 1:158; W. A Criswell, *Expository Sermons on Revelation* (Grand Rapids: Zondervan, 1975), 92.

[17] Hemer, *Letters to the Seven Churches*, 63–64; 231 n.28. Beale agrees that this view is possible but argues that it is not necessary as the connection with death and resurrection is made in the context. Beale, "Review of Colin J. Hemer," 110.

[18] Bernadette J. Brooten, *Women Leaders in the Ancient Synagogue: Inscriptional Evidence and Background Issues*, BJS (Atlanta, Ga.: Scholars Press, 1982), 5; Trebilco, *Jewish Communities in Asia Minor*, 104–13; Worth, Jr., *Greco-Asian Culture*, 82–84. The inscription is from the second century and may not be reflective of conditions in the first century.

2:10 *Be faithful, even to the point of death* is understood as a proverbial statement on Smyrna's faithfulness, attested to by an inscription.[19] 2:10 *Ten Days* of tribulation alluded to in local history, literature and an inscription.[20] 2:10 The *crown of life* is related to a halo crown of light.[21]	a Jewish taunt in Smyrna."[25]	cult, to the church.[28] 2:10 *Be faithful, even to the point of death* is understood against the background of Smyrna's faithfulness to Rome (Cicero *Phil.* 11.2.5),[29] and partially fulfilled in the martyrdom of Polycarp (*Mart. Pol.* 1.13; *FrgPol.* 64v.23).[30] 2:10 The *crown of life* is related to several allusions in coins, inscriptions, writings, victor's wreaths, and Mt. Pagus.[31] 2:10 The *crown of life* is related to a crown of athletic victory,[32] crown worn in cultic rites (Cybele or Bacchus),[33] honorary crowns[34] and a laurel crown depicted on coins.[35]

---

[22] Ford, *Revelation*, 393; W. O. E. Oesterley and T. H. Robinson, *A History of Israel* (Oxford: Oxford University Press, 1932), 424.

[23] Worth, Jr., *Greco-Asian Culture*, 84; Martin Hengel, *Judaism and Hellenism: Studies in Their Encounter in Palestine During the Early Hellenistic Period*, trans. John Bowde (Eugene, OR: Wipf & Stock, 2003), 308; W. W. Tarn, *Hellenistic Civilization*, 3d ed. (London: Arnold & Co., 1952), 225. Turner describes them as "some Judaeo-Gnostic sect." Cuthbert H. Turner, *Studies in Early Church History: Collected Papers* (Oxford: Oxford University Press, 1912), 202, 225.

[24] Kraabel, "Impact of the Discovery of the Sardis Synagogue," 180; John J. Pilch, "Lying and Deceit in the Letters to the Seven Churches: Perspectives from Cultural Anthropology," *Biblical Theology Bulletin* 22, no. 3 (1992): 131.

[26] Krodel, *Revelation*, 110; Worth, Jr., *Greco-Asian Culture*, 75. Both Ramsay and Hemer overlook this allusion.

[27] Ramsay, *The Letters to Seven Churches*, 251–2, 269–70. While Hemer questions the details of Ramsay's evidence for Smyrna's desolation, he still supports the basic thesis on more recent evidence. Hemer, *Letters to the Seven Churches*, 60–4, 76; Franz, "Propaganda, Power and the Perversion," 80; John Philip McMurdo Sweet, *Revelation*, T P I New Testament Commentaries (Valley Forge, PA: Trinity Press International, 1990), 651; Johnson, "Revelation," 617; Steve Gregg, *Revelation: Four Views: A Parallel Commentary* (Nashville, TN: Nelson, 1997), 66; David L. Barr, "The Apocalypse of John as Oral Enactment," *Int* 40, no. 3 (1986): 245 n. 9; M. Robert Mulholland, *Revelation: Holy Living in an Unholy World* (Grand Rapids: Asbury, 1990), 97–99. Moyise believes that this allusion is "extremely unlikely" but based on insufficient historical evidence. Steve Moyise, "Does the Author of Revelation Misappropriate the Scriptures?," *AUSS* 40, no. 1 (2002): 3–21.

[19] Hemer, *Letters to the Seven Churches*, 69, 77. Cadoux believes this to be a fanciful connection. Cecil J. Cadoux, *Ancient Smyrna: A History of the City from the Earliest Times to 224 A.D.* (Oxford: Basil Blackwell, 1938), 320 n. 1.

[20] Hemer acknowleged that the "possibility should not be pressed too far." Hemer, *Letters to the Seven Churches*, 69, 77.

[21] Beasley-Murray, *Revelation*, 83.

[25] Hemer, *Letters to the Seven Churches*, 75–77.

[28] Hemer, *Letters to the Seven Churches*, 65–68, 76; Osborne, *Revelation*, 131; Adela Yarbro Collins, "Vilification and Self-Definition in the Book of Revelation," *HTR* 79 (1986): 313; Kiddle, *Revelation*, 17:27; Frederick C. Grant, "Smyrna," in *DBib5*, 4:927; Mulholland, *Revelation*, 360.

[29] Ramsay, *The Letters to Seven Churches*, 275–6; Ford, *Revelation*, 395; Meinardus, *St. John of Patmos*, 62; Charles C. Whiting, *The Revelation of John: An Interpretation of the Book with an Introduction and a Translation* (Boston, MA: Gorham, 1918), 73; Charles Brown, *Heavenly Visions: An Exposition of the Book of Revelation* (Boston, MA: Pilgram, 1910), 63–64.

[30] Barclay, *Letters*, 31; Gregg, *Revelation: Four Views*, 66; Ramsay, *The Letters to Seven Churches*, 273; David S Clark, *The Message from Patmos: A Postmillennial Commentary on the Book of Revelation* (Grand Rapids: Baker, 1989), 35.

[31] Ramsay, *The Letters to Seven Churches*, 256–9; Hemer, *The Letters to the Seven Churches of Asia*, 60–75, 77. Cadoux believes Ramsay's connection of the garland and the city-buildings to be fanciful. Cadoux, *Ancient Smyrna*, 320 n. 1; Johnson, "Revelation," 618.

[32] Cadoux, *Ancient Smyrna*, 195–6; Metzger, *Breaking the Code*, 33; Jean Pierre Prévost, *How to Read the Apocalypse*, trans. John Bowden and Margaret Lydamore, The Crossroad Adult Christian Formation (New York: Crossroad, 1993), 73; Sweet, *Revelation*, 86; Swete, *Apocalypse*, lxi.

[33] Ramsay, *The Letters to Seven Churches*, 258; R. K. Harrison, *Archaeology of the New Testament: The Stirring Times of Christ and the Early Church Come to Life in the Latest Findings of Science* (Grand Rapids: Eerdmans, 1985), 53; Johnson, "Revelation," 618.

[34] Hemer, *Letters to the Seven Churches*, 73–74; 234 n. 58.

Pergamum	Unlikely	Possible	Likely
	2:13 *In the days of Antipas, my faithful witness, who was put to death in your city* according to the document *Acta Sanctorum,* Antipas was roasted to death in a bronze bull.[36] 2:13 *Satan's throne* is likened to the shape of the acropolis.[37] 2:13 *where Satan has his throne* represented by the immoral excesses displayed by Pergmum's citizens.[38] 2:17a. The *hidden manna* may also have its background in the pressures of the imperial cult.[39] 2:17a The *hidden manna* is understood as part of the Eucharist,[40] or granules of frankincense placed on temple altars.[41] 2:17b The *white stone with a new name written on it* is understood against the background of rewards for athletic victors,[42] discharged gladiators,[43] initiation to the service of Asclepius, the Greek god of healing, and permanent writings in contrast to impermanence of parchment.[44]	2:13 *where Satan has his throne* supports several possibilities in the cult of the Asklepieion (healing temple),[45] shape of the altar of Zeus,[46] and as Asia Minor's centre of Roman rule.[47] 2:13 *where Satan has his throne* represents outside sentiments and the "local hostility toward the Pergamene assembly [church]."[48] 2:17b The *white stone with a new name written on it* is understood against the background of a *tessera* which "served as a token for admission to the banquet"[49] and thus connected to the supper of the Lamb.[50] 2:17b The *white stone with a new name written on it* is understood against the background of jurors using white stones to cast votes of acquittal (Plutarch *Mor.* 186).[51] 2:17c. *A new name written on it* is understood against the background of the ancient near eastern belief that to give another their name was to possess (intimate relationship)	2:12, 16 *Sharp two-edged sword* is contrasted with the right and power of the sword of the Roman proconsul in the city where Antipas was one of its victims (as an *ius gladii* Lat. for "enemies of the state").[55] 2:13 *where Satan has his throne* is understood against the background of Pergamum being Asia Minor's centre of the imperial cult at the temple of Augustus, Severus and Trajaneum.[56] 2:13 *where Satan has his throne* represented as the collective polytheistic groups.[57] 2:14 *The teaching of Baalem. . .eating food sacrificed to idols and by committing sexual immorality* refers literally to the pagan feasts.[58] 2:17a The *hidden manna* is used in conjunction with Jewish tradition where the manna (Exod 16:1-36; Num 11:1-9) would be hidden under Mount Sinai, in the ark of the covenant, only to be revealed at the return of the Messiah (2 Macc 2:4–7; *2 Bar.* 6.7–8; 29.8;

---

[35] Barclay, *Letters*, 38–39.

[36] Eusebius, who mentions other martyrs of Pergamum, does not mention Antipas (Eusebius *Hist. eccl.* 2.4.15). Tait, *Messages to the Seven Churches*, 232.

[37] Peter Wood, "Local Knowledge of the Letters of the Apocalypse," *ExpTim* 73 (1962 1961): 264; Charles, *Revelation*, 1:61. Hemer believes this to be only picturesque and the argument better suites Smyrna. Hemer, *Letters to the Seven Churches*, 84. Beasley-Murray raises this as a possibility but prefers the altar of Zeus as his primary connection. Beasley-Murray, *Revelation*, 84.

[38] Specific evidence is not provided by these authors. J. A Seiss, *The Apocalypse* (Colorado Springs, Colo.: Cook, 1906), 100–101; Tait, *Messages to the Seven Churches*, 229; John T. Hinds, *A Commentary on the Book of Revelation*, New Testament Commentaries (Gospel Advocate) (Nashville, TN: Gospel Advocate, 1974), 34.

[39] Hemer, *Letters to the Seven Churches*, 94–95, 105.

[40] Pierre Prigent, *Apocalypse et Liturgie*, Cahiers Théologiques 52 (Lausanne: Delachaux et Niestlé, 1964), 22; *L'Apocalypse de saint Jean*, Commentaire du Nouveau Testament (Lausanne: Delachaux et Niestlé, 1981), 54; Philip Edgcumbe Hughes, *The Book of the Revelation: A Commentary* (Grand Rapids: Eerdmans, 1990), 46; Mulholland, *Revelation*, 109.

[41] Krodel, *Revelation*, 120–21; Court, *Myth and History*, 32–33.

[42] Hanns Lilje, *The Last Book of the Bible: The Meaning of the Revelation of St. John*, trans. Olive Wyon (Philadelphia, PA: Muhlenberg, 1957), 82.

[43] Ramsay dismisses this analogy for failing to make the essential points of comparison and not drawing on the familiarity of the reader's experience. Ramsay, *The Letters to Seven Churches*, 303; Barclay, *Letters*, 54; Ford, *Revelation*, 400.

[44] Ramsay, *The Letters to Seven Churches*, 302–306; Hemer, *Letters to the Seven Churches*, 96–103, 105.

[45] Here there are two possibilities. First, the Christian's aversion to calling the Greek god of healing, Asclepius, God-saviour (Gr. *theos soter*), and the Asclepion emblem of the serpent, associated by Christians as Satan (12:9), both would justify calling Pergamum the seat of Satan. Tait, *Messages to the Seven Churches*, 228; Ramsay, *The Letters to Seven Churches*, 285–86; Esther Onstad,

	that person (*Odes Sol.* 42:8, 9, 20; *1 En.* 69:14–19).[52] 2:17b The ***white stone with a new name written on it*** is understood against the background of Anatolian religious superstition where to know the name of a divine being or demon was to possess magical power over that supernatural being (i.e., Egyptian Scarab)[53] therefore, a spiritual union of the name of the victorious Christian with	*Sib. Or.* 7.149).[59] 2:17b The ***white stone with a new name written on it*** is associated with the OT High Priest's Urim and Thummim[60] or two onyx stones with names written on them worn on his ephod (Exod 28:9–12; *T. Levi* 8.12–14).[61] 2:17b ***A new name*** is connected to the historical setting of the new name given to Octavius of

Courage for Today, Hope for Tomorrow: A Study of the Revelation (Minneapolis, MN: Augsburg, 1993), 19. However, Barclay dismisses these connections, since Laodicea also had a similar connection but the phrase was not used for Laodicea. Barclay, *Letters*, 42–43.

[46] Deissmann, *Light from the Ancient East*, 85, 281 n. 3; Ford, *Revelation*, 393. Blaiklock combines the serpent allusions and the Saviour (Gr. *soter*) reference to conclude "perhaps," in reference to the physical appearance of the structure. Edward M. Blaiklock, *Cities of the New Testament* (New York: Revell, 1965), 105. While Blaiklock is tentative in his earlier work he uses the stronger "must" to argue for the throne of Zeus in Blaiklock, *Archaeology of the NT*, 126–8; Michael Avi-Yonah, ed., *Views of the Biblical World: The New Testament*, vol. 5 (Jerusalem: International, 1961), 271; Kelshaw, *Send This Message*, 93–94.

[47] Adela Yarbro Collins, *Crisis and Catharsis: The Power of the Apocalypse* (Louisville, KY: Westminster/Knox, 1984), 101–102; Charles, *A Critical and Exegetical Commentary on the Revelation of St John*, 1:60–61. Hemer legitimately challenges Ramsay's defence of Pergamum as the official capital of Asia Minor in favour of its rival Ephesus. Hemer, *Letters to the Seven Churches*, 82–84; Ramsay, *The Letters to Seven Churches*, 289; "Pergamum," in *DBib*, 3:750; Tait, *Messages to the Seven Churches*, 225–6; Farrer, *Revelation*, 73.

[48] Friesen, "Satan's Throne," 365.

[49] James M Efird, *Revelation For Today: An Apocalyptic Approach* (Nashville, TN: Abingdon, 1989), 57; Wilfrid J Harrington, *Revelation*, ed. Daniel J Harrington, Sacra Pagina Series 16 (Collegeville, Minn.: Liturgical, 2008), 62; Mounce, *The Book of Revelation*, 83. "That the banquet meal is in mind is supported by the reference to 'manna'" Beale, *The Book of Revelation*, 252–3; Johnson, "Revelation," 620; Hemer, *The Letters to the Seven Churches*, 98; Charles Homer Giblin, *The Book of Revelation: The Open Book of Prophecy*, Good News Studies 34 (Collegeville, Minn.: Liturgical, 1991), 57.

[50] Charles, *Revelation*, 1:66–67; Swete, *Apocalypse*, 40–41.

[51] Walter Bauer *et al.*, eds., "ψηφος," BDAG, 892; *NewDocs* 1:84; Avi-Yonah, ed., *Views of the Biblical World: NT*, 272; Barclay, *Letters*, 53–54. While, for Ramsay, the voting ballots analogy by itself is unsatisfactory, he accepts them as a useful visual connection for the custom innovation of the white stone. Ramsay, *The Letters to Seven Churches*, 302–306. See Hemer for further allusions. Hemer, *The Letters to the Seven Churches*, 242 n. 85. Osborne admits, "It is impossible to know for certain which of these is the best source for the imagery. . . . the best background would be a combination of the stone given victors at the games for entrance into a feast and possibly overtones of a vote of acquittal" Osborne, *Revelation*, 148–9.

[55] In contrast, Jesus possessed the power of life and death. Ramsay, *The Letters to Seven Churches*, 291–2; Hemer, *Letters to the Seven Churches*, 82–84, 104; Osborne, *Revelation*, 140; Mulholland, *Revelation*, 105; Whiting, *Revelation of John*, 78; Mounce, *Revelation*, 79; *What Are We Waiting For?: A Commentary on Revelation.* (Eugene, OR: Wipf & Stock, 2004), 9; James T. Draper, Jr., *The Unveiling: Inspirational Expositions of the Book of Revelation from a Premillennial Viewpoint* (Nashville, TN: Broadman, 1984), 54; Ford, *Revelation*, 398.

[56] Ramsay, *The Letters to Seven Churches*, 294–6; Hemer, *Letters to the Seven Churches*, 85, 87, 104; Franz, "Propaganda, Power and the Perversion," 80; Boring, *Revelation*, 91; Mounce, *Revelation*, 79; Charles, *Revelation*, 1:61; Kiddle, *Revelation*, 17:30; Swete, *Apocalypse*, 34; Osborne, *Revelation*, 141–3; Barclay, *Letters*, 44–45; Aune, *Revelation 1-5*, 183–4. Certainly, the allusion within the other temples of Zeus and Asclepius may also be relevant. Friesen contends, "that there are no references to imperial cults anywhere in Rev. 2–3." Friesen, "Satan's Throne," 366. Brent finds allusions to the imperial cult throughout the seven messages. Brent, *The Imperial Cult*, 178–90; Pfleiderer, *Primitive Christianity*, 415.

[57] Martin, *The Seven Letters*, 69; Lilje, *The Last Book of the Bible*, 79–80; Wood, "Local Knowledge of the Letters of the Apocalypse," 264; Caird, *Revelation*, 37; Tait, *Messages to the Seven Churches*, 225; Metzger, *Breaking the Code*, 35; Swete, *Apocalypse*, 34–35. Johnson defends this view by arguing that there was a concentration of polytheism in Pergamum compared with other polytheistic centres. Johnson, "Revelation," 619–20.

[58] Mounce places the emphasis on the literal understanding of the phrases while Caird argues that they could both be metaphorical and literal. The Balaam practice was similar to the beliefs of the Nicolaitans. Mounce, *Revelation*, 81; Caird, *Revelation*, 39; Barclay, *Letters*; Beale, *The Book of Revelation*, 251; Tait, *Messages to the Seven Churches*, 236–40, 243; Gordon Franz, "'Meat Offered to Idols' in Pergamum and Thyatira." *Bible and Spade* 14, no. 4 (2001): 105–110.

[52] Walther Eichrodt, *Theology of the Old Testament*, Old Testament Library (Louisville, KY: Westminster/Knox, 1967), 2:40–45; 310–11; H. Bietenhard, "Ονομα," ed. Gerhard Kittel and Gerhard Friedrich, trans. Geoffrey W. Bromiley, *Theological Dictionary of the New Testament* (Grand Rapids: Eerdmans, 1985), 5:253–8; Beale, *The Book of Revelation*, 254; Johnson, "Revelation," 620.

[53] Barclay prefers the protection of the amulet as the best association. Barclay, *Letters to the Seven Churches*, 54.

		the name of God written on the white *tessera*.[54]	Augustus.[62]

Thyatira	Unlikely	Possible	Likely
	2:20 *Jezebel* is identified as the wife of an Asiarch (ruler of Asia)[63] or the woman, Lydia (Acts 16:14).[64] 2:28 The *morning star* refers to the planet Venus as the symbol of Roman authority or Lucifer's battle of the stars (Isa 14:12; *Sib. Or.* 5.516, 527).[65]	2:18 *The Son of God who has eyes like flaming fire* and *feet like fine brass* is contrasted with Apollo, the Son of Zeus, as seen on coins grasping the hand of the Emperor[66] and the fact that the brass guild thrived in Thyatira.[67] 2:20 *Jezebel* is identified as Sibyl Sambathe, a local female soothsayer, whose shrine was "before the city" (*CIG* 2:3509)[68] 2:28 While the *morning star* is primarily referring to Christ (22:16)[69] there may be an allusion to Statius' comparing	2:18 *feet are like burnished bronze* is identified as a metal[72] familiar to the local bronze guild[73] and identified as a copper-zinc produced by a special distillation process.[74] 2:20 *tolerate that woman Jezebel, who calls herself a prophetess. . .* promoting *sexual immorality and the eating of food sacrificed to idols* is identified with the trade-guilds immorality practices and idolatry.[75] 2:22 *Those who commit adultery* are identified with the tradeguilds practice of immorality.[76]

[59] Ramsay, *The Letters to Seven Churches*, 308; Charles, *Revelation*, 1:65; Hemer, *Letters to the Seven Churches*, 96–102; Barclay, *Letters*, 53; Bruce J. Malina, *The Palestinian Manna Tradition: The Manna Tradition in the Palestinian Targums and its Relationship to the New Testament Writings*, Arbeiten zur Geschichte des spateren Judentums und des Urchristentums 7 (Leiden: Brill, 1968); Mounce, *Revelation*, 82; Osborne, *Revelation*, 148; Caird, *Revelation*, 42; Beale, *The Book of Revelation*, 252; Tait, *Messages to the Seven Churches*, 247–8.

[60] Tait dismisses Trench's application of the Urim and Thummim. Tait, *Messages to the Seven Churches*, 249–50.

[61] Beale, *The Book of Revelation*, 253, 258; Moses Stuart, *A Commentary on the Apocalypse* (Whitefish, MT: Kessinger, 2007), 2:78–79; Chilton, *Days of Vengeance*, 110; Donald D. Guthrie, *The Apostles* (Grand Rapids: Zondervan, 1992), 390; Marcus L Loane, *They Overcame: An Exposition of the First Three Chapters of Revelation* (Grand Rapids: Baker, 1981), 63–64.

[54] Ramsay, *The Letters to Seven Churches*, 306–308. Beale points out that believers all receive the same name and it is not a secret magical name just given to overcomers. However, he does entertain the possibility "that the magical background of secret, incantional divine names additionally enhanced the meaning of the concluding phrase in 2:17." Beale, *The Book of Revelation*, 258.

[62] Worth, Jr., *Greco-Asian Culture*, 152–3; William Barclay, *The Revelation of John: Chapters 1 to 5*, vol. 1, NDSB (Louisville, KY: Westminster/Knox, 2004), 1:99; Ramsay, *The Letters to Seven Churches*, 306–11.

[63] Edward Carus Selwyn, *The Christian Prophets and the Prophetic Apocalypse* (New York: MacMillan, 2009), 123 n. 1.

[64] Hemer, *Letters to the Seven Churches*, 250 n. 50.

[65] Ernst Lohmeyer, *Die Offenbarung Des Johannes*, Handbuch Zum Neuen Testament 16 (Tübingen: Siebeck, 1926), 30; Eduard Lohse, *Die Offenbarung Des Johannes*, Das Neue Testament Deutsch 11 (Göttingen: Vandenhoeck & Ruprecht, 1960), 28. Kistemaker points out that Christ's sovereignty would clash with this view. Kistemaker, *Book of Revelation*, 142 n. 70; Johann Lepsius, "Dr. Johann Lepsius on the Symbolic Language of the Apocalypse," ed. William M. Ramsay, trans. H. Ramsay, *The Expositor* 8, no. 1 (1911): 153–71; Robert W. Wall, *Revelation*, ed. W. Ward Gasque, New International Biblical Commentary (Peabody, MA: Hendrickson, 2002), 79.

[66] Mounce, *Revelation*, 85.

[67] Ramsay, *The Letters to Seven Churches*, 235; Franz, "Propaganda, Power and the Perversion," 84; Caird, *Revelation*, 43; Meinardus, *St. John of Patmos*, 94; Ford, *Revelation*, 405.

[68] Emil Schürer, *Die Prophetin Isabel in Thyatira, Offen. Joh., II, 20 , 11.*, ed. A. V. Harnack, Theologische Abhandlungen: Carl von Weizsäcker Zu Seinem Siebzigsten Geburtstage (Freiburg, Germany: Mohr Siebeck, 1892), 39–58; Arthur S. Peake, *The Revelation of John* (London: Johnson, 1919), 246–47 n. 1; Swete, *Apocalypse*, 42–43. Ramsay remarks that this theory is "as yet a mere tantalising possibility." Ramsay, *The Letters to Seven Churches*, 323. Charles and Beckwith rejected it because the sibylline priestess would not be a church member. Charles, *Revelation*, 1:70; Beckwith, *Apocalypse*, 466. Hemer on the other hand, argues, "This view deserves consideration." Hemer, *Letters to the Seven Churches*, 117.

[69] Charles, *Revelation*, 1:77; Swete, *Apocalypse*, 47; Richard C. Trench, *Commentary on the Epistles to the Seven Churches in Asia: Revelation 2, 3*, 2nd ed. (London: Parker, Son & Bourn, 1861), 154–55; Edward Hayes Plumptre, *A Popular Exposition of the Epistles to the Seven Churches of Asia* (London: Hodder & Stoughton, 1887), 149–50; Ticonius, *The Turin Fragments of Tyconius' Commentary on Revelation*, ed. Francesco Lo Bue, Texts and Studies: Contributions to Biblical and Patristic Literature (Cambridge: Cambridge University Press, 2009), 58; Hendriksen, *More than Conquerors*, 72–73.

	of Domitian with the morning star (Statius *Silv.* 4.1.1–4).[70] 2:28 The *morning star* alludes to Balaam's words in Numbers 24:17 as both a sceptre and a star.[71]	2:24 *Satan's so-called deep secrets* is an allusion to the proto-Gnostics identified with Jezebel and their deep secrets (mysteries).[77] 2:27 *Iron sceptre and dash them to pieces like pottery* (Ps 2:9) are understood against the background of the products of local industry.[78]

Sardis	Unlikely	Possible	Likely
	3:1–2 *but you are dead* is understood against the background of the impressive necropolis (city of death) and temple of Artemis.[79] 3:5 *Be dressed in white* is understood based upon the practice of wearing white for baptism candidates or members of the Essene community.[80]	3:5 *Be dressed in white.* White garments were proper attire for worship,[81] festal occasions,[82] and the Gymnasium.[83] 3:5 *Be dressed in white* is understood against the invention of dying wool attributed to Sardis.[84] 3:5 *I will not erase his name from the book of life* is explained against the practice of blotting out the names of criminal offenders from the list of citizens.[85]	3:2 *Be watchful,* (KJV) and 3:3 *I will come like a thief* are understood against the historical background of the acropolis twice falling to the enemies of Sardis (Cyrus and Antiochus III) due to a lack of vigilance among the city's defenders.[86] 3:3 *I will come like a thief, and you will not know at what time I will come to you.* Understood against the history of four sudden earthquakes in twelve years

[72] Charles, *Revelation*, 1:29; Swete, *Apocalypse*, 17; Moffatt, *Revelation*, 244–45; Beckwith, *Apocalypse*, 438–39.

[73] Kiddle, *Revelation*, 17:37; Caird, *Revelation*, 43. Plumptre rejects this connection on the basis that "the imagery had already been used without reference to any local coloring." Plumptre, *The Seven Churches of Asia*, 135. However, as Hemer points out this misunderstands the nature of the unity of the structure (compare 1:15 and 2:18). Hemer, *Letters to the Seven Churches*, 111.

[74] Hemer argues primarily from a political, economic, and geographical position (*IGR* 4:1259). Hemer, *Letters to the Seven Churches*, 111–17, 127. A Greek inscription mentions the Thyatiran guild of *Chalkos* (Lat. *aes*, brass). Kistemaker, *Revelation*, 136.

[75] While there is no direct identification of Jezebel with an individual, the practices correlate to the trade-guilds. Hemer, *Letters to the Seven Churches*, 128; Charles, *Revelation*, 1:70–71; Ramsay, *The Letters to Seven Churches*, 346–49; Kiddle, *Revelation*, 17:39. The parallel between Jezebel's seduction of Israel from her worship of Yahweh through syncretism with Baal (2 Kgs 9:22) and the first-century potential for syncretism with the imperial cult is striking. Caird, *Revelation*, 44–45.

[76] Hendriksen, *More than Conquerors*, 71; Barclay, *Letters*, 61.

[70] Hemer doubts that any one of these offers proof but rather "each furnish materials for conjecture, but none which offers a secure background for the thought of the passage. . . . It is because it needed no amplification that we are given no context." Hemer, *The Letters to the Seven Churches*, 126, 128, 253 n. 75.

[71] Hendriksen, *More than Conquerors*, 73; Kistemaker, *Revelation*, 142; Hughes, *The Book of the Revelation*, 52–53; Sweet, *Revelation*, 97.

[77] Wall, *Revelation*, 78–79; Barclay, *Letters*, 66.

[78] Wall, *Revelation*, 77.

[79] Johnson, "Revelation," 626; Wood, "Local Knowledge," 264. Worthy dismisses this connection since it would require a "limiting of the description to *one apparently specific location*." Worth, Jr., *Greco-Asian Culture*, 192.

[80] Martin, *The Seven Letters*, 90–91; Collins, *The Apocalypse*, 25; Guthrie, *The Relevance of John's Apocalypse*, 80.

[81] Ramsay, *The Letters to Seven Churches*, 386; Ford, *Revelation*, 409; Metzger, *Breaking the Code*, 39; Blaiklock, *Cities of the New Testament*, 117; Johnson, "Revelation," 626.

[82] Blaiklock, *Cities of the New Testament*, 117; Meinardus, *St. John of Patmos*, 106; Ramsay, *The Letters to Seven Churches*, 386.

[83] Kelshaw, *Send This Message*, 133–34.

[84] Ford, *Revelation*, 410; Johnson, "Revelation," 627–28; Mounce, *Revelation*, 112.

[85] Barclay, *Revelation of John*, 1:47; Kiddle, *Revelation*, 17:47; Hemer, *Letters to the Seven Churches*, 148–49.

		(AD 17–29).[87]

Philadelphia	Unlikely	Possible	Likely
	3:12 *I will make him a pillar in the temple of My God … and I will write upon him the name of My God.* Understood against the background of the Imperial Cult where the high priest carved his name into a bust which was placed in the temple.[88]	3:12 *Pillar in the temple of my God* connected with the temple pillars and the stability necessary for a city plagues by earthquakes.[89] 3:12 *I will make him a pillar in the temple of My God … and I will write upon him the name of My God.* Understood against the background of cutting inscriptions into pillars.[90]	3:8 *I have placed before you an open door that no-one can shut.* Understood against Philadelpia's cultural position as the door to the east in the spread of Greek culture.[91] 3:12 *Never again will he leave it* is understood against the background of the city being evacuated following the earthquake in AD 17 and 23 (Strabo *Geogr.* 12.8.18; 13.4.10).[92] 3:12 *I will write on him the name of my God and the name of the city of my God, the New Jerusalem* is understood in light of the city adopting two new names: Neocaesarea and Flavia.[93]

Laodicea	Unlikely	Possible	Likely
		3:18 *I counsel you to buy from me gold refined in the fire, so that you can become rich.* The wealth of Laodicea (a banking centre), was well known, as they refused funds from the Romans to rebuild following the earthquake of AD 17.[94] 3:18 *white garments, that you may clothe yourself, and that the shame of your nakedness may not be revealed.*	3:15–16 *neither cold nor hot… because you are lukewarm–neither hot nor cold–I am about to spit you out of my mouth.* This is well accepted to be an allusion to the local water supply[98] from the surrounding region.[99] 3:17 *You say "I am rich," have become wealthy and have need of nothing* is connected to the affluence and self sufficiency

[86] Mounce, *Revelation*, 93; Caird, *Revelation*, 47; Krodel, *Revelation*, 133; Worth, Jr., *Greco-Asian Culture*, 184–88; Wood, "Local Knowledge," 264.

[87] Mitten, "A New Look at Ancient Sardis," 61.

[88] L. van Hartingsveld, *Revelation: A Practical Commentary*, trans. John Vriend (Grand Rapids: Eerdmans, 1985), 23–24; Barclay, *Revelation of John*, 1:134–35; Ford, *Revelation*, 417. However, Hemer points out that there is no evidence of this custom and the Imperial Cult rank of *neocorate* was not given to Philadelphia until AD 213. Hemer, *Letters to the Seven Churches*, 268.

[89] Kiddle, *Revelation*, 17:53.

[90] Hemer, *Letters to the Seven Churches*, 268.

[91] Ford, *Revelation*, 415; Meinardus, *St. John of Patmos*, 115; Brown, *Heavenly Visions*, 105–106.

[92] Hemer, "Unto the Angels of the Churches," 171–73; Franz, "Propaganda, Power and the Perversion," 84; Caird, *Revelation*, 55; Krodel, *Revelation*, 135; Harrington, *Revelation*, 71; Charles W. Budden and Edward Hastings, *The Local Colour of the Bible* (Edinburgh: T&T Clark, 1925), 3:329–30.

[93] Ramsay, *The Letters to Seven Churches*, 397–98; Franz, "Propaganda, Power and the Perversion," 84; Edward M. Blaiklock, *The Seven Churches: An Exposition of Revelation Chapters Two and Three* (London: Marshall, Morgan & Scott, 1951), 64.

[94] Worth, Jr., *Greco-Asian Culture*, 218–19; Hemer, *Letters to the Seven Churches*, 191–96, 208; Charles, *Revelation*, 1:93. Unger connects their wealth with their proximity to several major trade routes. Merrill F. Unger, *Archaeology and the New Testament* (Grand Rapids: Zondervan, 1975), 267.

	Contrasted with Laodicea's dependence on the black wool clothing trade.[95] 3:20 *I stand at the door and knock.* The door of the four city gates, important aspects of the city being on a trade route.[96] 3:21 *I will give the right to sit with me on my throne.*The throne of Laodicea awarded to the orator Zeno, and the Zenonids family who defended the city and defeated Labienus Parthicus in 40 BC.[97]	of the city. It declined aid from the government following the earthquake of AD 60.[100] 3:17 *you are blind. . . buy. . .eye salve to anoint your eyes, that you may see.* Connected to the Phrygian eye powder or salve produced in Hierapolis.[101]

[98] Porter argues that the water supply was from the hot springs in Hierapolis based on the calcification in the terracotta water pipes found by archaeologists. Porter, "Why the Laodiceans Received Lukewarm Water (Rev 3:15–18)," 147.

[99] Rudwick and Green, "The Laodicean Lukewarmness," 176–78; Bruce, "Colossian Problems, Part 1: Jews and Christians in the Lycus Valley," 3–15; Sweet, *Revelation*, 107; Yamauchi, *NT Cities*, 141; Court, *Myth and History*, 40; Mounce, *Revelation*, 123; Johnson, "Laodicea and Its Neighbors," 1–18; Hemer, *Letters to the Seven Churches*, 277; Harrington, *Revelation*, 74; Chilton, *Days of Vengeance*, 134; Beasley-Murray, *Revelation*, 105; Giblin, *The Book of Revelation*, 65; Swete, *Apocalypse*, 60; Kelshaw, *Send This Message*, 165.

[95] Hemer, *Letters to the Seven Churches*, 247; Ramsay, *The Letters to Seven Churches*, 234; Ford, *Revelation*, 419; Sweet, *Revelation*, 108; Worth, Jr., *Greco-Asian Culture*, 217–18.

[96] Ramsay does not believe that verse 20 is part of the message to Laodicea but identified it as an added epilogue; however Hemer disagrees, arguing that it must have a conclusion like all the other messages. Ramsay, *The Letters to Seven Churches*, 236; Hemer, *Letters to the Seven Churches*, 204.

[97] Hemer, *Letters to the Seven Churches*, 205–206, 209.

[100] Franz, "Propaganda, Power and the Perversion," 84.

[101] Hemer, *Letters to the Seven Churches*, 196–99; Ramsay, *Cities and Bishoprics of Phrygia*, 2:52; Harrington, *Revelation*, 75; Rudwick and Green, "The Laodicean Lukewarmness," 176; Sweet, *Revelation*, 118; Wilcock, *Message of Revelation*, 56–57; Yamauchi, *NT Cities*, 145–46; Blaiklock, *Cities of the New Testament*, 125.

CHART 14: PROPOSED DATING FOR THE PATRIARCHS[1]

Period	Proponents	Dates BC	Evidence
Early Bronze 3 2800–2500 BC 3rd Millenium BC	D. N. Freedman	2650–2350[2]	Support the SST Ebla tablets Destruction of Bâb edh-Dhrâ` in 2350 BC
Intermediate Bronze 1 and 2 (MB 1) 2500–1950 BC (formerly under the early chronology EB 4 and MB 1) Late 3rd, Early 2nd Millenium BC	W. van Hattem K. Kenyon R. Price B. Wood J. Walton & R. Price E. Hindson & E. Towns J. Bimson N. Glueck E. Merrill	2400–2300[3] 2300–1900[4] 2275–2000[5] 2166–1991 (Abraham)[6] 2166–1805[7] 2166–1806[8] 2150–1992[9] 2100–1900[10] 2100–1700[11]	Literal biblical chronology based on a mid- fifteenth cent. BC date for the Exodus Antiquity of Accounts (Gen 14). Geopolitical conditions and climate of region. Nomadism-migration Personal names & places Texts from Egypt, Ur, Mari, Ebla, Nuzi and Hittites (twentieth to eighteenth cent. BC)

[1] Adapted from Price and House, *Zondervan Handbook of Biblical Archaeology*, 77. Also, see Chart 2 for different dates for the archaeological periods used by various scholars.

[2] Freedman states, "If Abraham and Lot had anything to do with the Cities of the Plain, then that link could only have existed in the Early Bronze Age, certainly not in the Middle Bronze Age." Freedman, "The Real Story of the Ebla Tablets," 157; Shanks, "BAR Interviews Giovanni Pettinato," 47; Albright, "The Jordan Valley in the Bronze Age," 58–61. Pettinato replied to Freedman's dating the Patriarchal Age to the third millennium as "impossible."

[3] Willem C. van Hattem, "Once Again: Sodom and Gomorrah," *BA* 44, no. 2 (Spring 1981): 90.

[4] Kenyon identifies the patriarchs with a Canaanite migration and "invasion of Palestine by nomad tribes of Amorites." Kathleen M. Kenyon, "Excavations in Jerusalem, 1965," *PEQ* 98, no. 1 (1966): 75; *Amorites and Canaanites*, Schweich Lectures on Biblical Archaeology (Oxford: Oxford University Press, 1967), 76; Paul W. Lapp, *The Dhahr Mirzbaneh Tombs: Three Intermediate Bronze Age Cemeteries in Jordan* (Philadelphia, PA: American Schools of Oriental Research, 1966), 114.

[5] Price and House, *Zondervan Handbook of Biblical Archaeology*, 41.

[6] Wood claims that the date for the destruction of Sodom is ca. 2070 BC based on a 1446 BC date for the Exodus. Randall Price, in the *Zondervan Handbook* (p. 41), places the destruction of Sodom and Gomorrah in 2067 BC. The date of the destruction of Bab edh-Dhra according to Rast and Schaub is 2350 BC. Wood, "Discovery of the Sin Cities," 1999, 78; "Locating Sodom: A Critique of the Northern Proposal," 81.

[7] John H. Walton, *Chronological and Background Charts of the Old Testament* (Grand Rapids: Zondervan, 1994), 15; Price, *The Stones Cry Out*, 92; *Zondervan Handbook of Biblical Archaeology*, 74.

[8] Ed Hindson and Elmer L. Towns, *Illustrated Bible Survey: An Introduction* (Nashville, TN: B&H, 2013), 36.

[9] Bimson, "Archaeological Data," 84–85.

[10] Nelson Glueck, *Rivers in the Desert: A History of the Negev* (New York: Farrar, Straus and Cudahy, 1959), 61–84; *The Other Side of the Jordan*, 15–16.

[11] Merrill, *Kingdom of Priests*, 47–48, 83–96; "Texts, Talls, and Old Testament Chronology," 20–21.

Period	Proponents	Dates BC	Evidence
Middle Bronze 2A/B	K. Kitchen, A. Millard	1991–1786[12]	13th cent. BC date for the Exodus. Hyksos in Egypt
1950–1650 BC	W. Albright, N. Glueck, S. Schultz, G. Wright, J. Hoffmeier	2000–1700[13]	Pottery in Negev
Late 2nd Millenium BC	S. Collins	2000–1600[14]	Beni-Hasan mural (1890 BC)
	J. P. Free, A. Hoerth & J. McRay	2000–1500[15]	Egyptian chronology (middle kingdom)
	G. Archer	2100–1500[16]	Geopolitical conditions (Genesis 14)[20]
	B. Walke, J. Goldingay, W. La Sor	1950–1550[17]	Price of slaves and covenant structure
	B. Arnold	1800–1650[18]	Amorite Hypothesis
	J. Holden & N. Geisler	1800–1550[19]	
Middle Bronze 2B/C	A. Mazar	1750–1550[21]	Remembered traditions
1750–1550 BC			Mari/Nuzi archives
1st Millenium BC			Properous urban culture
			Hyksos Dynasty
Late Bronze	C. Gordon	1550–1200[22]	Cuneiform and Egyptian parallels
1550–1200 BC			Amarna and Nuzi Tablets
1st Millenium BC			

[12] Kenneth A. Kitchen and T. C. Mitchell, "Chronology of the Old Testament," ed. I. Howard Marshall *et al.*, *NBD* (Downers Grove, IL: InterVarsity, 1996), 190; Millard, "Methods of Studying the Patriarchal Narratives as Ancient Texts," 43–58.

[13] Albright states on the basis of the evidence at Bab edh-Dhra that "it does suggest very strongly that the date of Abraham cannot be placed earlier than the nineteenth century BC" (1900 to 1801 BC). Albright, *The Archaeology of Palestine and the Bible*, 10; "A Revision of Early Hebrew Chronology," *JPOS* 1 (1921): 68, 79; Glueck, *Rivers in the Desert*, 61–84; *The Other Side of the Jordan*, 15–16; Samuel J. Schultz and Gary V. Smith, *Exploring the Old Testament* (Wheaton, IL: Crossway, 2001), 209; Wright, *Biblical Archaeology*, 50; Hoffmeier, *The Archaeology of the Bible: Reassessing Methodologies and Assumptions*, 68. Hoffmeier narrows the date to 1800-1540 in his *Israel in Egypt* book.

[14] Collins has a slightly narrower date of 1950–1550 in his response to Bryant Wood. Collins, "A Response to Bryant G. Wood," 27; "Sodom: The Discovery of a Lost City," *BS* 20, no. 3 (2007): 72.

[15] Free and Vos, *Archaeology and Bible History*, 64; Hoerth and McRay, *Bible Archaeology*, 101.

[16] Archer identifies these dates as the Middle Bronze Age. Gleason L. Archer, *A Survey of Old Testament Introduction*, Rev Upd (Chicago, IL: Moody, 1996), 184.

[17] Bruce K. Waltke and Cathi J. Fredricks, *Genesis: A Commentary* (Grand Rapids: Zondervan, 2001), 30; Goldingay, "The Patriarchs in Scripture and History," 11; William Sanford La Sor *et al.*, *Old Testament Survey: The Message, Form, and Background of the Old Testament*, 2nd ed. (Grand Rapids: Eerdmans, 1996), 38–43.

[18] Bill T. Arnold, *Encountering the Book of Genesis* (Grand Rapids: Baker, 2003), 86.

[19] Geisler and Holden base part of their arguments on the Excavations at Tall el-Ḥammâm. Geisler and Holden, *Popular Handbook of Archaeology and the Bible*, 191.

[20] Sarna, "The Patriarchs Genesis 12-36," 118.

[21] Mazar, *Archaeology of the Land of the Bible*, 1:225–226; Amihai Mazar, "The Patriarchs, Exodus and Conquest Narratives in Light of Archaeology," in *The Quest for the Historical Israel*, ed. Israel Finkelstein and Brian B. Schmidt, Archaeology and Biblical Studies 17 (Atlanta, Ga.: Society of Biblical Literature, 2007), 59.

[22] Cyrus H. Gordon, "The Patriarchal Narratives," *JNES* 13 (1954): 56–59; *Introduction to Old Testament Times* (Ventnor, NJ: Ventnor, 1953), chapter 8; "Biblical Customs and the Nuzu Tablets," 1–12; "The New Amarna Tablets," *Orientalia* 16 (1947): 1–21; "Hebrew Origins in the Light of Recent Discovery," in *Biblical and Other Studies*, ed. Alexander Altmann (Cambridge, MA: Harvard University Press, 1963), 5–6.

Period	Proponents	Dates BC	Evidence
Iron 1A 1200–1000 BC 1st Millenium BC	B. Mazar Y. Aharoni Z. Herzog	1250–1150[23]	Remembered in monarchy Excavations at Beersheba (no MB) Anarchronisms in Gen Account Mention of Philistines and Arameans
Persian/Greek tradition 400–165 BC Exilic–Post-Maccabean	T. L. Thompson J. Van Seeters S. M. Warner	400–165[24]	Literary and oral tradition Use of folklore

[23] Benjamin Mazar, *The World History of the Jewish People: Ancient Times: Patriarchs*, vol. 2 (London: Rutger's University Press, 1970), 169–87, 276–78; Aharoni, *The Land of the Bible*, 133–90; Ze'ev Herzog, "Deconstructing the Walls of Jericho," *Ha'aretz Magazine*, 1999, 4–5.

[24] Thompson, *Historicity of the Patriarchal Narratives*, 89; Seters, *Abraham in History and Tradition*; S. M. Warner, "The Patriarchs and Extra-Biblical Sources," *JSOT* 2 (1977): 50–61.

TIMELINES

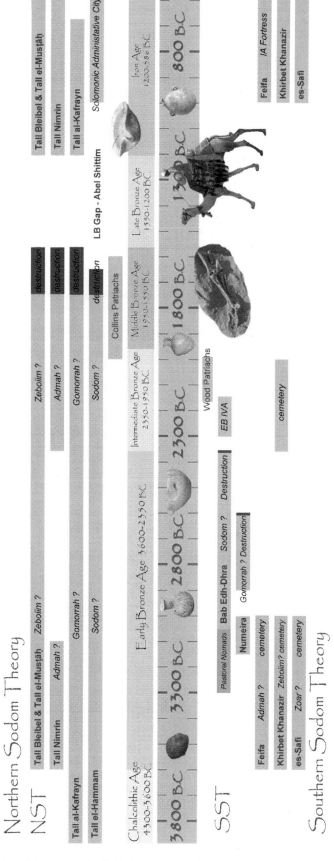

208. **Chart 15:** Timeline for the proposed location of the sites associated with the Northern and Southern Sodom Theories.

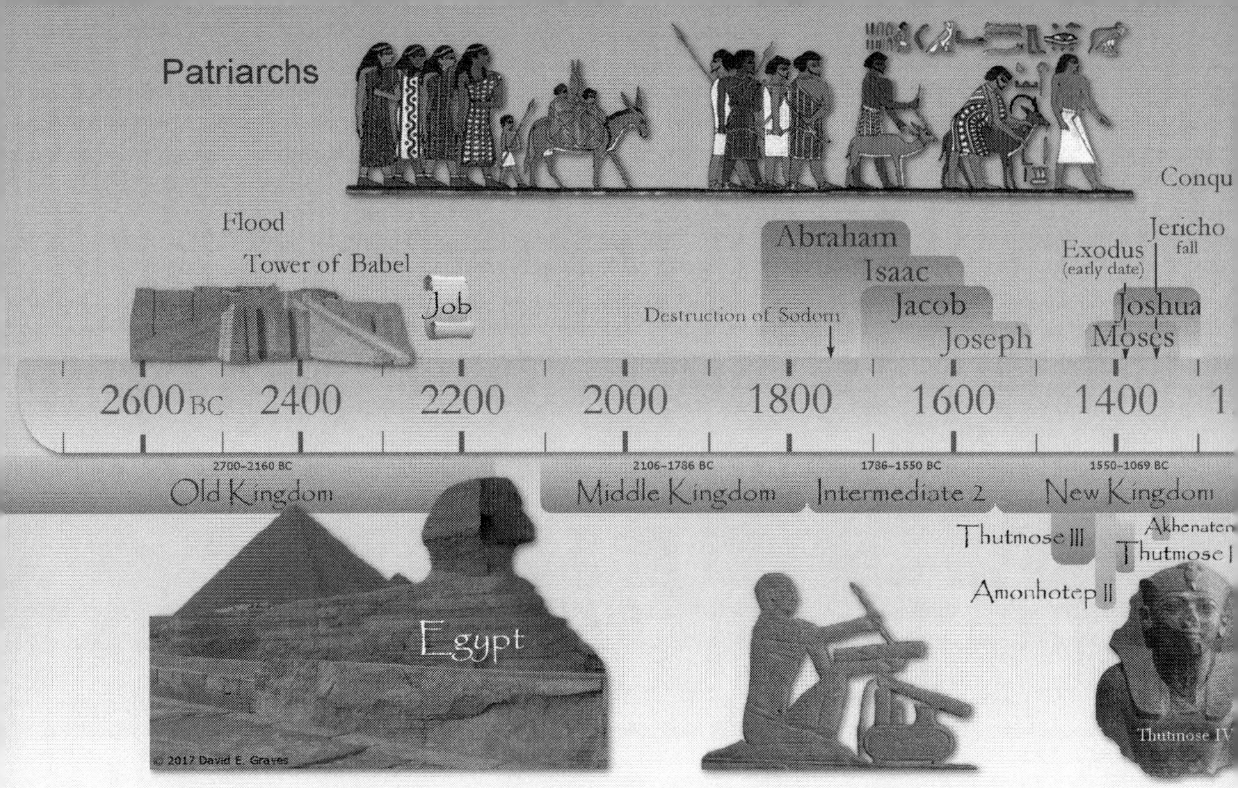

209. Timeline of the period of the patriarchs. Some scholars (i.e., Bryant Wood, J. Walton, N. Glueck, and E. Merrill, etc.) place the patriarchs between 2166–1700 BC, based on the dates in 1 Kgs 6:1 and Exod 12:40–41 taken literally. This has produced an early date for the exodus between 1491–1430 BC. The early date proposed here is 1396 BC based on current archaeological research being done at Tall el-Hammam (Sodom), under the direction of Dr. Steven Collins (Trinity Southwest University), and Tell Jericho, under the direction of Dr. Lorenzo Nigro (La Sapienza University, Rome). For the late date for the exodus, see The Judges Timeline.

210. Timeline of conquering judges and the suppressing nations.

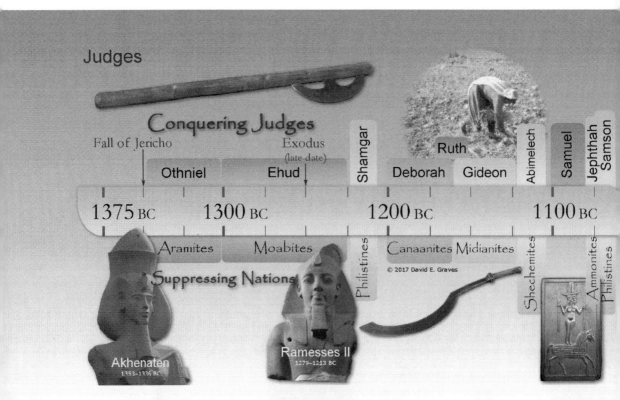

211. Timeline of the United Monarchy of Israel from Samuel (1094-1014 BC) to Solomon (970–928 BC).

Israel's United Monarchy
Samuel
Samson
Saul
David
Solomon
1100 BC
1050
1000
950 BC
Psalms
Song of Songs
Proverbs
Ecclesiastes
Kinnor harp on a Bar Kokhba revolt coin 2nd cent. AD
© 2017 David E. Graves

212. Timeline of the divided kingdom with the kings of Israel and Judah, along with the supporting prophets and some of the significant Assyrian and

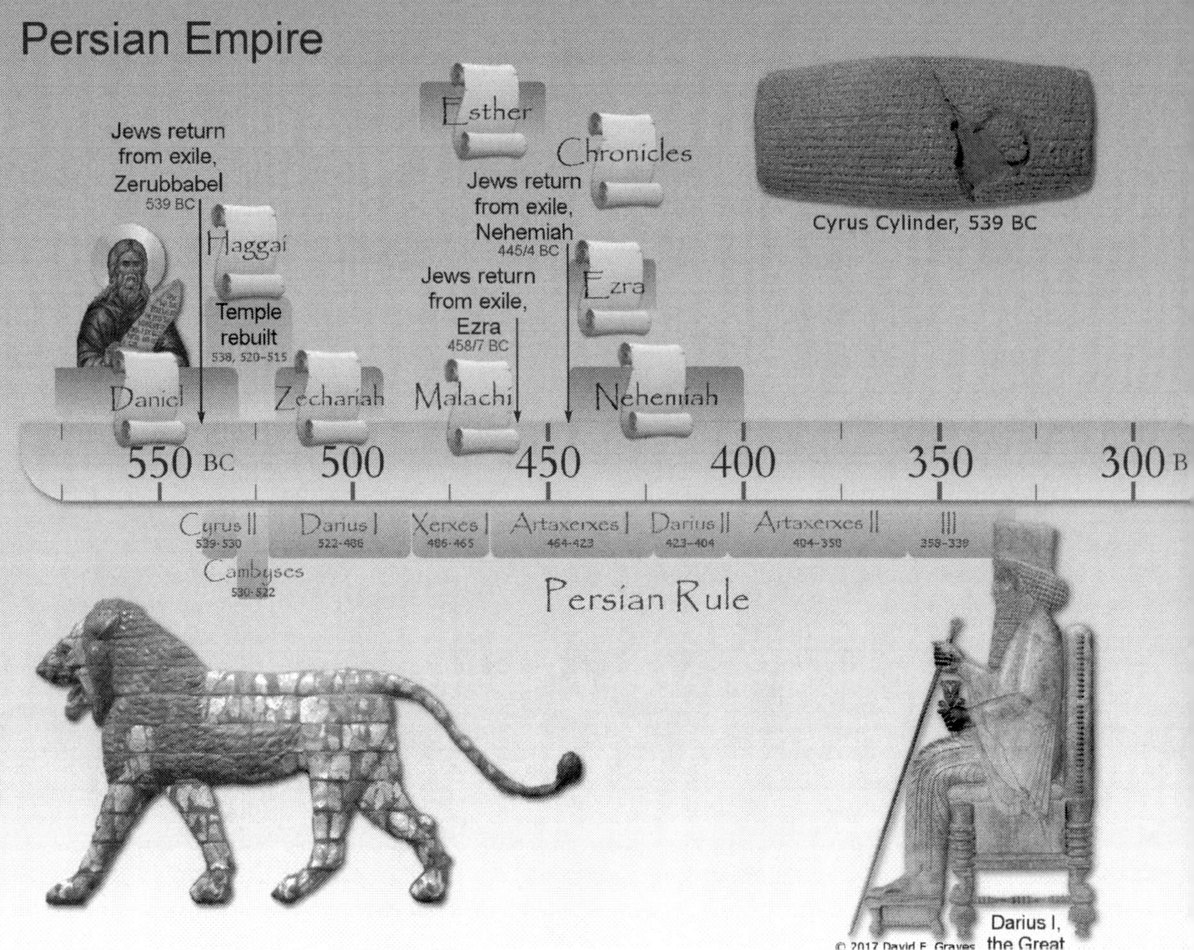

213. Timeline of the Persian Empire's control of Israel and the return from exile.

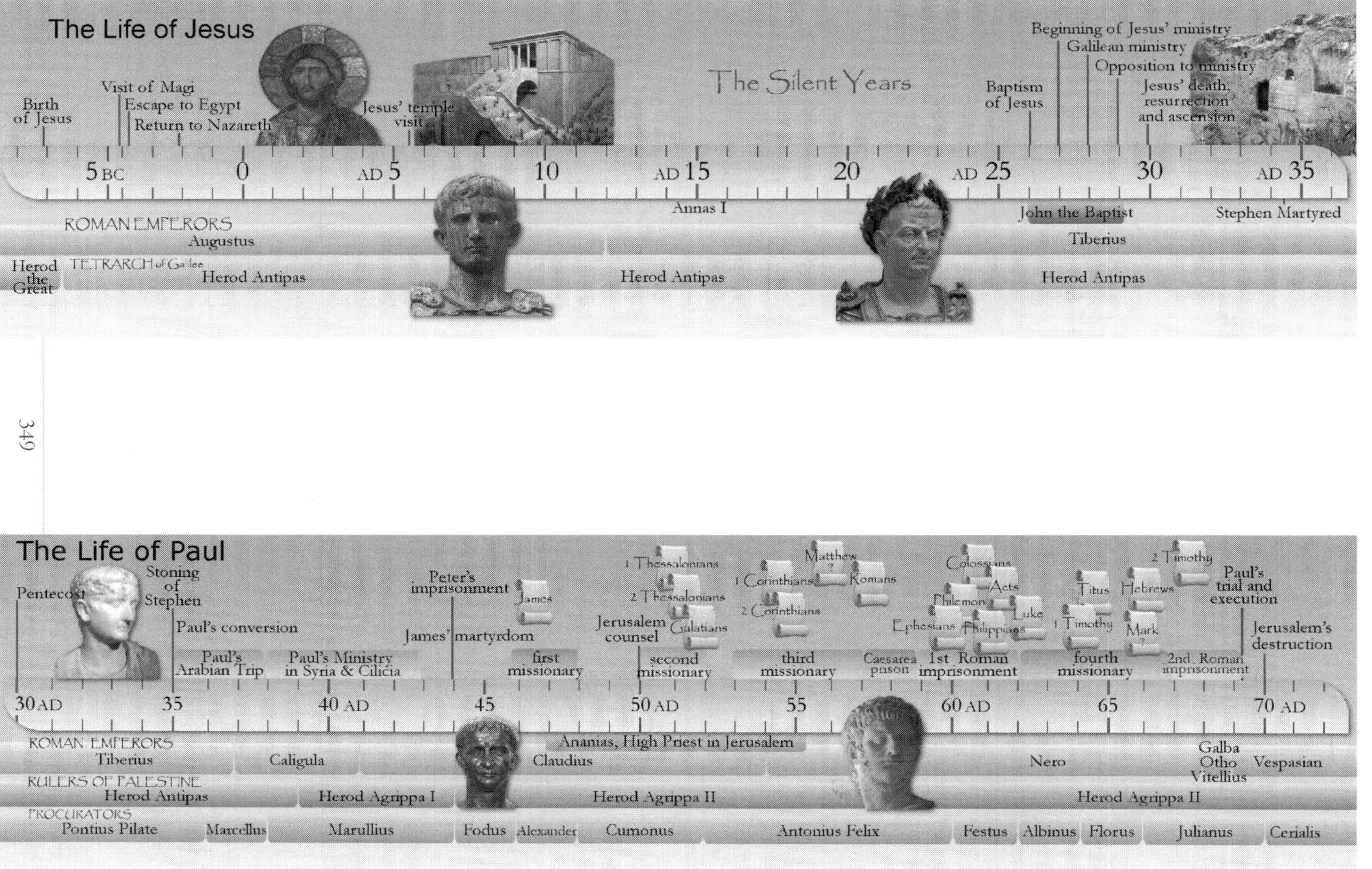
The Life of Jesus
Birth of Jesus
Visit of Magi
Escape to Egypt
Return to Nazareth
Jesus' temple visit
The Silent Years
Baptism of Jesus
Beginning of Jesus' ministry
Galilean ministry
Opposition to ministry
Jesus' death, resurrection and ascension
5 BC
0
AD 5
10
AD 15
20
AD 25
30
AD 35
Annas I
John the Baptist
Stephen Martyred
ROMAN EMPERORS
Augustus
Tiberius
Herod the Great
TETRARCH of Galilee
Herod Antipas
Herod Antipas
Herod Antipas
The Life of Paul
Pentecost
Stoning of Stephen
Paul's conversion
Paul's Arabian Trip
Paul's Ministry in Syria & Cilicia
Peter's imprisonment
James' martyrdom
James
first missionary
1 Thessalonians
2 Thessalonians
Galatians
Jerusalem counsel
second missionary
1 Corinthians
2 Corinthians
Matthew ?
Romans
third missionary
Caesarea prison
Colossians
Philemon
Acts
Ephesians
Philippians
Luke
1st Roman imprisonment
Titus
1 Timothy
Hebrews
Mark ?
2 Timothy
fourth missionary
2nd. Roman imprisonment
Paul's trial and execution
Jerusalem's destruction
30 AD
35
40 AD
45
50 AD
55
60 AD
65
70 AD
ROMAN EMPERORS
Ananias, High Priest in Jerusalem
Tiberius
Caligula
Claudius
Nero
Galba
Otho
Vitellius
Vespasian
RULERS OF PALESTINE
Herod Antipas
Herod Agrippa I
Herod Agrippa II
Herod Agrippa II
PROCURATORS
Pontius Pilate
Marcellus
Marullius
Fodus
Alexander
Cumonus
Antonius Felix
Festus
Albinus
Florus
Julianus
Cerialis

GLOSSARY

Abecedary An inscription consisting of the letters of an alphabet that is generally used to teach students the alphabet.

Acropolis The highest elevation of a city where often the most important public structures, fortifications, and especially temples and palaces are built.

Agora (Ἀγορά) The central market place or forum of a city where administrative, commercial, and cultic activities were performed.

Amphitheater (ἀμφιθέατρον *amphitheatron* from ἀμφί *amphi* "on both sides" or "around" + θέατρον *theatron* "place for viewing") A two-sided open-air venue used for entertainment, performances, and sports common to the Greco-Roman world. This is distinct from a theater, which consists of half of the same structure.

Amphora(e) (ἀμφιφορεύς *amphiphoreus* from ἀμφί *amphi* "on both sides" or "around" + φέρειν *pherein*, "to carry") Large storage jar with two handles and a pointed bottom; used for storing and transporting wine, oil, grapes, olive oil, olives, grain, fish, and other commodities.

Ankh (Egyptian *ʿnḫ)*, also known as *crux ansata* (Lat. "cross with a handle") An ancient Egyptian hieroglyphic ideograph symbolizing "life".

Antediluvian The period before the flood or pre-flood history.

Apocalypse (ἀποκάλυψις *apokalypsis, apokalyptein* "to unveil, reveal, or disclose" from ἀπο *apo* "from" + κάλυψειν *kalyptein* "to cover") The Greek name for the Book of Revelation. It means an unveiling or a revelation of Jesus Christ (Rev 1:1).

Apocrypha (ἀπόκρυφος *apókruphos* "hidden", "obscure", or "spurious") Non-canonical books that contain figures from Scripture. Some writings found a place in the Septuagint (LXX) and the Latin Vulgate version of the OT but not in the Jewish or Protestant Bibles.

Apostle (ἀπόστολος *apostolos* "person sent forth or messenger sent by another person") It generally refers to the disciples of Jesus ("the twelve" Matt 10:1–5; Mark 3:14; 6:7; Luke 6:13; 9:1) who were used to organize the church and spread the gospel (Matt 10:2–4; Mark 3:16; Luke 6:14; Acts 1:13). To qualify as an apostle one must have been a witness of the risen Christ (John 15:27; Acts 1:21, 22; 1 Cor 9:1; Acts 22:14, 15) and called by Jesus to this office (Luke 6:13; Gal 1:1). Their office was validated by their ability to perform miracles (Mark 16:20; Acts 2:43; 1 Cor 12:8–11).

Aqueduct Water channel usually associated with high arches to traverse a ravine, though they can also run along the ground.

Aramaic (אֲרָמָיָא *Arāmāyā)* A language or group of languages belonging to the Northwest group of Semitic languages of the ancient Near East, that originated in Aram (modern Syria) and became the international language of the Persians.

Ark of the Covenant (also ark of the testimony). The central piece of furniture in the OT tabernacle and only piece of furniture in the Holy of holies. The cloud of God's glory, the manifestation of God's presence, rested over the Ark of the Covenant between two heavenly creatures called cherubim. It was believed that this was where God dwelt. The box contained the copy of the Ten Commandments, manna and Aaron's rod which budded. The lid of the box called the *kapporeth* or mercy seat was sprinkled with the blood of the sacrifice (propitiation) indicating that God's grace would intervene between the holiness of God's presence in the cloud and the witness of man's sin in the law underneath the mercy seat.

Artifact A man-made object made from stone, metal, clay or other substance (e.g., coins, flint, figurines, pottery).

Asherah (אֲשֵׁרָה) A cultic object in female form (e.g., pillar-base fig- urines) representing fertility. In the ancient Near East Asherah functioned as a goddess (different goddesses in different religions), but in ancient Israel she was recognized as the consort of the Canaanite deity Baal. The Asherah is often depicted as a carved tree (Asherah pole) set in a high place. In the OT the Asherah was denounced as a false god and idol that corrupted Israel.

Ashlar Large, finely dressed, square-cut stone masonry used as a facing on walls.

Asiarchs (Ἀσιάρχης *Asiarchēs)* Most scholars believe that this is the title equivalent to the bishop (ἀρχιερεύς *archiereus)* of Asia that described an office applied to the head of the imperial cult in the Roman province of Asia, in the second cent. AD (Acts 19:31). Others believe that it was used to describe those who presided over the provincial festivals and games, while others maintain that it was a life-long office.

Asiatic Semite Semitic originates from the Hebrew for Noah's son Shem. The term is used for a people group originating from the region of the Levant including Israel, Syria, and the Fertile Crescent.

Assemblage A group of artifacts of different types found near one another and in the same stratum.

Atonement The act of providing satisfaction for sin or wrongdoing which results in reconciliation and peace between two wronged parties (Exod 32:30; Lev 4:26; 5:16; Num 6:11). In a stricter sense atonement means the effects and satisfaction which flows from the obedience, suffering, and death of Jesus Christ resulting in redemption for God's people.

Autograph The actual manuscript written by an individual.

Babylonian Chronicle A series of Babylonian historiographical cuneiform tablets chronicling the early years of the Babylonian ruler Nebuchadnezzar II and his capture of Jerusalem in 597/6 BC.

Balk (baulk) The vertical wall of a square left to preserve and read strata. This includes a one meter strip of unexcavated earth left in place on the north and east sides between squares.

Bar-Kokhba Revolt The second Jewish resistance to Roman rule by the Jews of the Roman province of Judea led by Simon bar Kokhba (AD 132–36).

Basalt A hard common grey/black igneous volcanic rock common in the region of Galilee and Jordan.

Basilica A rectangular building or hall with a central nave and two side aisles. The Romans used them for administrative buildings while the Christians converted them for churches.

Bedouin A member of a nomadic Arab tribe that still inhabits the desert regions of much of the Middle East.

Bema (βῆμα *bēma* "a step") A raised platform or podium from which orators addressed people in the market; often associated with a place of judgment (2 Cor 5:10). It was later applied to the platform around the altar of a church or synagogue for the clergy and choir.

Benchmark The "primary" benchmark is a point on a high secure surface that is set by the surveyor at the start of the excavation with an assigned and recorded elevation reference. This is the mark used to take all level readings within the square. It may be assigned to one of the corner stakes for the square.

Berosus (Βήρωσσος from Akk. *Bēl-rē'u-šu*, "Bel is his shepherd') A Hellenistic-era Babylonian priest of Bel Marduk and astronomer who wrote books on Babylonian history in *Kōine* Greek from 290 to 278 BC.

Bichrome Ware Two-colored (red and black) pottery found during the Middle Bronze 2, Late Bronze 1 (Cypriot and Syro/Canaanite), and Iron Aage (Phoenician) with geometric designs.

Body sherd Broken pottery that typically cannot be used as a diagnostic sherd.

Bulla (Lat. pl. bullae). A small seal impression with the sender's name that was attached to pottery or documents.

Canon (κανών *kanōn* "rule, measuring stick, or pattern". Heb. *qaneh* reed) To meet a standard or being complete. Theologically it refers to the authoritative list of books accepted by the church and regarded as Scripture; understood as the OT and NT.

Capital The top decorative section of a column (or pilaster). In classical architecture there are three types Doric, Ionic, and Corinthian.

Casemate A thick defensive (double) wall with rooms or compartments between the walls for storage, defense, or dwelling.

Ceramic typology The careful observation of changing pottery (ceramic) forms to determine the chronological dating sequence.

Chalcolithic (χαλκός *chalkos* "copper" + λίθος *lithos* "stone"). The first archaeological period to use copper.

Circus (Lat. "circle"; κίρκος *kirkos* "ring") A Roman oblong arena with curves at one or both ends with public seating and used for chariot races and other games. The Greeks called it a *Hippodrome* (ἱππόδρομος *hippodromos* from ἵππος *hippos* "horse" + δρόμος *dromos* "course").

Cistern A natural or man-made opening used for the scorage of water.

Codex (pl. *codices;* Lat. *caudex* "tree trunk", "book", or "notebook") A ancient bound manuscript (distinguished from a scroll) comprising a collection of single pages stitched together with a binding to form a book.

Colonnade A long row of columns either part of a building or free-standing. When the door to a building is closed in it is called a *portico* and when enclosing an open court, it is called a *peristyle.*

Copper Scroll Two scrolls of pure copper (originally joined to form a plaque) from the Second Temple period discovered on a ledge in Cave 3 at Qumran. The scroll contains a list of sixty-six hiding places of treasure thought to be in various locations in the Judean desert and the Jerusalem area.

Coptic The latest stage of the Egyptian languge that replaced demotic, originally based on the Greek alphabet. The religious writing of the Egyptian Coptic Church are written in Coptic.

Covenant A legal contract between two parties. In the ancient Near East and the OT it refers to binding parties through an intensified oath, sometimes ratified by a sacrifice (cf. Gen 15:9–11, 17–18). In the NT the term may carry the same meaning (e.g., new covenant) and signify an agreement, testament, or will.

Cuneiform (Lat. *cuneus* "wedge") Cursive wedge-shaped writing created by using a cut reed or stylus on set clay, dating to 3000 BC. The method is attested in Summerian, Hittite, Ugaritic, Elamite, and Akkadian texts.

Cyrus Cylinder A barrel-shaped baked clay cylinder

written in Babylonian cuneiform concerning the conquest of Babylon by the Persian monarch Cyrus in 539 BC and his royal edicts (539–530 BC).

Damnatio memoriae (Lat. "condemnation of memory") Judgment by the Roman Senate, as a form of dishonour upon a person or emperor, who has discredited the Roman State. Their names were often chiselled out of monuments and removed from official documents. It was not used by the Romans and is a modern designation.

Decalogue (δεκάλογος *dekálogos* "ten words") The Ten Commandments or ten words given to Moses on Mt. Sinai and written by the finger of God on two tablets of stone (Exod 20; 31:18; 32:15; Deut 5:22). The tablets were stored in the Ark of the Covenant (Exod 40:20; Deut 10:5).

Demotic (δημοτική *dēmotikē* "people of the town") An abbreviated and simplified form of the Egyptian Hieratic character invented to quickly write hieroglyphics, used for literary and commercial purposes. It was one of the translations found on the Rosetta Stone.

Dendrochronology A method based on examining the number, width, and densicy of the annual growth of tree rings.

Destruction layer The ash layer between strata that is indicative of a historical destruction and is important for dating the site in relation to documented history.

Destruction of Mankind Ancient Egyptian text from 1323 BC, also known as *The Book of the Cow of Heaven,* that describes the reasons for the imperfect state of the world in terms of humankind's rebellion against the supreme sun god Ra and the divine punishment inflicted on mankind through the goddess Hathor.

Diagnostic sherds Pieces of pottery, such as rims, handles, bases and painted body sherds, that identify the structure of the whole vessel.

Didache or *The Teaching of the Twelve Apostles* (διδαχή *didachē* "teaching") Also known as *The Teaching of the Twelve Apostles.* It is a short early (late first/second cent. AD) Christian document discovered in 1873, which contains three sections: including Christian ethics, ordinances (baptism and Eucharist) and church structure. Parts of the document are formulated as a catechism. Protestants do not consider it to be part of the NT, but it is included in the writings of the Apostolic Fathers.

Documentary hypothesis A hypothesis of biblical textual composition proposed by Julius Wellhausen that the Torah was derived from originally independent, parallel, an complete narratives, which were subsequently combined into the current form by a series of editors.

Dunam (Arabic *dönüm*) Used in the Ottoman Empire for a unit of land area to represent the amount of land that could be plowed in a day. The area was calculated by forty paces long and wide.

Elephantine papyri A collection of ancient Jewish documents from a Jewish community at Elephantine (an Egyptian border fortress) in the fifth century BC that includes letters and legal contracts from family.

Ephebe (ἔφηβος *ephebes;* pl. ἔφηβοι *epheboi)* A young male adolescent usually from an aristocratic family who is being trained *Ephebe* for civic leadership.

Epigraphy (ἐπιγραφή *epigraphē* from ἐπι *epi* "on" + γράφειν *graphein* "to write") The study of ancient languages based on their written form.

Eschaton (ἔσχατον "last things") A theological term for the study of the end of the age (the *eschaton*) and the consummation of world history.

Essenes (Ἐσσαῖου *essaiou* the "silent" or "reticent" ones) A Jewish sect identified by Josephus and Pliny residing around the Dead Sea (Josephus *J.W.* 2.119; Pliny *Nat.* 5.17). There were different groups of Essenes over time and many scholars identify the inhabitants of the Qumran community as Essenes, or "Essenic," despite the fact that sectarian documents among the Dead Sea Scrolls refer to the community as the *Yahad.*

Execration Texts Egyptian texts (MB II) inscribed with the curses upon cities, towns, and people from Palestine and Syria.

Fertile Crescent The crescent shaped region from Canaan to Mesopotamia (sometimes includes parts of Egypt) that distinquishes the more fertile area from the desert regions. The term was first coined by James Breasted.

Field The area of excavation on a tel composed of a unit of one or more squares.

Fill A mixed matrix of soil, gravel, rubbish and pottery used to level an area such as a floor or wall.

First Jewish Revolt The Jewish resistance to Roman rule from AD 66–70, especially in the city of Jerusalem.

First Temple period The period from the building of Solomon's Temple to its destruction by the Babylonians (ca. 966–587/6 BC).

Flavius Josephus First-century Jewish historian who wrote for the Romans an account of Jewish history including the Roman assault and conquest of Jerusalem and the Temple Mount.

Fulgurite Glass created from sand by means of a lightning strike.

Gematria (Heb. *gimatria;* Aramaic *gīmatrěyā,* γεωμετρία *geōmetria*). A traditional Jewish numerical system used to assign values to words or phrases in the Hebrew language. Many commentators believe that 666 represents Emperor Nero's name.

Genizah is a temporary repository or archive storage area in a Jewish synagogue or cemetery designated for the storage of worn-out or copies of Hebrew texts with mistakes.

Genre A category of literary composition characterized by similarities in form, style, or subject matter (e.g., history, poetry, wisdom, apocalyptic literature).

Glacis (French for "freezer, slip") A natural or artificial slope found in ancient fortified cities, usually employed for defensive purposes.

Gnostic (γνωστικός *gnōstikos* "having knowledge") A sect that infiltrated the early church and believed that the cosmos emanated from a transcendent god and that salvation was achieved through acquiring secret knowledge (γνῶσις, *gnōsis*).

Graffito(i) (γράφω, *graphō*, "to write", Italian *graffiare,* "to scratch") Any writing, slogan, figure or inscription scratched into a surface, often on a wall or public building. Examples found in Pompeii among other sites.

Hermeneutics (ἑρμηνεύω *hermēneuō* "translate, interpret") The science of interpreting the Bible utilizing historical, grammatical, and literary principles to help understand the meaning of the text.

Herodian The time period or architectural structures connected with Herod the Great or his family (Herodian dynasty).

Hieroglyphics (ἱερογλυφικός *hieroglyphikos* from ἱερός *hieros* "sacred" + γλύφω *glyphō* "to carve, write or engrave") Ancient Egyptian script (fourth millennium BC) using the form of over 600 pictures or symbols that represent sounds, syllables and words. Nearly all Egyptian state and ceremonial documents that were to be seen by the public were written in this script. Also, funerary and religious texts were copied using the script.

Hoard A group of coins or other small artifacts discovered together.

Hyksos (Ὑκσώς, Ὑξώς, *Hyxōs* or Ὑκουσσώς, *Hykussōs,* Egyptian *heqa khaseshet,* "ruler(s) of the foreign countries") An ethnically mixed group of Western Asiatic Semite people who overthrew the Egyptian Thirteenth Dynasty and formed the Fifteenth and Sixteenth Dynasties in Egypt (*ca.* 1674–1548 BC). The Hyksos are known for introducing new tools of warfare into Egypt including the composite bow and the horse-drawn chariot.

in situ (Lat. "in position" or "on site.") The precise location of an artifact in its original location. This is critical for the dating and interpretation of the strata and important for the provenance and interpretation of the artifact or structure itself.

Installation An archaeological structure that served a special function.

Islamic Waqf A charitable trust that maintains jurisdiction over holy sites in Israel and areas under Palestinian authority, including the Temple Mount in Jerusalem. Construction work carried out by the Waqf on the Temple Mount resulted in a large amount of archaeologically rich debris, some of which was collected by Israeli archaeologists connected with the Temple Mount Sifting Project.

Isopsephy (ἴσος *isos* "equal" + ψῆφος *psēphos* "pebble, used for counting") The Greek practice of assigning values to letters in a name and then adding up the numbrers to give a single number, a common practice in antiquity. Closely related was the Jews [Kabbalistic] numerical system called *gemetria.*

Jerusalem Prism See *Taylor Prism.*

Khirbet (Arabic "ruin" or "ruin on a hill"=mound) The Arabic equivlent of the Hebrew tel.

Klinker (clinker) A piece of brick or pottery that is melted or burned under high temperature.

Koine (ἡ κοινὴ διάλεκτος *he koinē dialektos* "the common dialect") The common Greek language of the NT period used in the Septuagint, The New Testament, and other commercial and private documents.

Krater A large bowl used for mixing wine and food.

Leningrad Codex (*Codex Leningradensis*) The oldest complete manuscript of the Hebrew Bible (ca. AD 1008) including the Masoretic Text and Tiberian vocalization.

Levant The eastern Mediterranean countries of Israel, Jordan, Palestine, Syria, Lebanon, Turkey, Cyprus, Egypt and Greece.

Level A surveyor term to indicate the height above sea level and used to designate a layer or stratum. It can also be used to indicate a locus.

Lisan (Arabic for "tongue") The small peninsula on the eastern side of the Dead Sea which separates the North and the South basins (Josh 15:2).

Locus (pl. *loci)* The feature in an archaeological square, such as a wall, pit, or installation that is different from a previous feature. It can be as minute as the difference in soil or as large as a room.

Madaba Map Sixch-century AD mosaic map of the Holy Land discovered on the floor of a Greek Orthodox church from the Byzantine period in the town of Madaba, Jordan. This is considered the oldest map of the Holy Land and has been significant in locating ancient sites and features depicted on the map.

Manual of Discipline (IQS, Community Rule) An important sectarian document of the Qumran Community that is definitive for classifying other compositions as sectarian or non-sectarian and describes the unique rules and practices of the community including the communal meal.

Martyrium Early churches with a specific architectural form centered on a central element and built on a central plan, circular, octagonal, or cruciform shape.

Masoretic Text The traditional (accepted) Hebrew text

of the Bible (ca. AD 1000) composed by the Masoretes, a group of scribes in Tiberias who developed a vowel system (critical apparatus) so the text could read with confidence.

Mastaba (Egyptian "eternal house") The earliest form of pyramid building by the Egyptians.

Maximalist Those who maximize (or prioritize) the biblical data with respect to the archaeological data and do not limit the historicity of the biblical accounts.

Mesha Inscription (also Moabite Inscription) An inscribed stone (stele) of King Mesha of Moab (ca. 840 BC) describing how the Moabite god Chemosh allowed the Moabites to be subjugated to Omri, King of Israel, but later restored the lands of Moab.

Messiah (Heb. *Mashiah,* LXX *Christos,* meaning "anointed") Within Judaism the promised deliverer, who will bring a kingdom of peace and justice (Dan 9:25, 26). For Christians the term refers to Jesus who is regarded as the fulfillment of the Jewish prophecy of a deliverer (John 1:41; 4:25) and thus called the Christ (Matt 26:54; Mark 9:12; Luke 18:31; 22:37; John 5:39; Acts 2; 16:31; 26:22, 23).

Minimalists Those who minimalize the biblical data in deference to the archaeological data and limit the historicity of biblical accounts.

Miqveh (pl. *miqva'ot,* "ritual bath") Stepped immersion pool for Jews to perform their ritual cleansing (immersion) either at home or in public. Most *miqvaot* have a rock cut division (small wall) down the center of the steps to separate pre-and post-ritual immersion.

Mishnah (Heb. pl. *Mishnayot;* "study by repetition" or "(oral) instruction" from *shanah,* "to repeat, to study and review") The first major written redaction of Jewish oral traditions (oral law) and the first work of rabbinic literature (Rabbi Judah the Patriarch, third cent. AD), which are part of the Talmud.

Monolith (Lat. *monolithus;* μονόλιθος *monolithos* from μόνος *monos* "one" or "single" + λίθος *lithos* "stone"). A large, single-cut stone.

Monotheism (μόνος *monos* "single" + θεός *Theos* "god") The belief that there is only one God.

Mosaic (Ital. *mosaic, mosaicus;* μούσειος *mouseios* "belonging to the Muses") Pictures or inscriptions made from small cut pieces of coloured stone called tessera (pl. tesserae).

Necropolis (νεκρόπολις *nekropolis* "city of the dead," pl. *necropoli*) A large ancient cemetery with tomb monuments located outside a city.

Neokoros (νεωκόρος "temple warden") A temple official; from the late first cent. AD formalized as a title for a city which held a provincial temple to the Roman emperor.

Neolithic (νεῖος *neios* "new" + λίθο, *lithos* "stone") The new Stone Age period (*ca.* 10,200– 4,500/2,000 BC).

Northwest Semitic A division of the Semitic language family comprising the indigenous languages of the Levant from the Bronze Age through the Iron Age (i.e., Amorite, Ugaritic, Old Aramaic, and Canaanite languages, including Phoenician and Hebrew).

Numismatic (νόμισμα, *nomisma* "current coin, money, usage", Lat. *Numismatis*). The science and study of coins.

Obelisk (ὀβελίσκος *obeliskos* derived from ὀβελός *obelos* "spit, nail, pointed pillar") A four-sided stone pillar with a tapered pyramidal point.

Obsidian (Lat. *obsidianus* from *Obsianus lapis* "[stone] of Obsius") A hard dark volcanic glass formed from lava.

Onomasticon (ὀνομαστικόν *onomastikon "belonging to names")* An alphabetical list of geographical places mentioned in the Bible, most often identified with the one written by Eusebius and translated by Jerome.

Ophel Denotes a fortified hill and describes a prominent feature of Jerusalem's topography, the extended portion of the City of David (the oldest part of Jerusalem) up to the foot of the Temple Mount (See 2 Chr 27:3; 33:14; Neh 3:26; 11:21).

Oracle (Lat. *oraculum* "to speak" from *orare* "pray, plead") A announcement from a god, through divine inspiration (χρησμοί *khrēsmoi,* i.e., Sibylline Oracles) or place where oracles are given (i.e., Delphi).

Oriental Institute Prism See *Taylor Prism.*

Ossuary (Lat. *ossuarium* from *ossuarius,* "for bones") A limestone box used to store the bones of the dead (secondary burial) after the flesh has decayed from the bones.

Ostracon (ὄστρακον *ostracon;* pl. ὄστρακα *ostraka* "a shard of pottery") A piece of pottery or other substance with an inscription on it.

Otzer (Heb. "treasure") A small pool that feeds "living" water to a *miqveh.*

Paleoethnobotany (παλαιός *palaiós* "old" from *ethnology* "study of culture" and *botany* "study of plants") The study of ancient plants and cultures (also archaeobotany).

Paleography (παλαιός *palaiós* "old" + γράφω *graphō* "to write") The study of ancient writing and texts.

Palimpsest: (Lat. *palimpsestus* from παλίμψηστος *palimpsēstos* "again scraped") A manuscript that has been scraped clean of the writing or washed off and ready to be used again.

Palynology (παλύνω *palunō* "strew, sprinkle") The analysis of particles that are strewn such as dust or pollen.

Papyrus (Lat. from πάπυρος *papyrus;* Lat. pl. *papyri).* A type of paper made from the Egyptian papyrus reed which grows along the Nile River. Papyri were used as writing material during the Old and New Testament periods and the early church.

Parable (παραβολή *parabolē* "a placing alongside of") A story drawn from nature or common life placed alongside a spiritual truth to illustrate its meaning.

Paraenesis (παραινέ *paraineō* "to exhort" or "admonish") A series of encouraging persuasive exhortations or admonitions, which do not necessarily refer to concrete situations.

Parchment (Περγαμηνός *pergamenos* "of Pergamon") Writing material made from animal skins (vellum) that originated in the city of Pergamum, Asia Minor.

Parousia (παρουσία *Parousia* "presence", "arrival", or "official visit") It is generally understood in the NT to mean the second coming or second advent of Jesus Christ.

Parthenon (Gr. "temple of the virgin goddess" from παρθένος *parthenos* "virgin, maiden, girl") A Greek temple built on the Athenian acropolis from 447 to 432 BC and dedicated to the goddess Athena, the city's patron, whose huge statue filled the interior of the building.

Patriarchs (from πατριά *patria* "lineage, family"; πατηρ *patēr* "father" + ἄρχειν *archein* "to rule"; Heb. אבות *Avot* or *Abot)* The term refers to the three biblical patriarchs of the people of Israel: Abraham, Isaac, and Jacob.

Pentateuch (πεντάτευχος *pentateuchos* "five scrolls") The first five books of the OT: Genesis, Exodus, Leviticus, Numbers and Deuteronomy.

Pentecost (Πεντηκοστή [ἡμέρα] *Pentēkostē [hēmera]*, "the fiftieth [day]") The Jewish "Feast of Weeks" (Exod 34:22 Deut 16:10) or the "Feast of Harvest" (Exod 23:15–22) that was seven weeks (fiftieth day) after Passover. It marked the end of the barley harvest and the beginning of the wheat harvest (Num 28:26–31).

Period A time of occupation in the history of a site or stratum (i.e., Early Bronze Age, Iron Age, etc.). Sometimes it is used to refer to sub-periods or phases of sites (i.e., IIa or IVb).

Pharisee (Φαρισαῖος *pharasaios*; Aramaic פְּרִישַׁיָּא *perishaiya*; Heb. פָּרוּשׁ *parush* "separated") A Jewish sect who required a strict interpretation of the written law. While accepting the oral law they adhered to many doctrines that were not found in the Law of Moses such as angels, the afterlife and the resurrection. They were opposed to the Sadducees.

Phase A subdivision of a period or stratum of occupation. It is sometimes used as a temporary designation during excavation before the stratigraphy is clear.

Pilgrim flask (Lat. *ampullae*) A small metal, glass, or ceramic vial shaped like a flattened canteen with one or two small handles on the side and a small spout. It was used by pilgrims in antiquity to carry water or oil.

Pithos (πίθος; pl. πίθοι *pithoi)* An exceptionally large storage jar.

Polytheism (πολυθεϊσμός *polytheismos;* πολυς *polys* "many" + theos "god[s]") The belief and worship of multiple deities, usually assembled into a pantheon of gods and goddesses.

Potsherd (sherd) Broken pieces of pottery may be used to date an archaeological strata.

Prefect The governor of a Roman province with low rank.

Probe An exploratory trench or square dug to determine the extent or nature of a locus for future excavation.

Procurator (Lat. "manager, overseer, agent, deputy") The governor of a Roman province with high rank.

Prophets (προφήτης, *prophētēs*) Individuals raised up by God, to speak on his behalf (2 Pet 1:21). They stood as counterparts to soothsayers and those practicing divination (Deut 18:15–18).

Propitiation (Lat. *propitiationem, propitiare* "appease, propitiate"; ἱλαστήριον *hilasterion;* Rom 3:25; Heb 9:5) An atonement whereby God is gracious toward sinners and favourably inclined or disposed to bless them. Propitiation does not make God loving or secure his love but makes his love consistent with his character. The term is used for the "mercy-seat" or the cover to the Ark of the Covenant (Exod 25:17; 25; 30:6). God is reconciled to man through the blood of a sacrifice.

Provenance The place of origin or earliest known history of some thing (see *in-situ*). In archaeology, it is crucial that provenance is known for an artifact to be useful as a diagnostic tool or in the interpretation of a site's history. Unprovenanced artifacts, usually coming from secondary sources outside a licensed excavation, such as the antiquity market, have limited value as educational examples of the material culture during the archaeological periods.

Pseudepigrapha (ψευδής *pseudēs* "false" + επιγραφή *epigraphē* "to inscribe or write") Commonly refers to works of Jewish religious literature written between 200 BC and AD 200. Many are lost and only mentioned by other writers.

Qumran An archaeological site located on a plateau north northwest of the Dead Sea that hosted a Jewish community from the Iron Age II through the end of the Second Temple Period (until the destruction by the Romans in AD 68). The Jewish community of the Second Temple period produced and preserved the Dead Sea Scrolls.

Rabbah (Abbr. *Rab.*) A Jewish collection of ancient rabbinical interpretations usually on one of the

Books of the Pentateuch (i.e., Rabbah; *Rab.* Gen 3:15).

Radiocarbon dating (also carbon dating or carbon-14 dating) A method for determining the age of an object containing organic material by using che properties of radiocarbon (C-14), a radioactive isotope of carbon.

Relative dating The science of determining the relative order of past events (the age of an object in comparison to another) as opposed to absolute dating (determining the estimated age).

Revetment A structure (dirt, stone or mudbrick) placed against a wall to provide strength and prevent erosion often used as a defensive structure.

Imperial cult An element of Roman state religion in which emperors and members of their families were regarded as gods.

Sadducee (Lat. pl. *Sadducaei;* Σαδδουκαῖοι, *Saddoukaioi; Heb.* צְדוּקִים *Ṣĕdûqîm)* An aristocratic Jewish sect affiliated with the high priests and which rejected most of the Jewish oral tradition held by the Pharisees and others.

Sanhedrin (Heb. סַנְהֶדְרִין *sanhedrín* "[great] council"; Συνέδριον *synedrion* "assembly sitting together") A term designating the Jewish political assembly at Jerusalem that represented the highest magistracy of the country (Josephus *Ant.* 14.5.4). It was also an assembly of twenty to twenty-three men appointed in every city in the biblical land of Israel (*m. Sanh.* 1:1).

Sarcophagus (σαρκοφάγος *sarkophagos* "flesh-eating" from σάρξ *sarx* "flesh" + φαγεῖν *phagein* "to eat"; pl. *sarcophagi)* A stone coffin with inscriptions and decorations.

Scarab (κάραβος *karabos* "beetle") An Egyptian seal made in the shape of a scarab beetle.

Scriptorium (Lat. *scriptōrius* "pertaining to writing"; pl. *scriptoria)* A formal facility used by scribes to produce and copy documents.

Sealed A locus that is free of contamination by another locus.

Sebastos (Lat. *Sebastianus* "from Sebastia", the city of Sivas, in modern Turkey. Σεβαστός *sebastos* "venerable one", from σέβας *sebas* "awe, reverence, dread"; pl. *Sebastoi)* Sebastos was an ancient Greek honorific term for Roman emperors used in the first cent. onward in place of Augustus. Temples of the Sebastoi only venerated the family of the Emperor (the family of Vespasian, Titus and Domitian).

Second Jewish Revolt (Bar Kokhba Revolt) Jewish resistance to Roman rule in the Roman province of Judea led by Simon bar Kosib a (also known as Bar Kokhba, "son of a scar") from A D 132–136.

Second Temple Period (536 BC–AD 70) The period from the return of the Babylonian exiles co rebuild the temple to its destruction by the Romans.

Septuagint (abbr. LXX, Lat. *septuaginta* "The Seventy") The Koine Greek translation of the Hebrew textual tradition that included certain texts which were later included in the canonical Hebrew Bible (Old Testament) made in Alexandria, Egypt by Jewish scholars (ca. 280–150 BC).

Shaft tomb A type of vertical underground burial chamber dug down into a deep rectangular burial structure. Such tombs were often built with a stone floor and lined with mudbrick, masonry, or wood.

Sherd (also *shard)* A fragment of pottery or other artifact.

Shofar Ram's horn used as a trumpet to call to prayer or other special occasions.

Sifting The process of filtering soil samples through wire mesh with mounted or hand-held screens to separate out small artifacts such as coins, beads, bits of glass, and metal. Dry involves using only the screens while wet sifting includes the addition of water to separate lighter organic material from heavier non-organic material.

Slip The thin clay coating applied to pottery by dipping the pot into a thick clay liquid, then firing it.

Spolia (Lat. "spoils") The repurposing of building materials for new construction elsewhere.

Square The basic area of excavation developed for precise documentation of the location of artifacs within a numbered grid system. The standard size is 5 meters x 5 meters, leaving a 1 meter unexcavated balk on the north and east sides (making 6 m x 6 m).

Squeeze Process of pressing a soft substance (plaster, plastic, etc.) into an impression (i.e., inscription or relief) to make a reliable reproduction for interpretation and preservation.

Stele or **stela** (στήλη *stēlē* "pillar, upright rock; or column"; pl. στῆλαι *stelai or stelae*) An upright stone pillar often containing an inscription to commemorate a military victory, boundary or tombstone.

Stoa (στοά; pl. *stoae* "base stand") A long covered hallway, to protect the public from the elements, supported with a colonnade of pillars, often with a portico (Lat. *porticus* "porch") and wall on one side.

Strabo A Greek geographer, philosopher, and historian who lived in Asia Minor during the transitional period of the Roman Republic into the Roman Empire (44 BC–AD 18). He wrote *Historical Sketches* comprising the history of the known world beginning from the conqust of Greece by the Romans and *Geography* in which he recounts ancient sites.

Stratification The layers (strata) of a tel created by successive destructions. Consists of archaeological deposits identified as periods of occupation containing artifacts.

Stratum (Lat. "a spread for a bed, quilt, or blanket"; pl. *strata)* A horizontal layer of soil containing artifacts and debris representing a particular time period and dated by using pottery and coins.

Suzerain-vassal treaty A form of an ancient Near Eastern legal document that includes a preamble, identifying the parties involved in the treaty: the king or dominant party, the subjugated people, and a prologue that lists the deeds already performed by the suzerain on behalf of the vassal. It also contained stipulations and blessings and curses sealed by witnesses.

Synagogue (συναγωγή *synagogē* from συν *syn* "together" + αγωγή *agogé* "learning or training"; Heb. בית כנסת *Bet Kenesset* "house of assembly" or בית תפילה, *beyt t'fila,* "house of prayer") A Jewish house of prayer and worship. Their exact date of origin is uncertain, although they appear after the Babylonian Exile.

Synoptic (Lat. *synopticus;* συνοπτικός *sunoptikos* "seeing the whole together at a glance" from σύνοψις *súnopsis* "a general view, synopsis" from σύν *sun* "the same" + ὄψις *ópsis* "to see or view") Used to refer to the four Gospels that provide a similar view of the life of Jesus.

Tacitus Roman senator and historian of the Roman Empire. His major, works include *Annals* and *Histories,* which examine the Roman emperors beginning, with the death of Augustus (AD 14) through the reigns of Tiberius, Claudius, and Nero to the first years of the Jewish Revolt against Rome (AD 66–69).

Talmud (Heb. *talmud* "instruction") The collection of rabbinic writings that form the authoritative body of Jewish tradition comprising Jewish civil and ceremonial law, including the Mishnah (abbr. *m.*). There are two versions of the Talmud: the Babylonian Talmud (abbr. *b.* which dates from the fifth cent. AD, but includes earlier material) and the earlier Palestinian or Jerusalem Talmud (abbr. *y.*).

Targum (Heb. "translation", or "interpretation"). Aramaic translation of the Hebrew Bible *(Tanakh).* Collected over a five-hundred-year period, it is difficult to date individual passages. Fragments were found at Qumran among the Dead Sea Scrolls.

Taylor Prism A hexagonal clay prism in Assyrian cuneiform recording the annals of the Assyrian king Sennacherib, including his attack on the cities of Judah and his attempted siege of Jerusalem. Three versions have survived (all with the same text): The Taylor Prism in the British Museum, the Oriental Institute Prism in the Oriental Institute of Chicago, and the Jerusalem Prism in the Israel Museum in Jerusalem.

Tel or **Tell** (Heb. תֵּל "mound or hill"; Arabic تل, tall used in Arabic countries). An unnatural mound created by the repeated destruction and rebuilding of ancient cities.

Temple Mount Sifting Project An archaeological project undertaken by the Israeli Antiquities Authority to sift and reclaim artifacts from some 20,000 tons of soil and debris dumped in the Kidron Valley by the Islamic Waqf as a result of their construction of the Al-Marwani Mosque in the area of Solomon's Stables.

Terracotta (also terra-cotta or terra cotta; Italian from *terra* "earth" + *cotta* "baked" i.e., "baked earth") Reddish clay or unglazed ceramic pottery.

Tessera (τέσσερα, "four"; pl. *tesserae*) Small, individual square stones, ivory, or wood used to create a picture or mosaic. Also, a ticket, or token.

Tetragrammaton (Heb. "having four letters") It has become a technical term for the name Y H W H (יהוה) in the Bible. Ancient Hebrew words did not contain vowels.

Tetrarch (Lat. *tetrarches*) A governor of the fourth part of a province in Ancient Rome, first instituted by Diocletan (AD 292).

Theophany (θεοφάνεια *theophaneia* "appearance of a god" from Θεός *Theos* "god" + φαίνω *phainō* "I show or shine") A term that refers to the divine manifestation or the appearance of deity to man.

Tosefta (Heb. "supplement") A large collection of writings, written in Mishnaic Hebrew, that are similar to the Mishnah but not as authoritative for religious Jews.

Trinitite The glassy residue created when sand was exposed to the affects of the Trinity nuclear bomb test in 1945.

Typology The study and comparison of the various shapes of artifacts for their classification.

Tyropoeon Valley (Heb. *ha gay*) The name for Jerusalem's transverse valley between the Hinnom Valley and Kidron Valley. Also called the Cheesemaker's Valley.

Ugaritic The Northwest Semitic language of Ugarit, spoken by the people of Ugarit (Ras Shamra).

Umayyad The first Arab dynasty of caliphs who ruled the Jerusalem Empire (AD 661–750) and whose capital was Damascus.

Uncial A style of manuscript writing that used capital letters and was common in Greek and Latin manuscripts from the fourth to eighth centuries AD.

Uruk The leading city of its day in ancient Mesopotamia founded by King Enmerkar ca. 4500 BC. Located in the southern region of Sumer, it was most famous for its king, Gilgamesh, and the epic tale of his quest for immortality recorded in the Gilgamesh Epic.

Vellum (Fr. *vélin* from *vel* "veal") A fine parchment prepared from the skin of a calf or lamb and used by scribes to write documents, such as biblical manuscripts.

Votive (Lat. *vōtīvus* from *vōtum* "vow") An object dedicated in fulfillment of a vow for a religious purpose.

Wadi (Arabic وَادِي *wādī* "valley, ravine") A dried up waterbed or gully which only flows during the rainy season.

Waqf (Arabic). Islamic council and fund which supervises the endowment of land and specifies that it be used for religious purposes.

Zealots A rebellious Jewish sect who opposed Roman domination during the intertestamental period. A sect of the Zealots was founded by Judas the Galilean, who led the Jewish revolt against Rome in AD 6 (Josephus *J.W.* 2.117; *Ant.* 18.1.2–6). Other notable Zealots include the Maccabean leaders, Mattathias and his sons and followers (1 Macc. 2:24–27), Menahem, who attempted to seize the leadership of the anti-Roman revolt in AD 66 (Josephus *J.W.* 2.433), and Eleazar ben Yar, leader of the Jewish revolt at Masada (AD 66–73; Josephus *J.W.* 7.8.6). Simon, one of the twelve apostles, was also a Zealot (Luke 6:15; Acts 1:13), along with the apostle Paul (Acts 22:3; Gal 1:14).

Ziggurat (Akk. *ziqqurratu* from *zaqāru* "to build high") A Mesopotamian pyramid like mound of mud brick constructed with a temple on top.

Bibliography

Primary Sources

Abegg, Jr., Martin G., Michael O. Wise, and Edward M. Cook. *The Dead Sea Scrolls: A New Translation.* San Francisco, CA: HarperCollins, 2005.

Abegg, Jr., Martin G., Peter Flint, and Eugene Ulrich. *The Dead Sea Scrolls Bible: The Oldest Known Bible Translated for the First Time into English (QBE).* New York: HarperCollins, 2002.

Aeschines. *Speeches.* Translated by C. D. Adams. LCL 106. Cambridge, MA: Harvard University Press, 1919.

Ameling, Walter, Hannah M. Cotton, Werner Eck, Benjamin Isaac, Alla Kushnir-Stein, Haggai Misgav, Jonathan Price, and Ada Yardeni, eds. *Corpus Inscriptionum Iudaeae/Palaestinae: Caesarea and the Middle Coast: Nos. 1121-2160.* Vol. 2. 7 vols. Corpus Inscriptionum Iudeaeae/Palaestinae. Berlin: Walter de Gruyter, 2011.

Ampelius, Lucius. *Lucii Ampelii Liber Memorialis.* Translated by Edidit Erwin Assmann. Leipzig: Teubner, 1935.

Appian. *Roman History: The Civil Wars, Books 3.27-5.* Translated by Horace White. Vol. 4. 4 vols. LCL 5. Cambridge, MA: Harvard University Press, 1913.

Apuleius. *Metamorphoses (The Golden Ass): Books 7–11.* Translated by J. Arthur Hanson. Vol. 2. 2 vols. LCL 453. Cambridge, MA: Harvard University Press, 1989.

Aristides, P. Aelius. *The Complete Works: Orations.* Translated by Charles A. Behr. 2 vols. Leiden: Brill, 1981, 1986.

Athenaeus. *The Learned Banqueters: Books 1-3.106e.* Edited and translated by S. Douglas Olson. Vol. 1. 7 vols. LCL 204. Cambridge, Mass.: Harvard University Press, 2007.

Aulock, Hans von, and Gerhard Kleiner. *Sylloge Nummorum Graecorum, Vol. 1: Pontus, Paphlagonia, Bithynia, Mysia, Troas, Aiolis, Lesbos, Ionia.* Berlin: Gebr. Mann, 1957.

Böeckh, August, Johannes Franz, Ernst Curtius, and Adolf Kirchhoff. *Corpus Inscriptionum Graecarum.* 4 vols. Berolini, Italy: Officina academica, 1877.

Burnett, Andrew, Michel Amandry, and Pere Pau Ripollés Alegre, eds. *Roman Provincial Coinage.* 9 vols. London: British Museum Press, 2003.

Buckler, William Hepburn, and David M. Robinson, eds. *Sardis: Greek and Latin Inscriptions.* Vol. 1. ASES 7. Leiden: Brill, 1932.

Cassius, Dio. *Roman History: Books 56–60.* Translated by Ernest Cary and Herbert B. Foster. Vol. 7. 9 vols. LCL 175. Cambridge, MA: Harvard University Press, 1924.

———. *Roman History: Books 61–70.* Translated by Ernest Cary and Herbert B. Foster. Vol. 8. 9 vols. LCL 176. Cambridge, MA: Harvard University Press, 1924.

Chaniotis, Angelos, Thomas Corsten, Nikolaos Papazarkadas, and Rolf Tybout, eds. *Supplementum Epigraphicum Graecum.* 23 vols. Leiden: Brill, 1923.

Chrysostom, Dio. *Discourses 31–36.* Translated by J. W. Cohoon and H. Lamar Crosby. Vol. 3. 5 vols. LCL 358. Cambridge, MA: Harvard University Press, 1940.

Cicero, Marcus Tullius. *In Catilinam 1–4. Pro Murena. Pro Sulla. Pro Flacco.* Translated by C. Macdonald. Vol. 10. 29 vols. LCL 324. Cambridge, MA: Harvard University Press, 1976.

———. *Letters to Atticus.* Translated by D. R. Shackleton Bailey. Vol. 22. 29 vols. LCL 7. Cambridge, MA: Harvard University Press, 1999.

———. *Letters to Friends.* Translated by D. R. Shackleton Bailey. Vol. 27. 29 vols. LCL 230. Cambridge, MA: Harvard University Press, 2001.

———. *Philippics 7-14.* Edited by John T. Ramsey and Gesine Manuwald. Translated by D. R. Shackleton. Vol. 15b. 29 vols. LCL 507. Cambridge, MA: Harvard University Press, 2010.AristidesP. Aelius. The Complete Works: Orations. Translated by C. A. Behr. 2 vols. Leiden: Brill, 1981.

———. *Pro Quinctio. Pro Roscio Amerino. Pro Roscio Comoedo. On the Agrarian Law.* Translated by J. H. Freese. Vol. 6. 29 vols. LCL 240. Cambridge, MA: Harvard University Press, 1930.

———. *The Orations of Marcus Tullius Cicero.* Translated by Charles D. Yonge. 4 vols. London, UK: Bell & Sons, 1913.

Comfort, Philip W., and David P. Barrett, eds. *The Text of the Earliest New Testament Greek Manuscripts.* Corrected and Enlarged ed. Wheaton, IL: Tyndale, 2001. BibleWorks. v.8.

———. *The Complete Text of the Earliest New Testament Manuscripts.* Grand Rapids: Baker, 1999.

Comfort, Philip W. *Encountering the Manuscripts: An Introduction to New Testament Paleography & Textual Criticism.* Nashville: Broadman & Holman Academic, 2005.

Corsten, Thomas. *Die Inschriften von Laodikeia Am Lykos.* IGSK 49. Bonn: Habelt, 1997.

Cook, B. F. *Greek Inscriptions.* 3rd ed. Berkeley, CA: University of California Press, 1987.

Demosthenes. *Orations 18-19: De Corona, De Falsa Legatione.* Translated by C. A. Vince and J. H. Vince. Vol. 2. 7 vols. 155. Cambridge, MA: Harvard University Press, 1926.

Dionysius of Halicarnassus. *Critical Essays: Volume I, Ancient Orators. Lysias. Isocrates. Isaeus. Demosthenes. Thucydides.* Translated by Stephen Usher. Vol. 8. 9 vols. LCL 465. Cambridge, MA: Harvard University Press, 1974.

Dittenberger, Carl Friedrich Wilhelm, Johann Gaertringen, Johannes E. Kirchner, Joannes Pomtow, Georg Wissowa, and Erich Ziebarth, eds. *Orientis Graeci Inscriptiones Selectae: Supplementum Sylloges Insciptionum Graecarum.* 3rd ed. 4 vols. Leipzig: Nachdruck der Ausgabe, 1915.

Edson, Charles F., ed. *Inscriptiones Epiri, Macedoniae, Thraciae, Scythiae, II, Inscriptiones Macedoniae, Fasc. 1, Inscriptiones Thessalonicae et Viciniae.* 2 vols. Inscriptiones Graecae 10. Berlin: de Gruyter, 1972.

Epiphanius of Salamis. *Panarion: Book II and III (Sects 47-80, De Fide).* Translated by Frank Williams. Leiden: Brill, 1993.

Eusebius, Pamphilus, and Jerome. *The Bodleian Manuscript of Jerome's Version of the Chronicles of Eusebius.* Edited by John Knight Fotheringham. Oxford, UK: Clarendon, 2012.

Eusebius, Pamphilus. *De Praeparatio Evangelica.* Translated by Edward Hamilton Gifford. Grand Rapids: Baker, 1981.

———. *Ecclesiastical History: Books 1–5.* Translated by Kirsopp Lake. Vol. 1. 2 vols. LCL 153. Cambridge, MA: Harvard University Press, 1926.

———. *Ecclesiastical History: Books 6–10.* Translated by J. E. L. Oulton. Vol. 2. 2 vols. LCL 265. Cambridge, MA: Harvard University Press, 1932.

———. *The Onomasticon of Eusebius Pamphili: Compared with the Version of Jerome and Annotated.* Edited by Noel C. Wolf. Translated by C. Umhau Wolf. Washington, DC: Catholic University of America Press, 1971.

Eustathius. *Commentarii Ad Homeri Iliadem et Odysseam.* Edited by Gottfried Stallbaum. Reprint of 1825–1830 edition. 4 vols. Hildesheim: Olms, 1830.

Felix, Minucius, and Tertullian. *Apology. De Spectaculis. Octavius.* Translated by T. R. Glover and Gerald H. Rendall. LCL 250. Cambridge, MA: Harvard University Press, 1931.

Finkelstein, Louis. *Sifra on Leviticus.* 4 vols. New York: Jewish Theological Seminary of America, 1991.

Fränkel, Max, Ernst Fabricius, and Carl Schuchhardt. *Die Inschriften von Pergamon.* Vol. 8. Sonderausgabe Aus Den Altertümern von Pergamon. Berlin: Spemann, 1890.

Freedman, H., and Maurice Simon, eds. *Midrash Rabbah.* 10 vols. London, UK: Soncino, 1992.

Freeman-Grenville, G. S. P., and Joan E. Taylor, eds. *The Onomasticon by Eusebius of Caesarea and the Liber Locorum of Jerome: Palestine in the Fourth Century AD.* Translated by G. S. P. Freedman-Grenville. Jerusalem: Carta, 2003.

Frey, P. Jean-Baptiste. *Corpus Inscriptionum Iudaicarum: Recueil Des Inscriptions Juives Qui Vont Du IIIe Siècle de Notre Ère.* Vol. 3. Rome: Pontifico Istituto di Archeologa Cristiana, 1936.

Gabba, Emilio. *Iscrizioni Greche E Latine per Lo Studio Della Bibba.* Torino: Marietti, 1958.

Gagarin, Michael, ed. *The Oxford Encyclopedia of Ancient Greece and Rome.* 7 vols. New York: Oxford University Press, 2010.

Galen. *Galen on Anatomical Procedures: De Anatomicis Administrationibus.* Translated by Charles Singer. London, UK: Oxford University Press, 1956.

George, Andrew R. *The Babylonian Gilgamesh Epic: Introduction, Critical Edition and Cuneiform Texts HELP.* Vol. 1. 2 vols. Oxford, UK: Oxford University Press, 2003.

Goldwurm, Hersh, and Nosson Scherman, eds. *The Talmud. Schottenstein Edition.* 73 vols. Brooklyn, NY: Mesorah, 1990.

Head, Barclay Vincent. *Catalogue of the Greek Coins of Ionia in the British Museum.* Bologna, Italy: Forni, 1964.

Heberdey, Rudolf, ed. *Tituli Pisidiae Linguis Graeca et Latina Conscripti, 1. Tituli Termessi et Agri Termessensis.* TAM, III.1. Vienna: ÖAW, 1941.

Hesiod. Theogony. *Works and Days. Testimonia.* Translated by Glenn W. Most. Vol. 1. 3 vols. LCL 57. Cambridge, MA: Harvard University Press, 2007.

Herrmann, Peter, ed. *Tituli Lydiae Linguis.* TAM, 5/2. Vienna: ÖAW, 1989.

Herodotus. *Historia: The Persian Wars.* Translated by Alfred Denis Godley. 4 vols. LCL 117-120. Cambridge, MA: Harvard University Press, 1920-1925.

Heron of Alexandria. *Druckwerke Und Automatentheater: Pneumatica Et Automata.* Translated by Wilhelm Schmidt. Griechisch und Deutsch. 5 vols. Stuttgart, Germany: Teubner, 1976.

Homer. *Iliad: Books 13-24.* Edited by William F. Wyatt. Translated by A. T. Murray. Vol. 2. 2 vols. LCL 171. Cambridge, MA: Harvard University Press, 1925.

Hornblower, Simon, and Anthony J. S. Spawforth, eds. *The Oxford Classical Dictionary.* 3rd ed. Oxford: Clarendon, 2003.

Jacoby, Felix. *Die Fragmente Der Griechischen Historiker.* 3 vols. Leiden: Brill Academic, 2004.

Jerome. *On Illustrious Men.* Edited and translated by Thomas P. Halton. Washington, DC: Catholic University of America Press, 1999.

Josephus, Flavius. *Jewish Antiquities: Volume I, Book 1–3.* Translated by H. St. J. Thackeray. Vol. 5. 13 vols. LCL 242. Cambridge, MA: Harvard University Press, 1930.

———. *Jewish Antiquities: Volume III, Books 7–8.* Translated by Ralph Marcus. Vol. 7. 13 vols. LCL 281. Cambridge, MA: Harvard University Press, 1934.

———. *Jewish Antiquities: Volume IX, Book 20.* Translated by Louis H. Feldman. Vol. 13. 13 vols. LCL 456. Cambridge, MA: Harvard University Press, 1965.

———. *Jewish Antiquities: Volume V, Books 12–13.* Translated by Ralph Marcus. Vol. 9. 13 vols. LCL 365. Cambridge, MA: Harvard University Press, 1943.

———. *Jewish Antiquities: Volume VI, Books 14–15.* Translated by Ralph Marcus and Allen Wikgren. Vol. 10. 13 vols. LCL 489. Cambridge, MA: Harvard University Press, 1943.

———. *Jewish Antiquities: Volume VII, Books 16–17.* Translated by Ralph Marcus and Allen Wikgren. Vol. 11. 13 vols. LCL 410. Cambridge, MA: Harvard University Press, 1963.

———. *Jewish Antiquities: Volume VIII, Books 18–19.* Translated by Louis H. Feldman. Vol. 12. 13 vols. LCL 433. Cambridge, MA: Harvard University Press, 1965.

———. *The Jewish War: Volume I, Books 1–2.* Translated by H. St. J. Thackeray. Vol. 2. 13 vols. LCL 203. Cambridge, MA: Harvard University Press, 1927.

———. *The Jewish War: Volume II, Books 3–4.* Translated by H. St. J. Thackeray. Vol. 3. 13 vols. LCL 487. Cambridge, MA: Harvard University Press, 1927.

———. *The Jewish War: Volume III, Books 5–7.* Translated by H. St. J. Thackeray. Vol. 4. 13 vols. LCL 210. Cambridge, MA: Harvard University Press, 1928.

———. *The Life. Against Apion.* Translated by H. St. J. Thackeray. Vol. 1. 13 vols. LCL 186. Cambridge, MA: Harvard University Press, 1926.

———. *The Works of Josephus: Complete and Unabridged.* Translated by William Whiston. New Updated. Peabody, MA: Hendrickson, 1980.

Kent, John Harvey. *The Inscriptions, 1926 to 1950: Corinth.* Vol. 8, Part 3. Athens: American School of Classical Studies at Athens, 1966.

Kitchen, Kenneth A. *Ramesside Inscriptions—Translated and Annotated, Translations, Vol. IV: Merenptah and the Late Nineteenth Dynasty.* Vol. 4. Oxford, UK: Wiley-Blackwell, 2003.

Klose, Dietrich O. A. *Die Münzprägung Von Smyrna in Der Römischen Kaiserzeit.* Berlin: de Gruyter, 1987.

Kutscher, Edward Yechezkel. *The Language and Linguistic Background of the Isaiah Scroll: 1QIsa[a].* Studies on the Texts of the Desert of Judah 6. Leiden: Brill, 1974.

Lafaye, Georges, René Cagnat, J. Toutain, and Victor Henry, eds. *Inscriptiones Graecae Ad Res Romanas Pertinentes.* 4 vols. Paris: Leroux, 1911–1927.

Lehmann, Clayton Miles, and Kenneth G. Holum. *The Greek and Latin Inscriptions of Caesarea Maritima.* Edited by Robert J. Bull and David Larrimore Holland. BASOR: Supplemental Studies. Issue 19. The Joint Expedition to Caesarea Maritima 5. Missoula, MT: Scholars Press, 1975.

LeMaire, André. *Inscriptions Hébraïques. I. Les Ostraca.* Vol. 1. Littératures Anciennes Du Proche-Orient 9. Paris: Les Éditions du Cerf, 1977.

Lipman, Eugene J., ed. *The Mishnah; Oral Teachings of Judaism.* Berlin: Schocken, 1974.

Llewelyn, Stephen R., and J. R. Harrison. *New Documents Illustrating Early Christianity: A Review of the Greek and Other Inscriptions and Papyri Published Between 1988 and 1992.* Edited by E. J. Bridge. Vol. 10. Grand Rapids: Eerdmans, 2012.

Lubetski, Meir, and Edith Lubetski, eds. *New Inscriptions and Seals Relating to the Biblical World.* Atlanta, Ga.: SBL, 2012.

Lucian of Samosata. *Anacharsis or Athletics. Menippus or The Descent into Hades. On Funerals. A Professor of Public Speaking. Alexander the False Prophet. Essays in Portraiture. Essays in Portraiture Defended. The Goddesse of Surrye.* Translated by A. M. Harmon. Vol. 4. 8 vols. LCL 162. Cambridge, MA: Harvard University Press, 1925.

———. *The Dead Come to Life or The Fisherman. The Double Indictment or Trials by Jury. On Sacrifices. The Ignorant Book Collector. The Dream or Lucian's Career. The Parasite. The Lover of Lies. The Judgement of the Goddesses. On Salaried Posts in Great Houses.* Translated by A. M. Harmon. Vol. 3. 8 vols. LCL 130. Cambridge, MA: Harvard University Press, 1921.

———. *The Downward Journey or The Tyrant. Zeus Catechized. Zeus Rants. The Dream or The Cock. Prometheus. Icaromenippus or The Sky-Man. Timon or The Misanthrope. Charon or The Inspectors. Philosophies for Sale.* Translated by A. M. Harmon. Vol. 2. LCL 54. Cambridge, Mass.: Harvard University Press, 1915.

———. *The Passing of Peregrinus. The Runaways. Toxaris or Friendship. The Dance. Lexiphanes. The Eunuch. Astrology. The Mistaken Critic. The Parliament of the Gods. The Tyrannicide. Disowned.* Translated by A. M. Harmon. Vol. 5. 8 vols. LCL 302. Cambridge, MA: Harvard University Press, 1936.

Martial, Marcus Valerius. *Epigrams, Spectacles: Books 1–5.* Edited and translated by D. R. Shackleton-Bailey. Vol. 1. 3 vols. LCL 94. Cambridge, MA: Harvard University Press, 1993.

Martial, Marcus Valerius. *Epigrams: Books 11–14.* Edited and translated by D. R. Shackleton-Bailey. Vol. 3. 3 vols. LCL 480. Cambridge, MA: Harvard University Press, 1993.

Mommsen, Theodor. *Corpus inscriptionum latinarum.* 20 vols. Berlin: De Gruyter, 1974.

Müller, Karl, Theodor Müller, and Victor Langlois. *Fragmenta historicorum graecorum.* Paris: Ambrosio Firmin Didot, 1841.

McCabe, Donald F. *Smyrna Inscriptions: Texts and List.* Edited by Tad Brennan and Neil Elliott R. Princeton, NJ: Princeton Institute for Advanced Study, 1988.

Merlin, Alfred, ed. *L'Année Épigraphique.* Villejuif: Collège de France, 1963–2010.

Meyer, Marvin, and James M. Robinson, eds. *The Nag Hammadi Scriptures: The Revised and Updated Translation of Sacred Gnostic Texts Complete in One Volume.* New York: HarperCollins, 2009.

Mommsen, Theodor. *Corpus inscriptionum latinarum.* 20 vols. Berlin: De Gruyter, 1974.

Müller, Karl, Theodor Müller, and Victor Langlois. *Fragmenta historicorum graecorum.* Paris: Ambrosio Firmin Didot, 1841.

Musurillo, Hebert, ed. *The Acts of the Christian Martyrs.* Translated by Hebert Musurillo. Oxford, UK: Clarendon, 1972.

Ovid. *Metamorphoses: Books 1–8.* Edited by J. P. Goold. Translated by Frank Justus Miller. Vol. 1. 6 vols. Loeb Classical Library 42. Cambridge, MA: Harvard University Press, 1916.

Paton, William R., ed. *Inscriptiones Graecae, XII. Inscriptiones Insularum Maris Aegaei Praeter Delum: 2. Inscriptiones Lesbi, Nesi, Tenedi.* Vol. 12. Berlin: De Gruyter, 1899.

Pausanias. *Description of Greece, Books 1–2: Attica and Corinth.* Translated by Henry A Ormerod and W. H. S. Jones. Vol. 1. 5 vols. LCL 93. Cambridge, MA: Harvard University Press, 1918.

———. *Description of Greece, Books 3–5: Laconia, Messenia, Elis 1.* Translated by W. H. S. Jones and Henry A Ormerod. Vol. 2. 5 vols. LCL 188. Cambridge, MA: Harvard University Press, 1926.

———. *Description of Greece, Books 6–8.21: Elis 2, Achaia, Arcadia.* Translated by W. H. S. Jones. Vol. 3. 5 vols. LCL 272. Cambridge, MA: Harvard University Press, 1933.

Peek, Werner., ed. *Griechische Vers-Inschriften.* Grab-Epigramme 1. Berlin: Hakkert, 1955.

Petronius, Seneca. *Satyricon. Apocolocyntosis.* Edited by E. H. Warmington. Translated by Michael Heseltine and W. H. D. Rouse. LCL 15. Cambridge, MA: Harvard University Press, 1913.

Pettinato, Giovanni, and A. Alberti. *Catalogo Dei Testi Cuneiformi Di Tell Mardikh-Ebla.* Materiali Epigrafici Di Ebla 1. Naples: Istituto Universitario Orientale di Napoli, 1979.

Petzl, Georg. *Tituli Lydiae Linguis Graeca et Latina Conscripti: Fasciculus III, Philadelpheia et Ager Philadelphenus.* TAM, V,3. Vienna: ÖAW, 2007.

Philo. *Every Good Man Is Free. On the Contemplative Life. On the Eternity of the World. Against Flaccus. Apology for the Jews. On Providence.* Translated by F. H. Colson. Vol. 9. 10 vols. LCL 363. Cambridge, MA: Harvard University Press, 1941.

———. *On Abraham. On Joseph. On Moses.* Translated by F. H. Colson. Vol. 6. 10 vols. LCL 289. Cambridge, MA: Harvard University Press, 1935.

———. *On Flight and Finding. On the Change of Names. On Dreams.* Translated by F. H. Colson and G. H. Whitaker. Vol. 5. 10 vols. LCL 275. Cambridge, MA: Harvard University Press, 1934.

———. *On the Confusion of Tongues. On the Migration of Abraham. Who Is the Heir of Divine Things? On Mating with the Preliminary Studies.* Translated by F. H. Colson and G. H. Whitaker. Vol. 4. 10 vols. LCL 261. Cambridge, MA: Harvard University Press, 1932.

———. *On the Embassy to Gaius. General Indexes.* Edited by J. W. Earp. Translated by F. H. Colson. Vol. 10. 10 vols. LCL 379. Cambridge, MA: Harvard University Press, 1962.

———. *The Works of Philo Judaeus: The Contemporary of Josephus.* Translated by C. D. Yonge. 3 vols. Whitefish, MT: Kessinger, 2007.

Philostratus, Flavius. *Life of Apollonius of Tyana: Books 1–4.* Translated by Christopher P. Jones. Vol. 1. 4 vols. LCL 16. Cambridge, MA: Harvard University Press, 2005.

. *Life of Apollonius of Tyana: Books 5–8.* Edited and translated by Christopher P. Jones. Vol. 2. 4 vols. LCL 17. Cambridge, MA: Harvard University Press, 2005.

Plato. *Republic: Volume I, Books 1–5.* Edited and translated by William Preddy and Chris Emlyn-Jones. Vol. 5. LCL 237. Cambridge, MA: Harvard University Press, 2013.

Plautus, Titus Maccius. *Amphitryon. The Comedy of Asses. The Pot of Gold. The Two Bacchises. The Captives.* Translated by Wolfgang David Cirilo de Melo. Vol. 1. 5 vols. LCL 60. Cambridge, MA: Harvard University Press, 2011.

———. *Casina. The Casket Comedy. Curculio. Epidicus. The Two Menaechmuses Plautus.* Edited and translated by Wolfgang David Cirilo de Melo. Vol. 2. 5 vols. LCL 61. Cambridge, MA: Harvard University Press, 2011.

———. *The Little Carthaginian. Pseudolus. The Rope.* Edited and translated by Wolfgang David Cirilo de Melo. Vol. 4. 5 vols. LCL 260. Cambridge, MA: Harvard University Press, 2012.

Pliny the Elder. *Natural History: Books 1–2.* Translated by H. Rackham. Vol. 1. 10 vols. LCL 330. Cambridge, MA: Harvard University Press, 1938.

———. *Natural History: Books 12–16.* Translated by H. Rackham. Vol. 4. 10 vols. LCL 370. Cambridge, MA: Harvard University Press, 1945.

———. *Natural History: Books 28–32.* Translated by William H. S. Jones. Vol. 8. 10 vols. LCL 418. Cambridge, MA: Harvard University Press, 1963.

———. *Natural History: Books 33–35.* Translated by William H. S. Jones. Vol. 9. 10 vols. LCL 394. Cambridge, MA: Harvard University Press, 1952.

———. *Natural History: Books 36–37.* Translated by D. E. Eichholz. Vol. 10. 10 vols. LCL 419. Cambridge, MA: Harvard University Press, 1962.

———. *Natural History: Books 3–7.* Translated by H. Rackham. Vol. 2. 10 vols. LCL 352. Cambridge, MA: Harvard University Press, 1942.

Pliny the Younger. *Letters, Books 8–10: Panegyricus.* Translated by Betty Radice. Vol. 2. 2 vols. LCL 59. Cambridge, MA: Harvard University Press, 1969.

Plutarch. *Moralia: Love Stories. That a Philosopher Ought to Converse Especially With Men in Power. To an Uneducated Ruler. Whether an Old Man Should Engage in Public Affairs. Precepts of Statecraft. On Monarchy, Democracy, and Oligarchy. That We Ought Not to Borrow. Lives.* Translated by Harold North Fowler. Vol. 10. 16 vols. LCL 321. Cambridge, MA:Harvard University Press, 1936.

———. *Moralia: Sayings of Kings and Commanders. Sayings of Romans. Sayings of Spartans. The Ancient Customs of the Spartans. Sayings of Spartan Women. Bravery of Women.* Translated by Frank Cole Babbitt. Vol. 3. 16 vols. LCL 245. Cambridge, MA:Harvard University Press, 1931.

Polybius. *The Histories: Books 28–39. Fragments.* Edited by F. W. Walbank, Christian Habicht, and S. Douglas Olson. Translated by William R. Paton and S. Douglas Olson. Vol. 6. 6 vols. LCL 161. Cambridge, MA: Harvard University Press, 2012.

Pritchard, James Bennett. *Ancient Near Eastern Texts Relating to the Old Testament with Supplement.* 3rd ed. Princeton, NJ: Princeton University Press, 1969.

Rahmani, L. Y. *A Catalogue of Jewish Ossuaries: In the Collections of the State of Israel.* Jerusalem: Israel Academy of Sciences and Humanities, 1994.

Rawlinson, Henry C. *The Persian Cuneiform Inscription at Behistun, Decyphered and Translated; With a Memoir on Persian Cuneiform Inscriptions in General, and on That of Behistun in Particular.* Journal of the Royal Asiatic Society of Great Britain and Ireland, 1848.

Rhomiopoulou, K. "New Inscriptions in the Archaeological Museum, Thessaloniki." In *Ancient Macedonian Studies in Honor of Charles F. Edson*, edited by Harry J. Dell, 299–305. Belgrade, Serbia: Institute for Balkan Studies, 1981.

Roberts, Alexander, James Donaldson, Philip Schaff, and Henry Wace, eds. *Ante-Nicene Fathers.* New Ed. 10 vols. Peabody, MA: Hendrickson, 1994.

———. *Nicene and Post-Nicene Fathers, Series I.* 14 vols. Peabody, MA: Hendrickson, 1994.

———. *Nicene and Post-Nicene Fathers, Series II.* 14 vols. Peabody, MA: Hendrickson, 1994.

Robinson, James M., ed. *The Nag Hammadi Library: A Translation of the Gnostic Scriptures.* London, UK: HarperCollins, 1990.

Rodkinson, Michael L. *New Edition of the Babylonian Talmud: Original Text, Edited, Corrected, Formulated and Translated into English.* 20 vols. Boston, MA: The Talmud Society, 1918.

Sanders, J. A. *The Psalms Scroll of Qumran Cave 11.* DJD 4. Oxford, UK: Oxford University Press, 1965.

Seneca, Lucius Annaeus. *Natural Questions: Books 1–3.* Translated by Thomas H. Corcoran. Vol. 7. 10 vols. LCL 450. Cambridge, MA: Harvard University Press, 1971.

Statius. *Silvae.* Translated by D. R. Shackleton Bailey. Vol. 1. 3 vols. LCL 206. Cambridge, MA: Harvard University Press, 2003.

Strabo. *Geography: Books 10–12.* Translated by Horace Leonard Jones. Vol. 5. 8 vols. LCL 211. Cambridge, MA: Harvard University Press, 1928.

———. *Geography: Books 13–14*. Translated by Horace Leonard Jones. Vol. 6. 8 vols. LCL 223. Cambridge, MA: Harvard University Press, 1929.

Suetonius Tranquillus, Gaius. *Lives of the Caesars: Claudius. Nero. Galba, Otho, and Vitellius. Vespasian. Titus, Domitian. Lives of Illustrious Men: Grammarians and Rhetoricians. Poets (Terence. Virgil. Horace. Tibullus. Persius. Lucan). Lives of Pliny the Elder and Passienus Crispus*. Translated by J. C. Rolfe. Vol. 2. LCL 38. Cambridge, MA: Harvard University Press, 1914.

Sukenik, Eleazar Lipa. *The Dead Sea Scrolls of the Hebrew University*. Jerusalem: Hebrew University Press Magnes, 1955.

Sutherland, Carol Humphrey Vivian. *Coinage in Roman Imperial Policy, 31 B.C.–A.D. 68*. London: Methuen & Company, 1951.

Tacitus, Cornelius. *Annals: Books 13–16*. Translated by John Jackson. Vol. 5. 5 vols. LCL 322. Cambridge, MA: Harvard University Press, 1937.

———. *Annals: Books 4–6, 11–12*. Translated by John Jackson. Vol. 4. 5 vols. LCL 312. Cambridge, MA: Harvard University Press, 1937.

———. *Books 4–5. Annals: Books 1–3*. Translated by Clifford H. Moore. Vol. 3. 5 vols. LCL 249. Cambridge, MA: Harvard University Press, 1931.

Tacticus, Aeneas, Asclepiodotus, and Onasander. *Aeneas Tacticus, Asclepiodotus, and Onasander*. Translated by Illinois Greek Club. LCL 156. Cambridge, MA: Harvard University Press, 1923.

Theodosius. "Topografia: The Topography of the Holy Land." In *Jerusalem Pilgrims Before the Crusades*, edited by John Wilkinson, 103–16. Oxford, UK: Aris & Phillips, 2002.

Victorinus, Apringius of Beja, Caesarius of Arles, and The Venerable Bede. *Latin Commentaries on Revelation: Victorinus of Petovium, Apringius of Beja, Caesarius of Arles and Bede the Venerable*. Edited and translated by William C. Weinrich. Ancient Christian Texts. Downers Grove, IL: IVP Academic, 2012.

Vitruvius. *On Architecture: Books 1–5*. Translated by Frank Granger. Vol. 1. 2 vols. LCL 251. Cambridge, MA: Harvard University Press, 1931.

———. *On Architecture: Books 6–10*. Translated by Frank Granger. Vol. 2. 2 vols. LCL 280. Cambridge, MA: Harvard University Press, 1934.

Wankel, Hermann, ed. *Die Inschriften von Ephesos*. 8 vols. Inschrifien griechischer Stadte aus Kleinasien 11.1-17.4. Bonn: Habelt, 1979.

Wroth, Warwick. *A Catalogue of the Greek Coins in the British Museum: Mysia*. Edited by Reginald Stuart Poole. London: Quaritch, 1892.

Wright, William. *Apocryphal Acts of the Apostles*. 2 vols. London, UK: Williams & Norgate, 1871.

Xenophon of Ephesus. *Hellenica: Books 1–4*. Translated by Carleton L. Brownson. Vol. 1. 7 vols. LCL 88. Cambridge, MA: Harvard University Press, 1918.

Xenophon of Ephesus, and Longus. *Daphnis and Chloe. Anthia and Habrocomes*. Edited and translated by Jeffrey Henderson. LCL 69. Cambridge, MA: Harvard University Press, 2009.

Zlotnick, Dov. *The Tractate "Mourning" (Semahot): Regulations Relating to Death, Burial and Mourning*. Yale Judaica Series. New Haven: Yale University Press, 1966.

SECONDARY SOURCES

Adams, Edward. "The Ancient Church at Megiddo: The Discovery and an Assessment of Its Significance." *ExpTim* 120, no. 2 (2008): 62–69.

Adam-Veleni, P. "Thessalonike." In *Brill's Companion to Ancient Macedon: Studies in the Archaeology and History of Macedon, 650 BC– 300 AD*, edited by Robin J. Fox and Robin Lane Fox, 545–62. Leiden: Brill, 2011.

Adler, Noam. *Oil Lamps of the Holy Land from the Adler Collection.* Jerusalem: Old City, 2005.

Agnes, Michael E. *Webster's New World College Dictionary.* 4th ed. Cleveland, Ohio: Webster's New World, 1999.

Aharoni, Yohanan. "Iron Age Pottery of the Timna' and 'Amram Area." *PEQ* 94 (1962): 66–67.

———. *The Land of the Bible: A Historical Geography.* Translated by Anson F. Rainey. 2nd ed. Louisville, KY: Westminster/Knox, 1981.

Ahlstrom, Gosta W. *The History of Ancient Palestine.* Edited by Diana Edelman. Minneapolis, MN: Augsburg Fortress, 1993.

Akşit, İlhan. *Pamukkale Hierapolis.* Istanbul: Akşit, 2003.

Aktüre, Zynep. "Reading into the Mysteries of Artemis Ephesia." In *Curating Architecture and the City*, edited by Sarah Chaplin and Alexandra Stara, 145–63. New York: Routledge, 2009.

Akurgal, Ekrem. *Ancient Civilizations and Ruins of Turkey from Prehistoric Times until the End of the Roman Empire.* Translated by John Whybrow and Mollie Emre. 2nd ed. Istanbul: Mobil Oil Turk A. S., 1985.

———. "Smyrna." Edited by Richard Stillwell, William L. MacDonald, and Marian Holland. *Princeton Encyclopaedia of Classical Sites.* Princeton, NJ: Princeton University Press, 1976.

Aland, Kurt, and Barbara Aland. *The Text of the New Testament an Introduction to the Critical Editions and to the Theory and Practice of Modern Textual Criticism.* Translated by Erroll F. Rhodes. 2nd ed. Grand Rapids: Eerdmans, 1995.

Alberti, Maria Emanuela. "Murex Shells as Raw Material: The Purple-Dye Industry and Its By-Products. Interpreting the Archaeological Record." *Kaskal* 5 (2008): 73–90.

Albright, William F. "Archaeological Discovery and the Scriptures." *Christianity Today* 12, no. 19 (June 21, 1968): 3–5.

———. "A Revision of Early Hebrew Chronology." *JPOS* 1 (1921): 49–79.

———. "From the Patriarchs to Moses. 1. From Abraham to Joseph." *BA* 36 (1973): 5–33.

———. "New Light from Egypt on the Chronology and History of Israel and Judah." *BASOR* 130 (April 1, 1953): 4–11.

———. *The Archaeology of Palestine.* London, UK: Taylor & Francis, 1956.

———. *The Biblical Period from Abraham to Ezra.* New York: Harper & Row, 1963.

———. "The Danish Excavations at Shiloh." *BASOR* 9 (11923): 10–11.

———. *The Excavation of Tell Beit Mirsim in Palestine, Vol. 1, The Pottery of the First Three Campaigns.* AASOR 12. Cambridge, MA: American Schools of Oriental Research, 1932.

———. "The Gezer Calendar." *BASOR* 92 (1943): 16–26.

———. "The Jordan Valley in the Bronze Age." *AASOR* 6 (1926): 13–74.

———. "The Site of Bethel and Its Identification." In *The Excavation of Bethel (1934-1960)*, edited by James Leon Kelso and William F. Albright, 1–3. AASOR 39. Cambridge, MA: American Schools of Oriental Research, 1968.

———. "Toward a More Conservative View: Interview with W. F. Albright." *Christianity Today*, January 18, 1963.

Albright, William F., J. L. Kelso, and J. P. Thorley. "Early Bronze Age Pottery from Bab-Ed-Dra in Moab." *BASOR* 95 (1944): 1–13.

Albright, William F., and Benno Landsberger. "Scribal Concepts of Education." In *City Invincible: A Symposium on Urbanization and Cultural Development in the Ancient Near East. Held at the Oriental Institute of the University of Chicago, December 4-7, 1958*, edited by Carl H. Kraeling and Robert M. Adams, 94–123. Chicago, IL: University of Chicago Press, 1960.

Albright, William Foxwell. *The Archaeology of Palestine and the Bible.* The Richards Lectures Delivered at the University of Virginia. New York: Flavell, 1935.

Alexander, David, and Pat Alexander, eds. *Zondervan Handbook to the Bible.* 3rd ed. Grand Rapids: Zondervan, 1999.

Alexander, L. C. A. "Chronology of Paul." Edited by Gerald F. Hawthorne, Ralph P. Martin, and Daniel G. Reid. *Dictionary of Paul and His Letters.* Downers Grove, IL: InterVarsity, 1993.

Alford, Henry. *Hebrews-Revelation.* Edited by Everett F. Harrison. The Greek Testament: A Critical and Exegetical Commentary 4. Chicago, IL: Moody, 1968.

Aling, Charles F. *Egypt and Bible History: From Earliest Times to 1000 BC.* Baker Studies in Biblical Archaeology. Grand Rapids: Baker, 1981.

Allen, Susan Heuck. *Finding the Walls of Troy: Frank Calvert and Heinrich Schliemann at Hisarlik.* Berkeley, CA: University of California Press, 1999.

Alliata, Eugenio. "The Pilgrimage Routes during the Byzantine Period in Transjordan." In *The Madaba Map Centenary: Travelling Through the Byzantine Umayyad Period. Proceedings of the International Conference Held in Amman 7–9 April 1997*, edited by Michele Piccirillo and Eugenio Alliata, 121–24. Studium Biblicum Franciscannum Collectio Maior 40. Jerusalem: Studium Biblicum Franciscannum, 1999.

Allinger-Csollich, W. "Birs Nimrud I. Die Baukörper Der Ziqqurat von Borsippa. Ein Vorbericht." *Baghdader Mitteilungen* 22 (1991): 383–499.

Alloway, B. V., G. Larsen, D. J. Lowe, P. A. R. Shane, and J. A. Westgate. "Tephrochronology." In *Encyclopedia of Quaternary Science*, edited by Scott Elias and Cary Mock, 2nd ed., 4:277–304. Edinburgh: Elsevier, 2013.

Alt, A. "The Settlement of the Israelites in Palestine." In *Essays on Old Testament History and Religion*, edited by A. Alt, 133–69. Sheffield, UK: University of Sheffield, 1989.

Altman, R. I. "Some Notes on Inscriptional Genres and the Siloam Tunnel Inscription." *Antiquo Oriente* 5 (2007): 35–88.

Amiran, Ruth. *Ancient Pottery of the Holy Land: From Its Beginnings in the Neolithic Period to the End of the Iron Age.* New Brunswick, NJ: Rutgers University Press, 1970.

Andreae, Bernard. "Datierung Und Bedeutung Des Telephosfrieses Im Zusammenhang Mit Den Übrigen Stiftungen Der Ataliden von Pergamon." In *Der Pergamonaltar. Die Neue Präsentation Nach Restaurierung Des Telephosfrieses*, edited by Wolf-Dieter Heilmeyer, 60–78. Tübingen: Wasmuth, 1997.

Archer, Gleason L. *A Survey of Old Testament Introduction.* Rev Upd. Chicago, IL: Moody, 1996.

Archi, Alfonso. "The Archives of Ebla." In *Cuneiform Archives and Libraries*, edited by Klaas R. Veenhof, 72–86. Papers Read at the 30e Rencontre Assyriologique Internationale, Leiden, 4-8 July 1983. Leiden: Netherlands Institute for the Near East, 1986.

———. "The Epigraphic Evidence from Ebla and the Old Testament." *Biblica* 60, no. 4 (1979): 556–66.

Arnold, Bill T. *Encountering the Book of Genesis*. Grand Rapids: Baker, 2003.

Arundell, Francis Vyvian J. *A Visit to the Seven Churches of Asia with an Excursion into Pisidia*. London, UK: Rodwell, 1828.

Applebaum, Shimon. *Judaea in Hellenistic and Roman Times: Historical and Archaeological Essays*. Edited by Jacob Neusner. Leiden: Brill Academic, 1989.

Arnaoutoglou, Ilias. "Hierapolis and Its Professional Associations: A Comparative Analysis." In *Urban Craftsmen and Traders in the Roman World*, edited by Andrew Wilson and Miko Flohr, 278–98. Oxford: Oxford University Press, 2016.

Arnold, Clinton E. *Ephesians: Power and Magic: The Concept of Power in Ephesians in Light of Its Historical Setting*. SNTS 63. Cambridge, UK: Cambridge University Press, 1989.

Ascough, Richard S., Philip A. Harland, and John S. Kloppenborg, eds. *Associations in the Greco-Roman World: A Sourcebook*. Waco, TX: Baylor University Press, 2012.

Assmann, Jan. *The Mind of Egypt: History and Meaning in the Time of the Pharaohs*. Cambridge, MA: Harvard University Press, 2003.

Atac, A., N. Aray, and R. V. Yildirim. "Asclepions in Turkey." *Balkan Military Medical Review* 9, no. 2 (2006): 82–84.

Atalay, Erol. "Die Kurudağ-Höhle [Bei Ephesos] Mit Archäologischen Funden." *JÖAI* 52 (1980 1978): 33–44.

Athas, George. *The Tel Dan Inscription: A Reappraisal and a New Introduction*. JSOTSup 360. New York: Bloomsbury, 2006.

Aune, David E. *Revelation 1-5*. Word Biblical Commentary 52A. Dallas, Tex.: Word Books, 1997.

———. *Revelation 6-16*. Word Biblical Commentary 52B. Dallas, Tex.: Word Books, 1998.

———. "The Apocalypse of John and the Problem of Genre." In *Early Christian Apocalypticism: Genre and Social Setting*, 65–69. Semeia 36. Atlanta, Ga.: Scholars Press, 1986.

Avci, Murat. "'Noah's Ark': Its Relationship to the Telçeker Earthflow, Mount Ararat, Eastern Turkey." *Bulletin of Engineering Geology and the Environment* 66 (August 1, 2007): 377–80.

Aviam, Mordechai. "Regionalism of Tombs and Burial Customs in the Galilee During the Hellenistic, Roman and Byzantine Periods." In *Jews, Pagans and Christians in the Galilee: 25 Years of Archaeological Excavations and Surveys: Hellenistic to Byzantine Periods*, edited by Mordechai Aviam, 257–313. Land of Galilee 1. Rochester, NY: University of Rochester Press, 2004.

Avigad, Nahman. *Discovering Jerusalem*. Nashville: Nelson, 1983.

———. *Hebrew Bullae from the Time of Jeremiah: Remnants of a Burnt Archive*. Translated by Rafi Grafman. Jerusalem: Israel Exploration Society. 1986.

Avi-Yonah, Michael, ed. *Views of the Biblical World: The New Testament*. Vol. 5. Jerusalem: International, 1961.

Avi-Yonah, Michael, and Ephraim Stern, eds. *Encyclopedia of Archaeological Excavations in the Holy Land*. 3rd ed. 4 vols. New York: Prentice Hall, 1996.

Avner, Uzi. "Ancient Cult Sites in the Negev and Sinai Deserts." *Tel Aviv* 11 (1984): 115–31.

Badia, Leonard F. *The Qumran Baptism and John the Baptist's Baptism.* Lanham, MD: University Press of America, 1980.

Bagatti, Bellarmino, and Józef Tadeusz Milik. *Gli Scavi Del 'Dominus Flevit': Monte Oliveto-Gerusalemme.* Vol. 2. Jerusalem: Tipografia dei PP. Francescani, 1958.

Bagnall, Roger S. "Christianity." In *Graffiti from the Basilica in the Agora of Smyrna,* edited by Roger S. Bagnall, Roberta Casagrande-Kim, Akin Ersoy, and Cumhur Tanriver, 45–47. Institute for the Study of the Ancient World. New York, N.Y.: New York University Press, 2016.

———. *Early Christian Books in Egypt.* Princeton, NJ: Princeton University Press, 2009.

Bahat, Dan. *The Atlas of Biblical Jerusalem.* Jerusalem: Carta, 1994.

Bailey, Donald Michael. *A Catalogue of the Lamps in the British Museum.* 4 vols. London, UK: British Museum, 1975.

———. *Greek and Roman Pottery Lamps.* Rev. ed. London, UK: British Museum, 1972.

Bailey, Kenneth E. *Jesus Through Middle Eastern Eyes: Cultural Studies in the Gospels.* Downers Grove, IL: IVP Academic, 2008.

Ballance, M. "The Site of Derbe: A New Inscription." *AS* 7 (1957): 147–51.

Balme, Jane, and Alistair Paterson, eds. *Archaeology in Practice: A Student Guide to Archaeological Analyses.* Hoboken, NJ: Wiley & Sons, 2014.

Baney, Ralph E. *Search for Sodom and Gomorrah.* 2nd ed. Kansas City, MO: CAM Press, 1962.

Bar-Asher, Moshe. "Mishnaic Hebrew: An Introductory Survey." In *The Literature of the Sages: Second Part: Midrash, and Targum; Liturgy, Poetry, Mysticism; Contracts, Inscriptions, Ancient Science and the Languages of Rabbinic Literature*, edited by Shmuel Safrai, Ze'ev Safrai, Joshua Schwartz, and Peter J. Tomson, 567–96. Compendia Rerum Ludaicarum Ad Novum Testamentum. Minneapolis, MN: Fortress, 2006.

Barber, E. J. W. *Prehistoric Textiles: The Development of Cloth in the Neolithic and Bronze Ages with Special Reference to the Aegean.* Princeton, NJ: Princeton University Press, 1991.

Barclay, William. *Letters to the Seven Churches.* London, UK: SCM, 1957.

———. *The Revelation of John: Chapters 1 to 5.* Vol. 1. The New Daily Study Bible. Louisville, KY: Westminster/Knox, 2004.

Barkat, Amiram. "Archeologist: King Herod's Tomb Desecrated, but Discovery 'High Point.'" *Haaretz*, May 7, 2007. http://www.haaretz.com/news/archeologist-king-herod-s-tomb-desecrated-but-discovery-high-point-1.219914.

Barkay, Gabriel. *2nd Progress Report on the Temple Mount Antiquities Salvage Operation: A Hebrew Bulla from the Temple Mount.* The Temple Mount Sifting Project, August 11, 2005.

Barker, Don. "The Dating of New Testament Papyri." *NTS* 57, no. 4 (2011): 571–82.

Barker, Philip. *Techniques of Archaeological Excavation.* 3rd ed. London, UK: Routledge, 1993.

Barnes, Timothy David. "The Date of Herod's Death." *JTS* 19, no. 1 (1968): 204–19.

Barr, David L. "The Apocalypse of John as Oral Enactment." *Interpretation* 40, no. 3 (1986): 243–56.

Barrett, C. K. "Paul's Address to the Ephesian Elders." In *God's Christ and His PeoplE, Studies in Honour of Nils Alstrup Dahl,* edited by J. Jervell and W. A. Meeks, 107–21. Oslo: Univer sitetsforlaget, 1977.

Barr, James. "Why the World Was Created in 4004 BC: Archbishop Ussher and Biblical Chronology." *BJRL* 67 (85 1984): 575–608.

Barton, George Aaron. *Archaeology and the Bible.* Alexandria, Egypt: Library of Alexandria, 1933.

Bartosiewicz, László. "'There's Something Rotten in the State . . .': Bad Smells in Antiquity." *European Journal of Archaeology* 6, no. 2 (2003): 175–95.

BAR Staff. "First Temple Period 'Matanyahu' Seal Discovered in Jerusalem." *Bible History Daily,* May 2, 2012. https://www.biblicalarchaeology.org/daily/biblical-sites-places/temple-at-jerusalem/first-temple-period-matanyahu-seal-discovered-in-jerusalem.

Başaran, Cevat, Vedat Keleş, and Rex Geissler. "Mount Ararat Archaeological Survey." *Bible and Spade* 21, no. 1 (2008): 70–96.

Bauer, Walter, William F. Arndt, and F. Wilbur Gingrich, eds. *A Greek-English Lexicon of the New Testament, and Other Early Christian Literature.* 3rd ed. Chicago, IL: University of Chicago Press, 1957.

Baugh, Steven M., Peter H. Davids, David E. Garland, David W. J. Gill, George H. Guthrie, Moyer V. Hubbard, Andreas J. Köstenberger, et al. *Zondervan Illustrated Bible Backgrounds Commentary Set.* Edited by Clinton E. Arnold. 4 vols. Santa Rosa, CA: Zondervan, 2002.

Beagley, Alan James. *The "Sitz Im Leben" of the Apocalypse With Particular Reference to the Role of the Church's Enemies.* Berlin: De Gruyter, 1987.

Beale, Gregory K. "Review of Colin J. Hemer, The Letters to the Seven Churches of Asia in Their Local Setting." *Trinity Journal* 7, no. 2 (1986): 110.

———. *The Book of Revelation: A Commentary on the Greek Text.* New International Greek Testament Commentary 12. Grand Rapids: Eerdmans, 1998.

Bean, George E. *Aegean Turkey: An Archaeological Guide.* New York: Praeger, 1966.

———. *Turkey Beyond the Maeander.* 2nd ed. London, UK: Murray, 1989.

———. *Turkey's Southern Shore - An Archaeological Guide.* London, UK: Praeger, 1968.

Beasley-Murray, George R. *Book of Revelation.* NCB. Grand Rapids: Eerdmans, 1983.

Becker, Cornelia. "Did the People in Ayios Mamas Produce Purple Dye during the Middle Bronze Age? Considerations on the Prehistoric Production of Purple-Dye in the Mediterranean." In *Animals and Man in the Past: Essays in Honour of Dr. A.T. Clason,* edited by Hijlke Buitenhuis and Wietschke Prummel, 122–134. Groningen: Rijksuniversiteit, 2001.

Beckwith, Isbon T. *The Apocalypse of John.* New York: MacMillan, 1919.

Behr, Charles A. *Aelius Aristides and the Sacred Tales.* Amsterdam: Hakkert, 1968.

Bekkum, Koenraad van. "From Conquest to Coexistence: Ideology and Antiquarian Intent in the Historiography of Israel's Settlement in Canaan." Ph. D. diss., Theologische Universiteit Van De Gereformeerde Kerken, 2010.

Ben-Tor, Amnon. "Hazor and the Chronology of Northern Israel: A Reply to Israel Finkelstein." *BASOR* 317 (2000): 9–16.

———. "The Fall of Canaanite Hazor–The 'Who' and 'When' Questions." In *Mediterranean Peoples in Transition, 13th to 10th Centuries BC,* edited by Ephraim Stern, Seymour Gitin, and Amihai Mazar, 456–67. Jerusalem: Israel Exploration Society, 1998.

———. "The Sad Fate of Statues and the Mutilated Statues of Hazor." In *Confronting the Past: Archaeological and Historical Essays on Ancient Israel in Honor of William G. Dever,* edited by Seymour Gitin, J. Edward Wright, and J. P. Dessel, 3–16. Winona Lake, IN: Eisenbrauns, 2006.

———. "Who Destroyed Canaanite Hazor?" *BAR* 39, no. 4 (2013): 26–36, 58–60.

Ben-Yosef, Erez, Dafna Langgut, and Lidar Sapir-Hen. "Beyond Smelting: New Insights on Iron Age (10th c. BCE) Metalworkers Community from Excavations at a Gatehouse and Associated Livestock Pens in Timna, Israel." *Journal of Archaeological Science: Reports* 11 (February 2017): 411–26.

Ben-Yosef, Erez, Ron Shaar, Liza Tauxe, and Hagai Ron. "A New Chronological Framework for Iron Age Copper Production at Timna (Israel)." *BASOR* 367 (August 2012): 31–71.

Berdowski, Piotr. "Garum Of Herod The Great (Latin-Greek Inscription On The Amphora From Masada)." *Analecta Archaeologica Ressoviensia* 1 (2006): 239–57.

Ben-Dov, Jonathan. "A Presumed Citation of Esther 3:7 in 4Qdb." *Dead Sea Discoveries* 6, no. 3 (1999): 282–84.

Berenbaum, Michael, and Fred Skolnik, eds. *Encyclopedia Judaica.* 2nd ed. 22 vols. New York: MacMillan, 2006.

Berger, Adolf. *Encyclopedic Dictionary of Roman Law.* Reprint of the 1953 edition. Transactions of the American Philosophical Society, 43, Pt. 2. The Lawbook Exchange, 2002.

Bernabé, Alberto. "The Ephesia Grammata: Genesis of a Magical Formula." In *The Getty Hexameters: Poetry, Magic, and Mystery in Ancient Selinous,* edited by Christopher A. Faraone and Dirk Obbink, 71–96. Oxford, U.K.: Oxford University Press, 2013.

Bernegger, P. M. "Affirmation of Herod's Death in 4 B.C." *Journal of Theological Studies* 34, no. 2 (1983): 526–31.

Best, Robert M. *Noah's Ark and the Ziusudra Epic: Sumerian Origins of the Flood Myth.* Winona Lake, IN: Eisenbrauns, 1999.

Betylon, John W. "Numismatics and Archaeology." *The Biblical Archaeologist* 48 (1985): 162–65.

Beyer, Klaus. *Aramaic Language: Its Distribution and Subdivisions.* Göttingen: Vandenhoeck & Ruprecht, 1986.

Bickerman, Elias J. "The Warning Inscriptions of Herod's Temple." *The Jewish Quarterly Review* 37, no. 4 (1947): 387–405.

Bieber, Margarete. *The History of the Greek and Roman Theater.* Princeton, NJ: Princeton University Press, 1961.

Bienkowski, Piotr. *Jericho in the Late Bronze Age.* Ancient Near East. Warminster, Wiltshire: Aris & Phillips, 1986.

———. "Jericho Was Destroyed in the Middle Bronze Age, Not the Late Bronze Age." *BAR* 16, no. 5 (1990): 45, 46, 69.

Bienkowski, Piotr, and Alan R. Millard, eds. *Dictionary of the Ancient Near East.* Philadelphia, PA: University of Pennsylvania Press, 2000.

Bietak, Manfred. *Avaris and Piramesse: Archaeological Exploration in the Eastern Nile Delta.* Proceedings of the British Academy 65. Oxford, UK: Oxford University Press, 1981.

———. *Avaris, the Capital of the Hyksos: Recent Excavations at Tell El-Dab'a.* London, UK: British Museum Press, 1996.

———. "Egypt and Canaan during the Middle Bronze Age." *BASOR*, no. 281 (1991): 27–72.

Bietak, Manfred, and Irene Forstner-Müller. "Ausgrabung eines Palastbezirkes der Tuthmosidenzeit bei 'Ezbet Helmi/Tell el-Dab'a: Vorbericht für Herbst 2004 und Frühjahr 2005." *Ägypten und Levante / Egypt and the Levant* 15 (2005): 65–100.

Bietenhard, H. "Ὄνομα." Edited by Gerhard Kittel and Gerhard Friedrich. Translated by Geoffrey W. Bromiley. *Theological Dictionary of the New Testament.* Grand Rapids: Eerdmans, 1985.

Biggs, Robert D. "The Ebla Tablets: An Interim Perspective." *BA* 43, no. 2 (1980): 76–86.

Billington, Clyde E. "Tall el-Hammam Is Not Sodom." *Artifax*, Spring 2012, 1–3.

Bimson, John J. "Archaeological Data and the Dating of the Patriarchs." In *Essays on the Patriarchal Narratives*, edited by Alan R. Millard and Donald J. Wiseman, 59–92. Downers Grove, IL: InterVarsity, 1980.

———. "Merenptah's Israel and Recent Theories of Israelite Origins." *Journal for the Study of the Old Testament*, no. 49 (1991): 3–29.

Biran, Avraham, and Joseph Naveh. "An Aramaic Stele Fragment from Tel Dan." *IEJ* 43, no. 2/3 (January 1, 1993): 81–98.

———. "The Tel Dan Inscription: A New Fragment." *IEJ* 45, no. 1 (January 1, 1995): 1–18.

Birdsall, James Neville. *The Bodmer Papyrus of the Gospel of John.* Wheaton, IL: Tyndale, 1960.

Birge, Darice E. "Sacred Groves in the Ancient Greek World." Ph.D. diss., University of California-Berkely, 1982.

Blackburn, Bonnie, and Leofranc Holford-Strevens. *The Oxford Companion to the Year: An Exploration of Calendar Customs and Time-Reckoning.* Oxford, UK: Oxford University Press, 2003.

Black, Matthew. *The Scrolls and Christian Origins: Studies in the Jewish Background of the New Testament.* Brown Judaic Studies 48. Atlanta, Ga.: Scholars Press, 1983.

Blaiklock, Edward M., and R. K. Harrison, eds. *The New International Dictionary of Biblical Archaeology.* Grand Rapids: Zondervan, 1983.

Blaiklock, Edward M. *Cities of the New Testament.* New York: Revell, 1965.

———. *The Archaeology of the New Testament.* Grand Rapids: Zondervan, 1970.

———. *The Seven Churches: An Exposition of Revelation Chapters Two and Three.* London, UK: Marshall, Morgan & Scott, 1951.

Blanckenhorn, Max. *Entstehung und Geschichte des Toten Meeres: Beitraeg zur Geologie Palaestinas.* Zeitschrift des deutschen Palästina-Vereins 19. Leipzig: Baedeker, 1896.

Bliss, Frederick Jones, and A. C. Dickie. *Excavations at Jerusalem 1894-1897.* London, UK: PEF, 1898.

Blomberg, Craig L. *Making Sense of the New Testament: Three Crucial Questions.* Grand Rapids: Baker Academic, 2004.

Blue, Bradley B. "Acts and the House Church." In *Graeco-Roman Setting,* edited by David W. J. Gill and Conrad H. Gempf, 119–222. BAFCS 2. Eugene, OR: Wipf & Stock, 2000.

Boatwright, Mary T. "Theaters in the Roman Empire." *BA* 53, no. 4 (1990): 184–92.

Bock, Darrell L. *Breaking The Da Vinci Code: Answers to the Questions Everyone's Asking.* New York: Nelson, 2006.

———. *The Missing Gospels: Unearthing the Truth Behind Alternative Christianities.* Nashville: Nelson, 2006.

Bogucki, Peter. "Europe, Northern and Western: Bronze Age." In *Encyclopedia of Archaeology*, edited by Deborah M. Pearsall, 1:1216–26. San Diego, CA: Academic Press, 2008.

Bohstrom, Philippe. "Divers Find Unexpected Roman Inscription from the Eve of Bar-Kochba Revolt." *Haaretz*, November 30, 2016. http://www.haaretz.com/jewish/archaeology/1.756193.

Bolen, Todd. "Identifying King David's Palace: Mazar's Flawed Reading of the Biblical Text." *The Bible and Interpretation*, September 2010. http://www.bibleinterp .com/opeds/ident357928.shtml.

———. "Search for Sodom under Dead Sea." *BiblePlaces*, December 14, 2010. http://blog.bibleplaces.com/2010/12/search-for-sodom-under-dead-sea.html.

Bonani, Georges, Magen Broshi, Israel Carmi, J. Stugnell, and W. Woelfli. "Radiocarbon Dating of the Dead Sea Scrolls." *Tigot* 20 (1991): 27–32.

Bonani, Georges, Susan Ivy, Willy Wolfli, Magen Broshi, Israel Carmi, and John Strugnell. "Radiocarbon Dating of Fourteen Dead Sea Scrolls." *Radiocarbon* 34, no. 3 (2006): 843–49.

Bonz, Marianne Palmer. "Differing Approaches to Religious Benefaction: The Late Third-Cent. Acquisition of the Sardis Synagogue." *HTR* 86 (1993): 139–54.

Boring, Eugene M. *Revelation*. Louisville, KY: Westminster/Knox, 1989.

Botta, Paul-Émile, and Étienne Flandin. *Monument de Ninive découvert et décrit par M. P.-É. Botta, mesuré et dessiné par M. E. Flandin*. Paris: Impr. nationale, 1849.

Bowersock, G. W. *Roman Arabia*. Cambridge, MA: Harvard University Press, 1998.

Bousset, Wilhelm. *Die Offenbarung Johannis*. Göttingen: Vandenhoeck & Ruprecht, 1906.

Bowman, Alan K., Edward Champlin, and Andrew Lintott, eds. *The Cambridge Ancient History: The Augustan Empire, 44 BC–AD 70*. Vol. 10. Cambridge, UK: Cambridge University Press, 1996.

Bowman, Sheridan. *Radiocarbon Dating*. Berkeley, CA: University of California Press, 1990.

Brenk, Frederick E. "Artemis of Ephesos: An Avant Garde Goddess." *Kernos* 11 (1998): 157–71.

Brent, Allen. *The Imperial Cult and the Development of Church Order: Concepts and Images of Authority in Paganism and Early Christianity Before the Age of Cyprian*. Leiden: Brill, 1999.

Bridger, David, and Samuel Wolk. *The New Jewish Encyclopedia*. Springfield, NJ: Behrman, 1962.

Briggs, Charles A., Samuel R. Driver, and Francis Brown. *Hebrew-Aramaic and English Lexicon of the Old Testament. Complete and Unabridged*. Peabody, MA: Hendrickson, 1996.

Briggs, Peter. "Testing the Factuality of the Conquest of Ai Narrative in the Book of Joshua." In *Beyond the Jordan: Studies in Honor of W. Harold Mare*, edited by Glenn A. Carnagey Sr, Glenn Carnagey Jr, and Keith N. Schoville, 157–96. Eugene, Ore.: Wipf & Stock, 2005.

Brinks, C. L. "'Great Is Artemis of the Ephesians': Acts 19:23-41 in Light of Goddess Worship in Ephesus." *CBQ* 71, no. 4 (2009): 776–94.

Bromiley, Geoffrey W., ed. *The International Standard Bible Encyclopedia*. Revised. 4 vols. Grand Rapids: Eerdmans, 1995.

Brooten, Bernadette J. *Women Leaders in the Ancient Synagogue: Inscriptional Evidence and Background Issues*. Brown Judaic Studies. Atlanta, Ga.: Scholars Press, 1982.

Broughton, T. R. S. "Roman Asia Minor." In *An Economic Survey of Ancient Rome: Africa, Syria, Greece, Asia Minor*, edited by Tenney Frank, 4:499–916. Baltimore, MD: John Hopkins University Press, 1975.

Brown, Charles. *Heavenly Visions: An Exposition of the Book of Revelation*. Boston, MA: Pilgram, 1910.

Brown, Dan. *The Da Vinci Code*. London, UK: Bantam, 2003.

Brown, Raymond E., Joseph A. Fitzmyer, and Roland Murphy, eds. *New Jerome Biblical Commentary*. New York: Bloomsbury, 1995.

Bruce, F. F. "Colossian Problems, Part 1: Jews and Christians in the Lycus Valley." *BSac* 141 (1984): 3–15.

———. *New Testament History*. 2nd ed. New York: Doubleday, 1980.

———. *Paul, Apostle of the Heart Set Free*. Grand Rapids: Eerdmans, 2000.

Bruce, F. F., Philip W. Comfort, and James I. Packer. *The Origin of the Bible*. Wheaton, IL: Tyndale, 2003.

Brueggermann, Walter. *The Land.* Overtures to Biblical Theology. Philadelphia, PA: Fortress, 1977.

Bryce, Trevor. *Life and Society in the Hittite World.* Oxford, UK: Oxford University Press, 2004.

Bucarelli, Ottavio, and Martín Maria Morales, eds. *Paolo apostolo martyri: l'apostolo San Paolo nella storia, nell'arte e nell'archeologia.* Miscellanea Historiae Pontificiae 69. Rome: Gregorian and Biblical Press, 2009.

Buckler, W. H., William M. Calder, and C. W. M. Cox. "Asia Minor, 1924. I.--Monuments from Iconium, Lycaonia and Isauria." *JRS* 14 (January 1, 1924): 24–84.

Budden, Charles W., and Edward Hastings. *The Local Colour of the Bible.* 3 vols. Edinburgh, UK: T&T Clark, 1925.

Budge, E. A. Wallis. *Legends of the Gods The Egyptian Texts, Edited with Translations.* London, UK: Kegan Paul, Trench and Trubner & Co. Ltd., 1912.

———. *Rosetta Stone in the British Museum.* Whitefish, MT: Kessinger, 2003.

Buhl, Marie-Louise, and Svend Holm-Nielson, eds. *Shiloh, The Pre-Hellenistic Remains: The Danish Excavations at Tell Sailûn, Palestine, in 1926, 1929, 1932 and 1963.* Copenhagen: National Museum of Denmark and Aarhus University Press, 1969.

Bull, Robert J. "Caesarea Maritima: The Search for Herod's City." *BAR* 8, no. 3 (1982): 24–40.

———. "Pontius Pilate Inscription." *BAR* 8, no. 5 (1982).

Bultmann, Rudolph. *Jesus Christ and Mythology.* Upper Saddle River, NJ: Prentice Hall, 1981.

Bunimovitz, Shlomo. "How Mute Stones Speak, Interpreting What We Dig Up." *BAR* 21, no. 2 (1995): 58–67, 97.

Bunimovitz, Shlomo, and Zvi Lederman. "The Iron Age Fortifications of Tel Beth Shemesh: A 1990–2000 Perspective." *IEJ* 51, no. 2 (January 1, 2001): 121–47.

Burge, Gary M., Lynn H. Cohick, and Gene L. Green. *The New Testament in Antiquity: A Survey of the New Testament within Its Cultural Context.* Grand Rapids: Zondervan, 2009.

Burkert, Walter. *Greek Religion.* Cambridge, MA: Harvard University Press, 1985.

Burns, Ross. *Damascus: A History.* Cities of the Ancient World. London, UK: Routledge, 2005.

Burrell, Barbara. *Neokoroi: Greek Cities and Roman Emperors.* CCS 9. Leiden: Brill, 2004.

Burstein, Stanley Mayer. *The Babyloniaca of Berossus.* 2nd ed. Vol. 1. 5 vols. Sources from the Ancient Near East 1. Malibu: Undena Publications, 1978.

Burton, Ernest DeWitt. "The Politarchs." *American Journal of Theology* 2 (1898): 598–632.

Byers, Gary A. "Israel in Egypt." *Bible and Spade* 18, no. 1 (2005): 1–9.

Byrne, Ryan. "The Refuge of Scribalism in Iron I Palestine." *BASOR* 345 (2007): 1–31.

Byrne, Ryan, and Bernadette McNary-Zak. *Resurrecting the Brother of Jesus: The James Ossuary Controversy and the Quest for Religious Relics.* Raleigh, NC: The University of North Carolina Press, 2009.

Cadoux, Cecil J. *Ancient Smyrna: A History of the City from the Earliest Times to 224 A.D.* Oxford, UK: Basil Blackwell, 1938.

Cadwallader, Alan H., and Michael Trainor, eds. *Colossae in Space and Time: Linking to an Ancient City.* NTOA / SUNT. Göttingen: Vandenhoeck & Ruprecht, 2011.

Cahill, Jane M. "Jerusalem at the Time of the United Monarchy. The Archaeological Evidence." In *Jerusalem in Bible and Archaeology: The First Temple Period,* edited by Andrew G. Vaughn and Ann E. Killebrew, 13–80. SBL Symposium Series 18. Atlanta, Ga.: SBL, 2003.

Caird, G. B. *The Revelation of Saint John.* Peabody, MA: Hendrickson, 1993.

Calder, William M. "Studies in Early Christian Epigraphy: Two Episcopal Epitaphs from Laodicea Combusta." *JRS* 10 (1920): 42–59.

Callaway, Joseph A. "A New Perspective on the Hill Country Settlement of Canaan in Iron Age I." In *Palestine in the Bronze and Iron Ages: Papers in Honour of Olga Tufnell*, edited by Jonathan N. Tubb, 31–49. London: Institute of Archaeology, 2008.

———. "Dame Kathleen Kenyon, 1906 -1978." *The Biblical Archaeologist* 42, no. 2 (1979): 122–25.

———. "Excavating Ai (Et-Tell): 1964-1972." *BA* 39 (1976): 18–31.

———. "New Evidence on the Conquest of ‹Ai." *JBL* 87, no. 3 (September 1, 1968): 312–20.

———. "Was My Excavation of Ai Worthwhile?" *BAR* 11, no. 2 (1985): 68–69.

Calpino, Teresa J. "Lydia of Thyatira's Call." In *Women, Work and Leadership in Acts,* 181–226. Tübingen: Mohr Siebeck, 2014.

Campbell, Douglas A. "An Anchor for Pauline Chronology: Paul's Flight from 'The Ethnarch of King Aretas' (2 Corinthians 11:32-33)." *Journal of Biblical Literature* 121, no. 2 (2002): 279–302.

———. "Possible Inscriptional Attestation to Sergius Paulus (Acts 13:6–12) and the Implications for Pauline Chronology." *JTS* 56, no. 1 (2005): 1–29.

Campbell, Thomas H. "Paul's 'Missionary Journeys' as Reflected in His Letters." *Journal of Biblical Literature* 74, no. 2 (1955): 80–87.

Cancik, Hubert, and Helmuth Schneider, eds. *Brill's New Pauly, Antiquity Volumes Online.* Translated by Christine F. Salazar and Francis G. Gentry. 22 vols. Leiden: Brill, 2006.

Chandler, Richard. *Travels in Asia Minor, and Greece: Or An Account of a Tour Made at the Expense of the Society of Dilettanti.* 2 vols. London, UK: Booker & Priestley, 1817.

Cansdale, Lena. *Qumran and the Essenes: A Re-Evaluation of the Evidence.* Texte Und Studien Zum Antiken Judentum 60. Tübingen: Siebeck, 1997.

Carroll, Kevin Killan. *The Parthenon Inscription.* Edited by Kent J. Rigsby. Greek, Roman, and Byzantine Studies Monographs 9. Durham, N.C.: Duke University, 1982.

Carter, John M. "A New Fragment of Octavian's Inscription at Nicopolis." *ZPE* 24 (1977): 227–30.

Carter, Warren. *Pontius Pilate: Portraits of a Roman Governor.* Interfaces Series. Collegeville, Minn.: Liturgical, 2003.

Casey, Christopher. "'Grecian Grandeurs and the Rude Wasting of Old Time': Britain, the Elgin Marbles, and Post-Revolutionary Hellenism." *Foundation* 3, no. 1 (2008): 31–64.

Ceram, C. W. *Gods, Graves & Scholars: The Story of Archaeology.* Translated by E. B. Garside and Sophie Wilkins. 2d Revised Edition. New York: Vintage, 1986.

Chambers, Roger. "Greek Athletics and the Jews: 165 BC–AD 70." Ph.D. diss., Miami University, 1980.

Chapman III, Rupert L. "Putting Sheshonq I in His Place." *PEQ* 141, no. 1 (2009): 4–17.

Charles, Robert H. *A Critical and Exegetical Commentary on the Revelation of St John.* 2 vols. The International Critical Commentary. Edinburgh, UK: T&T Clark, 1963.

Charlesworth, James H. "Archaeology, Jesus, and Christian Faith." In *What Has Archaeology to Do with Faith?*, edited by James H. Charlesworth and Walter P. Weaver, 1–22. Faith & Scholarship Colloquies. Philadelphia, PA: Trinity Press International, 1992.

———. , ed. *Jesus and the Dead Sea Scrolls*. New Haven, CT: Yale University Press, 1992.

———. *The Dead Sea Scrolls: Hebrew, Aramaic, and Greek Texts With English Translations*. Louisville, KY: Westminster/Knox, 2000.

———. *The Old Testament Pseudepigrapha: Apocalyptic Literature and Testaments*. Vol. 1. 2 vols. Peabody, MA: Hendrickson, 1983.

———. *The Old Testament Pseudepigrapha: Expansions of the Old Testament and Legends, Wisdom and Philosophical Literature, Prayers, Psalms, and Odes, Fragments of Lost Judeo-Hellenistic Works*. Vol. 2. 2 vols. Anchor Bible Reference Library. New York: Doubleday, 1985.

———. "The Tale of Two Pools: Archaeology and the Book of John." *Near East Archaeological Society Bulletin* 56 (2011): 1–14.

Charitonidou, Angeliki. "Epidaurus: The Sanctuary of Asclepius." In *Temples and Sanctuaries of Ancient Greece*, edited by Evi Melas, 89–99. London: Thames & Hudson, 1973.

Chavalas, Mark W., and K. Lawson Younger, eds. *Mesopotamia and the Bible: Comparative Explorations*. Grand Rapids: Baker Academic, 2002.

Chesson, Meredith S., and Morag M. Kersel. "Tomato Season In The Ghor Es-Safi: A Lesson in Community Archaeology." *NEA* 76, no. 3 (2013): 159–65.

Chesson, Meredith S., and R. Thomas Schaub. "Death and Dying on the Dead Sea Plain: Fifa, Al- Khanazir and Bab Adh-Dhra` Cemeteries." In *Crossing Jordan: North American Contributions to the Archaeology of Jordan*, edited by Thomas Evan Levy, P. M. Michèle Daviau, Randall W. Younker, and May Shaer, 253–60. London, UK: Equinox, 2007.

———. "Life in the Earliest Walled Towns on the Dead Sea Plain: Numayra and Bab Edh-Dhra`." In *Crossing Jordan: North American Contributions to the Archaeology of Jordan*, edited by Thomas Evan Levy, P. M. Michèle Daviau, Randall W. Younker, and May Shaer, 245–52. London, UK: Equinox, 2007.

Chilton, David. *The Days of Vengeance: An Exposition of the Book of Revelation*. Fort Worth: Dominion, 1987.

Cimok, Fatih. *Guide To The Seven Churches*. Istanbul: Tuttle, 1999.

Clair, William St. *Lord Elgin and the Marbles: The Controversial History of the Parthenon Sculptures*. 3rd ed. Oxford, UK: Oxford University Press, 1998.

Claridge, Amanda. *Rome*. 2nd ed. An Oxford Archaeological Guide. Oxford, UK: Oxford University Press, 2010.

Clark, David S. *The Message from Patmos: A Postmillennial Commentary on the Book of Revelation*. Grand Rapids: Baker, 1989.

Clarke, Andrew D. "Another Corinthian Erastus Inscription." *Tyndale Bulletin* 42 (1991): 146–51.

———. *Secular and Christian Leadership in Corinth: A Socio-Historical and Exegetkal Study of 1 Corinthians 1-6*. Leiden: Brill, 1993.

Cleland, Liza, Glenys Davies, and Karen Stears, eds. *Colour in the Ancient Mediterranean World*. BARI 1267. Oxford, U.K.: John and Erica Hedges, 2004.

Clerc, Michel Armand Edgar Anatole. *De rebus Thyatirenorum commentatio epigraphica*. Paris: Picard, 1893.

Clermont-Ganneau, Charles S. "The Discovery of a Tablet from Herod's Temple." *PEQ* 3, no. 1 (1871): 132–33.

Cline, Eric H. *From Eden to Exile: Unraveling Mysteries of the Bible*. Tampa, Fla.: National Geographic, 2007.

Cockburn, Andrew. "The Judas Gospel." *National Geographic* 209, no. 9 (2006): 78–95.

Codex Sinaiticus: Facsimile Prints. Greek Edition. Ancient Greek Edition. Peabody, MA: Hendrickson, 2011.

Cohen, Rudolf, and Yigal Yisraeli. "The Excavations of Rock Shelter XII/50 and in Caves XII/52-53." *Atiqot* 41, no. 2 (2002): 207–13.

Colless, Brian Edric. "Interpreting the Qeiyafa Ostracon." *Collesseum,* 2013. https://sites.google.com/site/collesseum/qeiyafa-ostracon-1.

———. "The Lost Link: The Alphabet in the Hands of the Early Israelites." *ASOR Blog,* 2013. http://asorblog.org/the-lost-link-the-alphabet-in-the-hands-of-the-early-israelites/.

Collins, Adela Yarbro. *Crisis and Catharsis: The Power of the Apocalypse.* Louisville, KY: Westminster/Knox, 1984.

———. *The Apocalypse.* New Testament Message: A Biblical-Theological Commentary Series. Wilmington, Del.: Michael Glazier, Inc., 1979.

———. "Pergamon in Early Christian Literature." In *Pergamon-Citadel of the Gods,* edited by Helmut Koester, 163—84. HTS 46. Harrisburg, PA: Trinity Press International, 1998.

———. "Vilification and Self- Definition in the Book of Revelation." *Harvard Theological Review* 79 (1986): 308–20.

Collins, John Joseph. *The Apocalyptic Imagination: An Introduction to Jewish Apocalyptic Literature.* 2nd ed. The Biblical Resource Series. Grand Rapids: Eerdmans, 1998.

Collins, John Joseph, and Daniel C. Harlow, eds. *The Eerdmans Dictionary of Early Judaism.* Grand Rapids: Eerdmans, 2010.

Collins, L. D., and David Fasold. "Bogus 'Noah's Ark' from Turkey Exposed as a Common Geologic Structure." *Journal of Geoscience Education* 44 (1996): 439–44.

Collins, Steven. "2005-2006 Season Summary." *Digging the Past: Voice of the Tall el-Hammam Excavation Project, Jordan,* 2006.

———. "A Chronology for the Cities of the Plain." *BRB* 2, no. 8 (2002): 1–9.

———. "A Response to Bryant G. Wood's Critique of Collins' Northern Sodom Theory." *Biblical Research Bulletin* 7, no. 7 (2007): 1–36.

———. "Explorations on the Eastern Jordan Disk." *BRB* 2, no. 18 (2002): 1–28.

———. "Rethinking the Location of Zoar: An Exercise in Biblical Geography." *BRB* 4, no. 1 (2006): 1–5.

———. "Sodom: The Discovery of a Lost City." *Bible and Spade* 20, no. 3 (2007): 70–77.

———. "Tall el-Hammam Is Sodom: Billington's Heshbon Identification Suffers from Numerous Fatal Flaws." *Artifax* 27, no. 3 (Summer 2012): 16–18.

———. "Tall el-Hammam Is Still Sodom: Critical Data-Sets Cast Serious Doubt on E. H. Merrill's Chronological Analysis." *BRB* 13, no. 1 (2013): 1–31.

———. "The Architecture of Sodom." *BRB* 2, no. 14 (2002): 1–9.

———. "The Geography of the Cities of the Plain." *Biblical Research Bulletin* 2, no. 1 (2002): 1–17.

———. "Where Is Sodom? The Case for Tall el-Hammam." *BAR* 39, no. 2 (2013): 32–41, 70–71.

Collins, Steven, Gary A. Byers, Carroll M. Kobs, David E. Graves, Phil Silvia, Khalid Tarawneh, and Khalid al Hawawrah. "Tall El-Hammam Season Ten, 2015: Excavation, Survey, Interpretations And Insights." *BRB* 15, no. 1 (2015): 1–37.

Collins, Steven, Gary A. Byers, Michael C. Luddeni, and John W. Moore. *The Tall Al-Hammam Excavation Project End of Season Activity Report Season Two: 2006/2007 Excavation and Exploration.* Submitted to the Department of Antiquities of the Hashemite Kingdom of Jordan, 2007.

Collins, Steven, Khalil Hamdan, and Gary A. Byers. "Tall el-Hammam: Preliminary Report on Four Seasons of Excavation (2006–2009)." *ADAJ* 53 (2009): 385–414.

Collins, Steven, Carroll Kobs, and Phillip J. Silvia. *Tall el-Hammam Excavation Project Field Manual.* Albuquerque, N.M.: TSU Press, 2013.

Collins, Steven, and Latayne C. Scott. *Discovering the City of Sodom: The Fascinating, True Account of the Discovery of the Old Testament's Most Infamous City.* New York: Simon & Schuster, 2013.

Collins, Steven, Khalid Tarawneh, Gary A. Byers, and Carroll M. Kobs. "Tall el-Hammam Season Eight, 2013: Excavation, Survey, Interpretations and Insights." *BRB* 13, no. 2 (2013): 1–20.

Conder, Claude Reignier, Horatio Herbert Kitchener. *The Survey of Western Palestine: Memoirs 2, Sheets VII–XVI, Samaria.* London: Palestine Exploration Fund, 1882.

Connah, Graham. *Writing about Archaeology.* Cambridge, UK: Cambridge University Press, 2010.

Constantinou, Eugenia Scarvelis. "Andrew of Caesarea and the Apocalypse in the Ancient Church of the East: Studies and Translation." Ph.D. diss., Université Laval, 2008.

Conzelmann, Hans. *Acts of the Apostles: A Commentary on the Acts of the Apostles.* Hermeneia: A Critical and Historical Commentary on the Bible. Philadelphia, PA: Fortress, 1987.

Coogan, Michael D., Marc Z Brettler, Carol A. Newsom, and Pheme Perkins, eds. *The New Oxford Annotated Bible with Apocrypha: New Revised Standard Version.* 4th ed. Oxford, UK: Oxford University Press, 2010.

Coote, Robert B., and Keith W. Whitelam. *The Emergence of Early Israel in Historical Perspective.* Social World of Biblical Antiquity Series. Sheffield: Sheffield Phoenix, 2010.

Corban, B. J. *The Explorers of Ararat and the Search for Noah's Ark.* Edited by Rex Geissler. Long Beach, CA: Great Commission Illustrated Books, 1999.

Corcoran, Simon. *The Empire of the Tetrarchs: Imperial Pronouncements and Government, AD 284-324.* Oxford: Clarendon, 2000.

Cornuke, Robert. *Ark Fever: Legend Chaser.* Wheaton, IL: Tyndale, 2005.

Cornuke, Robert, and David Halbrook. *In Search of the Lost Mountains of Noah: The Discovery of the Real Mt. Ararat.* Nashville: Broadman & Holman, 2001.

———. *In Search of the Mountain of God: The Discovery of the Real Mt. Sinai.* Nashville: Broadman & Holman, 2000.

Coulston, Jon C., and Hazel Dodge, eds. *Ancient Rome: The Archaeology of the Eternal City.* Monograph 54. Oxford, UK: Oxford University School of Archaeology, 2000.

Court, John M. *Myth and History in the Book of Revelation.* Louisville, KY: Westminster/Knox, 1979.

Court, John M. *The Book of Revelation and the Johannine Apocalyptic Tradition.* Sheffield, UK: Sheffield Academic, 2000.

Crawford, Sidnie White. "Has Esther Been Found at Qumran? 4QProto-Esther and the Esther Corpus." *Revue de Qumrân* 17, no. 1/4 (65/68) (November 1996): 307–25.

———. "Has Every Book of the Bible Been Found Among the Dead Sea Scrolls?" *Revue de Qumrân* 12 (October 1996): 28–33, 56.

Criswell, W. A. *Expository Sermons on Revelation.* Grand Rapids: Zondervan, 1975.

Cross, Frank Leslie, and Elizabeth A. Livingstone, eds. *The Oxford Dictionary Of The Christian Church.* Oxford, UK: Oxford University Press, 2005.

Cross, Frank Moore. "The Hebrew Inscriptions from Sardis." *HTR* 95, no. 1 (2002): 3–19.

Cross, Frank Moore, and Lawrence E. Stager. "Cypro-Minoan Inscriptions Found in Ashkelon." *IEJ* 56, no. 2 (January 1, 2006): 129–59.

Crouse, Bill, and Gordon Franz. "Mount Cudi: The True Mountain of Noah's Ark." *Bible and Spade* 19 (2006): 99–112.

Custance, Arthur C. *The Flood, Local or Global?.* The Doorway Papers 9. Grand Rapids: Zondervan, 1985.

Dąbrowa, Edward. "M. Paccius Silvanus Quintus Coredius Gallus Gargilius Antiquus et son cursus honorum." In *Nunc de suebis dicendum est: studia archaeologica et historica Georgio Kolendo ab amicis et discipulis dicata,* edited by Aleksander Bursche and Jerzy Kolendo, 99–102. Warsaw: Instytut Archeologii Uniwersytetu Warszawskiego, 1995.

Dahari, Uzi. *Final Report Of The Examining Committees For the Yehoash Inscription and James Ossuary.* Israeli Antiquities Authority, 2011.

Dalley, Stephanie. *Myths from Mesopotamia: Creation, the Flood, Gilgamesh, and Others.* Revised. Oxford World's Classics. Oxford, UK: Oxford University Press, 2009.

Daly, Okasha El. *Egyptology: The Missing Millennium. Ancient Egypt in Medieval Arabic Writings.* London: Cavendish, 2005.

Dancey, William S. *Archaeological Field Methods: An Introduction.* Minneapolis, MN: Burgess, 1981.

D'Ancona, Matthew, and Carsten Thiede. *The Jesus Papyrus.* New York: Doubleday, 2000.

D'Andria, Francesco, Mustafa Büyükkolancı, and Lorenzo Campagna. "The Castellum Aquae of Hierapolis of Phrygia." In *Cura Aquarum In Ephesus: Proceedings of the Twelfth International Congress on the History of Water Management and Hydraulic Engineering in the Mediterranean Region (Ephesus-Selçuck, October 2-10, 2004), Part 1,* edited by Gilbert Wiplinger, 359–61. BABesch Suppl. 12. Leuven, Belgium: Peeters, 2006.

Daniels, T. Scott. *Seven Deadly Spirits: The Message of Revelation's Letters for Today's Church.* Grand Rapids: Baker Academic, 2009.

Darnell, John Coleman, and Colleen Manassa. *Tutankhamun's Armies: Battle and Conquest During Ancient Egypt's Late Eighteenth Dynasty.* Hoboken, NJ: Wiley, 2007.

Davies, Graham I. *The Way of the Wilderness a Geographical Study of the Wilderness Itineraries in the Old Testament.* The Society for Old Testament Study Monographs 5. Cambridge, UK: Cambridge University Press, 1979.

Davies, John K. "The Reliability of the Oral Tradition." In *The Trojan War: Its Historicity and Context,* edited by Lin Foxhall and John Kenyon Davies, 87–110. Papers of the First Greenbank Colloquium, Liverpool, 1981. Bristol: Bristol Classical, 1984.

Davies, Paul E. "The Macedonian Scene of Paul's Journeys." *BA* 26, no. 3 (1963): 91–106.

Davies, Philip R. *In Search of "Ancient Israel": A Study in Biblical Origins.* The Library of Hebrew Bible/OT Studies. London, UK: Continuum International, 2006.

———. *Memories of Ancient Israel: An Introduction to Biblical History--Ancient and Modern.* Louisville, KY: Westminster/Knox, 2008.

Davies, William David, Louis Finkelstein, and Steven T. Katz. *The Cambridge History of Judaism: The Late Roman-Rabbinic Period.* Vol. 4. 4 vols. Cambridge University Press, 1984.

Davis, E. J. *Anatolia: or The Journal of a Visit to Some of the Ancient Ruined Cities of Caria, Phrygia, Lycia and Pisidia.* London, UK: Grant & Co., 1874.

Davila, James R. *The Provenance of the Pseudepigrapha.* Leiden: Brill, 2005.

Davis, Ellen N. "A Storm in Egypt during the Reign of Ahmose." In *Thera and the Aegean World III*, edited by David A. Hardy and A. C. Renfrew, 3:232–35. Proceedings of the Third International Congress, Santorini, Greece, 3–9 September 1989. London, UK: The Thera Foundation, 1990.

Davis, Thomas W. *Shifting Sands: The Rise and Fall of Biblical Archaeology: The Rise and Fall of Biblical Archaeology.* Oxford, UK: Oxford University Press, 2004.

———. "Theory and Method in Biblical Archaeology." In *The Future of Biblical Archaeology: Reassessing Methodologies and Assumptions*, edited by James K. Hoffmeier and Alan R. Millard, 20–28. Grand Rapids: Eerdmans, 2008.

Declercq, Georges. *Anno Domini: The Origins of the Christian Era.* Brepols Essays in European Culture 1. Turnhout, Belgium: Brepols, 2000.

DeConick, April D. *The Original Gospel of Thomas in Translation: With a Commentary and New English Translation of the Complete Gospel.* The Library of New Testament Studies. New York: Bloomsbury, 2006.

Dehandschütter, Boudewijn. "The Martyrium Polycarpi: A Century of Research." Edited by Wolfgang Haase and Hildegard Temporini. *Aufstieg Und Niedergang Der Römischen Welt: Geschichte Und Kultur Roms Im Spiegel Der Neueren Forschung* 27, no. 2 (1993): 485–522.

———. "The Meaning of Witness in the Apocalypse." In *L'Apocalypse Johannique et L' Apocalyptique Dans Le Nouveau Testament*, edited by Jan Lambrecht, 283–88. Gembloux, Belgium: Louvain University Press, 1980.

Deissmann, Gustav Adolf. *Light from the Ancient East.* Translated by Lionel R. M. Strachan. New York: Harper & Brothers, 1927.

———. *St Paul: A Study in Social and Religious History.* Translated by Lionel R. M. Strachan. Charleston, SC: BiblioBazaar, 2011.

De Lassus, Alain-Marie. "Le Septénaire Des Lettres de L'apocalypse de Jean: De La Correction Au Témoignage Militant." Ph.D. diss., University of Strasbourg, 2005.

Demoss, Matthew S. *Pocket Dictionary for the Study of New Testament Greek.* Downers Grove, IL: InterVarsity, 2001.

Demsky, Aaron. "An Iron Age IIA Alphabetic Writing Exercise from Khirbet Qeiyafa." *IEJ* 62, no. 2 (2012): 186–99.

Derwbear, Thomas. "Secret of Ancient Graffiti." *US Daily EU News,* July 22, 2003. www.turks.us/article.php?story=20030722090305725.

De Troyer, Kristin. "Once More, the So-Called Esther Fragments of Cave 4." *Revue de Qumrân* 19, no. 3 (75) (June 2000): 401–22.

Dever, William G. *Archaeology and Biblical Studies: Retrospects and Prospects: William C. Winslow Lectures, 1972.* Evanston, IL: Seabury-Western Theological Seminary, 1974.

———. "Retrospects and Prospects in Biblical and Syro-Palestinian Archeology." *The Biblical Archaeologist* 45, no. 2 (April 1, 1982): 103–7.

———. "Syro-Palestinian and Biblical Archaeology Ca. 1945-1980." In *The Hebrew Bible and Its Modern Interpreters*, edited by Douglas A. Knight and Gene M. Tucker, 31–74. Chicago, IL: Scholars Press, 1985.

———. "The Current School of Revisionist and Their Nonhistories of Ancient Israel." In *What Did the Biblical Writers Know, and When Did They Know It?*, 23–52. Grand Rapids: Eerdmans, 2001.

———. "The Impact of the 'New Archaeology' on Syro-Palestinian Archaeology." *Bulletin of the American Schools of Oriental Research*, no. 242 (April 1, 1981): 15–29.

———. "The Patriarchal Period." In *Israelite and Judaean History*, edited by John H. Hayes and J. Maxwell Miller, 102–20. Philadelphia, PA: Westminster, 1977.

———. "The Western Cultural Tradition Is At Risk." *BAR* 32, no. 2 (2006): 26, 76.

———. "Two Approaches to Archaeological Method-the Architectural and the Stratigraphic." *Eretz-Israel* 11 (1973): 1–8.

———. "Whatchmacallit: Why It's So Hard to Name Our Field." *BAR* 29, no. 4 (2003): 56–61.

———. *What Did the Biblical Writers Know, and When Did They Know It?*. Grand Rapids: Eerdmans, 2001.

———. "What Remains of the House That Albright Built?" *BA* 56, no. 1 (March 1993): 25–35.

———. *Who Were the Early Israelites and Where Did They Come From?*. Grand Rapids: Eerdmans, 2003.

———. "'Will the Real Israel Please Stand up?' Part I: Archaeology and the Religions of Ancient Israel." *BASOR*, no. 297 (1995): 61–80.

Dever, William G., and H. Darrell Lance, eds. *A Manual of Field Excavation: Handbook for Field Archaeologists*. Jerusalem: Hebrew Union College Press, 1978.

De Vries, Bert, ed. "Archaeology in Jordan, 1991." *AJA* 95, no. 2 (1991): 253–80.

DeVries, LaMoine F. *Cities of the Biblical World: An Introduction to the Archaeology, Geography, and History of Biblical Sites*. Eugene, OR: Wipf & Stock, 2006.

DeWitt, Dale S. "The Historical Background of Gen 11:1–9: Babel or Ur?" *Journal of the Evangelical Theological Society* 22, no. 1 (n.d.): 15–26.

Diamond, A. S. *The Earliest Hebrew Scribes*. New York: Jewish Book Council, 1960.

Dines, Jennifer Mary, and Michael Anthony Knibb. *The Septuagint*. New York: T&T Clark, 2004.

Diringer, David. *Le Iscrizioni Antico-Ebraiche Palestinesi*. Florence, Italy: Le Monnier, 1934.

———. "The Biblical Scripts." In *The Cambridge History of the Bible*, edited by Peter R. Ackroyd and Craig F. Evans, 1:, From the Beginnings to Jerome:11–29. Cambridge, UK: Cambridge University Press, 1975.

Dittenberger, Carl Friedrich Wilhelm, Johann Friedrich Wilhelm Rudolf August Hiller Von Gaertringen, Johannes E. Kirchner, Joannes Pomtow, Georg Wissowa, and Erich Ziebarth, eds. *Orientis Graeci Inscriptiones Selectae: Supplementum Sylloges Insciptionum Graecarum*. 3rd ed. 4 vols. Leipzig: Nachdruck der Ausgabe, 1915.

Dixon, Suzanne. *Childhood, Class and Kin in the Roman World*. New York: Routledge, 2005.

Djuric, Srdjan. *Ancient Lamps from the Mediterranean*. Toronto: Eika, 1995.

Donahue, Michelle Z. "Found: Fresh Clues to Mystery of King Solomon's Mines." *National Geographic*, April 2, 2017. https://news.nationalgeographic.com/2017/03/king-solomon-mines-bible-timna-dung.

Donati, Angela. *Pietro E Paolo La Storia Il Culto La Memoria Nei Primi Secoli.* Catalogo Della Monstra. Milan: Electa, 2000.

Donfried, Karl Paul. *Paul, Thessalonica, and Early Christianity.* Grand Rapids: Eerdmans, 2002.

Donner, Herbert. *The Mosaic Map of Madaba. An Introductory Guide.* Palaestina Antiqua 7. Kampen: Kok Pharos, 1992.

Doudna, G. "Dating the Scrolls on the Basis of Radiocarbon Analysis." In *Dead Sea Scrolls After Fifity Years,* edited by Peter W. Flint and James C. VanderKam, 1:430–71. Leiden: Brill Academic, 1999.

Dougherty, Raymond P. "Writing upon Parchment and Papyrus among the Babylonians and the Assyrians." *Journal of the American Oriental Society* 48 (January 1, 1928): 109–35.

Downey, Glanville. *A History Of Antioch In Syria: From Seleucus To The Arab Conquest.* Literary Licensing, LLC, 2012.

———. "The Gate of the Cherubim at Antioch." *The Jewish Quarterly Review,* New Series, 29, no. 2 (October 1, 1938): 167–77.

Downing, F. Gerald. "Pliny's Prosecutions of Christians." *Journal for the Study of the New Testament* 34 (1988): 105–23.

Draper, Jr., James T. *The Unveiling: Inspirational Expositions of the Book of Revelation from a Premillennial Viewpoint.* Nashville: Broadman, 1984.

Draper, Robert. "David and Solomon, Kings of Controversy." *National Geographic* 12 (December 2010): 85–87.

Drinkard, Joel F., Gerald L. Mattingly, and J. Maxwell Miller, eds. *Benchmarks in Time and Culture: An Introduction to Palestinian Archaeology.* ASOR/SBL Archaeology And Biblical Studies. Atlanta, Ga.: Scholars Press, 1988.

Drogula, Fred K. "The Office of the Provincial Governor under the Roman Republic and Empire [to AD 235]: Conception and Tradition." Ph. D. diss., University of Virginia, 2005.

Drower, Margaret S. *Flinders Petrie: A Life in Archaeology.* Madison, Wisc.: University of Wisconsin Press, 1995.

Dunbabin, Katherine M. D. "Wine and Water at the Roman Convivium." *JRA* 6 (1993): 116–41.

———. *The Roman Banquet: Images of Conviviality.* Cambridge, U.K.: Cambridge University Press, 2010.

Dunn, James D. G. *Jesus Remembered.* Grand Rapids: Eerdmans, 2003.

Dvorjetski, Estee. *Leisure, Pleasure, and Healing: Spa Culture and Medicine in Ancient Eastern Mediterranean.* Supplements to the Journal for the Study of Judaism 116. Leiden: Brill, 2007.

Eck, Werner, and Andreas Pangerl. "Syria Unter Domitian Und Hadrian: Neue Diplome Für Die Auxiliartruppen Der Provinz." *Chiron* 36 (2006): 205–47.

Eck, Werner. "Jahres- Und Provinzialfasten Der Senatorischen Statthalter von 69/70 Bis 138/139, 1. Teil." *Chiron* 12 (1982): 281–362.

———. "Jahres- Und Provinzialfasten Der Senatorischen Statthalter von 69/70 Bis 138/139. 2. Teil." *Chiron* 13 (1983): 147–237.

Edelstein, Emma Jeannette Levy, and Ludwig Edelstein. *Asclepius: A Collection and Interpretation of the Testimonies.* 2 vols. Baltimore, MD: Johns Hopkins Press, 1998.

Edersheim, Alfred. *The Life and Times of Jesus the Messiah.* New updated ed. Peabody, MA: Hendrickson, 1993.

Edwards, Douglas. "Galilean Archaeology and the Historical Jesus Quest." In *Biblical Archaeology: From the Ground Down: DVD*, edited by Hershel Shanks, n.p. Atlanta, Ga.: Biblical Archaeology Society, 2003.

Editor. "Governor of Jerusalem's Seal." *Artifax* 33, no. 1 (Winter 2018): 4.

Efird, James M. *Revelation For Today: An Apocalyptic Approach.* Nashville: Abingdon, 1989.

Egeria. *The Pilgrimage of Etheria.* Translated by M. L. McClure and C. L. Feltoe. London, UK: Society for Promoting Christian Knowledge, 1919.

Ehrenberg, Victor, Arnold H. M. Jones, and David L. Stockton, eds. *Documents Illustrating the Reigns of Augustus and Tiberius.* 2nd ed. Oxford, UK: Clarendon, 1976.

Ehrman, Bart D. "Christianity Turned on Its Head: The Alternative Vision of the Gospel of Judas." In *The Gospel of Judas*, edited by Rodolphe Kasser, Marvin Meyer, Gregor Wurst, and Bart D. Ehrman, 77–120. Washington, DC: National Geographic, 2008.

Ehrman, Bart D., and Michael W. Holmes, eds. *The Text of the New Testament in Contemporary Research: Essays on the Status Quaestionis. Second Edition.* Leiden: Brill, 2012.

Eichrodt, Walther. *Theology of the Old Testament.* 2 vols. Old Testament Library. Louisville, KY: Westminster/Knox, 1967.

Eisenbud, Daniel K. "IAA Refutes Authenticity Accusations of 'Jerusalem' Papyrus Inscription." *The Jerusalem Post,* October 30, 2016. http://www.jpost.com/Israel-News/IAA-refutes-authenticity-accusations-of-Jerusalem-papyrus-inscription-471239.

Elitzur, Yoel. *Ancient Place Names in the Holy Land: Preservation and History.* Jerusalem, Israel: The Hebrew University Magnes Press, 2004.

———. "The Siloam Pool-- 'Solomon's Pool-- Was a Swimming Pool'." *PEQ* 140, no. 1 (2008): 17–25.

Elitzur, Yoel, and Doron Nir-Zevi. "A Rock-Hewn Altar Near Shiloh." *PEQ* 135, no. 1 (2003): 30–36.

Elliott, J. K. "Review of the Jesus Papyrus by Carsten Peter Thiede; Matthew d'Ancona; Gospel Truth? New Light on Jesus and the Gospels by Graham Stanton." *NovT* 38, no. 4 (1996): 393–99.

Elliott, Keith, and Ian Moir. *Manuscripts and the Text of the New Testament: An Introduction for English Readers.* Edinburgh, UK: T&T Clark, 1996.

Elwell, Walter A., ed. *Evangelical Dictionary of Theology.* 2nd ed. Baker Reference Library. Grand Rapids: Baker Academic, 2001.

Elwell, Walter A., and Robert W. Yarbrough. *Readings from the First-Century World: Primary Sources for New Testament Study.* Encountering Biblical Studies. Grand Rapids: Baker Academic, 1998.

Enmarch, Roland. *Dialogue of Ipuwer and the Lord of All.* Oxford, UK: Griffith Institute, 2005.

Enmarch, Ronald. "The Reception of a Middle Egyptian Poem: The Dialogue of Ipuwer and the Lord of All in the Ramesside Period and beyond." In *Ramesside Studies in Honour of K. A. Kitchen*, edited by Mark Collier and Steven R. Snape, 169–75. Bolton, UK: Rutherford, 2011.

Evans, Craig A. *Fabricating Jesus: How Modern Scholars Distort the Gospels.* Downers Grove, IL: InterVarsity, 2006.

———. *Jesus and His World: The Archaeological Evidence.* London, UK: SPCK, 2012.

———. *Jesus and the Ossuaries: What Burial Practices Reveal about the Beginning of Christianity.* Waco, Tex.: Baylor University Press, 2003.

———. "The Family Buried Together Stays Together: On the Burial of the Executed in Family Tombs." In *The World of Jesus and the Early Church: Identity and Interpretation in Early Communities of Faith*, edited by Craig A. Evans, 87–96. Peabody, MA: Hendrickson, 2011.

———. , ed. *The World of Jesus and the Early Church: Identity and Interpretation in Early Communities of Faith.* Peabody, MA: Hendrickson, 2011.

Evans, Craig A., and Stanley E. Porter, eds. *Dictionary of New Testament Background: A Compendium of Contemporary Biblical Scholarship.* Downers Grove, IL: InterVarsity, 2000.

Ewald, Georg Heinrich. *History of Israel: Introduction and Preliminary History.* Edited and translated by Russell Martineau. 2nd ed. Vol. 1. 8 vols. London, UK: Longmans, Green, & Company, 1869.

Facaros, Dana, and Linda Theodorou. *Greece.* Country & Regional Guides - Cadogan. London, UK: Cadogan Guides, 2003.

Fagan, Brian. *The Rape of the Nile: Tomb Robbers, Tourists, and Archaeologists in Egypt.* Revised and Updated. New York: Basic Books, 2009.

Fagan, Brian M. *Return to Babylon: Travelers, Archaeologists and Monuments in Mesopotamia.* Boston, MA: Little, Brown & Co., 1979.

Faiman, David. "From Horeb to Kadesh in Eleven Days." *The Jewish Bible Quarterly* 22 (1994): 91–102.

Falkener, Edward. *Ephesus, and the Temple of Diana.* London, U.K.: Day & Son, 1862.

Falkenstein, A. *Die Neusumerische Gerichtsurkunden.* Vol. I. Munich: Beck, 1956.

Fant, Clyde E., and Mitchell G. Reddish. *A Guide to Biblical Sites in Greece and Turkey.* Oxford, UK: Oxford University Press, 2003.

Farrer, Austin M. *The Revelation of St. John the Divine: Commentary on the English Text.* Oxford, UK: Clarendon, 1964.

Faust, Avraham. "Did Eilat Mazar Find David's Palace?" *BAR* 38, no. 5 (2012): 47–52, 70.

———. "The Rural Community in Ancient Israel during Iron Age II." *BASOR* 317 (2000): 17–39.

Faust, Avraham, and Shlomo Bunimovitz. "The Four Room House: Embodying Iron Age Israelite Society." *NEA* 66, no. 1/2 (2003): 22–31.

Feder, Kenneth L. *Encyclopedia of Dubious Archaeology: From Atlantis to the Walam Olum.* Santa Barbara, CA: Greenwood, 2010.

Feeney, Denis. *Caesar's Calendar: Ancient Time and the Beginnings of History.* Oakland, Calf.: University of California Press, 2007.

Fehlmann, Marc. "Casts & Connoisseurs: The Early Reception of the Elgin Marbles." *Apollo* 165, no. 544 (June 2007): 44–51.

Feinman, Peter Douglas. "Methodism and the Origins of Biblical Archaeology: The William Foxwell Albright Story." *AUSS* 47, no. 1 (2009): 61–72.

———. *William Foxwell Albright and the Origins of Biblical Archaeology.* Berrien Springs, Mich.: Andrews University Press, 2004.

Feldman, Louis H. *Jewish Life and Thought Among Greeks and Romans: Primary Readings.* New York: Continuum International, 1996.

———. *Studies in Hellenistic Judaism.* Leiden: Brill, 1996.

Fellows, Richard. "Erastus (Rom 16:23) Was Erastus (Acts 19:22)." *Paul and Co-Workers*, June 25, 2010. http://paulandco-workers.blogspot.pt/2010/06/erastus-rom-1623-was-erastus-acts-1922.html.

Fensham, F. Charles. "Salt as a Curse in the Old Testament and the Ancient Near East." *Biblical Archaeologist* 25, no. 1 (February 1962): 48–50.

Ferguson, Everett. *Backgrounds of Early Christianity.* 3rd ed. Grand Rapids: Eerdmans, 2003.

———. *Encyclopedia of Early Christianity.* 2nd ed. New York: Routledge, 2013.

Fierman, Floyd S. "Rabbi Nelson Glueck: An Archaeologist's Secret Life in the Service of the OSS." *BAR* 12, no. 5 (1986): 18–22.

Filmer, W. E. "The Chronology of the Reign of Herod the Great." *JTS* 17 (1966): 283–98.

Fine, Steven, and Leonard Victor Rutgers. "New Light on Judaism in Asia Minor During Late Antiquity: Two Recently Identified Inscribed Menorahs." *JSQ* 3, no. 1 (1996): 1–23.

Fine, Steven. *Art and Judaism in the Greco-Roman World: Toward a New Jewish Archaeology.* Revised. Cambridge, UK: Cambridge University Press, 2010.

Finegan, Jack. *The Archeology of the New Testament: The Life of Jesus and the Beginning of the Early Church.* Revised. Princeton, NJ: Princeton University Press, 2014.

Finegan, Jack, E. Jerry Vardaman, and Edwin M. Yamauchi, eds. *Chronos, Kairos, Christos.* Winona Lake, IN: Eisenbrauns, 1989.

Finkel, Asher. *The Pharisees and the Teacher of Nazareth: A Study of Their Background, Their Halachic and Midrashic Teachings, the Similarities and Differences.* Arbeiten Zur Geschichte Des Spa¨tjudentums Und Urchristentums 4. Leiden: Brill, 1964.

Finkelstein, Israel. "Hazor and the North in the Iron Age: A Low Chronology Perspective." *BASOR* 314 (1999): 55–70.

———. "Philistine Chronology: High, Middle or Low?" In *Mediterranean Peoples in Transition, 13th to 10th Centuries BC*, edited by Ephraim Stern, Seymour Gitin, and Amihai Mazar, 140–47. Jerusalem: Israel Exploration Society, 1998.

———. "Shiloh Yields Some, But Not All, of Its Secrets: Location of Tabernacle Still Uncertain." *BAR* 12, no. 1 (1986): 22–41.

———. "The Archaeology of the United Monarchy: An Alternative View." *Levant* 28, no. 1 (January 1996): 177–87.

———. "The Date of the Philistine Settlement in Canaan." *Tel Aviv* 22 (1995): 213–39.

———. "The Emergence of Israel: A Phase in the Cyclic History of Canaan in the Third and Second Millennia BCE." In *From Nomadism to Monarchy: Archaeological and Historical Aspects of Early Israel*, edited by Israel Finkelstein and Nadav Na'aman, 150–78. Jerusalem: Israel Exploration Society, 1994.

———. "The Finds from the Rock-Cut Pool in Jerusalem and the Date of the Siloam Tunnel: An Alternative Interpretation." *Semitica et Classica* 6 (2013): 279–84.

Finkelstein, Israel, and Alexander Fantalkin. "Khirbet Qeiyafa: An Unsensational Archaeological and Historical Interpretation." *Tel Aviv* 39 (2012): 38–63.

Finkelstein, Israel, and Amihai Mazar. *The Quest for the Historical Israel.* Edited by Brian B. Schmidt. Archaeology and Biblical Studies 17. Atlanta, Ga.: SBL, 2007.

Finkelstein, Israel, and Nadav Na'aman, eds. *From Nomadism to Monarchy: Archaeological and Historical Aspects of Early Israel.* Jerusalem: Israel Exploration Society, 1994.

Finkelstein, Israel, Lidar Sapir-Hen, Guy Bar-Oz, and Yuval Gadot. "Pig Husbandry in Iron Age Israel and Judah New Insights Regarding the Origin of the 'Taboo.'" *ZDPV* 129 (2013): 1–20.

Finkelstein, Israel, and Neil Asher Silberman. *David and Solomon: In Search of the Bible's Sacred Kings and the Roots of the Western Tradition.* New York: Free Press, 2007.

———. *The Bible Unearthed: Archaeology's New Vision of Ancient Israel.* New York: Touchstone, 2002.

Finkelstein, Israel, Lily Singer-Avitz, David Ussishkin, and Ze'ev Herzog. "Has King David's Palace in Jerusalem Been Found?" *Tel Aviv* 34, no. 2 (2007): 142–64.

Finkelstein, Israel, Shelomoh Bunimovits, Zvi Lederman, and Baruch Brandl, eds. *Shiloh: The Archaeology of a Biblical Site.* Monograph Series of the Institute of Archaeology 10. Tel Aviv, Israel: Institute of Archaeology of Tel Aviv University, 1993.

Finney, D. J. *Probit Analysis. A Statistical Treatment of the Sigmoid Response Curve.* Cambridge, UK: Cambridge University Press, 1947.

First, Michell. "Can Archaeology Help Date the Psalms?" *BAR* 38, no. 4 (2012).

Fiorelli, Giuseppe. *Descrizione di Pompei.* Napoli: Tipografia Italiana, 1875.

Fischer, David Hackett. *Historians' Fallacies: Toward a Logic of Historical Thought.* New York: Harper & Row, 1970.

Fishwick, Duncan. *The Imperial Cult in the Latin West. Studies in the Ruler Cult of the Western Provinces of the Roman Empire,* 2.1. Leiden: Brill Academic, 2005.

Fitzmyer, Joseph A. "The Pauline Letters and the Lucan Account of Paul's Missionary Journeys." *Society of Biblical Literature Seminar Papers* 27 (1988): 82–89.

Fitzmyer, Joseph A. *The Semitic Background of the New Testament.* Grand Rapids: Eerdmans, 1997.

Fitzpatrick, Simon. "Simplicity of the Philosophy of Science." *Internet Encyclopedia of Philosophy: A Peer-Reviewed Academic Resource*, August 13, 2014. http://www.iep.utm.edu/simplici.

Flanagan, James W. "Chiefs in Israel." *JSOT* 20 (1981): 47–73.

Flanagan, James W., David W. McCreery, and Khair N. Yassine. "Tall Nimrin: Preliminary Report on the 1995 Excavation and Geological Survey." *ADAJ* 40 (1996): 271–92.

———. "Tell Nimrin: Preliminary Report on the 1993 Season." *ADAJ* 38 (1994): 205–44.

Flegg, Graham. *Numbers: Their History and Meaning.* Mineola, NY: Dover, 2002.

Flohr, Miko. "Textiles, Trade and the Urban Economies of Roman Asia Minor." In *Wirtschaft Als Machtbasis: Beiträge Zur Rekonstruktion Vormoderner Wirtschaftssysteme in Anatolien: Drittes Wissenschaftliches Netzwerk Der Abteilung Istanbul Des Deutschen Archäologischen Instituts,* edited by Katja Piesker, 21–42. BYZAS 22. Istanbul: Ege Yayinlari, 2016.

Flint, Peter W., and James C. VanderKam, eds. *The Dead Sea Scrolls After Fifty Years: A Comprehensive Assessment.* Vol. 2. Leiden: Brill, 1999.

Forbes, Robert J. *Studies in Ancient Technology.* Leiden: Brill, 1993.

Ford, J. Massyngberde. *Revelation: Introduction, Translation and Commentary.* AYBC 38. New York: Doubleday, 1985.

Fouts, David M. "A Defense of the Hyperbolic Interpretation of Large Numbers in the Old Testament." *JETS* 40 (1997): 377–87.

———. "The Demographics of Ancient Israel." *BRB* 7, no. 2 (2007): 1–10.

Fox, Tiffany. "A Scarab from a Biblical Pharaoh." *Artifax* 29, no. 4 (August 2004): 4–5.

France-Presse, Agence. "Jericho's Ancient Gates Found." *The New York Times.* November 28, 1998.

France, Richard Thomas. "Herod and the Children of Bethlehem." *NovT* 31, no. 2 (1979): 98–120.

Franken, H. J. "Tell Es-Sultan and Old Testament Jericho." *Oudtestamentische Studiën* 14 (1965): 189–200.

Franz, Gordon. "Is Mount Sinai in Saudi Arabia?" *Bible and Spade* 13, no. 4 (2000): 101–13.

———. "'Meat Offered to Idols' in Pergamum and Thyatira." *Bible and Spade* 14, no. 4 (2001): 105–110.

———. "Mt. Sinai Is Not at Jebel El-Lawz in Saudi Arabia." In *ETS/NEAS Meetings*, 1–10. Broadmoor Hotel, Colorado Springs, Colo., 2001.

———. "Propaganda, Power and the Perversion of Biblical Truths: Coins Illustrating the Book of Revelation." *Bible and Spade* 19, no. 3 (2006): 73–87.

———. "The Birth Date of Jesus." *Bible and Spade* 26, no. 1 (2013): 2–3.

Franz, Gordon, and Stephanie Hernandez. "The Most Important Discovery Was the People: An Interview with Dr. Gabriel Barkay." *Bible and Spade* 22, no. 1 (2009): 3–8.

Fraser, Christian. "St Paul's Tomb Unearthed in Rome." *BBC News, Rome*, December 7, 2006, sec. Europe. http://news.bbc.co.uk/2/hi/6219656.stm.

Freedman, David Noel. "The Real Story of the Ebla Tablets: Ebla and the Cities of the Plain." *BA* 41 (1978): 143–64.

Freedman, David Noel, Allen C. Myers, and Astrid B. Beck, eds. *Eerdmans Dictionary of the Bible.* Grand Rapids: Eerdmans, 2000.

Freedman, David Noel, Gary A. Herion, David F. Graf, and John David Pleins, eds. *The Anchor Yale Bible Dictionary.* 6 vols. New York: Doubleday, 1996.

Free, Joseph P., and Howard F. Vos. *Archaeology and Bible History.* Grand Rapids: Zondervan, 1992.

Frend, William H. C. *Martyrdom and Persecution in the Early Church: A Study of a Conflict from the Maccabees to Donatus.* Oxford, UK: Blackwell, 1965.

———. "The Persecutions: Some Links between Judaism and the Early Church." *Journal of Ecclesiastical History* 9 (1958): 141–58.

Friberg, Jöran. "Numbers and Measures in the Earliest Written Records." *Scientific American* 250, no. 2 (1984): 110–18.

Frick, Frank S. *The Formation of the State in Ancient Israel: A Survey of Models and Theories.* Social World of Biblical Antiquity Series 4. Sheffield, UK: Sheffield Academic, 1985.

Friedman, Matti. "Ancient Seal Found in Jerusalem the Times of Israel." *The Times of Israel,* May 1, 2012. http://www.timesofisrael.com/ancient-seal-found-in-jerusalem.

Friesen, Steven J. "Ephesus: Key to a Vision in Revelation." *BAR* 19, no. 3 (1993): 24–37.

———. "Satan's Throne, Imperial Cults and the Social Settings of Revelation." *JSNT* 27, no. 3 (2005): 351–73.

———. "Myth and Symbolic Resistance in Revelation 13." *JBL* 123 (2004): 281–313.

———. "Revelation, Realia, and Religion: Archaeology in the Interpretations of the Apocalypse." *Harvard Theological Review* 88, no. 3 (1995): 291–314.

———. "The Cult of the Roman Emperors in Ephesos: Temple Wardens, City Titles, and the Interpretation of the Revelation of John." In *Ephesos Metropolis of Asia: An Interdisciplinary Approach to Its Archaeology, Religion, and Culture*, edited by Helmut Koester, 229–50. HTS 41. Valley Forge, PA: Trinity, 1995.

———. "The Wrong Erastus: Ideology, Archaeology, and Exegesis." In *Corinth in Context: Comparative Studies on Religion and Society*, edited by Steven J. Friesen, Daniel N. Schowalter, and James Walters, 231–56. Leiden: Brill, 2010.

———. *Imperial Cults and the Apocalypse of John: Reading Revelation in the Ruins.* Oxford: Oxford University Press, 2001.

———. *Twice Neokoros: Ephesus, Asia and the Cult of the Flavian Imperial Family.* Leiden: Brill Academic, 1993.

Friesen, Steve, Daniel N. Schowalter, and James Walters, eds. *Corinth in Context: Comparative Studies on Religion and Society.* Supplement to Novum Testamentum 134. Leiden: Brill, 2010.

Fritz, Volkmar. "Conquest or Settlement? The Early Iron Age in Palestine." *BA* 50 (1987): 84–100.

Frymer-Kensky, Tikva. "What the Babylonian Flood Stories Can and Cannot Teach Us About the Genesis Flood." *BAR* 4, no. 4 (December 1978): 32–41.

Furnish, Victor Paul. "Corinth in Paul's Time—What Can Archaeology Tell Us?" *BAR* 14, no. 3 (1988): 14–27.

Galil, Gershon. "The Hebrew Inscription from Khirbet Qeiyafa/Neta'im: Script, Language, Literature and History." *UF* 41 (2009): 193–242.

Gera, Dov, and Hannah M. Cotton. "A Dedication from Dor to a Governor of Syria." In *Governors and Their Personnel on Latin Inscriptions from Caesarea Maritima,* edited by Hannah M. Cotton and Werner Eck, 497–500. Proceedings of the Israel Academy of Sciences and Humanities 7. Jerusalem, Israel: Israel Academy of Sciences and Humanities, 2001.

———. "A Dedication from Dor to a Governor of Syria." *IEJ* 41, no. 4 (1991): 258–66.

Garbini, Giovanni. *Myth and History in the Bible.* The Library of Hebrew Bible/OT Studies. London, UK: Sheffield Academic Press, 2003.

Gardiner, Alan H. "Davies's Copy of the Great Speos Artemidos Inscription." *JEA* 32 (1946): 43–56.

Garfinkel, Yosef. "A Minimalist Disputes His Demise: A Response to Philip Davies." *Bible History Daily: Biblical Archaeology Society*, June 13, 2012. http://www.biblicalarchaeology.org/uncategorized/a-minimalist-disputes-his-demise-a-response-to-philip-davies/.

———. "Christopher Rollston's Methodology of Caution." *BAR* 38, no. 5 (2012): 58–59.

Garfinkel, Yosef, Mitka R. Golub, Haggai Misgav, and Saar Ganor. "The ʾIšbaʿal Inscription from Khirbet Qeiyafa." *BASOR* 373 (2015): 217–33.

Garfinkel, Yosef, and Saar Ganor, eds. *Khirbet Qeiyafa: Excavation Report 2007-2008.* Vol. 1. Jerusalem, Israel: Israel Exploration Society, 2010.

———. "Khirbet Qeiyafa: Shaaraim." *The Journal of Hebrew Scriptures* 8, no. 22 (2010): 2–10.

———. "Site Location and Setting and History of Research." In *Khirbet Qeiyafa: Excavation Report 2007-2008*, edited by Yosef Garfinkel and Saar Ganor, 1:28–32. Jerusalem, Israel: Israel Exploration Society, 2010.

Garfinkel, Yosef, Florian Klimscha, Sariel Shalev, and Danny Rosenberg. "The Beginning of Metallurgy in the Southern Levant: A Late 6th Millennium CalBC Copper Awl from Tel Tsaf, Israel." *PLoS ONE* 9, no. 3 (March 26, 2014): e96882.

Garstang, John. *The Foundations of Bible History: Joshua, Judges.* Grand Rapids: Kregel, 1978.

Garstang, John, and J. B. E. Garstang. *The Story of Jericho.* New revised edition. London, UK: Marshall, Morgan & Scott, 1948.

Gaster, Theodor Herzl, and James G. Frazer. *Myth, Legend, and Custom in the Old Testament: A Comparative Study with Chapters from Sir James G. Frazer's Folklore in the Old Testament.* New York: Harper & Row, 1975.

Gates, Charles. *Ancient Cities: The Archaeology of Urban Life in the Ancient Near East and Egypt, Greece, and Rome.* New York: Routledge, 2003.

Gathercole, Simon. "The Gospel of Judas." *ExpTim* 118, no. 5 (February 2007): 209–15.

Geisler, Norman L, and Joseph M. Holden. *The Popular Handbook of Archaeology and the Bible.* Eugene, OR: Harvest House, 2013.

Gentry, Kenneth L., Jr. *Before Jerusalem Fell: Dating the Book of Revelation.* Powder Springs, GA: American Vision, 1998.

George, Sony, Ana Maria Grecicosei, Erik Waaler, and Jon Yngve Hardeberg. "Spectral Image Analysis and Visualisation of the Khirbet Qeiyafa Ostracon." In *Image and Signal Processing: 6th International Conference, ICISP 2014, Cherbourg, France, June 30 - July 2, 2014 ; Proceedings,* edited by Abderrahim Elmoataz, Olivier Lezoray, Fathallah Nouboud, and Driss Mammass, 272–279. Lecture Notes in Computer Science Image Processing, Computer Vision, Pattern Recognition 8509. Cham: Springer, 2014..

Gera, Dov, and Hannah M. Cotton. "A Dedicatory Inscription to the Ruler of Syria [Hebrew]." *Qadmoniot* 22, no. 1/2 (1989): 42.

Geva, Hillel, ed. *Ancient Jerusalem Revealed.* Jerusalem, Israel: Israel Exploration Society, 1994.

Gibbon, Guy E. *Critically Reading the Theory and Methods of Archaeology: An Introductory Guide.* Lanham, MD: AltaMira, 2014.

Giblin, Charles Homer. *The Book of Revelation: The Open Book of Prophecy.* Good News Studies 34. Collegeville, Minn.: Liturgical, 1991.

Gibson, Shimon. "The Pool of Bethesda in Jerusalem and Jewish Purification Practices of the Second Temple Period." *Proche-Orient Chrétiens* 55 (2005): 270–93.

Gill, David W., and Conrad H. Gempf, eds. *The Book of Acts in Its Graeco-Roman Setting.* Vol. 2. BAFCS 2. Grand Rapids: Eerdmans, 1994.

Gill, David W. J. "Erastus the Aedile." *Tyndale Bulletin* 40 (1989): 293–301.

Gitin, Seymour, Trude Dothan, and Joseph Naveh. "A Royal Dedicatory Inscription from Ekron." *IEJ* 47, no. 1/2 (January 1, 1997): 1–16.

Giveon, Raphael. "Three Fragments from Egyptian Geographical Lists." *Eretz Israel* 15 (1981): 81, 137–39, Plate 22.1.

Glueck, Nelson. *Explorations in Eastern Palestine IV. Part 1.* 4 vols. AASOR 25-28. New Haven, CT: ASOR, 1945.

———. "On the Trail of King Solomon's Mines." *National Geographic* 85, no. 2 (1944): 233–56.

———. *Rivers in the Desert: A History of the Negev.* New York: Farrar, Straus and Cudahy, 1959.

———. "Some Ancient Towns in the Plains of Moab." *BASOR* 91 (1943): 7–26.

———. *The Other Side of the Jordan.* New Haven, CT: ASOR, 1970.

Gnuse, Robert Karl. "BTB Review of Current Scholarship: Israelite Settlement of Canaan: A Peaceful Internal Process - Part 1." *BTB* 21, no. 2 (1991): 56–66.

———. "BTB Review of Current Scholarship: Israelite Settlement of Canaan: A Peaceful Internal Process - Part 2." *BTB* 21, no. 3 (1991): 109–17.

———. *No Other Gods: Emergent Monotheism in Israel.* JSOTSup 241. A&C Black, 1997.

Goedicke, Hans. "Hatshepsut's Temple Inscription at Speo Artemidos." *BAR* 7, no. 5 (1981): 42.

Gökgöz, Ali. "Geochemistry of the Kizildere-Tekkehamambuldan-Pamukkale Geothermal Fields, Turkey." *Geothermal Training Programme The United Nations University Reports* 5 (1998): 115–56.

Golb, Norman. *Who Wrote the Dead Sea Scrolls?: The Search for the Secret of Qumran.* New York: Scribner's Sons, 1995.

Goldingay, John E. "The Patriarchs in Scripture and History." In *Essays on the Patriarchal Narratives*, edited by Donald J. Wiseman and Alan R. Millard, 11–42. Winona Lake, IN: Eisenbrauns, 1983.

Goldman, Hetty. *Excavations at Gözlü Kule, Tarsus.* 3 vols. Institute for Advanced Studies. Princeton. Princeton, NJ: Princeton University Press, 1956.

Goldsmid, Frederic J. "Obituary: The Right Honourable Sir Henry Austen Layard, G. C. B." *The Geographical Journal* 4, no. 4 (October 1, 1894): 370–73.

Goodenough, Erwin R. "The Crown of Victory in Judaism." *Art Bulletin* 28 (1946): 139–59.

Goodman, Jeffrey. *The Comets Of God: New Scientific Evidence for God: Recent Archeological, Geological and Astronomical Discoveries That Shine New Light on the Bible and Its Prophecies.* Tuscon, AR: Archeological Research Books, LLC. 2010.

Goranson, Stephen. "An inkwell from Qumran." *Michmanim* 6 (1992): 37–40.

———. "Qumran: A Hub of Scribal Activity." *BAR* 20, no. 5 (1994): 36–39.

Gordon, Cyrus H. "Biblical Customs and the Nuzu Tablets." *BAR* 2 (1964): 21–33.

———. "Hebrew Origins in the Light of Recent Discovery." In *Biblical and Other Studies*, edited by Alexander Altmann, 3–14. Cambridge, MA: Harvard University Press, 1963.

———. *Introduction to Old Testament Times.* Ventnor, NJ: Ventnor, 1953.

———. "The New Amarna Tablets." *Orientalia* 16 (1947): 1–21.

———. "The Patriarchal Narratives." *JNES* 13 (1954): 56–59.

Görg, Manfred. "Israel in Hieroglyphen." *Biblische Notizen* 106 (2001): 21–27.

———. "Israel in Hieroglyphen." In *Mythos und Mythologie: Studien zur Religionsgeschichte und Theologie*, 251–58. Agypten Und Altes Testament 70. Wiesbaden: Harrassowitz, 2011.

———. *Untersuchungen zur hieroglyphischen Wiedergabe palästinischer Ortsnamen.* Bonner Orientalische Studien NS 29. Bonn: Selbstverlag des Orientalischen Seminars der Universität, 1974.

Görg, Manfred, Peter van der Veen, and Christoffer Theis. "Israel in Canaan (Long) Before Pharaoh Merenptah? A Fresh Look at Berlin Statue Pedestal Relief 21687." *Journal of Ancient Egyptian Interconnections* 2, no. 4 (2010): 15–25.

Gottwald, N. K. *The Tribes of Yahweh: A Sociology of the Religion of Liberated Israel 1250-1050 B. C. E.* New York: Knoll, 1979.

Gounaris, Georgios, and Emmanuela Gounari. *Philippi: Archaeological Guide.* Translated by Sophia Tromara. Thessaloniki: Thessaloniki University Studio Press, 2004.

Govier, Gordon. "Biblical Archaeology's Top Ten Discoveries of 2013." *Christianity Today*, December 31, 2013. http://www.christianitytoday.com/ct/2013/december-web-only/biblical-archaeologys-top-ten-discoveries-of-2013.html.

Grabbe, Lester L. *Ahab Agonistes: The Rise and Fall of the Omri Dynasty*. New York: Continuum International, 2007.

———. *Ancient Israel: What Do We Know and How Do We Know It?*. New York: Bloomsbury, 2008.

Graf, David F. "Zoora Rises from the Grave: New Funerary Stelae from Palaestina Tertia." *Journal of Roman Archaeology* 22 (2009): 752–58.

Grainger, John D. *Nerva and the Roman Succession Crisis of AD 96–99*. Roman Imperial Biographies. New York: Routledge, 2003.

Grant, Michael. *Herod the Great*. New York: American Heritage, 1971.

Graser, Elsa R. "A Text and Translation of the Edict of Diocletian." In *An Economic Survey of Ancient Rome: Rome and Italy of the Empire*, edited by Tenney Frank, 5:307–421. Baltimore, Md.: John Hopkins University Press, 1975.

Graves, David E. *Biblical Archaeology: Famous Discoveries That Support the Reliability of the Bible. Vol. 2*. Toronto, , Ont.: Electronic Christian Media. 2015.

———. "Fresh Light on the Governors of Judea." *BS* 30, no. 3 (2017): 58–68.

———. *Jesus Speaks to Seven of His Churches: A Commentary on the Messages to the Seven Churches in Revelation*. Toronto, Ont.: Electronic Christian Media, 2017

———. *Key Facts for the Location of Sodom Student Edition: Navigating the Maze of Arguments*. Toronto, Ont.: Electronic Christian Media, 2014.

———. *Key Themes of the New Testament: A Survey of Major Theological Themes*. Toronto, Ont.: Electronic Christian Media, 2013.

———. "Local References in the Letter to Smyrna (Rev 2: 8–11), Part 2: Historical Background." *Bible and Spade* 19, no. 1 (2006): 23–31.

———. "Local References in the Letter to Smyrna (Rev 2: 8–11), Part 3: Jewish Background." *Bible and Spade* 19, no. 2 (2006): 41–47.

———. "Local References in the Letter to Smyrna (Rev 2: 8–11), Part 4: Religious Background." *Bible and Spade* 19, no. 3 (2007): 88–96.

———. "Sodom And Salt in Their Ancient Near Eastern Cultural Context." *NEASB* 61 (2016): 15–32.

———. *The Seven Messages of Revelation and Vassal Treaties: Literary Genre, Structure, and Function*. Gorgias Dissertations Biblical Studies 41. Piscataway, NJ: Gorgias, 2009.

———. "What Is the Madder with Lydia's Purple? A Re-Examination of the Purpurarii in Thyatira and Philippi." *NEASB* 62 (2017): 3–29.

Graves, David E., and D. Scott Stripling. "Identification of Tall el-Hammam on the Madaba Map." *Bible and Spade* 20, no. 2 (2007): 35–45.

———. "Re-Examination of the Location for the Ancient City of Livias." *Levant* 43, no. 2 (2011): 178–200.

Grayson, Albert Kirk. *Assyrian Rulers of the Early First Millennium BC I (858-745 BC)*. Vol. 1. The Royal Inscriptions of Mesopotamia: Assyrian Periods 2. Toronto, Can.: University of Toronto Press, 1991.

Green, Joel B., Scot McKnight, and I. Howard Marshall, eds. *Dictionary of Jesus and the Gospels*. Downers Grove, IL: InterVarsity, 1992.

Gregg, Steve. *Revelation: Four Views: A Parallel Commentary*. Nashville: Nelson, 1997.

Grena, George M. *LMLK--A Mystery Belonging to the King*. Vol. 1. Redondo Beach, CA: 4000 Years of Writing History, 2004.

———. "What Are Lmlk Stamps and What Were They Used For?" *Bible and Spade* 18, no. 1 (2005): 19–24.

Grenfell, Bernard Pyne, and Arthur Surridge Hunt. *The Oxyrhynchus Papyri*. 75 vols. London, UK: Egypt Exploration Society, 2009.

Griffiths, J. Gwyn. "Review of Der Ägyptische Mythos von Der Himmelskuh. Eine Ätiologie Des Unvollkommenen by Erik Hornung." *The Journal of Egyptian Archaeology* 74 (January 1, 1988): 275–77.

Grimal, Nicolas. *A History of Ancient Egypt*. Oxford, UK: Wiley-Blackwell, 1994.

Grisanti, Michael A. "Recent Archaeological Discoveries That Lend Credence to the Historicity of the Scriptures." *Journal of Evangelical Theological Society* 56, no. 3 (2013): 475–97.

Gutfeld, Oren, and J. Randall Price. "Hebrew University Archaeologists Find 12th Dead Sea Scrolls Cave." *The Hebrew University of Jerusalem*, February 8, 2017. https://new.huji.ac.il/en/article/33424.

Guthrie, Donald D. *The Apostles*. Grand Rapids: Zondervan, 1992.

———. *The Relevance of John's Apocalypse*. Exeter, UK: Paternoster, 1987.

Guthrie, William K. C. *The Greeks and Their Gods*. Ariadne Series. Boston, MA: Beacon, 1950.

Habermas, Gary R. *The Secret of the Talpiot Tomb: Unraveling the Mystery of the Jesus Family Tomb*. Nashville: Holman Reference, 2008.

Hagelia, Hallvard. *Tel Dan Inscription: A Critical Investigation of Recent Research on Its Palaeography & Philology*. Studia Semitica Upsaliensia 22. Uppsala: Uppsala Universitet, 2006.

Halpern, Baruch. "Erasing History: The Minimalist Assault on Ancient Israel." *Bible Review* 11, no. 6 (December 1995): 26–35, 47.

Hamilton, William John. "Extracts from Notes Made on a Journey in Asia Minor in 1836 by W. I. [=J.] Hamilton." *JRGS* 7 (1837): 34–61.

———. *Researches in Asia Minor, Pontus and Armenia: With Some Account of Their Antiquities and Geology*. 2 vols. London, UK: Murray, 1842.

———. William John. *Researches in Asia Minor, Pontus and Armenia: With Some Account of Their Antiquities and Geology*. 2 vols. London, UK: Murray, 1842.

Hanfmann, George M. A., Nelson Glueck, and Jane C. Waldbaum. *New Excavations at Sardis and Some Problems of Western Anatolian Archaeology*. High Wycomb: University Microfilms, 1975.

Hanfmann, George M. A., William E. Mierse, and Clive Foss, eds. *Sardis from Prehistoric to Roman Times: Results of the Archaeological Exploration of Sardis, 1958-1975*. Cambridge, MA: Harvard University Press, 1983.

Hanfmann, George M. A., G. F. Swift, and Crawford H. Greenewalt, Jr. "The Ninth Campaign at Sardis (1966)." *BASOR*, no. 187 (1966): 17–52.

Hanfmann, George M. A., William E. Mierse, and Clive Foss, eds. *Sardis from Prehistoric to Roman Times: Results of the Archaeological Exploration of Sardis, 1958–1975*. Cambridge, MA: Harvard University Press, 1983.

Hanfmann, George M. A., and Jane C. Waldbaum. *A Survey of Sardis and the Major Monuments Outside the City Walls*. Cambridge, MA: Harvard University Press, 1975.

———. "New Excavations at Sardis and Some Problems of Western Anatolian Archaeology." In *Near Eastern Archaeology in the Twentieth Century: Essays in Honor of Nelson Glueck*, edited by James A. Sanders, 307–26. Garden City, NY: Doubleday, 1970.

Hanfmann, George M. A. *Letters from Sardis.* Cambridge, MA: Harvard University Press, 1972.

Hanson, J. W. "The Urban System of Roman Asia Minor and Wider Urban Connectivity." In *Settlement, Urbanization, and Population,* edited by Alan Bowman and Andrew Wilson, 229–75. OSRE. Oxford: Oxford University Press, 2011.

Har-El, Menashe. *The Sinai Journeys: The Route of the Exodus.* San Diego: Ridgefield, 1981.

Harland, James Penrose. "Sodom and Gomorrah Part II: The Destruction of the Cities of the Plain." *BA* 6, no. 3 (1943): 41–52.

Harland, Philip A. "Acculturation and Identity in the Diaspora: A Jewish Family and 'Pagan' Guilds at Hierapolis." *JJS* 57, no. 2 (2006): 222–44.

———. *Associations, Synagogues, and Congregations: Claiming a Place in Ancient Mediterranean Society.* 2nd ed. Kitchener, Ont.: Harland, 2011.

———. "Imperial Cults within Local Cultural Life: Associations in Roman Asia." *Ancient History Bulletin* 17, no. 1–2 (2003): 85–107.

Harrington, Wilfrid J. *Revelation.* Edited by Daniel J Harrington. Sacra Pagina Series 16. Collegeville, Minn.: Liturgical, 2008.

Harrison, R. K. *Archaeology of the New Testament: The Stirring Times of Christ and the Early Church Come to Life in the Latest Findings of Science.* Grand Rapids: Eerdmans, 1985.

Harris, R. Laird, Gleason L. Archer, Jr., and Bruce K. Waltke, eds. *Theological Wordbook of the Old Testament.* 2 vols. Chicago, IL: Moody, 1980.

Harris, Stephen L., and Robert Platzner. *The Old Testament: An Introduction to the Hebrew Bible.* New York: McGraw-Hill, 2002.

Hart, Gerald David. *Asclepius: The God of Medicine.* New York: Royal Society of Medicine, 2000.

Hartingsveld, L. van. *Revelation: A Practical Commentary.* Translated by John Vriend. Grand Rapids: Eerdmans, 1985.

Hasel, Michael G. "Israel in the Merneptah Stela." *BASOR*, no. 296 (November 1, 1994): 45–61.

———. "New Excavations at Khirbet Qeiyafa and the Early History of Judah." In *Do Historical Matters Matter to Faith?: A Critical Appraisal of Modern and Postmodern Approaches to Scripture*, edited by James K. Hoffmeier and Graham A. Magary, 477–96. Wheaton, IL: Crossway Books, 2012.

Hasson, Nir. "Archaeological Stunner: Not Herod's Tomb after All?" *Haaretz*, October 11, 2013. http://www.haaretz.com/archaeology/.premium-1.551881.

Hastings, James, and John A. Selbie, eds. *A Dictionary of the Bible: Dealing with Its Language, Literature and Contents Including the Biblical Theology.* 5 vols. New York: Scribner's Sons, 1911.

Hastings, James, and John A. Selbie, eds. *A Dictionary of the Bible.* Single Volume. New York: Scribner's Sons, 1909.

Hattem, Willem C. van. "Once Again: Sodom and Gomorrah." *BA* 44, no. 2 (Spring 1981): 87–92.

Hauser, Alan J. "Israel's Conquest of Palestine: A Peasants' Rebellion." *JSOT*, no. 7 (1978): 2–19.

Hawkins, Ralph K., and Shane Buchanan. "The Khirbet Qeiyafa Inscription and 11th–10th Century BCE Israel." *Stone-Campbell Journal* 14, no. 2 (2011): 219–34.

Hawthorne, Gerald F., Ralph P. Martin, and Daniel G. Reid, eds. *Dictionary of Paul and His Letters.* Downers Grove, IL: InterVarsity, 1993.

Hayes, John. *A Supplement to Late Roman Pottery.* Rome: British School at Rome, 1980.

Hayes, John W. *Late Roman Pottery*. Rome: British School at Rome, 1972.

Hayes, J. W. *Ancient Lamps in the Royal Ontario Museum a Catalogue. 1 Greek and Roman Clay Lamps*. Toronto: Royal Ontario Museum, 1980.

Head, Peter M. "Additional Greek Witnesses to the New Testament." In *The Text of the New Testament in Contemporary Research: Essays on the Status Quaestionis. Second Edition*, edited by Bart D. Ehrman and Michael W. Holmes, 429–60. Leiden: Brill, 2012.

———. "The Date Of The Magdalen Papyrus Of Matthew (P. Magd. Gr. 17 = P64): A Response To C. P. Thiede." *Tyndale Bulletin* 46 (1995): 251–85.

Heidel, Alexander. *Gilgamesh Epic and Old Testament Parallels*. 2nd ed. Chicago, IL: University Of Chicago Press, 1970.

Heilpern, Will. "Biblical King's Seal Discovered in Dump Site." *CNN*, December 4, 2015. https://www.cnn.com/2015/12/03/middleeast/king-hezekiah-royal-seal

Heinisch, H. F. "Ancient Purple, an Historical Survey." *Fibre Engineering and Chemistry, Great Britain* 18, no. 6 (1957): 203–6.

Heiser, Michael S. "Evidence Real and Imagined: Thinking Clearly About the 'Jesus Family Tomb.'" *Www.michaelsheiser.com*, 2008, 1–22.

Hekster, Olivier Joram, and Nicholas Zair. *Rome and Its Empire: Ad 193-284*. Edinburgh, UK: Edinburgh University Press, 2008.

Hellholm, David, and Kungl Vitterhets. *Apocalypticism in the Mediterranean World and the Near East: Proceedings of the International Colloquium on Apocalypticism, Uppsala, August 12-17, 1979*. Tübingen: Siebeck, 1989.

Hellwing, Shlomo, Moshe Sade, and Vered Kishon. "Faunal Remains." In *Shiloh: The Archaeology of a Biblical Site*, edited by Israel Finkelstein, Shelomoh Bunimovits, Zvi Lederman, and Baruch Brandl, 309–50. Monograph Series of the Institute of Archaeology 10. Tel Aviv, Israel: Institute of Archaeology of Tel Aviv University, 1993.

Hemer, Colin J. "Seven Cities of Asia Minor." In *Major Cities of the Biblical World*, edited by R.K. Harrison, 234–48. Nashville: Nelson, 1985.

———. *The Letters to the Seven Churches of Asia in Their Local Setting*. The Biblical Resource Series. Grand Rapids: Eerdmans, 2001.

———. "The Speeches of Acts: I. The Ephesian Elders at Miletus." *Tyndale Bulletin* 40, no. 1 (1989): 77–85.

———. "Unto the Angels of the Churches." *Buried History* 11 (1975): 4–27, 56–83, 110–35, 164–90.

Hemer, Colin J., and Conrad H. Gempf, eds. *The Book of Acts in the Setting of Hellenistic History*. WUNT 49. Winona Lake, IN: Eisenbrauns, 1990.

Hendel, Ronald S. "Biblical Views: Is There a Biblical Archaeology?" *BAR* 32, no. 4 (2006): 20.

Hendriksen, William. *More than Conquerors*. Grand Rapids: Baker, 1982.

Hengel, Martin. *Judaism and Hellenism: Studies in Their Encounter in Palestine During the Early Hellenistic Period*. Translated by John Bowde. Eugene, OR: Wipf & Stock, 2003.

Herr, Larry G., Gary L. Christopherson, Randall W. Younker, and David Merling. *Excavation Manual: Madaba Plains Project*. Revised. Berrien Springs, Mich.: Andrews University Press, 1998.

Herr, Larry G., and D. R. Clark. "Excavating the Tribe of Reuben: A Four Room House Provides a Clue to Where the Oldest Israelite Tribe Settled." *BAR* 27, no. 2 (2001): 36–47, 64–66.

Herzog, Isaac. "Semitic Porphyrology (The Dyeing of Purple in Ancient Israel) I: Tekhelet." D. Litt. diss., University of London, 1919.

Herzog, Ze'ev. *Archaeology of the City: Urban Planning in Ancient Israel and Its Social Implications.* Tel Aviv: Tel Aviv University, Institute of Archaeology, 1997.

———. "Deconstructing the Walls of Jericho." *Ha'aretz Magazine*, 1999, 1–9.

Hess, Brian. "Pig Lovers and Pig Haters: Patterns of Palestinian Pork Production." *Journal of Ethnobiology* 10 (1982): 195–225.

Hesse, Brian, and Paula Wapnish. "Can Pig Remains Be Used for Ethnic Diagnosis in the Ancient Near East?" In *The Archaeology of Israel: Constructing the Past, Interpreting the Present*, edited by Neil Asher Silberman and David B. Small, 238–70. JSOTSup 237. Sheffield, UK: T&T Clark, 1997.

Hess, Richard S. "Archaeology." In *Zondervan Pictorial Encyclopaedia of the Bible*, edited by Merrill C. Tenney and Moisés Silva, Revised, Full-Color Edition., 1:293–313. Grand Rapids: Zondervan, 2009.

———. "Early Israel in Canaan: A Survey of Recent Evidence and Interpretations." *PEQ* 125, no. 2 (1993): 125–42.

———. "Literacy in Iron Age Israel." In *Windows into Old Testament History: Evidence, Argument, and the Crisis of Biblical Israel*, edited by V. Philips Long, David W. Baker, and Gordon J. Wenham, 82–102. Grand Rapids, Mich: Eerdmans, 2002.

———. "The Jericho and Ai of the Book of Joshua." In *Critical Issues in Early Israelite History*, edited by Richard S. Hess, Gerald A. Klingbeil, and Paul J. Ray Jr., 33–46. Bulletin for Biblical Research Supplement 3. Winona Lake, Ind: Eisenbrauns, 2008.

———. "Writing about Writing: Abecedaries and Evidence for Literacy in Ancient Israel." *VT* 56, no. 3 (2006): 342–46.

———. "Yahweh's 'Wife' and Belief in One God in the Old Testament." In *Do Historical Matters Matter to Faith?: A Critical Appraisal of Modern and Postmodern Approaches to Scripture*, edited by James K. Hoffmeier and Graham A. Magary, 459–76. Wheaton, IL: Crossway Books, 2012.

Hicks, E. L. "Inscriptions from Thyatira." *The Classical Review* 3, no. 3 (1889): 136–38.

Hill, Carol A. "Making Sense of the Numbers of Genesis." *Perspectives on Science and Christian Faith* 55, no. 4 (2003): 239–51.

Hill, J. N., and Evans. "A Model for Classification and Typology." In *Models in Archaeology*, edited by David L. Clarke, 231–74. London: Methuen, 1972.

Hinds, John T. *A Commentary on the Book of Revelation.* New Testament Commentaries (Gospel Advocate). Nashville: Gospel Advocate, 1974. Commentary on Revelation.

Hindson, Ed, and Elmer L. Towns. *Illustrated Bible Survey: An Introduction.* Nashville: B&H, 2013.

Hirschfeld, Yizhar. *Qumran in Context: Reassessing the Archaeological Evidence.* Grand Rapids: Baker Academic, 2004.

Hirschfeld, Yizhar, and G. Solar. "The Roman Thermae at Hammat-Gader: Preliminary Report of Three Seasons of Excavations." *IEJ* 31, no. 3/4 (1981): 197–219.

Hizmi, Hananya, and Reut Livyatan-ben-Arie. "The Excavations at the Northern Platform of Tel Shiloh the 2012-2013 Seasons [Translated from Hebrew]." Edited by D. Scott Stripling and David E. Graves. Translated by Hillel Richman. *NEASB* 62 (2017): 35–52.

Hodoyan, Katia Lopez. "The Mysteries Surrounding the Tomb of St. Paul." *Rome Reports TV News Agency*, February 5, 2012. http://www.romereports.com/palio/the-mysteries-surrounding-the-tomb-of-st-paul-english-5996.html.

Hoehner, Harold W. *Herod Antipas: A Contemporary of Jesus Christ.* Grand Rapids: Zondervan Academie Books, 1980.

———. "The Date of the Death of Herod the Great." In *Chronos, Kairos, Christos*, edited by Jack Finegan, Jerry Vardaman, and Edwin M. Yamauchi, 101–32. Winona Lake, IN: Eisenbrauns, 1989.

Hoerth, Alfred J. *Archaeology and the Old Testament.* Grand Rapids: Baker, 1999.

Hoerth, Alfred J., and John McRay. *Bible Archaeology: An Exploration of the History and Culture of Early Civilizations.* Grand Rapids: Baker, 2006.

Hoffmann, Adolf. "The Roman Remodeling of the Asklepieion." In *Pergamon-Citadel of the Gods: Archaeological Record, Literary Description, and Religious Development,* edited by Helmut Koester, 41–61. HTS 46. Harrisburg, PA: Trinity Press International, 1998.

Hoffmeier, James Karl. *Ancient Israel in Sinai: The Evidence for the Authenticity of the Wilderness Tradition.* Illustrated edition. Oxford, UK: Oxford University Press, USA, 2005.

———. *Israel in Egypt: The Evidence for the Authenticity of the Exodus Tradition.* Oxford, UK: Oxford University Press, 1999.

———. "Sinai." Edited by Avraham Negev and Shimon Gibson. *Archaeological Encyclopedia of the Holy Land.* New York: Continuum International, 2001.

———. , ed. *The Archaeology of the Bible: Reassessing Methodologies and Assumptions.* Oxford, UK: Lion Hudson, 2008.

———. "The Evangelical Contribution to Understanding the (Early) History of Ancient Israel in Recent Scholarship." *Bulletin for Biblical Research* 7 (1997): 77–90.

———. "The North Sinai Archaeological Project's Excavations at Tell El-Borg (Sinai): An Example of the 'New' Biblical Archaeology?." In *The Future of Biblical Archaeology: Reassessing Methodologies and Assumptions*, edited by James K. Hoffmeier and Alan R. Millard, 53–68. Grand Rapids: Eerdmans, 2004.

———. "What Is the Biblical Date for the Exodus? A Response to Bryant Wood." *JETS* 50, no. 2 (2007): 225–47.

Hoffmeier, James Karl, and Alan R. Millard, eds. *The Future of Biblical Archaeology: Reassessing Methodologies and Assumptions.* The Proceedings of a Symposium, August 12-14, 2001 at Trinity International University. Grand Rapids: Eerdmans, 2004.

Hoff, Viviane, Catherine Metzger, and Christiane Lyon-Caen. *Catalogue Des Lampes En Terre Cuite Grecques et Chrétiennes.* Musée Du Louvre. Département Des Antiquités Grecques et Romaines. Paris: Ministère de la Culture et de la Communication, 1986.

Holden, Joseph M. "The James Ossuary: The Earliest Witness to Jesus and His Family?" *Bible Translation Magazine*, July 2012.

Holladay, John S. "The Eastern Nile Delta during the Hyksos and Pre-Hyksos Periods: Towards a Systemic/Socio-Economic Understanding." In *The Hyksos: New Historical and Archaeological Perspectives*, edited by Eliezer D. Oren, 183–252. Philadelphia, PA: University of Pennsylvania Museum Publication, 1997.

Holloway, Ross R. *The Archaeology of Early Rome and Latium.* New York: Routledge, 1996.

Holmes, Arthur F. *All Truth Is God's Truth.* Downers Grove, IL: InterVarsity, 1983.

Holum, Kenneth G. "Caesarea Palaestinae: Inscriptions of the Imperial Revenue Office." In *The Roman and Byzantine Near East: Some Recent Archaeological Research*, edited by John H. Humphrey. Journal of Roman Archaeology Supplement Series 14. Ann Arbor, Mich.: Journal of Roman Archaeology, 1995.

Hooker, Morna D. "Artemis of Ephesus." *JTS* 64, no. 1 (2013): 37–46.

Hope-Simpson, Richard. "The Analysis of Data from Surface Surveys." *Journal of Field Archaeology* 11, no. 1 (April 1, 1984): 115–17.

———. "The Limitation of Surface Surveys." In *Archaeological Survey in the Mediterranean Area*, edited by Donald R. Keller and D. W. Rupp, 45–48. Bar International 155. Oxford, UK: British Archaeological Reports, 1983.

Horbury, William. "The Benediction of the 'Minim' and Early Jewish-Christian Controversy." *JTS* 33, no. 1 (1982): 19–61.

Horn, Cornelia B., and Robert R. Phenix Jr. *John Rufus: The Lives of Peter the Iberian, Theodosius of Jerusalem, and the Monk Romanus*. Atlanta, Ga.: Society of Biblical Literature, 2008.

Hornung, Erik. *Der ägyptische Mythos von der Himmelskuh: Eine Ätiologie des Unvollkommenen*. Orbis biblicus et orientalis 46. Göttingen: Vandenhoeck & Ruprecht, 1982.

———. *The Tomb of Pharaoh Seti I*. Zürich: Artemis & Winkler, 1991.

Hornung, Erik, Rolf Krauss, and David A. Warburton. *Ancient Egyptian Chronology*. Handbook of Oriental Studies Section One: The Near and Middle East 83. Leiden: Brill Academic, 2006.

Horsley, G. H. R., and Stephen R. Llewelyn, eds. *New Documents Illustrating Early Christianity*. 10 vols. NewDocs. Grand Rapids: Eerdmans, 1981–2012.

Horsley, G. H. R. "Appendix: The Politarchs." In *The Book of Acts in Its Graeco-Roman Setting*, edited by David W. Gill and Conrad H. Gempf, 2:419–31. BAFCS 2. Grand Rapids: Eerdmans, 1994.

———. "The Inscriptions of Ephesos and the New Testament." *NovT* 34, no. 2 (1992): 105–68.

———. "The Silversmiths at Ephesos." In *New Documents Illustrating Early Christianity*, 4:7–10. Grand Rapids: Eerdmans, 2001.

Horst, Pieter Willem van der. *Ancient Jewish Epitaphs: An Introductory Survey of a Millennium of Jewish Funerary Epigraphy (300 BCE–700 CE)*. Leuven, Belgium: Peeters, 1991.

Houston, George W. *Inside Roman Libraries: Book Collections and Their Management in Antiquity*. Raleigh, NC: University of North Carolina Press, 2014.

Hughes, Lisa. "Dyeing in Ancient Italy? Evidence for the Purpurarii." In *Ancient Textiles: Production, Craft and Society*, edited by Carole Gillis and Marie-Louise B. Nosch, 87–92. Oxford: Oxbow, 2007.

Hughes, Philip Edgcumbe. *The Book of the Revelation: A Commentary*. Grand Rapids: Eerdmans, 1990.

Hurtado, Larry W. "𝔓52 (P.Rylands Gr 457) and the Nomina Sacra; Method and Probability." *Tyndale Bulletin* 54, no. 1 (2003): 443–74.

Hutchison, John C. "Was John the Baptist an Essene from Qumran?" *BSac* 159 (2002): 187–200.

Huttner, Ulrich R. *Early Christianity in the Lycus Valley*. Translated by David Green. AJEC: ECAM, 85.1. Leiden: Brill, 2013.

Israelowich, Ido. *Patients and Healers in the High Roman Empire*. Baltimore, Md.: Johns Hopkins University Press, 2015.

———. *Society, Medicine and Religion in the Sacred Tales of Aelius Aristides*. Leiden: Brill, 2012.

Irwin, Dorothy. *Mytharion: The Comparison of Tales from the Old Testament and the Ancient Near East.* Alter Orient Und Altes Testament 32. Neukirchen-Vluyn: Neukirchener Verlag, 1978.

Jacobovici, Simcha, and Charles Pellegrino. *The Jesus Family Tomb: The Evidence Behind the Discovery No One Wanted to Find.* San Francisco, Calf.: HarperOne, 2008.

Jacobsen, Thorkild. "The Eridu Genesis." *JBL* 100, no. 4 (December 1, 1981): 513–29.

———. *The Sumerian King List.* Assyriological Studies. Chicago, IL: University of Chicago Press, 1939.

Jacobs, Joan, and Irwin Jacobs. *Dead Sea Scrolls.* Edited by Margaret Dykens. San Diego Natural History Museum. San Diego: San Diego State University Press, 2007.

Jayne, Walter Addison. *Healing Gods of Ancient Civilizations.* New Haven, CT: Yale University Press, 1925.

Jeffers, James S. *The Greco-Roman World of the New Testament Era: Exploring the Background of Early Christianity.* Downers Grove, IL: InterVarsity, 1999.

Jenkins, Ferrell. "Have No Fear of the Authorities." *Ferrell's Travel Blog: Commenting on Biblical Studies, Archaeology, Travel and Photography*, September 10, 2010. http://ferrelljenkins.wordpress .com/2010/09/10/.

Jensen, Lloyd B. "Royal Purple of Tyre." *JNES* 22 (1963): 104–18.

Jensen, Morten Hørning. "Herod Antipas in Galilee: Friend or Foe of the Historical Jesus?" *Journal for the Study of the Historical Jesus* 5, no. 1 (January 2007): 7–32.

———. *Herod Antipas in Galilee: The Literary and Archaeological Sources on the Reign of Herod Antipas and Its Socio-Economic Impact on Galilee.* Wissenschaftliche Untersuchungen Zum Neuen Testament. Tübingen: Siebeck, 2006.

Jewett, Robert. *A Chronology of Paul's Life.* Minneapolis, MN: Fortress, 1979.

Johns, C. H. W. *Assyrian Deeds and Documents Recording the Transfer of Property, Including the So-Called Private Contracts, Legal Decisions and Proclamations Preserved.* Cambridge, UK: Cambridge University Press, 1924.

Johnson, Alan F. "Revelation." In *Hebrews--Revelation*, edited by Tremper Longman and David E Garland, Revised. The Expositor's Bible Commentary 13. Grand Rapids: Zondervan, 2006.

Johnson, Dennis E. *Triumph of the Lamb: A Commentary on Revelation.* Phillipsburg, NJ: P&R, 2001.

Johnson, Douglas. "The Star of Bethlehem Reconsidered: A Refutation of the Mosley/Martin Historical Approach." *Planetarian* 10, no. 1 (1981): 14–16.

Johnson, Sherman E. "Asia Minor and Early Christianity." In *Judaism and Christianity in the Age of Constantine*, edited by Jacob Neusner, 2:77–145. Leiden: Brill, 1975.

———. "Laodicea and Its Neighbors." *BA* 13 (1950): 1–18.

———. "The Apostle Paul and the Riot in Ephesus." *LTQ* 14 (1979): 79–88.

Jolly, Karen Louise. *Tradition and Diversity: Christianity in a World Context to 1500.* New York: Routledge, 2015.

Jones, A. H. M. *The Cities of the Eastern Roman Provinces.* 2nd ed. Oxford University Press Academic Monograph. Eugene, OR: Wipf & Stock, 2004.

———. *The Greek City: From Alexander to Justinian.* Oxford, UK: Clarendon, 1940.

Jones, Christopher P. "Aelius Aristides and the Asklepieion." In *Pergamon-Citadel of the Gods: Archaeological Record, Literary Description, and Religious Development*, edited by Helmut Koester, 63–76. Harrisburg, PA: Trinity Press International, 1998.

Joshel, S. R. *Work, Identity and Legal Status at Rome: A Study of the Occupational Inscriptions.* Norman, OK: University of Oklahoma Press, 1992.

Kafafi, Zeidan A. "New Insights on the Copper Mines of Wadi Faynan/Jordan." *PEQ* 146, no. 4 (2014): 263–80.

Kaiser, Jr., Walter C. *History of Israel.* Nashville: Broadman & Holman, 2010.

Kaiser, Jr., Walter C., and Duane Garrett, eds. *NIV Archaeological Study Bible: An Illustrated Walk Through Biblical History and Culture.* Grand Rapids: Zondervan, 2006.

Kalman, Mattew. "Judge Mulls Verdict in Jesus Forgery Trial." *AOL News*, October 5, 2010. http://www.aolnews.com/2010/10/05/judge-considers-verdict-in-5-year-long-jesus-forgery-trial/.

Kapera, Zdzislaw Jan. "Archaeological Interpretations of the Qumran Settlement: A Rapid Review of Hypotheses Fifty Years After the Discoveries at the Dead Sea." In *Mogilany 1989: Papers on the Dead Sea Scrolls Offered in Memory of Jean Carmignac*, edited by Zdzislaw Jan Kapera, 15–33. Qumranica Mogilanensia. Krakow: Enigma, 1993.

Karageorghis, Vassos. *Excavating at Salamis in Cyprus, 1952-1974.* Athens: A.G. Leventis Foundation, 1999.

———. *Salamis in Cyprus.* New Aspects of Antiquity. London, UK: Thames & Hudson, 1970.

Karweise, Stefan. "Ephesos." *RE Supp* 12 (1970): 323–26.

Kasser, Rodolphe, Marvin Meyer, Gregor Wurst, and Bart D. Ehrman, eds. *The Gospel of Judas.* Washington, DC: National Geographic, 2008.

Kaufman, Asher S. "Fixing the Site of the Tabernacle at Shiloh." *BAR* 14, no. 6 (Nov–Dec 1988): 46–52.

Kavanagh, Barry F., and S. J. Glenn Bird. *Surveying: Principles and Applications.* 4th ed. Englewood Cliffs, NJ: Prentice Hall College Division, 1995.

Kee, Howard C. "Self-Definition in the Asclepius Cult." In *Jewish and Christian Self-Definition: Self-Definition in the Graeco-Roman World*, edited by Ben F. Meyer and E. P. Sander, 3:118–36. Philadelphia, PA: Fortress, 1982.

Keener, Craig S. *Acts: An Exegetical Commentary: 15:1–23:35.* Vol. 3. 3 vols. Grand Rapids: Baker Academic, 2014.

Kehati, Ron. "The Faunal Assemblage." In *Khirbet Qeiyafa: Excavation Report 2007-2008*, edited by Yosef Garfinkel and Saar Ganor, 1:201–98. Jerusalem, Israel: Israel Exploration Society, 2010.

Keil, Josef. "Die Erste Neokorie von Ephesos." *NZ* 48 (1919): 125–30.

Kekec, Tevhit. *Pergamon.* Istanbul: Hitit Color, 1987.

Kelhoffer, James A. *Miracle and Mission: The Authentication of Missionaries and Their Message in the Longer Ending of Mark.* WUNT 112. Tübingen: Mohr Siebeck, 2000.

Kelle, Brad E. "What's in a Name? Neo-Assyrian Designations for the Northern Kingdom and Their Implications for Israelite History and Biblical Interpretation." *JBL* 121, no. 4 (Winter 2002): 639–66.

Kelly, Kevin T. "Justification as Truth-Finding Efficiency: How Ockham's Razor Works." *Minds and Machines* 14 (2004): 485–505.

Kelly, Robert L., and David Hurst Thomas. *Archaeology.* Boston, MA: Cengage Learning, 2012.

Kelshaw, Terence. *Send This Message to My Church: Christ's Words to the Seven Churches of Revelation.* Nashville: Nelson, 1984.

Kenyon, Frederic G. *The Chester Beatty Biblical Papyri, Fasciculus III Supplement, Pauline Epistles.* London, UK: Walker, 1937.

Kenyon, Kathleen M. *Amorites and Canaanites.* Schweich Lectures on Biblical Archaeology. Oxford, UK: Oxford University Press, 1967.

———. *Archaeology in the Holy Land.* 5th ed. Nashville: Nelson, 1979.

———. *Digging up Jericho: The Results of the Jericho Excavations, 1952-1956.* London, UK: Praeger & Benn, 1957.

———. "Excavation Methods in Palestine." *PEQ* 71, no. 1 (1939): 29–37.

———. "Excavations in Jerusalem, 1965." *PEQ* 98, no. 1 (1966): 73–88.

———. *Palestine in the Time of the Eighteenth Dynasty: Volume 2, Part 1: The Middle East and the Aegean Region, c.1800–1380 BC.* 3rd ed. Cambridge Ancient History 69. Cambridge, MA: Cambridge University Press, 1973.

———. *The Bible and Recent Archaeology.* Edited by Peter R. S. Moorey. Rev Sub. Louisville, KY: Westminster/Knox, 1987.

———. "The Middle and Late Bronze Age Strata at Megiddo." *Levant* 1, no. 1 (1969): 25–60.

Kenyon, Kathleen M., and Thomas A. Holland. *Excavations at Jericho.* Vol. 3. Jerusalem: British School of Archaeology in Jerusalem, 1982.

———. *Excavations at Jericho, Vol. II (only): The Tombs excavated in 1955-8.* British School of Archaeology in Jerusalem, 1965.

Kerényi, Karl. *Asklepios: Archetypal Image of the Physician's Existence.* Princeton, NJ: Princeton University Press, 1959.

Khouri, Rami G. *Antiquities of the Jordan Rift Valley.* Manchester, MI: Solipsist, 1988.

Kiddle, Martin. *The Revelation of St. John.* Vol. 17. 17 vols. The Moffatt New Testament Commentary. London, UK: Hodder & Stoughton, 1952.

Kidger, Mark. *The Star of Bethlehem: An Astronomer's View.* Princeton, NJ: Princeton University Press, 1999.

Kikawada, Isaac M. "The Double Creation of Mankind in Enki and Ninmah, Atrahasis I 1–351, and Genesis 1–2." *Iraq* 45 (1983): 43–45.

Kim, Young Kyu. "Palaeographic Dating Of P46 To The Later First Century." *Biblica* 69 (1988): 248–57.

King, Philip J. *Jeremiah: An Archaeological Companion.* Louisville, KY: Westminster/John Knox, 1993.

King, Philip J., and Lawrence E. Stager. *Life in Biblical Israel.* Louisville, KY: Westminster/Knox, 2001.

Kistemaker, Simon J. *Exposition of the Book of Revelation.* NTC. Grand Rapids: Baker Academic, 2001.

Kitchen, Kenneth A. "Ancient Egyptian Chronology for Aegeanists." *Mediterranean Archaeology and Archaeometry* 2, no. 2 (2002): 5–12.

———. *Ancient Orient and Old Testament.* Wheaton, IL: Tyndale, 1966.

———. "A Possible Mention of David in the Late Tenth Century BCE, and Deity *Dod as Dead as the Dodo." *JSOT*, no. 76 (1997): 29–44.

———. "Egyptian Interventions in the Levant in Iron Age II." In *Symbiosis, Symbolism, and the Power of the Past: Canaan, Ancient Israel, and Their Neighbors from the Late Bronze Age Through Roman Palaestina,* edited by William G. Dever and Seymour Gitin, 113–32. Winona Lake, IN: Eisenbrauns, 2003.

———. *On the Reliability of the Old Testament.* Grand Rapids: Eerdmans, 2003.

———. "Regnal and Genealogical Data of Ancient Egypt (Absolute Chronology I) The Historical Chronology of Ancient Egypt, A Current Assessment." In *Synchronisation of Civilisations in Eastern Mediterranean in the Second Millennium B.C. II*, edited by Manfred Bietak, 39–52. Contributions to the Chronology of the Eastern Mediterranean: Denkschriften Der Gesamtakademie 29. Vienna: Austrian Academy of Sciences, 2003.

———. "The Basics of Egyptian Chronology in Relation to the Bronze Age." In *High, Middle Or Low?: Acts of an International Colloquium on Absolute Chronology Held at the University of Gothenburg, 20th-22nd August, 1987*, edited by Paul Åström, 1:37–55. Studies in Mediterranean Archaeology and Literature. Gothenburg: Åström, 1987.

———. "The Chronology of Ancient Egypt." *World Archaeology* 23, no. 2 (October 1, 1991): 201–8.

———. "The Patriarchal Age: Myth or History?" *BAR* 21, no. 2 (1995): 48–57, 89–95.

———. "The Patriarchs Revisited: A Reply to Dr. Ronald S. Hendel." *NEASB* 43 (1998): 49–58.

———. *The Third Intermediate Period in Egypt, 1100-650 BC.* 2nd ed. Egyptology. Warminster, UK: Aris & Phillips, 1996.

———. "The Victories of Merenptah, and the Nature of Their Record." *JSOT* 28, no. 3 (March 1, 2004): 259–72.

Kite, Marion, and Roy Thomson, eds. *Conservation of Leather and Related Materials.* Conservation and Museology. Boston, MA: Butterworth-Heinemann, 2005.

Kittel, Gerhard, and Gerhard Friedrich, eds. *Theological Dictionary of the New Testament.* Translated by Geoffrey W. Bromiley. Abridged. 10 vols. Grand Rapids: Eerdmans, 1985.

Kitzinger, E. "A Fourth Century Mosaic Floor in Pisidian Antioch." In *Mansel'e Armağan (Mélanges Mansel)*, edited by Arif Müfid Mansel, 385–95. Ankara: Türk Tarih Kurumu Basimeri, 1974.

Kjaer, Hans Andersen. "Shiloh a Summary Report of the Second Danish Expedition, 1929." *PEQ* 63, no. 2 (1931): 71–88.

———. "The Danish Excavation of Shiloh." *PEQ* 59, no. 4 (October 1927): 202–13.

———. "The Excavatin of Shiloh 1929: Preliminary Report." *JPOS* 10 (1930): 87–174.

Kloner, Amos. "A Tomb with Inscribed Ossuaries in East Talpiyot, Jerusalem." *Atiquot* 29 (1996): 15–22.

Knauf, Ernst Axel. "Low and Lower? New Data on Early Iron Age Chronology from Beth Shean, Tel Rehov and Dor." *BN* 112 (2002): 21–27.

———. "The Low Chronology and How Not to Deal with It." *BN* 101 (2000): 56–63.

Knipfing, John R. "The Libelli of the Decian Persecution." *HTR* 16, no. 4 (1923): 345–90.

Knohl, Israel. *Messiahs and Resurrection in "The Gabriel Revelation."* New York: Continuum International, 2009.

———. "The Messiah Son of Joseph 'Gabriel's Revelation' and the Birth of a New Messianic Model." *BAR* 34, no. 5 (2008).

Knoppers, Gary N. "The Vanishing Solomon: The Disappearance of the United Monarchy from Recent Histories of Ancient Israel." *JBL* 116, no. 1 (April 1, 1997): 19–44.

Kobs, Carroll M. *The Tall Al-Hammam Excavation Project 2005–2013: Volume One: Seven Seasons of Ceramics, Eight Seasons of Artifacts.* Albuquerque, N.M.: TSU Press, 2014.

Kochavi, Moshe. "An Ostracon of the Period of the Judges from 'Izbet Sartah." *Tel Aviv* 4 (1977): 1–13.

Koester, Helmut. *Ancient Christian Gospels: Their History and Development.* 2nd ed. New York: T&T Clark, 1992.

———. , ed. *Ephesos Metropolis of Asia: An Interdisciplinary Approach to Its Archaeology, Religion, and Culture.* HTS 41. Cambridge, MA: Harvard Divinity School, 1995.

———. *Philippi at the Time of Paul and after His Death.* Edited by Charalambos Bakirtzis. Eugene, OR: Wipf & Stock, 2009.

———. *Revelation: A New Translation with Introduction and Commentary.* Edited by John J. Collins. AYBC 38A. New Haven, CT: Yale University Press, 2014.

Kogan, Leonid, Natalia Koslova, Sergey Loesov, Sergey Tishchenko, and Leonid Kogan, eds. "The Etymology of Israel (with an Appendix on Non-Hebrew Semitic Names among Hebrews in the Old Testament)." In *Babel Und Bibel 3: Annual of Ancient Near Eastern, Old Testament, and Semitic Studies*, 237–55. Papers of the Institute of Oriental and Classical Studies 14. Winona Lake, IN: Eisenbrauns, 2006.

Kosmetatou, Elizabeth. "The Attalids of Pergamon." In *A Companion to the Hellenistic World*, edited by Andrew Erskine, 159–174. Blackwell Companions to the Ancient World. Oxford: Blackwell, 2003.

Kosmidou, Elpida. "Greek Coins from the Eastern Cemetery of Amphipolis." *NumC* 166 (2006): 415–31.

Köstenberger, Andreas J., L. Scott Kellum, and Charles L Quarles. *The Cradle, the Cross, and the Crown: An Introduction to the New Testament.* Nashville: Broadman & Holman Academic, 2009.

Koukouli-Chrysanthaki, Chaido. "Amphipolis." In *Brill's Companion to Ancient Macedon: Studies in the Archaeology and History of Macedon, 650 BC - 300 AD*, edited by Robin J. Fox and Robin Lane Fox, 409–36. Leiden: Brill, 2011.

———. "Excavating Classical Amphipolis." In *Excavating Classical Culture: Recent Archaeological Discoveries in Greece*, edited by Maria Stamatopoulou and Marina Yeroulanou, 57–73. Studies in Classical Archaeology, British Archaeological Reports British Series 1031. Oxford, UK: Archaeopress, 2002.

———. "Philippi." In *Brill's Companion to Ancient Macedon: Studies in the Archaeology and History of Macedon, 650 BC - 300 AD*, edited by Robin J. Fox and Robin Lane Fox, 437–52. Leiden: Brill, 2011.

———. "Politarchs in a New Inscription from Amphipolis." In *Ancient Macedonian Studies in Honor of Charles F. Edson*, edited by Harry J. Dell, 229–41. Belgrade, Serbia: Institute for Balkan Studies, 1981.

Kraabel, A. Thomas. "Impact of the Discovery of the Sardis Synagogue." In *Sardis from Prehistoric to Roman Times: Results of the Archaeological Exploration of Sardis, 1958-1975*, edited by George M. A. Hanfmann, William E. Mierse, and Clive Foss, 178–90. Cambridge, MA: Harvard University Press, 1983.

———. "The Diaspora Synagogue: Archaeological and Epigraphic Evidence since Sukenik." In *ANRW*, edited by Wolfgang Haase and Hildegard Temporini, 477–510. 2.19. Berlin: de Gruyter, 1979.

Kraay, Colin. "The Coinage of Nicopolis." *NumC*, Seventh Series, 16, no. 136 (1976): 235–47.

Kraeling, Carl H. "The Jewish Community at Antioch." *JBL* 51, no. 2 (June 1, 1932): 130–60.

Kraemer, Ross Shepard. *Women's Religions in the Greco-Roman World: A Sourcebook.* Oxford, UK: Oxford University Press, 2004.

Kraft, Heinrich. *Die Offenbarung Des Johannes.* HNT 16a. Tübingen: Siebeck, 1974.

Kramer, Samuel Noah. *Enmerkar and the Lord of Aratta: A Sumerian Epic Tale of Iraq and Iran.* Philadelphia, PA: University Museum, University of Pennsylvania, 1952.

———. "Man's Golden Age: A Sumerian Parallel to Genesis 11:1." *JAOS* 63 (1943): 191–94.

———. "The 'Babel of Tongues': A Sumerian Version." *JAOS* 88, no. 1 (1968): 108–11.

———. *The Sumerians: Their History, Culture, and Character.* Chicago, IL: University Of Chicago Press, 1971.

Kraybill, J. Nelson. *Apocalypse and Allegiance: Worship, Politics, and Devotion in the Book of Revelation.* Grand Rapids: Brazos Press, 2010.

———. *Imperial Cult and Commerce in John's Apocalypse.* JSNTSup 132. Sheffield, UK: Sheffield Academic, 1999.

Kreitzer, L. Joseph. "A Numismatic Clue to Acts 19:23–41: The Ephesian Cistophori of Claudius and Agrippina," *JSNT* 9, no. 30 (1987): 59–70.

Krodel, Gerhard A. *Revelation.* Minneapolis, MN: Augsburg Fortress, 1989.

Krosney, Herbert, and Bart D. Ehrman. *The Lost Gospel: The Quest for the Gospel of Judas Iscariot.* Washington, DC: National Geographic, 2007.

Kudlek, Manfred, and Erich H. Mickler. *Solar and Lunar Eclipses of the Ancient Near East from 3000 B.C. to 0 with Maps.* Neukirchen-Vluyn: Butzon & Bercker, 1971.

Kumsar, Halil, Ömer Aydan, Celal Şimşek, and Francesco D'Andria. "Historical Earthquakes That Damaged Hierapolis and Laodikeia Antique Cities and Their Implications for Earthquake Potential of Denizli Basin in Western Turkey." *Bulletin of Engineering Geology and the Environment* (September 10, 2015): 1–18.

Kunze, Max, and Volker Kästner. *Der Altar von Pergamon: Hellenistische Und Römische Architektur.* 2nd ed. Antikensammlung II: Fuhrer Durch Die Ausstellung Des Pergamon Museums. Berlin: Henschelverlag Kunst und Gesellschaft, 1990.

Kutscher, Edward Yechezkel. *A History of the Hebrew Language.* Jerusalem: The Hebrew University Magnes Press, 1982.

Laale, Hans Willer. *Ephesus (Ephesos): An Abbreviated History from Androclus to Constantine XI.* Bloomington, IN: WestBow, 2011.

Lacheman, Ernest René, M. P. Maidman, David I. Owen, and Gernot Wilhelm, eds. *Studies on the Civilization and Culture of Nuzi and the Hurrians.* 11 vols. Winona Lake, IN: Eisenbrauns, 1989.

Lambert, Wilfred G., Alan R. Millard, and Miguel Civil. *Atra-Hasis: The Babylonian Story of the Flood.* Winona Lake, IN: Eisenbrauns, 1999.

Lambrecht, Jan. "The Book of Revelation and Apocalyptic in the New Testament." In *L'Apocalypse Johannique et L' Apocalyptique Dans Le NouveauTestament*, edited by Jan lambrecht, 1–18. Leuven: Leuven University Press, 1980.

Lampe, Peter. "MEXPI THC CHMEPON: A New Edition of Matthew 27:64b; 28:13 in Today's Pop Science and a Salty Breeze from the Dead Sea." In *Neutestamentliche Exegese Im Dialog: Hermeneutik - Wirkungsgeschichte - Matthäusevangelium*, edited by Peter Lampe, Moisés Mayordomo, and Migaku Sato, 355–66. Festschrift Für Ulrich Luz Zum 70. Geburtstag: Neukirchener Verlag, 2008.

Lanciani, Rodolfo Amedeo. *Ancient Rome in the Light of Recent Discoveries.* New York: Houghton, Mifflin & Company, 1898.

Langlois, Michael. "How a 2,700-Year-Old Piece of Papyrus Super-Charged the Debate over UNESCO and Jerusalem." *The Conversation,* November 15, 2016. http://theconversation.com/how-a-2-700-year-old-piece-of-papyrus-super-charged-the-debate-over-unesco-and-jerusalem-68376.

Lapp, Eric Christian. "The Archaeology of Light: The Cultural Significance of the Oil Lamp from Roman Palestine." Ph.D., Duke University, 1997.

Lapp, Paul W. "Bab Edh-Dhra', Perizzites and Emim." In *Jerusalem Through the Ages: The Twenty-Fifth Archaeological Convention*, 1–25. Jerusalem: Israel Exploration Society, 1968.

———. "Bab Edh-Dhra' (RB 1966)." *RB* 73 (1966): 556–61.

———. "Bab Edh-Dhraʿ (RB 1968)." *RB* 75 (1968): 86–93, pls. 3–6a.

———. "Bab Edh-Dhraʿ Tomb A 76 and Early Bronze I in Palestine." *BASOR* 189 (1968): 12–41.

———. *Palestinian Ceramic Chronology, 200 B.C.-A.D. 70*. ASOR. New Haven, CT: American Schools of Oriental Research, 1961.

———. *The Dhahr Mirzbaneh Tombs: Three Intermediate Bronze Age Cemeteries in Jordan*. Philadelphia, PA: American Schools of Oriental Research, 1966.

Larsen, Mogens Trolle. *The Conquest of Assyria: Excavations in an Antique Land*. New York: Routledge, 1996.

La Sor, William Sanford. *Dead Sea Scrolls and the New Testament*. Grand Rapids: Eerdmans, 1983.

———. "Discovering What Jewish Mikva'ot Can Tell Us About Christian Baptism." *BAR* 13, no. 1 (1987): 52–59.

La Sor, William Sanford, David Allan Hubbard, Frederic William Bush, and Leslie C. Allen. *Old Testament Survey: The Message, Form, and Background of the Old Testament*. 2nd ed. Grand Rapids: Eerdmans, 1996.

Lassus, Jean. "Antioch on the Orontes." In *The Princeton Encyclopedia of Classical Sites*, edited by Richard Stillwell, William L. MacDonald, and Marian Holland McAllister, 62. Princeton, NJ: Princeton University Press, 1976.

Latham, James E. *The Religious Symbolism of Salt*. Theologie Historique 64. Paris: Beauchesne, 1982.

Lawler, Andrew. "First Churches of the Jesus Cult." *Archaeology* 60, no. 5 (2007): 46.

Layard, Austen Henry. "Nineveh and Its Remains." *The Southern Quarterly Review* 16, no. 31 (1849): 1–31.

———. *Nineveh and Its Remains: A Narrative of an Expedition to Assyria During the Years 1845, 1846 and 1847*. London, UK: J. Murray, 1867.

———. *The Monuments of Nineveh: From Drawings Made on the Spot*. Piscataway, NJ: Gorgias, 2004.

Lehmann, Karl. *Samothrace: A Guide to the Excavations and the Museum*. Edited by J. R. McCredie. 6th ed. Thessaloniki: Institute of Fine Arts, New York University, 1998.

Lehmann, Karl, Phyllis Williams Lehmann, and J. R. McCredie, eds. *Samothrace*. 12 vols. New York: Princeton University Press, 1998.

Lehmann, M. R. "Abraham's Purchase of Machpelah and Hittite Law." *BASOR* 129 (1953): 15–18.

LeMaire, André. "Burial Box of James the Brother of Jesus: Earliest Archaeological Evidence of Jesus Found in Jerusalem." *BAR* 28, no. 6 (2002): 24–33, 70.

———. "'House of David' Restored in Moabite Inscription." *BAR* 20, no. 3 (1994): 30–37.

Lemche, Niels Peter. *The Israelites in History and Tradition*. Library of Ancient Israel. Louisville, KY: Westminster/Knox, 1998.

———. *The Old Testament between Theology and History: A Critical Survey*. Louisville, KY: Westminster/Knox, 2008.

Lenski, Richard C. H. *The Interpretation of St. John's Revelation*. CNT. Minneapolis, MN: Augsburg Fortress, 1963.

———. *The Interpretation of the Acts of the Apostles*. CNT. Minneapolis, MN: Augsburg Fortress, 1961.

Lepsius, Johann. "Dr. Johann Lepsius on the Symbolic Language of the Apocalypse." Edited by William M. Ramsay. Translated by H. Ramsay. *The Expositor* 8, no. 1 (1911): 160–80.

Lernau, Omri, and H. Lernau. "Fish Remains." In *Excavations at the City of David 1978-1985 Directed by Yigal Shiloh*, edited by Donald T. Ariel and Alon De Groot, 3:131–48. Qedem 33. Jerusalem, Israel: Hebrew University, 1992.

Leval, Gerard. "Ancient Inscription Refers to Birth of Israelite Monarchy." *BAR* 38, no. 3 (June 2012): 41–43, 70.

Lev, David. "Russia Decides to Search for Sodom and Gomorrah-in Jordan." *Arutz Sheva 7: Israel National News*, December 14, 2010. http://www.israelnationalnews.com/News/News.aspx/141132.

Levin, Yigal. "The Identification of Khirbet Qeiyafa: A New Suggestion." *BASOR*, no. 367 (2012): 73–86.

Lev-Tov, Justin S. E. "Pigs, Philistines, and the Ancient Animal Economy of Ekron from Late Bronze to Iron Age II." Ph.D. diss., University of Tennessee, 2000.

Levy, Thomas E. "From Camels to Computers: A Short History of Archaeological Method." *BAR* 22, no. 4 (1995): 44–51.

Levy, Thomas E., Russell B. Adams, Mohammad Najjar, A. Hauptmann, J. D. Anderson, B. Brandi, M. A. Robinson, and Thomas Higham. "Reassessing the Chronology of Biblical Edom: New Excavations and 14C Dates from Khirbat En-Nahas (Jordan)." *Antiquity* 78, no. 302 (2004): 874–76.

Levy, Thomas E., and Thomas Higham, eds. *The Bible and Radiocarbon Dating: Archaeology, Text and Science.* London, UK: Routledge, 2014.

Levy, Thomas E., Thomas Higham, C. Bronk Ramsey, N. G. Smith, Erez Ben-Yosef, M. Robinson, Stefan Münger, et al. "High-Precision Radiocarbon Dating and Historical Biblical Archaeology in Southern Jordan." *Antiquity* 105 (2008): 16460–65.

Levy, Thomas E., Stefan Münger, and Mohammad Najjar. "A Newly Discovered Scarab of Sheshonq I: Recent Iron Age Explorations in Southern Jordan." *Antiquity*, 2014, http://journal.antiquity.ac.uk/projgall/levy341.

Levy, Thomas E., and Mohammad Najjar. "Edom & Copper: The Emergence of Ancient Israel's Rival." *BAR* 32, no. 4 (2004): 24–35, 70.

Levy, Thomas E., Mohammad Najjar, and Erez Ben-Yosef, eds. *New Insights into the Iron Age Archaeology of Edom, Southern Jordan: Surveys, Excavations and Research from the Edom Lowlands Regional Archaeology Project (ELRAP).* Monumenta Archaeologica. Los Angeles, Calf.: The Cotsen Institute of Archaeology, 2014.

———. "What Do We Mean by Jabneh?" *Journal of Bible and Religion* 32 (1964): 125–32.

Lewis, Naphtali, Jonas C. Greenfield, and Yigael Yadin, eds. *The Documents from the Bar Kokhba Period in the Cave of Letters, Greek Papyri.* Judaean Desert Series 2. Jerusalem: Israel Exploration Society, 1989.

Libby, Willard F. *Radiocarbon Dating.* Chicago, IL: University of Chicago Press, 1952.

Lichtheim, Miriam. *Ancient Egyptian Literature: The New Kingdom.* 2nd ed. Vol. 2. 3 vols. Berkeley, CA: University of California Press, 2006.

———. *Ancient Egyptian Literature: The Old and Middle Kingdoms.* 2nd ed. Vol. 1. 3 vols. Berkeley, CA: University of California Press, 2006.

Liddell, Henry George, and Robert Scott. *An Intermediate Greek-English Lexicon.* 9th ed. Oxford, UK: Clarendon, 1889.

LiDonnici, Lynn R. *The Epidaurian Miracle Inscriptions.* SFSHJ 36. Atlanta, Ga.: Scholars Press, 1995.

———. "The Images of Artemis Ephesia and Greco-Roman Worship: A Reconsideration." *HTR* 85, no. 4 (October 1992): 389–415.

Lieu, Judith M. "Accusations of Jewish Persecution in Early Christian Sources, with Particular Reference to Justin Martyr and the Martyrdom of Polycarp." In *Tolerance and Intolerance in Early Judaism and Christianity*, edited by Graham N. Stanton and Gedaliahu A. G Stroumsa, 279–95. Cambridge, UK: Cambridge University Press, 1998.

Lightfoot, Joseph B. *The Apostolic Fathers: Greek Texts and English Translations*. Edited by Michael W. Holmes. Translated by J. R. Harmer. 2nd ed. Rev. Grand Rapids: Baker Academic, 1989.

Lilje, Hanns. *The Last Book of the Bible: The Meaning of the Revelation of St. John*. Translated by Olive Wyon. Philadelphia, PA: Muhlenberg, 1957.

Lindberg, Christine A., Katherine M. Isaacs, and Ruth Handlin Manley, eds. *Oxford American Dictionary & Thesaurus*. 2nd ed. New York: Oxford University Press, USA, 2009.

Livingston, David. *Khirbet Nisya: The Search for Biblical Ai, 1979-2002*. Manheim, PA: Masthof, 2012.

Livingston, David P. "Excavation Report for Khirbet Nisya." *Bible and Spade* 12, no. 3 (1999): 95–96.

———. "Further Considerations on the Location of Bethel at El-Bireh." *PEQ* 126, no. 2 (1994): 154–59.

———. "Locating Biblical Ai Correctly." *Ancient Days*, 2003. http://davelivingston .com/ai15.htm.

———. "Nimrod: Who Was He? Was He Godly or Evil?" *Bible and Spade* 14, no. 3 (2001): 67–72.

———. "One Last Word on Bethel and Ai." *BAR* 15, no. 1 (1989): 11.

———. "The Location of Biblical Bethel and Ai Reconsidered." *Westminster Theological Journal* 33, no. 1 (1970): 20–44.

Llewelyn, Stephen R., and Dionysia van Beek. "Reading the Temple Warning as a Greek Visitor." *Journal for the Study of Judaism* 42, no. 1 (2011): 1–22.

Loane, Marcus L. *They Overcame: An Exposition of the First Three Chapters of Revelation*. Grand Rapids: Baker, 1981.

Loffreda, Stanislao. "Capernaum-Jesus' Own City." *Bible and Spade* 10, no. 1 (1981): 1–17.

———. *Light and Life: Ancient Christian Oil Lamps of the Holy Land*. Studium Biblicum. Jerusalem: Franciscan, 2001.

Lohmeyer, Ernst. *Die Offenbarung Des Johannes*. Handbuch Zum Neuen Testament 16. Tübingen: Siebeck, 1926.

Lohse, Eduard. *Die Offenbarung Des Johannes*. Das Neue Testament Deutsch 11. Göttingen: Vandenhoeck & Ruprecht, 1960.

Longenecker, Richard N. *Biblical Exegesis in the Apostolic Period*. 2nd ed. Grand Rapids: Eerdmans, 1975.

López, Raúl Erlando. "Temporal Changes in the Ageing of Biblical Patriarchs." *Journal of Creation* 14, no. 3 (2000): 109–17.

———. "The Antediluvian Patriarchs and the Sumerian King List." *Journal of Creation* 12, no. 3 (1998): 347–57.

Lubbock, Sir John. *Pre-Historic Times, as Illustrated by Ancient Remains, and the Manners and Customs of Modern Savages*. 2nd ed. London, UK: Williams & Norgate, 1869.

Lucas, Alfred, and J. R. Harris. *Ancient Egyptian Materials and Industries*. Mineola, NY: Dover, 1962.

Luijendijk, AnneMarie. *Greetings in the Lord: Early Christians and the Oxyrhynchus Papyri*. Cambridge, MA: Harvard University Press, 2009.

MacAlister, Robert A. S., and J. G. Duncan. *Excavations on the Hill of Ophel, Jerusalem 1923-1925*. PEF Annual 4. London, UK: Palestine Exploration Fund, 1926.

McDonagh, Bernard. *Blue Guide: Turkey*. 3rd ed. London: A & C Black, 2001.

MacDonald, Burton. *East of the Jordan: Territories and Sites of the Hebrew Scriptures*. Edited by Victor H. Matthews. ASOR Books 6. Boston, MA: American Schools of Oriental Research, 2000.

———. "EB IV Tombs at Khirbet Khanazir: Types, Construction, and Relation to Other EB IV Tombs in Syria-Palestine." *Studies in the History and Archaeology of Jordan* 5 (1995): 129–34.

MacDonald, Lee Martin. "Acts." In *The Bible Knowledge Background Commentary: Acts-Philemon*, edited by Craig A. Evans and Isobel A. Combes, 19–194. Colorado Springs, Colo.: Cook, 2004.

Magness, Jodi. "The Date of the Sardis Synagogue in Light of the Numismatic Evidence." *AJA* 109 (2005): 443–75.

Maeir, Aren M. "A New Interpretation of the Term `Opalim (עפלים) in Light of Recent Archaeological Finds from Philistia." *JSOT* 32, no. 1 (2007): 23–40.

———. , ed. *Tell Es-Safi / Gath I: The 1996 - 2005 Seasons: Part 1: Text*. Ägypten Und Altes Testament 69. Wiesbaden: Harrassowitz, 2012.

———. "The Historical Background and Dating of Amos VI 2: An Archaeological Perspective from Tell Es-Safi/Gath." *Vetus Testamentum* 54, no. 3 (July 1, 2004): 319–34.

Maeir, Aren M., and Carl S. Ehrlich. "Excavating Philistine Gath: Have We Found Goliath's Hometown?" *BAR* 27, no. 6 (2001): 22–31.

Maeir, Aren M., Stefan J. Wimmer, Alexander Zukerman, and Aaron Demsky. "A Late Iron Age I/Early Iron Age II Old Canaanite Inscription from Tell Es-Safi/Gath, Israel: Palaeography, Dating, and Historical-Cultural Significance." *BASOR*, no. 351 (August 1, 2008): 39–71.

Magen, Yitshak, and Yuval Peleg. *The Qumran Excavations 1993 - 2004: Preliminary Report*. 6. Jerusalem: Israel Antiquities Authority, 2007.

Magie, David. *Roman Rule in Asia Minor to the End of the Third Century After Christ*. Edited by T. James Luce. 2 vols. Roman History. New York: Arno, 1975.

Magness, Jodi. *Jerusalem Ceramic Chronology: Circa 200-800 CE*. JSOT/ASOR Monographs 9. Sheffield, UK: Sheffield Academic, 1993.

———. *The Archaeology of Qumran and the Dead Sea Scrolls*. Grand Rapids: Eerdmans, 2003.

Maier, Paul. "Herod and the Infants of Bethlehem." In *Chronos Kairos Christos II*, edited by E. Jerry Vardaman, 169–89. Macon, Ga.: Mercer University Press, 1998.

Maier, Paul L. "The Date of the Nativity and the Chronology of Jesus' Life." In *Chronos, Kairos, Christos*, edited by Jack Finegan, Jerry Vardaman, and Edwin M. Yamauchi, 113–32. Winona Lake, IN: Eisenbrauns, 1989.

Malina, Bruce J. *On the Genre and Message of Revelation: Star Visions and Sky Journeys*. Peabody, MA: Hendrickson, 1995.

———. *The Palestinian Manna Tradition: The Manna Tradition in the Palestinian Targums and its Relationship to the New Testament Writings*. Arbeiten zur Geschichte des spateren Judentums und des Urchristentums 7. Leiden: Brill, 1968.

Mallon, Alexis. "Voyage D'exploration Au Sud-Est de La Mer Morte." *Biblica* 10 (1929): 94–98.

Manetho. *History of Egypt and Other Works*. Translated by W. G. Waddell. Loeb Classical Library 350. Cambridge, MA: Harvard University Press, 1940.

Mansel, Arif Müfid. *Excavations and Researches at Perge*. Türk Tarih Kurumu. Yayinlarindan 8. Ankara: Türk Tarih Kurumu Basimevi, 1949.

Marchant, Jo. "Archaeologists Are Only Just Beginning to Reveal the Secrets Hidden in These Ancient Manuscripts." ***Smithsonian Magazine***, December 11, 2017. https://www.smithsonianmag.com/history/archaeologoists-only-just-beginning-reveal-secrets-hidden-ancient-manuscripts-180967455.

Marcos, Natalio Fernández, and Wilfred G. E. Watson. *The Septuagint in Context: Introduction to the Greek Version of the Bible*. Leiden: Brill, 2000.

Margalith, Othniel. "On the Origin and Antiquity of the Name 'Israel.'" *Zeitschrift Für Die Alttestamentliche Wissenschaft* 102, no. 2 (1990): 225–37.

Marienberg, Evyatar. "Mikveh." Edited by Judith R. Baskin. *The Cambridge Dictionary of Judaism and Jewish Culture*. Cambridge, UK: Cambridge University Press, 2011.

Mariette, Auguste. *Catalogue général des monuments d'Abydos découverts pendant les fouilles de cette ville*. Paris: L'Impr. nationale, 1880.

Mariette, Auguste, and Alphonse Mariette. *The Monuments of Upper Egypt, a Translation of the "Itinéraire de La Haute Égypte", of Auguste Mariette-Bey*. Cairo: A. Mourès, 1877.

Markschies, Christoph. *Gnosis: An Introduction*. New York: T&T Clark, 2003.

Marshall, I. Howard, Alan R. Millard, James I. Packer, and D. J. Wiseman, eds. *New Bible Dictionary*. 3rd ed. Downers Grove, IL: InterVarsity, 1996.

Martin, Ernest L. "The Nativity and Herod's Death." In *Chronos, Kairos, Christos*, edited by Jack Finegan, Jerry Vardaman, and Edwin M. Yamauchi, 85–92. Winona Lake, IN: Eisenbrauns, 1989.

Martinez, F. Garcia, and W. G. E. Watson. *The Dead Sea Scrolls Translated: The Qumran Texts in English*. 2nd ed. Leiden: Brill Academic, 1997.

Martin, Hugh. *The Seven Letters*. Philadelphia, PA: Westminster, 1956.

Martin, Ralph P. *2 Corinthians*. Edited by David A Hubbard and Glenn W Barker. Word Biblical Commentary 40. Dallas, Tex.: Word Books, 1998.

Maso, Leonardo B. Dal. *Rome of the Caesars*. Translated by Michael Hollingworth. Firenze, Italy: Bonechi Edizioni, 1983.

Mazar, Amihai. "Archaeology and the Biblical Narrative: The Case of the United Monarchy." In *One God - One Cult - One Nation: Archaeological and Biblical Perspectives*, edited by Reinhard Gregor Kratz and Hermann Spieckermann, 29–58. BZAW 405. Berlin: De Gruyter, 2011.

———. *Archaeology of the Land of the Bible: 10,000-586 B.C.E.* Vol. 1. The Anchor Yale Bible Reference Library. New Haven, CT: Yale University Press, 1992.

———. "Rehob." In *The Oxford Encyclopedia of the Bible and Archaeology*, edited by Daniel M Master, B. Alpert Nakhai, Avraham Faust, L. Michael White, and Jürgen K. Zangeberg, 221–30. New York: Oxford University Press, 2013.

———. "Tel Rehov, 1998-2001." *Excavations and Surveys in Israel* 114 (2002): 38–40.

———. "The 1997-1998 Excavations at Tel Rehov: Preliminary Report." *IEJ* 49 (1999): 1–42.

———. "The Debate over the Chronology of the Iron Age in the Southern Levant." In *The Bible and Radiocarbon Dating: Archaeology, Text and Science*, edited by Thomas E. Levy and Thomas Higham, 15–30. London, UK: Routledge, 2014.

———. "The Divided Monarchy: Comments on Some Archaeological Issues." In *The Quest for the Historical Israel*, edited by Israel Finkelstein and Brian B. Schmidt, 159–80. Archaeology and Biblical Studies 17. Atlanta, Ga.: SBL, 2007.

———. "The Iron Age I Period." In *The Archaeology of Ancient Israel*, edited by Amnon Ben-Tor, translated by R. Greenberg, 258–301. New Haven, CT: Yale University Press, 1994.

———. "The Patriarchs, Exodus and Conquest Narratives in Light of Archaeology." In *The Quest for the Historical Israel*, edited by Israel Finkelstein and Brian B. Schmidt, 57–67. Archaeology and Biblical Studies 17. Atlanta, Ga.: Society of Biblical Literature, 2007.

———. "The Search for David and Solomon: An Archaeological Perspective." In *The Quest for the Historical Israel*, edited by Israel Finkelstein and Brian B. Schmidt, 117–40. Archaeology and Biblical Studies 17. Atlanta, Ga.: Society of Biblical Literature, 2007.

———. "The Spade and the Text: The Interaction between Archaeology and Israelite History Relating to the Tenth-Ninth Centuries BCE." In *Understanding the History of Ancient Israel*, edited by H. G. M. Williamson, 143–71. Proceedings of the British Academy 143. Oxford, UK: Oxford University Press, 2007.

Mazar, Amihai, and Shmuel Ahituv. "The Inscriptions from Tel Reḥov and Their Contribution to Study of Script and Writing during the Iron Age IIA." In *"See, I Will Bring a Scroll Recounting What Befell Me" (Ps 40:8): Epigraphy and Daily Life from the Bible to the Talmud. Dedicated to the Memory of Professor Hanan Eshel*, edited by Esther Eshel and Yigal Levin, 39–68. Journal of Ancient Judaism. Supplements 12. Göttingen: Vandehoeck & Rupprecht, 2013.

Mazar, Amihai, and Ofer Bar-Yosef. "Israeli Archaeology." *World Archaeology* 13, no. 3 Regional Traditions of Archaeological Research II (February 1, 1982): 310–25.

Mazar, Amihai, and John Camp. "Will Tel Rehov Save the United Monarchy?" *BAR* 26, no. 2 (2000): 38–51.

Mazar, Amihai, Dvory Namdar, Nava Panitz-Cohen, Ronny Neumann, and Steve Weiner. "The Iron Age Beehives at Tel Rehov in the Jordan Valley: Archaeological and Analytical Aspect." *Antiquity* 82 (2008): 629–39.

Mazar, Amihai, and Nava Panitz-Cohen. "It Is the Land of Honey: Beekeeping in Iron Age IIA Tel Rehov - Culture, Cult and Economy." *NEA* 70, no. 4 (2007): 202–19.

Mazar, Benjamin. *The World History of the Jewish People: Ancient Times: Patriarchs*. Vol. 2. 2 vols. London, UK: Rutger's University Press, 1970.

Mazar, Eilat. "Did I Find King David's Palace?" *BAR* 32, no. 1 (2006): 16–27, 70.

———. "Excavate King David's Palace." *BAR* 23, no. 1 (1997): 50–57, 74.

———. *Preliminary Report on The City of David Excavations 2005 at the Visitors Center Area*. Jerusalem, Israel: Shalem Press, 2008.

———. *The Palace of King David Excavations at the Summit of the City of David: Preliminary Report of Seasons 2005-2007*. Jerusalem, Israel: Shoham Academic Research and Publication, 2009.

Mazar, Eilat, David Ben-Shlomo, and Shmuel Ahituv. "An Inscribed Pithos from the Ophel, Jerusalem." *IEJ* 63, no. 1 (2013): 39–50.

McCarter, P. Kyle, Jr. "The Historical David." *Interpretation* 40, no. 2 (1986): 117–29.

McConville, J. Gordon. *Exploring the Old Testament, Volume 4: A Guide to the Prophets*. Downers Grove, IL: IVP Academic, 2008.

McDowell, Josh, and Bob Hostetler. *The New Tolerance: How a Cultural Movement Threatens to Destroy You, Your Faith, and Your Children*. Wheaton, IL: Tyndale, 1998.

McGrath, Alister E. *Christian Theology: An Introduction.* Hoboken, NJ: Wiley-Blackwell, 2006.

McRay, John. "Archaeology and the Bible: How Archaeological Findings Have Enhanced the Credibility of the Bible." *4Truth.Net of the Southern Baptist Convention*, September 28, 2013. http://www.4truth.net/fourtruthpbbible.aspx?pageid=8589952738.

———. *Archaeology and the New Testament.* Grand Rapids: Baker, 1991.

———. *Paul: His Life and Teaching.* Grand Rapids: Baker Academic, 2007.

Megaw, A. H. S. "Archaeology in Cyprus, 1957." *AR* 4 (1957): 43–50.

Meggitt, Justin J. "The Social Status of Erastus (Ro. 16:23)." *NovT* 38, no. 3 (1996): 1–6.

Meiggs, Russell. *Roman Ostia.* Oxford: Clarendon Press, 1973.

Meinardus, Otto F. A. *St. John of Patmos and the Seven Churches of the Apocalypse.* New York: Caratzas, 1979.

———. "The Christian Remains of the Seven Churches of the Apocalypse." *BA* 37, no. 3 (September 1, 1974): 69–82.

Mellink, Machteld J. "Archaeology in Asia Minor." *AJA* 81, no. 3 (1977): 289–321.

Mellor, Ronald. *Thea Rhōmē: The Worship of the Goddess Roma in the Greek World.* Hypomnemata 42. Göttingen: Vandenhoeck & Ruprecht, 1975.

Mendelsohn, Isaac. *Slavery in the Ancient Near East; A Comparative Study of Slavery in Babylonia, Assyria, Syria, and Palestine From the Middle of the Third Millennium to the End of the First Millennium.* Oxford, UK: Oxford University Press, 1949.

Merkelbach, Reinhold. "Der Griechische Wortchatz Und Die Christen." *Zeitschrift Für Papyrologie Und Epigraphik* 18 (1975): 108–36.

Merker, Gloria S. "Some Recent Books on Cypriote Archaeology." *IEJ* 52, no. 1 (2002): 106–11.

Merling, David. "The Book of Joshua, Part I: Its Evaluation by Nonevidence." *Andrews University Seminary Studies* 39, no. 1 (2001): 61–72.

———. "The Relationship Between Archaeology and Bible: Expectations and Reality." In *The Future of Biblical Archaeology: Reassessing Methodologies and Assumptions*, edited by James Karl Hoffmeier and Alan R. Millard, 29–42. The Proceedings of a Symposium, August 12-14, 2001 at Trinity International University. Grand Rapids: Eerdmans, 2004.

Merrill, Eugene H. "Fixed Dates in Patriarchal Chronology." *BSac* 137, no. 547 (1980): 241–51.

———. *Kingdom of Priests: A History of Old Testament Israel.* 2nd ed. Grand Rapids: Baker Academic, 2008.

———. "Texts, Talls, and Old Testament Chronology: Tall el-Hammam as a Case Study." *Artifax* 27, no. 4 (2012): 20–21.

Merrill, Selah. "Modern Researches in Palestine." *Journal of the American Geographical Society of New York* 9 (1877): 109–25.

———. "Modern Researches in Palestine." *PEFSt.* 11, no. 1 (1879): 138–54.

Meshel, Ze'ev. *Sinai: Excavations and Studies.* Bar International. Oxford, UK: Archaeopress, 2000.

Metzger, Bruce M. "Antioch-on-the-Orontes." *BA* 11, no. 4 (1948): 69–88.

———. *Breaking the Code: Understanding the Book of Revelation.* Nashville: Abingdon, 1999.

———. *Manuscripts of the Greek Bible: An Introduction to Greek Palaeography.* Oxford, UK: Oxford University Press, 1981.

Metzger, Bruce M., and Bart D. Ehrman. *The Text of the New Testament: Its Transmission, Corruption, and Restoration.* 4th ed. Oxford, UK: Oxford University Press, 2005.

Meyer, Eduard, and Bernhard Luther. *Die Israeliten und ihre Nachbarstämme: Alttestamentliche Untersuchungen.* Halle: Max Niemeyer, 1906.

Meyer, Marvin. *The Gnostic Discoveries: The Impact of the Nag Hammadi Library.* New York: HarperCollins, 2005.

Meyers, Eric M., ed. *The Oxford Encyclopedia of Archaeology in the Near East.* 5 vols. Oxford, UK: Oxford University Press, 1997.

Meyers, Carol L., and Eric M. Meyers. "An Assessment of the Evidence for Writing in Ancient Israel." In *Biblical Archaeology Today, Proceedings of the International Congress on Biblical Archaeology, Jerusalem*, edited by Avraham Biran, 301–12. Jerusalem: Israel Exploration Society, 1985.

———. "In Praise of Ancient Scribes." *Biblical Archaeologist* 45, no. 3 (1982): 143–53.

———. "Methods of Studying the Patriarchal Narratives as Ancient Texts." In *Essays on the Patriarchal Narratives*, edited by Donald J. Wiseman and Alan R. Millard, 43–58. Winona Lake, IN: Eisenbrauns, 1983.

———. "The Ostracon from the Days of David Found at Khirbet Qeiyafa." *TynBul* 62, no. 1 (2011): 1–13.

———. "The Practice of Writing in Ancient Israel." *Biblical Archaeologist* 35, no. 4 (1972): 98–111.

———. "The Tell Dan Stele." In *The Context of Scripture: Canonical Compositions from the Biblical World*, edited by William W. Hallo and K. Lawson Younger, 2:161–62. Leiden: Brill Academic, 2002.

Millard, Allen R. *Reading and Writing in the Time of Jesus.* New York: Continuum International, 2004.

———. "The Persian Names in Esther and the Reliability of the Hebrew Text." *JBL* 96, no. 4 (December 1, 1977): 481–88.

Miller, James Maxwell, and John Haralson Hayes. *A History of Ancient Israel and Judah.* Louisville, KY. Westminster/Knox, 1986.

Miller, J. Maxwell. "Archaeology and the Israelite Conquest of Canaan: Some Methodological Observations." *PEQ* 109, no. 2 (July 1977): 87–93.

———. "Site Identification: A Problem Area in Contemporary Biblical Scholarship." *Zeitschrift Des Deutschen Palästina-Vereins (1953-)* 99 (January 1, 1983): 119–29.

Miller, J. Maxwell, and Gene M. Tucker. *The Book of Joshua.* The Cambridge Bible Commentary of the English Bible. Cambridge, MA: Cambridge University Press, 1974.

Milne, Joseph Grafton. *The Silver Coinage of Smyrna.* London, UK: Taylor & Walton, 1914.

Misgav, Haggai, Yosef Garfinkel, and Saar Ganor. "The Khirbet Qeiyafa Ostracon." In *New Studies in the Archaeology of Jerusalem and Its Region*, edited by David Amit, Gary D. Stiebel, and Orit Peleg-Barkat, 3:111–23. Jerusalem, Israel: Israel Antiquities Authority, 2009.

———. "The Ostracon." In *Khirbet Qeiyafa: Excavation Report 2007-2008*, edited by Yosef Garfinkel and Saar Ganor, 1:243–60. Jerusalem, Israel: Israel Exploration Society, 2010.

Mitchell, S., and A. W. McNicoll. "Archaeology in Western and Southern Asia Minor 1971-78." *Archaeological Reports*, no. 25 (1978): 59–90.

———. "Archaeology in Asia Minor 1979-84." *Archaeological Reports*, no. 31 (1984): 70–105.

———. *Gilgamesh: A New English Version.* New York: Free Press, 2006.

Mitchell, Stephen, and Marc Waelkens. *Pisidian Antioch: The Site and Its Monuments.* Oxford, UK: Classical Press of Wales, 1998.

Mitford, T. B. "Notes on Some Published Inscriptions from Roman Cyprus." *Annual of British School at Athens* 42 (1947): 201–6.

Mitten, David Gordon. "A New Look at Ancient Sardis." *Biblical Archaeologist* 29, no. 3 (1966): 38–68.

Moeller, Nadine, and Robert K. Ritner. "The Ahmose 'Tempest Stela', Thera and Comparative Chronology." *Journal of Near Eastern Studies* 73, no. 1 (April 1, 2014): 1–19.

Moffatt, James. *The Revelation of St. John the Divine.* Edited by W. Robertson Nicoll. Expositor's Greek Testament 5. London, UK: Hodder & Stoughton, 1910.

Monson, John M. "Enter Joshua: The 'Mother of Current Debates' in Biblical Archaeology." In *Do Historical Matters Matter to Faith?: A Critical Appraisal of Modern and Postmodern Approaches to Scripture*, edited by James K. Hoffmeier and Graham A. Magary, 427–58. Wheaton, IL: Crossway Books, 2012.

———. "The Role of Context and the Promise of Archaeology in Biblical Interpretation." In *The Future of Biblical Archaeology: Reassessing Methodologies and Assumptions*, edited by James Karl Hoffmeier and Alan R. Millard, 309–27. The Proceedings of a Symposium, August 12-14, 2001 at Trinity International University. Grand Rapids: Eerdmans, 2004.

Montgomery, John Warwick. *The Quest for Noah's Ark: A Treasury of Documented Accounts from Ancient Times to the Present Day of Sightings of the Ark.* 2nd ed. Ada, MI: Bethany Fellowship, 1974.

Moore, John. "Dr. John Moore and Dr. Steven Collins Reflect on TeHEP's First Nine Years." *Update: Tall el-Hammam Excavation Project, The Official Newsletter of TeHEP*, April 11, 2014.

Moorey, Peter R. S. "Kathleen Kenyon and Palestinian Archaeology." *PEQ* 111, no. 1 (1979): 3–10.

———. "What Do We Know About the People Buried in the Royal Cemetery?" *Expedition* 20, no. 1 (1977): 24–40.

Moreland, James Porter, and William Lane Craig. *Philosophical Foundations for a Christian Worldview.* InterVarsity, 2003.

Morkot, R., P. James, I. J. Thorpe, N. Kokkinos, and J. Frankish. *Centuries of Darkness: A Challenge to the Conventional Chronology of Old World Archaeology.* New Brunswick, NJ: Rutgers University Press, 1991.

Morrey, P. R. S. "Where Did They Bury the Kings of the IIIrd Dynasty of Ur?" *Iraq* 46, no. 1 (1984): 1–18.

Moscrop, John James. *Measuring Jerusalem: The Palestine Exploration Fund and British Interests in the Holy Land.* London, UK: Leicester University Press, 2000.

Mounce, Robert H. *The Book of Revelation.* Revised. NICNT 17. Grand Rapids: Eerdmans, 1997.

———. *What Are We Waiting For?: A Commentary on Revelation.* Eugene, OR: Wipf & Stock, 2004.

Moyise, Steve. "Does the Author of Revelation Misappropriate the Scriptures?" *AUSS* 40, no. 1 (2002): 3–21.

Mueller, Tom. "Herod: The Holy Land's Visionary Builder." *National Geographic*, 2008.

Muir, Steven. "Religion on the Road in Ancient Greece and Rome." In *Travel and Religion in Antiquity*, edited by Philip A. Harland, 29–48. ESCJ 21. Waterloo, Ont.: Wilfrid Laurier University Press, 2011.

Mulholland, M. Robert. *Revelation: Holy Living in an Unholy World.* Grand Rapids: Asbury, 1990.

Murat, Avci. "The Formation and Mechanisms of the Great Telçeker Earthflow Which Also Crept Noah's Ark at Mount Ararat." presented at the Mount Ararat and Noah's Ark Symposium, Dogubeyazit, Turkey, 2005.

Murphy-O'Connor, Jerome. "Lots of God-Fearers? Theosebeis in the Aphrodisias Inscription." *RB* 99 (1992): 418–24.

———. *St. Paul's Corinth: Text and Archaeology*. Good News Studies 6. Minneapolis, MN: Liturgical, 2002.

———. *St. Paul's Ephesus: Texts and Archaeology*. Minneapolis, MN: Liturgical, 2008.

Muss, Ulrike. "The Artemision at Ephesos: From Paganism to Christianity." In *Mustafa Büyükkolancı'ya Armağan: Essays in Honour of Mustafa Büyükkolancı*, edited by Celal Şimşek, Bahadır Duman, and Erim Konakçi, 413–22. Istanbul: Yayinlari, 2015.

Mussies, Gerard. "Artemis" In *Dictionary of Deities and Demons in the Bible*, edited by Karel van der Toorn, Bob Becking, and Pieter Willem van der Horst, 2nd ed., 91–97. Grand Rapids, Mich.: Eerdmans, 1999.

———. "Pagans, Jews, and Christians at Ephesus." In *Studies on the Hellenistic Background of the New Testament*, edited by Pieter Wilhelm van der Horst and Gerard Mussies, 177–94. Utrechtse Theologische Reeks 10. Utrecht: Theological Faculty Utrecht University, 1990.

Mykytiuk, Lawrence J. *Identifying Biblical Persons in Northwest Semitic Inscriptions of 1200-539 B.C.E.* Society of Biblical Lit, 2004.

Na'aman, Nadav. "Bethel and Beth-Aven: The Location of the Early Israelite Sanctuaries." *Zion* 50 (1985): 15–25.

———. "The Interchange Between Bible and Archaeology: The Case of David's Palace and the Millo." *BAR* 40, no. 1 (n.d.): 57–61.

Navarra, Fernand. *Noah's Ark: I Touched It*. Edited by Dave Balsiger. Needham, MA: Logos International, 1974.

Naveh, Joseph. "Some Considerations on the Ostracon from 'Izbet Sartah." *IEJ* 28, no. 1/2 (1978): 31–35.

Naylor, Michael. "The Roman Imperial Cult and Revelation." *CBR* 8, no. 2 (2010): 207–39.

Neev, David, and Kenneth O. Emery. *The Dead Sea: Depositional Processes and Environments of Evaporites*. Ministry of Development: Geological Survey 41. Jerusalem: Geological Survey of Israel, 1967.

———. *The Destruction of Sodom, Gomorrah and Jericho: Geological, Climatological and Archaeological Backgrounds*. Oxford, UK: Oxford University Press, 1995.

Negev, Avraham, and Shimon Gibson, eds. *Archaeological Encyclopedia of the Holy Land*. 3rd ed. 1 vols. New York: Continuum International, 1996.

Netzer, Ehud. *Architecture of Herod, the Great Builder*. Grand Rapids: Baker Academic, 2008.

———. "The Last Days and Hours at Masada." *BAR* 17, no. 6 (1991): 20–32.

Newman, Francis William. *A History of the Hebrew Monarchy: From the Administration of Samuel to the Babylonish Captivity*. London, UK: Chapman, 1853.

Newton, Charles Thomas. *The Collection of Ancient Greek Inscriptions in the British Museum*. Edited by E. L. Hicks. 5 vols. Oxford: Clarendon, 1874.

Ngo, Robin. "Rare Egyptian Sphinx Fragment Discovered at Hazor." *Bible History Daily: Biblical Archaeology Society*, July 12, 2013.

Niditch, Susan. *Oral World and Written Word: Ancient Israelite Literature*. Library of Ancient Israel. Louisville, KY: Westminster/Knox, 1996.

Nielsen, Marjatta. "Diana Efesia Multimammia: The Metamorphoses of a Pagan Goddess from the Renaissance to the Age of Neo-Classicism." In *From Artemis to Diana: The Goddess of Man and Beast*, edited by Tobias Fischer-Hansen and Birte Poulsen, 455–96. Acta Hyperborea 12. Copenhagen: Museum Tusculanum, 2009.

Nigro, Lorenzo, and Hamdan Taha, eds. *Tell Es-Sultan/Jericho in the Context of the Jordan Valley: Site Management, Conservation, and Sustainable Development.* Studies on the Archaeology of Palestine & Transjordan 2. Rome: University of Rome, "La Sapienza," 2006.

Nilsson, Martin Persson. *Geschichte Der Griechischen Religion.* 2nd ed. 2 vols. Handbuch Der Altertumswissenschaft, 5.2. Munich: Beck, 1955.

Nir-El, Yoram, and Magen Broshi. "The Black Ink of the Qumran Scrolls." *Dead Sea Discoveries* 3, no. 2 (1996): 157–67.

Nongbri, Brent. "The Use and Abuse of 𝔓52: Papyrological Pitfalls in the Dating of the Fourth Gospel." *Harvard Theological Review* 98, no. 1 (January 2005): 23–48.

Noth, Martin. *A History of Pentateuchal Traditions.* Upper Saddle River, NJ: Prentice-Hall, 1972.

———. *The History of Israel.* New York: Harper, 1960.

Novak, Ralph Martin. *Christianity and the Roman Empire: Background Texts.* Harrisburg, PA: Trinity, 2001.

Oesterley, W. O. E., and T. H. Robinson. *A History of Israel.* Oxford, UK: Oxford University Press, 1932.

Ogden, Jack. "Metals." In *Ancient Egyptian Materials and Technology*, edited by Ian Shaw and Paul T. Nicholson, 148–76. Cambridge England: Cambridge University Press, 2009.

Ogg, George. *The Chronology of the Life of Paul.* London, UK: Epworth, 1968.

Ohannes, Elliott R. "William Mitchell Ramsay: An Intellectual Biography." Ph.D., University of Washington, 2007.

Oliver, James H. "Octavian's Inscription at Nicopolis." *The American Journal of Philology* 90, no. 2 (1969): 178–82.

Olson, Craig. "A Proposal for a Symbolic Understanding of the Patriarchal Lifespans." Ph.D. diss., Dallas Theological Seminary, 2017.

———. "How Old Was Father Abraham? Re-Examining the Patriarchal Lifespans in Light of Archaeology." In *Evangelical Theological Society*, 1–26. Boston, MA, 2017.

Onstad, Esther. *Courage for Today, Hope for Tomorrow: A Study of the Revelation.* Minneapolis, MN: Augsburg Fortress, 1993.

Oren, Eliezer D. "The 'Ways of Horus' in North Sinai." In *Egypt, Israel, Sinai: Archaeological and Historical Relationships in the Biblical Period*, edited by Anson F. Rainey, 69–119. Tel Aviv University, 1987.

Ortiz, Steven M. "Deconstructing and Reconstructing the United Monarchy: House of David or Tent of David (Current Trends in Iron Age Chronology)." In *The Future of Biblical Archaeology: Reassessing Methodologies and Assumptions*, edited by James Karl Hoffmeier and Alan R. Millard, 121–47. The Proceedings of a Symposium, August 12-14, 2001 at Trinity International University. Grand Rapids: Eerdmans, 2004.

———. "The Archaeology of David and Solomon: Method or Madness?" In *Do Historical Matters Matter to Faith?: A Critical Appraisal of Modern and Postmodern Approaches to Scripture*, edited by James K. Hoffmeier and Graham A. Magary, 497–516. Wheaton, IL: Crossway Books, 2012.

Ortner, Donald J, and Bruno Frohlich. *The Early Bronze Age I Tombs and Burials of Bâb Edh-Dhrâ', Jordan.* Reports of the Expedition to the Dead Sea Plain, Jordan 3. Lanham, MD: AltaMira, 2008.

Osborne, Grant R. *Revelation.* BECNT. Grand Rapids: Baker Academic, 2002.

———. *The Hermeneutical Spiral: A Comprehensive Introduction to Biblical Interpretation.* Downers Grove, IL: InterVarsity, 2006.

Oster, Richard E. "Ephesus as a Religious Center Under the Principate, I: Paganism Before Constantine." *ANRW* 18, no. 3 (1990): 1661–1728.

———. "The Ephesian Artemis as an Opponent of Early Christianity." *JAC* 19 (1976): 24–44.

Özgenel, Lale. "A Tale of Two Cities: In Search of Ancient Pompeii and Herculaneum." *Middle East Technical University Journal of the Faculty of Architecture METU JFA* 2008, no. 25 (1-25): 1.

Padilla, Osvaldo. *The Speeches of Outsiders in Acts: Poetics, Theology and Historiography*. Cambridge, UK: Cambridge University Press, 2008.

Paley, Samuel M. *King of the World: Ashur-Nasir-Pal II of Assyria*. New York: Brooklyn Museum, 1976.

Palmer, Earl F. *1, 2, 3 John; Revelation*. Atlanta, Ga.: Nelson, 1982.

Palmer, Edward H. *The Desert of the Exodus: Journeys on Foot in the Wilderness of the Forty Years' of Wanderings Undertaken in Connexion with the Ordance Survey of Sinai and the Palestine Exploration Fund*. Vol. 1. 2 vols. Cambridge, UK: Deighton, Bell & Co., 1871.

Pandermalis, Dimitrios. *Dion, the Archaeological Site and the Museum*. Athens: Archaoelogical Receipts Fund, 1997.

———. *The Sacred City of the Macedonians at the Foothills of Mt. Olympus*. Athens: Archaoelogical Receipts Fund, 1987.

Paradise, J. "A Daughter and Her Father's Property at Nuzi." *Journal of Cuneiform Studies* 32 (1980): 189–207.

Parcak, Sarah H. *Satellite Remote Sensing for Archaeology*. New York: Routledge, 2009.

Parker, D. C. *An Introduction to the New Testament Manuscripts and Their Texts*. Cambridge, UK: Cambridge University Press, 2008.

———. "Was Matthew Written Before 50 CE? The Magdalen Papyrus Of Matthew." *Expository Times* 107 (1996): 40–43.

Parkinson, R. B., Whitfield Diffie, Mary Fischer, and R. S. Simpson. *Cracking Codes: The Rosetta Stone and Decipherment*. University of California Press, 1999.

Parrot, André, Georges Dossin, and Georges Boyer. *Archives Royales de Mari: Publiées Sous La Direction de André Parrot et Georges Dossin. Textes Juridiques: Transcrits, Traduits et Commentés Par Georges Boyer*. Vol. 8. 21 vols. Paris: Imprimerie Nationale, 1958.

Parslow, Christopher Charles. *Rediscovering Antiquity: Karl Weber and the Excavation of Herculaneum, Pompeii and Stabiae*. Cambridge: Cambridge University Press, 1998.

Patrich, Joseph, and Benjamin Arubas. "'Herod's Tomb' Reexamined: Guidelines for a Discussion and Conclusions." In *New Studies in the Archaeology of Jerusalem and Its Region*, edited by Gary D. Stiebel, Orit Peleg-Barkat, Doron Ben-Ami, Shlomit Weksler-Bdolahand, and Yuval Gadot, 7:287–300. Collected Papers. Jerusalem, Israel: Hebrew University, 2013.

Patterson, Stephen J., Hans-Gebhard Bethge, and James M. Robinson. *The Fifth Gospel: The Gospel of Thomas Comes of Age*. New York: Bloomsbury Academic, 1998.

Payton, Robert. "The Ulu Burun Writing-Board Set." *AS* 41 (1991): 99–106.

Peake, Arthur S. *The Revelation of John*. London, UK: Johnson, 1919.

Peek, Werner. "Die Hydrophore Vera von Patmos." *Rheinisches Museum Für Philologie*, 1964, 315–25.

Pedrini, Lura Nancy, and Duilio Thomas Pedrini. *Serpent Imagery and Symbolism: A Study of the Major English Romantic Poets*. New Haven, CT: College and University Press, 1966.

Pelekides, S. *Άπο Οήν Πολιτεία Χαί Χοινωνία Της Άρχαίας Θεσσαλονίχης*. Thessaloniki: Triantaphyllu, 1934.

Pellegrino, Charles R. *Return to Sodom and Gomorrah: Bible Stories from Archaeologists*. New York: Avon Books, 1995.

Perry, Jonathan S. "Sub-Elites." In *A Companion to Roman Italy*, edited by Alison E. Cooley, 498–512. Blackwell Companions to the Ancient World. New York: Wiley & Sons, 2016.

Petrovich, Douglas N. "The Ophel Pithos Inscription: Its Dating, Language, Translation, And Script." *PEQ* 147, no. 2 (June 2015): 130–45.

Petsalis-Diomidis, Alexia. *Truly Beyond Wonders: Aelius Aristides and the Cult of Asklepios*. Oxford: Oxford University Press, 2010.

Pfeiffer, Charles F. *Wycliffe Dictionary of Biblical Archaeology*. Peabody, MA: Hendrickson, 2000.

Pfleiderer, Otto. *Primitive Christianity: Its Writings and Teachings in Their Historical Connections*. Translated by W. Montgomery. 3 vols. London, UK: Williams & Norgate, 1910.

Pickering, S. R. "The Dating of the Chester Beatty-Michigan Codex of the Pauline Epistles (P46)." In *Ancient History in a Modern University: Volume II (Early Christianity, Late Antiquity And Beyond)*, edited by T. W. Hillard, R. A. Kearsley, C. E. V. Nixon, and A. M. Nobbs, 216–27. Ancient History Documentary Research Centre, Macquarie University, NSW Australia. Eerdmans, 1998.

Pilch, John J. "Lying and Deceit in the Letters to the Seven Churches: Perspectives from Cultural Anthropology." *Biblical Theology Bulletin* 22, no. 3 (1992): 126–35.

Pinkerton, John. *A General Collection of the Best and Most Interesting Voyages and Travels in All Parts of the World*. Vol. 10. London: Longman, Hurst, Rees, Orme, & Brown, 1811.

Plumptre, Edward Hayes. *A Popular Exposition of the Epistles to the Seven Churches of Asia*. London, UK: Hodder & Stoughton, 1887.

Pococke, Richard. *A Description of the East and Some Other Countries*. Vol. 2, Part 1. London: Bowyer, 1745.

Politis, Konstantinos D. "Death at the Dead Sea." *BAR* 38, no. 2 (2013): 42–54.

Politis, Konstantinos D., Amanda M. Kelly, Daniel Hull, and Rebecca Foote. "Survey and Excavations in the Ghawr as-Safi 2004." *ADAJ* 49 (2005): 313–26.

Politis, Konstantinos D., Adamantios Sampson, and Margaret O'Hea. "Ghawr As-Safi Survey and Excavations 2008-2009." *ADAJ* 53 (2009): 297–310.

Politis, Konstantinos D., Adamantios Sampson, Margaret O'Hea, and Georgios Papaioannou. "Survey and Excavations in the Ghawr as-Safi 2006–07." *ADAJ* 51 (2007): 199–210.

Pollard, Leslie N. "The Function of *loipos* in Contexts of Judgment and Salvation in the Book of Revelation." Ph.D., Andrews University, 2007.

Pollock, Susan. "Chronology of the Royal Cemetery of Ur." *Iraq* 47 (1985): 129–47.

Pons, Mariona Vernet. "The Etymology of Goliath in the Light of Carian PN Wljat/Wliat: A New Proposal." *Kadmos* 51 (May 2012): 143–64.

Porat, Roi, Rachel Chachy-Laureys, and Yakov Kalman. "The Continuation of the Activity of the Herodium Expedition for the Promotion of Research and Development of Herod." *The Institute of Archaeology: The Hebrew University of Jerusalem*, 1-11, July 2013.

Portefaix, Lilian. "The Image of Artemis Ephesia - A Symbolic Configuration Related to Her Mysteries?" In 100 *Jahre Österreichische Forschunge in Ephesos*, edited by Herwig Friesinger and Friedrich Krinzinger, 611–17. Archäologische Forschungen 1. Wien: VÖAW, 1999.

Porter, Stanley E. "Recent Efforts to Reconstruct Early Christianity on the Basis of Its Payrological Evidence." In *Christian Origins and Greco-Roman Culture: Social and Literary Contexts for the New Testament*, edited by Stanley E. Porter and Andrew W. Pitts, 71–84. Leiden: Brill, 2013.

———. "Why the Laodiceans Received Lukewarm Water (Rev 3:15–18)." *TynBul* 38 (1987): 143–49.

Poulter, Andrew G. *Nicopolis Ad Istrum: A Late Roman and Early Byzantine City: The Finds and the Biological Remains*. Vol. 3. Reports of the Research Committee of the Society of Antiquar 67. Oxford, UK: Society of Antiquaries of London, 2007.

———. *Nicopolis As Istrum: A Roman to Early Byzantine City: The Pottery and Glass*. Vol. 1. Reports of the Research Committee of the Society of Antiquar. London, UK: Bloomsbury, 1999.

Poulter, Andrew G., Thomas Blagg, and Judith Butcher. *Nicopolis Ad Istrum: A Roman, Late Roman and Early Byzantine City: Excavations 1985-1992*. Edited by J. Reynolds. Journal of Roman Studies Monograph 8. London, UK: Roman Society Publications, 1995.

Prag, Kay. "A Walk in the Wadi Hesban." *PEQ* 123, no. 1 (1991): 48–61.

———. "Preliminary Report on the Excavations at Tell Iktanu and Tall el-Hammam, Jordan 1990." *Levant* 23 (1991): 55–66.

———. "Tell Iktanu and Tell al-Hammam. Excavations in Jordan." *Manchester Archaeological Bulletin* 7 (1992): 15–19.

———. "The Excavations at Tell al-Hammam." *Syria* 70, no. 1–2 (1990): 271–73.

Prévost, Jean Pierre. *How to Read the Apocalypse*. Translated by John Bowden and Margaret Lydamore. The Crossroad Adult Christian Formation. New York: Crossroad, 1993.

Price, J. Randall, and H. Wayne House. *Zondervan Handbook of Biblical Archaeology: A Book by Book Guide to Archaeological Discoveries Related to the Bible*. Grand Rapids: Zondervan, 2018.

Price, J. Randall. *Rose Guide to the Temple*. Torrance, CA: Rose, 2012.

———. *The Dead Sea Scrolls Pamphlet: The Discovery Heard around the World*. Torrance, CA: Rose, 2005.

———. *The Stones Cry Out: What Archaeology Reveals About the Truth of the Bible*. Eugene, OR: Harvest House, 1997.

Price, Martin J., and Bluma L. Trell. *Coins and Their Cities: Architecture on the Ancient Coins of Greece, Rome, and Palestine*. Detroit, MI: Wayne State University Press, 1977.

Price, S. R. F. *Rituals and Power: The Roman Imperial Cult in Asia Minor*. Reprint. Cambridge, UK: Cambridge University Press, 1985.

Prigent, Pierre. *Apocalypse et Liturgie*. Cahiers Théologiques 52. Lausanne: Delachaux et Niestlé, 1964.

———. *L'Apocalypse de saint Jean*. Commentaire du Nouveau Testament. Lausanne: Delachaux et Niestlé, 1981.

Psychoyos, Dimitris K. "The Forgotten Art of Isopsephy and the Magic Number KZ." *Semiotica* 154, no. 1–4 (2005): 157–224.

Puech, Émile. "Le Tombeau de Siméon et Zacharie Dans La Vallée de Josaphat." *RB* 111 (2004): 563–77.

———. "L'ostracon de Khirbet Qeyafa et Les Débuts de La Royauté En Israël." *RB* 17 (2010): 162–84.

Puech, Émile, and Joseph Zias. "Le Tombeau de Zacharie et Siméon Au Monument Funéraire Dit d'Absalom Dans La Vallée de Josaphat." *RB* 110 (2003): 321–35.

Rabinovich, Abraham. "Operation Scroll: Recent Revelations about Qumran Promise to Shake up Dead Sea Scrolls Scholarship." *Jerusalem Post Magazine*, May 6, 1994.

Rainey, Anson F. "Historical Geography." In *Benchmarks in Time and Culture: An Introduction to Palestinian Archaeology*, edited by Joel F Drinkard, Gerald L Mattingly, and J. Maxwell, Callaway, Joseph A Miller, 353–68. ASOR/SBL Archaeology And Biblical Studies. Atlanta, Ga.: Scholars Press, 1988.

———. "Rainey's Challenge." *BAR* 17, no. 6 (1991): 56–60, 93.

———. "The 'House of David' and the House of the Deconstructionists." *BAR* 20, no. 6 (1994): 47.

———. "Watching for the Signal Fires of Lachis." *PEQ* 119 (1987): 149–51.

Rainey, Anson F, and R. Steven Notley. *The Sacred Bridge: Carta's Atlas of the Biblical World.* Jerusalem: Carta, 2005.

Rakicic, M. "The Bees of Ephesos." *The Celator* 8, no. 12 (1994): 6–12.

Ramage, Andrew, Crawford H. Greenewalt, Jr., and Faruk Akca. "The Fourteenth Campaign at Sardis (1971)." *BASOR*, no. 206 (1972): 9–39.

Ramsay, William M. *Cities and Bishoprics of Phrygia.* 2 vols. Oxford, UK: Oxford University Press, 1895.

———. *St. Paul the Traveler and Roman Citizen.* Edited by Mark W. Wilson. Reprinted from printing of 1897. Grand Rapids: Baker, 1966.

———. "Studies in the Roman Province Galatia: II. Dedications at the Sanctuary of Colonia Caesarea." *JRS* 8 (January 1, 1918): 107–45.

———. "Studies in the Roman Province Galatia. IX. Inscriptions of Antioch of Phrygia-towards-Pisidia (Colonia Caesarea)." *JRS* 16 (1926): 102–19.

———. "Studies in the Roman Province Galatia. VI.–Some Inscriptions of Colonia Caesarea Antiochea." *JRS* 14 (1924): 172–205.

———. *The Bearing of Recent Discovery on the Trustworthiness of the New Testament.* Classic Reprint 1911. Charleston, SC: Forgotten Books, 2012.

———. *The Church of the Roman Empire Before AD 170.* 3rd ed. London, UK: Hodder & Stoughton, 1894.

———. *The Cities of St. Paul: Their Influence on His Life and Thought, The Cities of Eastern Asia Minor.* Whitefish, MT: Kessinger, 2004.

———. *The Historical Geography of Asia Minor.* Cambridge, MA: Cambridge University Press, 2010.

———. *The Letters to Seven Churches of Asia and Their Place in the Plan of the Apocalypse.* London, UK: Hodder & Stoughton, 1904.

———. *The Letters to Seven Churches: Updated Edition.* Edited by Mark W. Wilson. Peabody, MA: Hendrickson, 1994.

Ramsey, George W. *The Quest for the Historical Israel.* Atlanta, Ga.: Knox, 1981.

Rapske, Brian M. "Exiles, Islands, and the Identity and Perspective of John in Revelation." In *Christian Origins and Greco-Roman Culture: Social and Literary Contexts for the New Testament*, edited by Stanley E. Porter and Andrew W. Pitts, 311–46. Texts and Editions for New Testament Study: Early Christianity in Its Hellenistic Context 1. Leiden: Brill, 2012.

Rast, Walter E. "Bab Edh-Dhraʿ and the Origin of the Sodom Saga." In *Archaeology and Biblical Interpretation: Essays in Memory of D. Glenn Rose*, edited by Leo G. Perdue, Lawrence E. Toombs, and Gary L. Johnson, 185–201. Atlanta, Ga.: John Knox, 1987.

———. "Bronze Age Cities along the Dead Sea." *Archaeology* 40, no. 1 (1987): 42–49.

———. "Settlement at Numeira." In *The Southeastern Dead Sea Plain Expedition: An Interim Report of the 1977 Season*, 35–44. AASOR 46. Cambridge: American Schools of Oriental Research, 1979.

———. "The Southeastern Dead Sea Valley Expedition, 1979." *BA* 43, no. 1 (1980): 60–61.

Rast, Walter E., and R. Thomas Schaub, eds. *Bab Edh-Dhra': Excavations in the Cemetery Directed by Paul W Lapp, 1965-1967*. Reports of the Expedition to the Dead Sea Plain, Jordan 1. Winona Lake, IN: Eisenbrauns, 1989.

———. "Expedition to the Southeastern Dead Sea Plain, Jordan, 1979." *American Schools of Oriental Research Newsletter*, no. 8 (1980): 12–17.

———. "Survey of the Southeastern Plain of the Dead Sea, 1973." *ADAJ* 19 (1974): 5–53, 175–85.

———. "The Dead Sea Expedition: Bab Edh-Dhra' and Numeira, May 24-July 10, 1981." *American Schools of Oriental Research Newsletter*, no. 4 (1982): 4–12.

Rast, Walter E., R. Thomas Schaub, David W. McCreery, Jack Donahue, and Mark A. McConaughy. "Preliminary Report of the 1979 Expedition to the Dead Sea Plain, Jordan." *BASOR* 240 (1980): 21–61.

Rautman, Marcus. "Sardis in Late Antiquity." In *Archaeology and the Cities of Late Antiquity in Asia Minor*, edited by Ortwin Dally and Christopher Ratté, 1–26. Ann Arbor, Mich.: Kelsey Museum of Archaeology, 2012.

Ray, J. D. *The Rosetta Stone and the Rebirth of Ancient Egypt*. Cambridge, MA: Harvard University Press, 2007.

Reese, David S. "Marine Invertebrates, Freshwater Shells, and Land Snails: Evidence from Specimens Mosaics, Wall Paintings, Sculputure, Jewelry, and Roman Authors." In *The Natural History of Pompeii*, edited by Wilhelmina Feemster Jashemski and Frederick G. Meyer, 292–314. Cambridge, UK: Cambridge University Press, 2002.

———. "The Industrial Exploitation of Murex Shells: Purple-Dye and Lime Production at Sidi Khrebish, Benghazi (Berenice)." *Libyan Studies* 11 (1980): 79–93.

Redford, Donald B. *A Study of the Biblical Story of Joseph: Genesis 37-50*. Leiden: Brill, 1970.

———. *Egypt, Canaan, and Israel in Ancient Times*. Princeton, NJ: Princeton University Press, 1993.

———. "Textual Sources for the Hyksos Period." In *The Hyksos: New Historical and Archaeological Perspectives*, edited by Eliezer D. Oren, 1–44. Philadelphia, PA: University of Pennsylvania Museum, 1997.

Regev, E. "Family Burial, Family Structure, and the Urbanization of Herodian Jerusalem." *PEQ* 136 (2004): 109–31.

Regev, Johanna, Pierre de Miroschedji, Raphael Greenberg, Eliot Braun, Zvi Greenhut, and Elisabetta Boaretto. "Chronology of the Early Bronze Age in the Southern Levant: New Analysis for a High Chronology." *Radiocarbon* 3–4 (2012): 525–66.

Reich, Ronny, and Eli Shukron. "Jerusalem, City of David." In *Hadashot Arkheologiyot: Excavations and Surveys in Israel*, edited by Zvi Ed Gal, 51–53. 115. Jerusalem, Israel: Israel Antiquities Authority, 2003.

———. "The Excavations at the Gihon Spring and Warren's Shaft System in the City of David." In *Ancient Jerusalem Revealed*, edited by Hillel Geva, 237–39. Jerusalem, Israel: Israel Exploration Society, 1994.

———. "The Siloam Pool in the Wake of Recent Discoveries." In *New Studies on Jerusalem*, edited by Eyal Baruch, Ayelet Levy-Reifer, and Avraham Faust, 137–39. 10. Jerusalem, Israel: Bar-Ilan University, 2004.

Reich, Ronny, Eli Shukron, and Omri Lernau. "Recent Discoveries in the City of David, Jerusalem." *IEJ* 57 (2007): 153–69.

———. "The Iron Age II Finds from the Rock-Cut 'Pool' near the Spring in Jerusalem: A Preliminary Report." In *Israel in Transition: From Late Bronze II to Iron IIA: (c. 1250-850 BCE): The Archaeology,* edited by Lester L. Grabbe, 1:138–43. The Library of Hebrew Bible/Old Testament Studies 491. New York: T&T Clark, 2008.

Reimer, Ivoni Richter. *Women in the Acts of Apostles: A Feminist Liberation Perspective.* Minneapolis, MN: Fortress, 1995.

Reinhold, Meyer. *History of Purple as a Status Symbol in Antiquity.* 116. Brussels: Latomus, 1970.

Rendsburg, Gary A. "Review of Literate Culture and Tenth-Century Canaan: The Tel Zayit Abecedary in Context by Ron E. Tappy; P. Kyle McCarter." *BASOR* 359 (August 1, 2010): 89–91.

Renfrew, Colin, and Paul G. Bahn. *Archaeology: Theories, Methods, and Practice.* 6th ed. New York: Thames & Hudson, 2012.

Rengstorf, Karl Heinrich. *Hirbet Qumran Und Die Bibliothek Vom Toten Meer.* Translated by J. R. Wilkie. Stuttgart, Germany: Kohlhammer, 1960.

Reymond, Robert L. *A New Systematic Theology of the Christian Faith.* 2nd ed. Nashville: Nelson, 1998.

Reynolds, Joyce. "New Evidence for the Imperial Cult in Julio-Claudian Aphrodisias." *Zeitschrift Für Papyrologie Und Epigraphik* 43 (1981): 317–27.

Richard, Suzanne, ed. *Near Eastern Archaeology: A Reader.* Winona Lake, IN: Eisenbrauns, 2003.

Rich, Claudius James. *Narrative of a Journey to the Site of Babylon in 1811.* London, UK: Duncan & Malcolm, 1839.

Ridgway, Brunilde Sismondo. *Hellenistic Sculpture II: The Styles of ca. 200–100 B.C.* Wisconsin Studies in Classics. Madison, WI: University of Wisconsin Press, 2000.

Riesner, Rainer. *Paul's Early Period: Chronology, Mission Strategy, Theology.* Translated by Douglas W. Stott. Grand Rapids: Eerdmans, 1998.

Ritmeyer, Leen. *The Quest: Revealing the Temple Mount in Jerusalem.* Jerusalem: Carta, 2006.

Ritti, Tullia. "Associazioni di mestiere a Hierapolis di Frigia." In *Viaggi e commerci nell'antichità,* edited by Bianca Maria Giannattasio, 65–84. Geneva: Università di Genova, Facoltà di Lettere, 1995.

Roach, John. "2,000-Year-Old Seed Sprouts, Sapling Is Thriving." *National Geographic News,* November 22, 2005. http://news.nationalgeographic. com/news/2005/11/1122_051122_old_seed.html.

Roberts, C. H. "An Early Papyrus of the First Gospel." *Harvard Theological Review* 46 (1953): 233.

———. *An Unpublished Fragment of the Fourth Gospel, in the John Rylands Library.* Manchester: Manchester University Press, 1935.

Roberts, Mark D. "Ancient Ephesus and the New Testament: How Our Knowledge of the Ancient City of Ephesus Enriches Our Knowledge of the New Testament." *Reflections on Christ, Church, and Culture,* 2011. http://www.patheos.com/blogs/markdroberts/series/ancient-ephesus-and-the-new-testament/.

Roberts, Richard. "The Tree of Life (Rev 2:7)." *Expository Times* 25 (1914): 332.

Robert, Louis. "Documents d'Asie Mineure." *BCH* 101, no. 1 (1977): 43–132.

Robinson, David M. "Roman Sculptures from Colonia Caesarea (Pisidian Antioch)." *The Art Bulletin* 9, no. 1 (1926): 5–69.

Robinson, Edward. *Later Biblical Researches in Palestine, and in the Adjacent Regions: A Journal of Travels in the Year 1852.* Boston, MA: Crocker and Brewster, 1856.

Robinson, George L. "Jordan." In *Dictionary of the Bible, One Vol.,* edited by James Hastings and John A. Selbie, 493–94. New York: Scribner's Sons, 1909.

Robinson, James M. *From the Nag Hammadi Codices to the Gospel of Mary and the Gospel of Judas*. Institute for Antiquity and Christianity Occasional Papers 48. Claremont, Calf.: Institute for Antiquity & Christianity, 2006.

———. "The Discovery of the Nag Hammadi Codices." *BA* 42, no. 4 (October 1, 1979): 206–24.

Robinson, John A. T. "The Baptism of John and the Qumran Community." In *Twelve New Testament Studies*, 11–17. Studies in Biblical Theology 34. London, UK: SCM, 1962.

Rogers, Guy MacLean. *The Mysteries of Artemis of Ephesos: Cult, Polis, and Change in the Greaeco-Roman World*. New Haven, CT: Yale University Press, 2012.

Rogers, Guy Maclean. *The Sacred Identity of Ephesos: Foundation Myths of a Roman City. Routledge Revivals*. New York: Routledge, 2014.

Rohde, Erwin. *Pergamon: Burgberg Und Altar*. Berlin: Henschelverlag, 1982.

Rohl, David M. *A Test Of Time: Volume One-The Bible-From Myth to History*. London, UK: Arrow, 2001.

———. *From Eden to Exile: The Five-Thousand-Year History of the People of the Bible*. Lebanon, Tenn.: Greenleaf, 2009.

———. *Pharaohs and Kings: A Biblical Quest*. New York: Three Rivers, 1997.

———. *The Lords Of Avaris: Uncovering the Legendary Origins of Western Civilisation*. Hawthorn, Australia: Cornerstone Digital, 2010.

Rollston, Christopher A. "The Khirbet Qeiyafa Ostracon: Methodological Musings and Caveats." *Journal of the Institute of Archaeology of Tel Aviv University* 38, no. 1 (2011): 67–82.

———. "The Phoenician Script of the Tel Zayit Abecedary and Putative Evidence for Israelite Literacy." In *Literate Culture and Tenth-Century Canaan: The Tel Zayit Abecedary in Context*, edited by Ron E. Tappy and P. Kyle McCarter Jr., 61–96. Winona Lake, IN: Eisenbrauns, 2008.

———. "What's the Oldest Hebrew Inscription?" *BAR* 38, no. 3 (June 2012): 32–40, 66–68.

Roloff, Jürgen. The Revelation of John. Translated by John E. Alsup. CC. Minneapolis, MN: Fortress, 1993.

Romer, John. *The History of Archaeology: Great Excavations of the World*. New York: Checkmark, 2001.

Roskams, Steve. *Excavation*. Cambridge Manuals in Archaeology. Cambridge, UK: Cambridge University Press, 2001.

Rothenberg, Beno. "Notes and News." *PEQ* 98 (1966): 3–7.

Rowley-Conwy, Peter. *From Genesis to Prehistory: The Archaeological Three Age System and Its Contested Reception in Denmark, Britain, and Ireland*. Oxford Studies in the History of Archaeology. Oxford, UK: Oxford University Press, 2007.

Rowley, Harold Henry. "The Baptism of John and the Qumran Sect." In *New Testament Essays*, edited by A. J. B. Higgins, 219–23. Manchester, MI: Manchester University Press, 1959.

Rudwick, M. J. S., and E. M. B. Green. "The Laodicean Lukewarmness." *ExpTim* 69 (1958): 176–78.

Rufus, John. "Vita Petri Iberi." In *Petrus Der Iberer. Ein Characterbild Zur Kirchen- Und Sittengeschichte Des Fünften Jahrhundert*, translated by Richard Raabe. Leipzig: J. C. Hinrichs'sche Buchhandlung, 1895.

Ruscillo, Deborah. "Reconstructing Murex Royal Purple and Biblical Blue in the Aegean." In *Archaeomalacology: Molluscs in Former Environments of Human Behaviour*, edited by Daniella Bar-Yosef Mayer, 99–106. Oxford: Oxbow Books, 2005.

Russell, J. C. *Late Ancient and Medieval Population*. APSP. Philadelphia, PA: American Philosophical Society, 1958.

Rummel, Stan. *Ras Shamra Parallels: The Texts From Ugarit and the Hebrew Bible.* Rome: Pontificium Institutum Biblicum, 1981.

Sabin, Philip, Hans van Wees, and Michael Whitby. *The Cambridge History of Greek and Roman Warfare: Volume 1, Greece, The Hellenistic World and the Rise of Rome.* Cambridge, UK: Cambridge University Press, 2007.

Sáenz-Badillos, Angel. *A History of the Hebrew Language.* Translated by John Elwolde. Cambridge, UK: Cambridge University Press, 1996.

Saffrey, H. D. "Relire l'Apocalypse À Patmos." *RB* 82 (1975): 385–417.

Safrai, Shemuel, M. Stern, and David Flusser. *The Jewish People in the First Century: Historical Geography, Political History, Social, Cultural and Religious Life and Institutions.* Assen, Netherlands: Uitgeverij Van Gorcum, 1974.

Saftner, Bernard. *Punctuated Equilibrium Featuring The Proepistrephomeniad.* Bloomington, Ind.: Xlibris, 2008.

Saldarini, Anthony D. "Babatha's Story." *BAR* 24, no. 2 (1998): 28–37, 72.

Salisbury, Edward E. "Colonel Rawlinson's Outlines of Assyrian History, Derived from His Latest Readings of Cuneiform Inscriptions." *Journal of the American Oriental Society* 3 (January 1, 1853): 486–90.

Sallon, S., E. Solowey, Y. Cohen, R. Korchinsky, M. Egli, I. Woodhatch, O. Simchoni, and M. Kislev. "Germination, Genetics, and Growth of an Ancient Date Seed." *Science* 320, no. 5882 (June 13, 2008): 1464.

Salt, Henry, Jean-François Champollion, and Thomas Young. *Essay on Dr. Young's and M. Champollion's Phonetic System of Hieroglyphics: With Some Additional Discoveries.* London, UK: Londman, Hurst, Rees, Orme, Brown & Green, 1823.

Sanders, Henry A. "The Number of the Beast in Revelation." *JBL*, 95-99, 37, no. 1 (1918).

Sanders, Seth L. "Writing and Early Iron Age Israel: Before National Scripts, beyond Nations and States." In *Literate Culture and Tenth-Century Canaan: The Tel Zayit Abecedary in Context*, edited by Ron E. Tappy and P. Kyle McCarter Jr., 97–112. Winona Lake, IN: Eisenbrauns, 2008.

Sarna, Nahum M. *Genesis: The Traditional Hebrew Text with the New JPS Translation.* JPS Torah Commentary. Philadelphia: Jewish Publication Society, 1989.

———. "The Patriarchs Genesis 12-36." In *Genesis: World of Myths and Patriarchs*, edited by Ada Feyerick, Cyrus Herzl Gordon, and Nahum M Sarna, 117–66. New York: New York University Press, 1996.

Sass, Benjamin. *The Alphabet at the Turn of the Millennium: West Semitic Alphabet CA 1150-850 BCE.* Tel Aviv Occasional Publications 4. Tel-Aviv: Institute of Archaeology, 2009.

Sauter, Megan. "Isaiah's Signature Uncovered in Jerusalem Evidence of the Prophet Isaiah?" *Bible History Daily: Biblical Archaeology Society*, February 22, 2018.

Sayce, A. H. *The Hittites the Story of a Forgotten Empire.* Classic Reprint. Charleston, SC: Forgotten Books, 2012.

Schäfer, Jörg. "Pergamon Mysia, Turkey." In *The Princeton Encyclopedia of Classical Sites,* edited by Richard Stillwell, William L. MacDonald, and Marian Holland McAllister, 688–91. Princeton, NJ: Princeton University Press, 1976.

Scham, Sandra. "An Apology for Judas." *Archaeology* 59, no. 4 (2006): 50–51.

Schaub, R. Thomas, and Walter E. Rast. *The Southeastern Dead Sea Plain Expedition: An Interim Report of the 1977 Season.* AASOR 46. Boston, MA: American Schools of Oriental Research, 1979.

Scherrer, Peter, ed. *Ephesus: The New Guide.* Turkey: Ege Yayinin, 2000.

Schick, C. "Phoenician Inscription in the Pool of Siloam." *PEQ* 12, no. 4 (1880): 238–39.

Schiffman, Lawrence H., ed. *Archaeology and History in the Dead Sea Scrolls: The New York University Conference in Memory of Yigael Yadin.* Vol. JSOT/ASOR Monographs 2. Journal for the Study of the Pseudepigrapha Supplement Series 8. Sheffield, UK: JSOT Press, 1990.

———. *Reclaiming the Dead Sea Scrolls: The History of Judaism, The Background of Christianity, The Lost Library of Qumran.* Anchor Bible Reference Library. New York: Doubleday, 1995.

Schlier, Heinrich. *Principalities and Powers in the New Testament.* New York: Herder & Herder, 1961.

Schmid, S. G. "Decline or Prosperity at Roman Eretria? Industry, Purple Dye Works, Public Buildings, and Gravestones." *JRA* 12 (1999): 273–93.

Schmidt, Evamaria. *The Great Altar of Pergamon.* Boston, MA: Boston Book and Art Shop, 1965.

Schnabel, Eckhard J. *Acts.* Edited by Clinton E. Arnold. ZECNT 5. Grand Rapids, Mich.: Zondervan, 2012.

Schoville, Keith N. "Top Ten Archaeological Discoveries of the Twentieth Century Relating to the Biblical World." *Stone Campbell Journal* 4, no. 1 (2001): 29–34.

Schuler, Carl. "The Macedonian Politarch." *Classical Philology* 55 (1960): 90–100.

Schultz, Samuel J., and Gary V. Smith. *Exploring the Old Testament.* Wheaton, IL: Crossway, 2001.

Schürer, Emil. *Die Prophetin Isabel in Thyatira, Offen. Joh., II, 20, 11.* Edited by A. V. Harnack. Theologische Abhandlungen: Carl von Weizsäcker Zu Seinem Siebzigsten Geburtstage. Freiburg, Germany: Mohr Siebeck, 1892.

———. *The History of the Jewish People in the Age of Jesus Christ (175 BC–AD 135).* Edited by G. Vermes, F. Miller, and M. Black. Rev. 4 vols. Edinburgh, UK: T&T Clark, 1979.

Scobie, Charles H. "Local References in the Letters to the Seven Churches." *NTS* 39, no. 4 (1993): 606–24.

Scroggs, Robin. "The Sociological Interpretation of the New Testament: The Present State of Research." *NTS*, Sociological Interpretation of the NT, 26 (1980): 164–79.

Seager, Andrew R. "The Building History of the Sardis Synagogue." *AJA* 76 (1972): 425–35.

Segal, Peretz. "The Penalty of the Warning Inscription from the Temple of Jerusalem." *IEJ* 39, no. 1/2 (1989): 79–84.

Seiss, J. A. *The Apocalypse.* 3 vols. Colorado Springs, Colo.: Cook, 1906.

Selman, M. J. "Comparative Customs and the Patriarchal Age." In *Essays on the Patriarchal Narratives*, edited by Alan R. Millard and Donald J. Wiseman, 2nd ed., 91–139. Downers Grove, IL: InterVarsity, 1983.

Selwyn, Edward Carus. *The Christian Prophets and the Prophetic Apocalypse.* New York: MacMillan, 2009.

Seters, John Van. *Abraham in History and Tradition.* New Haven, CT: Yale University Press, 1975.

———. *In Search of History: Historiography in the Ancient World and the Origins of Biblical History.* Winona Lake, IN: Eisenbrauns, 1997.

———. *The Biblical Saga of King David.* Winona Lake, IN: Eisenbrauns, 2009.

Shanks, Hershel. "BAR Interviews Giovanni Pettinato: Original Ebla Epigrapher Attempts to Set the Record Straight." *BAR* 6, no. 5 (1980): 46–52.

———. "Breaking News: Golan and Deutsch Acquitted of All Forgery Charges: Forgery Allegations Dismissed by James Ossuary Trial Verdict." *Bible History Daily: Biblical Archaeology Society*, March 14, 2012. http://www.biblicalarchaeology.org/ daily/breaking-news-golan-and-deutsch-acquitted-of-all-forgery-charges/.

———. "Newly Discovered: A Fortified City from King David's Time Answers—and Questions—at Khirbet Qeiyafa." *BAR* 35, no. 1 (2009): 38–42.

———. "Prize Find: Oldest Hebrew Inscription Discovered in Israelite Fort on Philistine Border." *BAR* 36, no. 2 (April 2010): 51–55.

———. "Ritual Bath or Swimming Pool?" *BAR* 34, no. 3 (2008): 18.

———. "The Exodus and the Crossing of the Red Sea, According to Hans Goedicke." *BAR* 7, no. 5 (1981): 42–50.

———. "The Sad Case of Tell Gezer." *BAR* 9, no. 4 (1983): 30–42.

———. "The Siloam Pool: Where Jesus Cured the Blind Man." *BAR* 31, no. 5 (2005): 17–23.

———. "Was Herod's Tomb Really Found?" *BAR* 40, no. 3 (2014).

———. "When Did Israel Begin? New Hieroglyphic Inscription May Date Israel's Ethogenesis 200 Years Earlier than You Thought." In *Ancient Israel in Egypt and the Exodus*, edited by Dorothy Resig, 31–37. Washington, DC: Biblical Archaeology Society, 2012.

———. "When Did Israel Begin? New Hieroglyphic Inscription May Date Israel's Ethogenesis 200 Years Earlier than You Thought." *BAR* 38, no. 1 (2012): 59–62, 67.

Shanks, Hershel, Niels Peter Lemche, Thomas L. Thompson, William G. Dever, and P. Kyle McCarter Jr. "Face to Face: Biblical Minimalists Meet Their Challenge." *BAR* 23, no. 4 (1997): 26–42, 66.

Shanks, Hershel, and Ben Witherington III. *The Brother of Jesus: The Dramatic Story and Meaning of the First Archaeological Link to Jesus and His Family*. Rev Upd. New York: HarperCollins, 2009.

Shea, William H. "Amenhotep II as Pharaoh of the Exodus." *Bible and Spade* 16 (2003): 41–51.

———. "Two Palestinian Segments from the Eblaite Geographical Atlas." In *Word of the Lord Shall Go Forth: Essays in Honor of David Noel Freedman in Celebration of His Sixtieth Birthday*, edited by Carol L. Meyers and M. O'Connor, 589–612. American Schools of Oriental Research. Winona Lake, IN: Eisenbrauns, 1983.

Shiloh, Yigael. "Elements in the Development of Town Planning in the Israelite City." *IEJ* 28 (1978): 36–51.

———. "The Four-Room House: Its Situation and Function in the Israelite City." *IEJ* 20, no. 3/4 (1970): 180–90.

———. "Torah Scrolls and the Menorah Plaque from Sardis." *IEJ* 18, no. 1 (1968): 54–57.

Shiloh, Yigal, and David Tarler. "Bullae from the City of David: A Hoard of Seal Impressions from the Israelite Period." *BA* 49, no. 4 (1986): 196–209.

Shoham, Yair. "Hebrew Bullae." In *Excavations at the City of David 1978-1985, Directed by Yigal Shiloh: Inscriptions,* edited by Donald T. Ariel, 6:33. Qedem 41. Jerusalem: Hebrew University of Jerusalem, 2000.

Shtull-Trauring, Asaf. "'Hammurabi-like' Cuneiform Discovered at Tel Hazor." *Haaretz*, July 27, 2010. http://www.haaretz.com/print-edition /news/hammurabi-like-cuneiform-discovered-at-tel-hazor-1.304266.

Silva, Moisés, and Karen Jobes. *Invitation to the Septuagint.* Grand Rapids: Baker Academic & Brazos, 2005.

Silverberg, Robert. *Great Adventures in Archaeology*. Lincoln, Neb.: University of Nebraska Press, 1964.

Silvia, Phillip J. "The Middle Bronze Age Civilization-Ending Destruction of the Middle Ghor." Ph.D. diss., Trinity Southwest University, 2016.

Şimşek, Celal, and Mustafa Büyükkolancı. "Die Aquäducte Und Das Wasserverteilungssystem von Laodikeia Ad Lycum." In *Cura Aquarum In Ephesus: Proceedings of the Twelfth International Congress on the History of Water Management and Hydraulic Engineering in the Mediterranean Region (Ephesus-Selçuck, October 2-10, 2004), Part 1,* edited by Gilbert Wiplinger, 137–46. BABesch Suppl. 12. Leuven, Belgium: Peeters, 2006.

Şimşek, Celal. "Ancient 'Water Law' Unearthed in Laodicea." *Hürriyet Daily News,* September 13, 2011. http://www.hurriyetdailynews.com/ancient-water-law-unearthed-in-laodicea-.aspx?pageID=238&nid=87259.

Singer-Avitz, Lily. "The Date of the Pottery from the Rock-Cut Pool Near the Gihon Spring in the City of David, Jerusalem." *ZDPV* 128 (2012): 10–14.

Singer, Isidore, Cyrus Adler, Gotthard Deutsch, Kaufmann Kohler, and Emil G. Hirsch, eds. *The Jewish Encyclopedia.* 12 vols. New York: Funk & Wagnalls, 1906.

Singer, Suzanne F. "Herod the Great—The King's Final Journey." *BAR* 39, no. 2 (2013): 14.

Sinopoli, Carla M. *Approaches to Archaeological Ceramics.* Berlin: Springer Science & Business Media, 1991.

Sire, James W. *The Universe Next Door: A Basic Worldview Catalog.* Downers Grove, IL: InterVarsity, 1997.

Sivan, Daniel. "The Gezer Calendar and Northwest Semitic Linguistics." *IEJ* 48, no. 1–2 (1998): 101–5.

Sivertsen, Barbara J. *The Parting of the Sea: How Volcanoes, Earthquakes, and Plagues Shaped the Story of Exodus.* Princeton, NJ: Princeton University Press, 2011.

Skinner, Christopher W. *What Are They Saying About the Gospel of Thomas?.* New York: Paulist, 2012.

Slootjes, Daniëlle. *The Governor and His Subjects in the Later Roman Empire.* Leiden: Brill, 2006.

Slingerland, H. Dixon. "Acts 18:1-18, the Gallio Inscription, and Absolute Pauline Chronology." *JBL* 110, no. 3 (1991): 439–49.

Smalley, Stephen S. *The Revelation to John: A Commentary on the Greek Text of the Apocalypse.* Downers Grove, IL: InterVarsity, 2005.

Smallwood, E. Mary. *Documents Illustrating the Principates of Gaius Claudius and Nero.* Bristol: Bristol Classical, 1983.

———. *The Jews Under Roman Rule: From Pompey to Diocletian: A Study in Political Relations.* SJLA 20. Leiden: Brill, 1981.

Smith, George E. *Assyrian Discoveries: An Account of Explorations and Discoveries on the Site on Nineveh, During 1878 and 1874.* New York: Scribner, Armstrong & Co., 1875.

Smith, Robert Houston. "The Household Lamps of Palestine in Intertestamental Times." *The Biblical Archaeologist* 27, no. 4 (December 1, 1964): 101–24.

———. "The Household Lamps of Palestine in New Testament Times." *The Biblical Archaeologist* 29, no. 1 (February 1, 1966): 2–27.

———. "The Household Lamps of Palestine in Old Testament Times." *The Biblical Archaeologist* 27, no. 1 (February 1, 1964): 2–31.

Smith, William, William Wayte, and George Elden Marindin, eds. *A Dictionary of Greek and Roman Antiquities.* 3rd ed. 2 vols. London, UK: Murray, 1891.

Soanes, Catherine, and Angus Stevenson. *Concise Oxford English Dictionary.* 11th ed. Oxford, UK: Oxford University Press, 2005.

Sober, Elliott. "Let's Razor Ockham's Razor." In *From a Biological Point of View: Essays in Evolutionary Philosophy*, edited by Elliott Sober, 136–57. Cambridge Studies in Philosophy and Biology. Cambridge, UK: Cambridge University Press, 1994.

Sogliano, Antonio. "Isopsephia Pompeiana." *Rendiconti Della Reale Academia Dei Lincei* 10 (1901): 256–59.

Southern, Pat. *The Roman Army: A Social and Institutional History.* Oxford, UK: Oxford University Press, 2007.

Spanier, Ehud, Nira Karmon, and Elisha Linder. "Bibliography Concerning Various Aspects of the Purple Dye." *Levantina* 37 (1982): 437–47.

Sparks, Brad C. *Egyptian Text Parallels to the Exodus*, Forthcoming.

———. "Egyptian Text Parallels to the Exodus: The Egyptology Literature." In *Out of Egypt: Israel's Exodus Between Text and Memory, History and Imagination Conference*, edited by Thomas E. Levy. University of California, San Diego, 2013. https://www.youtube .com/watch?v=F-Aomm4O794.

Sparks, Kenton L. *Ancient Texts for the Study of the Hebrew Bible: A Guide to the Background Literature.* Grand Rapids: Hendrickson, 2005.

Speidel, Michael. "The Roman Army in Judaea under the Procurators." In *Roman Army Studies*, edited by Michael Speidel, 224–32. Stuttgart: Gieben, 1992.

Speiser, E. A. *Genesis: Introduction, Translation, and Notes.* The Anchor Bible. New York: Doubleday, 1964.

———. "The Wife-Sister Motif in the Patriarchal Narratives." In *Biblical and Other Studies*, edited by Amnon Altman, 15–28. Cambridge, MA: Harvard University Press, 1963.

Spodek, Howard. *World's History: Combined Volume.* 4th ed. Upper Saddle River, NJ: Prentice Hall, 2010.

Staff, IMFA. "Unique Biblical Discovery at City of David Excavation Site." *Israel Ministry of Foreign Affairs*, August 18, 2008. http://www.mfa.gov.il/MFA/History/Early+History+-+Archaeology/Unique+biblical+discovery+at+City+of+David+excavation+site+18-Aug-2008.htm.

Staff "Noah's Ark? Boat like Form Is Seen near Ararat." *Life Magazine*, September 5, 1960.

Staff "'Oldest Hebrew Script' Is Found." *BBC*, October 30, 2008, sec. Middle East. http://news.bbc.co.uk/2/hi/middle_east/7700037.stm.

Staff. "Rare Find Reveals Previously Unknown Roman Ruler in Judea." *The Times of Israel* (blog), January 24, 2018. http://www.timesofisrael.com/rare-find-reveals-previously-unknown-roman-ruler-in-judea.

Stambaugh, John E., and David L. Balch. *The New Testament in Its Social Environment.* LEC 2. Philadelphia, PA: Westminster, 1986.

Steiner, Margreet L. "It's Not There: Archaeology Proves a Negative." *BAR* 24, no. 4 (1998): 26–33, 62–63.

———. "The 'Palace of David' Reconsidered in the Light of Earlier Excavations: Did Eilat Mazar Find King David's Palace? I Would Say Not." *The Bible and Interpretation*, September 2009. http://www.bibleinterp.com /articles/palace_2468.shtml.

Steinmann, Andrew E. *From Abraham to Paul: A Biblical Chronology.* St. Louis, Miss.: Concordia, 2011.

———. "The Mysterious Numbers Of the Book of Judges." *JETS* 48 (2005): 491–500.

Stern, Ephraim, and Ilan Sharon. "Tel Dor, 1986: Preliminary Report." *IEJ* 37, no. 4 (1987): 201–11.

Stern, Ephraim, Ayelet Levinson-Gilboa, and Joseph Aviram, eds. *The New Encyclopedia of Archaeological Excavations in the Holy Land.* 4 vols. New York: MacMillan, 1993.

Stern, Ephraim, Ilan Sharon, and Ayelet Gilboa. "Tel Dor 1987: Preliminary Report." *IEJ* 39, no. 1/2 (1989): 32–42.

Stetson, Brad, and Joseph G. Conti. *The Truth About Tolerance: Pluralism, Diversity and the Culture Wars*. Downers Grove, IL: InterVarsity, 2005.

Stewart, Andrew. "Pergamo Ara Marmorea Magna: On the Date, Reconstruction, and Functions of the Great Altar of Pergamon." In *From Pergamon to Sperlonga: Sculpture and Context,* edited by Nancy T. de Grummond and Brunilde Sismondo Ridgway, 32–57. Hellenistic Culture and Society. Berkeley, CA: University of California Press, 2001.

Stewart, Zeph. "Greek Crowns and Christian Martyrs." In *Mémorial André-Jean Festugière: Antiquité Païenne et Chrétienne*, edited by E. Lucchesi and H. D. Saffrey, 119–24. Geneva: Cramer, 1984.

Stiebing, Jr., William H. "Climate and Collapse: Did the Weather Make Israel's Emergence Possible?" *Bible Review* 10, no. 4 (1994): 18–27, 54.

———. *Out of the Desert?: Archaeology and the Exodus/Conquest Narratives*. Buffalo, NY: Prometheus, 1989.

———. "The End of the Mycenean Age." *BA* 43, no. 1 (1980): 7–21.

Stillwell, Richard, William L. MacDonald, and Marian Holland McAllister, eds. *The Princeton Encyclopedia of Classical Sites*. Princeton, NJ: Princeton University Press, 1976.

Stone, Michael E., ed. *Jewish Writings of the Second Temple Period: Apocrypha, Pseudepigrapha, Qumran Sectarian Writings, Philo, Josephus*. The Literature of the Jewish People of the Second Temple and the Talmud 2. Leiden: Brill Academic, 1984.

Strange, James F. "The Book of Joshua: A Hasmonean Manifesto?" In *History and Traditions of Early Israel: Studies Presented to Eduard Nielsen*, edited by André LeMaire and Benedikt Otzen, 136–41. VTSup 50. Leiden: Brill Academic, 1993.

Strange, James F., and Hershel Shanks. "Synagogue Where Jesus Preached Found at Capernaum." *BAR* 9, no. 6 (1983): 24–31.

Strange, John. "The Transition from the Bronze Age to the Iron Age in the Eastern Mediterranean and the Emergence of the Israelite State." *Scandinavian Journal of the Old Testament* 1, no. 1 (1987): 1–19.

Strelan, Rick. Paul, *Artemis, and the Jews in Ephesus*. Berlin: de Gruyter, 1996.

Stripling, D. Scott. "Have We Walked in the Footsteps of Jesus? Exciting New Possibilities at Khirbet El-Maqatir." *Bible and Spade* 27, no. 4 (2014): 88–94.

———. "The Israelite Tabernacle at Shiloh." *Bible and Spade* 29, no. 3 (2016): 88–94.

Stripling, D. Scott, Bryant G. Wood, Gary A. Byers, and Titus M. Kennedy. "Renewed Excavations at Khirbet El-Maqatir: Highlights of the 2009–2011 Seasons." In *Collected Studies of the Staff Office of Archaeology of Judea and Samaria*, Forthcoming. Judea and Samaria Publication 13. Jerusalem: Israel Antiquities Authority, 2014.

Stuart, Moses. *A Commentary on the Apocalypse*. 2 vols. Whitefish, MT: Kessinger, 2007.

Sussman, Varda. *Ornamented Jewish Oil Lamps: From the Destruction of the Second Temple through the Bar-Kokhba Revolt*. Reprint. Ancient Near East. Jerusalem: Aris & Phillips, 1983.

———. *Roman Period Oil Lamps in the Holy Land: Collection of the Israel Antiquities Authority*. Oxford: British Archaeological Reports, 2012.

Sweet, John Philip McMurdo. *Revelation*. T P I New Testament Commentaries. Valley Forge, PA: Trinity Press International, 1990.

Swete, Henry Barclay. *Commentary on Revelation*. Reprint 1906. Eugene, OR: Wipf & Stock, 1999.

———. *The Apocalypse of St. John*. 3rd ed. London: MacMillan & Co., 1917.

Tabachnick, Stephen Ely. "Lawrence of Arabia as Archaeologist." *Biblical Archaeology Society* 23, no. 5 (1997): 40–47, 70–71.

Tabor, James D. *The Jesus Dynasty: The Hidden History of Jesus, His Royal Family, and the Birth of Christianity.* New York: Simon & Schuster, 2007.

Tait, Andrew. *The Messages to the Seven Churches of Asia Minor: An Exposition of the First Three Chapters of the Book of the Revelation.* London, UK: Hodder & Stoughton, 1884.

Talmon, Shemarayahu. "Was the Book of Esther Known at Qumran?" *Dead Sea Discoveries* 2, no. 3 (November 1995): 249–67.

Tanriöver, Y. Ersel, and N. Orhan Baykan. "The Water Supply Systems of Caria." In *Cura Aquarum In Ephesus: Proceedings of the Twelfth International Congress on the History of Water Management and Hydraulic Engineering in the Mediterranean Region (Ephesus-Selçuck, October 2-10, 2004), Part 1,* edited by Gilbert Wiplinger, 127–32. BABesch Suppl. 12. Leuven, Belgium: Peeters, 2006.

Tappy, Ron E., and P. Kyle McCarter Jr., eds. *Literate Culture and Tenth-Century Canaan: The Tel Zayit Abecedary in Context.* Winona Lake, IN: Eisenbrauns, 2008.

Tappy, Ron E., P. Kyle McCarter Jr., Marilyn J. Lundberg, and Bruce Zuckerman. "An Abecedary of the Mid-Tenth Century B.C.E. from the Judaean Shephelah." *BASOR* 344 (2006): 5–46.

Tarn, W. W. *Hellenistic Civilization.* 3rd ed. London, UK: Arnold & Co., 1952.

Taslialan, Mehmet. "New Excavations and Restorations in the Agora of Smyrna." In *Paper Presented at Institut Für Archäologie, Abt. Archäologie Des Mittelmeerraumes.* University of Berne, Institute of Archaeology, June 24, 2004.

Tattersall, Ian, and Winfried Henke, eds. *Handbook of Paleoanthropology.* 3 vols. New York: Springer, 2007.

Taylor, James E. *Introducing Apologetics: Cultivating Christian Commitment.* Grand Rapids: Baker Academic, 2006.

Taylor, Jeremy, and Reginald Heber. *The Whole Works of the Right Rev. Jeremy Taylor: With a Life of the Author and a Critical Examination of His Writings.* London, U.K.: Rivington, 1828.

Taylor, R. E. *Radiocarbon Dating an Archaeological Perspective.* Amsterdam: Academic Press, 1987.

Ten Dam, A., and C. Erentöz. "Kizildere Geothermal Field — Western Anatolia." *Geothermics* 2 (January 1, 1970): 124–29.

Tenney, Merrill C., and Moisés Silva, eds. *Zondervan Pictorial Encyclopedia of the Bible.* Revised, Full-Color Edition. 5 vols. Grand Rapids: Zondervan, 2009.

Tenney, Merrill C. *New Testament Times: Understanding the World of the First Century.* Grand Rapids: Baker, 2004.

Tepper, Yotam, and Leah Di Segni. *A Christian Prayer Hall of the Third Century CE at Kefar 'Othnay (Legio): Excavations at the Megiddo Prison 2005.* Jerusalem: Israel Antiquities Authority, 2006.

Thiede, Carsten P. "Papyrus Magdalen Greek 17 (Gregory-Aland P64): A Reappraisal." *Tyndale Bulletin* 46 (1995): 29–42.

———. "Papyrus Magdalen Greek 17 (Gregory-Aland P64): A Reappraisal." *Zeitschrift Für Papyrologie Und Epigraphik* 105 (1995): 13–20.

Thiele, Edwin Richard. *The Mysterious Numbers of the Hebrew Kings: A Reconstruction of the Chronology of the Kingdoms of Israel and Judah.* Revised. Grand Rapids: Kregel Academic & Professional, 1994.

Thiering, B. E. "Inner and Outer Cleansing at Qumran as a Background to New Testament Baptism." *NTS* 26, no. 2 (1980): 266–77.

Thimmes, Pamela. "Women Reading Women in the Apocalypse: Reading Scenario 1, the Letter to Thyatira (Rev. 2:18–29)." *CBR* 2, no. 1 (2003): 128–44.

Thomas, Robert L. *Revelation 1-7 Commentary*. Chicago, IL: Moody, 1992.

Thommen, Geraldine. "The Sebasteion at Aphrodisias: An Imperial Cult to Honor Augustus and the Julio-Claudian Emperors." *Chronika* 2 (2012): 82–91.

Thompson, Henry O. *Biblical Archaeology: The World, the Mediterranean, the Bible*. New York: Paragon, 1987.

———. "Thoughts On Archeological Method." *BAR* 3, no. 3 (1977): 225–27.

Thompson, Leonard L. *The Book of Revelation: Apocalypse and Empire*. New York: Oxford University Press, USA, 1997.

Thompson, Thomas L. *Early History of the Israelite People: From the Written & Archaeological Sources*. Leiden: Brill, 2000.

———. *The Bible in History: How Writers Create a Past*. London: Jonathan Cape, 1999.

———. *The Historicity of the Patriarchal Narratives: The Quest for the Historical Abraham*. Valley Forge, PA: Trinity Press International, 2002.

———. *The Mythic Past: Biblical Archaeology And The Myth Of Israel*. New York: Basic Books, 2000.

Thompson, Thomas L., and Dorothy Irwin. "The Joseph and Moses Narratives." In *Israelite and Judaean History*, edited by John H. Hayes and J. Maxwell Miller, 149–212. Philadelphia, PA: Westminster, 1977.

Thomson, William M. *The Land and the Book: Lebanon, Damascus, and Beyond Jordan*. Vol. 3. 3 vols. New York: Harper & Brothers, 1886.

———. *The Land and the Book: Southern Palestine and Jerusalem*. Vol. 1. 3 vols. New York: Harper & Brothers, 1880.

Thorburn, William M. "The Myth of Occam's Razor." *Mind*, New Series, 27, no. 107 (July 1, 1918): 345–53.

Ticonius. *The Turin Fragments of Tyconius' Commentary on Revelation*. Edited by Francesco Lo Bue. Texts and Studies: Contributions to Biblical and Patristic Literature. Cambridge, UK: Cambridge University Press, 2009.

Tilborg, Sjef Van. *Reading John in Ephesus*. NovTSup 83. Leiden: Brill Academic, 1997.

Toker, Tarhan. *Pamukkale (Hierapolis)*. Denizli, Turkey: Haber Gazetecilik, 1976.

Tours, Gregory of. *Glory of the Martyrs [Liber in Gloria Martyrum]*. Translated by Raymond Van Dam. Translated Texts for Historians Latin Series 3. Liverpool, UK: Liverpool University Press, 2004.

Tov, Emanuel. *Textual Criticism of the Hebrew Bible*. Minneapolis, MN: Augsburg Fortress, 2001.

———. "The Copying of a Biblical Scroll." In *Hebrew Bible, Greek Bible and Qumran: Collected Essays*, edited by Emanuel Tov, 107–27. Texts and Studies in Ancient Judaism 121. Tübingen: Siebeck, 2008.

Trebilco, Paul R. "Asia." In *The Book of Acts in Its Graeco-Roman Setting*, edited by David W. Gill and Conrad H. Gempf, 2:291–362. BAFCS 2. Grand Rapids, Mich.: Eerdmans, 1994.

———. *Jewish Communities in Asia Minor*. Society for New Testament Studies Monograph Series 69. Cambridge, UK: Cambridge University Press, 2006.

———. *The Early Christians in Ephesus from Paul to Ignatius*. Grand Rapids: Eerdmans, 2007.

Trench, Richard C. *Commentary on the Epistles to the Seven Churches in Asia: Revelation 2, 3*. 2nd ed. London, UK: Parker, Son & Bourn, 1861.

Trinkl, Elisabeth. "Artifacts Related to Preparation of Wool and Textile Processing Found inside the Terrace Houses of Ephesus, Turkey." In *Ancient Textiles: Production, Craft and Society*, edited by Carole Gillis and Marie-Louise B. Nosch, 81–86. Oxford: Oxbow, 2007.

Tristram, Henry Baker. *The Land of Moab: Travels and Discoveries on the East Side of the Dead Sea and the Jordan.* New York: Harper & Brothers, 1873.

Tuckett, Christopher. "Thomas and the Synoptics." *NovT* 30, no. 2 (April 1, 1988): 132–57.

Tuckett, Christopher M. "𝔓[52] and Nomina Sacra." *NTS* 47, no. 4 (October 2001): 544–48.

Tupper, E. Frank. "The Revival of Apocalyptic in Biblical and Theological Studies." *Review and Expositor* 72, no. 3 (1975): 279–303.

Turner, Cuthbert H. *Studies in Early Church History: Collected Papers.* Oxford, UK: Oxford University Press, 1912.

Tzaferis, Vassilios. "Archaeological Views: From Monk to Archaeologist." *BAR* 32, no. 4 (2006): 22.

———. "Inscribed to 'God Jesus Christ': Early Christian Prayer Hall Found in Megiddo Prison." *BAR* 33, no. 2 (2007): 38–49.

Ulpian. *The Digest of Justinian.* Edited and translated by Alan Watson. Philadelphia: University of Pennsylvania Press, 1998.

Unger, Merrill F. "Archaeology and Paul's Tour of Cyprus, Part 1." *BSac* 117 (1960): 229–33.

———. *Archaeology and the New Testament.* Grand Rapids: Zondervan, 1975.

———. *Archaeology and the Old Testament.* Grand Rapids: Zondervan, 1954.

Unnik, W. C. van. *Tarsus or Jerusalem: The City of Paul's Youth.* Translated by George Ogg. Eugene, Ore.: Wipf & Stock, 2009.

Ustinova, Yulia. *The Supreme Gods of the Bosporan Kingdom: Celestial Aphrodite and the Most High God.* Leiden: Brill, 1999.

Ussishkin, David. "Solomon's Jerusalem: The Text and the Facts on the Ground." In *Jerusalem in Bible and Archaeology: The First Temple Period*, edited by Andrew G. Vaughn and Ann E. Killebrew, 103–16. Atlanta, Ga.: SBL, 2003.

Van Biema, David, and Tim McGirk. "Was Jesus' Resurrection a Sequel?" *Time Magazine.* July 7, 2008.

VanderKam, James C. *The Dead Sea Scrolls Today.* 2nd ed. Grand Rapids: Eerdmans, 2010.

VanderKam, James C., and Peter W. Flint. *The Meaning of the Dead Sea Scrolls: Their Significance for Understanding the Bible, Judaism, Jesus, and Christianity.* San Francisco, Calf.: Harper, 2002.

Van Der Steen, Eveline J., and Klaas A. D. Smelik. "King Mesha and the Tribe of Dibon." *JSOT* 32, no. 2 (n.d.): 139–62.

Van Elderen, Bastian. "Some Archaeological Observations on Paul's First Missionary Journey." In *Apostolic History and The Gospel Biblical and Historical Essays Presented to F. F. Bruce on His 60th Birthday*, edited by W. Ward Gasque and Ralph P. Martin, 150–61. Exeter, UK: Paternoster, 1970.

Van Oort, Johannes. "Irenaeus's Knowledge of the Gospel of Judas: Real or False? An Analysis of the Evidence in Context." *HTS Teologiese Studies* 69, no. 1 (January 2013): 1–8.

Vardaman, E. Jerry. "Jesus' Life: A New Chronology." In *Chronos, Kairos, Christos*, edited by Jack Finegan, E. Jerry Vardaman, and Edwin M. Yamauchi, 55–84. Winona Lake, IN: Eisenbrauns, 1989.

Vaughn, Andrew G., and Ann E. Killebrew, eds. *Jerusalem in Bible and Archaeology: The First Temple Period.* SBL Symposium Series 18. Atlanta, Ga.: SBL, 2003.

Vaux, Roland de. *Archaeology and the Dead Sea Scrolls*. Schweich Lectures of the British Academy, 1959. Oxford, UK: Oxford University Press, 1973.

———. "On Right and Wrong Uses of Archaeology." In *Near Eastern Archaeology in the Twentieth Century: Essays in Honor of Nelson Glueck*, edited by James A. Saners, 64–80. New York: Doubleday, 1970.

Venuti, Niccolò Marcello marchese. *A Description of the First Discoveries of the Ancient City of Heraclea*. Translated by Wickes Skurray. London, UK: Baldwin, 1750.

Vickers, Michael J. *The Roman World*. 2nd ed. The Making of the Past. New York: Peter Bedrick Books, 1989.

Victorinus, Apringius of Beja, Caesarius of Arles, and The Venerable Bede. *Latin Commentaries on Revelation: Victorinus of Petovium, Apringius of Beja, Caesarius of Arles and Bede the Venerable*. Edited and translated by William C. Weinrich. Ancient Christian Texts. Downers Grove, IL: IVP Academic, 2012.

Von Wahlde, Urban C. "The Pool of Siloam: The Importance of the New Discoveries For Our Understanding of Ritual Immersion in Late Second Temple Judaism and the Gospel of John." In *John, Jesus, and History: Aspects of Historicity in the Fourth Gospel*, edited by Paul N. Anderson, Felix Just, and Tom Thatcher, 155–73. Atlanta, Ga.: SBL, 2009.

Wace, Henry. *A Dictionary of Christian Biography: And Literature to the End of the Sixth Century A.D. With an Account of the Principal Sects and Heresies*. Peabody, MA: Hendrickson, 1994.

Walker, Peter. *In the Steps of Saint Paul: An Illustrated Guide to Paul's Journeys*. Oxford, UK: Lion Books, 2014.

Wallace, Daniel B. "Earliest Manuscript of the New Testament Discovered?" *The Center for the Study of New Testament Manuscripts*, February 10, 2012. http://www.csntm.org/.

Wall, Robert W. *Revelation*. Edited by W. Ward Gasque. New International Biblical Commentary. Peabody, MA: Hendrickson, 2002.

Waltke, Bruce K., and Cathi J. Fredricks. *Genesis: A Commentary*. Grand Rapids: Zondervan, 2001.

Walton, John H. *Ancient Israelite Literature in Its Cultural Context: A Survey of Parallels between Biblical and Ancient Near Eastern Texts*. 2nd ed. Library of Biblical Interpretation. Grand Rapids: Zondervan, 1990.

Walton, John H. *Chronological and Background Charts of the Old Testament*. Grand Rapids: Zondervan, 1994.

———. "The Antediluvian Section of the Sumerian King List and Genesis 5." *The Biblical Archaeologist* 44, no. 4 (October 1, 1981): 207–8.

Walton, John H., Victor H. Matthews, and Mark W. Chavalas. *The IVP Bible Background Commentary: Old Testament*. Downers Grove, IL: InterVarsity, 2000.

Waltzing, Jean Pierre. *Étude historique sur les corporations professionnelles chez les Romains depuis les origines jusqu'à la chute de l'Empire d'Occident*. Vol. 3. 4 vols. Louvain: Peeters, 1895.

Warner, S. M. "The Patriarchs and Extra-Biblical Sources." *JSOT* 2 (1977): 50–61.

Weber, G. "Die Hochdruck Wasserleitung von Laodicea Ad Lycum." *JDAI* 19 (1904): 95–96.

Webster, Daniel. *Random House Webster's Unabridged Dictionary*. New York: Random House Reference, 1999.

Webster, Thomas Bertram Lonsdale. *Hellenistic Poetry and Art*. London: Methuen, 1964.

Weeks, Lloyd. "Metallurgy." In *A Companion to the Archaeology of the Ancient Near East*, edited by D. T. Potts, 295–317. Hoboken, NJ: Wiley & Sons, 2012.

Weinstein, James M. "Radiocarbon Dating." In *Benchmarks in Time and Culture: An Introduction to Palestinian Archaeology*, edited by Joel F. Drinkard, Gerald L. Mattingly, and J. Maxwell Miller, 235–60. ASOR/SBL Archaeology And Biblical Studies. Atlanta, Ga.: Scholars Press, 1988.

Weippert, Manfred. *Settlement of the Israelite Tribes in Palestine.* Translated by J. D. Martin. Study in Bible Theology 21. London, UK: SCM, 1971.

Weiss, Daniel. "Conspicuous Consumption." *Archaeology*, October 16, 2017. https://www.archaeology.org/issues/275-1711/from-the-trenches/6002-trenches-israel-dyed-textiles.

Weiss, Harvey, ed. *Ebla to Damascus: Art and Archaeology of Ancient Syria: An Exhibition from the Directorate-General of Antiquities and Museums, Syrian Arab Republic.* Washington, DC: Smithsonian Institution Traveling Exhibition Service, 1985.

Werlin, Steven H. "Qumran." Edited by Judith R. Baskin. *The Cambridge Dictionary of Judaism and Jewish Culture.* Cambridge, UK: Cambridge University Press, 2011.

Westcott, Brooke Foss, and Fenton J. A. Hort. *The New Testament in the Original Greek.* New York: Macmillan, 1964.

Wetzel, Henning. *Antike Tonlampen.* Leipzig: Leipziger Universitätsverlag, 1997.

Whallon, R. *Essays on Archaeological Typology.* Evanston, Ill: Center for Amer Archeology Pr, 1982.

Wheeler, Mortimer. *Archaeology from the Earth.* Oxford, UK: Clarendon, 1956.

Whiting, Charles C. *The Revelation of John: An Interpretation of the Book with an Introduction and a Translation.* Boston, MA: Gorham, 1918.

Wickert, Ulrich. "Antioch." In *The Encyclopedia of Christianity*, edited by Erwin Fahlbusch, Geoffrey W. Bromiley, David B. Barrett, Jan Milic Lochman, and John Mbiti, 1:81–82. Grand Rapids: Eerdmans, 1998.

Wiemers, Galyn. *Jerusalem: History, Archaeology and Apologetic Proof of Scripture.* Waukee, Iowa: Last Hope Books, 2010.

Wilcock, Michael. *The Message of Revelation: I Saw Heaven Opened.* Bible Speaks Today. Downers Grove, IL: InterVarsity, 1975.

Wilcox, Donald J. *The Measure of Times Past: Pre-Newtonian Chronologies and the Rhetoric of Relative Time.* Chicago, IL: University of Chicago Press, 1989.

Wild, J. P. *Textile Manufacture in the Northern Roman Provinces.* CamCS. Cambridge, U.K.: Cambridge University Press, 1970.

Wilkinson, John, ed. *Egeria's Travels: Translated with Supporting Documents and Notes.* Translated by John Wilkinson. 3rd ed. Warminster: Aris & Phillips, 1999.

———. *Jerusalem Pilgrims Before the Crusades.* Oxford, UK: Aris & Phillips, 2002.

———. "The Pool of Siloam." *Levant* 10, no. 1 (January 1978): 116–25.

Williams, C. L. R. "A Model of the Mastaba-Tomb of Userkaf-Ankh." *The Metropolitan Museum of Art Bulletin* 8, no. 6 (1913): 125–30.

Williams, Ellen Reeder, and Suzanne Heim. "Ebla to Damascus: Art and Archaeology of Ancient Syria." *BA* 48, no. 3 (1985): 140–47.

Williams, Jay G. *Those Who Ponder Proverbs: Aphoristic Thinking and Biblical Literature.* Sheffield, UK: Almond, 1981.

William, S. H. "The Qeiyafa Ostracon." *UF* 41 (2009): 601–10.

Wilson, Charles W. "On the Site of Ai and the Position of the Altar Which Abram Built Between Bethel and Ai." *PEFSt.* 1, no. 4 (1869): 123–26.

———. "Shiloh." *PEFSt.*, no. 5–6 (1873): 37–39.

Wilson, Clifford A. *Ebla Tablets: Secrets of a Forgotten City: Revelations of Tell Mardikh*. Third, Enlarged and Updated. San Diego, CA: Creation-Life, 1981.

Wilson, John. *Caesarea Philippi: Banias, The Lost City of Pan*. New York: Tauris, 2004.

Wilson, Mark W. *Biblical Turkey: A Guide to Jewish and Christian Sites of Asia Minor.* Istanbul: Ege Yayinlari, 2010.

———. *Revelation*. Zondervan Illustrated Bible Backgrounds Commentary. Grand Rapids: Zondervan, 2007.

———. "The Early Christians in Ephesus and the Date of Revelation, Again." *Neotestamentica* 39, no. 1 (2005): 163–93.

Witherington III, Ben. "The Death and Resurrection of Messiah--- Written in Stone." *Ben Witherington*, July 5, 2008. http://benwitherington .blogspot.com/2008/07/death-and-resurrection-of-messiah.html.

———. "The Jesus Tomb? 'Titanic' Talpiot Tomb Theory Sunk From the Start." Blog. *Ben Witherington*, February 26, 2007. http://benwitherington .blogspot.ru/2007/02/jesus-tomb-titanic-talpiot-tomb-theory.html.

———. *What Have They Done with Jesus?: Beyond Strange Theories and Bad History–Why We Can Trust the Bible*. Reprint edition. New York: HarperOne, 2007.

Wood, Bryant G. "Dating Jericho's Destruction: Bienkowski Is Wrong on All Counts." *BAR* 16, no. 5 (1990): 45, 47–49, 68–69.

———. "Did the Israelites Conquer Jericho? A New Look at the Archaeological Evidence." *BAR* 16, no. 2 (1990): 44–58.

———. "Excavations at Kh. El-Maqatir 1995–2000, 2009–2013: A Border Fortress in the Highlands of Canaan and a Proposed New Location for the Ai of Joshua 7-8." *The Bible and Interpretation*, 2014, 1–16.

———. "Extra-Biblical Evidence for the Conquest." *Bible and Spade* 18, no. 4 (2005): 98–99.

———. "From Ramesses to Shiloh: Archaeological Discoveries Bearing on the exodus–Judges Period." In *Giving the Sense: Understanding and Using Old Testament Historical Texts*, edited by David M. Howard, Jr. and Michael A. Grisanti, 256–82. Grand Rapids: Kregel Academic & Professional, 2004.

———. "In Search of Mt. Sinai." *Associates for Biblical Research Electronic Newsletter* 7, no. 6 (2007): 1–3.

———. "Khirbet El-Maqatir, 1995-1998." *IEJ* 50, no. 1–2 (2000): 123–30.

———. "Khirbet El-Maqatir, 1999." *IEJ* 50, no. 3–4 (2000): 249–54.

———. "Khirbet El-Maqatir, 2000." *IEJ* 51, no. 2 (2001): 246–52.

———. "Locating Sodom: A Critique of the Northern Proposal." *Bible and Spade* 20, no. 3 (2007): 78–84.

———. "New Evidence Supporting the Early (Biblical) Date of the Exodus and Conquest." *Associates For Biblical Research*, November 11, 2011, 1–5.

———. "Pharaoh Merenptah Meets Israel." *Bible and Spade* 18, no. 3 (2005): 65–82.

———. "Recent Research on the Date and Setting of the Exodus." *Bible and Spade* 21, no. 4 (2008): 97–108.

———. "Researching Ai." *Bible and Spade* 22, no. 3 (2009): 75–78.

———. "Researching Jericho." *Bible and Spade* 22, no. 3 (2009): 82–84.

———. "The Biblical Date for the Exodus Is 1446 BC: A Response to James Hoffmeier." *JETS* 50, no. 2 (2007): 249–58.

———. "The Discovery of the Sin Cities of Sodom and Gomorrah." *Bible and Spade* 12, no. 3 (1999): 67–80.

———. "The Rise and Fall of the 13th-Century Exodus-Conquest Theory." *JETS* 48, no. 3 (2005): 475–89.

———. "The Search for Joshua's Ai." In *Critical Issues in Early Israelite History*, edited by Richard S. Hess, Gerald A. Klingbeil, and Paul J. Ray Jr., 205–40. Bulletin for Biblical Research Supplement 3. Winona Lake, IN: Eisenbrauns, 2008.

———. "The Search for Joshua's Ai: Excavations at Kh. El-Maqatir." *Bible and Spade* 12, no. 1 (1999): 21–32.

———. *The Sociology of Pottery in Ancient Palestine: The Ceramic Industry and the Diffusion of Ceramic Style in the Bronze and Iron Ages*. The Library of Hebrew Bible/OT Studies. New York: T&T Clark, 2009.

———. "The Sons of Jacob New Evidence for the Presence of the Israelites in Egypt." *Bible and Spade* 10, no. 3 (1997): 53–65.

———. "Thoughts on Jebel Al-Lawz as the Location of Mount Sinai." *Associates for Biblical Research Electronic Newsletter* 6, no. 4 (May 17, 2006): 1–3.

———. "To Dip or Sprinkle? The Qumran Cisterns in Perspective." *BASOR* 256 (1984): 45–60.

———. "What Do Mt. Horeb, the Mountain of God, Mt. Paran and Mt. Seir Have to Do with Mt. Sinai?" *Associates for Biblical Research Electronic Newsletter* 7, no. 5 (June 2007): 1–3.

Wood, Bryant G., and D. Scott Stripling. *Joshua's Ai at Khirbet El-Maqatir: History of a Biblical Site*. Houston, Tex.: Houston Baptist University Press, 2014.

Wood, John Turtle. *Discoveries at Ephesus: Including the Sites and Remains of the Great Temple of Diana*. London, UK: Longmans, Green & Company, 1877.

Wood, Peter. "Local Knowledge of the Letters of the Apocalypse." *Expository Times* 73 (1962 1961): 163–64.

Woolley, C. Leonard. *Discovering the Royal Tombs at Ur: Joint Expedition of the British Museum and of the Museum of the University of Pennsylvania to Mesopotamia*. New York: Macmillan, 1969.

Woolley, C. Leonard, and T. E. Lawrence. *The Wilderness of Zin*. 2nd Revised. London: Stacey International, 2003.

Woolley, C. Leonard, and M. E. L. Mallowan. *Ur Excavations*. 9 vols. Oxford, UK: Oxford University Press, 1927.

Woolley, C. Leonard, and Peter R. S. Moorey. *Ur "of the Chaldees."* Revised and Updated. Ithaca, NY: Cornell University Press, 1982.

Woolley, C. L., and E. A. Speiser. *Excavations at Ur: The Pottery of Tell Billa*. London, UK: Museum, 1933.

Worth, Jr., Roland H. *The Seven Cities of Apocalypse and Greco-Asian Culture*. New York: Paulist, 2002.

———. *The Seven Cities of the Apocalypse and Roman Culture*. New York: Paulist, 2002.

Wright, David F., Sinclair B. Ferguson, and James I. Packer, eds. *New Dictionary of Theology*. Downers Grove, IL: InterVarsity, 1988.

Wright, George Ernest. "The 'New' Archaeology: An Address Prepared to Be given at Idalion, Summer, 1974." *BA* 38, no. 3–4 (September 1, 1975): 104–15.

Wright, G. Ernest. *Biblical Archaeology*. Abridged. Philadelphia, PA: Westminster, 1960.

Wright, N. T. *Judas and the Gospel of Jesus: Have We Missed the Truth about Christianity?*. Grand Rapids: Baker, 2006.

Würthwein, Ernst. *The Text of the Old Testament: An Introduction to the Biblia Hebraica.* Translated by Erroll F. Rhodes. 2nd ed. Grand Rapids: Eerdmans, 1994.

Wyatt, Mary Nell. *The Boat-Shaped Object on Doomsday Mountain: Is This the Remains of Noah's Ark.* Cornersville, TN: Wyatt Archaeological Research, 2004.

Yadin, Yigael. *Bar-Kokhba: The Rediscovery of the Legendary Hero of the Last Jewish Revolt Against Imperial Rome.* London: Littlehampton, 1971.

———. "Biblical Archaeology Today: The Archaeological Aspect." In *Biblical Archaeology Today: Proceedings of the International Congress on Biblical Archaeology Jerusalem, April 1984*, edited by J. Amitai, 21–27. Jerusalem: Biblical Archaeology Society, 1985.

———. *Hazor: The Rediscovery of a Great Citadel of the Bible.* New York: Random House, 1975.

———. "More on Solomon's Mines (Hebrew)." *Haaretz*, 1966.

———. "The Excavation of Masada—1963/64: Preliminary Report." *IEJ* 15, no. 1/2 (January 1, 1965): 1–120.

———. "The Fourth Season of Excavations at Hazor." *BA* 22, no. 1 (1959): 1–20.

———. "The Judean desert expeditions, 1962. Expedition D. Cave of letters." *Yedot* 26 (1962): 204–36.

Yadin, Yigael, Jonas C. Greenfield, and Ada Yardeni. "Babatha's Ketubbah." *IEJ* 44, no. 1–2 (1994): 75–101.

Yadin, Yigael, Y. Hevrah, and Y. Meshorer. *Masada: The Aramaic and Hebrew Ostraca and Jar Inscriptions: The Coins of Masada.* Jerusalem: Israel Exploration Society, 1989.

Yamauchi, Edwin M. "Historic Homer: Did It Happen?" *BAR* 33, no. 2 (2007): 28–37, 76.

———. "Homer and Archaeology: Minimalists and Maximalists in Classical Context." In *The Future of Biblical Archaeology: Reassessing Methodologies and Assumptions*, edited by James K. Hoffmeier and Alan R. Millard, 69–90. Grand Rapids: Eerdmans, 2008.

———. *New Testament Cities in Western Asia Minor: Light from Archaeology on Cities of Paul and the Seven Churches of Revelation.* Eugene, OR: Wipf & Stock, 2003.

———. "Pre-Christian Gnosticism in the Nag Hammadi Texts?" *Church History* 48, no. 2 (June 1, 1979): 129–41.

———. *The Archaeology of New Testament Cities in Western Asia Minor.* Grand Rapids: Baker, 1980.

———. *The Stones and the Scriptures: An Introduction to Biblical Archaeology.* Grand Rapids: Baker, 1981.

Yardeni, Ada, and Binyamin Elitzur. "A Hebrew Prophetic Text on Stone from the Early Herodian Period: A Preliminary Report." In *Hazon Gabriel: New Readings of the Gabriel Revelation*, edited by Matthias Henze, 11–30. Atlanta, Ga.: Society of Biblical Literature, 2011.

———. "Document: A First-Century BCE Prophetic Text Written on a Stone: First Publication, (in Hebrew)." *Cathedra* 123 (2007): 155–66.

Yardeni, Ada, Jonas C. Greenfield, Yigael Yadin, and Baruch Levine, eds. *The Documents from the Bar Kokhba Period in the Cave of Letters: Hebrew, Aramaic and Nabatean-Aramaic Papyri.* Jerusalem: Israel Exploration Society, 2002.

Yassine, Khair, Moawiyah M. Ibrahim, and James A. Sauer. "The East Jordan Valley Survey 1975 (Part Two)." In *The Archaeology of Jordan: Essays and Reports*, edited by Khair Yassine, 159–89. Amman: Department of Archaeology, University of Jordan, 1988.

Yavelberg, Ilan, and Ela Kehat. "Ancient Inscription Permits, for the First Time, the Definite Identification of Gargilius Antiques as the Roman Prefect during the Period before the Bar Kochba Revolt." *University of Haifa*, January 24, 2018. http://www.haifa.ac.il/index.php/en/home-page3/2025.

Yeatts, John R. *Revelation*. Believers Church Bible Commentary. Harrisonburg, VA: Herald, 2003.

Yegül, Fikret K. "The Bath-Gymnasium Complex in Asia Minor During the Imperial Roman Age." Ph.D. diss., Harvard University, 1975.

Yurco, Frank J. "Merenptah's Canaanite Campaign." *Journal of the American Research Center in Egypt* 23 (January 1, 1986): 189–215.

Zahn, Theodor. *Die Offenbarung Des Johannes*. 2 vols. KZNT 17. Leipzig: Deichert, 1924.

Zeitlin, S. "The Warning Inscription of the Temple." *The Jewish Quarterly Review* 38, no. 1 (1947): 111–16.

Zettler, Richard L., and Lee Horne, eds. *Treasures from the Royal Tombs of Ur*. Philadelphia, PA: University of Pennsylvania Museum of Archaeology and Anthropology, 1998.

Ziegenaus, Oskar, and Gioia De Luca. *Altertümer von Pergamon*. Leiden: de Gruyter, 1968.

———. *Das Asklepieion*. Vol. 1–4. Altertümer von Pergamon 11. Berlin: Deutsches Archäologisches Institut, 1968.

Zion, Ilan Ben. "Temple Mount Archaeological Project Yields Treasure, Unearths Conflict." *The Times of Israel*, June 6, 2014. http://www.timesofisrael.com/temple-mount-project-yields-treasure-but-unearths-conflict/.

Zweig, Zachi Dvira. "Sifting by Volunteers Reveals Hidden Story." *Esra Magazine*, May 2013. http://www.esra-magazine.com/blog/post/temple-mount-archaeology.

Credits and Permissions

The following photographic credits indicate ownership of the original color prints and use with permission to publish in this work. The credits listed here are provided for the images used in the charts for each period. These image credits are provided here in alphabetical order for easy reference. For a detailed analysis of these finds see David E. Graves, *Biblical Archaeology: Famous Discoveries That Support the Reliability of the Bible.* Vol. 2. Toronto, Can.: Electronic Christian Media, 2015. All photographs throughout the text are by the author, unless otherwise indicated.

Abila Inscripiton Drawing of the Abila Inscription. Michael J. Fuller http://users.stlcc.edu/mfuller/abila/AbilaAreaA.html

Ahaz bulla Photo of replica by David E. Graves

Alexamenos Graffiti Rodolfo Amedeo Lanciani, *Ancient Rome in the Light of Recent Discoveries* (New York: Houghton, Mifflin & Company, 1898), 186/Wikimedia Commons

Altar of Jeroboam I Photo by Bukvoed/Wikimedia Commons

Altar of Zeus, Pergamum Pergamon Museum in Berlin, Germany © Photo by Raimond Spekking/Wikimedia Commons

Amarna Tablets Photo by David E. Graves. Courtesy of the British Museum (ME E29844)

Annals of Sargon II Photo by David E. Graves. Used with permission of Oriental Institute Museum

Arch of Titus Photo by Michael C. Luddeni

Areopagus on Mars Hill, Athens Photo by O. Mustafin/Wikimedia Commons

Atrahasis Epic Photo by David E. Graves. Courtesy of the British Museum (ME 7894)

Augustus statue, Rome, Italy Photo by David E. Graves

Azekah Inscription Drawing by David E. Graves

Babylonian Chronicles Chronicle 5 covering the years 605–595 BC. Photo by David E. Graves. Courtesy of the British Museum (ME 21946)

Balaam Inscription (see Deir 'Alla Inscription)

Basilica of St. John, Ephesus Photo by David E. Graves

Bauch Seal (see Bulla of Berachyahu ben Neriah)

Behistun Relief Inscription Photo by Hara1603/Wikimedia Commons

Bema Seat Photo courtesy of Ferrell Jenkins, BiblicalStudies.info

Beni-Hasan Tomb Painting Photo courtesy of Farell Jenkins, BiblicalStudies.info

Bethlehem Bulla Drawing by David E. Graves

Black Obelisk Photo by David E. Graves. Used with permission of Oriental Institute Museum

Bulla of Berachyahu ben Neriah http://articles.aish.com/Bulla.jpg/Wikimedia Commons. Background removed by David E. Graves

Burnt House with Menorah Drawing by David E. Graves

Caiaphas Ossuary Deror_avi/Wikimedia Commons

Capernaum Synagogue Photo by Eddie Gerald/Wikimedia Commons

Chester Beatty Papyri Wikimedia Commons

Code of Hammurabi Oriental Institute Museum (Sb8). Photo by David E. Graves

Codex Alexandrinus (A) The end of the Gospel of Luke. Wikimedia Commons

Codex Ephraemi Rescriptus (C) Photo by Bibliothèque Nationale, Paris, Département des manuscrits, Grec 9, fol. 60r/Wikimedia Commons

Codex Sinaiticus (א) Matt 6:4–32. Wikimedia Commons

Codex Vaticanus (B) 2 Thess 3:11-18, Heb 1:1–2, 2. Wikimedia Commons

Coin of deified Domitian Courtesy of CNG

Cyrus Cylinder Photo by David E. Graves. Courtesy of the British Museum (ME 1880)

Dead Sea Scrolls Photo of a portion of the book of Isaiah by Ardon Bar Hama, The Israel Museum, Jerusalem/Wikimedia Commons

Deir 'Alla Inscription Drawing by David E. Graves

Destruction of Mankind Papyrus Photo by Edward Piercy/Wikimedia Commons

Diploma granting Roman Citizenship Photo by Matthias Kabel/Wikimedia Commons

Ebla Tablets Used with permission courtesy of Bryant G. Wood

Ekron Royal Dedicatory Inscription Photo by Oren Rozen (Israel Museum, Jerusalem) /Wikimedia Commons

Elephantine Papyri Abhandlungen der Königlich Preussischen Akademie der Wissenschaft, Volume 1907, Sachau: drei aramaïsche Papyrusurkunden aus Elephantine

Enuma Elish Photo by David E. Graves. Courtesy of the British Museum (ME K3473)

Epic of Gilgamesh Photo by David E. Graves. Courtesy of the British Museum (ME K3375)

Eridu Genesis or Ziusudra Epic Used with permission courtesy of the University of Pennsylvania Museum of Archaeology and Anthropology (B 10673)

Esarhaddon Chronicle Drawing by David E. Graves. British Museum (BM 25091)

Execration Texts Photo by Naunakhte/Wikimedia Commons

Famine Stele as found by W. M. Flinders Petrie. Markh/Wikimedia Commons

Gabbatha Paving of Hadrian's forum, thought to have been the "lithostrotos" of John's gospel, Aelia Capitolina. Photo by Carole Raddato/Wikimedia Commons

Gezer Calender Photo by replica by Yoavd/Wikimedia Commons

God-fearers Inscription, Miletus theater Photo by David E. Graves

Ḫattuša Tablets Photo by David E. Graves. Courtesy of the Museum in Boğazköy, Turkey

Herod the Great Ostraca Drawing by David E. Graves

Herod's family tomb Photo by Alistair from Montreal, Canada/ Wikimedia Commons

Hezekiah Bulla Drawing by David E. Graves

Hezekiah's Tunnel Photo by Tamar Hayardeni /Wikimedia Commons

House of Yahweh Ostracon Drawing by David E. Graves (IAA 1967–669)
https://www.biodiversitylibrary.org/item/93093#page/329/mode/1up

Incirli stele of Tiglathpileser III Drawing by David E. Graves

Ipuwer Papyrus Wikimedia Commons

Jacob's Well Photo by Jeremiah K Garrett/Wikimedia Commons

James Ossuary The James ossuary was on display at the Royal Ontario Museum from November 15, 2002 to January 5, 2003. Paradiso/Wikimedia Commons

Jehoash Inscription Drawing by David E. Graves

Jehoiachin Ration Record Pergamum Museum Berlin, Germany (VAT 16378). Photo courtesy of Ferrill Jenkins, BiblicalStudies.info.

Jerusalem papyrus Reproduction by David E. Graves

Judaea Capta Bronze Sestertius coin Replica from Tower of David Museum. Photo by David E. Graves

Ketef Hinnom Silver Amulets (see Silver Scroll)

Kinneret Boat Photo by Travellers & Tinkers/Wikimedia Commons

Kurkh Stele Monolith Inscription Photo by David E. Graves. Courtesy of the British Museum (ME 118883)

Lachish Letters (see Lachish Ostraca)

Lachish Ostraca Photo of replica of the front of Letter III by NenyaAleks/Wikimedia Commons

Lachish Reliefs Photo by Mike Peel (www.mikepeel.net)/Wikimedia Commons

Lysanias Inscription (lost) Inscription on a Dori temple near Damascus is lost. No Photograph available

Madaba Map, Madaba Jordan Photo by David E. Graves

Magdalen Papyrus 𝔓64 Wikimedia Commons

Mamertine Prison, Rome Photo by David E. Graves

Mari Tablets Louvre, Department of Oriental Antiquities (AO 20161). Jastrow/Wikimedia Commons. Colorized by David E. Graves

Martin Bodmer Papyri Photo by http://www.bible-researcher.com/papyrus66.html/ Wikimedia Commons

Merenptah Stele Photo courtesy of Greg Gulbrandsen

Merenptah's Battle Reliefs Karnak Temple Photo by David E. Graves

Mesha Stele Photo by Mbzt 2012/Wikimedia Commons

Moussaieff Ostraca Drawing by David E. Graves

Nabonidus Chronicle Photo by David E. Graves. Courtesy of the British Museum (ME 35582)

Nabonidus Cylinder Photo by Osama Shukir Muhammed Amin FRCP(Glasg) The British Museum, London (ME 92238)/Wikimedia Commons

Nag Hammadi Papyri First page of the Gospel of Judas. Photo from Wolfgang Rieger, *The Gospel of Judas. Critical Edition.* Washington 2007), 33/Wikimedia Commons

Nash Papyrus *Proceedings of the Society of Biblical Archæology,* Volume 25 (January-December 1903), p. 56/Wikimedia Commons

Nazareth Inscription Drawing by David E. Graves

Nebuchadnezzar's Brick Royal Ontario Museum (Rom 912.32). Photo by David E. Graves

Nimrud Prism (see Annals of Sargon II)

Nuzi Tablet Semitic Museum at Harvard. Photo by Farell Jenkins, BiblicalStudies. info

Oxyrhynchus Papyri © used with permission courtesy of University of Glasgow Library, Special Collections

Persepolis Relief Central Relief of the North Stairs of the Apadana, Persepolis, now in the Archaeological Museum in Tehran (Iran). Courtesy of Oriental Institute Museum, University of Chicago. Photo by David E. Graves

Peter's House Photo courtesy of Bryant G. Wood

Pilate Inscription Photo by David E. Graves

Pomegranate Inscription Photo of replica by Wikikati/Wikimedia Commons

Pompeii Graffiti Giuseppe Fiorelli. *Descrizione di Pompei.* Tipografia Italiana, 1875), 312.

Pontius Pilate Inscription Caesarea Maritima. Photo by David E. Graves

Pool of Bethesda Photo by Berthold Werner/Wikimedia Commons

Portrait of Emperor Claudius Photo by Claudius Luis García/Wikimedia Commons

Portrait of Nero Reworking as Domitian (AD 81–96) but restoration as Nero (end of sixteenth beginning of seventeenth century) Rome, Musei Capitonili. Photo by Carole Raddato /Wikimedia Commons

Portrait of Tiberius, Ephesus Museum. Photo by David E. Graves

Praetoran Guard, Puteoli, Italy Photo by Albert Krantz/Wikimedia Commons

Prayer of Nabonidus (4Q242) Drawing by David E. Graves

Ras Shamra Tablets Photo by National Museum, Damascus, Syria

Rosetta Stone Photo of reproduction by David E. Graves

Royal Steward Inscription (see Shebna Inscription)

Rylands Papyrus Wikimedia Commons

Sarsekim Tablet Drawing by David E. Graves

Seal of Shema Drawing by David E. Graves

Second Temple Stone Inscription Photo by Yoav Dothan/Wikimedia Commons

Sennacherib Prism Photo by David E. Graves. Used with permission of Oriental Institute Museum (OIM A2793)

Shebna Inscription Photo by Mustafaa (British Museum WA 125205)/Wikimedia Commons

Sheshonq I Inscription Photo by Olaf Tausch/Wikimedia Commons

Siloam Inscription Photo of replica by David E. Graves

Silver Bowl of Artaxerxes I Exhibit in the Arthur M. Sackler Gallery, Washington, DC, USA. Photo by Daderot/Wikimedia Commons

Silver Scroll Photo by Tamar Hayardeni/Wikimedia Commons

St. Philip's Martyrium, Hierapolis Photo by David E. Graves

Statue of Ephesian Goddess Artemis Photo by David E. Graves

Sumerian King List Used with permission courtesy of Ashmonlean Museum, Oxford, UK

Synagogue Inscription, Corinth Archaeological Museum of Ancient Corinth. Photo courtesy of Ferrell Jenkins, BiblicalStudies.info

Tale of Two Brothers Papyrus Trustees of the British Museum/Wikimedia Commons

Taylor's Prism (see Sennacherib Prism)

Tel Dan Stele Photo by David E. Graves. Israel Museum (IAA 1993–3162/ 1996–125)

Temple of Artemis Photo by FDV/Wikimedia Commons

Theater of Ephesus Photo by David E. Graves

Three Shekel Ostraca (see Moussaieff Ostraca)

Tyrannus Inscription Drawing by David E. Graves

Ugarit Tablets (see Ras Shamra Tablets)

Uzziah Epitaph Photo by Yoav Dothan/Wikimedia Commons

Vespasian-Titus Inscription Drawing by David E. Graves

Winged Bull of Sargon II Photo by David E. Graves. Courtesy of the British Museum (ME 118809)

Yehohanan heel bone from Giv'at Ha-Mivtar, Jerusalem Courtesy of the Biblical Antiquities Reproduction Group Inc.

Ziggurat of Ur Photo by Hardnfast/Wikimedia Commons

Index of Subjects

A

B

C

D

E

H

Ḫ

H

I

J

K

L

M

N

O

P

Q

R

S

T

U

V

W

X

Y

Z

Made in United States
Troutdale, OR
06/01/2023

10381514R00251